McGRAW-H

MICROCOMPUTING
LABS

Edition B

Annual Edition

More Software Application Tutorials from Mitchell McGraw-Hill

SCHMITZ	*Practical DOS! 2nd Edition (2.0–5.0)*
SCHMITZ	*Using DOS 5.0*
FREDERICK/YASUDA	*Using Windows 3.0/3.1*
LARSEN/LEEBURG	*Using WordPerfect 5.0*
LARSEN/LEEBURG	*Using WordPerfect 5.1*
LEEBURG/LARSEN	*Using WordPerfect for Windows*
CLUCK	*Using Word for Windows*
PITTER/PITTER	*Using Lotus 1-2-3, Release 2.2*
PITTER/PITTER	*Using Lotus 1-2-3 for DOS, Release 3.1+*
WILLIAMS/WILLIAMS	*Beginning Lotus 1-2-3, Release 2.2*
WILLIAMS/WILLIAMS	*Advanced Lotus 1-2-3, Release 2.2*
WILLIAMS/WILLIAMS	*Beginning Lotus 1-2-3 for Windows*
WILLIAMS/WILLIAMS	*Advanced Lotus 1-2-3 for Windows*
AMOROSO	*Decision Making Using Lotus 1-2-3: Building Quality Applications*
SHUMAN	*Using Microsoft Excel 4.0 for Windows*
PITTER/PITTER	*Using Microsoft Excel 4.0 for Windows: The Basics*
ROSNER/SHUMAN	*Using Quattro Pro 2.0/3.0*
PRICE	*Using dBASE III PLUS*
GRAUER & BARBER	*Database Management Through dBASE III PLUS*
GRAUER & BARBER	*Database Management Using dBASE IV and SQL*
SHUMAN	*Using dBASE IV*
REISS	*Using Paradox 4.0*
EAKINS	*Desktop Publishing on PC Compatibles and the Macintosh: PageMaker 4.x*
ADAMS	*HyperCard and Macintosh: A Primer*
YASUDA/FREDERICK	*Using Microsoft Works 2.0 on the PC*
YASUDA/FREDERICK	*Using Microsoft Works 2.0 on the Mac*
YASUDA/FREDERICK	*Using Microsoft Works 3.0 on the Mac*

McGRAW-HILL

MICROCOMPUTING LABS

Edition B

Annual Edition

Timothy J. O'Leary
Arizona State University

Brian K. Williams
Linda I. O'Leary

Mitchell McGRAW-HILL

New York St. Louis San Francisco Auckland Bogotá Caracas
Lisbon London Madrid Mexico Milan Montreal New Delhi Paris
San Juan Singapore Sydney Tokyo Toronto Watsonville

McGraw-Hill Microcomputing Labs: Edition B Annual Edition

Copyright © 1993, 1992, 1991, 1990, 1989 by McGraw-Hill, Inc. All rights reserved. Printed in the United States of America. Except as permitted under the United States Copyright Act of 1976, no part of this publication may be reproduced or distributed in any form or by any means, or stored in a database or retrieval system, without the prior written permission of the publisher.

2 3 4 5 6 7 8 9 0   KGP KGP   9 0 9 8 7 6 5 4 3

ISBN 0-07-048891-6

Sponsoring editor: Roger Howell
Editorial assistant: Laurie Boudreau
Director of production: Jane Somers
Design: Merrill Haber and Cecelia Morales
Composition: Pat Rogondino
Production management: Elaine Brett
Printer: Kingsport Press, Inc.

ABOUT THE AUTHORS

Timothy J. O'Leary has been a professional educator since 1975. He is currently an Associate Professor in the department of Decision and Information Systems at Arizona State University. He has written several books and articles on computers and information systems.

Linda I. O'Leary is a professional trainer in the area of computers. She has developed computer training manuals for corporations and presented numerous seminars on the use of many computer software packages. She has also coauthored many computer lab manuals.

Brian K. Williams is a professional writer and has coauthored six books about computers. The holder of degrees from Stanford University, he was for many years an editor and manager for several book publishers before turning full time to writing. He lives in Incline Village, Nevada.

ABOUT THE BOARD

Bob Autrey, Chuck Riden, and Jerry Booher are members of the McGraw-Hill Microcomputing Advisory Board. They are university and community college instructors who teach microcomputing courses. Their input has been invaluable to the development of this project.

To
Pat and Tuff—T.J.O
The Lyons, Rusts, & Gerritsens—B.K.W.
My sister, Ann—L.I.O.

CONTENTS IN BRIEF

Preface   xi

DOS 3.3–5.0 with Introduction to the Labs   DOS1
Overview: Getting Started with Your Microcomputer
Lab 1   Using the Disk Operating System (DOS)
Lab 2   Managing Your Disk
Summary
Index

WordPerfect 5.1   WP1
Overview: Word Processing
Lab 1   Editing a Document
Lab 2   Creating and Formatting a Document
Lab 3   Merging and Refining Documents
Lab 4   Creating a Research Paper
Summary
Index

Lotus 1-2-3 Release 2.2   SS1
Overview: Electronic Spreadsheets
Lab 1   Creating a Worksheet: Part 1
Lab 2   Creating a Worksheet: Part 2
Lab 3   Managing a Large Worksheet
Lab 4   Creating and Printing Graphs
Lab 5   Creating Templates and Macros
Summary
Index

dBASE III PLUS   DB1
Overview: Database
Lab 1   Creating a Database
Lab 2   Modifying, Editing, and Viewing a Database
Lab 3   Sorting, Indexing, and Summarizing Data
Lab 4   Creating a Professional Report
Summary
Index

For detailed Table of Contents, refer to beginning of each individual application software tutorial.

This edition of *Microcomputing Labs Annual Edition* covers the most current versions of popular software applications: WordPerfect 5.1, Lotus 1-2-3 Release 2.2, and dBASE III PLUS.

Designed for students in an introductory computer or microcomputer course, this book assumes no prerequisites.

OUR PURPOSE: TO CREATE COMPUTER COMPETENCY

This book is intended to give students competency in computer-related knowledge and skills in order to support their academic pursuits and to be of immediate value to their employers. Our goal is to prepare students to be:

- **Microcomputer-literate -** able to employ microcomputers to increase their productivity and effectiveness.

- **Familiar with commercial software -** especially word processing, spreadsheet, and database management packages.

- **Grounded in fundamental concepts -** having a basic working vocabulary and knowledge of computing and information concepts.

DISTINGUISHING FEATURES AND BENEFITS

Key Feature #1: Flexibility

The modular design provides instructors with many opportunities to meet their particular course objectives. You are now holding one of the three standard book versions:

- **Text Only.** *McGraw-Hill Computing Essentials: Annual Edition 1993–1994* in 14 brief chapters describes basic computer and information concepts.

- **Labs Only.** *McGraw-Hill Microcomputing Labs: Annual Edition* is available in two configurations of software applications. Both are spiral bound for convenient use in a lab setting. *Edition A* includes *DOS 3.3–5.0, WordPerfect 5.1, Lotus 1-2-3 Release 2.3,* and *dBASE IV Version 1.1. Edition B* includes *DOS 3.3–5.0, WordPerfect 5.1, Lotus 1-2-3 Release 2.2,* and *dBASE III PLUS.*

- **Text Plus Labs.** *McGraw-Hill Microcomputing: Annual Edition 1993–1994* is a spiral-bound combination of the text and *Labs Edition A.*

Also available: your own "mix and match" combinations. If none of the above options meets your needs, *you can mix and match modules to create your own customized instructional package.* The following lab modules may be ordered—with or without *McGraw-Hill Computing Essentials*—in any combination, shrink-wrapped with or without a three-ring binder:

> *DOS 5.0*
> *DOS 3.3–5.0*
> *DOS 2.0–3.0*
> *Windows 3.1*
> *Windows 3.0*
> *WordPerfect for Windows*
> *WordPerfect 5.1*
> *WordPerfect 5.0*
> *WordPerfect 4.2**
> *WordStar 4.0*
> *Lotus 1-2-3 for Windows*
> *Lotus 1-2-3 Release 2.3*
> *Lotus 1-2-3 Release 2.2*
> *Lotus 1-2-3 Release 2.01*
> *Microsoft Excel 4.0 for Windows*
> *Quattro Pro 4.0*
> *Quattro**
> *SuperCalc 4**
> *dBASE IV Version 1.1*
> *dBASE III PLUS**
> *Paradox for Windows*
> *Paradox 4.0*
> *Microsoft Works Release 2.0 on the IBM PC*
> *Local Area Network (LAN)*

* Educational versions of WordPerfect 4.2, Quattro Training Edition 1.01, SuperCalc 4, and dBASE III PLUS can be shrink-wrapped with these lab modules.

Your McGraw-Hill sales representative will explain this customization feature in more detail.

Key Feature #2: Revised Annually

Being able to revise our materials every year allows us—and our readers—to keep pace in this dynamic field. In this edition we have upgraded each software package to include: WordPerfect 5.1, Lotus 1-2-3 Release 2.2, and dBASE III PLUS. The above list of modules that are now available shows how further updating is possible.

Key Feature #3: "Learn by Doing" Approach

The lab modules are based on an ongoing case study that simulates real-world use of the software and leads the student step by step to the solution to the problem. Each lab module includes the following additional learning aids:

- Conceptual Overview
- Objectives
- Step-by-Step Procedures

- Wealth of Screen Displays
- Key Terms
- Lab Review (Matching and/or Fill-In Questions)
- Practice Exercises
- Glossary of Key Terms
- Summary of Commands
- Index

THE SUPPORT PACKAGE

Teaching materials sets for each of the lab modules are available to adopters. Each set includes:

- Objectives
- Schedule
- Procedural Requirements
- Teaching Tips
- Command Summary
- Answers to Matching/Fill-In Problems
- Answers to Practice Exercises
- Transparency Masters
- Printed Test Bank
- 3-1/2" IBM Student Data Disk and Test Questions

Note: RHTest, a computerized test bank, is also available to adopters.

Other Support Materials

- Color Transparencies
- Documentary-Style Videotapes
- Hypercard Presentation Tool (Computer Resource Library)
- Computerized Glossary of Terms

If you would like information on how to obtain the last four supplements described above, please contact your McGraw-Hill sales representative.

GENERAL SYSTEM REQUIREMENTS

To complete the labs in this book, the following hardware and software are needed:

Hardware

- An IBM PC or compatible computer system with enough memory to support the specific software program
- A monochrome or color monitor and a keyboard
- A printer

Note: The directions and figures in this book assume these configurations. If your computer system deviates from this, your instructor will provide you with alternative directions.

Operating System Software

■ DOS version 3.3 or higher

Applications Software

■ Full-power versions of WordPerfect 5.1, Lotus 1-2-3 Release 2.2, and dBASE III PLUS.

ACKNOW-LEDGMENTS

We were fortunate to have a great deal of fine input and ongoing advice from the McGraw-Hill Microcomputer Advisory Board: Bob Autrey, Mesa Community College; Jerry Booher, Scottsdale Community College; and Chuck Riden, Arizona State University, Mesa Community College, and Dobson High School. A special thanks goes to the industry professionals who have given invaluable insights into the use of microcomputers in today's work life. They include Bill Bauer, Ernst & Young; Brian Corke and Gene Kunkle, Sun State Seafoods; Ernie Ziak, Western Reserve Family Sports Center; and Jim Price, The Sports Authority.

We are also grateful for the helpful comments from our reviewers: David Adams, Northern Kentucky University; Henry Altieri, Norwalk State Technical College; Gary Armstrong, Shippensburg University; Harvey Blessing, Essex Community College; Cathy Brotherton, Riverside Community College; Earline Cocke, Northwest Mississippi Community College; Mona Dalton, Tallahassee Community College; Tim De Clue, Southwest Baptist University; Kevin Duggan, Midlands Technical College; Lucie Dutfield, Seneca College; Sandra Dzakovic, Niagara College; Jeannine Englehart, Coastline College; Patrick Fenton, West Valley College; Roger Franklin, Richard Bland College; Tom Gallagher, Seneca College; Nancy Gillespie, Glassboro State College; Carla Hall, St. Louis Community College–Florissant Valley; Sue Henry, Cheridian College; Jim Higgins, Mohawk College; Lister Horn, Pensacola Junior College; Ann Houck, Pima Community College; Peter Irwin, Richland College; Ruth Jaglowitz, Seneca College; Barbara Jauken, Southeast Community College; Cynthia Kachik, Santa Fe Community College; Tom Kane, Centennial College; John Keeling, Seneca College; Shelley Langman, Bellevue Community College; Philip E. Lowry, University of Nevada–Las Vegas; Deborah Ludford, Glendale Community College; Brian Monahan, Iona College; Trudy Montoya, Aims Community College; Don Myers, Vincennes University; Pam Nelson, Panhandle State University; Paul Northrup, University of Colorado, Boulder; Dean Orris, Butler University; James Payne, Kellogg Community College; Allan Peck, Springfield Technical Community College; Carl Penzuil, Corning Community College; Diane Peterson, Wisconsin Indianhead Technical College; James Phillips, Helena Vocational Technical Center; Rick Phillips, Roosevelt University; Leonard Presby, William Paterson College; Herbert Rebhun, University of Houston; Lisa Rosner, Stockton State College; Paul Ross, Millersville University; Lorilee Sadler, Indiana University; Peg Saragina, Santa Rosa Junior College; Judith Scheeren, Westmoreland County Community College; Ruth Schmitz, University of Nebraska, Kearny; Faye Simmons, Canton College of Technology; Laurie Smith, University of South Carolina; Sandra Stalker, North Shore Community College; Hamilton Stirling, University of South Florida at Saint Petersburg; Glenna Stites, Johnson Community College; Margaret Thomas, Ohio University; Nancy Tinkham, Glassboro State College; Douglas Topham; Timothy Trainor, Muskegon Community College; Michael Trombetta, Queensborough Community College;

Jeannetta Williams, Piedmont Virginia Community College; Don Wilson, Georgian College; and Al Woodman, Seneca College; Mark Workman, Frank Phillips College; and Marilyn Zook, Mt. Hood Community College.

In addition, we are extremely appreciative of all the efforts of the Mitchell/ McGraw-Hill staff and others who worked on this book: Roger Howell, Erika Berg, Laurie Boudreau, and Steve Mitchell for their enthusiastic support of the 1993–1994 edition; Jane Somers for her production supervision; John Ambrose, Kris Johnson, and Judith Hug for their marketing support; and Karen Jackson, Eric Munson, and Seibert Adams for their past and present editorial and marketing support.

We are also grateful for the contributions of those outside McGraw-Hill and Mitchell: Jim Elam for his dedication and thoughtful suggestions; Colleen Hayes for her thorough software evaluation and recommendations; Christy Butterfield for her cover design; Mark Poe for the new practice exercises; Peg Sallade for permission to use parts of her research paper "Aquatic Fitness"; Susan Defosset for copy editing; Elaine Brett for project management; Pat Rogondino for composition; and Jane Granoff for her technical consultation.

Write to Us

We welcome your reactions to this book, because we would like it to be as useful to you as possible. Write to us in care of: Microcomputer Applications Editor, Mitchell McGraw-Hill, 55 Penny Lane, Watsonville, CA 95076.

Timothy J. O'Leary
Brian K. Williams
Linda I. O'Leary

DOS 3.3-5.0
with Introduction to the Labs

1 2 3 4 5 6 7 8 9 0 KGP KGP 9 0 9 8 7 6 5 4 3

ISBN 0-07-048887-8

Library of Congress Catalog Card Number 92-82695

CONTENTS

Introduction to the Labs   **L1**
Organization of the Lab Modules   L1
How the Case Study Explains Software   L2
Directions and Commands   L3
General System Requirements   L5
Installation   L5

Overview   **Getting Started with Your Microcomputer   DOS1**
Computer Hardware   DOS1
Input Devices   DOS2
Processor Unit   DOS4
Secondary Storage   DOS4
Output Devices   DOS7
Computer Software   DOS8
Naming a File   DOS9
Directories   DOS9
Introduction   DOS10
Before You Begin   DOS10

Lab 1   **Using the Disk Operating System (DOS)   DOS13**
Before You Begin   DOS13
Starting Your Computer and Loading DOS   DOS14
Loading DOS (Cold Boot)   DOS15
Loading DOS (Warm Boot)   DOS15
Entering the Date   DOS16
Entering DOS Commands   DOS20
Changing the Default Drive   DOS21
Displaying a Directory Listing (DIR)   DOS21
Using Directory Pause and Wide   DOS23
Clearing the Screen (CLS)   DOS25
Formatting a Disk (FORMAT) and Assigning a Volume Label (/V)   DOS26
Formatting a Disk and Copying the Operating System   DOS30
Copying a File (COPY) to Another Disk   DOS31

Copying Multiple Files   DOS34
Copying a File to the Same Disk   DOS37
Checking the Disk (CHKDSK)   DOS39
Renaming a File (REN)   DOS40
Erasing a File (ERASE or DEL)   DOS41
Printing the Display Screen   DOS42
Key Terms   DOS43
Command Summary   DOS43
Lab Review   DOS44
       Matching   DOS44
       Fill-In Questions   DOS44
       Practice Exercises   DOS45

Lab 2   **Managing Your Disk   DOS46**
Understanding Directories   DOS46
Creating Directories (MD)   DOS47
Changing Directories (CD)   DOS49
Changing the Command Prompt (PROMPT)   DOS50
Creating a Subdirectory   DOS51
Copying a File to a Directory   DOS54
Displaying Directory Structure (TREE)   DOS54
Displaying File Contents (TYPE)   DOS57
Removing Directories (RD)   DOS57
Creating a Batch File   DOS59
Executing a Batch File   DOS61
Key Terms   DOS62
Command Summary   DOS62
Lab Review   DOS63
       Matching   DOS63
       Fill-In Questions   DOS63
       Practice Exercises   DOS64

Summary   **DOS 3.3-5.0   DOS66**
Glossary of Key Terms   DOS66
Functional Summary of DOS Commands   DOS70

Index   **DOS71**

Each lab module in the *McGraw-Hill Microcomputing* series consists of a sequence of labs that each require about one hour to complete. They are designed to provide you with practical skills in using the following kinds of software, which are the most widely used in business and industry:

- Disk Operating System (DOS)
- Windows user interface
- Word processor
- Spreadsheet
- Database

The labs describe not only the most important commands and concepts, but also explain why and under what circumstances you will use them. By presenting an ongoing case study based on input from actual business managers, we show how such software is used in a real business setting.

Organization of the Lab Modules

The Lab Modules Are Organized in the Following Categories: Overview, Objectives/Competencies, Case Study, Lab Activities, Key Terms, Command Summary, Lab Review, Glossary of Key Terms, Functional Summary of Selected Commands, and Index.

Overview   The overview, which appears in the first of the succession of labs, describes (1) what the program can do for you, (2) what the program is, (3) the generic terms that this and all similar programs use (for example, all word processing programs, regardless of brand name), and (4) the case study to be presented in the labs covered by the program.

Objectives/Competencies   The objectives or competencies list appears at the beginning of each lab. They list the concepts and commands to be learned in that particular lab.

Case Study   The case study introduces the specific case covered by the particular lab—the general problems that the software activities will help you solve.

Lab Activities   The lab activities consist of detailed, step-by-step directions for you to follow in order to solve the problems of the case. Your progress through the lab activities is reinforced by the use of carefully placed figures that represent how your screen should appear after you complete a procedure. Labs should be followed in sequence, because each succeeding lab builds on the ones preceding it. In addition, the number of screen displays decreases and directions become less specific. This feature allows you to think about what you have learned, avoids simple rote learning, and reinforces earlier concepts and commands, helping you to gain confidence.

Key Terms   Terms that are defined in the labs appear in **boldface (dark) type**. They are also listed at the end of each lab in the order in which they were introduced.

Command Summary   All commands that are used in the lab and the action they perform are listed at the end of each lab in the order in which they were introduced.

Lab Review   Each lab concludes with a series of problems designed to reinforce concepts and commands that you have learned in the lab. The review material may include matching and fill-in questions that do not require the use of the computer. Hands-on practice exercises are also included that require the use of the microcomputer to complete.

Glossary of Key Terms   The glossary, which appears at the end of each lab module, defines all the key terms that appear in bold in the overview and throughout the labs for that particular kind of software.

Functional Summary of Selected Commands   Each lab module also concludes with a quick-reference source for selected commands for that particular software. The commands are listed in the order in which they appear in the application's menus. If there are no menus, they are listed by the type of function they perform.

Index   Each lab module contains an index for quick reference back to specific items within that module.

How the Case Study Explains Software

The Ongoing Case Studies Show How to Solve Real-World Business Problems Using a Word Processor, a Spreadsheet, and a Database Program.

The ongoing case studies were written with the help of real-world experience contributed by industry managers. The specific case study used in each lab module is explained in the overview section for the module. The reader follows the instructions in the labs to solve the case problems using the different software applications, as follows:

Disk Operating System   This module first describes the hardware of a microcomputer system. It then shows you how to use the Disk Operating System (DOS) to start the computer system, format disks, make back-up copies of program and data files, and perform other file management tasks. The labs also cover directories, paths, and batch files.

Windows User Interface   How Windows makes DOS easier to use and more powerful is demonstrated in this series of labs. The labs show how to use the Windows environment and many Windows application programs such as Write, Cardfile, and Calendar.

Word Processor   The features of a word processing program are explained by showing how to create, revise, format, save, and print a business letter. The features associated with creating a newsletter and a research paper are also covered.

Spreadsheet   Use of the spreadsheet program is shown by depicting how an operating budget is created and modified. The spreadsheet data are adjusted to attain a set profit margin. Business growth over five years is graphed. The use of templates and macros is introduced as a report is created to calculate employee bonuses.

Database   Creating, modifying, updating, and making a report of a database of employee and customer information is demonstrated. The software is also used to sort and index these data and summarize the information in a professional report.

Directions and Commands

Commands and Directions Are Expressed Through Certain Standard Conventions.

We have followed certain conventions in the labs for indicating keys, key combinations, commands, command sequences, and other directions.

Keys   Computer keys are expressed in abbreviated form, as follows:

Computer Keys	Display in Text
Alt (Alternate)	(ALT)
(←) (Backspace)	(Bksp)
Caps Lock (Capital Lock)	(CAPS LOCK)
Ctrl (Control)	(CTRL)

Cursor Movement

(↑) (Up)	(↑)
(↓) (Down)	(↓)
(←) (Left)	(←)
(→) (Right)	(→)
Del (Delete)	(DEL)
End	(END)
ESC (Escape)	(ESC)
(↵) (Enter/Return)	(↵)
Home	(HOME)
Ins (Insert)	(INS)
Num Lock (Number Lock)	(NUM LOCK)
Pg Dn (Page Down)	(PGDN)
Pg Up (Page Up)	(PGUP)
Prt Sc (Print Screen)	(PrtScr)
Scroll Lock	(SCROLL LOCK)
⇧ (Shift)	(SHIFT)
Tab or ⇄	(TAB)

Function Keys

F1 through F12	(F1) through (F12)

Key Combinations   Many programs require that you use a combination of keys for a particular command (for example, the pair of keys (CTRL) and (F4)). You should press them in the order in which they appear, from left to right, holding down the first key while pressing the second. In the labs, commands that are used in this manner are separated by a hyphen or a plus sign—for example: (CTRL) - (F4) or (CTRL) + (F4).

Key names separated by a comma (,) indicate that you must press the first key and release it, and then press the second key and release it. For example: (ALT), W.

Directions   In the labs, all directions that you are to perform appear in a highlighted block. Most directions appear on separate lines preceded by the words "Press," "Move to," "Type," "Select," or "Choose." These directions are defined as follows:

- *Press:* This means you should press or strike a key. Usually a command key will follow the direction (such as (DEL) for "Delete"). For example:

  Press: (DEL)

- *Move to:* This means you should move the cursor or cell pointer to the location indicated. For example, the direction to move to line 4, position 12, would appear as:

  Move to: Ln 4 Pos 12

- *Type:* This means you should type or key in certain letters or numbers, just as you would on a typewriter keyboard. Whatever is to be typed will appear in **boldface (dark) type**. For example:

  Type: **January**

- *Select:* Many programs use a sequence of selections to complete a command. In the beginning, we will introduce these commands separately. Later, as you become more familiar with the software, we will combine the commands on a single line. Each command will be separated by a slash (/) or a greater-than symbol (>). The command sequences will follow the word "Select." If the first letter of a command appears in **boldface**, you can select that command by typing the letter. Other parts of the command sequence that are to be typed will also appear in **boldface**. For example, the command to retrieve a WordPerfect 5.1 file may appear as:

  Select: **F**ile>**R**etrieve>**LETTER**(⏎)

  This means you should type the letter F to select the File menu, type the letter R to select the Retrieve command, type the filename LETTER, and press (⏎) to complete the command.

- *Select/Choose:* Many applications use both Select and Choose to complete a command sequence. Choose is used to indicate selecting a command that begins an action. Select is used to indicate selecting or marking an item from a list of available options. Selecting does not begin an action as Choose does. For example, the command sequence to open a file may appear as:

  Select: File
  Choose: **O**pen
  Select: LETTER
  Choose: OK

  When this sequence of commands appears on a single line, it will begin with Choose, because the ultimate response is an action. For example, the same sequence as above would appear as:

  Choose: File/**O**pen/**LETTER**/OK

Additionally, directions may appear in a highlighted block embedded within the main text. They appear like this only after the procedure to perform the directions is very familiar to the student. Follow the instruction using the appropriate procedure.

In many lab modules, you can use either a mouse or a keyboard to perform the same procedure. The instructions are marked with the mouse or keyboard icon as shown below.

 Introduces a procedure to be followed if you are using a mouse.

 Introduces a procedure to be followed if you are using a keyboard.

Additionally, there may be special instructions for hard-disk users and floppy-disk users. These appear as follows:

Hard-Disk Systems:

Insert the master data disk in the A drive.

Floppy-Disk Systems:

Insert the master data disk in the B drive.

Special Assumptions   Any special directions or hardware and software assumptions that have been made in the preparation of these lab modules are described in the overview for that particular software application module under the heading "Before You Begin," or as a note in the beginning of the first lab of the module.

General System Requirements

To complete the labs, the following hardware and software are needed:

- An IBM or IBM-compatible computer system with a hard disk and one or two floppy disk drives, or a floppy disk system with two disk drives. The amount of RAM memory your computer must have varies with the application software program you will be using. If you are using a networked system, your instructor will provide additional instructions as needed.

- MS or PC-DOS version 3.3 or higher.

- A monochrome or color monitor and a keyboard.

- A mouse is not required, but is very helpful when you are using certain application programs.

- A printer.

- Application software programs selected by your instructor.

- Student data disk containing the files needed to perform the labs and to complete the practice exercises; this disk is supplied by your instructor.

Installation

Programs Must Be "Installed" in Order to Run on Certain Equipment.

Most software has to be installed or "custom-tailored" to run with specific computers and printers. The documentation accompanying the software gives details. If you find that, for some reason, your software will not print out correctly and won't run on your microcomputer, ask your instructor for assistance.

Getting Started with Your Microcomputer

A **microcomputer system** is composed of five essential parts: people, procedures, software, hardware, and data. The end users (people) need to know how to operate the computer hardware and use the software programs to input and analyze data or information. To learn how to operate or use the software, hardware, and data, the end users follow procedures. Procedures consist of rules or guidelines contained in manuals. This overview will focus briefly on the hardware and software aspects of your computer system.

Computer Hardware

The physical part of the computer system, called **hardware**, consists of four parts: input devices, the processor unit, secondary storage devices, and output devices. The **input devices** take data and put it into a form the computer can process. The most common input devices are a keyboard and a mouse. The **processor unit**, also called the systems unit, consists of the main memory and the central processing unit (CPU). The processor unit executes the software program instructions, performs calculations, and temporarily stores data and programs. The most common form of **secondary storage** is a disk. It provides a place to permanently store information or data that is input into the computer. **Output devices** are equipment that translate the processed information from the CPU into a form that you can understand. A computer screen or monitor is used for temporary display. A printer is used to make a permanent copy of your data. A typical computer system is shown in Figure 1.

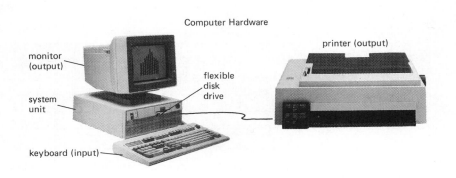

Computer Hardware

FIGURE 1

monitor (output)

printer (output)

flexible disk drive

system unit

keyboard (input)

Input Devices

Keyboard The **keyboard** is the most common type of input device. It allows you to communicate with the computer. It consists of four main areas: the function keys, the typewriter keys, the numeric keypad, and special-purpose keys. Two styles of keyboards are commonly found: the standard keyboard and the newer enhanced keyboard. Figure 2 shows a standard and an enhanced IBM keyboard.

The central area of the keyboard contains the standard typing keys and the spacebar. The standard keys consist of letters, numbers, and special characters such as the semicolon and the dollar sign, as they appear on a standard typewriter. You use these keys just like you would a normal typewriter. As you type, the characters appear on the computer screen rather than on paper. The **cursor**, a flashing symbol (usually an underline), identifies your location on the screen.

FIGURE 2

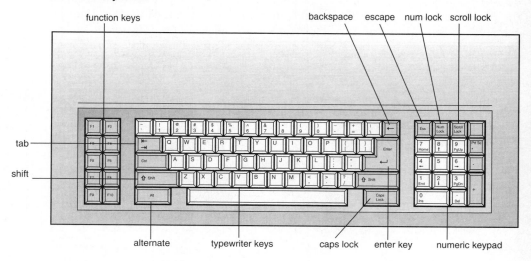

The other typing keys and their uses are described below.

Key	Action
(SHIFT) + letter	Types uppercase letter
(SHIFT) + number	Types symbol shown above number on that key
(CAPS LOCK)	Allows entry of all uppercase alphabetic characters without using (SHIFT)
(TAB)	Moves cursor preset number of spaces to the right
(SHIFT) + (TAB)	Moves cursor preset number of spaces to the left
(⏎)	Moves the cursor to the next line (same as on a typewriter); allows the user to enter data or command sequences

At the right side of the keyboard is the numeric keypad. It consists of nine keys with arrows and numbers on them. These keys can be used to enter numbers or to direct the movement of the cursor on the display screen. To use the numeric-keypad area to enter numbers, the (NUM LOCK) key must be on. To turn on (NUM LOCK), press the (NUM LOCK) key. When (NUM LOCK) is on, the indicator light on an enhanced keyboard is lighted. When (NUM LOCK) is off, use of the keys in the numeric keypad moves the cursor in the direction of the arrow. The (NUM LOCK) key acts like a toggle switch to switch control of the numeric keypad area between numeric entry and cursor movement. On the enhanced keyboard there is a separate directional keypad consisting of four arrow keys that are used exclusively to move the cursor.

There are also some keys in the numeric keypad with words on them: (HOME), (END), (PGUP), and (PGDN). These keys will have different meanings depending on the software program you are using. Typically you can use these keys to quickly move around through information on your screen.

Function keys are located across the top on the enhanced keyboard or on the left side of standard keyboards. They are labeled (F1), (F2), etc. They are used to send instructions to the software you are using, and therefore their use varies with the software program you are using. Frequently function keys are shortcuts for a long command. Instead of pressing several keys to perform a command, all you need to do is press one function key.

Scattered throughout the keyboard are special-purpose keys. The uses of these keys change with the type of work you are doing. Generally they have the following uses:

Key	Action
(ESC) (escape)	Quits or goes back one step in a program command; erases existing command
(CTRL) (control)	Used in combination with another key to perform a special task
(ALT) (alternate)	Assigns another function to a given key
(PrtScr)	Prints a hard copy of whatever is on the display screen when pressed. (Standard keyboards must hold down (SHIFT) in conjunction with (PrtScr).)
(SCROLL LOCK)	When pressed with the (↑) and (↓) keys, moves the document up or down on the screen
(Pause)	May let you stop a program for a short time

Key	Action
(CTRL)-(BREAK)	Stops a command from completing execution
(INS) (insert)	Allows you to insert characters between other characters
(DEL) (delete)	Erases the character the cursor is on
(←) or (Bksp) (backspace)	Moves cursor to left and erases character (this key may also appear as a left-facing arrow, (←), above the (←) key

FIGURE 3

Mouse   The **mouse** is an input device that is used in addition to the keyboard. It is a hand-held device that controls a pointer on the screen. Figure 3 shows an example of a mouse.

When you move the mouse around the desktop, the rubber-coated ball on the bottom of the mouse moves. The ball's movement is translated into signals that tell the computer how to move the onscreen pointer. On top of the mouse are two or three buttons that are used to make selections from items on the screen.

Processor Unit

The **processor unit**, also called the system unit, contains the central processing unit (CPU) and main memory. Figure 4 displays the parts of a processor unit.

The **central processing unit (CPU)** is the part of the computer system that does the actual computing. It contains the electronic circuitry through which data is processed and instructions are executed. In a microcomputer the CPU consists of a single silicon chip.

The **main memory,** or **primary storage** component, of the processor unit is where data and instructions are stored during processing by the microprocessor. Depending on the amount of memory your computer system has, the number of storage chips within the system unit will vary.

The amount of main memory is measured in **bytes**. A byte is a single memory location. Usually a byte stores one character. A **kilobyte (KB)** equals 1024 (or approximately 1000) bytes. A **megabyte (MB)** holds approximately one million bytes. The amount of main memory for computers varies from 64KB to several million bytes.

As Figure 4 shows, there are two types of main memory, **read-only memory (ROM)** and **random-access memory (RAM)**. The ROM area contains built-in instructions that direct the operations of the computer. ROM is not accessible to the user. The other type of memory, RAM, is accessible to the user. It is the computer's workplace. The RAM area holds the software programs and data that are loaded from the disk. RAM is also referred to as **temporary memory**, because whatever is in RAM is lost if the power is turned off.

Processor Unit

expansion slots to connect disk, monitor, printer, and other hardware

CPU

read-only memory (ROM) chip

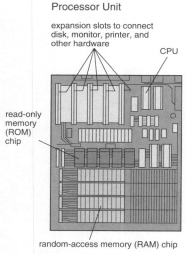

random-access memory (RAM) chip

FIGURE 4

Secondary Storage

Secondary storage devices provide a means of permanently storing the information contained in temporary memory. There are several types of secondary storage devices. The most common type of secondary storage is a **disk**. The disk is the permanent storage medium for either data (such as a business letter) or a software program (for example, a word processor, to edit that letter). The data and program information are stored on circular metal or plastic disks as a series of electromagnetic spots. The disk can be an internal **hard disk** that is housed within the processor unit, or an external **floppy disk**.

The amount of data a disk can hold is called **disk capacity**. Disk capacity, like main memory, is measured in kilobytes (KB) or megabytes (MB). A hard disk has a much greater capacity than a floppy disk.

Hard Disk The **hard disk** is a permanent fixture containing one or more circular metallic disks that are used to store data files and software programs. The internal hard disk is sealed in a container within the system unit to prevent any foreign matter from getting inside. It is usually referred to as the C drive. The **hard-disk drive** in the system unit provides the means for you to retrieve and save your data and programs onto the hard disk. The hard-disk drive contains an access arm and read-write heads for writing data to and reading data from the hard disk.

A microcomputer hard disk has a disk capacity from 20MB to over 300MB. The main advantages of a hard disk are that more information can be stored on the hard disk, and it is accessed more quickly than the information from a floppy disk.

Floppy Disk The second main type of secondary storage is the **floppy disk**, a flexible plastic disk. It allows the user to load instructions into the computer from disks containing software programs, and to save data onto and retrieve data from disks that contain information you create. The main advantage of floppy disks is that they are transportable.

Floppy disks come in several sizes. The most common sizes are 5-1/4 inch and 3-1/2 inch. The type of disk you will use depends on your computer hardware requirements. Figure 5 shows the 5-1/4- and 3-1/2-inch disks.

The 5-1/4-inch disks are contained within a jacket that protects the disk. The jacket is inserted in a paper envelope when it is not in use to further protect it. The write-protect notch can be covered with a removable tab, which comes with the disk when you buy it. This prevents the computer from accidentally writing over data that you want to keep.

A 3-1/2-inch disk has a hard plastic jacket. This makes the disk much more sturdy than a 5-1/4-inch disk. However, inside the hard jacket is the same type of soft plastic disk for storing data. The write-protect notch is covered by a sliding shutter. When the shutter is open, the write-protect hole is exposed, preventing information from being changed on the disk.

FIGURE 5

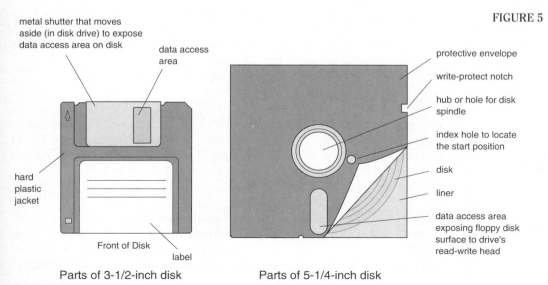

metal shutter that moves aside (in disk drive) to expose data access area on disk

data access area

hard plastic jacket

Front of Disk

label

Parts of 3-1/2-inch disk

protective envelope

write-protect notch

hub or hole for disk spindle

index hole to locate the start position

disk

liner

data access area exposing floppy disk surface to drive's read-write head

Parts of 5-1/4-inch disk

A **floppy-disk drive** is used to read information from the floppy disk to RAM and to write information from RAM to the disk. The floppy-disk drive also has an access arm and read-write heads. All microcomputers have at least one floppy-disk drive.

The floppy-disk drive is housed in the front of the computer as shown in Figure 1. A slot allows you to insert a floppy disk into the drive. The data is read from or written to the disk by the read-write head mechanism inside each drive.

If there are two floppy-disk drives, they are referred to as the A drive and the B drive. If the drives are positioned side by side, generally the A drive is on the left. If your drives are located one above the other, the A drive is the one on top. Usually the A drive contains the software program disk and the B drive contains the data disk.

When inserting a floppy disk into the disk drive, gently slide it into the drive with the end opposite the label first and label side up (or to the left if you have vertical drives). Some 5-1/4-inch floppy-disk drives have a lever that you need to push down or to the side after inserting the disk. With 3-1/2-inch disks, insert the disk into the drive until you hear a click. To remove the disk, if necessary lift up the drive lever on a 5-1/4-inch disk drive or press the button on the front of the 3-1/2-inch disk drive, and slide the disk out of the drive.

The capacity of floppy disks varies with the type of disk, from 360KB up to 2.88MB. Several factors control how much data can be stored on a floppy disk. If the disk is a single-sided disk, data can be stored on one side of the disk only. Double-sided disks store data on both sides of the disk. Most disks are double sided. Another factor that affects the amount of data that can be stored on a disk is the disk density. There are single-density, double-density, and high-density disks. Density refers to the number of bytes that can be recorded on the disk in a specified space. The higher density the disk is, the more data that can be stored. The chart below summarizes the different types and capacities of the most commonly used floppy disks.

Diameter (inches)	Description	Capacity (bytes)
5-1/4	Single-sided, double density	160KB/180KB
5-1/4	Double-sided, double density	320KB/360KB
5-1/4	Double-sided, high density	1.25MB
3-1/2	Double-sided, double density	720KB
3-1/2	Double-sided, high density	1.44MB

It is important to be aware of the density of disks because the disk drive on your computer must be able to support the disk capacity of the disk. Otherwise it will be unable to use the disk. A higher-density drive can read from and write to a lower-density disk, but a lower-density drive cannot read from or write to a higher-density disk.

Floppy Disk Care Since floppy disks contain a permanent copy of your work or program files that you use frequently, it is very important that this data not be lost or destroyed. If it is, you could lose a lot of time and effort. To help preserve your disks, there are some things you should know about their care and handling:

1. Excessive heat can melt or warp the disk. Do not, for example, expose your disk to excessive sunlight through the window of your car or to excessive heat by placing it on your heater.

2. Disks use magnetism to store data. Do not expose the disk to magnetic fields such as your telephone receiver, a loudspeaker, or a television. The magnetic fields from these machines can alter the data on your disk.

3. Do not touch the surface of the disk through the oval opening. Always handle the case only. The oils from your skin can damage the surface of the disk.

4. Store your disks standing up or in a vertical position. This way they will not bend or warp. Always place the 5-1/4-inch disk in its protective envelope.

5. Do not bend disks or place heavy objects on them.

6. Do not write on a 5-1/4-inch disk with a ballpoint pen. The pressure from the pen can crease the disk and damage it. If you must write on your disk, use a felt-tip pen. It is best, however, to write on the label before you place it on the disk.

Output Devices

The Computer Screen   The computer screen, or **monitor**, is how the computer communicates with you. The monitor displays instructions you send to the computer, as well as the information and results sent from the computer back to you. It relays program messages or instructions called prompts, and displays results of calculations, graphs, and text input.

The computer screen can be either a monochrome screen display or a color screen display. A monochrome screen uses only one color — usually white, green, amber, or black — to display text on a contrasting background. The color screen can display two or more colors, depending on the quality of the monitor. Many color screens are capable of displaying 256 colors at once from a selection of over 256,000 choices. If you have a color monitor or a monochrome monitor with a graphics board, you can view all of your work, including graphs, on your display screen.

The Printer   Along with the computer screen, a **printer** serves as a way for the computer to tell you what you have input and what it has done. The difference is that the printer generates a permanent hard copy of your work. Some printers can print both text and graphics (pictures). Others can print only text. If you have a printer that prints only text, you would need a device called a **plotter** to print graphs. Figure 6 on page 8 shows a printer (left) and a plotter (right).

Printers can produce hard copy that is either near letter (draft) quality or letter quality. Draft-quality print is formed by a series of dots and consequently may not appear solid. Letter-quality print is solid, like that produced by a typewriter.

The most popular type of printer that produces draft-quality print is the dot-matrix printer. Dot-matrix printers produce letters by a series of pins that press on a printer ribbon to produce dots in the form of the letter. These printers are fast and economical, but noisy.

Letter-quality print is produced by daisy-wheel, ink-jet, and laser printers. The daisy-wheel printer produces letters in ink from a thimble containing the characters (much like an electronic typewriter). The ink-jet printer sprays ink in the pattern of the character. The most recent type of printer used with microcomputers is the laser printer. It creates characters by means of an electronic charge. The laser printer is a high-resolution printer that produces typeset-quality text and graphics.

FIGURE 6

Although most printers can also print graphs, you may want to use a plotter to draw pictures and graphs. Most plotters use several pens of different colors to produce a multicolor drawing. The graphs and drawings produced by a plotter have much better line resolution and precision than graphs produced by a dot-matrix printer. A plotter produces professional presentation-quality graphs.

Computer Software

Software is the set of instructions that directs the computer to process information. These instructions are called **programs**. Without software, the computer cannot work. A commonly used analogy is that the computer hardware is the engine, while the software is the fuel that allows the engine to operate. Without software the hardware would be useless.

There are two types of software available for computers: systems software and applications software.

Systems Software   **Systems software** programs coordinate the operation of the various hardware components of the computer. The systems software or operating system program helps the user to actually operate the computer system. They are an interface between the user and the computer.

The operating system oversees the processing of the application programs and all input and output of the system. Without the operating system, you cannot use the applications software programs provided with this book. The operating system controls computer system resources and coordinates the flow of data to and from the microprocessor and to and from input and output devices such as the keyboard and the monitor.

Systems software is usually provided by the computer manufacturer. The various types of computers require different types of systems software programs in order to operate. Some of the most popular are MS-DOS, Apple-DOS, OS/2, and UNIX.

Applications Software   **Applications software** is a set of programs designed for specific uses or "applications," such as word processing, graphics, or spreadsheet analysis. Applications software can be custom-written but is usually purchased ready-made.

Normally, to use an application program like Lotus 1-2-3, a spreadsheet program, you load the program into the computer's main memory; execute (run) the program; and then create, edit, or update a file. When you have finished, you need to save the work you have done on a disk. If you don't save your work and you turn off the computer or exit the software program, your work is erased from memory and everything you have done will be lost.

The operating system acts as a communications link between the hardware and the application program. It is responsible for loading the applications software into memory and then starting the program. It also retrieves data files and saves them to disk when directed. When you have finished using the applications software, you are returned to the operating system.

Naming a File

The information your computer uses is stored in **files**. The instructions used to run a program are stored in program files. The information you create by using a program are stored in data files. In order to save your work as a file on the disk, you must assign it a **filename**.

Filenames consist of two parts: the filename the user creates, and an optional file **extension**. The two parts of a filename are separated by a period. They are shown in Figure 7.

A filename can be no longer than eight characters. It can contain only the letters A–Z, the numbers 0–9, and any of the following special characters: underscore (_), caret (^), dollar sign ($), tilde (~), exclamation point (!), number sign (#), percent sign (%), ampersand (&), hyphen (-), braces ({}), parentheses (), at sign (@), apostrophe ('), and the grave accent ('). It cannot contain spaces, commas, backslashes, periods, or any other special characters. A filename should be descriptive of the contents of the file. For example, the filename CHECKBK would be a good name for a file that contains your checking account information.

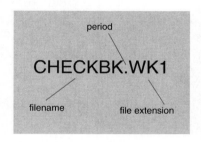

FIGURE 7

The file extension can be up to three characters long. The same restrictions regarding characters and spacing that apply to filenames apply to file extensions. Generally a file extension is used to identify the type of file. It is not always necessary to enter a file extension because many application programs automatically add an identifying file extension to any files created using the program. For instance, Lotus 1-2-3 Release 2.2 files have a file extension of "WK1." Thus when you see a file with that extension, you will know that it is used with Lotus 1-2-3 Release 2.2. The filename above would now read CHECKBK.WK1 if it had been created using Lotus 1-2-3 Release 2.2.

Directories

In addition to naming the files you create, you can create **directories** and **subdirectories** to organize the files into groups on your disk. If you do not create directories, all the files you save are stored in the **root directory** of the disk. Figure 8 is a graphical representation of directories and subdirectories.

All disks have a root directory that is created when the disk is prepared or formatted for use by the operating system program. If you do not create directories, the files are not organized on the disk, making it much more difficult to quickly locate a specific file. Using directories is essential to the organization of a hard disk. However, it is becoming increasingly important to use directories with floppy disks because of the increased disk capacity.

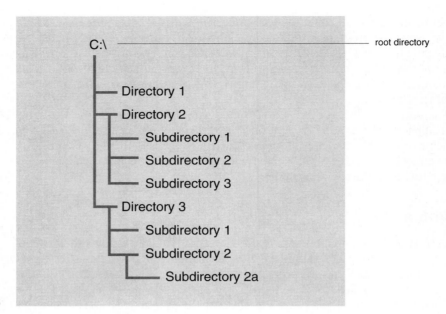

FIGURE 8

Directories are like file folders in which you store files that have something in common. Subdirectories are further subdivisions within a directory. The operating system program lets you format your disks and create directories. Like filenames, each directory must be assigned a unique name. The same rules apply to directory names as apply to filenames. However, a directory extension is not generally used, and is never supplied by the operating system.

The organization of directories and subdirectories and files is called the **directory tree**. All directories are branches from the root or main directory. Subdirectories are branches under a directory. Files can be stored in the root directory, a directory, or a subdirectory. Each file stored in a directory or subdirectory must have a unique filename. For example, if you give a new file the same filename as a file already in the same directory or subdirectory of the disk, the contents of the original file will be replaced by the contents of the new file. Many software programs have safeguards to prevent accidentally overwriting one file with another.

Introduction

The next two labs will explore the disk operating system (DOS) program. In the first DOS lab you will learn how to start your computer and how to use many basic and important DOS commands. In the second DOS lab you will learn how to organize the files on your disk and how to create a special file that makes DOS work for you.

Before You Begin

The following assumptions have been made:

- The version of DOS you are using is version 3.3 or higher.
- The initial or default command prompt is displayed.
- Most people are using DOS 3.3 and have a hard-disk system with two floppy-disk drives. Therefore, the screens in the labs display DOS 3.3

when a hard-disk system with two floppy disk drives is used. Hard-disk instructions are presented before floppy-disk instructions.

■ If you are using DOS 4.0 or 5.0, the DOS Shell does not load automatically when the computer is booted.

Throughout the labs you will see DOS 4.0 and 5.0 Notes. They appear whenever the DOS 4.0 and 5.0 screen displays slightly different information from the DOS 3.3 screen presented in the text. Wherever needed, supplemental screens specifically for DOS 4.0 and 5.0 are provided.

■ Your master data disk contains the files you will need to complete a series of labs as selected by your instructor.

■ If you have a hard-disk system, a DOS path command has been included in the AUTOEXEC.BAT file.

1 Using the Disk Operating System (DOS)

This lab provides instructions for starting your computer and loading and using the Disk Operating System (DOS). You will learn how to display the directory of files on a disk and how to prepare a new disk for use. You will create a backup copy of data files needed to run the labs selected by your instructor. Additionally, if necessary, you will create backup disks of the applications software programs you will be using. Finally, you will learn how to rename and erase files from a disk.

Before You Begin

Before you begin this lab, you will need the following:

- **Operating Software:** DOS version 3.3 or higher installed on your hard disk or on floppy disks.

If you have a floppy-disk system, the number of DOS disks and labels will vary depending upon the disk size (5 1/4- or 3 1/2-inch) and the type of DOS you are using (PC-DOS, MS-DOS, or DR-DOS). Generally, the number of disks and labels will be similar to those shown below:

Version	Disk Size	Number	Label
DOS 3.3	3.5	1	Program or Startup/Operating
	5.25	2	Program or Startup, Operating
DOS 4.0	3.5	2	Install, Operating
	5.25	2	Install, Operating
DOS 5.0	3.5	1	Startup/Support
	5.25	2	Startup, Support

Competencies

In this lab you will learn how to:

1. Start the computer system.
2. Change the default drive.
3. Display a directory listing.
4. Clear the display screen.
5. Format a disk.
6. Copy files.
7. Check a disk.
8. Rename files.
9. Erase files.

■ **Data files:** The data files you will need to complete the labs. They should be on a floppy disk supplied by your instructor. This disk will be referred to as the master data disk.

■ **A blank new disk:** Disks come in many different sizes and densities. Your instructor will tell you the size and density of disk you should purchase. Additionally, if you need more than one disk, your instructor will tell you how many.

The procedure you will follow in this lab varies with the type of computer system you have: hard-disk with one or two floppy-disk drives, or a floppy-disk system with two floppy-disk drives.

In a hard-disk-drive system, the hard disk is generally called the C drive. A computer system with a hard disk has either one or two external (floppy) disk drives. If your hard-disk system has two external drives, the upper or left drive is usually called the A drive and the lower or right drive is called the B drive.

If your hard disk system has one external drive, it acts as both the A and B drive. The A and B represent the disks that will be inserted into the drive rather than the physical drive location. You must switch disks each time DOS directs you to do so.

If your computer does not have a hard disk, you will most likely have two external or floppy-disk drives. The upper or left drive is called the A drive and the lower or right is called the B drive.

Throughout the labs directions are included for both computer systems. Follow the directions for your type of computer system. Hard-disk system directions are presented first, followed by directions for floppy-disk systems. Floppy-disk directions may appear in parentheses following hard-disk directions.

Note: If your school uses a local area network, your instructor will provide supplemental directions for the changes you need to make to complete the DOS labs.

Starting Your Computer and Loading DOS

The **operating system** program controls computer system resources and coordinates the flow of data to and from the system unit and to and from input and output devices like the keyboard and the display screen. It allows you to create and manage files and run applications software programs.

The operating system used on IBM and IBM-compatible microcomputers is DOS, which stands for disk operating system. The two main types of DOS are PC-DOS and MS-DOS. PC-DOS is IBM's version and MS-DOS is Microsoft's version. Both are very similar and can be used on all IBM-compatible computers. A third DOS system, DR-DOS produced by Digital Research, is also available. We will refer to all types of IBM operating systems simply as DOS.

DOS has three major functions: to control the input and output from your computer; to interpret and execute commands you enter from your keyboard or other input device; and to save and manage files on your disk. Three specific files—COMMAND.COM, IBMDOS.COM (MSDOS.SYS in Microsoft's DOS), and IBMBIO.COM (IO.SYS in Microsoft's DOS)—perform these functions.

COMMAND.COM is the program that reads whatever is typed at the keyboard and processes the commands given to the computer. It also contains the DOS commands that are most often used. The last two files handle input and output to and from the computer and manage the files on the disk. When you start your computer, these files are loaded into the main memory of your computer.

In addition, many DOS commands are stored in individual task files called **utility programs**. These files are not used as frequently and therefore are not loaded into RAM until they are executed.

Now you will start your computer and load DOS. Starting the computer and loading DOS is often called **booting** the system. If your computer is not on, turning on the computer and starting DOS is called a **cold start** or **cold boot**. If your computer is on, you can restart the computer without turning the power switch off and on again. This is called a **warm start** or **warm boot**.

If your computer is off, follow the directions to start your computer in the section "Loading DOS (Cold Boot)." If your computer is on, skip to the section "Loading DOS (Warm Boot)."

Loading DOS (Cold Boot)

Hard-Disk System:

The instructions to start your computer and load DOS assume that you already have DOS on the hard disk and that the hard-disk drive is the C drive.

1. The A drive should be empty and the drive door open.

2. Turn on the power switch.

3. If necessary, turn your monitor on and adjust the contrast and brightness.

Floppy-Disk System:

1. Insert the DOS disk (labeled Startup, Program, or Install, depending upon the type and version of DOS you are using), into drive A. If necessary, close the drive door.

2. Turn on the power switch.

3. If necessary, turn your monitor on and adjust the contrast and brightness.

Loading DOS (Warm Boot)

Hard-Disk System:

The instructions to start your computer and load DOS assume that you already have DOS on the hard disk and that the hard-disk drive is the C drive.

1. The A drive should be empty and the drive door open.

2. Press and hold down the (CTRL) and (ALT) keys with your left hand; then press the (DEL) key with your right hand. Release the three keys.

3. If necessary, turn your monitor on and adjust the contrast and brightness.

Floppy-Disk System:

1. Insert the DOS disk (labeled Startup, Program, or Install, depending upon the type and version of DOS you are using), into drive A. If necessary, close the drive door.

2. Press and hold down the (CTRL) and (ALT) keys with your left hand; then press the (DEL) key with your right hand. Release the three keys.

3. If necessary, turn your monitor on and adjust the contrast and brightness.

When you turn the computer on, it performs a memory check to determine if all the RAM locations are able to receive and store data correctly and initializes the equipment for use. (If you are doing a warm boot, the memory check is not performed.) Then it accesses the disk drive and reads the three DOS files into RAM.

After a few seconds you will hear the whirring sound of the disk in the drive, followed by a beep. Then the light near the C drive for a hard-disk system (or the A drive for a floppy-disk system) will blink on and off. When the light is on, the computer is either reading from or writing to the disk.

> *Caution:* Do not remove or insert a disk into the drive when the light is on. This can result in damage to the files on the disk.

Your screen should be similar to Figure 1-1.

FIGURE 1-1

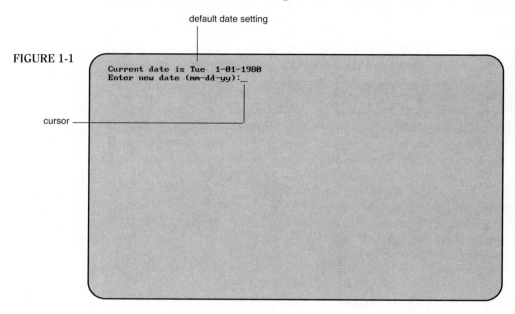

You have just completed the loading of your operating system and are now ready to continue by responding to the date and time prompts.

Note: If your screen displays an opening menu of items from which you need to select, your instructor will advise you of the procedures to follow to access the DOS program files.

Entering the Date

Note: Depending on your computer system, the DOS version you are using, and how DOS was installed if you have a hard disk, you may or may not be asked to enter the current date and time. If your screen displays a C> (or A>), as in Figure 1-3, read the section on entering the date and time but do not follow the instructions.

Note: The screens displayed in this lab reflect the use of MS-DOS Version 3.3 and a computer system with a hard disk and two floppy-disk drives. If you are using DOS

4.0 or 5.0 and a different computer configuration, your screens and some procedures may be slightly different. Follow the directions for your computer system. If
you are using DOS 4.0 or 5.0, read and follow the directions in the special notes for
those versions throughout the labs.

In Figure 1-1, DOS displays the current day of the week and date as Tues 1-01-
80. Your computer may display a different date (most likely the current date). If
your computer displays the current date, it is because your computer contains a
battery clock that maintains the correct day and time information even when the
computer is turned off. If your computer does not contain a battery clock, the date
will be the same as the date displayed in Figure 1-1.

The date that is displayed is the default date. A **default** setting is the setting
that is used by the program if it is not directed to use another. If you do not enter a
different date, the program assumes that you want to use the default date setting.

The second line of the message displays the prompt, "Enter new date (mm-dd-
yy):". A **prompt** is how a program tells you it is waiting for you to enter command,
respond to a question, or provide more information. In this case, the prompt asks
you to enter a new date. The flashing underscore following the prompt is called the
cursor. The cursor shows you where the next character you type will appear.

If the date displayed as the current date is correct, to accept it,

Press:　⟨⏎⟩

If the date displayed as the current date is not correct, you will want to enter
the current date. Entering the current date sets the date on the system clock. If you
leave your system on, the date will continue to advance. It is always a good practice
to enter the current date at the DOS date prompt, otherwise DOS will use the
default date. Whenever you create or update a file, the date you enter is recorded
along with the filename. This information can help you locate the most recent
version of a file.

The date is entered in the form month-day-year (mm-dd-yy) using one- or
two-digit numbers. The three parts of the date can be separated by hyphens (-),
slashes (/), or periods (.). Though the default date shows the day of the week, you do
not enter this information. DOS automatically determines the day of the week from
the date you enter.

Use the number keys at the top of the keyboard to enter your current date. The
figures in this lab will display the date 9-22-94. To enter your current date, replace
the date below (9-22-94) with your current date,

Type:　　9-22-94 (enter your current date)

If you make a mistake while typing, use the ⟨Bksp⟩ key to erase the characters to the
left of the cursor back to the error, and retype the entry correctly.

To indicate that you have completed the date and want to enter it into the
program,

Press:　⟨⏎⟩

Your screen should be similar to Figure 1-2.

FIGURE 1-2

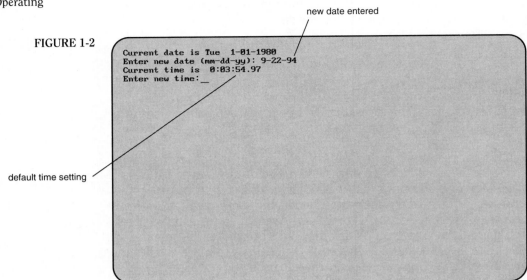

new date entered

```
Current date is Tue  1-01-1980
Enter new date (mm-dd-yy): 9-22-94
Current time is  0:03:54.97
Enter new time:_
```

default time setting

If the message "Invalid date" is displayed and the prompt to enter the date is displayed again, you entered the date incorrectly. Try again.

Next DOS displays the default time. The format for the time is hours:minutes:seconds.hundredths of seconds. The default time starts with 0 hours, 0 minutes, 0 seconds, and 0 one-hundredths of a second each time the computer is turned on. DOS uses a 24-hour clock that is similar to a military clock. 1:00 A.M. is the first hour on the 24-hour clock and 1:00 P.M. is the 13th hour.

DOS 4.0 and 5.0 note: The time is displayed using the standard 12-hour time format rather than military format. Following the time the letter "a" or "p" is displayed to indicate A.M. or P.M.

The current time displayed on your screen will reflect the amount of time that has elapsed since the computer was turned on, or the current time if your computer contains a battery clock. If the time displayed as the current time is correct, to accept it,

Press: ⎵⏎

If the time displayed as the current time is not correct, the correct time can be entered. To enter the time, type a number between 0 and 23 for the hour and a number between 0 and 59 for the minutes. It is not necessary to enter the seconds or hundredths of a second. Separate the hours and minutes by a colon (:).

DOS 4.0 and 5.0 note: You can enter the time using the standard 12-hour time format (a number between 0 and 12 is entered for the hour) rather than military format. When using the 12-hour format, DOS assumes an A.M. time unless you specify a P.M. time by typing a "p" following the time.

Use the number keys at the top of the keyboard to enter the current time. The figures in this lab will display the time as 10:15. To enter your current time, replace the time below (10:15) with your current time.

Type: **10:15** (enter your current time)

If you make a mistake while typing, use the (Bksp) key to erase the characters to the left of the cursor back to the error, and retype the entry correctly.

To indicate that you have completed the time and want to enter it into the program,

Press: (⏎)

Your screen should be similar to Figure 1-3.

FIGURE 1-3

```
Current date is Tue  1-01-1980
Enter new date (mm-dd-yy): 9-22-94
Current time is  0:03:54.97
Enter new time: 10:15 ─────────────────────────────── new time entered
C>_
```

─── DOS prompt

If the message "Invalid time" is displayed and the prompt to enter the time is displayed again, you entered the time incorrectly. Try again.

Depending upon how your DOS program was installed, immediately after DOS is loaded the version of DOS in use and the copyright information may be displayed.

Depending upon your computer system, the **command prompt**, C> or A>, will be displayed. C> is displayed if you booted from the hard disk, and A> if you booted from a floppy disk. The letter in the command prompt tells you which drive is the **default drive** or **current drive**. This is the drive that DOS will search to get a file or execute a program. The > is known as the **prompt character**. The C> sign then is known as the "C prompt." The command prompt is followed by the cursor. It means that DOS is waiting for you to enter **commands** or instructions for actions you want DOS to perform. The line containing the command prompt is called the **command line**.

Note: If your command prompt looks like C:\> or A:\>, do not be concerned. You will learn about customizing the command prompt in Lab 2.

Entering DOS Commands

A DOS command is entered following the command prompt. The name of the command is entered first. The command name states the action you want DOS to perform. For example, to display information about what version of DOS you are using, the VERSION command is used. The command name is shortened to VER.

The VER command is one of the commands contained in the COMMAND.COM file. This type of command is called an **internal command** because it stays in RAM until you turn off the system unit or load DOS again. When the computer is booted, the internal commands are copied into memory from the booting disk. Therefore, if you have a floppy-disk system, this command can be issued with or without the DOS disk in the drive.

Other DOS commands are not read into memory until they are used. These commands are used less often, so to save memory space DOS does not copy them into memory. They are called **external commands**. If you have a hard disk, the external commands are read from the hard disk into memory as they are used. If you have a floppy-disk system, the DOS disk must be in the drive when an external command is issued. External commands are cleared from memory after use.

DOS commands can be entered in either upper- or lowercase characters, or a combination of the two. Throughout the labs the commands will be displayed in uppercase characters. You press ⏎ when you are finished typing a command. If you enter a DOS command incorrectly, the command will not be executed and DOS will display an error message. One of the most common error messages is "Bad command or file name." If this message appears, look for a misspelled command or filename and reenter the command correctly.

To use the VER command to display information about the version of DOS you are using, at the C> (or A>),

Type: VER

Press: ⏎

Your screen should be similar to Figure 1-4.

FIGURE 1-4

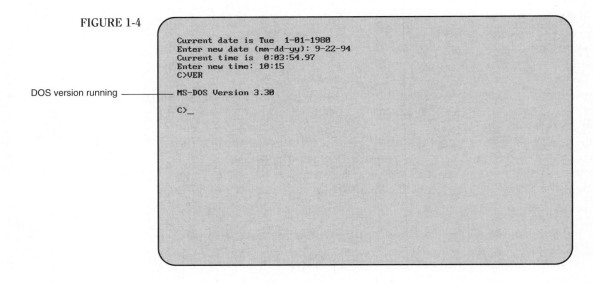

DOS version running

```
Current date is Tue  1-01-1980
Enter new date (mm-dd-yy): 9-22-94
Current time is  0:03:54.97
Enter new time: 10:15
C>VER

MS-DOS Version 3.30

C>_
```

In response to the command, DOS displays the version information for the version of DOS you are using. Below it the command prompt is displayed again.

Changing the Default Drive

Another simple command is to change the current disk drive to another disk drive. To change the current drive to another, simply type the letter of the drive you want to change to followed by a colon. If you do not include the colon, DOS does not interpret the command correctly. The drive letter followed by a colon is called the **drive specifier**.

You will change the current drive to the drive containing the master data disk.

Hard-Disk Systems:

Insert the master data disk in the A drive.

The current drive is C. To change to the drive containing the master data disk (A), at the C>,

Type: A:
Press: ⏎

The command prompt changes to A>.

Floppy-Disk Systems:

Insert the master data disk in the B drive.

The current drive is A. To change to the drive containing the master data disk, B, at the A>,

Type: B:
Press: ⏎

The command prompt changes to B>.

If the screen displays the error message "Disk error reading Drive A" followed by three choices, "Abort, Retry, Ignore?" (or "Abort, Retry, Fail?"), this means that DOS was unable to read the disk in the specified drive. Usually this is because there is no disk in the drive or the drive door or latch is open. Correct the problem and type R to retry the command. Do not change disks in the drive before retrying the command. You could also type A to abort the command. The last choice, I (or F), ignores the error condition if possible. This choice is not recommended, however.

Now DOS will use the current drive to read files from and write files to the disk in the drive.

Displaying a Directory Listing (DIR)

Frequently you will want to see a list of all the files on a disk. A portion of each disk is devoted to maintaining a list of all filenames. This listing is called a **directory**. To display a list of the filenames, the DIR (**DIR**ectory) command is used.

You will display the directory of files on the master data disk. The drive containing your master data disk should be the current drive.

At the A> on a hard-disk system (or B> on a floppy-disk system),

Type: **DIR**

Press:

Watch your screen carefully. The information and filenames listed at the beginning of the directory scroll off the top of the screen to allow the filenames at the bottom of the directory to be seen. This is because there are more files in the directory than can be displayed on the screen at one time.

Your screen should be similar to Figure 1-5A (or Figure 1-5B for DOS 4.0 and 5.0).

FIGURE 1-5A

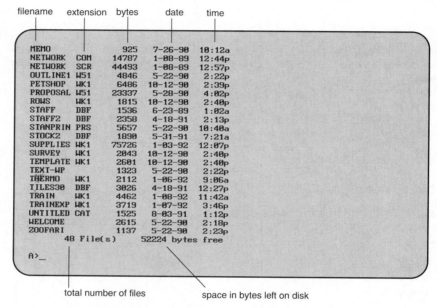

FIGURE 1-5B

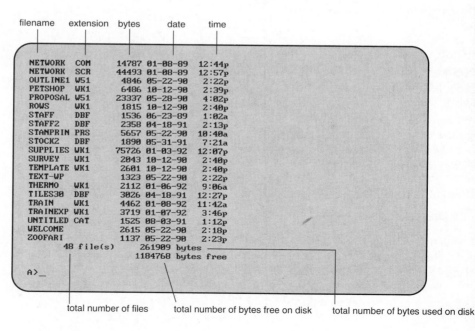

The DIR command displays the filename, the file extension, the size of the file in bytes, and the date and time the file was created or last updated. By entering the correct date and time when loading DOS, you can quickly determine when a file was created or updated. The total number of files and the number of free bytes (remaining space) on the disk are displayed at the bottom of the list of filenames. The number of bytes free will vary with the size and density of disk you are using.

Note: The number of files and filenames displayed on your screen may differ from the filenames shown in Figure 1-5 depending upon the software application programs you will be using.

DOS 4.0 and 5.0 note: Your screen will also display the number of used bytes at the end of the directory listing.

Next you will display a directory listing for the files on your hard disk or, for floppy-disk systems, the files on the A drive (the drive containing your DOS disk) without changing the current drive.

To do this you need to provide some additional information as part of the DIR command to tell DOS you want to see a directory listing for a drive other than the current drive. Most commands require more information, called **parameters**. Parameters define the object you want the command to act on. You specify parameters after the command name and separate it from the command name with a space. A space is a **delimiter**. A delimiter is used to indicate where one part of a command ends and another begins. Other characters that can be used as delimiters are the comma (,) semicolon (;), equals sign (=), and Tab key. A period is not a delimiter.

The current drive is still the drive containing your master data disk (A or B).

	Hard Disk	**Floppy Disk**
At the:	A>	B>
Type:	DIR C:	DIR A:

The drive specifier following the command name is a parameter. It tells DOS which drive to act on. It does not change the current drive. The space following the command name is the delimiter.

Press:

Your display screen should list all the files on the hard disk or the DOS disk in the A drive.

Again, if there are more files than can be shown at one time on the display screen, the files and information at the beginning of the directory scroll off the top of the screen to allow the files at the bottom of the directory to be seen. The current drive is still the drive containing your master data disk (A or B).

Using Directory Pause and Wide

As you noticed, when the screen was filled with filenames, the files listed at the beginning of the directory moved or scrolled off the top of the screen to allow the rest of the directory listing to be seen. This may be unsatisfactory because the filename you want to check may not be visible. The directory command can be altered so that it will pause, or stop the scrolling of filenames, when the screen is full. The command to do this is DIR/P (**DIR**ectory/**P**ause). The / is a **switch** character that is entered following the DIR command. It tells the command to handle a task in a different manner. A switch can be used in many DOS commands. The switch character is then followed by the appropriate switch letter or number, in this case P for pause.

To use this command to display the directory of files on your master data disk,

Type: DIR/P
Press: ⬅

When the screen is filled, the filenames do not continue to scroll off the top of the screen. Instead, the DIR command pauses the display of filenames. To continue viewing the filenames, following the directions on the bottom of the screen,

Press: any key

DOS 5.0 note: The message "(continuing A:\)" for hard-disk users or "(continuing B:\)" for floppy-disk users is displayed at the top of each continued screen of filenames.

Continue to press any key until all the filenames on the disk have been displayed and the command prompt A> (B>) appears on the screen again.

Another way to view a directory of filenames allows more files to be viewed on the display at one time. This is done by displaying the filenames across the width of the screen. This command is DIR/W (**DIR**ectory/**W**ide).

Type: DIR/W
Press: ⬅

Your screen should be similar to Figure 1-6.

FIGURE 1-6

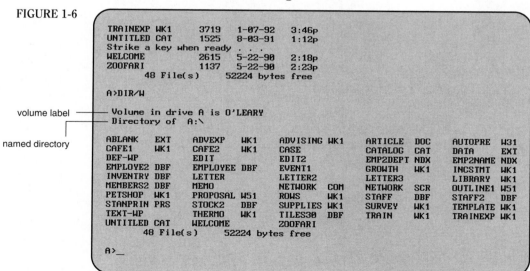

The files are listed across the screen. Notice that the file size, date, and time information are omitted. The lines of information above the list of filenames tell you whether the disk has been assigned a volume label and the name of the directory

being viewed. (The volume label on your disk may be different than the one in Figure 1-6.) You will learn about volume labels later in this lab and about directories in the next lab.

DOS 4.0 and 5.0 note: Your screen may show an additional line of information above the filenames. It will tell you the volume serial number assigned to the disk.

Next you will display a directory wide listing for the files on the C (or A) drive. When adding a parameter to a command, the switch character follows the parameter.

	Hard Disk	**Floppy Disk**
At the:	A>	B>
Type:	DIR C:/W	DIR A:/W
Press:	⏎	⏎

The directory listing for the files on the C (or A) drive is displayed. The default drive is still A (or B).

Clearing the Screen (CLS)

At times the display screen can get cluttered. This makes reading the screen difficult. For example, your display currently shows the end of the listing of files from the directory wide listing of the current drive and all the files in response to the directory wide listing of the files on the C (or A) drive. Although there is room at the bottom of the screen to enter further commands, it would be easier to read if the screen was erased or cleared first. The DOS command to erase the display screen is CLS (**CL**ear **S**creen). This is an internal command.

Type: CLS
Press: ⏎

Your screen should be similar to Figure 1-7.

FIGURE 1-7

A>_

home position

All information on the screen is erased, and the DOS prompt and cursor are placed in the upper left corner (**home** position) of the screen. Now when you issue the next command, the screen will be much easier to read.

To change your default drive back to C for hard-disk users and A for floppy-disk users,

	Hard Disk	**Floppy Disk**
Type:	C:	A:
Press:	⏎	⏎

Formatting a Disk (FORMAT) and Assigning a Volume Label (/V)

Before a new disk can be used, you must **format** or convert it from a generic state into a form that can be used by your computer. Disks are shipped from the manufacturer in a blank (**unformatted**) form so that they can be used by a variety of computers. You need to format a new disk so you can create a **backup,** or duplicate, copy of the master data disk for your own use.

The DOS command to format a new disk is FORMAT. The FORMAT command initializes or prepares a new disk to accept DOS information and files. Specifically, it sets up and labels the **tracks** (concentric rings where data is stored on the disk) and **sectors** (divisions of the tracks) on the disk to accept information. It checks the tracks for any bad spots that cannot be used to store information and marks off these areas so they cannot be used. It also sets up the area on the disk where the directory of files will be maintained.

Any disk, old or new, can be formatted. However, if you format a used disk, any files or information on it will be erased during formatting. Before formatting a disk, it is a good practice to display a directory listing of the disk to confirm that it does not contain any files, or that the files on the disk are files you no longer need.

The FORMAT command requires that you include the drive containing the disk you want to format as a parameter. For example, the command to format a disk in the A drive would be FORMAT A:. You can also specify that you want to assign the disk a volume name or identification. To tell the FORMAT command to perform the extra task of assigning a **volume label** to the disk, the switch /V is used. The command to format a disk in the A drive and to assign it a volume label would be FORMAT A:/V.

DOS 4.0 and 5.0 note: You do not need to add the /V switch to the FORMAT command. These versions automatically ask you to enter a volume label as part of FORMAT.

As discussed earlier, some DOS commands such as VER are stored in RAM memory and are called internal commands. Others require that the program statements are read into memory every time the command is used. They are called external commands. FORMAT is an external command.

You are now ready to format your first new disk. You will format the disk and assign it a volume label. The volume label could identify the contents of the disk or, as you will use it, the name of the owner of the disk. You will enter your last name as the volume label.

Note: Disks vary in size and density. Therefore the FORMAT command you may need to use may differ slightly from the one presented below. Your instructor will tell you what changes you need to make.

Hard-Disk System:

Remove the master data disk from the A drive.
You will tell DOS to format the blank disk, which will be located in the A drive, and assign it a volume label. The DOS files are stored in a division of the hard disk called a directory (you will learn about directories in Lab 2). You must be in the directory containing DOS when an external command is issued or your computer must be set up to accept DOS commands from any drive. This manual assumes that your computer has been set up to accept DOS commands from any drive or directory. If this is not the case, your instructor will provide you with additional instructions.
The command to format a disk in the A drive and assign it a volume name is FORMAT A:/V. If you need to format the disk in the B drive, replace the A: with B: in the following instructions. At the C>,

Type: **FORMAT A:/V**
Press: ⏎

Notice that the C-drive light goes on as the program to format a disk is read into memory.

> **Warning:** Be especially careful when formatting from a hard disk that you do not accidentally format the hard disk, because all your programs and files will be erased.

Floppy-Disk System:

Remove the master data disk from the B drive. When you issue an external command, the DOS disk should be in the A drive and the default drive must be the drive containing the DOS files.
Your DOS disk (labeled Program, Startup, or Install) should be in the A drive. If you are using 5-1/4-inch disks, place a write-protect tab over the write-protect notch of the DOS disk. If you are using 3-1/2-inch disks, open the window to write-protect the DOS disk. Write-protecting the disk will prevent accidental erasing or writing on the disk. However, files can still be read from the disk.
The A drive should be the default drive. If it is not, change the default drive to A.
You will tell DOS to format the blank disk, which will be located in the B drive, and assign it a volume label. The command to format a disk in the B drive and assign it a volume label is FORMAT B:/V. At the A>,

Type: **FORMAT B:/V**
Press: ⏎

Notice that the A-drive light goes on as the program to format a disk is read into memory.

Note: If the message "Bad command or file name" is displayed, you may have entered the command incorrectly. If so, try again. Alternatively, DOS may have been unable to locate the FORMAT program files on the disk. To correct this if you have a floppy-disk system, insert a different DOS disk (labeled Operating or Support) in the drive and try again. Otherwise, check with your instructor.

Your screen should be similar to Figure 1-8.

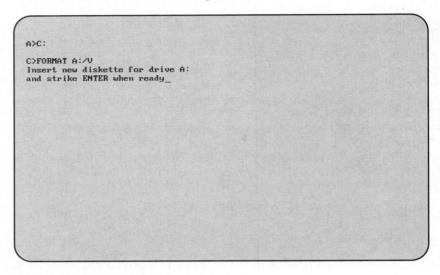

```
A>C:

C>FORMAT A:/V
Insert new diskette for drive A:
and strike ENTER when ready_
```

FIGURE 1-8

The message on the screen instructs you to insert the disk you want to format in the drive you specified. If the drive is not correct, you cancel the command by pressing (CTRL) - (BREAK). Following the directions on the screen, insert a new disk, label side up, in the A or B drive. If necessary, close the drive door. To continue the command,

Press: (↵)

While the disk is being formatted, a message is displayed on the screen. Depending upon your version of DOS, it may display "Head: 0 Cylinder: 0," "Formatting...," or "x percent of disk formatted." All these messages are telling you that the disk is in the process of being formatted.

DOS 5.0 note: Your screen will also display the message "Checking existing disk format" before formatting begins. If your disk is a different density than can be formatted using the default format settings, or if it has been previously formatted using different format settings, another message will be displayed: "Existing format differs from that specified. The disk cannot be unformatted. Proceed with Format?" Check with your instructor. If the format process begins, your screen will also tell you the density, such as 1.44MB, at which the disk is being formatted.

When formatting is complete, your screen should be similar to Figure 1-9.

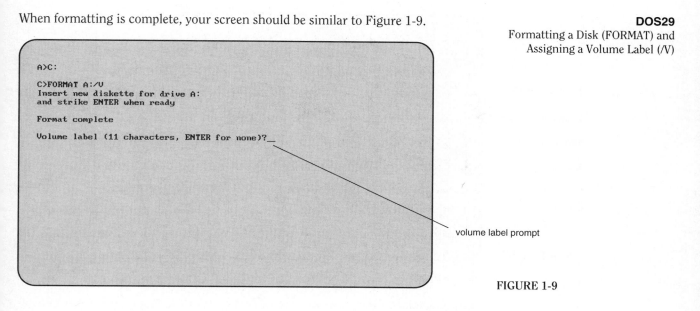

```
A>C:

C>FORMAT A:/U
Insert new diskette for drive A:
and strike ENTER when ready

Format complete

Volume label (11 characters, ENTER for none)?_
```
volume label prompt

FIGURE 1-9

The message "Format complete" is displayed.

The prompt "Volume label (11 characters, ENTER for none)?" is displayed. As you can see from the prompt, a volume label cannot be longer than 11 characters. If you did not want to enter a volume label after all, you could simply press ⏎ to leave the volume label blank.

To enter your last name as the volume label (in place of O'LEARY, type your last name),

Type: **O'LEARY** (type your last name)
Press: ⏎

Your screen should be similar to Figure 1-10A (or Figure 1-10B for DOS 4.0 and 5.0).

FIGURE 1-10A

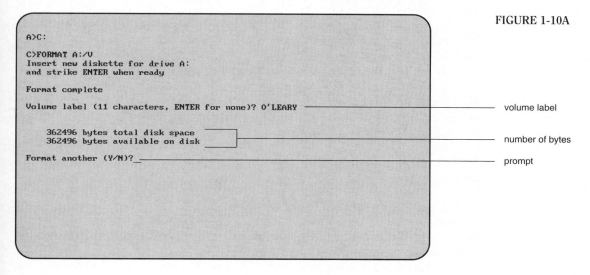

```
A>C:

C>FORMAT A:/U
Insert new diskette for drive A:
and strike ENTER when ready

Format complete

Volume label (11 characters, ENTER for none)? O'LEARY
```
volume label

```
   362496 bytes total disk space
   362496 bytes available on disk
```
number of bytes

```
Format another (Y/N)?_
```
prompt

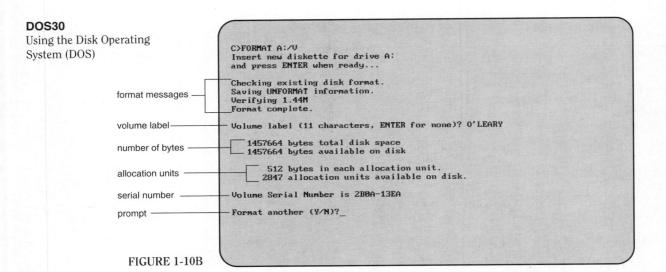

format messages

volume label

number of bytes

allocation units

serial number

prompt

```
C>FORMAT A:/V
Insert new diskette for drive A:
and press ENTER when ready...

Checking existing disk format.
Saving UNFORMAT information.
Verifying 1.44M
Format complete.
Volume label (11 characters, ENTER for none)? O'LEARY

  1457664 bytes total disk space
  1457664 bytes available on disk

    512 bytes in each allocation unit.
   2847 allocation units available on disk.
Volume Serial Number is 2B0A-13EA
Format another (Y/N)?_
```

FIGURE 1-10B

The volume label, your last name, is entered on the disk. The total number of bytes on the disk and bytes available for use are displayed.

DOS 4.0 and 5.0 note: In addition to the information about available bytes, your screen will tell you how many bytes are in bad sectors (if there are any), the number of bytes available in each allocation unit, how many allocation units were created (indicates how DOS has divided the available disk for file storage into groups of sectors), and the serial number.

Next DOS asks whether you want to format another disk. If you wanted to format another disk, you would type "Y" for "Yes." To end formatting using this command,

Type: N
Press: ⏎

The DOS prompt is displayed again. You have formatted your disk and it is now ready to be used. Remove the formatted disk from the A (or B) drive.

To show that this disk has been formatted, you will put a label on it. Before affixing the label to the disk, write your name and the words "DATA DISK" on the label. If you need to write on a label that is already on a 5 1/4-inch disk, use a felt-tip pen only. This disk will be used to hold the backup copy of the files from the master data disk. Place the label on the disk.

Formatting a Disk and Copying the Operating System

If your instructor wants you to format additional disks to hold backup copies of the application software programs you will be using in the labs, follow the instructions below to format additional disks. Otherwise read the information in this section, but do not follow the instructions.

If you have a floppy-disk system, you may also want the DOS FORMAT command to copy the three operating system files (COMMAND.COM, IBMDOS.COM or

MSDOS.SYS, and IBMBIO.COM or IO.SYS) from the DOS disk onto the disk you are formatting during the format procedure. Copying the DOS system files to your disk during formatting will make your disk bootable. That is, you will not need the DOS disk when starting the computer system. The /S (**System**) switch copies the three operating system files to the disk during the FORMAT command.

Generally, the operating system files are only copied to disks that will hold copies of your application software programs. Sometimes, however, the application software program is too large and there is not enough disk space to have both the DOS programs and the application software programs on one disk.

Hard-Disk System:

To format additional disks, follow the formatting procedure presented in the previous section, repeating it as many times as needed. When DOS asks if you need to format another disk, type "Y" to respond "Yes" to the prompt. Label the disks appropriately.

Floppy-Disk System:

You should format the disks using both the /V and /S switches. The command from the A> would be: **FORMAT B:/V/S.** When DOS asks if you need to format another disk, type "Y" to respond "Yes" to the prompt. Repeat the format procedure as many times as needed. Label the disks appropriately.

After formatting a disk using the /S switch, display a directory listing. You will see that there is an extra file on the newly formatted disk. It is the COMMAND.COM file that was copied to the disk while it was formatted with /S. The other two operating system files were also copied to the disk; however, they do not appear in the file directory because they are **hidden files**.

Copying a File (COPY) to Another Disk

Now that your disk has been formatted, it is ready to be used to store information. You will use the disk to hold a copy of the files from the master data disk. The master data disk contains all the files you will need to run labs selected by your instructor.

Whenever you copy a file, you are creating a backup or duplicate copy of the file. You can create a backup copy of a single file or as many files on a disk as you want. Because both floppy and hard disks can be damaged, thus making all or some of the files on them unreadable, it is important to make backup copies of files so that you do not have to recreate them if the disk is damaged.

The COPY command lets you copy a single file, several files, or all files from one disk to another. It is an internal command. Therefore, if you are using a floppy-disk system, the DOS disk does not need to be in the drive. The disk you want to copy files from is called the **source** disk. The source disk in this case will be the master data disk. The disk that you want to copy files to is called the **target** disk. The target disk will be your newly formatted blank disk.

To clear the display,

Type: **CLS**

Press: ⏎

Hard-Disk System:

The instructions that follow assume that you are copying your data files from one floppy disk to another. If you are copying your data files from the hard drive, your instructor will provide alternate instructions.

Place the master data disk in drive A. Change the default drive to A.
Place the formatted blank disk in drive B.

One disk drive note: If your computer system has a hard disk and only one floppy-disk drive, DOS will treat your single drive as both the A and B drives during the copy procedure. Begin the copy procedure with the master data disk in the drive.

Floppy-Disk System:

Remove the DOS disk from the A drive and place the master data disk in the A drive.
Place the formatted blank disk in the B drive.

First let's take a look at the files on the master data disk in the A drive. The A> should be displayed. If it is not, change the default to the A drive. At the A>,

Type: **DIR/W**
Press: ⏎

There are 48 files on this disk (the number of files on your data disk may be different). Notice that some files do not have a file extension. A file extension is not a required part of a filename. If there is a filename extension, it must be used when issuing a DOS command, such as the COPY command, that requires a filename as part of the command. (See the earlier Overview section on "Naming a File" for information on filenames.)

You will copy the file ABLANK.EXT from the source disk in the A drive to the target disk in the B drive.

The complete DOS command to copy this file would be written as shown in Figure 1-11A. The only two delimiters (spaces) used in this command are after the DOS command name (COPY) and before the target drive specifier. The filename and extension are separated by a period.

The same command can be entered without the source drive specified. If you do not enter a source drive, the default (current) drive would be assumed by DOS to be the drive containing the source disk. The command then would appear as in Figure 1-11B.

FIGURE 1-11A

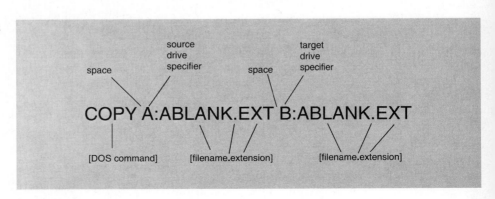

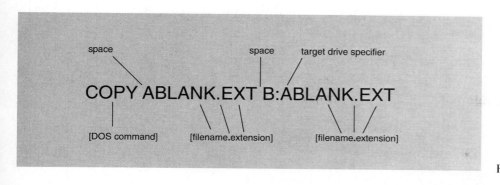

FIGURE 1-11B

It can be shortened even more by omitting the filename and extension following the target drive specifier. This is because DOS assumes that you want to copy the file using the same filename as on the source disk. The command then is written as in Figure 1-11C.

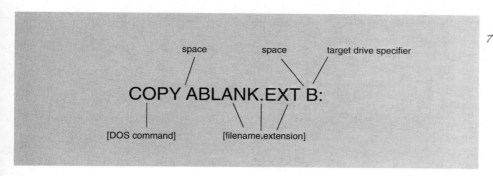

FIGURE 1-11C

At the A>, enter the COPY command exactly as shown below.

Type: **COPY ABLANK.EXT B:**
Press: ⌨

As the file is read from the disk in the A drive and copied to the disk in the B drive, first the A drive light goes on and then the B drive light goes on. Whenever drive A's light goes on, it is reading a file from that drive. Whenever drive B's light goes on, it is writing the file onto the disk.

One disk drive note: If you have a hard disk and only one floppy-disk drive, DOS will prompt you to insert a disk for the B drive. Remove the master data disk, insert the target disk in the drive, and press ⌨.

Your screen should be similar to Figure 1-12.

```
A>DIR/W

 Volume in drive A is O'LEARY
 Directory of  A:\

ABLANK    EXT     ADVEXP    WK1    ADVISING WK1     ARTICLE   DOC     AUTOPRE  W31
CAFE1     WK1     CAFE2     WK1    CASE             CATALOG   CAT     DATA     EXT
DEF-WP            EDIT             EDIT2            EMP2DEPT  NDX     EMP2NAME NDX
EMPLOYE2  DBF     EMPLOYEE  DBF    EVENT1           GROWTH    WK1     INCSTMT  WK1
INVENTRY  DBF     LETTER           LETTER2          LETTER3           LIBRARY  WK1
MEMBERS2  DBF     MEMO             NETWORK   COM    NETWORK   SCR     OUTLINE1 W51
PETSHOP   WK1     PROPOSAL  W51    ROWS      WK1    STAFF     DBF     STAFF2   DBF
STANPRIN  PRS     STOCK2    DBF    SUPPLIES  WK1    SURVEY    WK1     TEMPLATE WK1
TEXT-WP           THERMO    WK1    TILES30   DBF    TRAIN     WK1     TRAINEXP WK1
UNTITLED  CAT     WELCOME          ZOOFARI
          48 File(s)       52224 bytes free

A>COPY ABLANK.EXT B:
        1 File(s) copied

A>_
```

FIGURE 1-12

confirmation message

DOS tells you that one file has been copied, and the command prompt is displayed again.

Copying Multiple Files

You could continue to copy each file individually from the source disk to the target disk, but that would take a lot of time. A quicker method to copy all the files from one disk to another is to use DOS **global filename characters**, called wildcards, as part or all of the filename. **Wildcard characters** can be used in any DOS command that requires a filename as part of the command. The two wildcard characters are * and ?. They are interpreted as follows:

?   Match any one character in the filename

*   Match any number of characters in the filename

For example, to copy a file with the filename ART1.DOC, any character can be replaced with a ?. If the 1 in the filename is replaced with a ? (ART?.DOC), the command to copy this file is then written as COPY ART?.DOC B:. This command tells DOS to copy all files on the disk beginning with ART, having any next character (?), and having the file extension .DOC, from the default drive to the disk in the B drive. For example, this command would copy the files ARTS.DOC and ART2.DOC, but it would not copy a file named ARTICLE.DOC because there are too many characters.

To copy all the files with a filename extension of .DOC, the filename is replaced by an *. The command is then written as COPY *.DOC B: This command tells DOS to copy any filename (*) with a file extension of .DOC from the disk in the default drive to the disk in the B drive. For example, the files MEMO.DOC and ARTS.DOC would be copied, but ARTS.DOT would not because the file extension does not match.

Since you need to copy all the files from the disk in drive A to the disk in drive B, you can use a wildcard character in place of both the filename and the extension (*.*). The command to copy all the files is written as COPY *.* B:. This command tells DOS to copy every file (any filename and any filename extension) on the disk in the default drive (A) to the disk in the B drive.

Clear the display (CLS).

One disk drive note: If your computer system has a hard drive and only one floppy-disk drive, read the directions below; however, follow the alternate instructions in the "One disk drive note" below.

Type: **COPY *.* B:**

Press: ⏎

As each file is copied, the drive lights go on and off as the file is read from one drive and copied to the other. The name of each file is displayed after it is copied.

Your screen should be similar to Figure 1-13.

FIGURE 1-13

```
MEMO
NETWORK.COM
NETWORK.SCR
OUTLINE1.W51
PETSHOP.WK1
PROPOSAL.W51
ROWS.WK1
STAFF.DBF
STAFF2.DBF
STANPRIN.PRS
STOCK2.DBF
SUPPLIES.WK1
SURVEY.WK1
TEMPLATE.WK1
TEXT-WP
THERMO.WK1
TILES30.DBF
TRAIN.WK1
TRAINEXP.WK1
UNTITLED.CAT
WELCOME
ZOOFARI
     48 File(s) copied ───────────────────────── total files copied

A>_
```

When all the files are copied, a message tells you the number of files copied, and then the command prompt appears again.

When you use the COPY command, DOS reads each file individually from the source disk into memory and copies it to the target disk. It has to switch back and forth between the drives, making COPY rather slow when you are copying many files. Another, faster command that can be used to copy large numbers of files is XCOPY. XCOPY is an external command.

XCOPY reads as many files as it can store in memory at a time and then copies them as a batch to the target disk. This makes the copy procedure much faster. It also copies directories and subdirectories (you will learn about these features in Lab 2). The command to copy all files from the source disk in drive A to the formatted target disk in drive B would be XCOPY A:*.* B:.

One disk drive note: If you used the COPY command to copy your files, you would need to swap disks many times. To avoid this, use the XCOPY command. You will only need to swap disks a few times. From the C>, the command is: XCOPY A:*.* B:.

Once copying is complete, let's check to see if the files have actually been transferred to your newly created backup data disk.

Clear the display screen (CLS). With the master data disk in drive A, at the A>,

Type: **DIR/W**
Press: ⏎

The directory of the files on the master data disk is displayed.

One disk drive note: If your computer system has a hard disk and one floppy-disk drive, remove the master data disk from the drive and insert the backup data disk in the drive when directed to switch disks by DOS in the following instructions.

To compare the listing of files on the master data disk with the files on your newly created backup data disk in the B drive,

Type: **DIR B:/W**
Press: ⏎

Your screen should be similar to Figure 1-14.

FIGURE 1-14

volume label

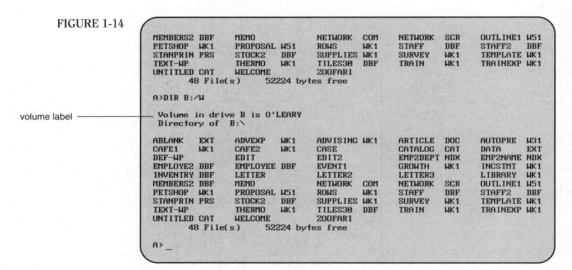

All the files that were on the master data disk are now on the previously blank disk in the B drive. Notice the volume label on your newly created data disk. Your last name should appear following the volume statement where O'LEARY appears in Figure 1-14. This is the volume label you entered as part of the FORMAT command.

Note: If you need to make backup copies of the application software programs you will be using, use the COPY *.* command as above to copy the program files to your additional blank, formatted disks. Label the disks appropriately.

Hard-Disk System:

Remove your newly created data disk from the B drive and place it in the A drive. Put the master data disk away.
   Clear the screen.

Floppy-Disk System:

Remove the master data disk from the A drive and put it away. Place the DOS disk in the A drive. Your newly created data disk should be in the B drive.
   Clear the screen.

Another DOS command, DISKCOPY, can also be used to copy all files from one floppy disk to another floppy disk. This command makes an exact duplicate of the source disk. First it formats the target disk. Then it duplicates the source disk onto the target disk. It cannot be used to copy floppy disks that are different sizes and densities. The advantages of using DISKCOPY are that it is faster than COPY and it formats at the same time. However, because DISKCOPY makes an exact duplicate of the source disk, there are several disadvantages.

The first problem has to do with disk fragmentation. When DOS saves a file to disk, it tries to locate enough empty space on the disk to hold the entire file. If it cannot find enough space, it saves the file in pieces in whatever areas on the disk it can locate. As a disk is used, the files become fragmented or scattered over different locations on the disk. This means it takes longer to retrieve all the parts of the file and results in unnecessary wear and tear on the disk and the drive heads and motor. The DISKCOPY command will copy the fragmented files exactly as they appear on the source disk to the target disk. In contrast, the COPY command copies each file individually; thus files that are fragmented on the source disk are most likely copied to contiguous locations, or "put back together," on the target disk.

The second problem is that DISKCOPY will write a copy of the data on the source disk onto bad sectors of the target disk. This happens even after the FORMAT command has roped off the bad sectors. When data is copied onto the bad sectors, the information on the copy in those areas is unusable.

For these reasons DISKCOPY is usually used only to make copies of commercial software. If you use this command, the format is DISKCOPY A: B:. The first drive specified is the source drive and the second is the target drive.

Copying a File to the Same Disk

You can also copy a file to the same disk; however, you must give the file a different filename.

First you will try to copy the file ABLANK.EXT to the same disk using the same filename.

Hard-Disk System:

At the A>,

Type: COPY ABLANK.EXT A:
Press:

Floppy-Disk System:

Change the current drive to B. At the B>,

Type: COPY ABLANK.EXT B:
Press:

Your screen should be similar to Figure 1-15.

error message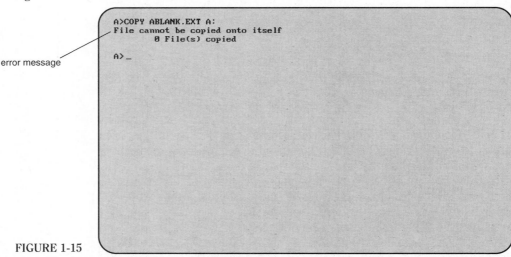

```
A>COPY ABLANK.EXT A:
File cannot be copied onto itself
        0 File(s) copied

A> _
```

FIGURE 1-15

The message "File cannot be copied onto itself" is displayed. Below this, a second message reads "0 file(s) copied."

The command could not be completed because the filename already exists on the disk. To correct this, you need to change the COPY command to include a new filename. Rather than retype the entire command again, you can have DOS retype the previous command for you. Then you can change (edit) the command. To try this,

Press: F3

The COPY command is displayed following the command prompt. The cursor is positioned at the end of the command (in this case, immediately following the target drive specifier). To correct the command, you will enter a different filename following the target drive specifier. You will copy the file ABLANK.EXT to ABLANK.BAK.

Type: ABLANK.BAK

If you have a hard-disk system, the command should now read, "COPY ABLANK.EXT A:ABLANK.BAK." (If you have a floppy-disk system, it should read, "COPY A BLANK.EXT B:ABLANK.BAK.") If your entry is not the same, correct it by pressing Bksp to delete incorrect characters to the left of the cursor, and then retype the entry correctly.

Press: ⏎

The COPY command is successfully completed.
To see both filenames, display a directory wide listing. ABLANK.BAK is the last file in the directory listing.
Clear the screen.

Checking the Disk (CHKDSK)

Another useful command, which reports in more detail than a DIR command on how much space is available on the disk, is the CHKDSK (**CH**ec**K** Di**SK**) command. This command provides a status report on both the disk and RAM memory. CHKDSK is an external command.

You will use this command to check your data disk.

Hard-Disk System:

At the A>,

Type: CHKDSK

Press: ⏎

Floppy-Disk System:

The DOS disk should be in the A drive. At the B>,

Type: A: CHKDSK B:

Press: ⏎

Note: If the message "Bad command or file name" is displayed, you may have entered the command incorrectly. If so, try again. Alternatively, DOS may have been unable to locate the CHKDSK program files on the disk. To correct this if you have a floppy-disk system, insert a different DOS disk (labeled Operating or Support) in the drive and try again. Otherwise, check with your instructor.

Your screen should be similar to Figure 1-16A (or Figure 1-16B for DOS 4.0 and 5.0).

FIGURE 1-16A

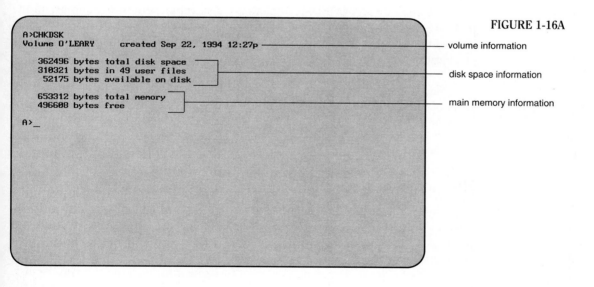

```
A>CHKDSK
Volume O'LEARY     created Sep 22, 1994 12:27p ———————————— volume information

    362496 bytes total disk space
    310321 bytes in 49 user files ———————————— disk space information
     52175 bytes available on disk

    653312 bytes total memory
    496608 bytes free     ———————————— main memory information

A>_
```

```
A>chkdsk

Volume O'LEARY      created 09-22-1994 11:59a ———————— volume information
Volume Serial Number is 3B47-1305 ———————————————— serial number

   1457664 bytes total disk space ┐
    310321 bytes in 49 user files  ├——————————————— disk space information
   1147343 bytes available on disk ┘

       512 bytes in each allocation unit ┐
      2847 total allocation units on disk ├———————— allocation unit information
      2313 available allocation units on disk ┘

    655360 total bytes memory ┐
    461376 bytes free         ├————————— main memory information
                              ┘

A>_
```

FIGURE 1-16B

The information CHKDSK displays is divided into several areas. The upper area displays information about the disk. The disk report tells you how many bytes can be stored on the disk (total disk space), the number of bytes used in files, and how much disk space is still available. If your disk has bad sectors or contains directories (you will learn about directories in Lab 2), CHKDSK will display the bytes used by these areas also.

The lower area displays information about main memory. Specifically, it tells you how much main memory your computer has and how much is available (free) for use.

DOS 4.0 and 5.0 note: CHKDSK displays the disk volume and serial number in the first two lines. In addition to the information about disk space, CHKDSK displays information about the number of bytes available in each allocation unit, the number of allocation units on the disk, and the number of available allocation units.

Additionally, if a problem has been detected by the CHKDSK command, instead of the disk status report DOS will display diagnostic messages. If this occurs, see your instructor.

Clear the screen.

Renaming a File (REN)

Sometimes a filename may be confusing to you or it may no longer be descriptive of the file contents. In that case you may want to rename it. DOS makes this easy for you to do. To change the name of a file, the RENAME (REN) command is used. This command is an internal command.

The new filename must be a different filename from any other files on the disk. If the filename already exists, DOS will not rename the file and will display the message "Duplicate filename or File not found." You do not include a target drive specifier when using the RENAME command because the command replaces the existing filename with the new filename on the same disk.

The ABLANK.EXT file is a file that does not contain information you will need to run the labs. You will change the filename ABLANK.EXT to EMPTY.EXT.

At the A> (or B>),

Type: **RENAME ABLANK.EXT EMPTY.EXT**

Press: (⏎)

DOS does not display a message confirming that the file was successfully renamed. To make sure the filename was changed, display a directory wide listing.

Your screen should be similar to Figure 1-17.

FIGURE 1-17

```
A>RENAME ABLANK.EXT EMPTY.EXT

A>DIR/W

 Volume in drive A is O'LEARY
 Directory of  A:\

EMPTY    EXT     ADVEXP   WK1     ADVISING WK1     ARTICLE  DOC     AUTOPRE  W31
CAFE1    WK1     CAFE2    WK1     CASE             CATALOG  CAT     DATA     EXT
DEF-WP           EDIT             EDIT2            EMP2DEPT NDX     EMP2NAME NDX
EMPLOYE2 DBF     EMPLOYEE DBF     EVENT1           GROWTH   WK1     INCSTMT  WK1
INVENTRY DBF     LETTER           LETTER2          LETTER3          LIBRARY  WK1
MEMBERS2 DBF     MEMO             NETWORK  COM     NETWORK  SCR     OUTLINE1 W51
PETSHOP  WK1     PROPOSAL W51     ROWS     WK1     STAFF    DBF     STAFF2   DBF
STANPRIN PRS     STOCK2   DBF     SUPPLIES WK1     SURVEY   WK1     TEMPLATE WK1
TEXT-WP          THERMO   WK1     TILES30  DBF     TRAIN    WK1     TRAINEXP WK1
UNTITLED CAT     WELCOME          ZOOFARI          ABLANK   BAK
        49 File(s)       52175 bytes free

A>_
```

renamed file

As you can see, the filename ABLANK.EXT no longer exists. It has been changed to EMPTY.EXT.

Rename the file ABLANK.BAK using the first eight characters of your last name as the filename and the first three characters of your first name as the file extension (i.e., LASTNAME.FST)

Erasing a File (ERASE or DEL)

A file that you no longer need can easily be removed from a disk by using the ERASE or DEL (**DEL**ete) command. Both commands perform the same task. Since you do not need the file EMPTY.EXT, you will remove it from your data disk.

At the A> (or B>),

Type: **ERASE EMPTY.EXT**

Press: (⏎)

DOS does not display a message confirming that the file was successfully deleted. To verify that the file was erased, display a directory wide listing.

Your screen should be similar to Figure 1-18.

```
 UNTITLED CAT     WELCOME         ZOOFARI        ABLANK    BAK
          49 File(s)      51200 bytes free

 A>RENAME ABLANK.BAK LASTNAME.FST

 A>ERASE EMPTY.EXT

 A>DIR/W

  Volume in drive A is O'LEARY
  Directory of  A:\

 ADVEXP    WK1    ADVISING WK1    ARTICLE  DOC    AUTOPRE  W31    CAFE1    WK1
 CAFE2     WK1    CASE            CATALOG  CAT    DATA     EXT    DEF-WP
 EDIT             EDIT2           EMP2DEPT NDX    EMP2NAME NDX    EMPLOYE2 DBF
 EMPLOYEE  DBF    EVENT1          GROWTH   WK1    INCSTMT  WK1    INVENTRY DBF
 LETTER           LETTER2         LETTER3         LIBRARY  WK1    MEMBERS2 DBF
 MEMO             NETWORK  COM    NETWORK  SCR    OUTLINE1 W51    PETSHOP  WK1
 PROPOSAL  W51    ROWS     WK1    STAFF    DBF    STAFF2   DBF    STANPRIN PRS
 STOCK2    DBF    SUPPLIES WK1    SURVEY   WK1    TEMPLATE WK1    TEXT-WP
 THERMO    WK1    TILES30  DBF    TRAIN    WK1    TRAINEXP WK1    UNTITLED CAT
 WELCOME          ZOOFARI         LASTNAME FST
          48 File(s)      52224 bytes free

 A> _
```

FIGURE 1-18

The file is no longer listed in the directory.

Printing the Display Screen

You can print a copy of your display screen if you have a printer connected to your computer. Before printing, if necessary turn the printer on and adjust the paper so that it is properly aligned.

Your screen should still display a directory wide listing of the files on your data disk. To print a copy of the information on your display screen, press (PrtScr) (on some keyboards you need to press (SHIFT)-(PrtScr)).

Press: (PrtScr)

Next, you will erase the file you renamed using your last and first name, using the DEL command. In place of the filename LASTNAME.FST in the command below, substitute the filename containing your last name and first name. At the A> (or B>),

Type: **DEL LASTNAME.FST**
Press: (⮐)

Finally, display a directory wide listing. You should now have 47 files (or one less file than you had originally) on your data disk.

You will continue to learn more about DOS in Lab 2.

Key Terms

operating system	current drive	format
utility program	prompt character	unformatted
booting	command	backup
cold start	command line	track
cold boot	internal command	sector
warm start	external command	volume label
warm boot	drive specifier	hidden file
default	directory	source
prompt	parameter	target
cursor	delimiter	global filename characters
command prompt	switch	wildcard characters
default drive	home	

Command Summary

Command	Action
VER	Displays the DOS version information
A:	Makes the A drive the current drive
B:	Makes the B drive the current drive
C:	Makes the C drive the current drive
DIR	Displays a directory listing
DIR/P	Displays a directory listing, pausing when the screen is full
DIR/W	Displays a directory listing across the width of the screen
CLS	Clears the screen display
FORMAT A:	Formats a disk in the A drive
FORMAT A:/V	Formats the disk and assigns it a volume label
FORMAT A:/S	Formats the disk and copies the system files to it
COPY A:<filename> B:	Copies the specified file from the A disk drive to the B disk drive
COPY A:*.* B:	Copies all files with any filename and file extension from the disk in drive A to the disk in drive B
XCOPY	Copies as many files at a time that can be read into memory from the source disk to the target disk
DISKCOPY	Creates an exact duplicate of the source disk on the target disk
CHKDSK	Provides a status report on both the disk and RAM
REN <filename> <new filename>	Assigns a new filename to the specified file
ERASE <filename>	Removes specified file from disk
DEL <filename>	Removes specified file from disk

Matching

1. A>   _____ **a.** retypes the previous DOS command
2. DOS   _____ **b.** pauses the screen display while displaying a directory listing
3. FORMAT/V   _____ **c.** clears the display screen
4. RENAME   _____ **d.** the default drive is A
5. ERASE   _____ **e.** the IBM disk operating system
6. DIR/P   _____ **f.** the disk whose files you want to copy
7. CLS   _____ **g.** command to assign a new name to a file
8. *.*   _____ **h.** wildcard characters that mean any filename and any file extension
9. source   _____ **i.** command to remove a file from the disk
10. F3   _____ **j.** prompts you to enter a volume label during formatting

Fill-In Questions

1. On the screen below, several items are identified by letter. In the spaces below the screen, enter the correct term for each item.

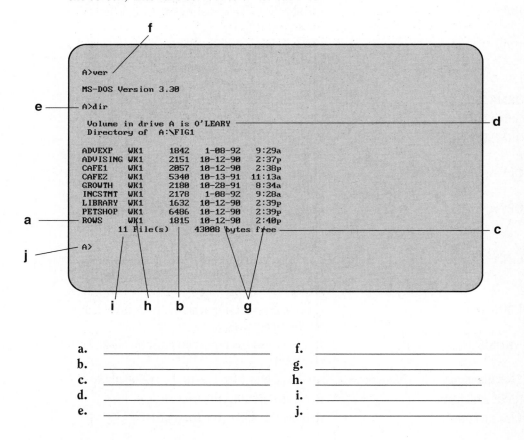

a. _____   f. _____
b. _____   g. _____
c. _____   h. _____
d. _____   i. _____
e. _____   j. _____

2. Complete the following sentences by filling the blank with the correct term.

    a. The _____ command displays the version of DOS that is running.

    b. DOS commands that are not copied into RAM when DOS is loaded are called _____.

    c. The / is a _____ that is entered following the DIR command.

    d. The command to clear the screen is _____.

    e. Before a new disk can be used, it must be _____.

    f. The _____ can be used to identify the disk's contents or the disk's owner.

    g. The disk you want to copy a file to is called the _____.

    h. The wildcard character _____ matches any one character in the filename.

    i. To change the name of a file, the _____ command is used.

    j. _____ or _____ can be used to remove a file from a disk.

Practice Exercises

1. With the computer turned off, perform a cold boot. Then perform a warm boot of the system.

2. Format a blank disk using the /S parameter. Display a directory listing. What is the name of the file displayed? How many bytes are used? Available? Format the disk again but do not use the /S parameter. Display a directory listing. Are any files displayed? How many bytes are used? Available?

3. With your data disk in the A drive,

    Display a directory of the files one screen at a time. Display a directory wide listing. Use wildcard characters to:

        Display all files beginning with the letter C. How many files are listed?

        Display all files with the file extension .DBF. How many files are listed?

        Display all files having any first four characters and a last character of 1 in the filename. How many files are listed?

        Display all files having a filename consisting of up to any five characters. How many files are listed?

4. Using your data disk, copy a file to the same disk using the same filename and the file extension .BAK. Rename the .BAK file using your first name as the filename. Display a directory wide listing. Print the screen. Erase the .BAK file from the disk.

5. Two other function keys, (F1) and (F2), perform similarily to the (F3) DOS function key. Pressing (F1) displays the last command you typed, character by character. (You can also use the (→) in place of (F1).) Pressing (F2) followed by one character of the command displays the command up to that character. The three function keys can also be used in combination. (F3) if used after (F1) or (F2) copies all remaining characters to the command line. Try out the three function keys using different variations of the DIR command.

Managing Your Disk

2

Competencies

In this lab you will learn how to:

1. Create and remove directories.

2. Change directories.

3. Specify paths to files.

4. Change the DOS prompt.

5. Copy a file to a directory.

6. Display the contents of a file.

7. Change directories.

8. Create a batch file.

In the first DOS lab you learned many of the basic DOS commands that allow you to manage the files on your disk. In this lab you will learn about several more complex DOS commands. Specifically, you will learn how to create and use subdirectories and batch files.

Understanding Directories

Load DOS (cold or warm boot). If necessary, respond to the date and time prompts. If you need help, refer to Lab 1.

The DOS prompt C> (or A>) should be displayed on your screen.

Place your data disk in the A (or B) drive. Change the default drive to the drive containing your data disk. Using the /W switch, display a directory listing of the files on your data disk.

The DIR command displays a list of the files on your data disk. All the files are contained in the main or **root directory** of your disk. It does not really have the name "ROOT," but it is called that because it is the point of origin of all other directories. The "Directory of" line on your screen displays the drive specifier followed by a backslash (\). The \ represents the root directory.

The root directory is created during formatting. All disks have a root directory. On a hard disk, the root directory contains the DOS COMMAND.COM file and the two hidden operating system files. On floppy disks, if the disk was formatted using the system switch (/S), these files are also located in the root directory.

As you add more files to the root directory, it gets very crowded and disorganized. This is especially true of hard disks, which can hold large amounts of data. To help organize files into like categories, you can create directories. A **directory** is a subdivision of the root directory. You can create further divisions within each directory by creating **subdirectories**. Technically, other than the root directory, all directories are subdirectories. However, to show relationships between two directories, the word *subdirectory* is used to refer to a directory created under another directory.

For example, you may want to store software programs, and the files you create using these programs, by the type of program. Alternatively, you might want to store your programs and information by project. Let's say that while you are taking this course you want to keep all the files you will be using with the spreadsheet program in a separate directory from the files for the word processing program. Furthermore, you want to separate the files you will be using in each lab by creating a subdirectory for each lab. You could do this in the following manner:

Root Directory:

    Directory 1: Spreadsheet Program Files

        Subdirectory A: Lab 1 data files
        Subdirectory B: Lab 2 data files

    Directory 2: Word Processing Program Files

        Subdirectory A: Lab 1 data files
        Subdirectory B: Lab 2 data files

Rather than keeping all of your files in the root directory and then wondering how all of them relate to each other, the use of directories and subdirectories allows you to organize the files on your disk.

This kind of a directory system is known as a **tree-structured directory**, since a root directory can have many directories, each of which in turn can have many subdirectories, and so on. Imagine the directory as a family tree with the original parents (root) as the base of the tree. Their children are branches (directories) on the tree, and then their grandchildren are branches (subdirectories) from the children (directories).

Graphically, the tree-structured directory (shown upside-down to make it easier to read) would look like this:

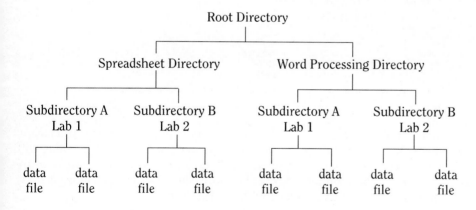

Creating Directories (MD)

To create a directory, you use the MKDIR (**MaKe DIRectory**) command. This command is an internal command and can be abbreviated as MD. You will try this command by creating a directory for the spreadsheet files. A directory, like a file, must be assigned a name. Directory names follow the same rules as filenames: a maximum of eight characters followed by a period, and an extension of one to three characters. Generally, a file extension is not added to a directory name. You will name this directory SSFILES.

Clear the screen. The command to make a directory on the current drive is MD SSFILES. The directory name can be entered in either upper- or lowercase characters.

At the A> (or B>),

Type: **MD SSFILES**
Press: ⏎

Drive A (or B) runs for a second while it records the information for the directory on the disk. To look at the directory,

Type: **DIR/P**
Press: ⏎

Your screen should be similar to Figure 2-1.

FIGURE 2-1

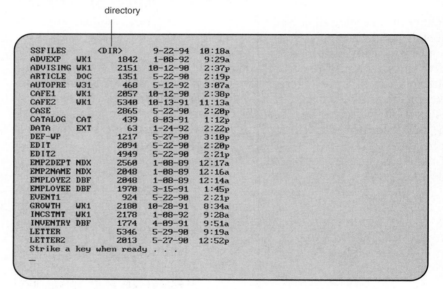

directory

```
SSFILES      <DIR>       9-22-94   10:18a
ADVEXP   WK1    1842     1-08-92    9:29a
ADVISING WK1    2151    10-12-90    2:37p
ARTICLE  DOC    1351     5-22-90    2:19p
AUTOPRE  W31     468     5-12-92    3:07a
CAFE1    WK1    2057    10-12-90    2:38p
CAFE2    WK1    5340    10-13-91   11:13a
CASE            2865     5-22-90    2:20p
CATALOG  CAT     439     8-03-91    1:12p
DATA     EXT      63     1-24-92    2:22p
DEF-WP          1217     5-27-90    3:10p
EDIT            2094     5-22-90    2:20p
EDIT2           4949     5-22-90    2:21p
EMP2DEPT NDX    2560     1-08-89   12:17a
EMP2NAME NDX    2048     1-08-89   12:16a
EMPLOYE2 DBF    2048     1-08-89   12:14a
EMPLOYEE DBF    1970     3-15-91    1:45p
EVENT1           924     5-22-90    2:21p
GROWTH   WK1    2180    10-28-91    8:34a
INCSTMT  WK1    2178     1-08-92    9:28a
INVENTRY DBF    1774     4-09-91    9:51a
LETTER          5346     5-29-90    9:19a
LETTER2         2013     5-27-90   12:52p
Strike a key when ready . . .
_
```

DOS automatically converts the directory name to all uppercase letters (if you entered the name in lowercase) and displays it as a file under the root directory along with the original data files. You can distinguish it from the other files because of the <DIR> message (abbreviation for directory) displayed in place of the file size data.

Press any key until all the files have been displayed.

Next you will create another directory under the root directory and will name it WPFILES. This directory will hold files created using a word processing program. To create another directory,

Type: **MD WPFILES**
Press: ⏎

To display a listing of the files,

Type: **DIR**

Press: ⏎

You should now have two directories on your disk, SSFILES and WPFILES in the root directory.

Changing Directories (CD)

Now you would like to further subdivide the SSFILES directory into two sub-directories, LAB1 and LAB2. A subdirectory is a subdivision created within a directory. To create a subdirectory under the SSFILES directory, you will first move to the SSFILES directory.

The command to move from one directory to another must include a "path." A **path** is a chain of directory names that tells DOS how to maneuver through the directories to find the directory you want. A path shows the directions for finding a directory or file on the disk. It reflects the organization of your directories. The path begins with the root directory. Backslashes separate the different parts of the path.

Even though you have created two directories, you are still in the root directory. The directory you are in is called the **current directory**. By default, when you first access a disk you are in the root directory, which is also the current directory. To change from the root directory to a directory or a subdirectory, you use the CHDIR (**CH**ange **DIR**ectory) command. This command is an internal command and can be abbreviated as CD.

You are now in the root directory of the data disk in the current drive. To enter the command to move into the SSFILES directory,

Type: **CD SSFILES**

Press: ⏎

The current directory is now SSFILES. This is the directory DOS will read and write files to unless instructed to use another directory. But how do you know that you are in this directory? The command prompt still simply displays the current drive letter and the prompt symbol (>).

Note: If your command prompt displays the name of the current directory (such as A:\SSFILES), your command prompt has been customized to display the directory path. You will learn about this feature shortly.

To verify that you are in the SSFILES directory,

Type: **DIR**

Press: ⏎

Your screen should be similar to Figure 2-2.

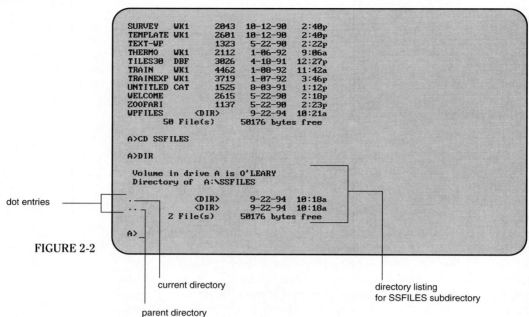

dot entries

FIGURE 2-2

current directory

parent directory

directory listing
for SSFILES subdirectory

The "Directory of" line of the directory listing displays the drive specifier followed by "\SSFILES." The message tells you that the current directory is SSFILES, immediately below the root directory (\). Below this information, two entries are listed as "." and ".." (dot and dot-dot entries). The dot entry represents the directory you are currently viewing. The dot-dot entry represents the **parent directory**, which is the directory one level above the current directory. In this case the root directory is the parent directory of the current directory, SSFILES.

That is:
      SSFILES   .
      Root   ..

You can use the .. entry in place of the directory name to view or move to a directory one level above the current directory. For example, to display a directory wide listing of the root directory files from the current directory, SSFILES,

Type: **DIR..\W**
Press: ⟨⏎⟩

You are now viewing the contents of the root directory. You have not, however, moved back into the root directory; the current directory is still SSFILES. Notice that in a directory wide listing the directory names are enclosed in brackets to distinguish them from filenames.

Changing the Command Prompt (PROMPT)

Displaying a directory listing is one way to find out your location within the directory organization of a disk. However, it is not very convenient. Another way to keep track of the directory you are in without having to type "DIR" is to change the command prompt to display the directory information. The standard command prompt (A>,B>, or C>) does not tell you if you are in a directory or in the root directory.

Note: Your computer may already display the directory information. Even if it does, complete this section to learn about the PROMPT command.

The default command prompt can be changed using the PROMPT command. This is an internal command and is shorthand for the SET PROMPT command. It will allow you to customize the command prompt using symbols called **prompt codes**. All prompt codes begin with a $ and are immediately followed by a prompt code symbol or character. (Your DOS manual provides a listing of all prompt code symbols.) For example, the initial command prompt uses the prompt codes NG. The $N symbol makes DOS display the current drive letter, and the $G symbol makes it display the greater-than (>) character.

The prompt code symbol that will display the current path is $P. To change the default command prompt to display the current path and the greater-than symbol, the prompt codes PG are used.

Clear the screen.

Type: **PROMPT PG**
Press: ⏎

Your screen should be similar to Figure 2-3.

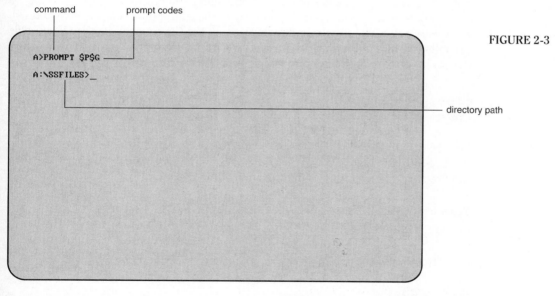

command   prompt codes

```
A>PROMPT $P$G
A:\SSFILES>_
```

directory path

FIGURE 2-3

Your command prompt should now appear as A:\SSFILES> (or B:\SSFILES). The path you have taken is now clearly visible. SSFILES is the current directory. This is helpful because you do not need to use the DIR command to confirm which directory you are in each time you change directories.

Creating a Subdirectory

Next you will create a subdirectory within the SSFILES directory to hold the data files used in Lab 1. This subdirectory will be named LAB1 and will be subordinate to the SSFILES directory. When creating a subdirectory, the current directory must be the directory in which the subdirectory will be created, or you must include the directory path in the MD command instructing DOS where to create the directory. Since the current directory is still SSFILES, you can simply enter the command as MD LAB1. DOS will assume that you want to create the subdirectory under the current directory.

Type: MD LAB1
Press: ⏎

Type: DIR
Press: ⏎

The directory listing now displays "LAB1 <DIR>" within the directory SSFILES. The SSFILES directory is still the current directory. Not until you change directories using the CD command does the current directory change.

Type: CD LAB1
Press: ⏎

LAB1 is now the current directory. You are two directory levels below the root directory. The DOS prompt should now show the path you have taken as A:\SSFILES\LAB1> (or B:\SSFILES\LAB1). From the root directory you moved to the SSFILES directory, and from there to the LAB1 subdirectory.

   Now that you have "pathed" your way to the appropriate subdirectory, you will work your way back to the root directory, using the CD command again. If you type CD followed by two periods (CD..), you will move from the current subdirectory (LAB1) to the parent directory immediately above it (SSFILES).

Type: CD..
Press: ⏎

You are now in the SSFILES directory, and the DOS prompt should be A:\SSFILES> (or B:\SSFILES>). While this is the current directory, you will create another subdirectory, named LAB2, under the current directory.

Type: MD LAB2
Press: ⏎

To move to the parent directory, in this case the root directory,

Type: CD..
Press: ⏎

You are now in the root directory, and the DOS prompt should be A:\> (or B:\>).

Next you want to move into the LAB2 subdirectory. Graphically, you want to flow through the directory as follows:

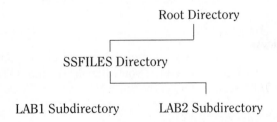

Root Directory

SSFILES Directory

LAB1 Subdirectory   LAB2 Subdirectory

To do this, you could enter the command CD SSFILES and then the command CD LAB2. A faster way, however, is to specify the complete path as part of the CD command.

Type: **CD SSFILES\LAB2**
Press: (←)

You instructed DOS to move from the root directory to the SSFILES directory and finally to the LAB2 subdirectory. The command prompt should now display A:\SSFILES\LAB2> (or B:\SSFILES\LAB2>).

A faster way to move back to the root directory is to type CD followed by a backslash (\). The \ symbol represents the root directory. This command will return you directly to the root directory from any subdirectory level. To return directly to the root directory,

Type: **CD**
Press: (←)

Your screen should be similar to Figure 2-4.

FIGURE 2-4

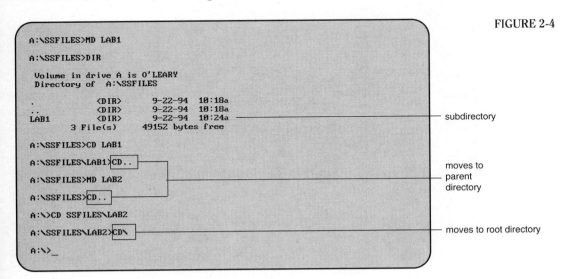

The command prompt should be A:\> (or B:\>), and the root directory is the current directory.

You can also use the \ symbol with many other DOS commands. For example, the command DIR\ will display a directory listing of the files in the root directory from any directory level on the disk without changing the current directory.

Copying a File to a Directory

To copy a file from the root directory into a directory or subdirectory, you must specify the path as part of the COPY command. First you will copy the file DATA.EXT from the root directory to the LAB1 subdirectory of the SSFILES directory. To do this,

Type: **COPY DATA.EXT SSFILES\LAB1**
Press: ⌁

The command instructed DOS to copy the specified file from the current directory (the current directory is assumed by DOS unless another is specified) to the subdirectory LAB1.

If the current directory was not the directory containing the file you wanted to copy, you would also need to specify the file location. For example, if the file you wanted to copy was in the root directory of the disk in drive A, and the current directory was the root directory of drive B, the command to copy the file would be COPY A:DATA.EXT B:\SSFILES\LAB1.

Displaying Directory Structure (TREE)

To verify that the file was copied into the correct directory, you could view a directory listing (DIR). Another way is to use the TREE command. The TREE command displays the relationship between directories and subdirectories on a disk beginning with the root directory if you are using version 3.3 or with the current directory if you are using version 4.0 or 5.0. The TREE command is an external DOS command; therefore, if you are using a floppy-disk system, make sure that the DOS disk is in drive A.

Clear the screen.

Hard Disk:	**Floppy Disk:**
Type: TREE	**A:TREE B:**
Press: ⌁	⌁

Note: If the message "Bad command or file name" is displayed, you may have entered the command incorrectly. If so, try again. Alternatively, if you are using a floppy-disk system, DOS may have been unable to locate the TREE program files on the disk. To correct this, insert a different DOS disk (labeled Operating or Support) in the drive and try again.

Your screen should be similar to Figure 2-5A (or Figure 2-5B for DOS 4.0 and 5.0).

FIGURE 2-5A

```
Sub-directories:   LAB1
                   LAB2


Path: \SSFILES\LAB1

Sub-directories:   None


Path: \SSFILES\LAB2

Sub-directories:   None


Path: \WPFILES

Sub-directories:   None



A:\>_
```

FIGURE 2-5B

```
A:\>TREE
Directory PATH listing for Volume O'LEARY
Volume Serial Number is 3B47-1305
A:.
├─────SSFILES
│     ├─────LAB1
│     └─────LAB2
└─────WPFILES

A:\>_
```

All the directory paths for the disk in drive A (or B) are displayed. As you can see, each of the subdirectories is listed, along with the path used to access each one.

DOS 4.0 and 5.0 note: The screen displays a graphic representation of the directory as a tree. The root directory is displayed at the top of the directory tree. The directories and subdirectories are displayed as branches from the root directory.

However, the files in the directories are not displayed. To list any files in the subdirectories and directories, the /F (Files) switch is used.

Clear the screen.

	Hard Disk	**Floppy Disk**
Type:	TREE /F	A:TREE B:/F
Press:	⏎	⏎

To stop the scrolling of the screen, press (CTRL)-S at any point (hold down (CTRL) and press S at the same time).

Your screen should be similar to Figure 2-6A (or Figure 2-6B for DOS 4.0 and 5.0).

FIGURE 2-6A

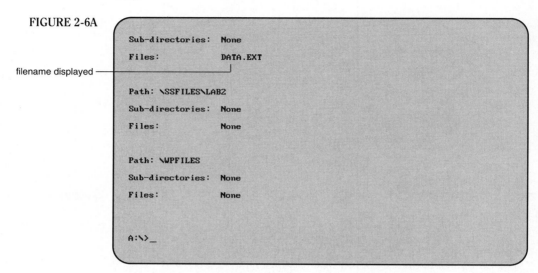

filename displayed

FIGURE 2-6B

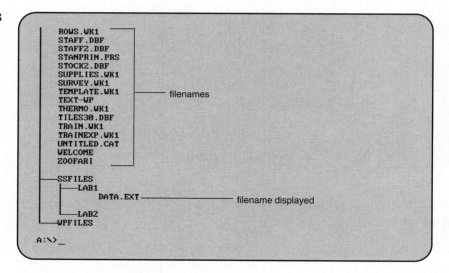

filenames

filename displayed

The directory tree displays all files in the root directory first. Then the directory paths and all files in each directory or subdirectory are listed. Now you can see that the file was copied into the correct directory.

The TREE command gives you a good look at how your disk is organized, and what files are located in the different directories. Whenever you are unfamiliar with the contents of a disk, using this command will let you quickly determine how it is organized.

Next you will move into the LAB1 subdirectory to access the file DATA.EXT. Clear the screen.

Type: **CD SSFILES\LAB1**
Press: ⬅

The DOS prompt shows that you have changed directories and that the current directory is LAB1.

Displaying File Contents (TYPE)

If you want to display the contents of a file while in DOS, you can use the TYPE command. This is an internal DOS command. Although the TYPE command will display the contents of a file on the screen, some files may not be readable. However, most text can be displayed in a legible format. To use this command to display the contents of DATA.EXT,

Type: **TYPE DATA.EXT**
Press: ⬅

Your screen should be similar to Figure 2-7.

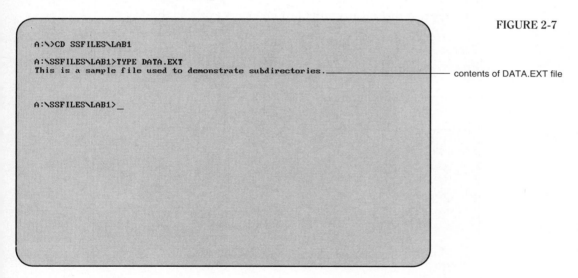

FIGURE 2-7

```
A:\>CD SSFILES\LAB1

A:\SSFILES\LAB1>TYPE DATA.EXT
This is a sample file used to demonstrate subdirectories.———————— contents of DATA.EXT file


A:\SSFILES\LAB1>_
```

The contents of this file consist of one sentence: "This is a sample file used to demonstrate subdirectories."

Removing Directories (RD)

At some point you may no longer need the subdirectories you have created, and you will want to remove them from the disk to save space. (Each directory requires a minimum of 1K, or 1024 characters, of storage.)

Unlike files, the ERASE or DEL commands cannot be used to remove a subdirectory from a disk. The command that will do this is RMDIR or RD (**R**emove **D**irectory). You will remove the LAB1 and LAB2 subdirectories.

Before removing a directory, all files and subdirectories within the directory must be deleted first. To erase the file DATA.EXT,

Type: **ERASE DATA.EXT**
Press: ⏎

The directory (or subdirectory) you want to remove cannot be the current directory. By default, the RD command will remove a subdirectory of the current directory. If you include a path or drive letter with the RD command, you can remove a directory from another location on the disk or from another disk. To move one directory level above the subdirectory you want to remove to make the SSFILES directory current,

Type: **CD..**
Press: ⏎

You should now be in the SSFILES directory.
To remove the subdirectory LAB1,

Type: **RD LAB1**
Press: ⏎

To verify that the subdirectory LAB1 no longer exists on the disk,

Type: **DIR**
Press: ⏎

Your screen should be similar to Figure 2-8.

FIGURE 2-8

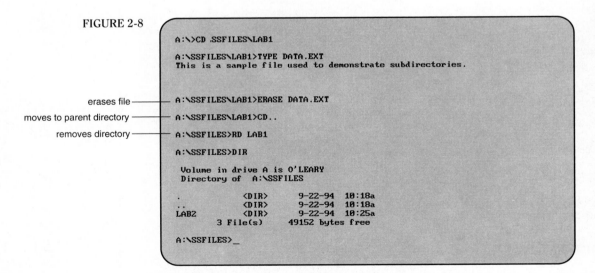

```
A:\>CD .SSFILES\LAB1

A:\SSFILES\LAB1>TYPE DATA.EXT
This is a sample file used to demonstrate subdirectories.


A:\SSFILES\LAB1>ERASE DATA.EXT          erases file

A:\SSFILES\LAB1>CD..                     moves to parent directory

A:\SSFILES>RD LAB1                       removes directory

A:\SSFILES>DIR

  Volume in drive A is O'LEARY
  Directory of   A:\SSFILES

  .            <DIR>        9-22-94  10:18a
  ..           <DIR>        9-22-94  10:18a
  LAB2         <DIR>        9-22-94  10:25a
         3 File(s)     49152 bytes free

A:\SSFILES>_
```

As you can see, the subdirectory LAB1 has been removed.
Remove the subdirectory LAB2.

Next you will remove the directories WPFILES and SSFILES. To do this, you will first make the root directory current, then you will enter the RD command.

Type: CD\
Press: (⏎)
Type: **RD WPFILES**
Press: (⏎)

In a similar manner, remove the SSFILES directory. Display a directory listing.

There should no longer be any subdirectories on your disk. The current directory should be the root directory.

Creating a Batch File

Up to this point you have learned how to use DOS. Now you are going to learn how to make DOS use *itself*. You can do this through the use of batch files.

A **batch file** is a series of DOS commands that are stored in a disk file. When instructed to do so, DOS will execute the commands in the batch file, one line at a time. These commands are executed just as they would be if they were typed in at the keyboard.

So what's the advantage of having a batch file? If you have a task that you will repeat over and over again, such as booting a program, it's better to put the commands in a batch file. This way you won't misspell one of the commands or make another kind of mistake. You can just type the commands once, save them, and then execute them as a batch file.

A batch file can be created in several different ways. One method is to use the COPY CON command. This is similar to the COPY command except, instead of copying a file from a disk or directory, you are copying input from the keyboard, or **con**sole. You specify the filename of the batch file as the target of the COPY command.

You will create a batch file named SAMPLE.BAT. All batch files have a file extension of .BAT. The batch file you will create will contain several of the commands you have learned in these labs, plus several new commands that are commonly used in batch files.

Clear the screen.

Type: **COPY CON SAMPLE.BAT**
Press: (⏎)

The cursor moves down to the next line. Now you can start typing the actual DOS commands you want to record in the batch file. The first command you want your batch file to perform is to clear the screen (CLS).

Type: **CLS**

Make sure you entered this command correctly. Once you press (⏎), you cannot go back and correct the error in the line.

Press: (⏎)

Next you want to display the DOS version.

Type: **VER**
Press:

The next command you will enter is DATE. This command will prompt you to enter the date.

Type: **DATE**
Press:

Next you will enter the command to display the text of the file named DATA.EXT.

Type: **TYPE DATA.EXT**
Press:

The last command you will enter will display a message following the command prompt, and then pause to let the user read and act on the message. To do this, the REMARK (REM) and PAUSE commands are used. REM tells DOS to display on the screen whatever follows the command. PAUSE halts the screen display by temporarily interrupting the execution of the batch file.

Type: **REM This batch program was written by Student Name** (type your name).
Press:
Type: **PAUSE**

That is the entire batch file. To tell DOS that this is the end of the batch file,

Press: (F6)

The (F6) key enters a ^Z character at the end of the batch file. This tells DOS that this is the end of the file and to save the file to disk under the filename specified in the COPY CON command (SAMPLE.BAT).

Press:

Your screen should be similar to Figure 2-9.

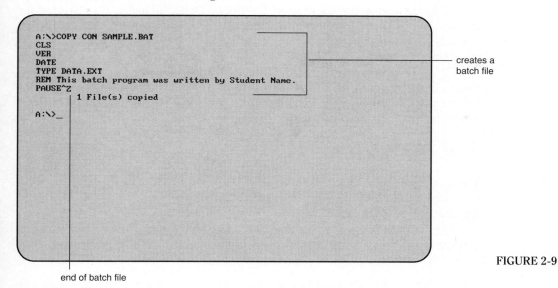

```
A:\>COPY CON SAMPLE.BAT
CLS
VER
DATE
TYPE DATA.EXT
REM This batch program was written by Student Name.
PAUSE^Z
          1 File(s) copied

A:\>_
```

creates a
batch file

end of batch file

FIGURE 2-9

The message "1 File(s) copied" is displayed. The batch file SAMPLE.BAT has been written to the data disk.

To check the contents of this file,

Type: **TYPE SAMPLE.BAT**

Press: ⏎

If you made an error entering the batch file commands, start over again by recreating the file.

A batch file can also be entered using the non-document mode of a word processing program, or with EDLIN (EDIT in DOS 5.0), the DOS line editor program that acts as a limited word processor. Using either of these methods, errors can be easily corrected.

Executing a Batch File

To tell DOS to execute the commands in a batch file, simply type the filename following the prompt. You do not need to enter the .BAT file extension. If you were not in the directory containing the batch file you would need to include the path before the file name. At the A:\> (B:\>),

Type: **SAMPLE**

Press: ⏎

Once DOS locates the file, it is executed one line at a time. First the screen is cleared, then the version information is displayed. Notice that the command as it appears in the batch file is displayed following the command prompt, just as if you had typed it in. The DATE command should be prompting you to enter the date. In response to the prompt, you could enter the date as described at the beginning of Lab 1. However, since the date displayed is acceptable,

Press: ⏎

As soon as you complete the response, the next command is executed. The screen should be displaying the contents of the file DATA.EXT. Finally, the message you entered following the REM command is displayed. Notice that the screen displays not only the message but also the REM command.

Now, in response to the PAUSE command, the screen displays the message "Strike a key when ready..." (DOS 4.0 and 5.0 message is "Press any key to continue..."). The batch program has temporarily suspended execution and is waiting for the user to respond. You can continue execution of the batch file, or cancel it with (CTRL) - (BREAK). To continue,

Press: any key

The command prompt is displayed again.

Using Print Screen, print a copy of your display screen showing the commands executed by the batch file.

Although this was a simple example of a batch file, you can see how batch files can save you time by executing frequently used sequences of DOS commands.

Key Terms

root directory	current directory
directory	parent directory
subdirectory	prompt code
tree-structured directory	batch file
path	

Command Summary

Command	Action
MKDIR or MD	Creates a new directory or subdirectory
CHDIR or CD	Changes directories
DIR..	Displays a directory listing of the parent directory
PROMPT <promptcode>	Changes the command prompt display
CD..	Changes to the parent directory
CD\	Changes to the root directory
TREE	Shows all directory relationships
TREE/F	Shows all directories and files
TYPE <filename>	Displays contents of text files
RMDIR or RD	Removes or deletes a directory or subdirectory
COPY CON <filename.BAT>	Begins creation of a batch file
REM	Records comments in a batch file
PAUSE	Temporarily suspends processing of a batch program
(F6)	Enters a ^Z character that marks the end of a batch file

LAB REVIEW

Matching

1. path
2. MD
3. DIR ..
4. CD
5. (F6)
6. PG
7. COPY CON <filename>
8. TREE
9. RD
10. DATE

_____ a. DOS command to create a directory

_____ b. command that displays directory paths

_____ c. command that displays a directory listing of parent directory

_____ d. chain of directory names used to move through directories and subdirectories

_____ e. removes a directory

_____ f. prompt codes

_____ g. copies entries from the keyboard to a file

_____ h. ends a batch file

_____ i. changes to another directory

_____ j. displays the date prompt

Fill-In Questions

1. On the screen below, several items are identified by letters. In the spaces below the screen, enter the correct term for each item.

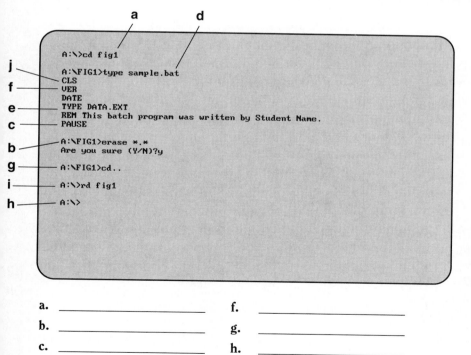

a. _____   f. _____

b. _____   g. _____

c. _____   h. _____

d. _____   i. _____

e. _____   j. _____

2.   Complete the following sentences by filling in the blanks.

   a.   The main DOS directory is called the _____.

   b.   To help you organize files into like categories, you can create _____.

   c.   To create a directory, you use the _____ command.

   d.   The directory you are in is called the _____.

   e.   The method DOS uses to let you access files in a directory is through the use of _____.

   f.   To get from the root directory to a directory, or from a directory to another directory, you use the _____ command.

   g.   The DOS prompt is customized using symbols called _____.

   h.   To verify that a file was copied into the correct directory, you could view a directory listing (DIR) or use the _____ command.

   i.   The _____ command can be use to display the contents of a file on the screen.

   j.   Before removing a directory, all files within the directory must first be _____.

Practice Exercises

1.   Create the following hierarchical directory on your data disk. Use directory names of your choice.

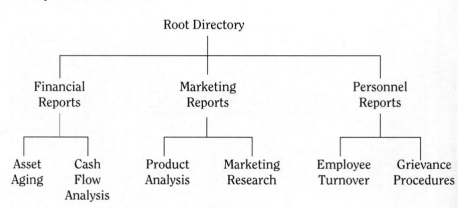

Once you've created this directory, use the TREE command to verify all your directory relationships.

2.   Create and execute a batch file that will copy the file DATA.EXT from the root directory into the Product Analysis directory you created in problem 1. Then have it display the file contents and, finally, erase the file from the subdirectory.

3. Use your data disk to complete the following steps.

    a. Create the following tree-structured directory.

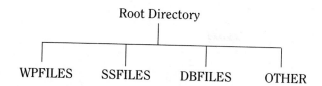

Root Directory

WPFILES   SSFILES   DBFILES   OTHER

    b. Copy the files that have a file extension of .DBF to the directory DBFILES. Make the DBFILES directory current. Display the files in this directory. Display the files in the root directory.

    c. Copy the files for your spreadsheet program to the directory SSFILES (ask your instructor for the file extension). Make the root directory current. Verify that the files are in the correct directory by using the TREE command.

    d. Copy the files with the file extensions .DOC to the WPFILES directory.

    e. Copy the files with the file extensions .BAT, .CAT, .PRS, and .COM to the OTHER directory. Verify that the files are in the correct directory by using the TREE command. *Note:* Use the (CTRL)-S key combination to temporarily halt the scrolling of the screen.

    f. Create a batch file that clears the screen, displays the DOS version, displays a line of text that includes your name, displays the contents of the file AUTOPRE.W31, and displays a directory wide listing for the root directory. Display the contents of the batch file and print the screen. Execute the batch file.

    g. Display a directory wide listing for the root directory. Print the screen. Remove the files from the directories. Remove the directories.

4. *Disk cleanup:* Remove all directories and subdirectories from your data disk. Erase the files DATA.EXT and AUTOPRE.W31 and all files with a .BAT file extension from the root directory.

DOS 3.3-5.0

GLOSSARY OF KEY TERMS

Application software: Computer programs that perform specific tasks, such as word processing.

Backup: A duplicate copy of a file or a disk.

Batch file: A series of DOS commands that are stored in a file with a .BAT file extension. When instructed, DOS will execute the commands in the batch file, one line at a time.

Boot: To start up the computer, loading the operating system software program.

Byte: The amount of space occupied by a single character on a disk.

Central processing unit (CPU): The electronic circuitry through which data is processed and instructions executed. Also called the processor.

Cold boot: To boot the computer system by turning on the computer. Also called a cold start.

Command: An instruction to perform a task or procedure.

Command line: The line containing the command prompt, where you enter commands.

Command prompt: The characters displayed by DOS to indicate it is ready to accept commands. It consists of the default drive letter followed by the > character, e.g., A>. It can be customized to display additional information.

Current directory: The active directory or the last directory you accessed using a CD command.

Current drive: The drive the program will use to get a file or execute a program. It is the same as the default drive.

Cursor: The blinking line or rectangle that shows where the next character you type will appear.

Default: The setting assumed by the program if no other setting is specified.

Default drive: The drive the program uses unless directed otherwise. It is the same as the current drive.

Delimeter: Used to indicate where one part of a command ends and other begins. Can be a space, comma, semicolon, equals sign, or a tab space.

Directory: A named division of the root directory that allows files to be grouped into related categories.

Directory tree: The graphic representation of the structure of a disk. The directories and subdirectories are shown as branches off the top level of the "tree," known as the root directory.

Disk: A plastic disk that stores data and program instructions as electromagnetic spots. The data on the disk can be read from the disk by the disk drive and loaded into RAM. Conversely, data in RAM can be written to the disk.

Disk capacity: The amount of data in bytes that a disk can hold.

Disk drive: The mechanical device in the system unit that reads from and writes to a disk.

Disk operating system (DOS): The operating system software program used by IBM and IBM-compatible computers.

Drive specifier: Used to indicate the drive to use. Consists of the drive letter followed by a colon.

Extension: The optional second part of a filename. It can be a maximum of three characters and is separated from the filename by a period.

External command: A DOS command that is read into memory from a floppy disk or the hard-disk drive when the command is entered.

File: The form in which information the computer uses is stored on a disk.

Filename: A unique and descriptive name assigned to each file on a disk. The filename can be a maximum of eight characters and can be followed by a period and an optional file extension.

Floppy disk: A removable plastic disk that stores data and program instructions as electromagnetic spots. The data on the disk can be read from the disk by the floppy disk drive and loaded into RAM. Conversely, data in RAM can be written to the disk.

Floppy-disk drive: The disk drive that reads and writes information to a floppy disk.

Format: The process of preparing a blank, unformatted disk for use by your computer system.

Global filename characters: The ? and * characters that are used to replace all or part of a filename in a DOS command. Also called wildcard characters.

Hard disk: A permanent fixture of the system unit that contains one or more magnetic disks used to store data and programs. Also called a fixed disk.

Hard-disk drive: The disk drive in the system unit that reads and writes information to the hard disk.

Hardware: The physical components and electronics of the computer consisting of input devices, processor unit, output devices, and secondary storage devices.

Hidden file: A file that is on the disk but that does not typically appear when a directory of filenames is displayed.

Home: The upper left corner of the screen.

Input device: A device (such as the keyboard) that allows the user to enter data or information into the computer in a form that the computer can process.

Internal command: A DOS command that can be used without the DOS disk in the drive. This is because the program statements to perform the command were copied into RAM when DOS was loaded.

Keyboard: An input device, very similar to a typewriter keyboard, that allows you to communicate with the computer.

Kilobyte: Approximately 1000 bytes (1024). Abbreviated as KB.

Main memory: Temporary storage area of the processor unit that holds data and instructions for use during processing by the CPU. Also called primary storage.

Megabyte: Approximately one million bytes. Abbreviated as MB.

Microcomputer system: People, procedures, software, hardware, and data.

Monitor: The output device that prints messages on a video display screen for temporary viewing by the user.

Operating system: A program that controls computer system resources and coordinates the flow of data to and from the system unit and to and from the input and output devices. DOS is an operating system.

Output device: A device through which the computer informs the user of what it has done. A monitor and printer are two common output devices.

Parameter: Defines the object the command is to act on. It is specified following the command name.

Parent directory: The directory level one level above the current directory.

Path: A description that tells DOS how to maneuver through the directories and subdirectories to locate a directory or file within the system. The path consists of a drive letter followed by a directory name, one or more subdirectory names if applicable, and a filename. The parts of the path are separated from each other by a backslash (\).

Plotter: A high-quality output device used mainly for line drawings, though it can also be used for text.

Primary storage: The part of the processor unit that temporarily holds data and programs. Also called main memory.

Printer: An output device that produces a printed copy of your work.

Processor unit: The part of the computer that contains the central processing unit (CPU) and main memory. Also called the system unit.

Program: The set of instructions that directs the computer to process information.

Prompt: A message, displayed by the program, that requires a user response.

Prompt character: The greater-than symbol (>) displayed in the command prompt.

Prompt codes: Special DOS symbols that begin with a $ character. They are used with the PROMPT command to allow you to customize the command prompt.

Random-access memory (RAM): The part of main memory that holds the data and instructions. Also called temporary memory.

Read-only memory (ROM): The part of main memory that controls the operations of the computer system.

Root directory: The main directory of a disk that is created when the disk is formatted. Directories can be created below the root directory.

Secondary storage: A device for permanently saving the data and instructions held in RAM. A disk is a common secondary storage device.

Sector: A basic unit of storage on a disk. Each sector holds half a kilobyte of information.

Software: The set of instructions (programs) that directs the computer to process information.

Source: The original disk you want to copy.

Subdirectory: A named subdivision of a directory.

Switch: The / character followed by the appropriate letter. It is used to tell DOS to perform a command in a different manner.

Systems software: The software programs that coordinate the operation of the hardware components of the computer.

Target: The disk that will hold the files copied from the source disk.

Temporary memory: The RAM area of main memory. It holds the data and instructions. It is called temporary memory because whatever is in RAM is lost when the power to the computer is turned off.

Track: Concentric rings of a disk that can hold information. The more tracks a disk has, the more information it can hold.

Tree-structured directory: The organization of a disk into directories and subdirectories; it resembles an upside-down family tree.

Unformatted: The way a new disk is shipped from the factory in a blank format so that it can be used by a variety of computer systems.

Utility programs: The external DOS commands.

Volume label: A label used to identify the disk. It is usually entered as part of the FORMAT command. It cannot exceed 11 characters.

Warm boot: Reloading DOS after the computer is already turned on, using (CTRL) + (ALT) and (DEL). Also called a warm start.

Wildcard characters: DOS global filename characters, ? and *, which give you greater flexibility when referring to filenames in a DOS command.

Functional Summary of DOS Commands

Command	Action
A:	Makes the A drive the current drive
B:	Makes the B drive the current drive
C:	Makes the C drive the current drive
CD <path\directory name>	Change directories
CD\	Changes to the root directory
CD..	Changes to the parent directory
CHKDSK	Provides a status report on both the disk and RAM memory
CLS	Clears the screen display
COPY A: <filename> B:	Copies the specified file from the disk in the A drive to the disk in the B drive
COPY *.* B:	Copies all files (any filename and extension) from the current directory to the disk in the B drive
COPY CON <filename.BAT>	Begin creation of a batch file
DEL <filename>	Removes specified file from disk
DIR	Displays a directory listing
DIR..	Displays a directory listing of the parent directory
DIR/P	Displays a directory listing, pausing when the screen is full
DIR/W	Displays a directory listing across the width of the screen
DISKCOPY	Creates an exact duplicate of the source disk on the target disk
ERASE <filename>	Removes specified file from the disk
FORMAT A:	Formats a disk in the A drive
FORMAT A:/V	Formats a disk in drive A and assigns it a volume label
FORMAT A:/S	Formats a disk in drive A and copies the system files to it
MD <directory name>	Creates a new directory or subdirectory
PAUSE	Temporarily suspends processing of a batch program
PROMPT <promptcode>	Changes the command prompt display
RD <directory name>	Removes or deletes a directory or subdirectory
REM	Records comments in a batch file
REN <filename> <new filename>	Assigns a new filename to the specified file
TREE	Shows all directory relationships
TREE/F	Shows all directories and files
TYPE <filename>	Displays contents of text files
VER	Displays the DOS version information
XCOPY	Copies as many files, including directories, at a time that can be read into memory from the source disk to the target disk

(ALT) key, DOS3
Applications software, DOS8

Backing up files, DOS26
Backslash (\), DOS46, DOS49
(Bksp) key, DOS4, DOS17
Bad command or file name, DOS20
Batch files, DOS59-DOS62
Booting in DOS, DOS15-DOS16
(BREAK) key, DOS4
Bytes, defined, DOS4

Central processing unit (CPU), DOS1,
    DOS4
CHDIR command, DOS49-DOS50
CHKDSK command, DOS39-DOS40
CLS command, DOS25-DOS26
Cold boot, DOS15
COMMAND.COM file, DOS14, DOS30,
    DOS46
Command line, DOS19
Command prompt, DOS19, DOS50-DOS51
Commands, DOS:
    CHDIR, DOS49-DOS50
    CHKDSK, DOS39-DOS40
    CLS, DOS25-DOS26
    COPY, DOS31-DOS38, DOS54
    COPY CON, DOS59
    DEL, DOS41-DOS42, DOS57
    DIR, DOS21-DOS25
    DISKCOPY, DOS37
    editing, DOS38
    entering, DOS19, DOS20
    ERASE, DOS41-DOS42, DOS57
    external, DOS20
    FORMAT, DOS26-DOS31
    internal, DOS20
    MD, DOS47-DOS49
    MKDIR, DOS47-DOS49
    PAUSE, DOS60, DOS62
    PROMPT, DOS50-DOS51
    REM, DOS60, DOS62
    RENAME, DOS40-DOS41
    RD, DOS57-DOS59
    TREE, DOS54-DOS57
    TYPE, DOS57
    VER, DOS20
    XCOPY, DOS35
Control key, DOS3, DOS4, DOS62

COPY command, DOS31-DOS38, DOS54
COPY CON command, DOS59
Copying files:
    to a directory, DOS54
    to another disk, DOS31-DOS37
    multiple, DOS34-DOS37
    to same disk, DOS37-DOS38
    system files, DOS30-DOS31
    using DISKCOPY, DOS37
    using XCOPY, DOS35
    with wildcard characters, DOS34-
        DOS36
CPU (central processing unit), DOS1,
    DOS4
(CTRL) key, DOS3, DOS4, DOS62
Current directory, DOS49
Current drive, DOS19, DOS21
Cursor, DOS2, DOS4

Date, entering, DOS16-DOS19
Defaults:
    command prompt, DOS51
    date settings, DOS17
    disk drive, DOS19, DOS21
DEL command, DOS41-DOS42, DOS57
(DEL) key, DOS4
Deleting:
    directories, DOS57-DOS59
    files, DOS41-DOS42
Delimiters, command, DOS23
Density, of disks, DOS6
DIR command, DOS21-DOS23
    with /P, DOS23-DOS24
    with /W, DOS24-DOS25
Directories, disk:
    changing, DOS49-DOS50
    checking with CHKDSK,
        DOS39-DOS40
    copying files to, DOS54
    current, DOS49
    deleting, DOS57-DOS59
    displaying, DOS21-DOS25,
        DOS54-DOS57
    dot entries in, DOS50
    making, DOS47-DOS49
    naming, DOS47-DOS48
    parent, DOS50
    paths in, DOS49
    removing, DOS57-DOS59

Directories, disk: (continued)
    root directory, DOS9-DOS10,
        DOS46
    subdirectories, DOS9, DOS46,
        DOS51-DOS54
    tree-structured, DOS9-DOS10,
        DOS47
    wide-screen, DOS24-DOS25
Disk drives, DOS5, DOS6, DOS16
    changing, DOS21
    current, DOS19
    default, DOS19
    letters for, DOS14
DISKCOPY command, DOS37
Disks, DOS4-DOS7
    backing up, DOS26
    bad sectors on, DOS40
    capacity of, DOS5, DOS6
    care of, DOS6-DOS7
    density of, DOS6
    formatting, DOS26-DOS31
    inserting and removing, DOS6
    listing files on, DOS21-DOS25
    parts of, DOS5
    source and target, DOS31
    tracks and sectors on, DOS26
    volume label on, DOS26-DOS30
    See also Hard disks
Display screens. See Screens
Displaying:
    directory structure, DOS54-DOS57
    file contents, DOS57
DOS (disk operating system):
    booting, DOS15-DOS16
    files for, DOS14, DOS30-DOS31
    loading, DOS14-DOS16
    utility programs in, DOS15
    versions of, DOS14
Dot entries in directory, DOS50
Double-density disks, DOS6
Drive specifier, DOS21, DOS46

Editing commands, DOS38
ERASE command, DOS41-DOS42, DOS57
Erasing files, DOS41-DOS42
(ESC) key, DOS3
External commands, DOS20

File extension, DOS9

Filenames in DOS, DOS9, DOS40-DOS41
Files:
  backing up, DOS26
  batch, DOS59-DOS62
  copying, DOS31-DOS38
  copying to directories, DOS54
  deleting, DOS41-DOS42
  displaying contents of, DOS57
  erasing, DOS41-DOS42
  fragmented, DOS37
  hidden DOS, DOS31, DOS46
  naming, DOS9
  renaming, DOS40-DOS41
  system, DOS14, DOS30-DOS31
Fixed-disk drives, DOS6
Floppy-disk drives, DOS14, DOS15
Floppy disks, DOS4, DOS5
FORMAT command, DOS26-DOS31
Formatting disks, DOS26-DOS31
  and copying system files,
    DOS30-DOS31
  with volume label, DOS26
Function keys, DOS2, DOS3
  (F3) to edit commands, DOS38
  (F6) (end of file), DOS60

Global filename characters, DOS34

Hard-disk drives, DOS4, DOS5
  booting with, DOS15
  letter for, DOS14
  organizing, DOS46-DOS47
Hardware components, DOS1-DOS8
Hidden files, DOS31, DOS46
High-density disks, DOS6
Home position, on screen, DOS26

IBMBIO.COM file, DOS14, DOS31
IBMDOS.COM file, DOS14, DOS30
Input devices, DOS1, DOS2-DOS4
(INS) key, DOS4
Internal commands, DOS20
IO.SYS file, DOS14, DOS31

Keyboard:
  enhanced and standard, DOS2
  function keys, DOS1, DOS2
  kinds of keys, L3, DOS2-DOS4
  numeric keypad, DOS2-DOS3
Kilobyte (KB), defined, DOS4

Loading DOS, DOS14-DOS16

Megabyte (MB), defined, DOS4
Memory:
  checking amount available,
    DOS39-DOS40
  RAM and ROM, DOS4
Microprocessor, DOS4
MKDIR or MD command, DOS47-DOS49
Monitors, DOS1, DOS7
Mouse, DOS4
MSDOS.SYS file, DOS14, DOS31

Naming directories, DOS47-DOS48
Naming files, DOS9
Num Lock key, DOS2, DOS3
Numeric keypad, DOS2, DOS3

Operating system, DOS14
  copying onto disks, DOS30-DOS31
Output devices, DOS1, DOS7

Parameters, command, DOS23
Parent directories, DOS50
Paths, DOS49
PAUSE command, DOS60, DOS62
Pause key, DOS3
Plotters, DOS7-DOS8
Primary storage, DOS4
Printers, DOS7-DOS8
Printing display screen, DOS42
Processor unit, DOS1, DOS4
Programs, software, DOS8
Prompt, DOS:
  changing, DOS50-DOS51
  character for, DOS19
  codes for, DOS51
  command, DOS19, DOS50-DOS51
PROMPT command, DOS50-DOS51
Prompts, DOS17
(PrtScr) key, DOS3, DOS42

Random-access memory (RAM), DOS4
RD command, DOS57-DOS59
Read-only memory (ROM), DOS4
REM command, DOS60, DOS62
RENAME command, DOS40-DOS41
Renaming files, DOS40-DOS41
Root directory, DOS9-DOS10, DOS46

Screens:
  clearing with CLS, DOS25-DOS26
  home position on, DOS26
  as output devices, DOS7
  pausing between, DOS60
  printing information on, DOS42
  stopping scrolling of, DOS56
(SCROLL LOCK) key, DOS3
Secondary storage, DOS1, DOS4-DOS7
Sectors, on disks, DOS26, DOS40
Software, DOS8-DOS9
Source disk, DOS31
Storage:
  primary, DOS4
  secondary, DOS1, DOS4-DOS7
Subdirectories:
  creating, DOS47-DOS49,
    DOS51-DOS54
  organizing files in, DOS9-DOS10
  paths to access, DOS49
  removing, DOS57-DOS59
Switch characters:
  /P (Pause), DOS24
  /S (System), DOS31, DOS46
  /V (Volume), DOS26
System files, DOS14, DOS30-DOS31
System requirements, L5
System unit, DOS1, DOS4
Systems software, L3, DOS8

Target disk, DOS31
Time, entering, DOS18-DOS19
Tracks, on disks, DOS26
TREE command, DOS54-DOS57
Tree-structured directories, DOS9-DOS10,
  DOS47
TYPE command, DOS57

Utility programs in DOS, DOS15

Version of DOS, DOS20
Volume label on disks, DOS26-DOS30

Warm boot, DOS15
Wildcard characters, DOS34-DOS36
Write-protect tabs, DOS5

XCOPY command, DOS35

WordPerfect 5.1

890 KPKP 909876543

/N 048806-1

RDER INFORMATION:
SBN 0-07-048806-1

WordPerfect 5.1 is a registered trademark of WordPerfect Corporation.
IBM, IBM PC, and PC DOS are registered trademarks of International Business Machines, Inc.

CONTENTS

Overview   Word Processing   WP3
Definition of Word Processing   WP3
Advantages of Using a Word Processor   WP3
Word Processing Terminology   WP4
Case Study for Labs 1–4   WP5

Lab 1   Editing a Document   WP6
Loading the WordPerfect 5.1 Program   WP6
    Starting WordPerfect on a Two-Disk System   WP6
    Starting WordPerfect on a Hard-Disk System   WP7
The Editing Screen   WP8
Entering WordPerfect 5.1 Commands   WP9
Using the Pull-Down Menu   WP9
Using a Mouse   WP13
Using the Function Keys   WP15
Retrieving a File   WP17
Moving the Cursor   WP19
Using the Mouse to Move the Cursor   WP27
Editing a Document   WP28
    Exercise 1.1 Deleting Characters: (BKSP)   WP29
    Exercise 1.2 Deleting Characters: (DEL)   WP31
    Exercise 1.3 Inserting Characters: Insert Mode   WP32
    Exercise 1.4 Inserting Characters: Typeover Mode   WP33
    Exercise 1.5 Deleting Words: (CTRL)-(BKSP)   WP35
    Exercise 1.6 Deleting from Cursor to End of Line:
        (CTRL)-(END)   WP36
    Exercise 1.7 Deleting Several Lines of Text: (ESC),
        (CTRL)-(END)   WP37
    Exercise 1.8 Inserting and Deleting Blank Lines   WP38
    Exercise 1.9 Undeleting Text   WP40
Clearing the Screen   WP41
Listing File Names   WP42
Editing the Welcome Letter   WP44
Saving and Replacing an Existing File   WP44
Printing a Document   WP45
Exiting WordPerfect 5.1   WP48
Key Terms   WP48
Matching   WP48
Practice Exercises   WP49

Lab 2   Creating and Formatting a Document   WP50
Creating a Document   WP50
Spell-Checking   WP52
Saving a New File   WP54
Combining Files   WP56
Moving Text   WP57
Using the Block Command   WP59
Using the Date Command   WP62
Aligning Text Flush with the Right Margin   WP63
Setting Margins   WP65
Using and Setting Tabs   WP67
Displaying Hidden Codes   WP70

Searching and Replacing Text   WP73
Setting Justification   WP75
Printing the Document   WP76
Saving the Document in a New File   WP77
Key Terms   WP78
Matching   WP78
Practice Exercises   WP78

Lab 3   Merging and Refining Documents   WP83
The Merge Feature   WP83
Entering Merge Codes in the Primary File   WP84
Creating the Secondary File   WP89
Merging the Primary and Secondary Merge Files   WP94
Centering and Boldfacing Text   WP95
Using Two Document Files   WP98
Creating a Split Screen   WP99
Moving Text Between Documents   WP100
Closing a Split Screen   WP101
Underlining Text   WP102
Defining Columns   WP103
Reformatting the Screen Display   WP106
Viewing the Document   WP107
Changing Justification   WP109
Using Hyphenation   WP109
Saving and Exiting Two Document Files   WP111
Key Terms   WP111
Matching   WP111
Practice Exercises   WP112

Lab 4   Creating a Research Paper   WP116
Creating an Outline   WP116
Editing the Outline   WP121
Creating Lines   WP125
Creating a Table of Contents   WP127
Creating Footnotes   WP134
Editing a Footnote   WP138
Numbering Pages   WP139
Suppressing Page Numbers   WP140
Centering Text Top to Bottom   WP141
Using Block Protection   WP142
Preventing Widows and Orphans   WP144
Printing the Report   WP146
Key Terms   WP146
Matching   WP147
Practice Exercises   WP147

Summary   WordPerfect 5.1   WP150
Glossary of Key Terms   WP150
Functional Summary of Selected WordPerfect Commands   WP15

Index   WP157

Word Processing

The most popular applications software used on a microcomputer today is a word processor. To put your thoughts in writing, from the simplest note to the most complex book, is a time-consuming process. Even more time-consuming is the task of editing and retyping the document to make it perfect. There was a time that perfection in written communication was difficult, if not impossible, to achieve. With the introduction of word processing, errors should be nearly nonexistent—not because they are not made, but because they are easy to correct. Word processors let you throw away the correction fluid, scissors, paste, and erasers. Now, with a few keystrokes, you can correct errors, move paragraphs, and reprint your document easily.

Definition of Word Processing

Word processing applications software is a program that helps you create any type of written communication via a keyboard. A word processor can be used to manipulate text data to produce a letter, a report, a memo, or any other type of correspondence. Text data is any letter, number, or symbol that you can type on a keyboard. The grouping of the text data to form words, sentences, paragraphs, and pages of text results in the creation of a document. Through a word processor you can create, modify, store, retrieve, and print part or all of a document.

Advantages of Using a Word Processor

The speed of entering text data into the computer depends on the skill of the user. If you cannot type fast, a word processor will not improve your typing speed. However, a word processor will make it easier to correct and change your document. Consequently, your completed document will take less time to create.

Where a word processor excels is in its ability to change, modify, or edit a document. Editing involves correcting spelling, grammar, and sentence-structure errors. With a word processor, the text is stored on a diskette. As errors are found, they are electronically deleted and corrected. Once the document is the way you want it to appear, it is printed on paper. Goodbye, correction fluid!

In addition to editing a document, you can easily revise or update it through the insertion or deletion of text. For example, a document that lists prices can easily be updated to reflect new prices. A document that details procedures can be revised by deleting old procedures and inserting new ones. This is especially helpful when a document is used repeatedly. Rather than recreating the whole document, only the parts that change need to be revised.

Revision also includes the rearrangement of pieces or blocks of text. For example, while writing a report, you may decide to change the location of a single word or several paragraphs or pages of text. You can do it easily by using Block and Move commands. Blocks of text can also be copied from one area of the document to another. This is a real advantage when the text includes many recurring phrases or words.

Combining text in another file with your document is another advantage of word processors. An example of this is a group term paper. Each person is responsible for writing a section of the paper. Before printing the document, the text for all sections, which is stored in different files, is combined to create the complete paper. The opposite is also true. Text that may not be appropriate in your document can easily be put in another file for later use.

Many word processors include special programs to further help you produce a perfect document. A spell checker will check the spelling in a document by comparing each word to a dictionary of words. If an error is found, the program will suggest the correct spelling. A syntax checker electronically checks grammar, phrasing, capitalization, and other types of syntax errors in a document. A thesaurus will display different words, each with a meaning similar to the word you entered.

After changes are made and the document appears ready to be printed, the word processor also makes it easy to change the design or appearance of the document. For example, a word processor lets you set the line spacing of a document. You can decide how large you want the right, left, top, and bottom margins. The number of lines printed on each page can be specified. In addition, you can quickly specify whether the pages will or will not be numbered and where (top or bottom, centered or not) the number will appear. Further, a word processor will let you enter headers and footers on each page or specified pages.

If, after reading the printed copy, you find other errors or want to revise or reformat the document, it is easy to do. Simply reload the document file, make your changes, and reprint the text! Now that saves time!

Word Processing Terminology

The following list of terms and definitions are generic in nature and are associated with most word processing programs.

Block: Any group of characters, words, lines, paragraphs, or pages of text.

Boldface: Produces dark or heavy print.

Center: Centers a line of text evenly between the margins.

Character string: Any combination of letters, numbers, symbols, and spaces.

Delete: To erase a character, word, paragraph, or block of text from the document.

Flush right: Aligns text on the right-hand margin.

Format: Defines how the printed document will appear; includes settings for underline, boldface, print size, margin settings, line spacing, etc.

Insert mode: Allows new text to be entered into a document between existing text.

Justified: The text has even left and right margins, produced by inserting extra spaces between words on each line.

Merge: Combine text in one document with text in another.

Overstrike: Causes the printer to print one character over another to make the type darker.

Search: Scans the document for all matching character strings.

Search and replace: Scans the document for all matching character strings and replaces them with others.

Template: A document, like a form letter, that contains blank spaces for automatic insertion of information that varies from one document to another.

Typeover mode: New text is entered in a document by typing over the existing text on the line.

Unjustified: The text has an even left margin and an uneven, or ragged, right margin.

Word wrap: Automatic adjustment of number of characters or words on a line while entering text; eliminates pressing the ⟨⟵⟩ (Return) key at the end of each line.

Case Study for Labs 1- 4

Karen Barnes is the membership assistant for the Sports Club. The club just purchased a word processing program. Her first assignment using the software package is to create a letter welcoming new members to the club.

In Lab 1, the rough draft of the letter entered by Karen is corrected. During this process, the basic cursor-movement keys and editing features are demonstrated.

Lab 2 continues with modifying the welcome letter by entering new text, combining files, and rearranging paragraphs and blocks of text. The print, line, and page formats are modified, and the completed document is printed.

In the third lab, the welcome letter is changed to a form letter using the Merge feature. Next, another document is created using text taken from the welcome letter. The Split Screen feature lets the user view both documents on the screen at the same time, greatly simplifying the process. Finally, the document is changed to column format to be used in the club newsletter.

In the final word processing lab, Peg, a student intern at the Sports Club, is writing a term paper. As part of this process you will learn how to create an outline, produce a table of contents, and enter footnotes. Several new format features are also demonstrated.

Editing a Document

1

OBJECTIVES

In this lab you will learn how to:

1. Load the WordPerfect 5.1 program.

2. Issue a WordPerfect 5.1 command.

3. Retrieve a file.

4. Move around a document.

5. Delete characters, words, and lines of text.

6. Undelete text.

7. Insert text in Insert and Typeover modes.

8. Insert and delete blank lines.

9. Clear the display.

10. List file names.

11. Save and replace a file.

12. Print a document.

13. Exit WordPerfect 5.1.

CASE STUDY

Karen Barnes, the membership assistant for the Sports Club, has been asked to create a letter welcoming new members to the club. The letter should briefly explain the services offered by the club. Karen has written a rough draft of the welcome letter using WordPerfect 5.1. However, it contains many errors. You will follow Karen as she uses WordPerfect 5.1 to correct and modify the letter.

Loading the WordPerfect 5.1 Program

Starting WordPerfect on a Two-Disk System

Boot the system by turning on the computer and loading DOS. After you have responded to the DOS date and time prompts, the A> should appear on your display screen.

Remove the DOS diskette and place the backup WordPerfect 1 diskette in the A drive and the backup data diskette in the B drive.

To load the WordPerfect 5.1 program, you will begin by changing the default disk drive to B. This tells the system that the diskette in the B drive will be used to save and retrieve files. At the A>,

Type: **B:**
Press:

To tell the system that the WordPerfect program diskette is in the A drive and to load the program into memory,

Type: A:WP
Press: ⏎

After a few moments, your display screen should provide copyright information, the version number of your copy, and the default drive that the system will use.

This screen also prompts you to insert the WordPerfect 2 disk. Follow these directions by removing the WordPerfect 1 disk from drive A, inserting the WordPerfect 2 disk, and pressing any key.

The editing screen is displayed. Skip to the section, "The Editing Screen," on the next page.

Starting WordPerfect on a Hard-Disk System

The WordPerfect program should have already been installed on your hard disk. It is assumed that the program files are on the C drive in the subdirectory \WP. If yours is in a different drive or subdirectory, substitute the appropriate drive and subdirectory name in the directions below.

The drive door(s) should be open. Turn on your computer and, if necessary, respond to the date and time prompts. The DOS C> should be displayed.

Put your data disk in drive A and, if necessary, close the door.

To load the WordPerfect 5.1 program, begin by changing the default disk drive to A. At the C>,

Type: A:
Press: ⏎

Drive A is now the default drive. This means that the diskette in the A drive will be used to save and retrieve files. Now you are ready to load the WordPerfect program. The command, WP, will load the program into memory. You must include the drive and subdirectory path as part of the command to tell the system where to find the WordPerfect files. To do this,

Type: C:\WP\WP
Press: ⏎

After a few moments, your screen should briefly display the opening screen. This screen contains copyright information, the version number of your copy, and the default drive that the system will use. This is quickly replaced with the Editing screen.

The Editing Screen

Your display screen should be similar to Figure 1-1.

cursor

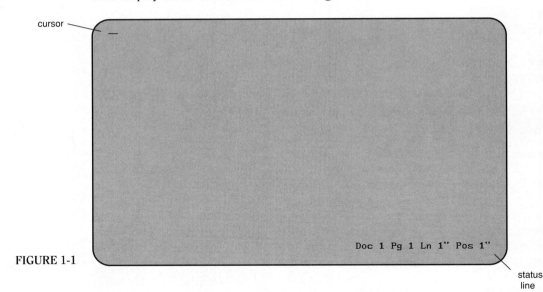

Doc 1 Pg 1 Ln 1" Pos 1"

FIGURE 1-1

status
line

This is a blank WordPerfect 5.1 Editing screen. The blinking line or dash in the upper left corner is the **cursor**. It shows you where the next character you type will appear.

The line of information at the bottom of the screen is the **status line**. It displays four items of information about the current location of the cursor:

Doc 1 This shows which **document** window displays the cursor. A **window** is an area of the screen which displays the document. You can enter and edit text in two separate windows at a time. These windows are displayed as Doc 1 or Doc 2 in the status line. Currently, the cursor is in the document 1 window, and the window occupies the entire screen.

Pg 1 This shows the number of the **page** the cursor is located on. A page refers to the physical page when a document is printed. It is currently on page 1.

Ln 1" This tells you the vertical distance in inches between the cursor and the top of the page. This is the **line** on which the cursor rests. The cursor is currently 1 inch from the top of the page.

Pos 1" This tells you the horizontal location, or **position** of the cursor on the line. The position is displayed in inches from the left edge of the page. The cursor is currently 1 inch from the left edge of the page.

The line and position locations of the cursor you see on your screen are **default,** or initial, WordPerfect 5.1 settings. WordPerfect comes with many default settings. These are generally the most commonly used settings. For example, the current position of the cursor at 1 inch from the left edge of the page is the default left margin setting. The right margin default setting is 1 inch from the right edge of the page. When the document is printed, the printed page will have 1-inch left and right margins. Other default settings include a standard paper-size setting of 8-1/2 by 11 inches, tab settings every .5 inch, and single line spacing. If you do not specify different settings, WordPerfect uses the default settings.

Entering WordPerfect 5.1 Commands

The WordPerfect 5.1 editing screen is blank, except for the status line. Commands are entered using the pull-down menus or the function keys. Both methods produce the same result.

Using the Pull-Down Menu

A **pull down menu** displays a list of commands in a box that are available for selection when the menu is selected. Using the pull-down menu lets you see the various commands and options available. This is particularly helpful to people who are just learning to use the program.

To activate the pull-down menu,

Press: (ALT) - = (hold down (ALT) while pressing =)

Your display screen should be similar to Figure 1-2.

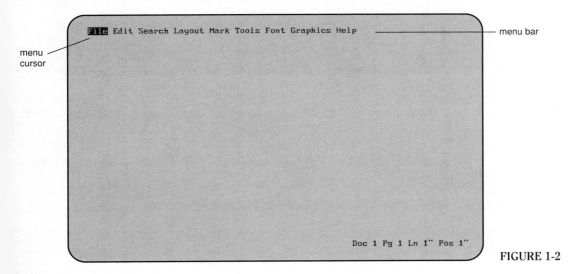

FIGURE 1-2

The top line of the screen displays the **menu bar**. It lists the names of nine menus which can be opened. The first menu name, File, is highlighted with the **menu cursor**. The (→) and (←) keys are used to move the menu cursor in the direction of the arrow from one menu name to the next.

Press: (→)

The menu cursor is positioned on Edit.

Press: (→) (8 times)

The menu cursor has moved to each menu name and in a circular fashion has returned to the File menu.

To activate the pull-down menu of commands associated with the highlighted menu,

Press: ⏎

Your display screen should be similar to Figure 1-3.

Pull-down menu

FIGURE 1-3

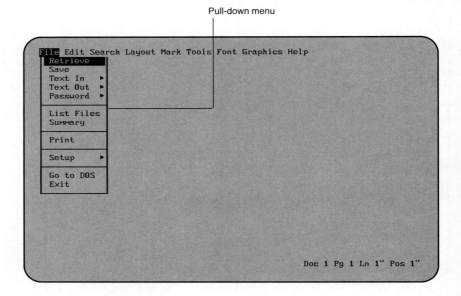

The pull-down menu of commands is displayed in a box below the File menu name, and the first pull-down menu command, Retrieve, is highlighted.

Note: Newer releases of WordPerfect 5.1 show function key command equivalents in the menus.

Now pressing → will move the menu cursor to the next pull-down menu.

Press: →

The Edit pull-down menu is displayed. Notice that the menu cursor is not positioned on the first command, Move; instead it is positioned on the third command, Paste. This is because the first two commands are not available for selection at this time. Pull-down menu commands which cannot be selected are surrounded by brackets ([]). Additionally the menu cursor cannot be positioned on a command that is not available for selection.

The ↑ and ↓ keys are used to move the menu cursor within the pull-down menu.

Press: ↓

The menu cursor has moved to the next available command, Undelete.

Press: ↓ (2 times)

Your display screen should be similar to Figure 1-4.

FIGURE 1-4

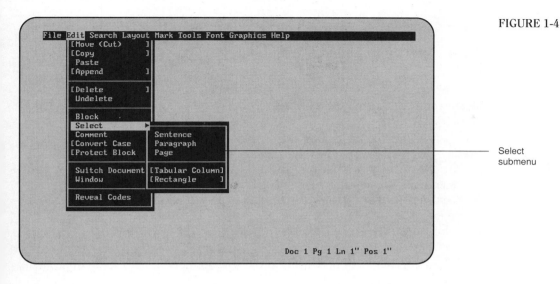

Select
submenu

The menu cursor is positioned on Select. Notice the > symbol following the command name. This symbol tells you that a **submenu** of options will be displayed when the command is highlighted. In this case, the submenu consists of the options displayed in the box to the right.

Press: ⟶

The menu cursor remains positioned on the pull-down command, Select, and another menu cursor highlights the first submenu option, Sentence. The ⬆ and ⬇ keys are used to move around the submenu.

Press: ⬇

The submenu cursor is positioned on Paragraph.

Press: ⟵

The submenu cursor is cleared.

Press: PGDN

The menu cursor is positioned on the last command in the Edit menu, Reveal Codes. Pressing PGDN or PGUP in a pull-down menu or submenu will quickly move the menu cursor to the first or last command in the menu.

Press: PGUP

The menu cursor is positioned back on Paste. To see what commands are available in the other menus,

Press: ⟶ (9 times)

The File pull-down menu should be displayed. To remove the pull-down menu,

Press: (ESC)

Pressing (ESC) when a menu is displayed "backs up," or cancels, the previous selection.

When a pull-down menu is not displayed a quick way to move the menu cursor to the last menu name in the menu bar from any location on the bar is to press (END).

Press: (END)

The menu cursor is positioned on Help. The same action could have been accomplished using (HOME), (→); however, it requires an extra keystroke.

Press: (←)

The menu cursor moved one menu to the left. To move quickly to the first menu, File,

Press: (HOME) , (←)

A quicker way to move to and activate a pull-down menu is to type the **mnemonic letter** (the highlighted letter associated with the menu name) of the menu you want to select. To select **H**elp,

Type: **H**

The Help menu is selected, and the pull-down menu of commands is displayed.

So far you have moved the menu cursor to highlight many commands. However, you have not yet selected or executed a command. A command is selected by highlighting the command with the menu cursor and pressing (⏎) , or by typing the mnemonic letter associated with the command.

Note: If you find that you have selected the wrong command, use Cancel ((F1)) to cancel the selection, or (ESC) to back out of a selected menu.

The menu cursor is over the first command, Help. Since this command is highlighted, it can be selected by pressing (⏎) . It can also be selected by typing the mnemonic letter "h."

Select: Help

Your display screen should be similar to Figure 1-5.

FIGURE 1-5

```
┌─────────────────────────────────────────────────────────────┐
│  Help            License #:  WP510137643       WP 5.1   01/19/90
│                                                                │
│      Press any letter to get an alphabetical list of features.│
│                                                                │
│          The list will include the features that start with that letter,
│          along with the name of the key where the feature is found.  You
│          can then press that key to get a description of how the feature
│          works.                                                │
│                                                                │
│      Press any function key to get information about the use of the key.
│                                                                │
│          Some keys may let you choose from a menu to get more information
│          about various options.  Press HELP again to display the template.
│                                                                │
│                                                                │
│                                                                │
│                                                                │
│  Selection: 0                       (Press ENTER to exit Help) │
└─────────────────────────────────────────────────────────────┘
```

You have executed the Help menu's Help command. A full screen of information about how the Help system works is displayed. You will use Help shortly for more information. For now, following the directions on the screen to exit Help,

Press: ⏎

You are returned to the blank Editing screen. Once a command is executed and completed, you are returned to the Editing screen rather than to the menu.

Using a Mouse

If you have a mouse attached to your computer, follow the instructions below. If you do not have a mouse, skip to the next section, "Using the Function Keys."

The mouse controls a pointer on your screen. As soon as you move the mouse the pointer appears.

Move the mouse in any direction.

The pointer appears as a solid rectangle. You move the pointer on the screen by moving the mouse over the desk top in the direction you want the pointer to move.

Move the mouse in all directions (up, down, left, and right) and note the movement of the pointer on the screen.

If you pick up the mouse and move it to a different location on your desk top, the pointer will not move on the screen. This is because the pointer movement is controlled by the rubber-coated ball on the bottom of the mouse. This ball must move within its socket in order for the pointer to move on the screen. The ball's movement is translated into signals that tell the computer how to move the on-screen pointer.

On top of the mouse are two or three buttons. These buttons are used to enter user input instructions. Quickly pressing and releasing a mouse button is called clicking. To activate the WordPerfect 5.1 menu bar, click the right mouse button.

The menu bar appears at the top of the screen, just as if you had used the keyboard equivalent, (ALT) - =. (See Figure 1-2.)

Move the mouse so that the pointer is within the menu bar.

Move the mouse to the right and left to move the pointer from one menu name to the next. This has the same effect as using the $\rightarrow$ and $\leftarrow$ keys to move the menu cursor within the menu bar.

Position the pointer anywhere within File on the menu bar. To activate the pull-down menu,

Click: Left button

Note: If the pointer is not on a menu name when you click the left button, the menu will be cleared from the screen. If this happens, click the right button again to display the menu bar and try again.

The pull-down menu of commands is displayed below the File menu name, and the menu cursor is positioned on Retrieve. This is the same as if you had pressed $\leftarrow\!\!\!\!\!\rule[0.4ex]{0.6em}{0.4pt}$ using the keyboard (See Figure 1-3).

With the pointer still in the menu bar, hold down the left mouse button and move the mouse slowly to the right along the menu bar. Do not release the left button until the pointer is positioned over Tools.

Note: If, when you release the left button, the pointer is not on a menu name, the menu bar is cleared from the screen. If this happens, click the right button again to re-display the menu bar and try again.

Note: Developing the skill for moving the mouse and correctly positioning the pointer takes some time. If you accidentally find yourself in the wrong location or in a command that you did not intend to select, click the right button on a two-button mouse or the center button on a three-button mouse. This action will cancel most selected commands.

The process of holding down the left button as you move the mouse is called **dragging**. After dragging the mouse through the menu bar, releasing the left button selects the menu the pointer is on. Dragging the mouse along the menu bar while the pull-down menu is displayed has the same effect as using the $\rightarrow$ and $\leftarrow$ keys to move from one menu to another when the pull-down menu is displayed.

Note: If, while dragging the menu, you decide you do not want to select a menu, move the pointer to any area outside the menu bar or submenu box and release the left button. The menu is cleared. Also, at any point you can cancel the menu by clicking the right button.

Move the pointer to Help and click the left button. You have now selected the Help menu. This action has the same effect as typing the mnemonic letter of the menu.

Use the mouse to move the pointer to each of the three pull-down menu commands.

To select a pull-down menu command, move the pointer to the command (anywhere on the line within the menu box) and click the left button. You can also drag the mouse within the pull down-menu. This way you can see the submenu options associated with the highlighted pull-down menu command. When you release the left button the option is selected. Be careful when dragging the menus that you have the menu cursor on the correct menu item before releasing the left button.

Either method has the same effect as selecting the pull-down command using the arrow keys to highlight the command and pressing ⏎ , or by typing the mnemonic letter.

To select the Help command, move the pointer to Help and press the left button. Your screen should look similar to Figure 1-5, shown earlier

Note: If the pointer is not on a pull-down menu command when you select it, the menu bar is cleared from the screen. If this happens, click the right button again to re-display the menu bar and try again.

You have executed the Help menu's Help command. To exit the Help screen,

Click: Right button

This has the same effect as pressing ⏎ .

Using the Function Keys

The other way to issue a WordPerfect 5.1 command is to use the function keys. WordPerfect provides a function key template to place over the function keys to tell you what command each function key performs. If you have a function template place the appropriate template for your keyboard over the function keys.

Each function key, alone or in conjunction with other keys, can perform four different commands. The template lists the four commands associated with each function key. Notice that the commands are displayed in four colors. These colors tell you the key combinations to use to perform that specific task or activity. The color code and key combinations are explained below:

Color	Press
red	(CTRL) and function key
green	(SHIFT) and function key
blue	(ALT) and function key
black	function key alone

For example, (F3) used alone or in combination with (CTRL), (SHIFT), or (ALT), accesses four different WordPerfect commands, as shown below:

Key Combination	Command
(CTRL) - (F3)	Screen
(SHIFT) - (F3)	Switch
(ALT) - (F3)	Reveal Codes
(F3)	Help

The Help command, (F3), accesses the Help system as if you had selected Help from the menu bar and then Help from the pull-down menu of commands. To show how you can access Help using the Function key,

Press: Help (F3)

The same screen of information (Figure 1-5) about how to use the WordPerfect Help system is displayed. This time you will use Help to display information about the function key template on the screen (in case you do not have a template or lose or forget your template in the future). Following the directions on the Help screen to display the template,

Press: Help F3

Your display screen should be similar to Figure 1-6.

FIGURE 1-6

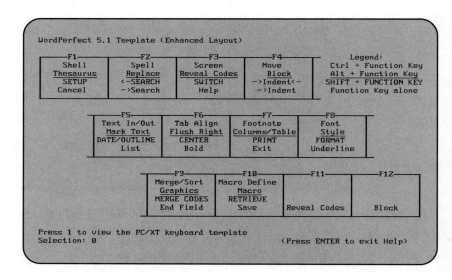

The Enhanced Layout template for keyboards whose function keys are above the typewriter keys is displayed.

If your function keys are located to the left of the typewriter section of the keyboard (PC/XT keyboard), following the directions on the screen,

Press: 1

The IBM PC/XT keyboard layout is displayed.

Depending upon your keyboard, the grid of 10 or 12 boxes displayed on the screen contains the WordPerfect commands that are associated with the function keys. Instead of a color code, the legend to the right lists the keys (CTRL, SHIFT and ALT) that are used in combination with the function key, or the function key alone.

The function key template could also have been displayed using the pull-down menu by selecting Help and then Template.

To leave the Help screen,

Press: ⏎

You are returned to the blank WordPerfect screen.

Note: If your template is a black and white photocopy of the template provided by WordPerfect, then use red, green, and blue highlight pens to color code your template.

Retrieving a File

Karen worked on the first draft of the welcome letter yesterday and saved it on the diskette in a file named LETTER.

To open a file in WordPerfect, the Retrieve command is used. To use the pull-down menu to select the Retrieve command,

Press: (ALT) - =

The Retrieve command is a command in the File menu. Because the menu cursor is already positioned over the File menu, to select it,

Press: ⏎

The pull-down menu of 11 commands associated with the File menu is displayed. The Retrieve command is highlighted. To select the Retrieve command,

Press: ⏎

Note: To cancel an incorrect menu selection, press (F1) (Cancel) to terminate the command, or (ESC) to back up one step in the command selection.

Your display screen should be similar to Figure 1-7.

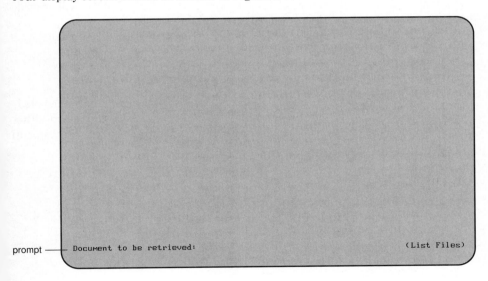

FIGURE 1-7

prompt —— Document to be retrieved: (List Files)

The cursor location information in the status line has been replaced by a WordPerfect prompt "Document to be retrieved." A **prompt** is the way the program tells you it needs more information. In this case the prompt wants you to enter the name of the file to be retrieved.

Before entering the file name, you will use Help for information about the Retrieve command. The WordPerfect Help system is **context-sensitive**. This means that whenever a command is in use, pressing Help ((F3)) will display information about that particular command.

Press: Help (F3)

Your display screen should be similar to Figure 1-8.

FIGURE 1-8

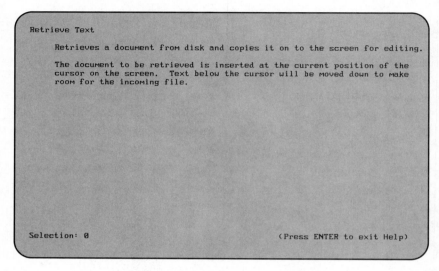

```
Retrieve Text

    Retrieves a document from disk and copies it on to the screen for editing.

    The document to be retrieved is inserted at the current position of the
    cursor on the screen.  Text below the cursor will be moved down to make
    room for the incoming file.
```

```
Selection: 0                                              (Press ENTER to exit Help)
```

This screen tells you how the Retrieve command works. Most importantly it tells you that when you retrieve a file, a copy is displayed on the screen while the original file remains unchanged on the disk. The WordPerfect Help feature will provide specific information about the command you are using.

To leave the Help screen,

Press: ⏎

You are returned to the same place you were before using Help. You are now ready to enter the name of the file to retrieve. The file name can be entered in either upper- or lowercase letters. However, WordPerfect will always display a file name in uppercase.

Type: A: **LETTER**
Press: ⏎

After a few moments your display screen should be similar to Figure 1-9.

FIGURE 1-9

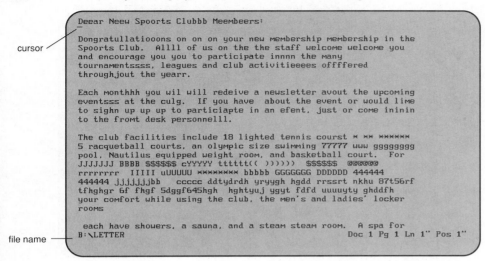

cursor

file name

The Retrieve command loads a copy of the file from the diskette into memory. The original file remains on the diskette. The first three paragraphs of the rough draft of the welcome letter are displayed on the screen. As you can see, it contains many errors, which you will correct in this lab.

In addition to the cursor location information, the status line displays the file name of the file in use. This information will sometimes be replaced with other WordPerfect messages. Often a prompt (like the one you responded to when retrieving the file) or a menu of choices to select from will be displayed in the status line as part of the command sequence. Again, if you find that you have entered an incorrect command and are accidentally in the wrong menu, press Cancel ((F1)) or (ESC). Then reenter the command correctly.

You could have also entered this command using the function key combination, (SHIFT) - (F10). Look on your template next to the (F10) key. The word "Retrieve" is printed in green letters. The top left-hand corner of the template displays the color code. Green means to use (SHIFT) in combination with the function key (hold down (SHIFT) and, while holding it down, press (F10)).

Moving the Cursor

The cursor can be moved around the screen by using the arrow keys or by using the mouse. The arrow keys, located on the numeric keypad or on the separate cursor key area, move the cursor one character space in the direction indicated by the arrow.

Note: Be careful to use only the keys specified as you are following the directions in this section. If you do, the instructions and figures in the text should be the same as what you see on your screen. Also, make sure the (NUM LOCK) (number lock) key is not on when using the numeric keypad area. If it is, numbers will be entered on the screen rather than the cursor moving through the text.

Press: (→) (6 times)

Your display screen should be similar to Figure 1-10.

FIGURE 1-10

cursor →

```
Deear Neeu Spoorts Clubbb Meembeers:

Dongratullatiooons on on on your new membership membership in the
Spoorts Club.  Allll of us on the the staff welcome welcome you
and encourage you you to participate innnn the many
tournamentssss, leagues and club activitieeees offffered
throughjout the yearr.

Each monthhh you wil will redeive a newsletter avout the upcoming
eventsss at the culg.  If you have  about the event or would lime
to sighn up up up to particiapte in an efent, just or come ininin
to the fromt desk personnel1.

The club facilities include 18 lighted tennis courst × ×× ××××××
5 racquetball courts, an olympic size swimming 77777 www ggggggggg
pool, Nautilus equipped weight room, and basketball court.  For
JJJJJJJ BBBB $$$$$$ cYYYYY tttttt(( )))))) $$$$$$ ©©©©©©
rrrrrrrr  IIIII uUUUUU ××××××× bbbbb GGGGGGG DDDDDD 444444
444444 jjjjjjjbb   ccccc ddtydrdh yryygh hgdd rrssrt nkhu 87t56rf
tfhghgr 6f fhgf 5dggf645hgh  hghtyuj ygyt fdfd uuuuyty ghddfh
your comfort while using the club, the men's and ladies' locker
rooms

 each have showers, a sauna, and a steam steam room.  A spa for
B:\LETTER                                 Doc 1 Pg 1 Ln 1" Pos 1.6"
```

→ new position value

The cursor moved six character spaces to the right along the line. It should be positioned under the "N" in "Neew." Notice how the status line reflects the change in the horizontal location of the cursor on the line. The position value increased to 1.6" as the cursor moved to the right along the line. The position value is displayed as a decimal. The current cursor location then is 1-6/10 inch from the left edge of the page.

Press: ⊕

The cursor moved down one line. Since this is a blank line, the cursor moved back to the left margin on the line. The status line reflects the change in the location of the cursor by telling you that the new vertical or line location of the cursor is Ln 1.17", and the horizontal location of the cursor is Pos 1". Like the position value, the line value is displayed as a decimal. Line numbers increase as you move down the page. The current line location of the cursor is 1-17/100 inch from the top of the page.

Press: ⊕

The cursor moved down to the next line and back to Pos 1.6". It should be on the "t" in "Dongratullatiooons." The cursor moved to position 1.6 because it was last located in a line containing text (line 1") at that position. The cursor will attempt to maintain its position in a line of text as you move up or down through the document.

By holding down either ← or →, the cursor will move quickly character by character along the line.

To see how this works, hold down → and move the cursor to the right along the line until it is under the "i" in the word "in."

The status line should show that the cursor is on Pos 6.9". If you moved too far to the right along the line of text, use ← to move back to the correct position.

This saves multiple presses of the arrow key. Many of the WordPerfect cursor movement keys can be held down to execute multiple moves.

Press: ⊕ (2 times)

The cursor moved up two lines and should be positioned at the end of the first line.
Using the arrow keys and the status line for cursor location reference,

Move to: Ln 3.17" Pos 7.4" (end of first line of third paragraph)

Note: Throughout the WordPerfect 5.1 labs you will be instructed to move the cursor to specific line and position locations (for example, Move to: Ln 3.17" Pos 7.4"). To confirm the appropriate cursor position, the location of the cursor in the text is described in parentheses (for example, "end of first line of third paragraph"). If your cursor is not at the described location, move it there before continuing.

The default right margin setting is 1 inch from the right side of the paper (Pos 7.5".) To see what happens when the cursor reaches the right margin,

Press: $\rightarrow$

The cursor automatically moved to the beginning of the next line. Unlike a typewriter, you did not need to press a return key to move from the end of one line to the beginning of the next. It is done automatically for you.
You can also move the cursor word by word in either direction on a line by using (CTRL) in combination with $\rightarrow$ or $\leftarrow$. (CTRL) is held down while pressing the arrow key.

Press: (CTRL) - $\rightarrow$ (5 times)

The cursor skipped to the beginning of each word and moved five words to the right along the line. It should be positioned on the "s" in the word "size."
To move back to the first word in this line,

Press: (CTRL) - $\leftarrow$ (5 times)

The cursor should be positioned on "5," the first character in the line. If the cursor is positioned in the middle of a word, (CTRL) - $\rightarrow$ will move the cursor to the beginning of the next word; however, (CTRL) - $\leftarrow$ will move the cursor to the beginning of the word it is on, rather than to the beginning of the preceding word.
The cursor can be moved quickly to the end of a line of text by pressing (END). To move to the end of this line,

Press: (END)

Pressing (HOME) and then $\rightarrow$ will have the same effect. But it requires the use of two keys rather than one.
Unfortunately, simply pressing (HOME) will not take you to the beginning of a line of text. Because (HOME) is used in combination with several other keys, you must use it followed by $\leftarrow$ to move to the beginning of a line.
To move back to the beginning of the line,

Press: (HOME)
Press: $\leftarrow$

The cursor should be back on the "5."

The letter is longer than what is currently displayed on the screen. To move to the bottom line of the screen, using ⊥,

Move to: Ln 4.83" Pos 1" (beginning of the first line of the fourth paragraph)

The screen can display only 24 lines of text at a time. If the cursor is positioned on either the top or bottom line of the screen, using ⊤ or ⊥ will move, or **scroll**, more lines of the document onto the screen. As you scroll up or down through the document, the lines at the top or bottom of the screen move out of view to allow more text to be displayed.

To scroll the rest of the letter into view on the screen,

Press: ⊥ (13 times)

The cursor should be at the beginning of the word "Sports" (Ln 7").

Your display screen should be similar to Figure 1-11.

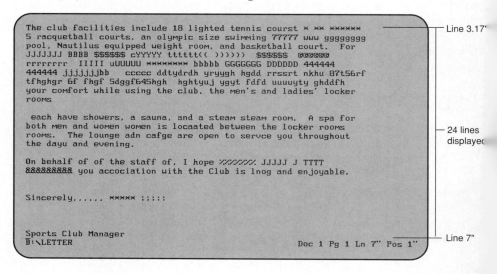

FIGURE 1-11

The first 13 lines of the letter are no longer visible on the screen. They scrolled off the top of the screen to allow the new lines at the bottom of the screen to be displayed.

Each time you pressed ⊥ a new line of text was brought into view at the bottom of the screen. At the same time a line of text scrolled out of view at the top of the screen.

The screen still displays only 24 lines of the letter. The cursor can be moved quickly to the top line of the screen by pressing (HOME) followed by ⊤. To move to the top line of the screen,

Press: (HOME)
Press: ⊤

The cursor should be at the beginning of Ln 3.17", on the "t" in "the."

(HOME) followed by (↓) will move the cursor to the last line of the screen.

Press: (HOME)
Press: (↓)

The cursor should be positioned back at the beginning of "Sports" on the last line (Ln 7") of the screen.

You can also move to the top or bottom of the screen by using the minus (-) or plus (+) signs located to the right of the numeric keypad. (Do not use the plus or minus signs located in the upper row of the keyboard.) To move to the top of the screen,

Press: -

The cursor is positioned back on the first line of text on the screen.

Press: +

The cursor is positioned back on the last line of the screen.

Using the plus or minus keys to move to the bottom or top of the screen requires fewer keystrokes than using (HOME) and (↑) or (↓).

The screen is positioned over 24 lines of text on page 1 of the document (see Figure 1-11). WordPerfect differentiates between a screen and a page. A screen can display only 24 lines of text, whereas the printed page can display many more lines of text.

The cursor can be moved to the top or bottom line of a page using the (CTRL) - (HOME) key combination (while holding down (CTRL) press (HOME)). This is called the Go to key because of the prompt you will see displayed in status line.

Press: (CTRL) - (HOME)

Your display screen should be similar to Figure 1-12.

FIGURE 1-12

```
The club facilities include 18 lighted tennis courst × ×× ××××××
5 racquetball courts, an olympic size swimming 77777 www gggggggg
pool, Nautilus equipped weight room, and basketball court.  For
JJJJJJJ BBBB $$$$$$ cYYYYY tttttt(( )))))  $$$$$$  @@@@@@
rrrrrrrr  IIIII uUUUUU ×××××××× bbbbb GGGGGGG DDDDDD 444444
444444 jjjjjjjbb   ccccc ddtydrdh yryygh hgdd rrssrt nkhu 87t56rf
tfhghgr 6f fhgf 5dggf645hgh  hghtyuj ygyt fdfd uuuuyty ghddfh
your comfort while using the club, the men's and ladies' locker
rooms

  each have showers, a sauna, and a steam steam room.  A spa for
both men and women women is locaated between the locker rooms
rooms.  The lounge adn cafge are open to seruce you throughout
the dayu and evening.

On behalf of of the staff of, I hope ///////. JJJJJ J TTTT
&&&&&&&&& you accociation with the Club is lnog and enjoyable.


Sincerely,,,,,, ×××× ;;;;;



Sports Club Manager
Go to _
```

prompt

The prompt "Go to" is displayed in the status line. A number, a character, ⬆ or ⬇ can be entered at this prompt.

To move to the top of the current page,

Press: ⬆

The cursor should be positioned on the first line (1") of page 1. The screen is positioned over the first 24 lines of text on this page.

To move the cursor to the last line of page 1,

Press: (CTRL) - (HOME)
Press: ⬇

The cursor should be positioned on the last line of page 1. The dashed line at the bottom of the screen shows the location of the end of page 1 and the beginning of page 2.

Press: ⬇

Your display screen should be similar to Figure 1-13.

FIGURE 1-13

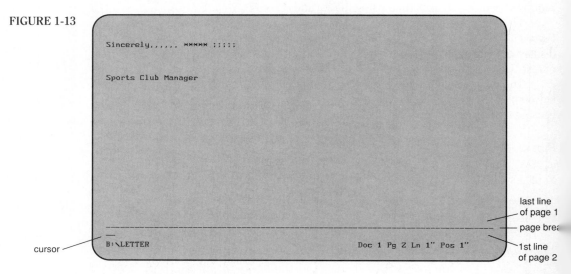

Sincerely.,.,.., ⋈⋈⋈⋈ ;;;;;

Sports Club Manager

last line of page 1
page break
1st line of page 2

cursor

B:\LETTER   Doc 1 Pg Z Ln 1" Pos 1"

The cursor should be positioned on the last line of the screen. This is the first line of page 2 in the document.

The cursor can also be quickly moved from one page of text to another using the (PGUP) (page up) and (PGDN) (page down) keys. The message "Repositioning" will appear briefly in the status line while the cursor moves to the new location.

To move back to the top of the previous page,

Press: (PGUP)

The cursor is positioned on the first line of page 1.

To move to the top of page 2,

Press: (PGDN)

Your display screen should be similar to Figure 1-14.

FIGURE 1-14

cursor

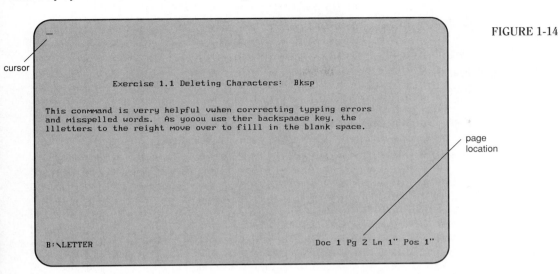

page
location

The cursor should be on the first line of page 2. The screen is positioned over the first 24 lines of page 2. Using (PGUP) or (PGDN) always positions the cursor on the left margin of the first line of the page.

To move through several pages of the document at once, you could press (PGDN) or (PGUP) multiple times. Or you can use the GoTo key combination again.

To move to page 5 of this document,

Press: (CTRL) - (HOME)

To respond to the "Go to" prompt, enter the page number. Use the number keys on the top line of the keyboard, above the alphabetic keys, as follows:

Type: 5
Press: ⏎

Your display screen should be similar to Figure 1-15.

FIGURE 1-15

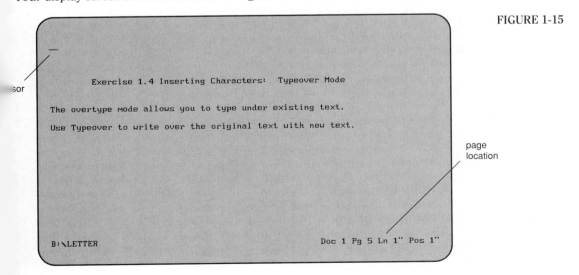

page
location

The cursor is positioned on the first line of page 5.

The biggest jump the cursor can make is to move to the beginning or end of a document. To move to the end of this document,

Press: (HOME)
Press: (HOME)
Press: (↓)

Your display screen should be similar to Figure 1-16.

FIGURE 1-16

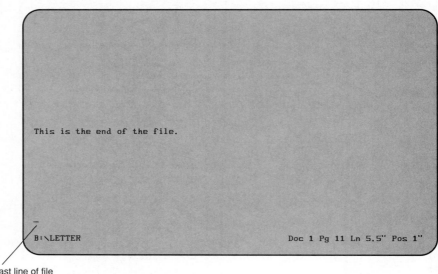

This is the end of the file.

B:\LETTER   Doc 1 Pg 11 Ln 5.5" Pos 1"

last line of file

The cursor should be positioned on a blank line. This line is the last line in the document.

To move quickly back to the first line of text in the document,

Press: (HOME)
Press: (HOME)
Press: (↑)

The cursor should be positioned on the first line of page 1 of this document.

To review, the following cursor movement features have been covered:

Key	Action
→	One character to right
←	One character to left
↑	One line up
↓	One line down
CTRL - →	One word to right
CTRL - ←	One word to left
HOME - →	Right end of line
END	Right end of line
HOME , ←	Left edge of screen
HOME , ↑	Top of screen
- (minus sign)	Top of screen
HOME , ↓	Bottom of screen
[+] (plus sign)	Bottom of screen
CTRL - HOME , ↑	Top of current page
CTRL - HOME , ↓	Bottom of current page
CTRL - HOME page number	Top of page number specified
PGUP	Top of previous page
PGDN	Top of next page
HOME , HOME , ↑	Beginning of document
HOME , HOME , ↓	End of document

Using the Mouse to Move the Cursor

If you do not have a mouse, skip to the next section, "Editing a Document." If you have a mouse, you can use it to move the cursor to a specific location in a document. To do this, position the mouse pointer at the location in the text where you want to move the cursor and click the left button. Using the mouse,

Move to: "y" of "your" (first line of first paragraph)

Notice the cursor has not moved and the status line information has not changed.

Click: left button

The cursor is now positioned under the "y," and the status line reflects its new location in the document (Ln 1.33" Pos 3.8").

Practice using the mouse to move the cursor by moving it to the following locations on the screen:

Move to: "E" in "Each" (first line of second paragraph)

Move to: "b" in "basketball" (third line of third paragraph)

Move to: "s" in "sauna" (last line on screen)

Try moving the mouse pointer to the next line of text.

It will not move beyond the displayed text on the screen. To scroll the text on the screen, with the mouse pointer positioned on either the top or bottom line of the text on the screen, hold down the right button and move the mouse slightly up or down. The screen will continue to scroll until you release the button.

To try this, with the mouse positioned on the last line of text on the screen (not the status line) hold down the right button and move the mouse downward. Be careful that you do not quickly click the right button, as this will cause the menu to be displayed. If this happens, click the right button again to cancel the menu.

After a moment to stop the scrolling, release the right button.

Upon releasing the right button, the cursor also moves to the mouse pointer location. If there is no text on the line where you stopped scrolling, the cursor will be positioned at the beginning of the line.

Scroll the document upward until you are back on the first line of text on page 1.

To review, the following mouse features have been covered:

Mouse	Action
In Editing screen:	
Click right button	Displays menu.
Click left button	Positions cursor.
Dragging - right button	Scrolls screen.
In pull-down menus:	
Click right button	Backs out of all menus and removes menu bar from screen.
Click left button	Displays menu choices for menu-bar item positioned on or selects menu item.
Dragging	Moves across menu-bar and displays pull-down menu for each of the nine menus.
	Moves down a pull-down menu, highlights each choice and displays submenu if available. Releasing the button selects the highlighted command.

Editing a Document

Now that you have learned how to move the cursor around the document, you are ready to learn how to **edit**, or correct errors in a document.

The next part of this lab contains a series of exercises. Each exercise will show you a WordPerfect editing feature and allow you to practice using the feature. As you read the text in the book you will be directed to use the editing feature to correct the exercise on your display screen. When you have completed the exercise, a figure in the book will show you how your display screen should appear. After completing each exercise press (PGDN) to go to the next exercise. To begin the exercise,

Press: (PGDN)

Exercise 1.1 Deleting Characters: (BKSP)

Your display screen should be similar to Figure 1-17.

FIGURE 1-17

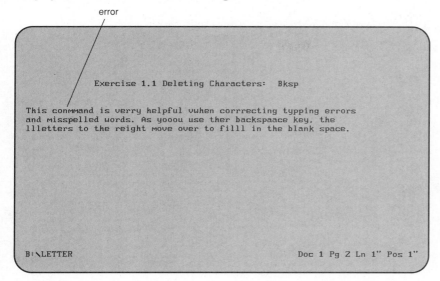

error

```
          Exercise 1.1 Deleting Characters:  Bksp

This conmmand is verry helpful vwhen corrrecting typping errors
and misspelled words. As yooou use ther backspaace key, the
llletters to the reight move over to filll in the blank space.
```

B:\LETTER   Doc 1 Pg Z Ln 1" Pos 1"

The first exercise, "Exercise 1.1 Deleting Characters: Bksp," should be on your display screen.

The (BKSP) (backspace) key will **delete,** or erase, a character to the left of the cursor. This key may be labeled with a left-facing arrow, the word "Backspace" or "Bksp," or a combination of the two. It is located above the (⏎) key.

The paragraph in the exercise on the display screen contains several errors that you will correct using the (BKSP) key. The first error on the screen is in the second word, "conmmand." The word should be "command." The "n" needs to be deleted.

To position the cursor to the right of the "n,"

Move to: Ln 2.33" Pos 1.8" (first "m" in "conmmand")

Note: If you are using the mouse to move the cursor, use the information in parentheses to tell you where to position the mouse pointer. Then verify the cursor position using the line and position information.

As a character is deleted, the text to the right will move over to fill in the space left by the deleted character. Watch your screen carefully as you

Press: (BKSP)

The character to the left of the cursor, in this case the "n", is deleted. The text to the right then moves over one space to fill in the space left by the character that was deleted.

There is now an extra space at the end of this line. As soon as you move the cursor to the right one space or down a line, WordPerfect will examine the line to see whether the word beginning on the next line ("and") can be moved up to fill in the space without exceeding the margin setting. This process of filling in the spaces is called **reformatting**. Watch your screen carefully as you correct the error in the word "verry."

Move to:	Ln 2.33" Pos 2.9" (second "r" in "verry")
Press:	(BKSP)
Press:	(→) (1 time)

Your display screen should look similar to Figure 1-18.

FIGURE 1-18

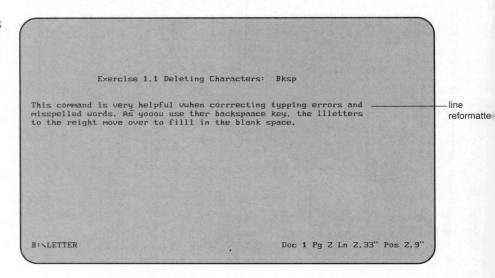

```
                    Exercise 1.1 Deleting Characters:  Bksp


This command is very helpful vwhen corrrecting typping errors and          ──── line
misspelled words. As yooou use ther backspaace key, the llletters                reformatte
to the reight move over to filll in the blank space.
```

```
B:\LETTER                                    Doc 1 Pg 2 Ln 2.33" Pos 2.9"
```

The word "and" from the beginning of the line below moved up to the end of the current line. The deletion of the extra characters created enough space for the whole word to move up a line. As you move the cursor through the text it will be automatically reformatted.

The automatic reformatting of text is the default setting in WordPerfect 5.1. As you move through the text the lines above the cursor will always display properly on the screen.

Continue this exercise by using (BKSP) to correct the text on the display. As you edit and move through the text, WordPerfect will constantly reexamine the margin space and reformat as needed.

When you are finished your display screen should be similar to Figure 1-19.

FIGURE 1-19

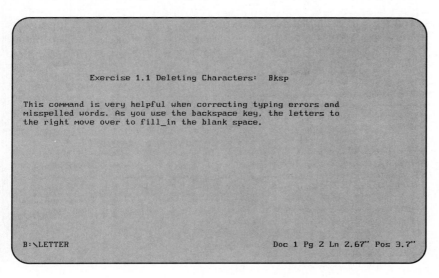

```
          Exercise 1.1 Deleting Characters:  Bksp

 This command is very helpful when correcting typing errors and
 misspelled words. As you use the backspace key, the letters to
 the right move over to fill_in the blank space.




 B:\LETTER                              Doc 1 Pg 2 Ln 2.67" Pos 3.7"
```

As you can see, each time you press (BKSP) the cursor "backs up" through the text, deleting the character to the left of the cursor. The text is reformatted as needed.

Exercise 1.2 Deleting Characters: (DEL)

To move to the next exercise,

Press: (PGDN)

The second exercise, "Exercise 1.2 Deleting Characters: Del," should be on your screen.

A second way to delete a character is with (DEL). On most keyboards the (DEL) key is at the right side of the keyboard beneath the numeric keypad. This key will delete the character the cursor is positioned under.

The first error is in the second word in the first line of the exercise, "**u**you."

Move to: Ln 2.67" Pos 1.5" (under the first "u" in "uyou")

To delete the "u,"

Press: (DEL)

The "u" was removed, and the text to the right moved over to fill in the blank space. The paragraph will be reformatted as needed.

Complete the exercise by using (DEL) to correct the text on the screen. When you are done your display screen should be similar to Figure 1-20 on the next page.

```
                    Exercise 1.2 Deleting Characters:   Del

When you use the Del key, the character under the cursor is
deleted. This command is useful when you see an error in the text
several lines back. Instead of using the backspace key and
deleting all the correct text, use the arrow keys to move the
cursor to the location of the error, and press Del.

As the characters are deleted, the text from the right fills in
the blank space.




B:\LETTER                                    Doc 1 Pg 3 Ln 3.33" Pos 4.3"
```

FIGURE 1-20

Exercise 1.3 Inserting Characters: Insert Mode

Press: PGDN

Text can be entered into a document in either the **Insert** or **Typeover modes**. The default setting for WordPerfect is the Insert mode. As you type in Insert mode, new characters are inserted into the existing text. The existing text moves to the right to make space for the new characters.

The first sentence on the screen should read: "The **Insert** mode allows new text **to** be entered into **a** document." The three missing words, "Insert," "to" and "a" can be easily entered into the sentence without retyping it.

To enter the word "Insert" before the word "mode" in the first sentence,

Move to: Ln 3" Pos 1.4" (under the "m" in "mode")
Type: **Insert**
Press: Space bar

The word "Insert" has been entered into the sentence by moving everything to the right to make space as each letter is typed.

Next, to enter the word "to" before the word "be,"

Move to: Line 3" Pos 4.2" (under the "b" in "be")
Type: **to**
Press: Space bar

Finally, to enter the word "a" before the word "document,"

Move to: Ln 3" Pos 6.1" (under the "d" in "document")
Type: **a**
Press: Space bar

Your display screen should be similar to Figure 1-21.

FIGURE 1-21

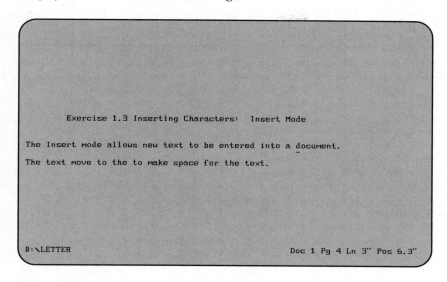

```
          Exercise 1.3 Inserting Characters:   Insert Mode

The Insert mode allows new text to be entered into a document.
The text move to the to make space for the text.
```

```
B:\LETTER                                    Doc 1 Pg 4 Ln 3" Pos 6.3"
```

As each new character was entered into the existing text, the text to the right moved over to make space.

In a similar manner, correct the second sentence on the screen to read: "The **old** text move**s** to the **right** to make space for the **new** text". Your display screen should be similar to Figure 1-22.

FIGURE 1-22

```
          Exercise 1.3 Inserting Characters:   Insert Mode

The Insert mode allows new text to be entered into a document.
The old text moves to the right to make space for the new text.
```

```
B:\LETTER                                    Doc 1 Pg 4 Ln 3.33" Pos 6.8"
```

Exercise 1.4 Inserting Characters: Typeover Mode

Press: (PGDN)

The second method of entering text in a document is to use the Typeover mode. In this mode, the new text types over the existing characters.

The (INS) (insert) key, located to the left of the (DEL) key, changes the mode from Insert to Typeover.

Press: (INS)

Your display screen should be similar to Figure 1-23.

FIGURE 1-23

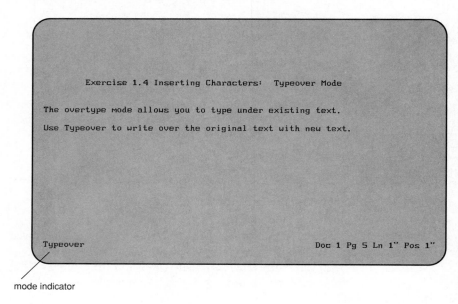

mode indicator

To tell you that the Typeover mode is on, the word "Typeover" appears on the left side of the status line.

The first sentence should read: "The **Typeover** mode allows you to type **over** existing text." To correct this sentence,

Move to: Ln 2.5" Pos 1.4" (beginning of "overtype")
Type: **Typeover**

As each character was typed, the character (or space) under it was replaced with the character being typed.

Next, to replace the word "under" with "over,"

Move to: Ln 2.5" Pos 4.7" (beginning of "under")
Type: **over**

Notice that there is still one extra character. To remove the extra "r,"

Press: (DEL)

Your display screen should be similar to Figure 1-24.

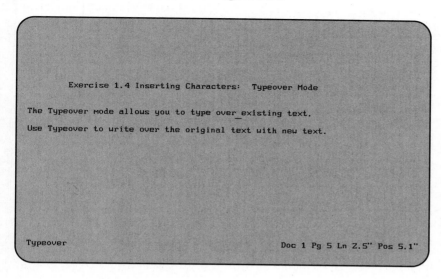

In a similar manner, correct the sentence to be: "**The** typeover **mode replaces the original text with new text.**"

To turn off the Typeover mode,

Press: (INS)

Exercise 1.5 Deleting Words: (CTRL) - (BKSP)

Press: (PGDN)

The (CTRL) - (BKSP) key combination is used to delete entire words. The cursor can be positioned on any character of the word to be deleted, or one space to the left of the word to be deleted.

The first line on the screen contains several duplicate words. It should read: "This command is very helpful for deleting unnecessary words.

To remove the first duplicate word, "command,"

Move to: Ln 2.67" Pos 1.5" ("c" of "command")
Press: (CTRL) - (BKSP)

The word the cursor is positioned on is deleted. Notice also that one blank space was deleted, leaving the correct number of spaces between words.

If the cursor is placed on a blank space immediately after a word, then using (CTRL) - (BKSP) deletes the word to the left of the cursor and the blank space the cursor is on.

Use (CTRL) - (BKSP) to delete the other duplicate words in the sentences on the screen. After completing the exercise, your display screen should be similar to Figure 1-25.

FIGURE 1-25

```
                    Exercise 1.5 Deleting Words:   Ctrl-Bksp


     This command is very helpful for deleting unnecessary words.
     Words such as these are obviously redundant, and therefore
     need not be written twice.




B:\LETTER                                              Doc 1 Pg 6 Ln 3" Pos 3"
```

The text to the right filled in the blank space when you deleted a word. The paragraph was reformatted as needed. You may have also noticed that any punctuation following a word is considered part of the word and is deleted also.

Exercise 1.6 Deleting from Cursor to End of Line: (CTRL) - (END)

Press: (PGDN)

The (CTRL) - (END) key combination will delete everything on a line from the cursor to the right. If the cursor is placed at the beginning of a line, all the text on the line is deleted.

You will delete the unnecessary text following the word "cursor" in the first line in this exercise.

Move to: Ln 2.67" Pos 4.5" (first "8" immediately following "cursor")
Press: (CTRL) - (END)

The text from the cursor to the right is deleted.

Continue this exercise by deleting the unnecessary characters at the end of the next two lines.

Next, delete the entire contents of the fourth line by placing the cursor on the first character in the line.

Your display screen should be similar to Figure 1-26.

```
    Exercise 1.6  Deleting From Cursor to End of Line:  Ctrl-End

 To delete the text from the cursor
 to the end of the line,
 move the cursor to the first character

 you want to delete and press Ctrl-End.




B:\LETTER                                  Doc 1 Pg 7 Ln 3.17" Pos 1"
```

FIGURE 1-26

Exercise 1.7 Deleting Several Lines of Text: (ESC), (CTRL) - (END)

Press: (PGDN)

Several lines of text can be deleted at once by using (ESC) followed by the (CTRL) - (END) key combination. To delete several lines of text, first move the cursor to the beginning of the line of text to be deleted.

To erase the lines which are labeled as lines 13, 14, and 15 on the screen, first,

Move to: Ln 3" Pos 1" (beginning of line 13)

Next, count the number of lines you want to erase. You want to delete three lines. To do this, you could use the (CTRL) - (END) command three times to erase the contents of each line. Or you can use (ESC) to tell WordPerfect to repeat a function a specified number of times.

Press: (ESC)

The status line displays the prompt "Repeat Value = 8." The number 8 is the default setting.

(ESC) acts as a **repeater** to specify the number of times to repeat a specified function. The number you enter tells WordPerfect how many times to repeat the function you will enter next. Do not press (⏎) after typing in your response to the prompt.

To repeat the function three times,

Type: 3

There are many functions which can be repeated. To move through a document you can press (ESC) and the (↑) and (↓) keys to move up or down a specified number of lines, (PGUP) or (PGDN) to move forward or backward by pages, (→) or (←) to move right or left character by character along a line. To delete text you can press (ESC) and (CTRL) - (BKSP) to remove a specified number of words, (CTRL) - (END) to remove lines of text, or (CTRL) - (PGDN) to delete pages. In this case, to remove the three lines of text,

Press: (CTRL) - (END)

Your display screen should be similar to Figure 1-27.

FIGURE 1-27

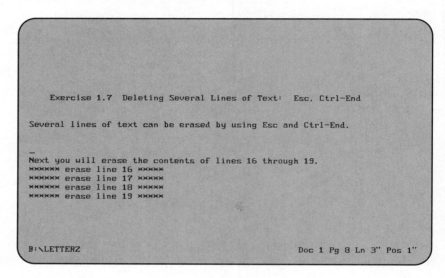

```
        Exercise 1.7  Deleting Several Lines of Text:  Esc, Ctrl-End

    Several lines of text can be erased by using Esc and Ctrl-End.


    _
    Next you will erase the contents of lines 16 through 19.
    xxxxxx erase line 16 xxxxx
    xxxxxx erase line 17 xxxxx
    xxxxxx erase line 18 xxxxx
    xxxxxx erase line 19 xxxxx



    B:\LETTER2                                      Doc 1 Pg 8 Ln 3" Pos 1"
```

The contents of lines 13, 14, and 15 have been deleted.
In a similar manner, erase lines 16 through 19.
(ESC) can be entered before using the arrow and (DEL) keys, (PGUP) , (PGDN) , (HOME)- (↓) and (HOME) - (↑), and (CTRL) - (←) and (CTRL) - (→) to tell WordPerfect to repeat the procedure the specified number of times. It can also be used to enter the same character into the text a number of times.

Exercise 1.8 Inserting and Deleting Blank Lines

Press: (PGDN)

The (⏎) key is used to insert a blank line into text or to mark the end of a paragraph. It is called a **hard carriage return**
If (⏎) is pressed in the middle of a line of text, all text to the right of the cursor moves to the beginning of the next line. For example,

Move to: Ln 2.5" Pos 5.3 ("m" of "middle" in the first line of this exercise)
Press: (⏎)

A hard carriage return is entered at the end of the first line, and the text from the cursor to the right moves down to the beginning of the next line.

If you press (BKSP) the hard carriage return at the end of the first line is deleted, and the text returns to its original location.

Press: (BKSP)

If ⏎ is pressed at the beginning of a line, a blank line is inserted into the document. To see how this works,

Move to: Ln 3" Pos 1" (beginning of "If" on the fourth line of this exercise)
Press: ⏎

A blank line is inserted into the text, forcing the line the cursor is on to move down one line.

If ⏎ is pressed at the end of a paragraph or line of text, the cursor moves to the beginning of the next line.

Move to: Ln 3.83" Pos 7.5" (end of last line in the exercise)
Press: ⏎

The cursor moves to the beginning of the next line.

To delete a blank line, position the cursor at the beginning of the blank line and press (DEL). To try this,

Move to: Ln 3.5" Pos 1" (beginning of blank line between second and third sentences)
Press: (DEL)

Your display screen should be similar to Figure 1-28.

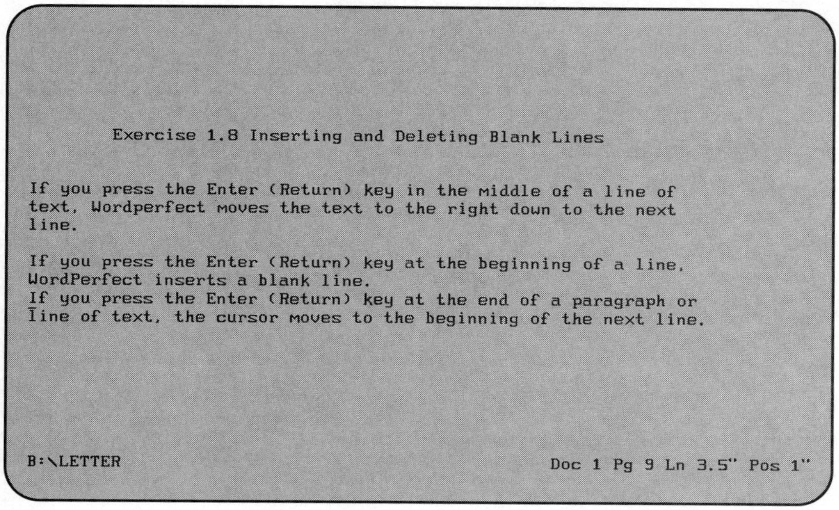

FIGURE 1-28

```
        Exercise 1.8 Inserting and Deleting Blank Lines

If you press the Enter (Return) key in the middle of a line of
text, Wordperfect moves the text to the right down to the next
line.

If you press the Enter (Return) key at the beginning of a line,
WordPerfect inserts a blank line.
If you press the Enter (Return) key at the end of a paragraph or
line of text, the cursor moves to the beginning of the next line.




B:\LETTER                              Doc 1 Pg 9 Ln 3.5" Pos 1"
```

The blank line is deleted, and the text below moves up one line.

Exercise 1.9 Undeleting Text

Press: (PGDN)

It is easy to accidentally delete text you did not intend to delete. Fortunately the Edit>Undelete, or Undelete (F1), command lets you restore your deletions. To do this, each time you delete text WordPerfect stores it in a special file called a **buffer**. Only the last three deletions are stored.

To see how this works, delete the three sentences numbered 1, 2, and 3 by moving to the beginning of each line and pressing (CTRL) - (END).

To restore the deleted text,

Select: Edit
Select: Undelete

Your screen should be similar to Figure 1-29.

FIGURE 1-29

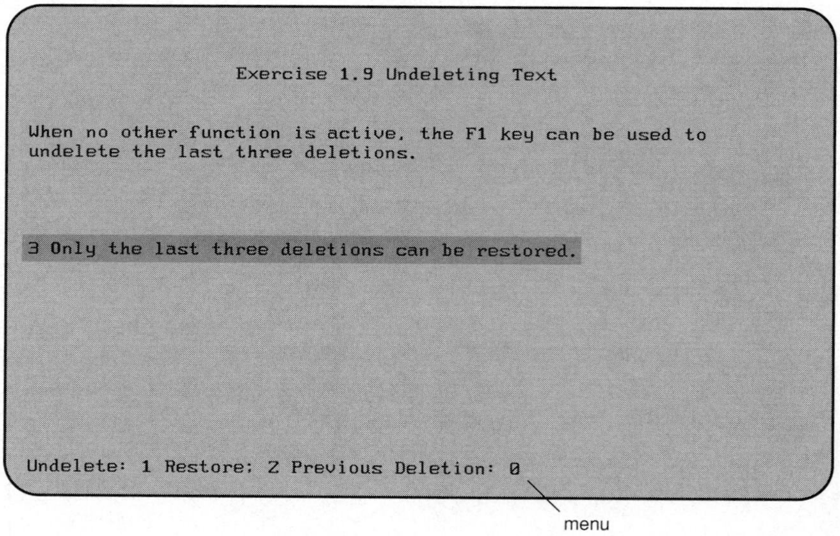

```
                    Exercise 1.9 Undeleting Text


  When no other function is active, the F1 key can be used to
  undelete the last three deletions.



  3 Only the last three deletions can be restored.





  Undelete: 1 Restore: 2 Previous Deletion: 0
```
                                                    menu

The most recently deleted text (sentence 3) appears highlighted on the screen. The undelete menu appears in the status line. It lets you restore the highlighted text or see the previous deletions. To see the previous deletion,

Select: Previous

The second deletion is displayed. You can also use the up and down arrow keys to display the deletions.

Press: (↑)

The first deletion is displayed.

Press: (↑)

The third deletion is displayed again. To restore the highlighted text,

Select: Restore

The third deletion is reentered at the cursor position.

Restore the first and second deletions in numerical order above sentence 3. To do this, first position the cursor in the location where you want the text displayed. Then select the Edit>Undelete command, display the deleted text, and select Restore. When you are done the screen should appear as it did before you deleted the sentences.

To review, the following editing keys have been covered:

Key	Action
(BKSP)	Deletes character to left of cursor
(DEL)	Deletes character at cursor
(INS) on	Inserts character into text
(INS) off	Uses Typeover mode to insert text
(CTRL) - (BKSP)	Deletes word cursor is on
(⏎)	Moves cursor to next line
	Inserts a blank line
(CTRL) - (END)	Deletes line of text from cursor to right
(ESC) # (function)	Repeats certain functions n times, where n= any number
Undelete (F1)	Restores the last three deletions

Clearing the Screen

Now that you know how to move around a document and how to use several different types of editing keys, you will correct the rough draft of the welcome letter Karen created. A copy of the rough draft is in another file named **LETTER2**.

Before retrieving a new file, you must clear the current document from the screen. If you do not clear the current document from the screen, the file you retrieve will combine with the document on the screen, creating a third document.

All WordPerfect 5.1 commands are issued by using the pull-down menu or the function key combination. As you use WordPerfect 5.1 commands throughout this series of labs, the command will be presented using both the function keys and the pull-down menus. The pull-down menu command sequence will be presented first. It will appear following the word "Select." Each menu command in the sequence will be separated with >, and the mnemonic letter will appear boldfaced. For example, the command to retrieve a file will appear as "Select: **F**ile>**R**etrieve."

The function key equivalent command will appear below the pull-down menu command sequence. It will be preceded with >> for example, the command to retrieve a file using the function key will appear as ">> Retrieve (SHIFT) - (F10)."

As you become familiar with the program you will probably rely less on the pull-down menus to issue commands and more on the function keys. This is because the function keys accomplish the same procedure with fewer keystrokes. Always have your function key template handy, as you will find is a very helpful reminder of the key combination to use.

To clear the current document from the screen, use the pull-down menu command, File Exit, or the function key Exit (F7) command,

Select: File>Exit
>> Exit (F7)

The prompt in the status line, "Save Document? Yes (No)," is asking whether you want to save the changes you made to the current file, LETTER, in memory to the diskette. In most cases, before you clear a document from the screen, you will want to save the work you have done onto a diskette. In this way you would be able to retrieve the file again and resume work on it if needed. Notice that following the prompt WordPerfect displays the response to the prompt as "Yes." This is the default response. To respond to the prompt, you can type the appropriate letter (Y or N) or you can position the mouse pointer on the option and click the left button. Additionally, you can simply press (↵) to accept the default response.

You do not want to save the edited version of the document. By responding "N" (No) to the prompt, the changes you made to the document file LETTER will not be saved. The original version of the file LETTER remains on the diskette unchanged. You can retrieve the file LETTER again and repeat the exercises for practice. To indicate that you do not want to save the document as it appears on the screen,

Type: N

The next prompt, "Exit WP? No (Yes)," is asking if you want to exit the WordPerfect program. This time the default response is "No." If you select Yes the screen clears, and the operating system prompt will appear in the lower left-hand corner of the display screen. You could then turn your computer off, load another program, or reload the WordPerfect 5.1 program. If you accept the default (No), the display screen will clear and you can continue using the WordPerfect 5.1 program by creating a new document or, as you will do, retrieving another document file. Since you want to continue working in WordPerfect,

Press: (↵)

The document LETTER is cleared from the screen, and a blank WordPerfect screen is displayed.

Listing File Names

The new file you want to use is named LETTER2. A listing of the files on the disk can be displayed by using the List Files or List (F5) command.

Select: File>List Files
>> List (F5)

The name of the current directory (B or A) is displayed in the status line. If you wanted to see a display of the files on a diskette in another drive, you could enter the name of the new directory. A listing of the files in that directory would then be displayed. The current drive, however, would not change. If you wanted to actually change the current directory to another directory, you would type =, as the prompt in the status line indicates. The current directory name would disappear. You could then enter the name of the directory you wanted to use. Since you simply want to see a listing of the files on the diskette in the current (A or B) drive,

Press: ⏎

Your display screen should be similar to Figure 1-30.

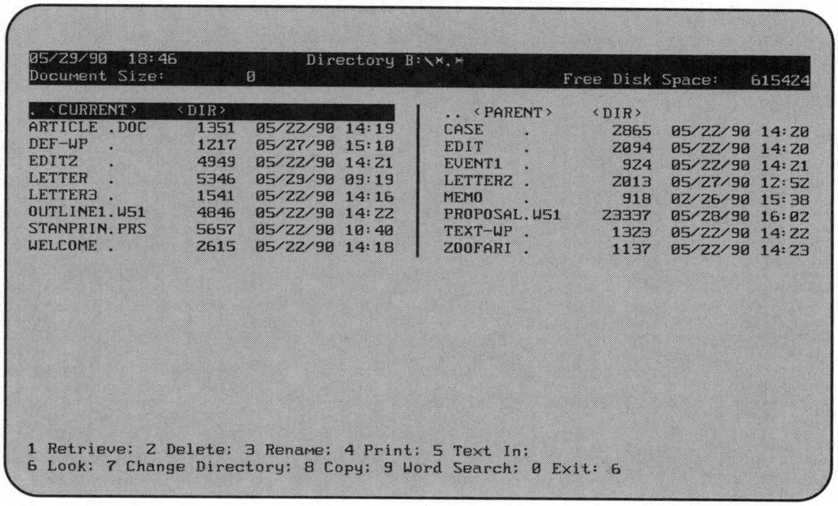

FIGURE 1-30

```
05/29/90  18:46              Directory B:\*.*
Document Size:          0                    Free Disk Space:     615424

.  <CURRENT>   <DIR>               ..  <PARENT>    <DIR>
ARTICLE .DOC     1351  05/22/90 14:19    CASE    .      2865  05/22/90 14:20
DEF-WP  .        1217  05/27/90 15:18    EDIT    .      2094  05/22/90 14:20
EDIT2   .        4949  05/22/90 14:21    EVENT1  .       924  05/22/90 14:21
LETTER  .        5346  05/29/90 09:19    LETTER2 .      2013  05/27/90 12:52
LETTER3 .        1541  05/22/90 14:16    MEMO    .       918  02/26/90 15:38
OUTLINE1.WS1     4846  05/22/90 14:22    PROPOSAL.WS1  23337  05/28/90 16:02
STANPRIN.PRS     5657  05/22/90 10:40    TEXT-WP .      1323  05/22/90 14:22
WELCOME .        2615  05/22/90 14:18    ZOOFARI .      1137  05/22/90 14:23




1 Retrieve; 2 Delete; 3 Rename; 4 Print; 5 Text In;
6 Look; 7 Change Directory; 8 Copy; 9 Word Search; 0 Exit: 6
```

The top of the screen displays the current date and time, the name of the directory being viewed, the size of the document you are currently working on, and the remaining free diskette space. Beneath this information is an alphabetized list of the files in the directory in two columns. The file names are alphabetized from left to right across the column and then down the column. The directory includes files which are not WordPerfect files. The files listed on your screen may differ from the files in Figure 1-30 depending upon the software programs selected by your instructor.

The file you want to retrieve, LETTER2, appears in the directory. The menu of **options** in the status line allows you to organize and work with the files on the disk. An option is selected by typing the number to the left of the option name, or typing the highlighted letter, or positioning the mouse pointer on the option and clicking the left mouse button. Notice the first menu option, 1 Retrieve. By selecting this option you can retrieve the WordPerfect file you want to use. To do this, first you need to move the highlight bar, by using the arrow keys or by dragging the mouse, over the file name you want to retrieve.

Move to: LETTER2

With the highlight bar over the file name you want to retrieve, to retrieve the file,

Select: Retrieve

The document LETTER2 is displayed on the screen. Using the List Files ((F5)) command to display a file directory and retrieve a file is very helpful when you are not sure of the name of the file you want to use. The result, retrieval of a file, is the same as if you used the Retrieve ((SHIFT) - (F10)) command or selected File>Retrieve from the menu.

Editing the Welcome Letter

The rough draft of the welcome letter is displayed on the screen. Using the editing features presented above, correct the letter on your screen. Refer to Figure 1-31 for missing words. Use it as a guide to how your screen should appear when you are done. Check that there is only one blank space between words and following a period.

Saving and Replacing an Existing File

The file saved on the diskette as LETTER2 does not include the editing changes you have just made to the document on the screen. When you are entering text, it is stored temporary memory (RAM) only. Not until you **save** the document to the diskette are you safe from losing your work due to power failure or other mishap.

To save the document to disk and continue working on the file, use the File>Save or (F10) command.

Select: File>Save   .
  >>   Save (F10)

The prompt "Document to be saved:" is dispalyed followed by the drive and filename of the file you are currently using.

You could save both the original version of the document and the revised document as two separate files. To do this, you would enter a new file name for the revised version at this prompt. However, you do not want to keep the original version. Instead you will **replace,** or write over, it with the current version of the document on the screen. To save the current version of the document on the display screen over the version currently on the diskette, using the same file name,

Press: (⏎)

Your display screen should be similar to Figure 1-31.

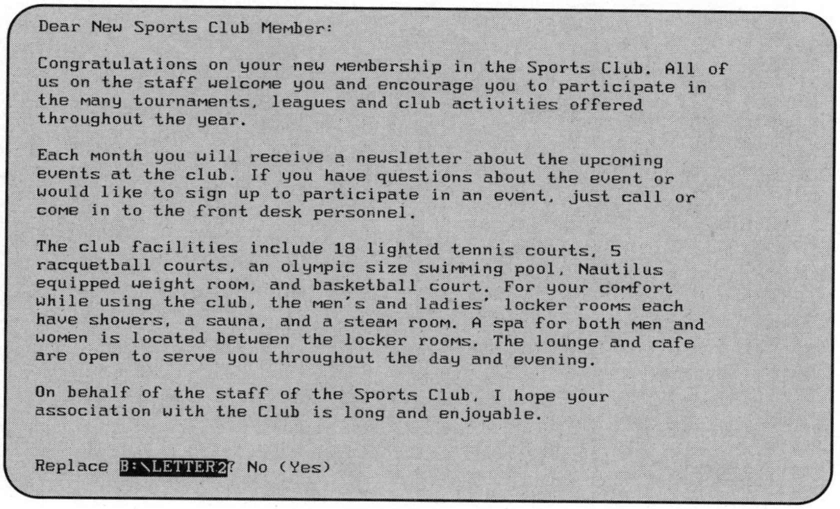

FIGURE 1-31

```
Dear New Sports Club Member:

Congratulations on your new membership in the Sports Club. All of
us on the staff welcome you and encourage you to participate in
the many tournaments, leagues and club activities offered
throughout the year.

Each month you will receive a newsletter about the upcoming
events at the club. If you have questions about the event or
would like to sign up to participate in an event, just call or
come in to the front desk personnel.

The club facilities include 18 lighted tennis courts, 5
racquetball courts, an olympic size swimming pool, Nautilus
equipped weight room, and basketball court. For your comfort
while using the club, the men's and ladies' locker rooms each
have showers, a sauna, and a steam room. A spa for both men and
women is located between the locker rooms. The lounge and cafe
are open to serve you throughout the day and evening.

On behalf of the staff of the Sports Club, I hope your
association with the Club is long and enjoyable.


Replace B:\LETTER2? No (Yes)
```

The next prompt , "Replace!," protects the user from accidentally writing over an existing file. It asks you to confirm that you want to replace the contents of the file on the diskette with the revised document on the display.

If you enter N (No), the "Document to be Saved:" prompt appears again to allow you to enter a new file name. Since you want to replace the original document on the diskette with the new document on the display,

Type: **Y**

The revised document writes over the original document saved on the diskette, and you are returned to the document.

Printing a Document

Karen wants to print a hard copy of the welcome letter to give to the Membership Coordinator. If you have printer capability you can print a copy of the document displayed on the screen.

Note: Please consult your instructor for printing procedures that may differ from the directions below.

The Print menu is accessed by selecting Print from the File menu or by pressing (SHIFT) - (F7) (Print).

Select: File>Print
   >>   Print (SHIFT) - (F7)

Your display screen should be similar to Figure 1-32.

FIGURE 1-32

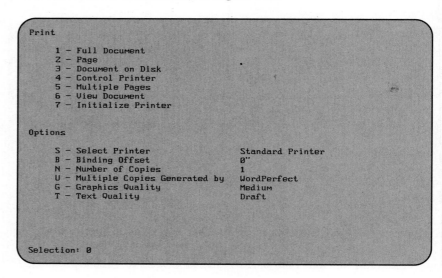

```
 Print
         1 - Full Document
         2 - Page
         3 - Document on Disk
         4 - Control Printer
         5 - Multiple Pages
         6 - View Document
         7 - Initialize Printer


 Options
         S - Select Printer             Standard Printer
         B - Binding Offset             0"
         N - Number of Copies           1
         U - Multiple Copies Generated by  WordPerfect
         G - Graphics Quality           Medium
         T - Text Quality               Draft



 Selection: 0
```

The document has been temporarily removed from the screen to display the Print
screen. This screen is divided into two menus, Print and Options. The Print menu
lets you print a document from the screen or from a document stored on a disk. The
Options menu lets you select the printer and make changes to the printer settings.

In the Options menu, notice that to the right of the menu options, the selected printer and printer settings are displayed. The selected printer is Standard
Printer. This is the **active printer**, or the printer that WordPerfect 5.1 expects to use
to print the document.

The active printer can be changed using the Select Printer option.

Select: Select Printer

The Select Printer screen is displayed. At the top of the screen is a list of printers
your school has defined. If Standard Printer is listed here, it will be highlighted, and
an asterisk (*) indicates that it is the active printer.

To select the appropriate printer, first move the highlight bar to the name of
the printer you want to use. The Select option (1) in the menu in the status line lets
you change the highlighted printer to the active printer.

Select: Select

You are returned to the Print screen, and the printer you selected should be displayed as the active printer.

Now you are ready to instruct WordPerfect to print the letter. If necessary turn
the printer on and adjust the paper so that the perforation is just above the printer
scale.

The first two Print menu options let you specify how much of the document
you want printed. If you wanted to print the full document, then option 1 Full
Document would be selected. If you wanted to print only the page the cursor is on,
then you would select **P**age.

To print a copy of the entire document,

Select: Full Document

Your printer should be printing out the document, and the letter is again displayed on your screen.

The printed copy of the welcome letter should be similar to Figure 1-33. It may not match exactly if you changed the active printer from Standard Printer to another printer. The number of words on a line in your printed document and the document on your screen may have changed. This is a result of the printer you selected.

FIGURE 1-33

```
Dear New Sports Club Member:

Congratulations on your new membership in the Sports Club. All of
us on the staff welcome you and encourage you to participate in
the many tournaments, leagues and club activities offered
throughout the year.

Each month you will receive a newsletter about the upcoming
events at the club. If you have questions about the event or
would like to sign up to participate in an event, just call or
come in to the front desk personnel.

The club facilities include 18 lighted tennis courts, 5
racquetball courts, an olympic size swimming pool, Nautilus
equipped weight room, and basketball court. For your comfort
while using the club, the men's and ladies' locker rooms each
have showers, a sauna, and a steam room. A spa for both men and
women is located between the locker rooms. The lounge and cafe
are open to serve you throughout the day and evening.

On behalf of the staff of the Sports Club, I hope your
association with the Club is long and enjoyable.

Sincerely,


Sports Club Manager
```

Notice that the right margins are even, rather than uneven or **ragged** as shown on the screen. This is one of WordPerfect's default print settings. You will look at several of these settings in the next lab.

Note: Documents created with WordPerfect 5.1 are printer-specific. That is, documents specify the active printer. All the document files supplied with the labs specify the Standard Printer as the active printer. To print any of these files, you may need to change the active printer to one appropriate for your particular micro-computer system.

Exiting WordPerfect 5.1

To leave WordPerfect 5.1 select File>Exit or Exit (F7).

Select: File>Exit
    >>   Exit (F7)

In response to the prompt to save the file, you can respond No, since no changes were made to the document since you last saved it.

Select: No

To exit WordPerfect 5.1,

Select: Yes

You are returned to the DOS prompt.

Always exit the WordPerfect 5.1 program using the File>Exit ((F7)) command. Never turn off your computer until you exit properly, or you may lose text.

KEY TERMS

cursor	scroll
status line	edit
document	delete
window	reformat
page	Insert mode
line	Typeover mode
position	repeater
default	hard carriage return
pull-down menu	buffer
menu bar	option
menu cursor	replace
submenu	save
mnemonic letter	active printer
prompt	ragged
context-sensitive	

MATCHING

1. (F7)   _____ **a.** displays a menu of command choices that can be selected

2. (ESC)   _____ **b.** cancels a command or exits a file

3. typeover   _____ **c.** a question or indicator from the program that requires input from the user

4. status line   _____ **d.** new text writes over old text in a document

5. (ALT) - =   _____ **e.** creates a hard carriage return

6. prompt   _____   **f.** retrieves a document file

7. ⏎   _____   **g.** deletes word cursor is on

8. (SHIFT) - (F10)   _____   **h.** displays cursor location information or menu and command prompts

9. (CTRL) - (BKSP)   _____   **i.** deletes several lines of text

10. (ESC) (CTRL) - (END)   _____   **j.** causes a command to repeat a specified number of times

PRACTICE EXERCISES

1. Retrieve the file EDIT. Follow the directions in the file to correct the sentences. Save the edited version of the file as EDIT. When you have completed the exercise print a copy of the file. Remember to select the appropriate printer for your microcomputer system.

2. Retrieve the file EDIT2. Follow the directions above the six paragraphs to correct the text in this file. Your corrected document should look like the text beginning on page WP3 in the section "Advantages of Using a Word Processor." Save the edited file as EDIT2. When you have completed the exercises print a copy of the file. Remember to select the appropriate printer for your microcomputer system.

3. Retrieve the file MEMO. This is a WordPerfect 5.1 document which is similar to the document you edited in Lab 1. It contains many errors. Edit the document using the commands you learned in this lab. Save the edited file as MEMO. Print a copy of the edited document. Remember to select the appropriate printer for your microcomputer system.

Your edited document should look like this:

TO: All Sports Club Employees

FROM: Ernie Powell, Sports Club Manager

DATE: December 1, 1992

The Sports Club will have the following holiday hours:

December 24, 1992	6:00 AM to 3:00 PM
December 25, 1992	closed all day
December 31, 1992	6:00 AM to 3:00 PM
January 1, 1993	closed all day

4. Retrieve the file CASE. Correct the text in this file using the commands you learned in this lab. Your corrected document should look like the text on page WP5, "Case Study for Labs 1-4." Save the corrected version of the file as CASE. Print the edited document. Remember to select the appropriate printer for your computer system.

Creating and Formatting a Document

2

OBJECTIVES

In this lab you will learn how to:

1. Create a new document.

2. Spell-check a document.

3. Save a document.

4. Combine files.

5. Move text.

6. Block text for copying and moving.

7. Enter the system date.

8. Align text flush with the right margin.

9. Set margins.

10. Use and set tabs.

11. Display hidden codes.

12. Search and replace text.

13. Set justification.

CASE STUDY

After editing the rough draft of the welcome letter, Karen showed it to the membership coordinator. The coordinator would like the letter to include information about monthly club fees and the new automatic fee payment program. We will follow Karen as she enters the new information into a file, combines it with the welcome letter, and adds some finishing touches to the letter.

Creating a Document

Boot the system by turning on the computer and loading DOS. Enter the current date when responding to the DOS date prompt. Load WordPerfect. If you are not sure of the procedure, refer to Lab 1, "Introduction to WordPerfect."

A blank WordPerfect screen is like a blank piece of paper you put into the typewriter. To create a new document, simply begin typing the text. When the cursor reaches the end of a line, however, do not press ⏎. WordPerfect will decide when to move the words down to next line based on the margin settings. This is called **word wrap**. The only time you need to press ⏎ is at the end of a paragraph or to insert blank lines.

As you type the text shown below, do not press ⏎ until you are directed to at the end of the paragraph. There should be one space following a period at the end of a sentence. If you make typing errors as you enter the text, use the editing features you learned in Lab 1 to correct your errors.

Type: The Sports Club is offering a new program to all its members which will save you writing a check each month. Upon your authorization, the bank will send payment of your monthly charges directly to the club. You will receive a copy of your monthly statement to confirm the accuracy of your bill. If you are interested in the automatic fee payment program, please contact the accounting department to make the necessary arrangements (931-4285 ext. 33).

Press: ⏎

Your display screen should be similar to Figure 2-1.

FIGURE 2-1

```
The Sports Club is offering a new program to all its members
which will save you writing a check each month. Upon your
authorization, the bank will send payment of your monthly charges
directly to the club. You will receive a copy of your monthly
statement to confirm the accuracy of your bill. If you are
interested in the automatic fee payment program, please contact
the accounting department to make the necessary arrangements
(931-4285 ext. 33)._
```

                                                    Doc 1 Pg 1 Ln 2.17" Pos 2.8"

The text on your screen may not exactly match the text in Figure 2-1. This is because the active printer your WordPerfect 5.1 program is using controls the font (print) size, which affects the number of characters WordPerfect can display on a line and where it will word wrap the line of text.

As you can see, the automatic word wrap feature makes entering text in a document much faster than typing. This is because a carriage return does not need to be pressed at the end of every line.

To insert a blank line,

Press: ⏎

To enter the second paragraph,

Type: The regular monthly membership fee is $45.00. Other expenses, such as league and lesson fees, pro-shop purchases, and charges at the Courtside Cafe can also be billed to your account. The charges will be itemized on your monthly statement and added to your regular monthly fee.

To end the second paragraph,

Press: ⏎

Your display screen should be similar to Figure 2-2.

FIGURE 2-2

```
The Sports Club is offering a new program to all its members
which will save you writing a check each month. Upon your
authorization, the bank will send payment of your monthly charges
directly to the club. You will receive a copy of your monthly
statement to confirm the accuracy of your bill. If you are
interested in the automatic fee payment program, please contact
the accounting department to make the necessary arrangements
(931-4285 ext. 33).

The regular monthly membership fee is $45.00. Other expenses,
such as league and lesson fees, pro-shop purchases, and charges
at the Courtside Cafe can also be billed to your account. The
charges will be itemized on your monthly statement and added to
your regular monthly fee.
```
```
                                        Doc 1 Pg 1 Ln 3.33" Pos 1"
```

Check that you have entered the two paragraphs correctly. Do not be concerned if there is a difference in where WordPerfect decided to word wrap. If you find any errors, correct them using the editing features you learned in Lab 1.

Spell-Checking

It is always a good idea to check your spelling in a document when you are finished working on it. To help you do this quickly, WordPerfect has a built-in dictionary that checks for spelling errors. Additionally it will look for words which are incorrectly capitalized and duplicate words.

To enter several intentional errors in this document,

Change the spelling of "Sports" to "Sprots" in the first line.
Enter a second "new" after the word "new" in the first line.
Change the word "program" to "pROgram" in the first line.

Now you will check the spelling of your document. If you are running WordPerfect from a two-disk system, remove your data disk from drive B and insert the Speller disk. If you have a hard-disk system, WordPerfect will automatically access the spell-check program on your disk.

Begin by positioning the cursor at the top of the document so that the entire document will be checked.

Press: (PGUP)

To begin spell-checking,

Select: **T**ools>Spell
   >>   Spell (CTRL) - (F2)

The menu in the status line lets you specify how much of the document you want to check. You can spell-check a word, a page, or a whole document. To check the document,

Select: **D**ocument

Your screen should be similar to Figure 2-3.

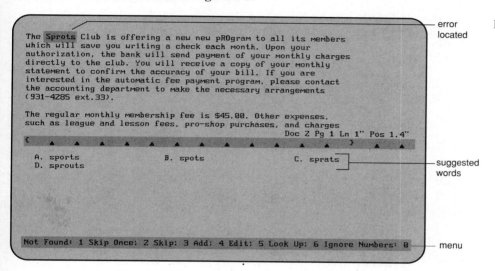

error located — FIGURE 2-3

suggested words

menu

The Speller has encountered the first word which is not in its dictionary. The word "Sprots" is highlighted. The lower half of the screen lists four suggested replacements. The menu options in the status line have the following effect:

Skip Once	accepts the word as correct for this occurrence only
Skip	accepts the word as correct throughout the spell-check of this document
Add Word	adds the word to the **supplementary dictionary**. The Speller uses the supplementary dictionary as a secondary dictionary whenever it does not encounter the word in the main dictionary. When a word is added to the supplemental dictionary, the Speller will always accept the added word as correct.
Edit	positions the cursor on the word so you can change the spelling directly
Look Up	looks up words that match a pattern
Ignore Numbers	does not check the spelling of words containing numbers

To change the spelling of the word to one of the suggested spellings, press the letter corresponding to the correct word in the list.

Press: A

The Speller replaces the misspelled word with the selected replacement and moves on to locate the next error. The double word error has been located. The menu options in the status line have the following effect:

Skip	leaves the words as they are
Delete 2nd	deletes the second occurrence of the word
Edit	positions the cursor on the second duplicate word so you can edit it
Disable Double Word Checking	ignores double-occurring words for the rest of the document

To delete the second duplicate word,

Select: 3 Delete 2nd

The next error the Speller locates is the capitalization error. To edit the word,

Select: 4 Edit

Correct the word to "program."

To resume spell-checking,

Press: Exit (F7)

Finally the Speller stops on the word "Courtside." Although this is the correct spelling for the word, the Speller dictionary does not contain this word. To leave the word as it is in the document,

Select: 2 Skip

There should be no other misspelled words. However, if the speller encounters others in your file, correct them as needed. When no others are located the word count is displayed. To exit the spell-checker,

Press: Space bar

Note: Two-disk users: Remove the Speller disk from drive B and insert your data disk.

Saving a New File

Next Karen needs to retrieve the file containing the welcome letter and add the new paragraphs to it. But first she needs to save the current document to the diskette and clear the screen.

You could use the File>Save or (F10) command to save the revised document. But as you saw in the previous lab, this command returns you to the document. Since Karen does not want to keep working on the same file, she will save the file while clearing the screen by using the File>Exit or (F7) command.

The difference between the Save command and the Exit command is:

Save   saves the document on the diskette and returns you to the current document.

Exit   saves the document on the diskette, clears the document from the screen (and memory), and lets you either continue working with WordPerfect by retrieving or creating another document, or leave the program.

To save the two paragraphs on the screen to a file on the diskette, use the File>Exit or (F7) command.

Select: File>Exit
>>   Exit (F7)

The prompt "Document to be saved:" appears in the status line. WordPerfect is prompting you to enter the name of the file. The file name should be descriptive of the contents of the file. It can consist of two parts.

The first part of the file name is required and can be up to eight characters long. There can be no spaces within it. If you want to use two words in the name, separate them with a hyphen or an underscore. You will use the file name AUTO-PAY.

The second part of the file name is the file extension. It can be up to three characters long and is separated from the first part of the file name by a period. It is not required. You will use the extension .DOC to show that this is a document file. The file name can be entered in either upper- or lowercase letters.

Type: AUTO-PAY.DOC
Press: ⏎

After a few moments the document is saved on the diskette and cleared from the screen. At this point you could leave the WordPerfect program by entering **Y** to the prompt, "Exit WP?." However, since you have a lot more to do, in response to the prompt,

Type: N

Next Karen will retrieve the welcome letter. A complete, corrected copy of the welcome letter is saved for you in a file named LETTER3.

Retrieve the file LETTER3 using either File>Retrieve (SHIFT) - (F10) or File>List Files (F5).

Combining Files

The welcome letter is displayed on the screen. After looking at the letter Karen decides she wants the two new paragraphs from the AUTO-PAY.DOC file to be entered following the third paragraph of the welcome letter.

Move to: Ln 4.17" Pos 1" (beginning of blank line separating paragraphs three and four)

The contents of two files can be combined easily be retrieving the second file without clearing the display screen of the current file. A copy of the contents of the retrieved file is entered at the location of the cursor into the document on the display screen.

To combine the text in the AUTO-PAY.DOC file with the current file (LETTER3) on the display, at the location of the cursor, retrieve the AUTO-PAY.DOC file using either File>Retrieve (SHIFT) - (F10) or File>List Files (F5). If you use List Files, respond Yes to the prompt in the status line to combine with the current document.

Your display screen should be similar to Figure 2-4.

FIGURE 2-4

```
Dear New Sports Club Member:

Congratulations on your new membership in the Sports Club. All of
us on the staff welcome you and encourage you to participate in
the many tournaments, leagues and club activities offered
throughout the year.

Each month you will receive a newsletter about the upcoming
events at the club. If you have questions about the event or
would like to sign up to participate in an event, just call or
come in to the front desk personnel.

The club facilities include 18 lighted tennis courts, 5
racquetball courts, an olympic size swimming pool, Nautilus
equipped weight room, and basketball court. For your comfort
while using the club, the men's and ladies' locker rooms each
have showers, a sauna, and a steam room. A spa for both men and
women is located between the locker rooms. The lounge and cafe
are open to serve you throughout the day and evening.
The Sports Club is offering a new program to all its members
which will save you writing a check each month. Upon your
authorization, the bank will send payment of your monthly charges
directly to the club. You will receive a copy of your monthly
statement to confirm the accuracy of your bill. If you are
B:\LETTER3                                          Doc 1 Pg 1 Ln 4.17" Pos 1"
```

AUTO-PAY.DOC text
combined with LETTER3

The two paragraphs from the AUTO-PAY.DOC file have been inserted into the welcome letter at the location of the cursor.

To separate paragraphs 3 and 4 with a blank line,

Press: (⏎)

To view the rest of the text, using the (↓) key,

Move to: Ln 8.17" Pos 1" (last line of letter)

Moving Text

After looking over the welcome letter Karen decides she would like to change the order of the paragraphs in the letter. She wants the paragraph about the automatic fee payment program (paragraph 4) to follow the paragraph about the monthly membership fees (paragraph 5).

A complete sentence, paragraph, or page of text can be moved by selecting Edit>Select from the menu or by using the Move (CTRL) - (F4) command. First the cursor must be positioned anywhere within the piece of text to be moved. You will place the cursor on the first character (T) of paragraph 4.

Move to: Ln 4.33" Pos 1" ("T" of "The" at beginning of paragraph 4)

Next, to use the pull-down menu to select the Move command,

Select: Edit>Select

There are three submenu options available for selection: Sentence, Paragraph, and Page. These options allow you to specify the area of text to be moved. To specify a paragraph,

Select: Paragraph

Your display screen should be similar to Figure 2-5.

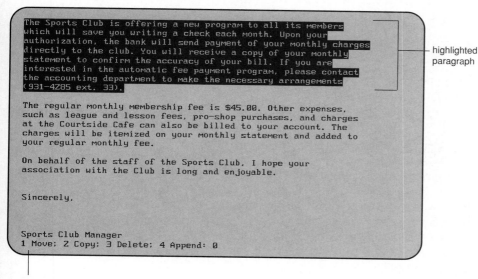

FIGURE 2-5

— highlighted paragraph

Move menu options

The entire paragraph is highlighted. Only one sentence, paragraph, or page of text can be marked (highlighted) for moving at a time.

The status line now displays four more menu options: Move, Copy, Delete, and Append. They have the following meanings:

Move allows you to remove the text from its present location so it can be moved to another location

Copy leaves the original text and moves a duplicate to another location

Delete permanently removes the text from the document

Append lets you add the text to the end of a file on the disk

The default option, 0, displayed at the end of the menu, allows you to cancel the command. A menu option which appears in the status line is selected by typing the number to the left of the option you want to use or by typing the highlighted letter. Rather than select the Move option at this time, you will cancel your command selections. This will allow you to see how the Move command works when using the function key equivalent, (CTRL) - (F4).

Press: ⏎

To reposition the cursor within the paragraph to be moved,

Press: ⬆ (2 times)

The cursor should be on Ln 5.55" Pos 1" (the "(" of the telephone number).
    To use the function key equivalent,

Press: (CTRL) - (F4)

The same three options, which let you specify the area of text to move (**S**entence, **P**aragraph, or Pa**g**e), appear in the status line.
    To specify the entire paragraph,

Select: Paragraph

Your screen should again look like Figure 2-5.

Now the same menu of four Move options appears in the status line. To continue the Move command by moving the paragraph from one location in the document to another, select Move as follows:

Select: Move

The marked paragraph is removed from the document and is stored in temporary memory until needed. The text below the deleted paragraph moves up. The status line now directs you to move the cursor and press ⏎ to retrieve the text.
    You will reenter the paragraph below the paragraph on the monthly fees. To do this,

Move to: Ln 5.33" Pos 1" ("O" of "On")
Press: ⏎

Your display screen should be similar to Figure 2-6.

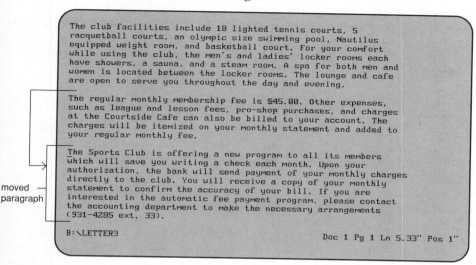

moved — paragraph

FIGURE 2-6

The marked paragraph is reentered into the document beginning at the cursor location. That was a lot quicker than retyping the whole paragraph!

Note: When the use of the function key command instruction requires a selection from a menu displayed in the status line, the instructions will appear separated by commas. For example: >> (CTRL) - (F4), **2 P**aragraph, **1 M**ove.

Using the Block Command

Next Karen wants to move the telephone number of the accounting department. She wants it to follow the reference to the accounting department in the same sentence. Because the telephone number is not a complete sentence, paragraph, or page of text, the Move command cannot be used by itself. Instead it is used along with the Block command.

The Block (Edit>Block or (ALT) - (F4)) command is used to mark an area, or **block**, of text. A block of text can be as short as a single letter or as long as several pages of text. The marked text can then be acted upon by the Move command.

Before using the Block command, the cursor must be placed on the first character in the block of text to be moved. In this case it is the opening parenthesis surrounding the telephone number.

Move to: Ln 6.5" Pos 1" ("(" at beginning of telephone number)

To access the Block command,

Select: Edit>Block
   >> Block (ALT) - (F4)

Note: Dragging the mouse across text automatically turns on the Block feature. Therefore, if you use the mouse to specify a block of text, you do not need to select Edit>Block or press (ALT) - (F4) first.

The message "Block on" flashes in the status line. This shows that the Block command is active. Next, the area of text to be moved must be identified. To do this the text is highlighted by moving the cursor using the cursor movement keys or dragging the mouse (hold down the left button while moving the mouse) to the end of the area of text to be moved. To highlight the telephone number, using ⟶ or dragging the mouse,

Move to: Ln 6.5" Pos 2.7" (")" of telephone number)

The highlight should cover the phone number through the closing parenthesis. The text to be moved is now defined. Once a block of text is defined many different WordPerfect commands can be used to manipulate the block. For example, it can be underlined, deleted, copied, or centered on the page.

Karen wants to move this block of text to another location in the document. To do this the Move (**E**dit>**M**ove or (CTRL) - (F4)) command is used.

Note: If you use (CTRL) - (F4) to issue this command you will need to select an option from the menus displayed in the status line. The three options in the first menu let you specify the type of text to be moved. Since you defined a block of text you will select **B**lock. A second menu appears which lets you tell the program what you want to do with the block. Since you want to move a block, you will select **M**ove.

Select: **E**dit>**M**ove (Cut)
  >>   Move (CTRL) - (F4), **B**lock, **M**ove

Your display screen should be similar to Figure 2-7.

FIGURE 2-7

```
The club facilities include 18 lighted tennis courts, 5
racquetball courts, an olympic size swimming pool, Nautilus
equipped weight room, and basketball court. For your comfort
while using the club, the men's and ladies' locker rooms each
have showers, a sauna, and a steam room. A spa for both men and
women is located between the locker rooms. The lounge and cafe
are open to serve you throughout the day and evening.

The regular monthly membership fee is $45.00. Other expenses,
such as league and lesson fees, pro-shop purchases, and charges
at the Courtside Cafe can also be billed to your account. The
charges will be itemized on your monthly statement and added to
your regular monthly fee.

The Sports Club is offering a new program to all its members
which will save you writing a check each month. Upon your
authorization, the bank will send payment of your monthly charges
directly to the club. You will receive a copy of your monthly
statement to confirm the accuracy of your bill. If you are
interested in the automatic fee payment program, please contact
the accounting department to make the necessary arrangements
.


Move cursor; press Enter to retrieve.          Doc 1 Pg 1 Ln 6.5" Pos 1"
```

The block of text is temporarily removed from the document. It will remain in temporary memory until ⏎ is pressed.

As long as you do not press ⏎ you can do other simple editing tasks before completing the Move command. For instance, notice that there is a space left before the period at the cursor location. While the cursor is positioned properly, you can delete the space before using the Move command. To delete the space,

Press: (BKSP)

You can now move the cursor to the location where you want the block to appear. Karen wants it to follow the word "department."

Move to: Ln 6.33" Pos 3.5" (blank space after "department")

You are now ready to retrieve the block. To do this,

Press: ⏎

Your display screen should be similar to Figure 2-8.

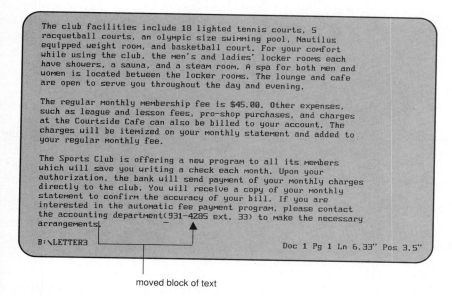

FIGURE 2-8

moved block of text

The telephone number for the accounting department now follows the reference to the department in the sentence.

To insert a space before the opening parenthesis of the telephone number,

Press: Space bar

After looking over the letter for a while, Karen decides she wants to make the following changes:

- enter the current date in the upper right-hand corner
- increase the margin width
- indent the first line of each paragraph
- replace the word "club" with "sports club"
- change the right margin to print ragged

You will follow Karen as she makes these changes to the Welcome letter.

Using the Date Command

Karen wants the date to be entered on the first line of the letter. To move to the top of the letter and insert a blank line,

Press: (PGUP)

Press: (⏎)

Press: (↑)

A blank line has been inserted at the top of the letter where the date will be entered.

The Date command (Tools>Date Code or Date (SHIFT) - (F5), Date Code) inserts the current date into your document. The date inserted into the document is the date you entered when responding to the DOS date prompt.

To use the Date command,

Select: Tools

>> Date (SHIFT) - (F5)

The three date options in the Tools menu (or if you use the function key command, in the menu displayed in the status line) are:

Date Text   inserts the current date as text into your document

Date Code   inserts a WordPerfect code, which automatically updates the date whenever the file is retrieved or printed

Date Format   allows changes to the default date format display

The welcome letter will be mailed to new members as they join the club. Karen wants the current date automatically entered whenever the letter is printed. To do this, the Date Code option is used.

Select: Date Code

Your display screen should be similar to Figure 2-9.

FIGURE 2-9

current date

```
March 20, 1992_
Dear New Sports Club Member:

Congratulations on your new membership in the Sports Club. All of
us on the staff welcome you and encourage you to participate in
the many tournaments, leagues and club activities offered
throughout the year.

Each month you will receive a newsletter about the upcoming
events at the club. If you have questions about the event or
would like to sign up to participate in an event, just call or
come in to the front desk personnel.

The club facilities include 18 lighted tennis courts, 5
racquetball courts, an olympic size swimming pool, Nautilus
equipped weight room, and basketball court. For your comfort
while using the club, the men's and ladies' locker rooms each
have showers, a sauna, and a steam room. A spa for both men and
women is located between the locker rooms. The lounge and cafe
are open to serve you throughout the day and evening.

The regular monthly membership fee is $45.00. Other expenses,
such as league and lesson fees, pro-shop purchases, and charges
at the Courtside Cafe can also be billed to your account. The
B:\LETTER3                                        Doc 1 Pg 1 Ln 1" Pos 2.4"
```

The current date is entered into the letter at the location of the cursor. It appears as text, not as a WordPerfect code. Whenever this file is retrieved or printed, the current system date will be displayed using this format. You will see shortly how the date is stored as a WordPerfect code.

Note: The date in Figure 2-9 will be different from the date that appears on your display. If you did not enter the current date at the DOS prompt, then the default system date will be used.

Aligning Text Flush with the Right Margin

Next Karen wants the date to end against the right margin or to be **flush right**. The Flush Right command (Layout>Align>Flush Right or Flush Right (ALT) - (F6)) is used to do this. For this command to work correctly the cursor must first be positioned on the first character of the text to be moved and there must be a hard carriage return at the end of the existing line of text. To position the cursor at the beginning of the date,

Press: (←)

Because the date is a WordPerfect code rather than text you entered character by character, the program considers the date a single character, and the cursor jumps quickly to Ln 1" Pos 1".

To move the date flush with the right margin and reformat the display, using the pull-down menu,

Select: Layout

The Layout menu options affect the design of the document. We will be using many of these options shortly. The Align option controls the placement of text on a line.

Select: Align

Your screen should be similar to Figure 2-10.

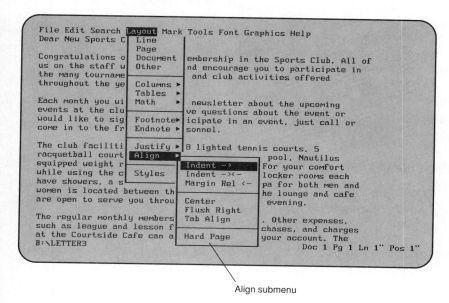

Align submenu

FIGURE 2-10

There are three submenu options which affect the placement of text on a line: Center, Flush Right, and Tab Align. To align the text located to the right of the cursor flush with the right margin,

Select: Flush Right

To reformat the display of the line,

Press: ⬇

Your display screen should be similar to Figure 2-11.

FIGURE 2-11

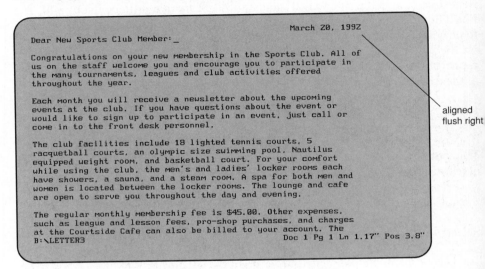

aligned
flush right

The date has moved flush with the right margin.

The function key command equivalent is simply Flush Right (ALT) - (F6). In this case, using the function key would be quicker than using the pull-down menus.

The Flush Right command can also be used before typing in new text that you want aligned with the right margin. As you type the text it is entered so that the last character in the line is even with the right margin.

Next Karen wants the date separated from the salutation by four blank lines. To move to the beginning of line 2 and insert four blank lines between the date line and the salutation,

Press: (HOME)
Press: (⟵)
Press: (⟸) (4 times)

The salutation begins on line 1.83".

Setting Margins

Karen would like to change the right and left margin widths from 1 inch (the default setting) to 1-1/2 inches. To change the left and right margin widths of a document, the Line Format (Layout>Line or Format (SHIFT) - (F8)) command is used. The new margin setting must be entered at the beginning of the document so that the entire document below the setting will be formatted to the new margin specifications.

To position the cursor at the top of the document,

Press: (PGUP)

This time, you will use the function key command to set the margins.

Press: Format (SHIFT) - (F8)

Your display screen should be similar to Figure 2-12.

FIGURE 2-12

```
Format

    1 - Line
            Hyphenation                 Line Spacing
            Justification               Margins Left/Right
            Line Height                 Tab Set
            Line Numbering              Widow/Orphan Protection

    2 - Page
            Center Page (top to bottom)  Page Numbering
            Force Odd/Even Page          Paper Size/Type
            Headers and Footers          Suppress
            Margins Top/Bottom

    3 - Document
            Display Pitch               Redline Method
            Initial Codes/Font          Summary

    4 - Other
            Advance                     Overstrike
            Conditional End of Page     Printer Functions
            Decimal Characters          Underline Spaces/Tabs
            Language                    Border Options

    Selection: 0
```

Line submenu

The document is replaced by a full-screen menu. This menu is divided into four submenus: 1 Line, 2 Page, 3 Document, and 4 Other. Below each submenu the options for that submenu are listed.

The Line, Page, and Other submenu options change the settings from the point they are entered into the document forward. The Document submenu options change the settings for the entire document.

The command to set margins is an option in the Line submenu.

Select: Line

Your display screen should be similar to Figure 2-13.

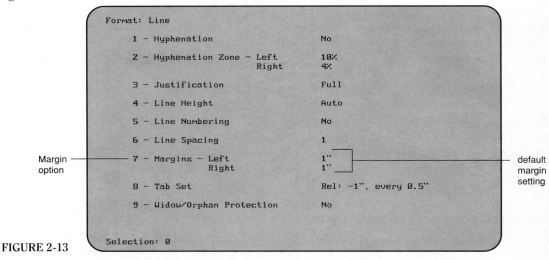

Format: Line

1 — Hyphenation	No
2 — Hyphenation Zone — Left	10%
Right	4%
3 — Justification	Full
4 — Line Height	Auto
5 — Line Numbering	No
6 — Line Spacing	1
7 — Margins — Left	1"
Right	1"
8 — Tab Set	Rel: -1", every 0.5"
9 — Widow/Orphan Protection	No

Selection: 0

Margin option → (7 — Margins)

default margin setting → (1" settings)

FIGURE 2-13

The Line Format menu is displayed. The left side of the menu lists the 9 options which affect line endings, spacing, numbering, length, and tabs. The right column displays the current settings, in this case the default settings, for each option. The Margins option lets you specify new left and right margins. The default margin settings provide 1 inch of space from the left and right edge of the paper.

Select: Margins

The cursor jumps to the right column under the setting for the left margin. The margin setting can be entered as a decimal or as a fraction. To change the left margin setting to 1-1/2 inches, you could enter either 1.5 or 1 1/2.

Type: 1.5
Press: ⏎

The cursor moves to the right margin setting. To change the right margin,

Type: 1 1/2
Press: ⏎

WordPerfect converts the fraction to a decimal.

If you wanted you could continue to select other Line Format options. However, Karen first wants to see how the document has changed with the new margin settings. To quickly leave the Line Format menu and return directly to the document, use the Exit command, (F7).

Press: Exit (F7)

The left margin now begins at Pos 1.5"; however, the right margin has not adjusted to the new right margin setting. To reformat the display of text on the screen,

Press: (HOME)
Press: (↓)

Your display screen should be similar to Figure 2-14.

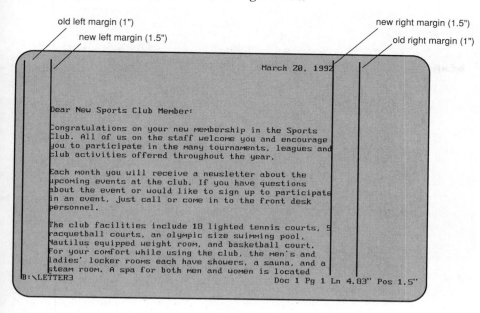

old left margin (1")
new left margin (1.5")
new right margin (1.5")
old right margin (1")

```
                              March 20, 1992

Dear New Sports Club Member:

Congratulations on your new membership in the Sports
Club. All of us on the staff welcome you and encourage
you to participate in the many tournaments, leagues and
club activities offered throughout the year.

Each month you will receive a newsletter about the
upcoming events at the club. If you have questions
about the event or would like to sign up to participate
in an event, just call or come in to the front desk
personnel.

The club facilities include 18 lighted tennis courts, 9
racquetball courts, an olympic size swimming pool,
Nautilus equipped weight room, and basketball court.
For your comfort while using the club, the men's and
ladies' locker rooms each have showers, a sauna, and a
steam room. A spa for both men and women is located
B:\LETTER3                      Doc 1 Pg 1 Ln 4.83" Pos 1.5"
```

FIGURE 2-14

The letter has been reformatted to fit within the new margin settings.
To return to the top of the letter,

Press: (HOME)

Press: (↑)

Using and Setting Tabs

Next Karen wants to indent the first line of each paragraph and the closing. The **Tab**
key lets you easily indent text on a line. WordPerfect has set the default tab setting
at every half inch. As with other default settings, the Tab spacing can also be set to
your needs. The Line Format command, (Layout>Line or (SHIFT) - (F8), Line), is used
to view and set tabs.

Select: Layout>Line

>>   Format (SHIFT) - (F8) Line

The Line Format menu is displayed. To display the current tab settings,

Select: Tab Set

Your display screen should be similar to Figure 2-15.

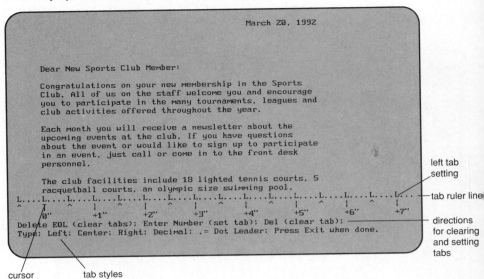

FIGURE 2-15

A Tab Ruler line is displayed at the bottom of the screen. The "L" marks the location of each tab stop from the left margin. The cursor can be moved along the ruler line using → and ←. For Help information about tabs,

Press: Help F3

Your screen should be similar to Figure 2-16.

FIGURE 2-16

```
Tab Set

     Sets the tab positions (tab stops) in the document.  Tab stops are
     initially set every half-inch.  To change the default, select this option.

     Tab settings in WordPerfect 5.1 are normally set relative to the left
     margin.  Press t for more information.

     You can determine how text is aligned on the tab stop (e.g., text can be
     centered).  For more information, press 1.

     You can delete the tab settings to the right of the cursor by pressing
     Delete to End of Line (Ctrl-End).  Pressing Del erases the tab setting at
     the cursor. To set a regular tab, enter the position number (e.g. 1.75").
     To set evenly spaced tabs, enter the position for the first tab setting,
     followed by a comma and the increment measurement (e.g., 1",2" sets the
     first tab at 1", the next one at 3", etc.)

     While the cursor is located on a tab setting, you can move the tab by
     holding down Ctrl and pressing the Left or Right Arrows.  Text on the
     screen will automatically move with the new tab position.  You can move
     from tab setting to tab setting using the Alt-Arrow or Ctrl-Arrow key
     combinations as well as the Up and Down Arrows.

     Selection: 0                              (Press ENTER to exit Help)
```

After reading the information on this screen about how to clear and set tabs, following the directions on the screen to obtain more information about tab styles,

Type: 1

This information describes the four styles or types of tabs you can create using the Tab menu.

To return to the document,

Press: ⟨⏎⟩

To review, the basic procedures for clearing and setting tabs are:

- Clear an individual tab setting by placing the cursor on the tab stop and pressing ⟨DEL⟩.

- Clear multiple tab settings by placing the cursor on the first tab stop to be deleted and using ⟨CTRL⟩ - ⟨END⟩ to delete all tab stops from the cursor to the right.

- Enter new left tab settings by moving the cursor to the tab stop and typing L, or by entering the number.

However, Karen is satisfied with the default tab settings and does not want to make any changes. To leave the settings as they are and return to the document,

Press: Cancel ⟨F1⟩ (3 times)

To indent the first line of the first paragraph,

Move to: Ln 2.17" Pos 1.5" (on "C" in "Congratulations")
Press: ⟨TAB⟩

Your display screen should be similar to Figure 2-17.

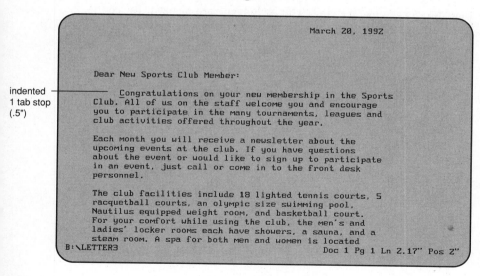

FIGURE 2-17

indented 1 tab stop (.5")

```
                                     March 20, 1992



        Dear New Sports Club Member:

               Congratulations on your new membership in the Sports
        Club. All of us on the staff welcome you and encourage
        you to participate in the many tournaments, leagues and
        club activities offered throughout the year.

        Each month you will receive a newsletter about the
        upcoming events at the club. If you have questions
        about the event or would like to sign up to participate
        in an event, just call or come in to the front desk
        personnel.

        The club facilities include 18 lighted tennis courts, 5
        racquetball courts, an olympic size swimming pool,
        Nautilus equipped weight room, and basketball court.
        For your comfort while using the club, the men's and
        ladies' locker rooms each have showers, a sauna, and a
        steam room. A spa for both men and women is located
B:\LETTER3                           Doc 1 Pg 1 Ln 2.17" Pos 2"
```

The first line is indented.

In a similar manner, indent the first lines of the next five paragraphs. Notice as you move down through the text that each paragraph is automatically reformatted.

To indent the closing lines,

Move to:	Ln 9.17" Pos 1.5" (on "S" in "Sincerely")
Press:	(TAB) (7 times)
Move to:	Ln 9.83" Pos 1.5" (on "S" of "Sports")
Press:	(TAB) (7 times)
Press:	(↓)

Notice that the last line of the letter is on the last line of the page. Karen feels this does not look good and decides to reset the right and left margins back to the default setting of 1 inch.

Displaying Hidden Codes

Press:	(PGUP)

Karen could reset the margins using the Line Format menu. There is another way, however, to return the margins to their original settings.

WordPerfect places hidden **codes** in the document whenever a feature is used that controls the format and display of the document. The codes consist of symbols that tell WordPerfect and the printer what to do. When the program reads the code, it reformats all the text in the document from that point on to the new setting. The codes are hidden so that your document on the display screen looks as close as possible to the text as it will appear when printed. Because the codes are hidden, your display is not cluttered.

The code is entered into the document at the location of the cursor when the command is issued. WordPerfect lets you see the hidden codes in the document so that you can remove the codes you no longer want or need. To see the hidden codes, use the Reveal Codes command (Edit>Reveal Codes or Reveal Codes (ALT) - (F3)).

Select:	Edit>Reveal Codes
>>	Reveal Codes (ALT) - (F3)

Your display screen should be similar to Figure 2-18.

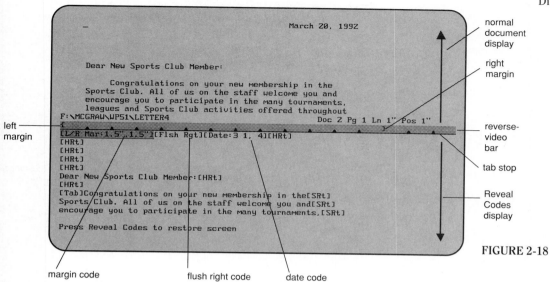

FIGURE 2-18

The screen is divided into two windows by a reverse-video bar, which shows the left ({) and right (}) margins and tab (^) settings. The upper window displays the document as it normally appears. The lower window displays the same text with the hidden codes revealed. This is the Reveal Codes screen. The codes are always displayed in brackets ([]).

The first code displayed in the Reveal Codes screen is [L/R Mar: 1.5",1.5"]. This code controls the left and right margin settings. The first part of the code is an abbreviation of the command used. The selected settings are displayed next. Since the cursor is on this code, it is highlighted.

The next code [Flsh Rgt] is the Flush Right code which aligns the date flush with the right margin. The code [Date:3 1, 4] tells the program to enter the current date into the document. The last code [HRt] stands for a hard carriage return. This code is entered whenever you press ⏎ .

To delete a code, the (BKSP) or (DEL) key is used. The (BKSP) key will delete codes to the left of the cursor, and the (DEL) key will delete codes the cursor is highlighting.

Karen wants to delete the margin code. Since this code is highlighted, to remove it,

Press: (DEL)

Your display screen should be similar to Figure 2-19.

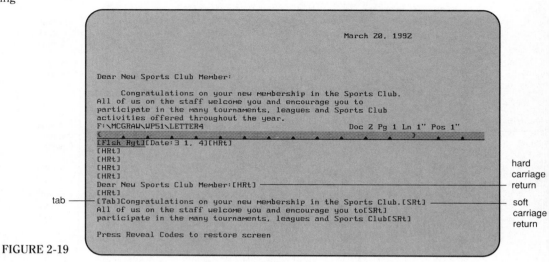

FIGURE 2-19

The code is deleted from the document. When a code is deleted, the document acts as if the code had never been entered. The removal of the margin code causes the margin settings to return to the default settings of one inch. Look in the upper window and you can see that the text is now displayed using the new margin settings.

A code also can be deleted from the document while you are in normal document display mode. That is, you do not have to use the Reveal Codes screen to remove codes. However, if you have forgotten where the code was entered in the text, then it is best to use the Reveal Codes screen while deleting codes. In either display mode, first move the cursor to the location of the code in the document. Then use (BKSP) to delete codes to the left of the cursor and (DEL) to delete codes the cursor is highlighting.

Let's look at the other codes displayed in the Reveal Codes screen. Each of the blank lines between the date and salutation is coded with the [HRt] symbol. The code that tells WordPerfect to indent the paragraph is [Tab]. At the end of each line of the first paragraph a [SRt] code is displayed. This code identifies the location of a **soft carriage return**. As WordPerfect reformats the text on the screen, it enters a [SRt] code at the end of a line. This code shows the location where WordPerfect decided to automatically word wrap to the next line.

When the Reveal Codes screen is in use you can type characters or use any WordPerfect features. The text in the Reveal Codes screen may not wrap the same as the text in the document Editing screen, however. This is because it contains the format codes.

To return to normal document display and hide the codes again, you must reselect the Reveal Codes command. To do this quickly using the function key command,

Press: Reveal Codes (ALT) - (F3)

To see where the letter ends on the page,

Press: (HOME) (HOME) (↓)

As you can see, because the margin widths were decreased, more text can be displayed on a line. Consequently, the last line of the letter is now on Ln 9".

Press: (PGUP)

Searching and Replacing Text

Next Karen wants to find all occurrences of the word "club" in the letter and change it to "Sports Club" where appropriate. The Replace (Search>Replace or Replace (ALT) - (F2)) command will help do this quickly. You will use the pull-down menu to perform this task.

Select: Search

Your screen should be similar to Figure 2-20.

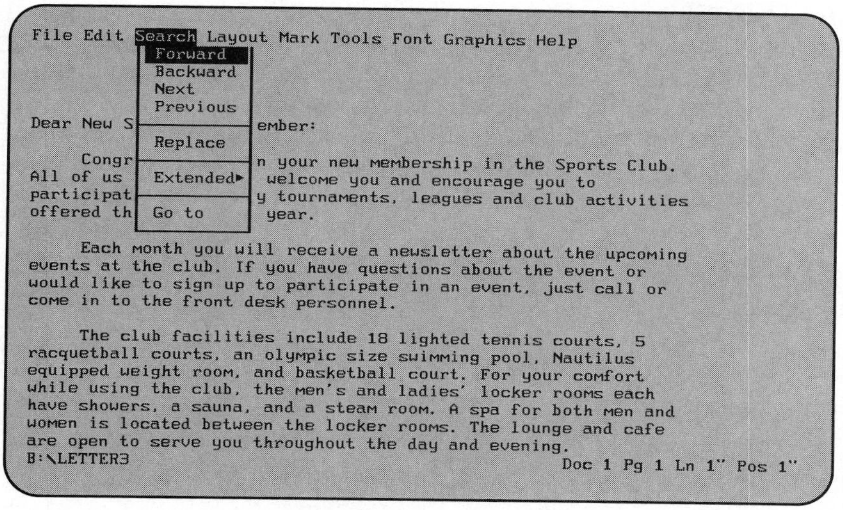

FIGURE 2-20

WordPerfect has several commands for **searching** through a file to find a **string**, or specific combination of characters and/or codes. The first two Search menu options, Forward and Backward, move the cursor either forward or backward through the document to locate the first occurrence of the combination of letters, characters or numbers specified. The function key equivalent to the Search>Forward command is Search (F2), and for the Search>Backward command it is Search (SHIFT) - (F2).

The second two options, Next and Previous, tell the program to continue the search by moving to the next occurrence or to the previous occurrence of the matching string.

The next Search menu option, Replace, moves the cursor forward through a document to locate the specified string and replaces it with another. You cannot use Replace to search backward through the text.

Replace is the command Karen wants to use.

Select: **R**eplace

The prompt "W/Confirm? No (Yes)" is displayed in the status line. If you respond **Yes** to the prompt, WordPerfect will display the matching string and ask for confirmation before replacing it. If you respond **N**o, WordPerfect will automatically replace every occurrence of the word with the new string.

To selectively replace the word,

Type: Y

The "—> Srch:" prompt is displayed on the status line. The word or phrase you want to find is entered following the prompt. When entering the search string, lowercase letters will match both upper- and lowercase letters in the text. However, if you enter the search string in uppercase letters, only uppercase matches will be found. After entering the search string, do not press ⏎.

Type: club

Next, to search forward in the document,

Press: Search (F2)

The prompt "Replace with" is displayed next. If no replacement string were entered at this prompt, the word "club" would be deleted at every occurrence. You want to replace "club" with "Sports Club." The replacement string must be entered exactly as you want it to appear in your document. Do not press ⏎ after typing the replace string.

Type: **Sports Club**
Press: Search (F2)

Your display screen should be similar to Figure 2-21.

FIGURE 2-21

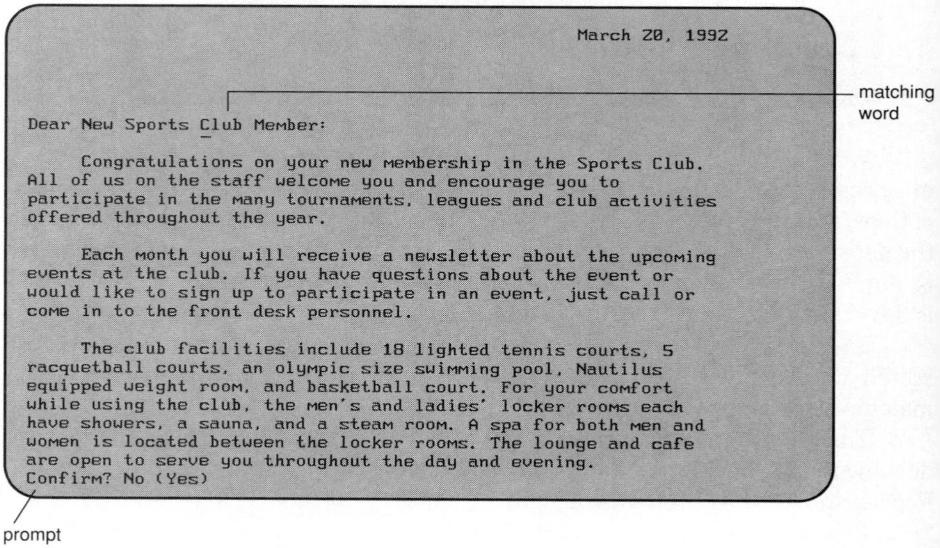

March 20, 1992

— matching word

Dear New Sports Club Member:

    Congratulations on your new membership in the Sports Club. All of us on the staff welcome you and encourage you to participate in the many tournaments, leagues and club activities offered throughout the year.

    Each month you will receive a newsletter about the upcoming events at the club. If you have questions about the event or would like to sign up to participate in an event, just call or come in to the front desk personnel.

    The club facilities include 18 lighted tennis courts, 5 racquetball courts, an olympic size swimming pool, Nautilus equipped weight room, and basketball court. For your comfort while using the club, the men's and ladies' locker rooms each have showers, a sauna, and a steam room. A spa for both men and women is located between the locker rooms. The lounge and cafe are open to serve you throughout the day and evening.
Confirm? No (Yes)

prompt

Immediately the cursor moves to the first word matching the search string "club." Notice that the cursor is positioned on "Club." This is because the search string was entered in all lowercase letters, and WordPerfect does not distinguish between upper- and lowercase letters when searching the text for matching strings.

The prompt "Confirm? No (Yes)" is displayed in the Status line. The first occurrence is acceptable as it is (you do not want to replace it),

Type: N (or press ⏎)

The cursor skips to the next occurrence of the word "club" and waits for your response. Again, it is already correct.

Type: N

The cursor moves to the third occurrence of the word "club" and waits for your response. This time Karen wants to replace it with "Sports Club."

Type: Y

The word "club" is replaced with the word "Sports Club." The cursor moves to the next match.

Respond to the remaining prompts to replace "club" with "Sports Club" when needed. When no more matches are located the search ends.

Setting Justification

On the screen the welcome letter has even left margins and uneven, or ragged right, margins. But, as you noted at the end of Lab 1, when the letter is printed the text is aligned evenly with both the left and right margin settings. This is called **justification**. To justify text, WordPerfect inserts extra spaces between some of the words on a line to force the line to end even with the right margin setting. Printing a document so that the text aligns against the right and left margins is the default setting in WordPerfect.

Karen wants the welcome letter to be printed with ragged right margins (as it is displayed on the screen). The command to change justification is on the Line Format menu (Layout>Line or Format (SHIFT) - (F8), Line). Using this command inserts a code in the document to control the printing of the text. The code should be entered at the beginning of the document so that the entire letter will be printed with a ragged right margin. If it is not entered at the beginning of the document, the new justification setting will begin at the cursor location and will continue until you insert another code that changes the setting.

To move the cursor to the beginning of the welcome letter and to display the Line Format menu,

Press: (PGUP)
Select: Layout>Line
   >>   Format (SHIFT) - (F8), Line

The default justification setting is Full, meaning that both the left and right margins are aligned or justified.

Select: Justification

The Justify menu at the bottom of the screen displays four justification settings. They have the following effect:

Left   aligns text against left margin, leaving right margin ragged
Center   centers each line of text between the left and right margins
Right   aligns text against right margin, leaving left margin ragged
Full   aligns text against the right and left margins

To change justification to have even left margins and ragged right margins,

Select: Left

The new justification setting "Left" is displayed in the Format Line menu.
To quickly exit the Format Line menu and return to the document,

Press: Exit (F7)

Nothing looks different on the screen. But when the document is printed the right margin will be uneven, as it is displayed.

Note: The pull-down menu option, Layout>Justify, also lets you set the justification of text in your document. It has the same four choices and produces the same effect as using Layout>Line>Justify.

Printing the Document

To print a copy of the welcome letter,

Select: **File>Print**
   >>   Print (SHIFT) - (F7)

The Print menu is displayed.
Let's take a moment to look at the Print options you have not used yet. The second option, Binding Offset, allows you to move the printed document to the right or left side of the paper to allow space for binding. The current setting of 0" is the default. The third option, Number of Copies, allows you to print multiple copies of a document. The default is to print 1 copy. The fourth option, Multiple Copies Generated by, is an option used by some laser printers to print more than one copy of the current print job. The default (1) lets WordPerfect control the number of copies. The last two options, Graphics Quality and Text Quality, allow you to set the quality level at which the graphics or text are printed. The lower quality settings produce a "rough" copy and print faster. The default settings for these options are displayed in the right column.
If necessary, use the Select Printer option to select the printer which is appropriate for your computer system.
To print the letter Karen could select either Full Text or Page from the Print menu, since the welcome letter is only one page long. If the text were longer than a single page, selecting Page would print only the page the cursor is positioned on.

Select: Page

Your printed letter should be similar to Figure 2-22.

FIGURE 2-22

```
                                        March 20, 1992


Dear New Sports Club Member:

      Congratulations on your new membership in the Sports Club.
All of us on the staff welcome you and encourage you to
participate in the many tournaments, leagues and Sports Club
activities offered throughout the year.

      Each month you will receive a newsletter about the upcoming
events at the Sports Club. If you have questions about the event
or would like to sign up to participate in an event, just call or
come in to the front desk personnel.

      The Sports Club facilities include 18 lighted tennis courts,
5 racquetball courts, an olympic size swimming pool, Nautilus
equipped weight room, and basketball court. For your comfort
while using the Sports Club, the men's and ladies' locker rooms
each have showers, a sauna, and a steam room. A spa for both men
and women is located between the locker rooms. The lounge and
cafe are open to serve you throughout the day and evening.

      The regular monthly membership fee is $45.00. Other
expenses, such as league and lesson fees, pro-shop purchases, and
charges at the Courtside Cafe can also be billed to your account.
The charges will be itemized on your monthly statement and added
to your regular monthly fee.

      The Sports Club is offering a new program to all its members
which will save you writing a check each month. Upon your
authorization, the bank will send payment of your monthly charges
directly to the Sports Club. You will receive a copy of your
monthly statement to confirm the accuracy of your bill. If you
are interested in the automatic fee payment program, please
contact the accounting department (931-4285 ext. 33) to make the
necessary arrangements.

      On behalf of the staff of the Sports Club, I hope your
association with the Sports Club is long and enjoyable.

                              Sincerely,



                              Sports Club Manager
```

Saving the Document in a New File

Karen would like to save the edited version of the welcome letter that is displayed on the screen in a new file named LETTER4. This will allow the original file, LETTER3, to remain unchanged on the diskette in case you would like to repeat the lab for practice. She is also ready to exit the WordPerfect program. To both save the document and exit the program, use the **F**ile>**E**xit (Exit (F7)) command.

Select: File>Exit
>>   Exit (F7)

To respond Yes to the prompt to save the document,

Press: ⏎

To enter the new file name following the "Document to be Saved:" prompt,

Type: LETTER4
Press: ⏎

The revised letter has been saved on the disk as LETTER4. The printer specifications which were active when the file was saved were also saved with this file. If you were to retrieve this file again, the printer you made active would appear on the Print screen as the selected printer.

To indicate you are ready to exit the WordPerfect program,

Type: Y

KEY TERMS

word wrap
supplementary dictionary
block
flush right
code

soft carriage return
search
string
justification

MATCHING

1. word wrap   ———— a. saves file and resumes edit
2. F10   ———— b. automatic adjustment of words on a line
3. [HRt]   ———— c. displays the Line Format menu
4. CTRL - F4   ———— d. turns on the Block feature
5. ALT - F6   ———— e. moves the cursor a set number of spaces
6. SHIFT - F5   ———— f. displays the Date menu
7. margin   ———— g. hidden code for hard carriage return
8. TAB   ———— h. displays the Move menu
9. SHIFT - F8   ———— i. border of white space around the printed document
10. ALT - F4   ———— j. moves text flush with the right margin

PRACTICE EXERCISES

1. This problem will give you practice in creating, combining, and rearranging text.

- Enter the first paragraph from the "Overview to WordProcessing" into a WordPerfect document.

- Save the file as OVER-WP.

- Combine the text in the file DEF-WP (on your data diskette) with your file OVER-WP. The text in the file DEF-WP should be entered at the end of the text in OVER-WP.

- Rearrange the paragraphs in the text so they are in numerical order.

- Rearrange the order of sentence 4. It should read, " The grouping of text data to form words, sentences, paragraphs and pages of text results in the creation of a document."

- Set the justification to have a ragged right margin.

- Enter your name on the last line of the document.

- Print the document.

- Save this new document as OVER-WP.REV.

2. You are the public relations assistant at the local zoo and you are working on a news release about the various fund-raising activities at the zoo.

- Enter the three paragraphs below. Save the file as EVENTS, but do not exit the file. Print the file.

    The zoo Wine Tasting Event is sponsored by the zoo Wine Tasting Society. The second annual event was a 1978 Cabernet Sauvignon tasting party. It raised $3,600 to top off the Roadrunner Exhibit campaign.

    The Aid-to-Zoo National Horse Show is the major fund-raising activity of the Friends of the zoo Auxiliary. This event has raised funds for numerous exhibits throughout the zoo, including the Nocturnal Exhibit, Elephant Exhibit, Galapagos Exhibit, and the Graphic Signage and Deer Exhibit in the Children's zoo. Proceeds from the 1992 Horse Show exceeded $100,000, and were directed toward the Educational Graphics Exhibit.

    The Black-Tie Ball, an annual event held under the stars at the zoo, is sponsored by the men's Wildest Club in Town. Proceeds from the 1992 Black-Tie Ball amounted to $24,000 and are earmarked for architectural drawings for a proposed Bear Exhibit. Past proceeds have gone toward such projects as the Animal Nursery in the Children's zoo.

- Combine the text in the file ZOOFARI (on your data diskette) with the current file. The text in this file should be inserted below the second paragraph. There should be a blank line between paragraphs.

- Change the order of the paragraphs so that the first paragraph is about the Horse Show event, the second paragraph is about the Black-Tie Ball event, the third paragraph is about the Wine Tasting event, and the last paragraph is about the Zoo-Fari. Again, there should be a blank line between paragraphs.

■ Find and replace all occurrences of the word "zoo" with "Zoo".

■ Enter your name on line 1 and the current date using the Date command on line 2. Leave one blank line below the date.

■ Print the completed document. Save and replace the file as EVENTS. Exit WordPerfect.

3.   You are the managing director of the local zoo. Every quarter you need to update the zoo Advisory Board about the current status of the zoo.

■ Enter the memo below using margin settings of Left = 1.2", Right = 1.6", Tabs of 1.7" and 2.2" only, and justification left.

```
TO:          Advisory Board
FROM:        [Your Name], Managing Director
DATE:        [Enter current date using Date command]
```

One year after creating a Marketing Department, we are seeing excellent results. We are not budgeting for advertising, and our public relations, promotions, and publications are rapidly improving. With this boost in our profile, we believe that 912,500 attendance figure is within reach and we hope to cross 1,000,000 mark soon.

The major construction project for this quarter continues to be the new Children's Zoo. We expect completion of the project in the next quarter. It has been the largest construction project since our opening twenty-five years ago. Every department at the Zoo has helped in its planning and construction. We are looking forward to its opening scheduled for next quarter.

The other major project this quarter has been the updating of the Zoo Master Plan. The architectural firm and the Society Board have produced a well thought out plan to guide us through the next decade. We hope to begin the renovation of the Arizona exhibit using these guidelines in the next quarter.

The animal inventory has increased this quarter making our collection to this date 292 specimens from 1,280 species. Our collection is well-cared for and its health is excellent. Our breeding success is above normal and our animals enjoy an excellent quality of life, a reflection of our feeding and veterinary programs.

This quarter has been very productive and exciting as we near the completion of the Children's Zoo project.

- Indent each paragraph 1 tab stop.
- Delete the second sentence in the second paragraph using the Move command.
- The animal inventory figures in the fourth paragraph are incorrect. They should be switched to be "1,280 specimens from 292 species." Use the Block/Move command to make these changes.
- Print the memo. Save the file as STATUS.

4. In this problem you will create and format a document.

- Clear the screen for creation of a new document.
- Set justification to ragged right.
- Set margins to left = 2" and right = 1.5".
- Clear all tab settings. Enter new tab settings of .5" and 3" (save with Exit (F7)).
- Enter the letter below as follows:

Begin the letter approximately 2.17" from the top of the page.

Enter the current date using the Date command.

Display the date flush with the right margin.

Enter the letter using the approximate line values as a guide.

Indent each paragraph 5 spaces.

Closing begins approximately on position 6.33".

Use your name in the closing.

(Ln 2.17")   Current Date

(Ln 2.83")   Ms. Peg Mitchell
                 Admissions Department
                 Arizona State University
                 Tempe, AZ 85257

(Ln 3.67")   Dear Ms. Mitchell:

(Ln 4")   Thank you for taking the time to speak with me yesterday about the possibility of employment in your department.

                      I feel my professional background in personnel services and my educational background in higher education would meet many of your requirements.

                      I am enclosing a complete resume and hope that if a position becomes available in the near future you will consider my credentials.

(Ln 6.33")   Sincerely,

(Ln 7.0")   (your name)

- Reveal hidden codes.
- Delete the previous margin setting code.
- Enter new margin settings of left = 1.5", right = 1.5".
- Print the letter.
- Save the letter using the file name JOB.

Merging and Refining Documents

3

CASE STUDY

Karen Barnes, the membership assistant, submitted the final copy of the welcome letter to the membership coordinator. The membership coordinator is very pleased with the content and form of the welcome letter. However he would like it to be more personalized. He wants to include the first name of the new member and an inside address. Karen will create a form letter using WordPerfect's Merge feature to personalize each welcome letter.

As a second project, he would like Karen to write an article for the club newsletter about the new automatic fee payment program. You will follow Karen as she works on these two projects.

The Merge Feature

Boot the system and if necessary, enter the current date at the DOS date prompt. Load the WordPerfect program.
Retrieve the file WELCOME.

This is the same as the welcome letter you saved as LETTER4 in Lab 2. Notice that the date in the letter is the same as the system date you entered at the DOS prompt. Each time this letter is retrieved or printed, the date will display the system date. This is because of the date code you entered in the document.

Karen needs to change the welcome letter so that each letter sent to a new member is more personal. The welcome letter will include the new member's first name in the salutation and his or her full name and address as the inside address. To do this Karen will use the Merge feature of WordPerfect.

The Merge feature will combine a list of names and addresses that are contained in one file with a form letter in another file. The names and addresses are

OBJECTIVES

In this lab you will learn how to:

1. Use the Merge command.
2. Create primary and the secondary merge files.
3. Merge the primary and secondary files.
4. Center, boldface, and underline text.
5. Open two document files.
6. Create a split screen or open a window.
7. Move text between two documents.
8. Define newspaper-style columns.
9. Reformat the screen display.
10. Use the View Document command.
11. Change justification.
12. Use the Hyphenation feature.
13. Save and exit two document files.

WP83

entered (merged) into the form letter in the blank spaces provided. The result is a personalized form letter.

Merge usually requires the use of two files: a **primary file** and a **secondary merge file**. The primary file contains the basic form letter. It directs the merge process through the use of **merge codes**. The merge codes control what information is used from the secondary merge file and where it is entered in the document in the primary file. The welcome letter will be modified to be the primary file.

The secondary merge file, sometimes called an **address file**, contains the information needed to complete the form letter in the primary file. It will contain the new member's name and address data. Each piece of information in the secondary merge file is called a **field**. For example, the member's full name is a field of data, the street address is another field of data, the city a third field of data, and so forth. All the fields of data that are needed to complete the primary document are called a **record**.

The secondary file you will create will contain the following fields of information for each record: Full Name, Street Address, City, State, Zipcode, and First Name. WordPerfect takes the field information from the secondary merge file and combines or merges it into the primary file.

First Karen will modify the welcome letter to accept information from the secondary merge file. Then she will create the secondary merge file, which will hold the new members' names and addresses to be entered into the primary file.

Entering Merge Codes in the Primary File

The welcome letter needs to be modified to allow entry of the name and address information for each new member from the secondary merge file. The inside address will hold the following three lines of information:

> Full Name
> Street Address
> City State Zipcode

The first line of the inside address, which will hold the new member's full name, will be entered as line 5 of the welcome letter.

Move to: Ln 1.67" Pos 1" (blank line above salutation)

How will WordPerfect know to enter the member's full name from the secondary file at this location in the primary file? WordPerfect uses a series of codes, called merge codes, which direct the program to accept information from the secondary merge file at the specified location in the primary file. To display the menu of merge codes use the Tools>Merge Codes or (SHIFT) - (F9) command.

Select: Tools>Merge Codes
>>   **Merge Codes** (SHIFT) - (F9)

Your display screen should be similar to Figure 3-1.

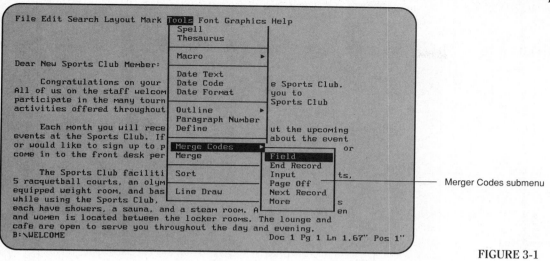

Merger Codes submenu

FIGURE 3-1

The Merge Codes submenu (displayed in the status line if you used the function key) consists of five commonly used merge codes. The sixth option, More, allows you to select other merge codes not listed on the menu.

The Merge Codes submenu options have the following meanings:

Field	identifies the field to be inserted from the secondary document into the primary document
End Record	marks the end of a record in the secondary file
Input	stops the merge and waits for keyboard input
Page Off	instructs WordPerfect not to place page breaks after each primary file
Next Record	instructs WordPerfect to move to the next secondary file record during the merge

A Field merge code needs to be entered in the primary file for each field of data you want copied from the secondary file. The location of the Field merge code directs WordPerfect where to enter the data. The cursor is positioned on the line where the new member's full name will appear as the first line of the inside address. The first field you will identify, then, is the Full Name field.

Select: Field

The prompt "Enter field:" is displayed in the status line. Following the prompt you must enter the name you want to assign to the first Field merge code. A field name should be short and descriptive of the contents of the field. You will use the field name "Name."

Type: Name
Press: ⏎

Your display screen should be similar to Figure 3-2.

FIGURE 3-2

merge code
field name
tilde

March 20, 1992

{FIELD}Name~

Dear New Sports Club Member:

    Congratulations on your new membership in the Sports Club.
All of us on the staff welcome you and encourage you to
participate in the many tournaments, leagues and Sports Club
activities offered throughout the year.

    Each month you will receive a newsletter about the upcoming
events at the Sports Club. If you have questions about the event
or would like to sign up to participate in an event, just call or
come in to the front desk personnel.

    The Sports Club facilities include 18 lighted tennis courts,
5 racquetball courts, an olympic size swimming pool, Nautilus
equipped weight room, and basketball court. For your comfort
while using the Sports Club, the men's and ladies' locker rooms
each have showers, a sauna, and a steam room. A spa for both men
and women is located between the locker rooms. The lounge and
B:\WELCOME   Doc 1 Pg 1 Ln 1.83" Pos 1"

The Field merge code, {FIELD}, followed by the name you assigned the field is displayed at the cursor location. The ~ (tilde) at the end of the field name tells WordPerfect where the field name ends. When the command to merge the documents is used, the information for the new member's full name from the secondary merge file will be entered at this location in the primary file.

The next line of the inside address will contain the street address. To create and move to the next line,

Press:

To enter the Field merge code for the street address,

Select: **T**ools>**M**erge Codes>**F**ield
  >> Merge Codes (SHIFT) - (F9), **F**ield

This time, in response to the field name prompt,

Type: **Address**
Press:

The second Field merge code is displayed in the welcome letter.

The next line of the inside address will display three fields of data from the secondary file: city, state, and zipcode. They will be identified by the field names City, State, and Zip.

Press:

To enter the merge code for the next field of data,

Select: **T**ools>Merge Codes>**F**ield
   >>   Merge Codes (SHIFT) - (F9), Field

Type: **City**
Press: (⏎)

To separate the City field from the next field,

Press: Space bar

The State field will be entered on the same line as the City field.

Select: **T**ools>Merge Codes>**F**ield
   >>   Merge Codes (SHIFT) - (F9), Field
Type: **State**
Press: (⏎)

To separate the State field from the next field, Zipcode, and enter the field name,

Press: Space bar (2 times)
Select: **T**ools>Merge Codes>**F**ield
   >> Merge Codes (SHIFT) - (F9), **F**ield
Type: **Zip**
Press: (⏎)

To enter a blank line between the inside address and the salutation,

Press: (⏎)

Your display screen should be similar to Figure 3-3.

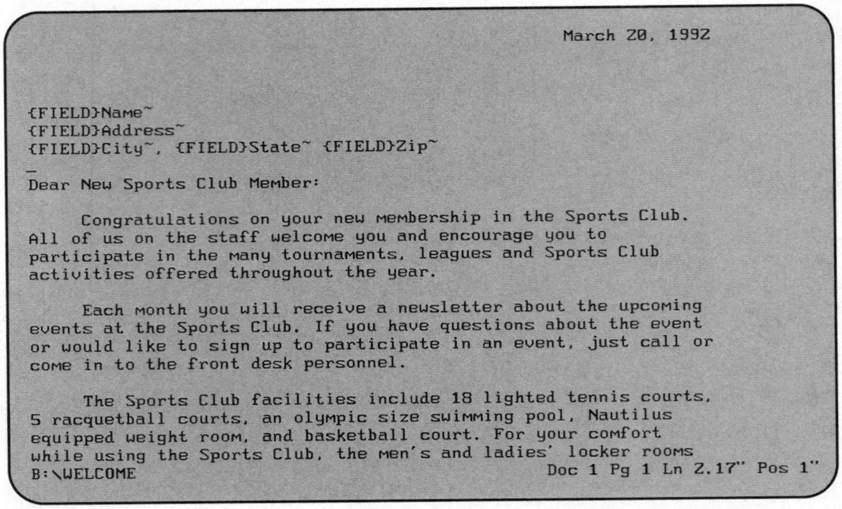

```
                                                  March 20, 1992



{FIELD}Name~
{FIELD}Address~
{FIELD}City~, {FIELD}State~ {FIELD}Zip~

Dear New Sports Club Member:

     Congratulations on your new membership in the Sports Club.
All of us on the staff welcome you and encourage you to
participate in the many tournaments, leagues and Sports Club
activities offered throughout the year.

     Each month you will receive a newsletter about the upcoming
events at the Sports Club. If you have questions about the event
or would like to sign up to participate in an event, just call or
come in to the front desk personnel.

     The Sports Club facilities include 18 lighted tennis courts,
5 racquetball courts, an olympic size swimming pool, Nautilus
equipped weight room, and basketball court. For your comfort
while using the Sports Club, the men's and ladies' locker rooms
B:\WELCOME                                 Doc 1 Pg 1 Ln 2.17" Pos 1"
```

FIGURE 3-3

The merge codes to enter the inside address data from the secondary merge file are now complete. If you have made an error, you can edit the merge codes just like any other text entry.

The last field of information (field 6) that needs to be entered in the primary file is the new member's first name in the salutation. First the words "New Sports Club Member" need to be deleted.

Move to: Ln 2.33" Pos 1.5" ("N" of "New")
Press: (CTRL) - (END)

To enter the merge code for the first name (field 6) into the salutation,

Select: **T**ools>Merge Codes>**F**ield
\>> Merge Codes (SHIFT) - (F9), **F**ield
Type: **FirstName**
Press: (↵)

To end the salutation with a colon,

Type: **:**

Once all the merge codes that are needed in the primary file are correctly entered, the file must be saved.

A few notes about entering field merge codes in the primary document before saving the file:

- A field name can be used more than one time in the primary document. For example, the Name field could be used again in the letter without assigning it a new field name.

- The field name should be short and descriptive. It can be a single word or multiple words. If you enter multiple words use a hyphen or underscore to separate the words. Do not use a blank space between words.

- Not all the fields in the secondary file need to be used in the primary file.

To save the primary file as **WELCOME.PF** (the extension .PF identifies the file as a primary file) and clear the screen in preparation for creating the secondary merge file,

Select:	File>Exit
>>	**Exit** (F7)
Type:	**Y**
Type:	**WELCOME.PF**
Press:	(⏎)
Type:	**N**

Creating the Secondary File

A blank Wordperfect screen is ready to be used to enter the fields and records for the secondary merge file. The secondary merge file will hold the six fields of data about each new member. The six fields of data for each new member form a record of information.

The primary file calls for the following six fields of data for each record:

Field Number	Field Name
Field 1	Name
Field 2	Address
Field 3	City
Field 4	State
Field 5	Zip
Field 6	FirstName

When entering the data for the secondary merge file, the following rules must be observed:

- At the beginning of the document enter a merge code which identifies the names of each field used in the primary file.

- The order of fields in the primary file determines what order the fields of data should be listed in the secondary merge file. For example, the FirstName field in the primary file is the sixth field of data in a record from the secondary merge file.

- The end of a field of data is marked with an **End Field** merge code.

- The end of a record is marked with an **End Record** merge code.

- Each field of data must be entered in the same sequence for all records and must contain the same type of information.

- The same number of fields must appear in each record.

To enter the merge code that identifies the field names,

Select: Tools>Merge Codes>More
   >>   Merge Codes (SHIFT) - (F9), **M**ore

Your display screen should be similar to Figure 3-4.

FIGURE 3-4

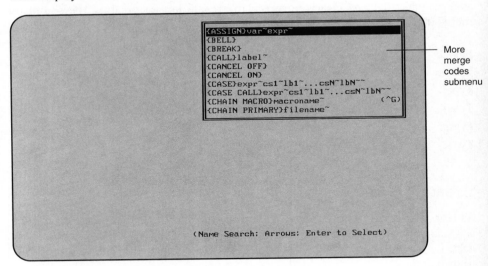

More
merge
codes
submenu

A submenu of other merge codes is displayed. They are listed in alphabetical order. You can use the ↑ and ↓ keys to move the highlight bar through the list of codes, or you can use the mouse. If you use the mouse, position the mouse pointer inside the Merge Codes selection box and drag the mouse to move the highlight. The list will scroll as you drag the mouse. You can also move by "pages" using the (PGDN) or (PGUP) keys.

Using any of these methods, move the highlight to {FIELD NAMES}. To select it,

Press: (↵) (or press the right mouse button)

The prompt "Enter Field 1:" appears in the status line. In response to the prompt you need to enter the field name of the first field. The field name must be entered exactly as you typed it in the primary file.

Type: **Name**
Press: (↵)

WordPerfect displays a prompt asking you to enter the name of the second field.

Type: **Address**
Press: (↵)

Continue to define the remaining four field names (City, State, Zip, and FirstName). When WordPerfect prompts you to enter the field name for the seventh field,

Press: (↵)

This tells WordPerfect that you are finished. When you are done your screen should be similar to Figure 3-5.

FIGURE 3-5

```
{FIELD NAMES}Name~Address~City~State~Zip~FirstName~~{END RECORD}
===============================================================================
 _




Field: Name                              Doc 1 Pg 2 Ln 1" Pos 1"
```

The {FIELD NAMES} definition code is displayed on the first line of the screen. The name of each field as you typed it and a tilde at the end of each field name are included. The code ends with an extra tilde and an {END RECORD} merge code. WordPerfect treats this merge code as a special record in the secondary file. The page break line separates this record from the other records you will be entering into the document next.

The first record begins immediately below the special record. Your cursor should be on the first line of page 2. Notice that the status line displays "Field: Name." This tells you WordPerfect is ready for you to enter the first field of data, the new member's full name.

Type: **Mr. Anthony R. Myers** (do not press ⏎)

To tell the program that this is the end of the first field of data, you must enter the End Field merge code. This code can be entered easily using the (F9) key, or it can be entered using Tools>Merge Codes> More>{End Field}. Since pressing (F9) is much easier, to enter this code,

Press: End Field (F9)

The End Field code is entered after the first field, and the cursor moves down one line. WordPerfect displays "Field: Address" in the status line to tell you it expects you to enter the data for this field next.

Type: **1452 Southern Ave.**
Press: End Field (F9)

Enter the information for the remaining fields as follows:

Type: **Mesa**
Press: End Field (F9)

Type: AZ
Press: End Field (F9)

Type: 85202
Press: End Field (F9)

Type: Anthony
Press: End Field (F9)

The six fields of information, corresponding to the six field merge codes used in the inside address and saluatation in the primary file, are complete for the first record in the secondary merge file.

To separate this record from the next record and to indicate a page break between documents, the End Record merge code is entered. To enter this code,

Select: **T**ools>Mer**g**e Codes>**E**nd Record
>> Merge Codes (SHIFT) - (F9), **E**nd Record

Your display screen should be similar to Figure 3-6.

FIGURE 3-6

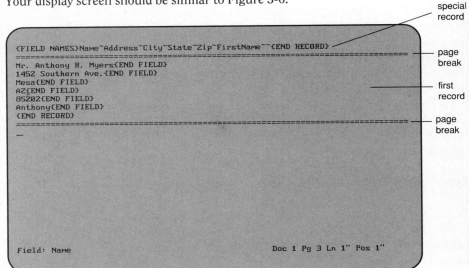

An {END RECORD} code is entered on the line, and the cursor moves to the next line in the file. A double dashed line separates each record. This line indicates a page break. It tells WordPerfect to begin a new page following the page break.

Never separate fields or records with an extra hard carriage return. Also do not insert spaces following the last word in a field and a End Record merge code.

Enter the field information for the second record as follows:

Type: Miss Allycin Miller
Press: End Field (F9)

Type: 128 Forest Ave.
Press: End Field (F9)

Type:	Tempe
Press:	End Field (F9)

Type:	AZ
Press:	End Field (F9)

Type:	85285
Press:	End Field (F9)

Type:	Allycin
Press:	End Field (F9)

Select:	Tools>Merge Codes>End Record
>>	Merge Codes (SHIFT) - (F9), End Record

Your display screen should be similar to Figure 3-7.

FIGURE 3-7

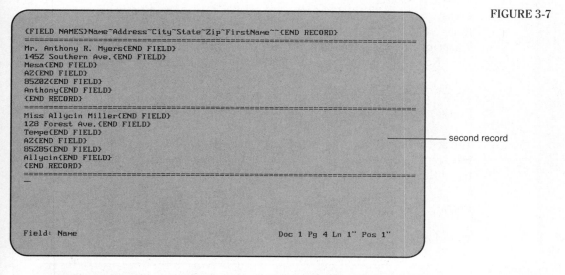

```
{FIELD NAMES}Name~Address~City~State~Zip~FirstName~~{END RECORD}
===============================================================
Mr. Anthony R. Myers{END FIELD}
1452 Southern Ave.{END FIELD}
Mesa{END FIELD}
AZ{END FIELD}
85202{END FIELD}
Anthony{END FIELD}
{END RECORD}
===============================================================
Miss Allycin Miller{END FIELD}
128 Forest Ave.{END FIELD}
Tempe{END FIELD}
AZ{END FIELD}
85285{END FIELD}
Allycin{END FIELD}
{END RECORD}
===============================================================
—



Field: Name                        Doc 1 Pg 4 Ln 1" Pos 1"
```

— second record

Enter your name and address as the third record in the secondary file.

Check your screen and make any corrections as needed. Make sure each field ends with an End Field code and that each record ends with an End Record code.

The number of records you enter into the secondary file is limited only by your diskette space.

To save the secondary file using the file name WELCOME.SF (the file extension .SF identifies this file as the secondary file) and clear the screen in preparation for merging the primary file with the secondary merge file,

Select:	File>Exit
>>	Exit (F7)
Press:	Y
Type:	WELCOME.SF
Press:	(↵)
Type:	N

A blank WordPerfect screen is ready for use.

Merging the Primary and Secondary Merge Files

Now that you have created and saved the primary and secondary merge files, you are ready to combine them to create the new personalized welcome letter.

During this process a third file is created. The original primary and secondary files are not altered or affected in any way. The third file is the result of the merging of the primary and secondary files. It is very important to clear the screen of any document before merging files.

Select: Tools>Merge
    >>   Merge (CTRL) - (F9), **Merge**

In response to the prompt to enter the name of the primary file,

Type: **WELCOME.PF**
Press: (↵)

The primary file is retrieved into the computer's memory.

Next respond to the prompt to enter the name of the secondary file:

Type: **WELCOME.SF**
Press: (↵)

The status line displays the message "* Merging *." At the completion of the merge, the document containing the three letters is displayed on the screen. To move to the top of the document,

Press: (HOME) (HOME) (↑)

Your display screen should be similar to Figure 3-8.

FIGURE 3-8

```
                                                          March 20, 1992
    —

    Mr. Anthony R. Myers
    1452 Southern Ave.
    Mesa, AZ 85202

    Dear Anthony:

        Congratulations on your new membership in the Sports Club.
    All of us on the staff welcome you and encourage you to
    participate in the many tournaments, leagues and Sports Club
    activities offered throughout the year.

        Each month you will receive a newsletter about the upcoming
    events at the Sports Club. If you have questions about the event
    or would like to sign up to participate in an event, just call or
    come in to the front desk personnel.

        The Sports Club facilities include 18 lighted tennis courts,
    5 racquetball courts, an olympic size swimming pool, Nautilus
    equipped weight room, and basketball court. For your comfort
    while using the Sports Club, the men's and ladies' locker rooms
                                            Doc 1 Pg 1 Ln 1" Pos 1"
```

The personalized letter to Anthony Myers is displayed. The fields of data from the secondary merge file have been entered into the primary file at the location of the merge codes.

To see the letter using the data for the second record,

Press: ⬚PGDN⬚

Finally, to see the letter containing your name and address information,

Press: ⬚PGDN⬚

Now each time Karen needs to send welcome letters, all she needs to do is to create the new member secondary merge file and issue the Merge command. Because the Date command was used, the date will automatically reflect the date the letter was created.

Save ⬚F10⬚ the current document of three welcome letters as WELCOME.MRG. The letters can be printed like any other document. **Print the letter containing your name and address information only.** Remember to select the appropriate printer for your microcomputer system first.

To leave the document and clear the screen,

Select:	**File>Exit**
>>	**Exit** ⬚F7⬚
Type:	**N**
Type:	**N**

To review, the steps in creating a customized form letter are:

1. Create the primary file. Enter Field merge codes in the document to tell WordPerfect where and what fields of information to use from the secondary merge file. Save the document as the primary file.

2. Create the secondary merge file. It will contain the special record which identifies the field names used in the primary file and the variable data or information needed to complete the primary file for each record. Each field of data must end with an End Field code. Each record must end with an End Record code. As many records as diskette space will allow can be entered in this file.

3. Use the Merge command to combine the primary and secondary files to create a customized document for each record in the secondary merge file.

Centering and Boldfacing Text

The second project Karen needs to work on is the article for the newsletter about the new automatic fee payment program. The membership coordinator already has a file started which contains another article to be entered in the newsletter. He has asked Karen to enter her article at the end of this document.

Retrieve the file ARTICLE.DOC. Your display screen should be similar to Figure 3-9.

FIGURE 3-9

```
  —              ** NEW MEMBER **
                    ORIENTATION
                      MEETING


A New Member Orientation meeting will be held on Thursday
evening, November 19 from 7:00 to 8:30 PM in the Adult Lounge.
All new members are encouraged to attend this meeting. Your
picture for the identification card can be taken at this time.
The tennis and racquetball Pro staff will be discussing their
programs, sign-up procedures and costs. The Sports Club
management will also present information on other club events and
programs, procedures and costs. This is your opportunity to meet
the people who can help you make the most of your membership.

This meeting is also open to old members who may have questions
or suggestions to improve the Sports Club. We would like to see
and meet you all!

Refreshments will be served following the meeting.


B:\ARTICLE.DOC                              Doc 1 Pg 1 Ln 1" Pos 1"
```

An article concerning a new member orientation meeting is displayed on the screen.

Karen will begin the article about the automatic fee payment program three lines below the end of the first article. To move to this location,

Press: (HOME) (HOME) (↓)

The cursor should be on Ln 4.67" Pos 1" (three blank lines below the last line of text).

She would like to enter a title for her article similar to the title in the article on the display screen. Notice that each line of this title is centered between the margins. If you have a color monitor, you will also note that it is displayed in color. This is because it has been formatted to be printed in boldface print.

The title for her article is: NEW PROGRAM AUTOMATIC PAYMENT. She will enter it on three lines.

To turn on the capability to enter text in all capital letters,

Press: (CAPS LOCK)

Notice in the status line that "POS" is displayed in uppercase letters. This is how WordPerfect tells you that the (CAPS LOCK) key is on. The (CAPS LOCK) key affects only alphabet keys. Other characters will require that you use the (SHIFT) key.

To **center** text between the margins, the Center (Layout>Align>Center or (SHIFT)-(F6)) command is used. The cursor must be positioned on the left margin before using the command. Otherwise the text will be centered between the cursor location and the right margin.

Select: Layout>Align>Center
>>   Center (SHIFT) - (F6)

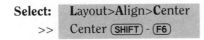

The cursor jumps to the middle of the screen. As text is typed, it will be centered between the current margin settings.

Karen also wants the title to be printed in **boldface** characters. Boldface text is printed darker than normal text. On the screen it is displayed brighter than surrounding text or in color if you have a color monitor. The command to produce boldfaced text is Bold, (Font>Appearance>Bold or (F6)). To mark the area in the document to begin bold text and enter the first line of the title,

Select: Font>Appearance>**Bold**
>> Bold (F6)
Type: ** NEW PROGRAM **
Press: (⏎)

The text is displayed brighter on your screen or in color if you have a color monitor, to show the area that is to be printed in bold text. If yours is not brighter, you may need to adjust the contrast and brightness of your monitor.

Before entering the second line of the heading, the Center command must be used again. Each line you want centered must begin with the Center command. The Bold command continues in effect until turned off by selecting the command again. Since it is quicker to use the function key to initiate the Center command, to center this line,

Press: Center (SHIFT) - (F6)
Type: AUTOMATIC
Press: (⏎)
Press: Center (SHIFT) - (F6)
Type: PAYMENT

To end boldfacing using the function key command and turn off all capital letters,

Press: Bold (F6)
Press: (CAPS LOCK)

Karen will begin the text of the article two lines below the heading. To create the blank lines and move to this location,

Press: (⏎) (3 times)

Your cursor should now be on Ln 5.5" Pos 1". Your display screen should be similar to Figure 3-10.

FIGURE 3-10

```
A New Member Orientation meeting will be held on Thursday
evening, November 19 from 7:00 to 8:30 PM in the Adult Lounge.
All new members are encouraged to attend this meeting. Your
picture for the identification card can be taken at this time.
The tennis and racquetball Pro staff will be discussing their
programs, sign-up procedures and costs. The Sports Club
management will also present information on other club events and
programs, procedures and costs. This is your opportunity to meet
the people who can help you make the most of your membership.

This meeting is also open to old members who may have questions
or suggestions to improve the Sports Club. We would like to see
and meet you all!

Refreshments will be served following the meeting.


                        ** NEW PROGRAM **
                           AUTOMATIC
                            PAYMENT



B:\ARTICLE.DOC                              Doc 1 Pg 1 Ln 5.5" Pos 1"
```

Using Two Document Files

Now Karen could begin typing the information about the automatic fee payment program into the document. However, she doesn't want to retype the same information that is in the welcome letter. Instead she will copy the paragraph about the automatic fee payment program from the WELCOME file into the document on the display.

To do this she will use the WordPerfect Switch feature. This feature will let her use two document files at the same time. It does this by creating a new screen for the second document file.

To create a new screen and switch to that screen, the Switch (Edit>Switch Document or (SHIFT) - (F3)) command is used.

Select: Edit>Switch Document
   >>   Switch (SHIFT) - (F3)

The screen is blank. The status line indicates, however, that you are in document 2. The ARTICLE.DOC file is still in the computer's memory as document 1, although it is not displayed.

At this point new text could be entered to create a new document, or an existing document can be retrieved. Karen will retrieve the WELCOME file into the new screen.

Retrieve WELCOME.

The welcome letter is displayed on the screen as document 2. Two files are now open and can be used at the same time.

To see and use the file ARTICLE.DOC in the document 1 screen, use Edit>Switch Document or Switch (SHIFT) - (F3) again. It now acts as a toggle to move between the two document screens. Since the function key is quicker,

Press: (SHIFT) - (F3)

The file ARTICLE.DOC is displayed in the document 1 screen.

The two files can be seen and used by switching from one document screen to another using (SHIFT)-(F3) or Edit>Switch Document.

Creating a Split Screen

It would be even more convenient for Karen if she could see both documents at the same time on the display screen. This can be done by splitting the display screen into two parts, or **windows**, using the Screen (Edit>Window or (CTRL) - (F3)) command.

Select: Edit>Window
>> Screen (CTRL) - (F3), Window

The prompt "Number of lines in this window: 24" is displayed in the status line. This is the default window-size setting for a full screen of 24 lines. To divide the full screen into two equal halves,

Type: 12
Press: ⏎

Your display screen should be similar to Figure 3-11.

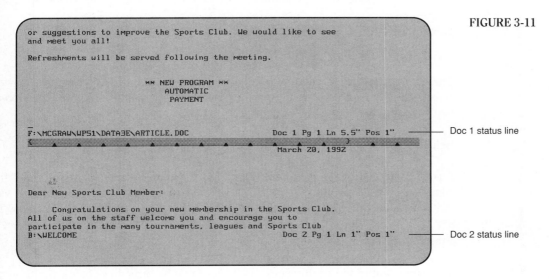

FIGURE 3-11

The screen is divided into two equal parts by a reverse-video bar marked by tri-angles, which represent the tab stops. Document 1 is displayed in the top window. Document 2 is displayed in the bottom window. The status line at the bottom of each window identifies the file and cursor location.

The cursor is currently located in document 1. You could now edit the file in this window without affecting the file in document 2. To switch into document 2,

Press: Switch (SHIFT) - (F3)

The cursor has jumped into document 2.

Note: Mouse users can click on the window to switch from one document to another.

Now you could edit the document in this window without affecting the file in the other window. Notice as you switch from one window to the other that the triangles within the reverse video bar change direction. They point upward when the cursor is in the upper window and downward when the cursor is in the lower window.

The cursor movement keys and command keys operate as they would if only one window or one file was open.

Moving Text Between Documents

Now Karen is ready to move a copy of the paragraph on the automatic fee payment program from the WELCOME file (document 2) into the ARTICLE.DOC file (document 1).

The paragraph to be copied is the fifth paragraph. Using the ⬇ key and the status line in document 2 to locate your cursor position,

Move to: Ln 6.17" Pos 1" (left margin of first line of fifth paragraph)

Next, to issue the Move command,

Select: Edit>Select>Paragraph
    >>   Move (CTRL) - (F4), Paragraph

The whole paragraph is highlighted. The menu displayed in the Status line lets you select whether you want to cut, copy, or delete the marked (highlighted) section of text. To copy the block,

Select: Copy

A copy of the paragraph is stored in temporary memory. Karen wants to insert the copy of the paragraph into the ARTICLE.DOC file in document 1. To do this you will switch into document 1 and then retrieve the paragraph from temporary memory.

Press: Switch (SHIFT) - (F3)

The cursor jumps back into document 1. It should be three lines below the heading (Ln 5.5" Pos 1"). If it is not there, before continuing, move it to that location.

To retrieve the paragraph into document 1,

Press: (⏎)

The paragraph is copied into the file in document 1. To see the rest of the paragraph,

Move to: Ln 6.67" Pos 1" (last line of paragraph)

Your display screen should be similar to Figure 3-12.

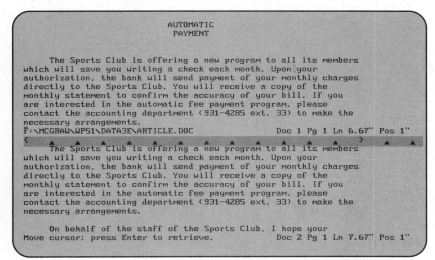

FIGURE 3-12

The copy of the paragraph has been copied from the file in document 2 and inserted into the file in document 1. Using the Split Screen feature to view both documents at the same time made this process very easy.

The documents in each window operate independently of each other. The changes that are made in one document do not affect the other. You can also use the split screen to view two different parts of the same document at the same time.

Closing a Split Screen

Karen no longer needs to see the WELCOME file in document 2. To return to displaying a single document on the screen at one time, the process of creating a window is reversed.

Select: Edit>Window
   >>   Screen (CTRL) - (F3), Window

To return to a full screen of 24 lines,

Type: 24
Press: (⏎)

Your display screen should be similar to Figure 3-13.

```
                        AUTOMATIC
                        PAYMENT

        The Sports Club is offering a new program to all its members
which will save you writing a check each month. Upon your
authorization, the bank will send payment of your monthly charges
directly to the Sports Club. You will receive a copy of the
monthly statement to confirm the accuracy of your bill. If you
are interested in the automatic fee payment program, please
contact the accounting department (931-4285 ext. 33) to make the
necessary arrangements.




B:\ARTICLE.DOC                                    Doc 1 Pg 1 Ln 6.67" Pos 1"
```

FIGURE 3-13

The screen display returns to a single window of 24 lines, and document 1 occupies the whole screen. Both documents, however, are still open. But document 2 is not visible on the display. When closing a window, the document the cursor is positioned in is the document that will be displayed.

To continue her work on the article, Karen wants to remove the indentation from the first line in the paragraph. To do this she could use the Reveal Codes screen to locate the position of the tab code and then delete it. However, she is sure the tab code is located at the beginning of the line that is indented. So she will remove the code while in normal document display.

Move to: Ln 5.5" Pos 1" (left margin of first line)
Press: (DEL)

The tab code has been deleted, and the line is no longer indented.

Underlining Text

Finally, Karen wants to **underline** the accounting department telephone number. To underline text which is already entered in a document, the area of text to be underlined must first be defined using the Block feature.

To position the cursor under the "9" in the telephone number, and to turn Block on,

Move to: Ln 6.5" Pos 4.5" ("9" in telephone number)
Select: Edit>Block
  >> Block (ALT)-(F4)

To define the block of text to be underlined (the entire telephone number),

Move to: Ln 6.5" Pos 6.1" (the "3" at end of telephone number)

The telephone number is highlighted on the screen.

To mark this block of text to be underlined, the Underline (Font>Appearance>Underline or F8) command is used.

Select: Font>Appearance>Underline
   >>   Underline F8

Your display screen should be similar to Figure 3-14.

FIGURE 3-14

```
                    AUTOMATIC
                    PAYMENT

     The Sports Club is offering a new program to all its members
which will save you writing a check each month. Upon your
authorization, the bank will send payment of your monthly charges
directly to the Sports Club. You will receive a copy of the
monthly statement to confirm the accuracy of your bill. If you
are interested in the automatic fee payment program, please
contact the accounting department (931-4285 ext. 33) to make the
necessary arrangements.




B:\ARTICLE.DOC                            Doc 1 Pg 1 Ln 6.5" Pos 6.1"
```

The marked block of text is underlined, highlighted, or displayed in color, depending upon your monitor. When it is printed, it will be underlined. The hidden code to turn underlining on and off is placed at the beginning and end of the block.

If you want to underline text as you enter it into the document, simply select Underline before typing the text. It then must be turned off by selecting Underline again at the end of the text to be underlined. It is much quicker to use the function key, F8, to initiate this command than it is to use the pull-down menus.

Defining Columns

The articles will appear in the newsletter as long newspaper-style columns. The WordPerfect Columns (Layout>Columns or ALT - F7) command lets you easily set the text format of a document into columns.

As with many WordPerfect commands, a hidden code is entered into the document to control the display of the text. The location of the hidden code indicates the point in the document at which the command will take effect. Since both articles need to be displayed in a column format, move the cursor to the top of page 1.

Press: PGUP
Select: Layout>Columns
   >>   Columns/Table ALT - F7, Columns

The Columns submenu (displayed in the status line if you used the function key command) lists three options: On, Off, and Define. They have the following effect:

On   turns columns on at the cursor position
Off   turns columns off at the cursor position
Define   defines the type, spacing, and number of columns

To use the Columns feature, you must first define the column settings.

Select: Define

Your display screen should be similar to Figure 3-15.

FIGURE 3-15

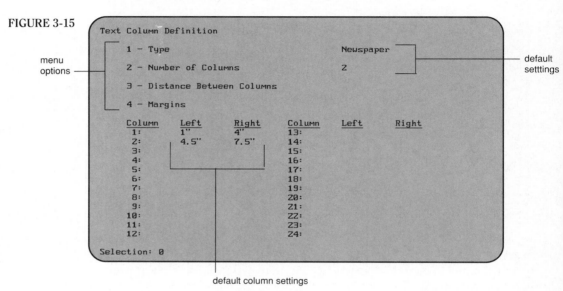

default column settings

The Text Column Definition menu replaces the document on the screen. Four menu options are displayed in the upper portion of the screen. The default settings are displayed in the column to the right of each option. The lower portion of the screen shows the right and left margins for the columns based upon the default settings.

The first menu option, Type, lets you specify the type of column you want to create.

Select: Type

The three types of columns which can be created are displayed in the menu in the status line: 1 Newspaper, 2 Parallel, and 3 Parallel with Block Protect. With **newspaper columns**, text runs vertically up and down the page through the columns. With **parallel columns**, text runs horizontally across the page. One of the columns may spill over to the next page while the other does not. The third type of column, Parallel with Block protect, is the same as parallel columns, except that text is protected from being split between two pages.

The default setting is Newspaper. Since the default setting is acceptable, this option does not need to be changed. To leave this menu without changing the default,

Press:

The second option, 2 Number of Columns, lets you specify how many columns of text you want across the width of the page. The Sports Club newsletter has three columns.

Select: Number of Columns

The cursor is positioned under the default setting. To change the number of columns to three,

Type: 3

Press: ⏎

Your display screen should be similar to Figure 3-16.

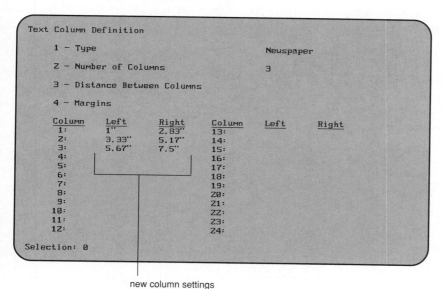

FIGURE 3-16

new column settings

Wordperfect automatically calculates and displays the new left and right margins for the three columns in the lower portion of the screen. The first column will begin at the left default margin of 1" and end at 2.83". The second column will begin at 3.33" and end at 5.16" . The third column will begin at 5.67" and end at the right default margin setting of 7.5".

The next option, 3 Distance Between Columns, lets you specify how much space you want between the columns.

Select: Distance Between Columns

The default setting of .5" is displayed. Karen thinks the default setting will be suitable, and decides to leave it as it is.

Press: ⏎

You can also change the default left and right margins by selecting the Margins option. However, for our purposes, the default settings are acceptable. To save the column definitions and exit the menu,

Press: F7 or ⏎

The column settings have been defined. A hidden code, [Col Def], containing the column definitions has been entered into the document.

The Columns menu is displayed in the status line again. It allows you to continue making selections. Next you need to direct the program to display the document using the column settings defined. This will enter a [Col on] code in the document. To turn the display of columns on,

Select: On

Reformatting the Screen Display

It appears that nothing has happened. To reformat the display of the text to the new column settings, you could move down through the document using (PGDN) or the cursor movement keys. However, a faster way is to use the Rewrite command, an option in the Screen menu.

Press: Screen (CTRL) - (F3)
Select: Rewrite

The text is reformatted so that it is in newspaper-style columns. Your display screen should be similar to Figure 3-17.

FIGURE 3-17

```
 ** NEW MEMBER **        meeting.
    ORIENTATION
    MEETING
                         ** NEW PROGRAM **
                            AUTOMATIC
A New Member                PAYMENT
Orientation
meeting will be
held on Thursday     The Sports Club is
evening, November    offering a new
19 from 7:00 to      program to all its
8:30 PM in the       members which will
Adult Lounge. All    save you writing a
new members are      check each month.
encouraged to        Upon your
attend this          authorization, the
meeting. Your        bank will send
picture for the      payment of your
identification       monthly charges
card can be taken    directly to the
at this time. The    Sports Club. You
tennis and           will receive a
racquetball Pro      copy of the
staff will be        monthly statement
B:\ARTICLE.1                         Col 1 Doc 1 Pg 1 Ln 1" Pos 1"
```

The two articles appear on the screen as two columns of text. Using this option quickly reformats the screen display to the new settings.

To move to the bottom of the page,

Press: (CTRL) - (HOME) (↓)

The cursor is positioned on the last line of the second column. The second column ends before the last line of the page. If there were more text in the second column, it would wrap to the top of the third column.

The following keys can be used to move around the document while in column format:

Key	Action
⬆, ⬇, or PGDN	scroll all columns at the same time
→, ←, or HOME	move cursor inside a column
CTRL - HOME →	move cursor from one column to another
CTRL - HOME ←	
PGUP	move cursor to top of first column

Try moving the cursor around the columns. When you are done, use PGUP to return to the top of the first column.

To edit text while in column format, the delete keys all work within a single column. As in regular document display, the text is automatically reformatted on a line when insertions and deletions are made. You can use most WordPerfect features when in column format, with the exception of Column Definition, Document Comments, Footnotes, and Margins.

In some cases it may be easier to turn off the display of columns, do the editing and changes to the text that are needed, and then turn the column display back on. The display of columns is turned off by selecting the Columns Off/On option in the Columns menu. A [Col off] code is hidden in the document to control the display.

Note: Be careful when turning columns on or off. If the command is not entered in the proper location in the document, any text located between the on and off codes is formatted in columns. The original column definition settings remain in effect in the document unless the code is deleted or another column definition is entered.

Viewing the Document

Before Karen prints the article she wants to view it on the screen as it will appear when printed. The View Document option in the Print menu lets you see how different formats and settings will appear when the document is printed.

To see how the columns will appear when printed,

Select: File>Print>View Document
   >> Print (SHIFT) - (F7), View Document

After a few moments, the text is generated and displayed in the view document screen. Your display screen should be similar to Figure 3-18 on the next page.

The full page is displayed as close in appearance as possible to the printed page. WordPerfect can display the entire page by changing to a graphics display mode rather than the text display mode.

Note: If your computer does not have graphics capabilities, the View Document feature displays the document in text mode. The instructions in the rest of this

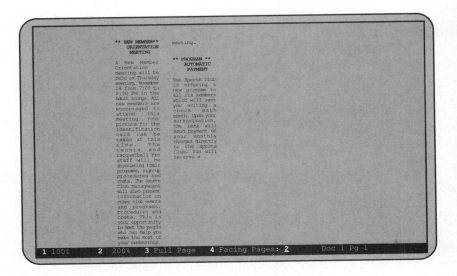

FIGURE 3-18

section do not apply to your computer system. Instead, to see the lower half of the document press (CTRL) (HOME) (↓). To leave the View screen press (F7). Continue the lab by skipping to the next section, "Changing Justification."

The menu at the bottom of the screen lets you enlarge the viewed document. To view the document at its actual size (100%),

Press: 1

Your display screen should be similar to Figure 3-19.

FIGURE 3-19

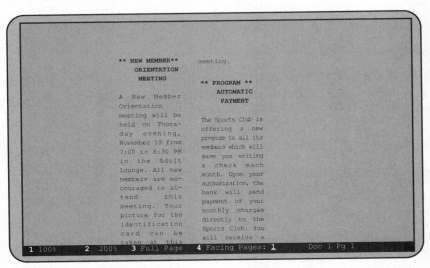

Now the text is large enough to read easily. Because most monitors are not large enough to display an entire page at full size, only the upper postion of the article is visible. To move to the bottom of the page,

Press: (CTRL) - (HOME) (↓)

Karen is not pleased with how the articles will appear when printed. She does not like the large gaps which appear between words. The gaps occur because the justification setting is Full, forcing the program to insert spaces between words to make the right and left margins even. She also does not like how the last line of the first article appears at the top of the second column.

To leave the View screen,

Press: Exit (F7)

Changing Justification

Karen would like to see how the document will appear if the justification setting is changed to Left. To make this change,

Press: (PGUP)
Select: Layout>Line>Justification>Left
  >>   Format (SHIFT) - (F8), Line> Justification>Left
Press: Exit (F7)

The change in the justification setting does not affect the screen display since the text is displayed with left justification only. When printed, the right margins will be printed as they appear on the screen.

If your computer has graphics capabilities, view the change in the document by selecting File>Print>View Document or Print (SHIFT)-(F7), View Document. You will see that the right margins are no longer even and the large gaps between words have been eliminated. However, now the large gap appears at the right margin, making the right margin too ragged. To leave the View screen, press Exit (F7).

On lines of text where there are several short words, the wrapping of text to the next line is not a problem. On lines where there are long words, the long word is wrapped to the next line, leaving a large gap on the previous line. Hyphenating a long word at the end of a line will help solve this problem.

Using Hyphenation

WordPerfect's Hyphenation feature fits as much of a word as possible on a line before hyphenating the word. The balance of the word wraps to the next line. Hyphenation is set to off by default. To turn it on,

Select: Layout>Line> Hyphenation>Yes
  >>   Format (SHIFT) - (F8), Line>Hyphenation>Yes

To leave the Line Format menu,

Press: Exit (F7)

To reformat the screen display,

Press: Screen (CTRL) - (F3), Rewrite

Your screen should be similar to Figure 3-20.

```
 ** NEW MEMBER **        ** NEW PROGRAM **
    ORIENTATION             AUTOMATIC
      MEETING                PAYMENT


A New Member Ori-       The Sports Club is
entation meeting        offering a new
will be held on         program to all its
Thursday evening,       members which will
November 19 from        save you writing a
7:00 to 8:30 PM in      check each month.
the Adult Lounge.       Upon your authori-
All new members         zation, the bank
are encouraged to       will send payment
attend this meet-       of your monthly
ing. Your picture       charges directly
for the identifi-       to the Sports
cation card can be      Club. You will
taken at this           receive a copy of
time. The tennis        the monthly state-
and racquetball         ment to confirm
Pro staff will be       the accuracy of
discussing their        your bill. If you
programs, sign-up       are interested in
B:\ARTICLE.DOC                              Col 1 Doc 1 Pg 1 Ln 1" Pos 1"
```

FIGURE 3-20

WordPerfect adds hyphenation to the document. The hyphenation points are determined automatically, based upon the U.S spelling dictionary rules. This dictionary is included in the WordPerfect 5.1 program. If WordPerfect cannot determine how to hyphenate a word, it will prompt you to position the hyphen in any long word that needs hyphenation. The prompt "Position hyphen; Press (ESC)" appears in the status line. Following the prompt the word requiring hyphenation is displayed with the suggested hyphenation. To accept the hyphenation as displayed, press (ESC). To change the hyphenation, move the hyphen with the arrow keys to the correct location and press (ESC). If the word cannot be appropriately hyphenated, press (F7) to cancel hyphenation for that word.

Hyphenating the newsletter has made the right margins much less ragged. Additionally, because more words were able to fit on a line, the last line of the first article now ends at the bottom of the first column, and the second article begins at the top of the second column. Karen is pleased with the appearance of the articles now.

Note: If your computer can display graphics, view the document again using **File**>**P**rint>**V**iew Document or Print (SHIFT) - (F7), **V**iew Document. To leave the View screen, press Exit (F7).

Move to the bottom of the second column and enter your name.
If you have printer capability, print a copy of the article. If necessary, select the appropriate printer for your microcomputer system first.

Saving and Exiting Two Document Files

When there are two documents in use, both need to be saved (if needed) and exited from before leaving the WordPerfect program. To save the current document,

Select: File>Exit
>> Exit (F7)
Type: Y
Type: COLUMNS.DOC
Press: (⏎)

The next prompt, "Exit Doc 1?," is new. Whenever there are two open documents at one time, each document needs to be exited.

Type: Y

Document 2, the welcome letter, is displayed on the screen. Since no changes were made to this document, it is not necessary to save the file. To close this document and exit WordPerfect,

Select: File>Exit
>> Exit (F7)
Type: N
Type: Y

The DOS prompt appears on your display screen.

KEY TERMS

primary file   field   window
secondary merge file record   underline
merge codes   center   newspaper columns
address file   boldface

MATCHING

1. End Record~   _____ a. boldfaces text
2. (SHIFT) - (F8) 2   _____ b. merges files
3. Field~   _____ c. displays merge codes
4. (F9)   _____ d. identifies field name
5. (CTRL) - (F9) 1   _____ e. switches to other document
6. (SHIFT) - (F9)   _____ f. displays Columns/Table menu
7. Layout>Align>Center   _____ g. displays Page Format menu
8. (F6)   _____ h. identifies end of field
9. (SHIFT) - (F3)   _____ i. identifies end of record
10. (ALT) - (F7)   _____ j. centers text

PRACTICE EXERCISES

1. To complete this problem you must first have completed problem 4 in Lab 2 You will change this letter into a form letter and create a secondary file.

- Create a secondary file. Each record will contain seven fields of data Enter the following records:

    1. Mr. Paul Simone
       Advising Department
       Arizona State University
       Tempe
       AZ
       85257
       Mr. Simone

    2. Mr. Phil Miller
       Southern Telephone Corp.
       56 Highland Way
       Phoenix
       AZ
       85001
       Mr. Miller

    3. Your first and last name
       Your Major Department
       Your School
       City
       State
       Zipcode
       Your last name

- Save the secondary file as JOB.SF.
- Modify the letter in JOB to accept the seven fields of information. Save the primary file as JOB.PF. Print the file.
- Merge the primary and secondary files and print the three letters.

2. The local zoo acknowledges all gifts and donations with a personalized form letter that includes the following fields of data:

Field 1 - full name
Field 2 - street address
Field 3 - city
Field 4 - state
Field 5 - zipcode
Field 6 - donation
Field 7 - designation

■ Create a secondary merge file using the data shown below for each of the records.

1. Mr. and Mrs. Brian Matheson
   1432 Winding Way
   Scottsdale
   AZ
   86942
   $1,000
   Bear Exhibit

2. Mr. and Mrs. Charles Larson
   732 Decatur St.
   Mesa
   AZ
   85287
   $500
   Otter Exhibit

3. Your first and last name
   Street
   City
   State
   Zipcode
   Donation
   Designation

■ Save the secondary merge file as DONATION.SF.

■ The thank you letter for donations is shown on the next page. Create a primary file by entering this letter and the appropriate merge codes reflecting the fields of data in the secondary merge file.

```
[Date Command]


[Field 1]
[Field 2]
[Field 3], [Field 4] [Field 5]

Dear [Field 1]:

The zoo would like to thank you for your generous
donation of [Field 6]. As you specified, your
donation will go toward the [Field 7].

The zoo is continually building new exhibits and
structures, renovating old structures and exhibits,
and upgrading the zoo grounds. It is through the
generosity of donations such as yours that we are
able to continue to improve and grow.

Your gift is greatly appreciated.



Development Director
```

- Save the thank you letter as DONATION.PF. Print the file.
- Merge the primary and secondary files and print the letters.

3. To complete this problem you must first have completed problem 1 in Lab 2. Retrieve the file OVER-WP.REV.

- Enter the title OVERVIEW OF WORD PROCESSING on the first line of the document. It should be in all capital letters and boldfaced. Enter a blank line below the title.
- Underline the title DEFINITION OF WORD PROCESSING.
- Split the screen into two windows of 12 lines each.
- Move into document 2 and retrieve the file TEXT-WP.
- Copy the entire page into document 1. It should be entered at the end of document 1 above your name. Leave two blank lines above the heading "Advantages of Using a Word Processor."
- Clear the window.
- Change this document to be displayed as newspaper-style columns with four columns separated by .3 inches.
- Print the document
- Save the new document as TEXT-WP.REV.

4. To complete this problem, you must first have completed problem 2 in Lab 2. Retrieve the file EVENTS. The text in this file will be used in the zoo member newsletter.

- Enter the heading shown below for the article, centered and in bold, as two lines. (Leave a blank line below your name and date, and two blank lines below the heading.)

  Special Zoo

  Events

- Boldface the name of each event in the first line of each paragraph.

- The article needs an introductory paragraph. This has already been created and saved for you as EVENT1. Create a second window on the screen of 12 lines. Move into the Doc 2 window and retrieve this file. Copy the entire contents of the text in Doc 2 into Doc 1. It should be the first paragraph of the article.

- Clear the window.

- Change the text in Doc 1 to be displayed as two newspaper-style columns. They should be separated by 1 inch.

- Add hyphenation.

- Save the article as EVENT2.

- Print the document.

Creating a Research Paper

4

[handwritten note: LOOK AT BLOCK COMMAND FOR NEXT TEST]

OBJECTIVES

In this lab you will learn how to:

1. Create and edit an outline.
2. Draw lines.
3. Generate a table of contents.
4. Enter and edit footnotes.
5. Specify page numbering.
6. Suppress page numbering.
7. Center text top to bottom on a page.
8. Use Block Protection.
9. Prevent widows and orphans.

CASE STUDY

Peg is a senior recreation major at a local university. As part of her degree requirements she must work one semester in an approved internship program. To fulfill this requirement she worked at the Sports Club as an assistant in the swimming program.

As part of the requirements of the internship program, she must write a proposal on how to improve the swimming program. Her proposal is that the club offer an aquatic fitness program. In this lab we will follow Peg as she creates an outline and writes a paper on this topic.

Creating an Outline

Peg has already completed the research she needs and has thought about how the club could begin an aquatics fitness program. She needs to organize her thoughts and topics. To do this she decides to create an outline of the topics she plans to cover in her paper.

Boot the system and load the WordPerfect program.

The WordPerfect Automatic Outlining feature will help her prepare the outline for her proposal. This feature is accessed by selecting the Tools>Outline or Date/Outline (SHIFT) - (F5) command.

Note: If you use the function key command, the Date/Outline menu appears in the status line. The fourth option, Outline, then displays the Outline menu.

Select: **T**ools>**O**utline
    >>   Date/Outline (SHIFT) - (F5), **O**utline

To turn on the Automatic Outlining feature,

Select: On

The WordPerfect screen is unchanged except for the message "Outline" displayed in the status line. This tells you that the Outline mode is on. WordPerfect will remain in this mode until you select this option again.

Peg has decided to divide her paper into three sections. In this lab you will learn how to create the outline for the first section of the paper as shown in Figure 4-1.

FIGURE 4-1

I.   Introduction

    A.   Statement of purpose
        1.   Justification for proposal
        2.   Organization of proposal
    B.   Reasons for aquatic exercise programs
        1.   Popularity of swimming
        2.   Benefits of aquatic exercise
            a.   Adaptable to many people
            b.   Less damaging to joints and bones
            c.   Improves cardiovascular system
    C.   Determining Target Heart Rate (THR)
        1.   Define THR
        2.   Measure THR
            a.   Direct
            b.   Indirect
                (1) Karvonen formula
                (2) Percentage of Maximum Heart Rate (MHR)

In Outline mode the and (TAB) keys perform specific functions. You will see how they perform differently as you create the outline. To begin outlining,

Press:

The Roman numeral "I." appears on the second line of the page. This is called a **paragraph number**. While in Outline mode the key, in addition to inserting a blank line in the text, automatically displays a paragraph number. The Roman numeral I indicates that this is the first level of the outline.

To enter the text for the first line of the outline,

Press: Indent (F4)

The cursor has moved over one tab stop on the line. The Indent key ((F4)) moves the cursor along the line one tab stop. In normal text entry mode, the Indent key ((F4)) will align all text with the left tab stop until is pressed. You may wonder why you did not use the (TAB) key to do this. As you will see shortly, the (TAB) key in Outline mode performs a different function.

To enter the text for this line,

Type: **Introduction**
Press:

Your screen should be similar to Figure 4-2.

paragraph number ——

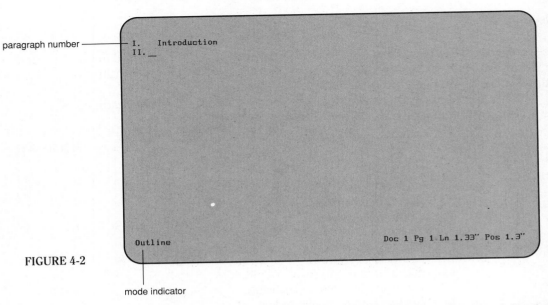

I.   Introduction
II. _

Outline   Doc 1 Pg 1 Ln 1.33" Pos 1.3"

FIGURE 4-2

mode indicator

The Roman numeral "II." is displayed on the next line. Peg wants a blank line below the first outline level. Once a paragraph number is entered on a line, the ⏎ key can be used to insert a blank line.

Press: ⏎

A blank line is created, and Roman numeral II has moved down one line.

Next Peg needs to change the outline level from Roman numeral II to the second level of the outline, A. To do this,

Press: (TAB)

The cursor moved along the line one tab space, and "II." changed to "A." While outline mode is on, using (TAB) both changes the outline level number and tabs in one tab stop along the line.

Each time you press (TAB) the paragraph number advances to the next outline level. Instead of pressing (TAB), you could press Space bar five times to advance the cursor to the next tab stop, and the paragraph number would also automatically advance.

Note: If you press (TAB) too many times and find yourself in the wrong outline level, to back up a tab stop press Margin Release ((SHIFT) - (TAB)). The outline number will automatically adjust. If you press (BKSP) the automatic paragraph number for that line will be deleted. If that happens you will need to press ⏎ at the correct location to insert a new paragraph number.

To indent and enter the text for this level,

Press: (F4)
Type: **Statement of purpose**

WordPerfect inserts a hidden code in the outline at each tab location. These codes control the outline levels. To see the hidden paragraph number codes,

Select: Edit>Reveal Codes
>>   Reveal Codes (ALT) - (F3)

Your screen should be similar to Figure 4-3.

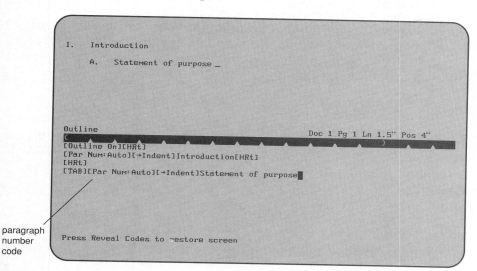

FIGURE 4-3

paragraph
number
code

The first code, [Outline On], was entered when you turned on the Automatic Outlining feature. The hidden code [Par Num:Auto] is automatically entered following a [TAB] or [HRt] code when in Outline mode. The number of tabs along the line determines the paragraph number level that is displayed in the outline. When you delete a [Par Num:Auto] code, the paragraph number disappears. To leave the Reveal Codes screen,

Select: Edit>Reveal Codes
>>   Reveal Codes (ALT) - (F3)

To continue the outline,

Press: (⏎)

The new paragraph number is "B." When you press (⏎) the new paragraph number is created at the same level as the previous number. In this case, however, the next line of the outline begins at the third level. To change the paragraph number to this level,

Press: (TAB)

The paragraph level number "1." is displayed. To indent and enter the text,

Press: Indent (F4)
Type: **Justification for proposal**
Press: (⏎)

The paragraph number "2." appears on the line to allow you to enter the second topic at this outline level. Since this is the correct level for the next line of the outline, you are ready to enter the text for this level.

Press: Indent (F4)
Type: **Organization of proposal**
Press: (⏎)

A third-level paragraph number is displayed again. The next outline level to be entered is a second level. To change the level in the opposite direction, or to back up a level, Margin Release ((SHIFT) - (TAB)) is used. This is just the opposite of pressing (TAB) to increase the number's level.

Press: (SHIFT) - (TAB)

The outline number level has decreased one level and is now "B." To enter the text for this level,

Press: (F4)
Type: **Reasons for aquatic exercise programs**
Press: (⏎)

Complete the first section of the outline by entering the remaining outline levels as shown in Figure 4-4 using the (⏎), (TAB), (SHIFT) - (TAB), and Indent ((F4)) keys. Don't forget to indent before entering the text for each line. If you do forget to indent, you can use the cursor movement keys to move to the first character on the line and then press (F4). The editing and cursor movement keys can be used to correct the text in the outline in the same manner as in regular document entry.

When you are done your screen should be similar to Figure 4-4.

FIGURE 4-4

```
I.    Introduction

      A.   Statement of purpose
           1.   Justification for proposal
           2.   Organization of proposal
      B.   Reasons for aquatic exercise programs
           1.   Popularity of swimming
           2.   Benefits of aquatic exercise
                a.   Adaptable to many people
                b.   Less damaging to joints and bones
                c.   Improves cardiovascular system
      C.   Determining Target Heart Rate (THR)
           1.   Define THR
           2.   Measure THR
                a.   Direct
                b.   Indirect
                     (1)  Karvonen formula
                     (2)  Percentage of Maximum Heart Rate_




Outline                                          Doc 1 Pg 1 Ln 4" Pos 6.7"
```

If you have not done so already, after typing the last line press (⏎).
To change the paragraph number to "II,"

Press: (SHIFT) - (TAB) (4 times)

To insert a blank line between section I and II of the outline,

Press: ⟨⏎⟩

The next two sections of the outline have already been completed for you and saved on the file OUTLINE1.W51. **To combine the files, with your cursor positioned immediately after the "II.", retrieve the file OUTLINE1.W51.**

The completed outline consists of three sections. The second topic area discusses the parts of an aquatic fitness routine. The third area discusses how an aquatic fitness program should be modified for people with different physical limitations. **To see the complete outline use ⟨↓⟩ to move to the end of the document.**

Editing the Outline

After looking over her completed outline Peg wants to move a section of the outline to another location. It is easy to edit and move text within an outline while Outline mode is on. To move to the area of the outline that she wants to change,

Press :   ⟨HOME⟩ - ⟨↑⟩ (2 times)

Your screen should look similar to Figure 4-5.

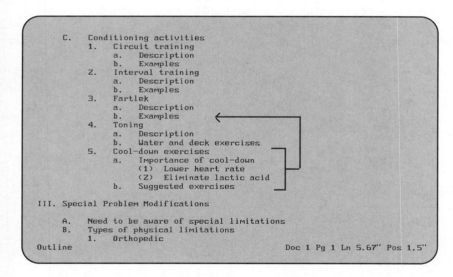

FIGURE 4-5

She wants to move the entire outline section "5. Cool-down exercises" above the section "4. Toning." She also wants to decrease the outline level of section 5 by one level, to level D.

Sections of an outline are grouped into **families**. A family consists of the outline level on the line where the cursor is located, plus any subordinate or lower levels. To move to the first line of the family to be moved,

Move to: Ln 7.83" Pos 1" (outline level "5. Cool-down exercises")
Select: **Tools>Outline**
    >>   Date/Outline ⟨SHIFT⟩ - ⟨F5⟩, **Outline**

Note: If you used the function key to issue this command, the outline menu will appear in the status line.

Your screen should be similar to Figure 4-6.

FIGURE 4-6

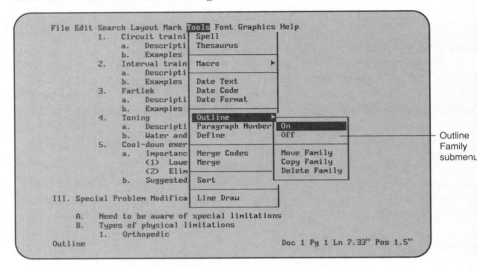

Outline
Family
submenu

An outline family can be moved, copied, or deleted while in Outline mode using one of the three Family commands displayed in the submenu.

Select: Move Family

Outline level "5. Cool-down exercises" and the two sublevels below it should be highlighted. The highlighted outline family can be moved vertically or horizontally within the outline using the arrow keys.

Peg wants to move the family above the section of the outline beginning with "4. Toning." To move the outline family to this location,

Press:

Your screen should be similar to Figure 4-7.

FIGURE 4-7

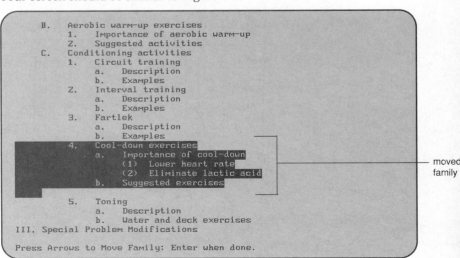

moved
family

After a few seconds, the family moves up within the hierarchy of the outline and is now "4. Cool-down exercises," and the family below it has changed to "5. Toning."

Peg now wants to change the family from outline level 4 to level D. To do this, the paragraph number level needs to be lowered one level. Moving the highlighted family one level to the left will accomplish this task.

Press: (⟵)

The outline family has moved one outline level to the left (horizontally), and all outline level numbers within the family have adjusted appropriately. Notice that the outline levels in the family below it have also adjusted. The new number, "3. Toning," however, is not how Peg wants it to be. She will correct this next.

To fix the highlighted family in place,

Press: (⏎)

Next Peg wants to change the outline family beginning at level "3. Toning" to level E.

Move to: Ln 8.33" (outline level "3. Toning")
Select: Tools>Outline>Move Family
>> Date/Outline (SHIFT) - (F5), Outline>Move Family

Press: (⟵)
Press: (⏎)

The family moved over one tab space on the line, and the paragraph number changed from "3." to "E." All sublevels below it have adjusted appropriately.

Finally, delete the blank line above this outline level by deleting the [HRt] following the word "Exercises" and add a blank line above outline level III. Be careful that you place the cursor correctly before deleting the line or pressing (⏎) to create a blank line. Use Reveal Codes to make sure you are deleting the correct codes.

Your screen should be similar to Figure 4-8.

FIGURE 4-8

```
       C.   Conditioning activities
            1.   Circuit training
                 a.    Description
                 b.    Examples
            2.   Interval training
                 a.    Description
                 b.    Examples
            3.   Fartlek
                 a.    Description
                 b.    Examples
       D.   Cool-down exercises
            1.   Importance of cool-down
                 a.    Lower heart rate
                 b.    Eliminate lactic acid
            2.   Suggested exercises
       E.   Toning
            1.   Description
            2.   Water and deck exercises

III. Special Problem Modifications

       A.   Need to be aware of special limitations
       B.   Types of physical limitations
            1.   Orthopedic
Outline                              Doc 1 Pg 1 Ln 8.83" Pos 1.5"
```

This same task could be accomplished by deleting or adding [Tab] codes to reduce or increase the paragraph number level, and by using the Block feature to move sections of the outline. When using the Block feature to move a section of the outline, be careful to include all appropriate codes in the block, so that when it is moved the outline levels will adjust appropriately. However, the outline Family feature does the same thing more quickly and accurately. Use Block if the paragraphs you want to manipulate are not a family or if you are not in Outline mode.

Peg feels the outline will help her to organize the topics in her paper. To turn off Outline mode, place the cursor at the end of the outline, and then select Outline Off. To do this,

Press: (HOME) (HOME) (↓)
Select: Tools>Outline>Off
>>   Date/Outline (SHIFT) - (F5), Outline>Off

The "Outline" indicator in the status line is no longer displayed indicating Outline mode is not on. An [Outline Off] code has been inserted into the document. Now you could continue typing normal text, and the (↵) and (TAB) keys will act as they normally do. However, if you move the cursor into the area of text between the [Outline on] and [Outline Off] codes, the (↵) and (TAB) keys will work as they do in Outline mode.

Peg wants to enter a centered title at the beginning of the outline. To do this,

Press: (PGUP)
Press: Center (SHIFT) - (F6)
Type: **OUTLINE FOR AQUATIC FITNESS PROPOSAL**
Press: (↵)

On the next line center your name and the current date.

To separate the two title lines from the beginning of the outline,

Press: (↵) (2 times)

Your screen should be similar to Figure 4-9.

FIGURE 4-9

```
                OUTLINE FOR AQUATIC FITNESS PROPOSAL
                       Student Name    Date


I.    Introduction

      A.    Statement of purpose
            1.    Justification for proposal
            2.    Organization of proposal
      B.    Reasons for aquatic exercise programs
            1.    Popularity of swimming
            2.    Benefits of aquatic exercise
                  a.    Adaptable to many people
                  b.    Less damaging to joints and bones
                  c.    Improves cardiovascular system
      C.    Determining Target Heart Rate (THR)
            1.    Define THR
            2.    Measure THR
                  a.    Direct
                  b.    Indirect
                        (1)  Karvonen formula
                        (2)  Percentage of Maximum Heart Rate


II.   Aquatic Fitness Routine
                                          Doc 1 Pg 1 Ln 1.33" Pos 1"
```

Using Save (F10), save the outline as OUTLINE2.
Print the outline. If necessary select the printer that is appropriate for your computer system.
Clear the screen (Exit (F7)). Do not exit WordPerfect.

Creating Lines

After several days, Peg has written the body of the internship proposal using WordPerfect 5.1 and has saved it on the diskette as PROPOSAL.W51.
To see what she has done so far, retrieve PROPOSAL.W51.
The title page of the report should be displayed on your screen. The first thing Peg would like to do is to draw a line below the title of the report. WordPerfect's Line Draw feature lets you draw lines, boxes, graphs, and other illustrations in your document. The Line Draw feature is an option that is accessed through the Tools menu or (CTRL) - (F3).

Select: Tools>Line Draw
   >>   Screen (CTRL) - (F3), Line Draw

Your screen should be similar to Figure 4-10.

FIGURE 4-10

```
                    A PROGRAM IN

                   AQUATIC FITNESS

                  FOR THE SPORTS CLUB




 1 |: 2 ||: 3 *: 4 Change: 5 Erase: 6 Move: 1        Ln 1" Pos 1"
```

The Line Draw menu is displayed in the status line. This menu lets you create a single line (1), double line (2), or a line composed of asterisks (3). Change, option 4, lets you change the style of option 3 to something other than an asterisk from a selection of choices. The default is a single line.
Lines are created by using the arrow keys. Once this menu is displayed the arrow keys will automatically begin creating a line if they are pressed. To move the cursor without creating a line, the Move option (6) must be selected. Since Peg wants to create a line below the title, she needs to move the cursor to the line and position where the line is to begin. To do this,

Select: Move

The Line Draw menu is still displayed. Following the colon at the end of the menu, the selected option is displayed. Now the cursor can be moved without creating a line. She wants the line to be two lines below the last line of the title. Using the arrow keys,

Move to: Ln 2.83" Pos 2.6"

Peg wants to create a double line. To do this,

Select: 2

The menu remains on the screen, with the selected option, 2, displayed following the colon in the menu.
    To create the line, using the ⟶ key,

Move to: Ln 2.83" Pos 6.5"

Your screen should be similar to Figure 4-11.

FIGURE 4-11

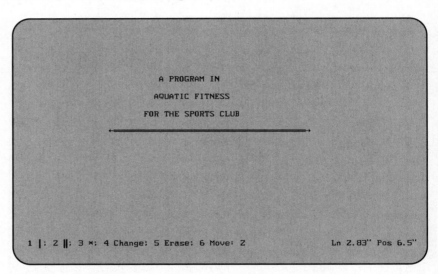

```
                        A PROGRAM IN

                      AQUATIC FITNESS

                   FOR THE SPORTS CLUB
        ◄──────────────────────────────────────►



  1 | ; 2 ‖; 3 ×; 4 Change; 5 Erase; 6 Move; 2          Ln 2.83" Pos 6.5"
```

The line has been created. However, Peg thinks the line is too long. The Erase menu option will let you erase a line or a part of a line.

Select: Erase

To delete part of the line, using ⟵,

Move to: Ln 2.83" Pos 5.8"

The line is shortened. To turn off the Line Draw feature,

Press: Exit (F7)

You are returned to the document, and the Line Draw menu is no longer displayed.

After looking at the title, Peg thinks that another line above the title would look good.

Move to:	Ln 1.5" Pos 2.6" (Use Space bar to move to Pos 2.6")
Select:	**Tools>Line Draw**
>>	Screen (CTRL) - (F3), **Line Draw**

This time she wants to create a single line.

Select:	**1**
Move to:	Ln 1.5" Pos 5.8"

Peg is happy with how the line appears and does not want to make any other changes. To leave the Line Draw feature,

Press: **Exit** (F7)

When the lines are printed the arrows at the beginning and end of the lines will not be printed.

Complete the title page by entering "By your name" on line 5.67". On line 5.83" enter the title of the course, and on the next line enter the current date as code using the Date command (Tools>Date Code or (SHIFT) - (F5), Date Code). All three lines should be centered on the page.

Creating a Table of Contents

Next Peg needs to create a table of contents for the report. Using ⊕,

Move to: Pg 2 Ln 1.5"

The second page of the report contains the heading "TABLE OF CONTENTS" centered on the page. The table of contents can be generated automatically by WordPerfect from text within the document. There are three steps to creating a table of contents:

Step 1 The text to be used in the table of contents is marked.
Step 2 The location where the table is to be displayed is specified.
Step 3 The table is generated or created.

Step 1: Marking Text for the Table of Contents

The Mark menu, or Mark Text (ALT) - (F5), marks the text to be used in the table of contents. Before selecting the command you must first highlight the text to be used as the table of contents heading.

The first heading to be marked is "INTRODUCTION." To move to the top of page 3,

Press: (PGDN)

When a block is defined that will be used in a table of contents, any codes that are included in the block will be included in the table of contents when it is created. Since this heading is in bold and centered, if the [Center] and [BOLD] codes are also included when the block is defined, the heading in the table of contents will appear both boldfaced and centered. Therefore you must be careful when highlighting a block of text to include in a table of contents, that only the codes you want are specified.

To display the codes while blocking the text,

Select: File>Reveal Codes
>> Reveal Codes (ALT) - (F3)

The cursor is positioned on the [Center] code, as you can see in the Reveal Codes portion of the window. Peg does not want to include either the [BOLD] code or the [Center] code in the block. To move the cursor to the right of the codes,

Press: (CTRL) - (→)

The cursor should be on the "I" in "INTRODUCTION." Next you need to highlight the word "INTRODUCTION," which will be used in the table of contents. While in Reveal Codes screen you can use the Block feature to highlight text; or you can use the mouse.

To turn on the Block feature,

Select: Edit>Block
>> Block (ALT) - (F4)

"Block on" flashes in the status line of the upper part of the window, and a [Block] code is displayed in the Reveal Codes area. To highlight "INTRODUCTION,"

Press: (→) (12 times) or drag the mouse

Your screen should be similar to Figure 4-12.

FIGURE 4-12

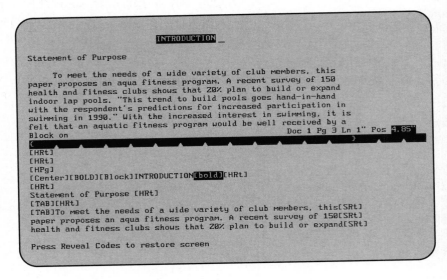

"INTRODUCTION" is highlighted in the upper screen, and the cursor is positioned on the ending [bold] code in the Reveal Codes screen. None of the codes surrounding the text will be included in the block.

To leave the Reveal Codes screen,

Select: Edit>Reveal Codes
   >>   Reveal Codes (ALT) - (F3)

The Block On feature should still be active.

Next, to tell WordPerfect that this block of text is to be used in a table of contents, it must be marked. The Mark menu, or Mark Text (ALT) - (F5), lets you specify the type of text you want to identify.

Select: Mark
   >>   Mark Text (ALT) - (F5)

Your screen should be similar to Figure 4-13. (If you used the function key command (ALT) - (F5) the menu is displayed in the status line.)

FIGURE 4-13

```
File Edit Search Layout Mark Tools Font [Graphics] Help
                        Index
Statement of Purpose    Table of Contents
                        List
      To meet the needs o [Cross-Reference     ]  members, this
paper proposes an aqua f  Table of Authorities▶  survey of 150
health and fitness clubs                         build or expand
indoor lap pools. "This  [Define               ]  s hand-in-hand
with the respondent's pr                          participation in
swimming in 1990." With  [Generate             ]  n swimming, it is
felt that an aquatic fit                          ll received by a
wide variety of club mem [Master Documents     ]
      The program present [Subdocument          ]  ually adaptable
to almost any individual                          asing number of
bone and joint problems  [Document Compare     ]  s. There are also
many people with other s                          regards fitness
and exercise, who try to make the best of their bodies. Aqua
fitness can help these people, as well as those without any
physical impairments, to improve their cardiorespiratory systems.
      This report is designed to present enough information to
begin an aqua program for any fitness level participant. All of
the activities are monitored for intensity by a percentage of
each participants own heart rate. Since participants will be
listening to their own bodies for when to speed up or slow down,
Block on                              Doc 1 Pg 3 Ln 1" Pos 4.85"
```

As you can see from the menu, text can also be marked to create a list, an index, a cross reference, or a table of authorities. The ToC option will mark a block for use in a table of contents by placing a [Mark] code at the beginning of the block and an [End Mark] code at the end of the block of text.

Select: Table of Contents
   >>   ToC

The prompt "ToC Level:" is displayed.

A table of contents can have up to five levels of heads. The selection of the level of heads determines how the table of contents will look. A **level one head** is the main head. A blank line is placed before all first-level entries. The **level two head** is subordinate to the level one head and is not separated from it by blank lines. Level two heads appear indented under the level one head. For example:

> This is a level one head.
>> This is a level two subhead.
>> This is a level two subhead.

> This is a level one head.
>> This is a level two subhead.

Peg wants to create a table of contents that will display the three main topics (I, II, and III in the outline) as level one heads. To identify the blocked text as a level one head,

Type: `1`
Press: `⏎`

You are returned to the document. The heading "INTRODUCTION" has been marked to be part of the table of contents.

The next heading to be marked is "Statement of Purpose" on line 1.33". Since there are no codes surrounding this block of text, you can simply highlight the block. This heading will be a second-level head in the table of contents.

Move to: Pg 3 Ln 1.33" Pos 1" (on "S" in "Statement")
Select: Edit>**B**lock
　　>> Block (ALT) - (F4)

Highlight "Statement of Purpose". The cursor should be on Pos 3".

Then, to mark the text as a second-level head in the table of contents,

Select: Mark>**T**able of **C**ontents
　　>> Mark Text (ALT) - (F5), To**C**
Type: 2
Press: `⏎`

To see the hidden codes marking the text for level one and level two table of contents heads,

Select: Edit>**R**eveal Codes
　　>> Reveal Codes (ALT) - (F3)

Your screen should be similar to Figure 4-14.

```
                    INTRODUCTION

Statement of Purpose _

     To meet the needs of a wide variety of club members, this
paper proposes an aqua fitness program. A recent survey of 150
health and fitness clubs shows that 20% plan to build or expand
indoor lap pools. "This trend to build pools goes hand-in-hand
with the respondent's predictions for increased participation in
swimming in 1990." With the increased interest in swimming, it is
felt that an aquatic fitness program would be well received by a
B:\PROPOSAL.W51                          Doc 1 Pg 3 Ln 1.33" Pos 3"
```
```
[HPg]
[Center][BOLD][Mark:ToC,1]INTRODUCTION[End Mark:ToC,1][bold][HRt]
[HRt]
[Mark:ToC,2]Statement of Purpose[End Mark:ToC,2] [HRt]     ——— level one table of contents code
[TAB][HRt]                                                 ——— level two table of contents code
[TAB]To meet the needs of a wide variety of club members, this[SRt]
paper proposes an aqua fitness program. A recent survey of 150[SRt]
health and fitness clubs shows that 20% plan to build or expand[SRt]
indoor lap pools. "This trend to build pools goes hand[-]in[-]hand[SRt]
with the respondent's predictions for increased participation in[SRt]

Press Reveal Codes to restore screen
```

The mark text codes are displayed surrounding the text to be used in the table of contents. The two levels are also differentiated within the codes. If you needed to delete a table of contents heading, you would simply delete the code surrounding the text.

To return to the document,

Select: Edit>Reveal Codes
   >>   Reveal Codes (ALT) - (F3)

Mark the next two headings as level two table of contents heads. They are:

Reasons for Aquatic Exercise Program - Pg 3 Ln 6.5"
Determining Target Heart Rate (THR) - Pg 4 Ln 1.83"

Next mark AQUATIC FITNESS ROUTINE (Pg 5 Ln 8") as a level one table of contents head. Be careful not to include the center and bold codes when blocking the heading.

Finally, mark the next two headings as level two table of contents heads:

Warm-up Stretches - Pg 6 Ln 1"
Aerobic Warm-up Exercises - Pg 6 Ln 4.67"

Note: You will complete marking the remaining table of contents heads in a practice exercise at the end of this lab.

Step 2: Define Table of Contents Location

The second step is to define where the table of contents is to be inserted into the document.

Move to: Pg 2 Ln 1.5" Pos 1" (3 lines below the heading "TABLE OF CONTENTS")

The Mark menu (or (ALT) - (F5)) option Define lets you specify the location for
the table.

Select: **M**ark>**D**efine

>>   Mark Text (ALT) - (F5), **D**efine

Your screen should be similar to Figure 4-15.

FIGURE 4-15

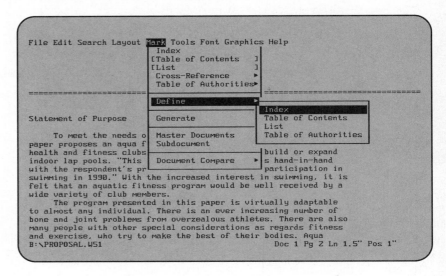

Note: If you used the function key to issue this command, the document is
replaced by a full-screen menu of five options. They are the same choices which are
available in the Define submenu.

Select: Table of **C**ontents

>>   Define Table of **C**ontents

Your screen should be similar to Figure 4-16.

FIGURE 4-16

```
Table of Contents Definition

    1 - Number of Levels           1

    2 - Display Last Level in      No
          Wrapped Format

    3 - Page Numbering - Level 1   Flush right with leader
                         Level 2
                         Level 3
                         Level 4
                         Level 5

















Selection: 0
```

A full-screen menu is displayed. This is the Table of Contents Definition menu. Option 1 Number of Levels displays the default setting of 1 as the number of levels used in the table of contents. Since you defined two levels in the table of contents, change this setting to 2.

Select: Number of Levels

Type: 2

The second option lets you specify whether you want the second-level entries to wrap, or to each be displayed on a separate line. You want each level to be displayed on a separate line. This is the default, and requires no adjustment.

The third option lets you select the page numbering style for each level. The default will display the page numbers flush with the right side of the page with a series of dots, or **leaders**, between the header and the page number. To select this option,

Select: Page Numbering

The five numbering styles are displayed in the status line. To leave the page numbering style as it is for both levels and to exit this menu,

Press: Exit (F7)

To leave the Table of Contents Definition menu,

Press: (⏎)

You are returned to the document. To see the codes,

Select: Edit>Reveal Codes
>> Reveal Codes (ALT) - (F3)

The code [Def Mark ToC,2:5,5] has been entered into the document at this location. This code will tell WordPerfect where to place the table of contents when it is generated.

Select: Edit>Reveal Codes
>> Reveal Codes (ALT) - (F3)

Step 3: Generate the Table of Contents

Finally, you are ready for WordPerfect to do a little work. Once all the headings are marked and the table of contents definitions completed, the table of contents can be generated.

Select: Mark>Generate
>> Mark Text (ALT) - (F5), Generate

The Mark Text: Generate menu is displayed. To generate the table of contents,

Select: Generate Tables, Index, Cross-References, etc.

The prompt at the bottom of the screen asks you to confirm that you want any existing tables deleted. Since there are no other tables created in this document, you can accept the default response of Yes.

Type: **Y**

The message displayed at the bottom of the screen tells you that generation has started. The "Pass:" and "Page:" indicators help you keep track of its progress. When complete the table of contents should be displayed.

Your screen should be similar to Figure 4-17.

FIGURE 4-17

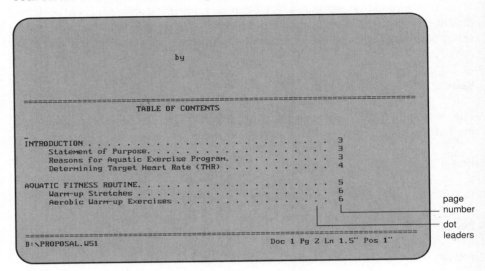

The table of contents for the first few pages of the report is displayed. A blank line separates the first-level heads. The level two heads appear indented under the level one heads. The page numbers are displayed flush with the right side of the page. A series of dots, or leaders, separates the heads from the page numbers, as specified.

Creating Footnotes

Next Peg needs to enter footnotes into her paper. WordPerfect can help her do this by automatically numbering the footnotes and placing them properly at the bottom of the page. The Footnote (Layout>Footnote or Footnote (CTRL) - (F7), 1) command is used to create footnotes.

Before using the Footnote command, the cursor must be positioned in the text where the footnote number is to be inserted. Peg's first footnote will appear following the quote in the first paragraph of the Statement of Purpose on page 3.

Press: (PGDN)
Move to: Ln 2.5" Pos 2.8" (after the quotes (") on the sixth line of the first paragraph of page 3)

Select: Layout
   >>   Footnote (CTRL) - (F7)

The Layout menu options, Footnote and Endnote (displayed in the status line if you used the function key), let you create and edit footnotes or endnotes. The procedure for both is very similar. The difference is that footnotes are printed at the bottom of the page where the reference is made, and endnotes are compiled as a list at the end of the document.

To create a footnote,

Select: Footnote

Your screen should be similar to Figure 4-18.

FIGURE 4-18

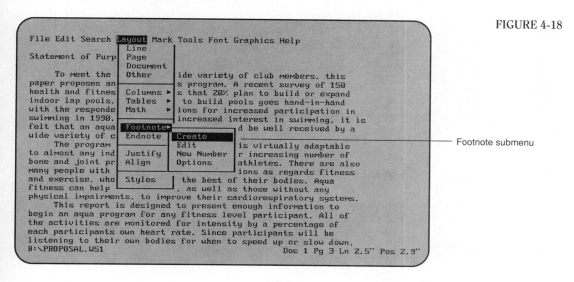

Footnote submenu

The four Footnote submenu options (displayed in the status line if you used the function key command) let you create and edit footnotes. To create a footnote,

Select: Create

The text has been replaced by a nearly blank screen. This is a special editing screen used to enter the text for the endnote or footnote. The note can be up to 16,000 lines long. The number 1 displayed on the screen shows that this is the first footnote entered in the text.

To enter a space after the number and before the text of the footnote,

Press: Space bar

When entering a footnote, the same commands and features you use in the normal document editing can be used.

Type: **"Participation Up, Swimming Forecast Looks Strong,"** <u>**Athletic Business**</u>**, July 1988, p. 37.** (do not press Enter)

Your screen should be similar to Figure 4-19.

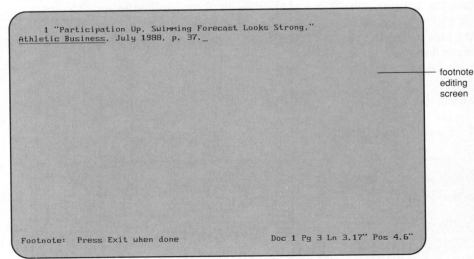

footnote
editing
screen

FIGURE 4-19

To save the footnote and return to the document,

Press: Exit (F7)

Your screen should be similar to Figure 4-20.

footnote number

FIGURE 4-20

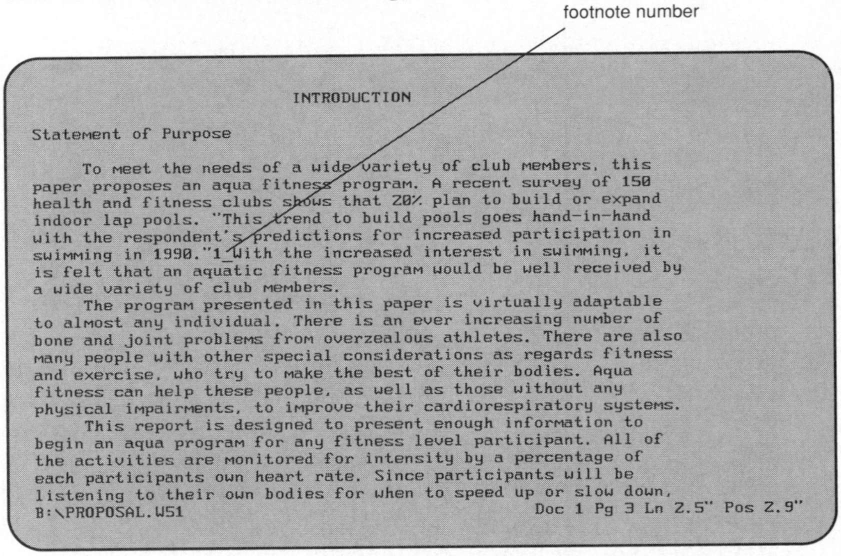

The footnote number, 1, is entered in the text at the location of the cursor. On some screens it may appear highlighted or superscripted. It will appear as a superscript number when printed. The footnotes will not appear on the screen. When the page or entire report is printed, they will be automatically printed on the bottom of the page containing the footnote number.

To enter the second footnote,

Move to: Pg 3 Ln 8.67" Pos 4.8" (space after "water." on third line of sixth paragraph)

| **Select:** | Layout>Footnote>Create |
| **>>** | Footnote (CTRL) - (F7), Footnote>Create |

Notice that the footnote number on the screen is 2.

Press:	Space bar
Type:	**President's Council on Physical Fitness and Sports, <u>Aqua Dynamics:</u> <u>Physical Conditioning Through Water Exercises</u>, p. 1.**
Press:	**Exit** (F7)

The second footnote number is entered in the text.

Peg forgot to enter a footnote earlier in the text.

Move to:	Pg 3 Ln 7.33" Pos 6.8" (space after the word "activity." on fourth line of fifth paragraph)
Select:	Layout>Footnote>Create
>>	Footnote (CTRL) - (F7), Footnote>Create

Notice that this footnote is number 2. WordPerfect automatically adjusted the footnote numbers when the new footnote was inserted.

Press:	Space bar
Type:	**Ibid.**
Press:	**Exit** (F7)

Notice that both footnotes are still displayed as footnote 2. To update the screen display using the Rewrite feature,

| **Select:** | Screen (CTRL) - (F3), Rewrite |
| **Move to:** | Pg 4 Ln 1" |

Your screen should be similar to Figure 4-21.

FIGURE 4-21

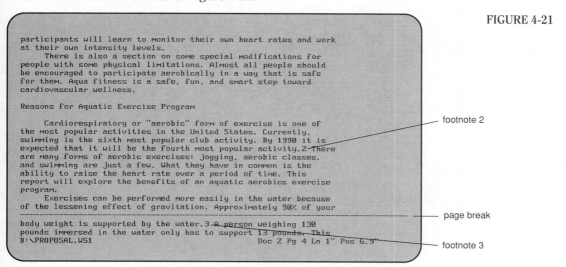

The footnote number for the third footnote changed to 3. Also notice that the sentence containing the third footnote moved to the top of page 4. This is because WordPerfect determined there would not be enough space at the bottom of page 3 to display two footnotes and the associated text.

Editing a Footnote

Peg realizes that she forgot to enter the date in the footnote text for the third footnote. The Edit option in the Footnote submenu lets you change the information in an existing footnote. To edit a footnote you can be anywhere within the document. To edit footnote 3,

Select: Layout>Footnote>Edit

>>   Footnote (CTRL) - (F7), Footnote>Edit

The prompt to enter the number of the footnote that you want to edit is displayed. If the correct footnote number is displayed following the prompt you can press (↵) to accept it. Otherwise you must type in the footnote number following the prompt. Since you want to edit footnote number 3,

Type: 3
Press: (↵)

The text for footnote 3 is displayed on the screen. To add the date before the page number of the footnote,

Move to: Ln 1.67" Pos 6.7"
Type: 1981,
Press: Space bar
Press: Exit (F7)

Now Peg wants to see how the page containing the footnotes will appear when printed. To see how the footnotes on page 3 will appear when printed move to anywhere within page 3, then

Select: File>Print> View Document

>>   Print (SHIFT) - (F7), View Document

After a few moments page 3 is generated and displayed in the View Document screen.

Note: If your computer does not have graphics capabilities, your screen cannot display the entire page. Instead it will display the first 24 lines of the page with the margins and other print options as close as possible to how it will appear when printed. The instructions that follow do not apply to your computer system. Instead, to see the footnotes as they will appear when printed, press (CTRL) - (HOME) (↓). The footnotes will appear as they will be printed; however, the footnote numbers will not appear in super-script. To leave the View screen, press (F7). Continue the lab by skipping to the next section, "Numbering Pages."

If you are not viewing the bottom of the page and your View screen is not 100%,

Select: 1 100%
Press: (HOME) ⬇

The text is large enough to read easily. Notice that the footnote number is displayed in superscript, and the footnotes appear at the bottom of the page as they will be printed.

To leave the View screen,

Press: Exit (F7)

Numbering Pages

Next Peg wants to instruct WordPerfect to print page numbers for each page in the report. The code to create page numbering is entered on the page where you want page numbering to begin. Generally this is the beginning of the document. To move to the top of page 1,

Press: (HOME) (HOME) ⬆

The Layout>Page, or Format (SHIFT) - (F8), Page, command is used to specify page numbering.

Select: Layout>Page
  >> Format (SHIFT) - (F8), Page

The Page Format menu is displayed. The Page Numbering option lets you specify the placement of numbers on the pages.

Select: Page Numbering

The Format: Page Numbering menu is displayed. The four options let you control how and where page numbers are inserted. To turn on page numbering from the cursor position forward, you need to specify where you want the page number placed on the page. The Page Number Position option shows the default is to display no page numbers. To change this setting and specify where you want the number placed,

Select: Page Number Position

Your screen should be similar to Figure 4-22.

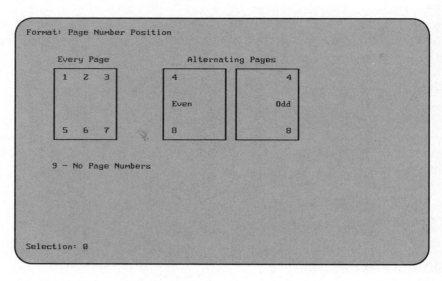

FIGURE 4-22

The Format: Page Number Position menu is displayed. The numbers displayed on the page layout let you specify where the page number will appear. The option number corresponds to its position on the page layout. Peg wants each page number centered on the bottom of every page (option 6),

Select: 6

The new page number position, bottom center, is displayed. To return to the document,

Press: Exit (F7)

The page numbers will not appear on the screen. However, when the document is printed the page numbers will appear on the margin of the location specified. If new pages are inserted or others deleted, WordPerfect will automatically renumber the pages.

Suppressing Page Numbers

Peg realizes that she really does not want the title and table of contents pages to be numbered. She can turn off the page numbering for specified pages using the Page Format menu. To do this, the cursor must be positioned at the beginning of the page to be unnumbered.

The cursor should already be on the first line of page 1. If it is not, move it there.

Select: Layout>Page
>>   Format (SHIFT) - (F8), Page

The option "Suppress (this page only)" will turn off page numbering for the page the cursor is on.

Select: Suppress (this page only)

Your screen should be similar to Figure 4-23.

FIGURE 4-23

```
Format: Suppress (this page only)

     1 - Suppress All Page Numbering, Headers and Footers

     2 - Suppress Headers and Footers

     3 - Print Page Number at Bottom Center   No

     4 - Suppress Page Numbering              No

     5 - Suppress Header A                    No

     6 - Suppress Header B                    No

     7 - Suppress Footer A                    No

     8 - Suppress Footer B                    No




Selection: 0
```

A menu of eight options is displayed. The options allow you to suppress or temporarily turn off different page format settings. To turn off page numbering and return to the document,

Select: Suppress **P**age Numbering
Type: **Y**
Press: Exit (F7)

Use the Reveal Codes screen to look at the codes inserted at this location in your document. It should display [Pg Numbering:Bottom Center][Suppress:PgNum]. **Exit the Reveal Codes screen.**
Following the procedure above, suppress the page numbering for the Table of Contents page (page 2).

Centering Text Top to Bottom

Next Peg would like the text on the title page to be centered between top and bottom margins of the page. Before this command is used the cursor needs to be positioned at the top left margin of the page to be centered.

Press: (HOME) (HOME) (↑)

The cursor should be on the left margin of the first line of page 1. The Center Page option (1) in the Page Format menu will automatically center the text vertically on a page.

Select:	Layout>**P**age
>>	Format (SHIFT) - (F8), **P**age
Select:	**C**enter Page (top to bottom)
Type:	**Y**
Press:	Exit (F7)

Again, not until you print or view the page will you see how the text is centered on the page. It will position the text on this page so that an equal number of blank lines lie above and below the first and last line of text.

Center the text on the table of contents page. Use the Reveal Codes screen to view the codes entered at this location.

Using Block Protection

Peg has one last concern. She wants to make sure that text that should remain together on one page, such as a table or a long quote, is not divided over two pages. This situation frequently occurs because WordPerfect automatically calculates the length of each page and inserts a **soft page break** when needed without discrimination as to the text. The position of a soft page break will change as text is added or deleted.

To control where a page ends you could enter a **hard page break** to make WordPerfect begin a new page. A hard page break is entered by pressing (CTRL) - (←). However, if you continue to edit the document by adding and deleting text that affects the length of the document, the location of the hard page break may no longer be appropriate. Then you would need to delete the hard page break code and reenter it at the new location. To do this is time consuming.

One solution is to use the Block Protection command (Edit>Protect Block or Block (ALT) - (F4), Format (SHIFT) - (F8)) to keep a specified block of text together on a page. Before using Block Protection, the block of text must be marked. The area of text which Peg does not want to be split between two pages is on page 5.

Move to:	Pg 5 Ln 1.5" Pos 1" ("W" in "With")

To specify the first block of text to protect,

Select:	**E**dit>**B**lock
>>	Block (ALT) - (F4)

Highlight the text on lines 1.5" through 2.33". The highlight should cover the lead-in sentence and the following three lines of formulas.

Select:	**E**dit>**P**rotect Block

To see the hidden codes entered into the text as a result of using this command,

Select: **E**dit>**R**eveal Codes
   >>   Reveal Codes (ALT) - (F3)
Press: (↑) (2 times)

Your screen should be similar to Figure 4-24.

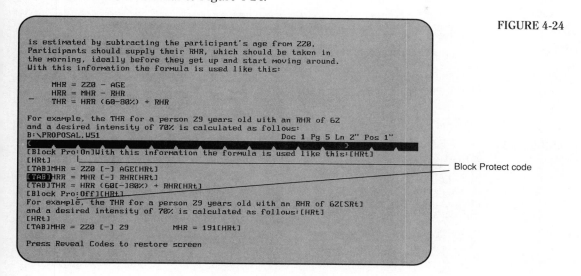

FIGURE 4-24

Block Protect code

A [Block Pro:On] code is inserted at the beginning of the block, and a [Block Pro:Off] code is inserted at the end of the block. Now, when WordPerfect formats this page for printing, the text between these codes will never be divided between two pages. If there is not enough space on a page to accommodate the entire block of text a page break is inserted above the [Block Pro:On] code, and the entire block is moved to the next page.

However, in this case it appears that there are enough lines left on this page to keep the entire block of text together, and no page break is inserted. It is always a good idea to turn on Block Protection even though it currently may appear that it is not needed. Later editing of the document may change the location of the block in the text, resulting in a split between two pages.

To remove the Reveal Codes screen,

Select: **E**dit>**R**eveal Codes
   >>   Reveal Codes (ALT) - (F3)

The next block to be protected begins on Pg 5 Ln 2.5" through Ln 3.33". This block begins with the words "For example" and ends after the third line of formulas. Block this area of text.

To protect this block, you will use the function key equivalent this time. It is (SHIFT) - (F8).

Select: Format (SHIFT) - (F8)

The prompt "Protect Block?" appears in the status line. To turn on protection,

Type: Y

As Peg looks through the document she notices that a chart which begins on page 5 is divided between two pages. To move to the bottom of page 5,

Press: CTRL - HOME ↓

As you can see, the fitness table which begins on page 5 continues on page 6.

Following the above procedure, protect the table and lead-in sentence (beginning with the word "Once") to prevent the text from appearing on separate pages. (The block should extend through Pg 6 Ln 1.5".)

Your screen should be similar to Figure 4-25.

FIGURE 4-25

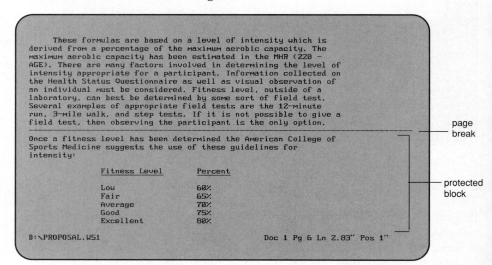

This time a page break is inserted by the program so that the entire block begins on the following page. Using Block Protection Peg could add more lines of data within the block codes, and the protection would remain in effect.

Preventing Widows and Orphans

The second way to control how text is divided between two pages is to turn on Widow/Orphan Protection. When the first line of a paragraph is the last line on a page it is called a **widow**. When the last line of a paragraph appears at the top of a new page it is called an **orphan**. To prevent this type of problem from occurring, the Widow/Orphan Protection command is used.

The Widow/Orphan Protection command (Layout>Line>Widow/Orphan Protection or SHIFT - F8, Line>Widow/Orphan Protection) should be entered at the beginning of the document so that all the following text will be affected. To move back to the beginning of the document and to use this command,

Press: (HOME) (HOME) (↑)
Select: **Layout>Line**
>> Format (SHIFT) - (F8), **L**ine

The Line Format menu is displayed. The last option, 9, Widow/Orphan, will turn on this protection.

Select: **W**idow/Orphan Protection

The cursor moved to the default for this option. To turn on Widow/Orphan Protection,

Type: **Y**
Press: Exit (F7)

To see the hidden codes,

Select: **E**dit>**R**eveal Codes
>> Reveal Codes (ALT) - (F3)

Your screen should be similar to Figure 4-26.

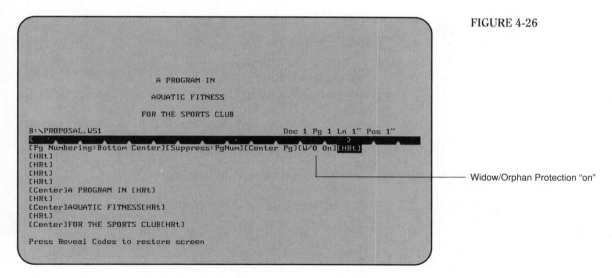

FIGURE 4-26

Widow/Orphan Protection "on"

The four page-format codes you entered at the beginning of the document are displayed. The code [W/O on] will will automatically determine when it is necessary to adjust the text on a page to eliminate widows and orphans. This protection applies only to traditional paragraphs, however.

Select: **E**dit>**R**eveal Codes
>> Reveal Codes (ALT) - (F3)

Printing the Report

Although Peg has a lot more work to do on the report, she wants to print out the first few pages of the text to see how the page settings and footnotes will appear.

Select: File>Print
   >>   Print (SHIFT) - (F7)

Next select the printer you want to use to print this document.
The option Multiple Pages will let you specify which pages of the on-screen document to print.

Select: Multiple Pages

The prompt "Page(s):" allows you to print the entire document (All), which is the default, individual pages, or any range of pages.

To print pages 1 through 3, 5, and 6,

Type: 1-3,5,6
Press: (↵)

The prompt "Document may need to be generated. Print?" is displayed. In response to this prompt,

Type: Y

The specified pages should be printing.
Check to see that the page numbers are displayed as specified, that the first two pages are centered, and that the footnotes are correct.
To leave the Print menu,

Press: (↵)

Save the edited report as FITNESS and exit WordPerfect.

Key Terms

paragraph number
family
level one head
level two head
leader
soft page break
hard page break
widow
orphan

Matching

1. (SHIFT) - (F5), 4 _____ **a.** allows you to specify the placement of page numbers
2. [Par Num:Auto] _____ **b.** turns on the Outline feature
3. (CTRL) - (F3), 3 _____ **c.** reformats the display of the screen
4. (ALT) - (F5),1, 2 _____ **d.** the View Document command
5. (ALT) - (F5), 6 _____ **e.** the code for an outline paragraph number
6. (CTRL) - (F7), 1 _____ **f.** creates a footnote
7. (CTRL) - (F3), 2 _____ **g.** centers a page top to bottom
8. (SHIFT) - (F7), 6 _____ **h.** generates a table of contents

9. (SHIFT) - (F8), 2, 1 _____ **i.** accesses the Line Draw feature
10. (SHIFT) - (F8), 2, 6 _____ **j.** creates a second level table of contents head

Practice Exercises

1. Retrieve the file FITNESS (created at the end of the lab). You will complete the table of contents for the report.

■ Continue marking the level one and two heads as shown below. Do not include bold, center, or underline codes.

Level one head:

Special Problem Modifications

Level two heads:

Conditioning Activities
Cool-Down Activities
Toning
Orthopedic
Diabetes
Asthmatic
Obesity
Hypertension
Seizures
Elderly

- Return to page 2 of the report and delete the table of contents definition marker code [DefMark ToC,2].

- Enter a new definition marker code at this location. This time specify that the page numbers are displayed flush right but without dot leaders.

- Generate the new table of contents. Make sure that you respond "Yes" to the prompt to confirm that you want any previous tables deleted.

- Print the table of contents page only.

- Save the revised report as FITNESS1.

2. Retrieve the file FITNESS1 created in problem 1. You will enter several more footnotes in the report.

- Enter the fourth footnote at the end of the sentence on Pg 4 Ln 5". The footnote is:

  > Judy Seigel, "Children's Target Heart Rate Range," <u>Journal of Physical Education, Recreation & Dance</u>, 59, April 1988.

- Enter the fifth footnote at the end of the sentence on Pg 5 Ln 4.33". The footnote is:

  > Joseph McEnvoy, <u>Fitness Swimming: Lifetime Programs</u>, 1985, p. 12.

- Enter another footnote at the end of the first sentence on Pg 4 Ln 8. This footnote is:

  > <u>Ibid</u>.

  What number is this footnote? Use the Rewrite feature to update the footnote numbering. What number is the footnote in the middle of page 5?

- Edit footnote number 4. It needs the page reference, "p. 78," added to the end of the footnote.

- Save the report as FITNESS2.

- Print pages 4 and 5.

3. In the next two problems you will create an outline for a paper and write a short paper using WordPerfect. The paper can be any paper you have written in the past.

- Create an outline for your paper. The outline for your paper should have a minimum of three main topic heads (I., II., III.).

- Under the three topic heads you must have a minimum of two subheads (A., B.).

- You must show at least two paragraph level three and level four numbers (1., 2., and a., b.).

Minimally, your outline should look like this:

```
I.
        A.
                1.
                2.
                        a.
                        b.
        B.

II.
        A.
        B.

III.
        A.
        B.
```

4. Write a paper based upon the outline you created in problem 3. The paper can be a paper you have written in the past. It must be a minimum of five pages. You must demonstrate the following:

- Title page

    The title of the paper must be centered and boldfaced.

    The title must have a double line above and below it.

    Your name and the current date (using the Date command) must appear near the bottom of the title page. They must be centered.

    The entire title page should be centered top to bottom.

- Table of contents

    The heading on this page should be centered and boldfaced.

    The table of contents should show the three main headings from the outline as level one heads. The structure of your report will determine the number of level two heads.

    The page numbers should appear right justified. There should not be any dot leaders before the page numbers.

- Body of the report

    There must be a minimum of three pages of text.

    You must enter a minimum of four footnotes.

- The report must have pages numbered on the top right of every page. Suppress page numbering for the title page and the table of contents.

- Turn on Widow/Orphan Protection.

- Turn right justification off.

- Print the report.

WordPerfect 5.1

Glossary of Key Terms

Active printer: The selected printer used to print the document.

Address file: The secondary merge file used in a merge. It typically contains name and address data to be combined with the primary file document.

Block: A selected area of text, which can vary in size from a single character to the entire document, that is to be copied, moved, or deleted.

Boldface: Printed text that appears darker than surrounding text as a result of printing over the text several times.

Buffer file: A temporary file used to store the last three deletions made to the document.

Center: To position text in a line evenly between the margins.

Code: A hidden symbol entered in the text when a command that affects the format of the text—such as justification, margins, and boldfacing—is used.

Context sensitive: The ability of the Help system to automatically display information about the command in use.

Cursor: A flashing underscore or box that indicates where the next character you type will appear on the screen.

Default: The predefined program settings used initially by the program. Generally, these settings are the most commonly used settings.

Delete: To erase or remove a character, word, or block of text from the document.

Document: A WordPerfect file containing text and codes.

Edit: To correct or change the text or format of a document file.

Endnote: A note of reference in a document displayed at the end of the text.

Family: A section of an outline that consists of the outline level at the cursor location and any subordinates or lower levels.

Field: Each piece of data contained in a record of information in the secondary merge file for use in the merge process.

File extension: The last one to three characters of a filename following a period. Some software packages use this to identify which files were created using that package.

Filename: A unique name for identifying different documents and programs. Each filename consists of from one to eight characters, followed by a period (.) and an optional file extension.

Flush right: Positions a line of text so that the rightmost character is aligned with the right margin.

Footnote: A note of reference in a document displayed at the bottom of the page where the reference occurs.

Hard carriage return: Moves the cursor to the beginning of the next line or inserts a blank line into a text file when ⏎ is pressed.

Hard page break: A page break entered by pressing ((CTRL) - (⏎)). A new page will begin following a hard page break regardless of the amount of text on the page.

Insert mode: Allows new text to be entered in a document at the cursor location by moving all existing text to the right.

Justification: When on, the text is aligned with both the left and right margins, producing even or straight margins on both the right and left sides of the document.

Leader: A series of dots or other characters between the header and the page number in the table of contents.

Level one head: The main head used in the table of contents.

Level two head: The second level head used in the table of contents.

Line: A single row of text. The WordPerfect default setting is 54 lines to a printed page.

Menu bar: The top line of the screen which, when activated by pressing (ALT) - = , displays the nine menus that can be opened.

Menu cursor: The highlight that covers the name of the selected menu.

Merge codes: WordPerfect codes entered in the primary file that control which fields are used from the secondary merge file and where they are entered in the primary file.

Mnemonic letter: The highlighted letter associated with the menu or submenu name.

Move: To remove a marked block of text from one location in a document and place it in a different location.

Newspaper columns: Columns of text that are read down the page and wrap to the top of the next column on the same page, like a newspaper.

Option: A list of command menu choices from which the user selects.

Orphan: The last line of a paragraph that is printed as the first line of a new page.

Page: The number of lines that can be printed on a single sheet of paper.

Paragraph number: The lettering/numbering system used in the Outline command to identify the topic levels and define the structure of the outline.

Parallel columns: Columns of text that are read across a page of text rather than down.

Position: The location of the cursor on a line.

Primary file: The file containing the form letter or master document that controls the merge process using merge codes.

Prompt: A question or other indication that the computer is waiting for a response from the user.

Pull-down menu: A list of commands displayed in a box below the selected menu that are available for selection.

Record: All the fields of data in the secondary merge file that may be used to complete the primary file during the merge process.

Reformat: Automatic readjustment of the text on a line after the text has been changed so that the justification is reestablished.

Repeater: The (ESC) key in WordPerfect causes a command or function to be repeated a certain number of times.

Replace: To substitute a new version of a document for the old version when saving.

Repositioning: The message displayed in WordPerfect when the cursor is directed to move to a new location.

Save: To write the current document to a diskette so that when the computer is turned off, the document will remain intact.

Scroll: To move quickly line by line, screen by screen, or page by page through the document.

Search: To move backward or forward through a document to locate a specified character string in the document.

Secondary merge file: A file used in a merge. It typically contains name and address data to be combined with the primary file document.

Soft carriage return: Carriage return entered automatically by the word wrap feature, which determines when a line of text should end.

Soft page break: A page break automatically entered by the program when the entire page is filled. The location of the page break changes automatically as text is added or deleted.

Status line: The bottom line of the screen display, which displays the document number, page, line, and position of the cursor in the document. It may also display a menu or program prompts if a command is issued.

String: A specific combination of characters and/or codes.

Submenu: Another list of commands available for selection when a command that displays a > symbol following the command name is selected.

Supplementary dictionary: A secondary dictionary used by the Speller consisting of words added by the user. Whenever the Speller does not locate the word in the main dictionary, it will check the supplemental dictionary.

Switch: To move from one document into another document file when two documents are in use at one time.

Typeover mode: Activated by pressing the (INS) key. In the typeover mode, new text replaces the existing text by typing over it.

Underline: An underscore appears under every character or space in the selected block of text.

Widow: The first line of a paragraph that is printed as the last line of a page.

Window: Division of the display screen into two parts, which allows you to view two different documents at the same time or two parts of the same document at the same time.

Word wrap: Feature that automatically determines when to begin the next line of text. The user does not press (⏎) at the end of a line unless it is the end of a paragraph or to insert a blank line.

Functional Summary of Selected WordPerfect Commands

To start WordPerfect: WP
To display Menu bar: (ALT) - =

Function	Command	Action
Cursor movement	(→)	One character right
	(←)	One character left
	(↑)	One line up
	(↓)	One line down
	(CTRL) - (→)	One word right
	(CTRL) - (←)	One word left
	(HOME) - (→) or (END)	Right end of line
	(HOME) (←)	Left edge of screen
	(HOME) (↑) or - (minus sign)	Top of screen
	(HOME) (↓) or + (plus sign)	Bottom of screen
	(CTRL) - (HOME) (↑)	Top of current page
	(CTRL) - (HOME) (↓)	Bottom of current page
	(CTRL) - (HOME) page n	Top of the page n specified
	(PGUP)	Top of previous page
	(PGDN)	Top of next page
	(HOME) (HOME) (↑)	Top of document
	(HOME) (HOME) (↓)	Bottom of document
	(CTRL) - (HOME) (→)	One column right
	(CTRL) - (HOME) (←)	One column left
	(ESC) n, command	Repeat command n times
	(ESC) n, arrow	Move cursor n spaces or lines
Insert	(INS) on	Insert text
	(INS) off	Typeover text
	(↵)	Insert blank line/end line
Delete	(DEL)	Delete at cursor
	(BKSP)	Delete left of cursor
	(CTRL) - (BKSP)	Delete word
	(CTRL) - (END)	Delete to end of line
	(CTRL) - (PGDN)	Delete to end of page
Retrieve	(SHIFT) - (F10) File>Retrieve	Retrieve a file
Save	(F10) File>Save>Y	Save file, resume edit
	(F7) **Y** File>Exit>Y	Save file, clear screen
Blocks	(ALT) - (F4) Edit>Block	Block on/off
	(CTRL) - (F4) Edit>Select	Move, copy, delete, or append a sentence, paragraph, page

WP154
Summary: WordPerfect

Function	Command	Action
Format	(F6) Font>Appearance>Bold	Bold on/off
	(F8) Font>Appearance>Underline	Underline on/off
	(SHIFT) - (F6) Layout>Align>Center	Center text
	(ALT) - (F6) Layout>Align>Flush Right	Flush right
	(SHIFT) - (F8), **1 7** Layout>Line>Margins	Set margins
	(SHIFT) - (F8), **1 8** Layout>Line>Tab Set	Set tabs
	(SHIFT) - (F8), **1 3** Layout>Line>Justification	Set justification
Print	(SHIFT) - (F7) **1** File>Print>Full Document	Print full document
	(SHIFT) - (F7) **2** File>Print>Page	Print a page
	(SHIFT) - (F7) **6** File>Print> View Document	View Document
	(SHIFT) - (F7) **S** File>Print>Select Printer	Selects printer
Outline	(SHIFT) - (F5) **4 1** Tools>Outline>On	Outline mode on
	(SHIFT) - (F5) **4 2** Tools>Outline>Off	Outline mode off
	(SHIFT) - (F5) **4 3** Tools>Outline>Move Family	Move family
	(SHIFT) - (F5) **4 4** Tools>Outline>Copy Family	Copy family
	(SHIFT) - (F5) **4 5** Tools>Outline>Delete Family	Delete family
Line Draw	(CTRL) - (F3) **2** Tools>Line Draw	Begins Line Draw
	(CTRL) - (F3) **2 1** Tools>Line Draw>1	Creates single line
	(CTRL) - (F3) **2 2** Tools>Line Draw>2	Creates double line
	(CTRL) - (F3) **2 3** Tools>Line Draw>3	Creates line of asterisks
	(CTRL) - (F3) **2 4** Tools>Line Draw>Change	Creates line of your design
	(CTRL) - (F3) **2 5** Tools>Line Draw>Erase	Erases a line
	(CTRL) - (F3) **2 6** Tools>Line Draw>Move	Moves the cursor without creating a line
Table of Contents	(ALT) - (F5) **1** Mark>Table of Contents	Marks selected text to be used in TOC
	(ALT) - (F5) **5** Mark>Define>Table of Contents	Specifies location and design for TOC

Function	Command	Action
Table of Contents (*continued*)	(ALT) - (F5) 6 5 Mark>Generate>Generate	Generates TOC Tables, Indexes, Cross-References, etc.
Footnotes	(CTRL) - (F7) 1 Layout>Footnote>Create	Allows entry of footnote references and specifies location of footnote in text
	(CTRL) - (F7) 2 Layout>Endnote>Create	Allows entry of endnote references and specifies location of endnote in text
	(CTRL) - (F7) 1 2 Layout>Footnote>Edit	Allows you to edit footnote references
Page Format	(SHIFT) - (F8) 2 6 Layout>Page>Page Numbering	Specifies placement of page numbers
	(SHIFT) - (F8) 2 8 Layout>Page>Suppress	Surpresses page numbering
	(SHIFT) - (F8) 2 1 Layout>Page>Center Page	Centers text vertically on a page
	(SHIFT) - (F8) 1 9 Layout>Line>Widow/ Orphan Protection	Turns on Widow/Orphan protection
	(SHIFT) - (F8) Edit>Protect Block	Turns on block protection for a selected block of text
Merge	(SHIFT) - (F9) 1 Tools>Merge Codes>Field	Define field names
	(SHIFT) - (F9) 2 Tools>Merge Codes> End Record	End of record
	(SHIFT) - (F9) 6 Tools>Merge Codes>More	Advanced Merge Codes
	(F9) Tools>Merge Codes> More>{End of Field}	End field
	(CTRL) - (F9) 1 Tools>Merge	Merge primary and secondary files
Columns	(ALT) - (F7) 1 3 Layout>Columns>Define	Define column settings
	(ALT) - (F7) 1 1 Layout>Columns>On	Turn on column settings
	(ALT) - (F7) 1 2 Layout>Columns>Off	Turn off column settings
Search	(F2) Search>Forward	Search forwards
	(SHIFT) - (F2) Search>Backward	Search backwards
	(ALT) - (F2) Search>Replace	Search and replace
Utilities	(SHIFT) - (F3) Edit>Switch Document	Switch to document 2
	(F3) Help>Help	Help

Function	Command	Action
Utilities (*continued*)	(F5) File>List Files	List files
	(ALT) - (F3) Edit>Reveal Codes	Reveal codes
	(F1) Edit>Undelete	Cancel/Undelete
	(CTRL) - (F3) 1 Edit>Window	Windows
	(SHIFT) - (F5) 1 Tools>Date Text	Date text
	(SHIFT) - (F5) 2 Tools>Date Code	Date as code
	(SHIFT) - (F5) 3 Tools>Date Format	Date Format
	(CTRL) - (F2) Tools>Spell	Begins Spell Checking
	(ALT) - (F1) Tools>Thesaurus	Begins Thesaurus
	(CTRL) - (F3) 3	Rewrites display of text on the screen
	(CTRL) - (⏎)	Hard page break
Exit	(F7)>**NY**	Abandons file without saving and exits WP
	(F7) **Y Y** File>Exit **Y Y**	Saves file and exits WP

Address files:
    creating, WP89-93
    defined, WP84, WP150
    merging with letter files, WP94-95
Aligning flush right, WP63-64
Appending text, defined, WP58

Binding, allowing for in printing,
    WP76-77
Block protection, WP142-43
Blocks:
    defined, WP4, WP150
    marking, WP59-60
    marking for contents, WP127-31
    marking for underline, WP102-3
    moving, WP59-61
    moving, in Outline mode, WP121
    summary of commands, WP153
    See also Block protection
Boldfacing:
    defined, WP4, WP150
    text, WP95-WP97
Booting up, WP6
Brackets, for codes, WP72

Canceling menu selections, WP12
Caps Lock key, WP96
Carriage returns:
    hard, WP38, WP71, WP150
    soft, WP72, WP150
    and word wrap, WP52
Centering:
    defined, WP4, WP150
    text, WP95-97
    text top to bottom, WP141-42
Character string:
    defined, WP4
    text, WP73-74
Characters:
    deleting, WP29-31
    inserting, WP32-35
    repeating, WP37
Codes:
    for Block Protect, WP143
    for columns, WP103
    defined, WP150
    deleting, WP72

displaying, WP70-72
hiding, WP72
merge, WP84-89, WP151
in Outline mode, WP119, WP122-24
removing Reveal Codes, WP119
for tables of contents, WP127-28
Columns:
    commands for, WP155
    defining, WP103
    editing in column format, WP107
    newspaper style, WP104
    parallel, WP104
    turning settings on/off, WP106
Commands:
    Block, WP59-61, WP124
    Block Protect, WP142-44
    Bold, WP97
    canceling, WP12
    Center, WP96
    for columns, WP155
    Date, WP62-63
    Delete, WP153
    Exit, WP42, WP48
    Flush Right, WP71
    Footnote, WP155
    Format, WP65-67
    formatting, WP66
    and function key template, WP8
    GOTO, WP24, WP25
    for Line Draw, WP125-27
    Line Format, WP67, WP75
    List Files, WP42-43
    Math/Columns, WP103-6
    Merge, WP94
    Merge Codes, WP84
    Move, WP57-59
    Page Format, WP155
    Print, WP45
    Replace, WP73-75
    Retrieve, WP10
    Reveal Codes, WP70-72
    Rewrite, WP106-7, WP109
    Save, WP49, WP55
    Screen, WP99, WP101
    Search Backward, WP73
    Search Forward, WP73
    summary of, WP153

Switch, WP98-99
for tables of contents, WP154
Underline, WP102
for utilities, WP155
Widow/Orphan Protect, WP144-45
Contents, table of:
    creating, WP127-34
    defining location of, WP131-34
    generating, WP134-35
    leaders in, WP133
    levels of heads in, WP129
    marking text for, WP127-31
    summary of commands, WP154
Copying text:
    between documents, WP98-99
    within a document, WP58
Cursor:
    defined, WP8, WP150
    jumping to beginning, WP24
    jumping to end, WP24
    moving, WP19-27
    moving between columns, WP107
    position, in Status Line, WP8
    summary of commands, WP153
    using a mouse, WP27-28
Customizing form letters. *See* Merging

Dates:
    code for, WP62
    Date/Outline menu options, WP62
    entering into documents, WP62
    entering when booting, WP6
Default settings:
    defined, WP8
    justification, WP75
    left margin, WP21
    line spacing, WP21
    right margin, WP21
    tabs, WP21
Deleting:
    blank lines, WP38-39
    characters with backspace key, WP29-31
    characters with Del, WP31
    codes, WP70
    in column format, WP107
    defined, WP4, WP58, WP150
    to end of line, WP36

several lines, WP37-38
summary of commands, WP153
tabs, WP69
words, WP35-36
Directory, listing files in, WP42-43
Displaying:
formatted footnotes, WP137-38
Help screens, WP12
hidden codes, WP70-72
pages on screen, WP137-38
tab settings, WP67-70
Documents:
creating, WP50-52
defined, WP150
editing, WP28-41
exiting, WP42, WP48
footnotes in, WP134-38
moving text between, WP100-1
printing, WP45-47, WP76-77,
WP146
saving, WP44-45
saving and exiting two, WP111
saving in a new file, WP77-78
using two, WP98-99
viewing on screen, WP107-9,
WP138-39
See also Files
Drawing lines, WP125-27

Editing:
in column format, WP107
defined, WP150
deleting characters, WP29-31
deleting words, WP35-36
documents, WP28-41
footnotes, WP138
inserting text, WP32-35
summary of keys used, WP27, WP41
Endnotes:
creating and editing, WP135
defined, WP150
summary of commands, WP155
Erasing. *See* Deleting
(ESC) key as repeater, WP37-38, WP151
Exiting a document:
with Exit command, WP42,
WP44-45, WP48, WP77, WP156
with two documents in use, WP111
Extensions in file names:
defined, WP43
.PF for primary files, WP89, WP94
.SF for secondary files, WP94

Fields:
in address files, WP85, WP89
defined, WP150
File names:
defined, WP150

entering, WP42
extensions, WP43, WP89, WP91,
WP150
rules for, WP42
Files:
combining, WP56, WP98-99
jumping to beginning/end, WP26
listing, WP42-44
merging, WP94-95
opening, WP11-WP12
primary merge, WP84-89, WP94-95
replacing, WP44-45
retrieving, WP17-19
saving, WP44-45
saving and exiting two, WP111
saving in a new file, WP77-78
secondary merge, WP89-93
using two, WP98-99
See also Address files; Documents
Flush right:
aligning text, WP63-64
code for, WP71
defined, WP4, WP150
Footnotes:
creating, WP134-38
defined, WP150
displaying, WP137-38
editing, WP138
numbering, WP135
saving, WP136
summary of commands, WP155
Form letters. *See* Merging
Formatting:
in columns, WP103-7
defined, WP5
summary of commands, WP154
Function keys:
combining with other keys, WP27
(F1) (Cancel), WP12, WP17, WP69
(F2) (Search Forward), WP73
(F3) (Help), WP12, WP16
(F5) (List Files), WP42-WP43
(F7) (Exit), WP41-42, WP48
(F8) (Underline), WP102
(F10) (Save), WP42-43
template for, WP8-9
See also Commands

GOTO command, WP24, WP25

Hard carriage returns, WP38, WP71,
WP150
Hard page breaks, WP142
Heads, in tables of contents, WP129,
WP151
Help screen:
clearing, WP13
displaying, WP12

Hidden codes:
for columns, WP103
displaying, WP70-72
hiding, WP72
Home key, WP21-23
Hyphenation, WP109-10

Indenting first line of paragraph, WP69
Insert mode:
defined, WP151
editing in, WP32-33
Inserting:
blank lines, WP38-39
in Insert mode, WP32-33
summary of commands, WP153
in Typeover mode, WP34-35

Justifying:
changing, WP109
defined, WP5, WP151
setting margins for, WP75-76

Keys:
arrow, WP19-24
(BACKSPACE), to delete, WP29-31,
WP71, WP118
(CAPS LOCK), WP96
for cursor movement, WP19-27
(DEL), WP31, WP38, WP71
for deleting, WP29-31, WP35-36, WP107
editing, WP36, WP41
(END), WP21
(ESC), WP37-38
for GOTO, WP24, WP25
(HOME), WP21-26
Indent, WP117
(INS), WP41
Mark Text, WP116, WP129
(NUM LOCK), WP19
in Outline mode, WP116-24
(PGDN), WP24-25, WP27
(PGUP), WP24-25, WP27
summary of functions, WP153-56
(TAB), WP118, WP120
See also Commands; Function keys

Leaders, in tables of contents, WP133
Letters, personalized. *See* Merging
Line Draw feature:
to draw boxes, WP125-27
summary of commands, WP154
Lines:
blank, inserting and deleting, WP38-39
creating, WP125-27
and cursor position, WP8
defined, WP151
deleting, WP37-38
double, WP126

Listing file names, WP42-44
Loading WordPerfect, WP6-9

Margins:
 aligning flush right, WP63-64
 code for, WP70
 justifying, WP5, WP75, WP151
 left, default for, WP21
 ragged right, WP75, WP76
 right, default for, WP21
 setting, WP65-67
Memory, temporary, WP152
Menus:
 Date/Outline, WP62
 Footnote, WP135
 Format, WP65
 Line Draw, WP126
 Line Format, WP75
 List Files, WP42
 Mark Text, WP116, WP132
 Math/Columns, WP103-6
 Merge/Sort, WP94
 Move, WP57-59, WP60
 options in, WP43
 Page Numbering, WP139
 Print, WP45, WP76-77
 Screen, WP124
 Pull-Down, WP9-13
 Table of Contents Definition, WP132-33
 Text Column Definition, WP103-5
Merging:
 addresses with form letter, WP83-95
 codes for, WP84-89, WP151
 defined, WP5
 summary of commands, WP155
 See also Primary files; Secondary
  files
Modes:
 Insert, WP4, WP32-33, WP151
 Outline, WP116-46
 Typeover, WP5, WP34-35, WP152
Mouse, using a, WP13-17
 to move the cursor, WP27-28
Moving the cursor, WP19-28
Moving text:
 between documents, WP100-1
 with Block command, WP59-61
 defined, WP151
 with Move command, WP57-59
 in Outline mode, WP121

Newspaper-style columns, WP104, WP151
Numbering:
 footnotes, WP135-36
 pages, WP139-40
 paragraphs in outlines, WP117
 suppressing, WP140-41
Numeric keypad, and NumLock, WP19

Opening files, WP11-12
Options. *See* Commands; Menus
Orphans:
 defined, WP144, WP151
 preventing, WP144-45
Outlines, creating, WP116-23
Overstriking, defined, WP5

Page breaks:
 hard, WP142
 preventing, WP142-44
Page Format, commands for, WP155
Pages:
 centering top to bottom, WP141-42
 defined, WP151
 displaying on screen, WP138-39
 numbering, WP139-40
 preventing page breaks, WP142-44
 and Status Line, WP8
 suppressing numbering, WP140-41
 See also Formatting
Paragraph numbers, WP117, WP151
Parallel columns, WP104, WP151
Primary files, for merging:
 creating, WP84-89
 defined, WP84, WP151
 merging with secondary files, WP89-93
Printing documents:
 allowing for binding, WP76-77
 merged letters, WP95
 with Print command, WP45-47
 using Print Options menu, WP76-77
 specifying range of pages, WP146
 summary of commands, WP154
Prompts, WP17, WP151
Protecting blocks from page breaks,
  WP142-44

Ragged-right margins, setting, WP75-76
Records, in address files, WP84, WP151
Reformatting:
 in columns, WP106-7
 defined, WP151
 display of text, WP66
Repeater, (ESC) key as, WP37-38,
  WP151
Replacing character string, WP73-75
Replacing existing files, WP44-45,
  WP151
Repositioning message, WP24, WP151
Research paper, creating, WP116-46
Retrieving files, WP17-19, WP153
Revealing codes:
 removing Reveal Codes, WP119
 on screen, WP70-72
Ruler line, tab, WP68

Saving documents:
 commands for, WP153
 defined, WP152
 and exiting, WP55
 and exiting two documents, WP111
 with (F10), WP42-43
 in a new file, WP77-78
 and replacing files, WP44-46
 with two documents in use, WP111
Saving footnotes, WP136
Screens:
 clearing, WP41-42
 closing split screens, WP101-2
 components of, WP8
 creating split screens, WP90-100
 reformatting in columns, WP106-7
 updating footnote numbers on,
  WP138-39
 View Document, WP138-39
Scrolling between columns, WP107
Search and replace, WP5
Searching:
 backward and forward, WP73
 defined, WP5, WP152
 summary of commands, WP155
Secondary merge files:
 creating, WP89-93
 defined, WP84, WP152
 fields in, WP84, WP89
 merging with primary file, WP89-93
Soft carriage returns, WP72, WP152
Split screens:
 closing, WP101-2
 creating, WP99-100
 to reveal hidden codes, WP70
 and Status Line, WP8
Status Line:
 and cursor location, WP8
 defined, WP152
 information in, WP12
Strings:
 defined, WP73
 upper- and lowercase in, WP74
Suppressing page numbers, WP140-41
Switching between documents, WP98-99,
  WP152

Tab ruler line, WP68
Table of contents:
 creating, WP127-34
 defining location of, WP131-33
 generating, WP134-35
 leaders in, WP133
 levels of heads in, WP129
 marking text for, WP127-31
 summary of commands, WP154

Tabs:
 default settings for, WP8
 deleting, WP69
 displaying current settings, WP67,
  WP69
 in Outline mode, WP117-19,
  WP124-25
 removing, WP69
 setting, WP67-70
Templates:
 defined, WP5
 function key, WP8
Temporary memory, WP152
Text:
 aligning flush right, WP63-64
 appending, WP58
 boldfacing, WP95-97
 centering, WP95-97
 centering top to bottom, WP141-42
 in column format, WP103-7
 copying, WP58
 deleting, WP58

 entering, WP50-52
 indenting, WP69
 justified, WP5, WP75, WP151
 moving, WP57-59
 moving, between documents, WP100-1
 moving, in Outline mode, WP121
 protecting from page breaks, WP142-44
 ragged right, WP75
 reformat display of, WP66
 underlining, WP102-3
 unjustified, WP75
 See also Formatting
Typeover mode:
 defined, WP5, WP152
 editing in, WP34-35

Underlining text, WP102-3, WP152
Unjustified text, defined, WP5
Utilities, summary of, WP155-6

Viewing documents on screen, WP107-9,
  WP138-39

Widows:
 defined, WP144, WP152
 preventing, WP144-45
Windows. *See* Split screens
Word processing:
 advantages of using, WP3-4
 defined, WP3
 terminology, WP4
Word wrap, WP5, WP50, WP152
WordPerfect:
 exiting, WP39, WP42, WP156
 Help system for, WP8
 loading, WP6-9
Words, deleting, WP35-36

Lotus 1-2-3
Release 2.2

567890 KPKP 909876543

P/N 048808-8

ORDER INFORMATION:
ISBN 0-07-048808-8

CONTENTS

Overview   Electronic Spreadsheets   SS3
Definition of Electronic Spreadsheets   SS3
Advantanges of Using an Electronic Spreadsheet   SS3
Electronic Spreadsheet Terminology   SS4
Case Study for Labs 1–5   SS5

Lab 1   Creating a Worksheet: Part 1   SS6
Loading the Lotus 1-2-3 Program   SS6
Examining the Worksheet   SS7
Moving Around the Worksheet   SS8
Using the Function Keys   SS11
Using Scroll Lock   SS12
Entering Labels   SS13
Editing a Cell Entry   SS17
Using the UNDO Feature   SS22
Using 1-2-3 Menus   SS23
Using the Help System   SS25
Retrieving a File   SS26
Entering Values   SS29
Entering Formulas   SS31
Recalculating the Worksheet   SS32
Saving a Worksheet   SS33
Printing a Worksheet   SS35
Key Terms   SS37
Matching   SS37
Practice Exercises   SS38

Lab 2   Creating a Worksheet: Part 2   SS42
Using the Copy Command   SS42
Highlighting a Range   SS45
Copying Formulas   SS48
Entering an @Function   SS51
Using the Erase Command   SS53
Changing Column Widths   SS54
Formatting a Value   SS57
Inserting Rows   SS61
Using the Repeat Label Prefix Character   SS61
Inserting Columns   SS63
Saving and Replacing a File   SS64
Printing a File   SS65
Key Terms   SS66
Matching   SS66
Practice Exercises   SS66

Lab 3   Managing a Large Worksheet   SS69
Locating and Correcting a Circular Reference   SS69
Freezing Titles   SS72
Creating and Scrolling Windows   SS75
Displaying a Percent   SS77
Using What-If Analysis   SS79
Using an Absolute Cell Reference   SS82
Extracting Worksheet Data   SS85
File Linking   SS87
Entering the System Date   SS90
Justifying Text   SS92

Using Compressed Printing   SS94
Key Terms   SS96
Matching   SS96
Practice Exercises   SS97

Lab 4   Creating and Printing Graphs   SS101
Using the Access System   SS101
Selecting the Type of Graph   SS104
Labeling the X Axis   SS106
Specifying the Data to Be Graphed   SS107
Viewing the Graph   SS107
Entering Graph Titles   SS108
Naming the Graph Settings   SS113
Saving Graphs for Printing   SS114
Switching the Graph Type   SS114
Resetting Graph Specifications   SS115
Defining Multiple Data Ranges   SS116
Entering Legends   SS117
Creating a Stacked-Bar Graph   SS118
Creating a Pie Chart   SS120
Shading the Pie Slices   SS121
Exploding a Slice of the Pie   SS123
Recalling Named Graphs   SS125
Saving the Worksheet   SS126
Printing a Graph   SS127
Key Terms   SS130
Matching   SS130
Practice Exercises   SS130

Lab 5   Creating Templates and Macros   SS134
Naming a Range   SS134
Using the @IF Function   SS139
Creating a Template   SS141
Creating an Interactive Macro   SS141
Planning the Macro   SS142
Entering the Macro   SS143
Naming the Macro   SS145
Testing the Macro   SS146
Editing the Macro   SS147
Using a Repetition Factor   SS150
Documenting the Macro   SS152
Using the Learn Feature   SS153
Protecting Cells   SS159
Creating an Autoexecute Macro   SS160
Key Terms   SS162
Matching   SS162
Practice Exercises   SS163

Summary   Lotus 1-2-3 Release 2.2   SS167
Glossary of Key Terms   SS167
Functional Summary of Selected Lotus 1-2-3
   Commands   SS170
Function Keys   SS173

Index   SS174

Electronic Spreadsheets

In contrast to a word processor, which manipulates text, an electronic spreadsheet manipulates numerical data. The first electronic spreadsheet software program (Visi-Calc) was offered on the market in 1979. Since then more than 5 million electronic spreadsheet programs of differing brands have been sold. In a 10-year period, spreadsheets have revolutionized the business world.

Definition of Electronic Spreadsheets

The electronic spreadsheet, or worksheet, is an automated version of the accountant's ledger. Like the accountant's ledger, it consists of rows and columns of numerical data. Unlike the accountant's ledger, which is created on paper using a pencil and a calculator, the electronic spreadsheet is created using a computer system and an electronic spreadsheet applications software program.

The electronic spreadsheet eliminates the paper, pencil, and eraser. With a few keystrokes the user can quickly change, correct, and update the data. Even more impressive is the spreadsheet's ability to perform calculations—from very simple sums to the most complex financial and mathematical formulas. The calculator is replaced by the electronic spreadsheet. Analysis of data in the spreadsheet has become a routine business procedure. Once requiring hours of labor and/or costly accountants' fees, data analysis is now available almost instantly using electronic spreadsheets.

Nearly any job that uses rows and columns of numbers can be performed using an electronic spreadsheet. Typical uses of electronic spreadsheets are for budgets and financial planning in both business and personal situations.

Advantages of Using an Electronic Spreadsheet

Like a word processor, the speed of entering the data into the worksheet using the keyboard is not the most important advantage gained from using an electronic spreadsheet. This is because the speed of entering data is a function of the typing speed of the user and the user's knowledge of the software program. The advantages are in the ability of the spreadsheet program to quickly edit and format data, perform calculations, create graphs, and print the spreadsheet.

The data entered in an electronic spreadsheet can be edited and revised using the program commands. Numeric or text data is entered into the worksheet in a location called a cell. These entries can then be erased, moved, copied, or edited. Formulas can be entered that perform calculations using data contained in specified cells. The results of the calculations are displayed in another cell.

The design and appearance of the spreadsheet can be enhanced in many ways. There are several commands which control the format or display of a numeric entry in a cell. For instance, numeric entries can be displayed with dollar signs or with a set number of decimal places. Text or label entries in a cell can be displayed centered or left- or right-justified (aligned) to improve the spreadsheet appearance. Columns and rows can be inserted and deleted. The cell width can be changed to accommodate entries of varying lengths.

You have the ability to "play" with the values in the worksheet, to see the effect of changing specific values on the worksheet. This is called "what-if," or sensitivity, analysis. Questions that once were too expensive to ask or took too long to answer can now be answered almost instantly, and with little cost. Planning that was once partially based on instinct has been replaced to a great extent with facts. However, any financial planning resulting from the data in a worksheet is only as accurate as that data and the logic behind the calculations. Incorrect data and faulty logic only produce worthless results.

Most electronic spreadsheets also have the ability to produce a visual display of the data in the form of graphs. As the values in the worksheet change, a graph referencing those values automatically reflects the new values. The graphs produced by most spreadsheet programs are a tool for visualizing the effects of changing values in a worksheet. Thus, they are analytic graphs. An electronic spreadsheet program is not designed to produce graphs exclusively, as many presentation graphics programs are. As a result the graphs may appear crude compared to those produced by a pure graphics software program.

Electronic Spreadsheet Terminology

Absolute cell reference: The cell address in a formula does not change when the formula is copied to another cell. A $ character entered before the row number and/or column letter causes absolute addressing.

Arithmetic operators: Special characters assigned to basic numerical operations (e.g., + for addition, * for multiplication).

Automatic recalculation: The recalculation of all formulas in a worksheet whenever a value in a cell changes.

Cell: The space created by the intersection of a horizontal row and a vertical column. It can contain a label, value, or formula.

Circular reference: A formula in a cell that directly or indirectly references itself.

Column: The vertical line on the spreadsheet identified by letters.

Copy: A spreadsheet command that duplicates the contents of a cell or range of cells to another location in the worksheet.

Format: The feature that controls how values in the spreadsheet are displayed (currency, percent, number of decimal places, etc.).

Formula: A numeric computation containing cell references and arithmetic operators.

Freeze: A spreadsheet feature that stops the scrolling of specified rows and/or columns on the display.

Function: A set of built-in or preprogrammed formulas.

Global: Command that affects all rows and columns in the spreadsheet.

Graph: The visual representation of ranges of data in the worksheet. Some graph types are line, bar, stacked-bar, and pie chart.

Justification: The alignment of a label in a cell to the left, centered, or right in the cell space.

Label: A text entry in a cell used to describe the data contained in the row or column.

Manual recalculation: Recalculation of the formulas in a worksheet is performed only when specified by the user.

Mode: Displays the status or condition the program is currently operating in. The three main categories of operation are READY, EDIT, and MENU.

Move: The command which relocates the contents of a cell(s) to another area in the worksheet.

Range: A cell or rectangular group of adjoining cells.

Relative cell reference: The adjustment of the cell address in a formula to reflect its new location in the spreadsheet when copied.

Row: The horizontal line on the worksheet identified by numbers.

Value: A number displayed in a cell.

What-if analysis: A process of evaluating the effect of changing the contents of one or more cells in the spreadsheet to help in decision making and planning.

Case Study for Labs 1–5

Paula Nichols is the manager of the Courtside Cafe at the Sports Club. She has proposed expanding the menu of the cafe and has been asked by the board of directors to prepare a budget for the first 6 months of operation.

In Lab 1, Paula learns how to use a spreadsheet program to assist her in preparing this budget. She enters descriptive row and column titles and enters the values for the expected sales for food and beverages. She also enters a formula to compute a total value.

Lab 2 continues the building of the cafe budget by entering the values for expenses using copying. Functions are introduced. The worksheet is formatted to display currency.

In Lab 3, Paula expands the cafe budget to cover a 1-year period. The problems of managing a large worksheet are handled in this lab by freezing titles and creating windows. What-if analysis on the worksheet is used to achieve the objectives of a 20 percent profit margin by the end of a year of operation.

Lab 4 deals exclusively with creating graphs. It requires that the computer can display and print graphs. The case used in this lab follows Fred Morris as he prepares several graphs to show trends in membership growth of the Sports Club over 5 years. A line, bar, stacked-bar, and pie chart are created.

In Lab 5, Fred creates a bi-weekly membership enrollment report which uses macros to help speed up the data entry and report generation process. You will learn how to create, test, and edit macro commands.

Creating a Worksheet: Part 1

1

OBJECTIVES

In this lab you will learn how to:

1. Move around the worksheet.

2. Enter labels.

3. Edit worksheet entries.

4. Use the UNDO feature.

5. Use the Main menu.

6. Use the Help system.

7. Enter values.

8. Enter formulas.

9. Save a worksheet file.

10. Print a file.

CASE STUDY

Paula Nichols is the manager of the Courtside Cafe at the Sports Club. She has proposed that the menu of the Courtside Cafe be expanded. The board of directors, before approving the expansion, want her to prepare a budget for the first 6 months of the proposed cafe expansion.

During the next three labs, you will follow Paula as she creates and uses a worksheet for the cafe budget using Lotus 1-2-3. In this lab, you will follow Paula as she learns to enter descriptive row and column titles for the worksheet. She will enter the expected sales values for food and beverages. A simple formula to calculate the expected sales total value will also be entered.

Loading the Lotus 1-2-3 Program

To load the Lotus 1-2-3 Release 2.2 program, boot the computer with the DOS diskette in drive A. After you respond to the DOS date and time prompts, the A> should be on your display. Remove the DOS diskette. Place the Lotus 1-2-3 System Disk in drive A and your data diskette in drive B.

Note: If you have a hard disk or network system, consult your instructor for instructions.

At the A>,

Type: 123
Press: ⏎

The computer loads the Lotus 1-2-3 Release 2.2 program into memory. After a few moments your display should be similar to Figure 1-1.

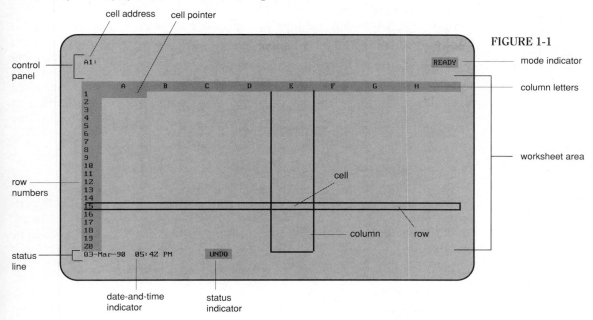

FIGURE 1-1

Examining the Worksheet

Figure 1-1 is a blank Lotus 1-2-3 **worksheet**. It is similar to a financial spreadsheet in that it is a rectangular grid of rows and columns used to enter data.

The worksheet screen is divided into three areas: the worksheet area, the control panel, and the status line.

The **worksheet area** is located in the center of the display screen and occupies the largest amount of space on the screen. The worksheet consists of a rectangular grid of **rows** and **columns**. The border of **row numbers** along the left side of the worksheet area identifies each row in the worksheet. The border of **column letters** across the top of the worksheet area identifies the columns.

The intersection of a row and column creates a **cell**. The cell that is highlighted on your display is A1. The highlight box is called the **cell pointer**. It identifies the **current cell**, which is the cell your next entry or procedure affects.

The **control panel** is located above the column letters. It consists of three lines that display information about the worksheet. On the left side of the first line, the **cell address** of the current cell is displayed. The cell address always consists of the column letter followed by the row number of the current cell. Since the cell pointer is located in cell A1, the cell address displays "A1." The highlighted box on the right side of the first line is the **mode indicator**. It tells you the current **mode**, or state, the 1-2-3 program is in. The current mode is READY. When READY is displayed, you can move the cursor, make a cell entry, use the function keys, or initiate a command. There are 14 different modes of operation. As you are using the program, the mode indicator will display the current mode. The other modes will be discussed as they appear throughout the labs.

The control panel shows other information in the second and third lines as commands are executed and entries are made in the worksheet. You will be referring to this area of the worksheet often throughout this series of labs.

The bottom line of the display screen contains the **status line**. This line is used to display the date-and-time indicator, status indicators, and error messages. Currently the **date-and-time** indicator is displayed on the left side of the status line. This indicator shows the date and time as maintained by DOS. As you are using the program, **error messages** may replace the date-and-time indicator to tell you the program detects an error or cannot perform a task. The highlighted box containing the word "UNDO" is a **status indicator**. (If UNDO is not displayed, this feature has been turned off on your system.) Status indicators tell you that a certain key or program condition is in effect. Currently it tells you that the UNDO feature is in effect. Other status indicators will be displayed as they are activated and will be discussed as they appear throughout the labs.

Moving Around the Worksheet

The arrow keys, (HOME), (END), (PGUP), (PGDN), and (TAB) keys allow you to move the cell pointer around the worksheet. They are called the **pointer-movement keys**. The arrow keys on the numeric keypad move the cell pointer in the direction indicated by the arrow.

To move the cell pointer to cell E3,

Press: (→) (4 times)
Press: (↓) (2 times)

Your display screen should be similar to Figure 1-2.

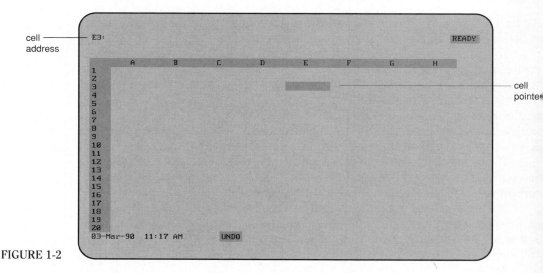

FIGURE 1-2

The cell pointer is in cell E3, making this cell the current cell. The control panel reflects the new location of the cell pointer in the worksheet by displaying the cell address E3 (column E row 3).

Press: (←) (5 times)

The computer beeped, because the cell pointer cannot be moved beyond the limits of the row or column borders.

To practice moving around the display screen using the four arrow keys,

Move to: E10
Move to: C6
Move to: G18

To return quickly to the upper left-hand corner, cell A1, of the worksheet,

Press: (HOME)

Wherever you are in the worksheet, pressing (HOME) will move the cell pointer to the upper left-hand corner of the worksheet.

The worksheet is much larger than the part you are viewing on your display screen. The worksheet actually extends many columns to the right and many rows down. The worksheet in Lotus 1-2-3 has 256 columns and 8192 rows.

The part of the worksheet you see on your display screen is called a **window**. The current window shows rows 1 through 20 and columns A through H.

To move one full window to the right of the current window,

Press: (TAB)

Your display screen should be similar to Figure 1-3.

FIGURE 1-3

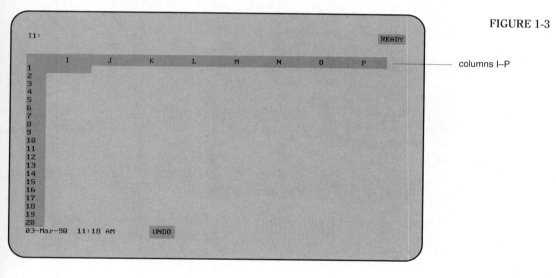

columns I–P

The window is now positioned over columns I through P and rows 1 through 20 of the worksheet.

To return to the previous window,

Press: (SHIFT) - (TAB)

The window is now positioned over columns A through H again.

The same movement of the window can be made using (CTRL) - (→) instead of (TAB), and (CTRL) - (←) instead of (SHIFT) - (TAB).

To move down one full window on the worksheet,

Press: (PGDN)

Your display screen should be similar to Figure 1-4.

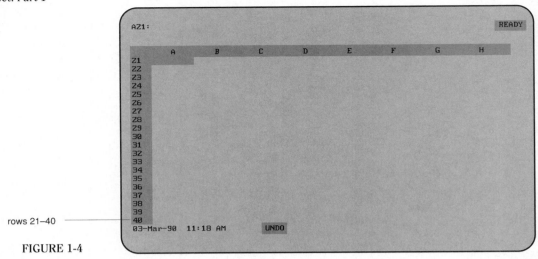

rows 21–40

FIGURE 1-4

The window is positioned over rows 21 through 40 of the worksheet. Columns A through H have remained the same.

To move up a window on the worksheet,

Press: `PGUP`

The window is positioned over rows 1 through 20 of the worksheet again.

If you hold down the arrow keys, the `TAB` or `SHIFT` - `TAB` keys, or the `PGUP` or `PGDN` keys, you can quickly move through the worksheet. This is called **scrolling**. You will try this by holding down `TAB` for several seconds. Watch your display screen carefully as the columns quickly change window by window.

Press: `TAB` (hold down for several seconds)

To quickly return to cell A1,

Press: `HOME`

The `END` key followed by an arrow key will move the cell pointer to the last cell of that row or column. To quickly move the cell pointer to the last row of column A in the worksheet,

Press: `END`

Notice the word "END" displayed in the status line. This is a status indicator. The status line will display different status indicator messages about a particular program or key condition as they are used. In this case it tells you the `END` key is on.

Press: `↓`

The cell pointer moved to the last row, 8192, of column A in the worksheet.

To move to the rightmost column in row 8192,

Press: (END)
Press: (→)

Your display screen should be similar to Figure 1-5.

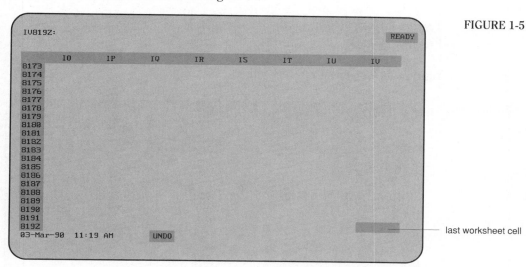

FIGURE 1-5

last worksheet cell

The cell pointer is positioned in cell IV8192. This is the last cell in the Lotus 1-2-3 worksheet. Columns are labeled A to Z, AA to AZ, BA to BZ, and so forth, through IA to IV.

Using the Function Keys

The function keys on your keyboard (located to the left of the typewriter keys or above the typewriter keys, depending upon your computer keyboard) perform special operations. Each function key, except the (F6) key, performs two operations. One operation is executed by pressing the function key alone, another by pressing the (ALT) key and the function key in combination. The function keys are named according to the operation they perform. The function keys and their operations are listed in Table 1-1 below.

TABLE 1-1

HELP	EDIT	NAME	ABS	GOTO	WINDOW	QUERY	TABLE	CALC	GRAPH
(F1)	(F2)	(F3)	(F4)	(F5)	(F6)	(F7)	(F8)	(F9)	(F10)
(ALT)	(ALT)	(ALT)	(ALT)	(ALT)		(ALT)	(ALT)	(ALT)	(ALT)
(F1)	(F2)	(F3)	(F4)	(F5)		(F7)	(F8)	(F9)	(F10)
COMPOSE	STEP	RUN	UNDO	LEARN		APP1	APP2	APP3	APP4

The GOTO function key ((F5)) will move the cell pointer to a specific cell in a worksheet.

Press: (F5) GOTO

Notice the second line in the control panel. It displays the prompt, "Enter address to go to:" followed by the address of the current cell pointer position. A **prompt** is how the program tells you it is waiting for a user response. In this case, the prompt is asking the user to enter the cell address that you want to move the cell pointer to. The cell address you want to move the cell pointer to is entered in either upper- or lowercase letters. To move the cell pointer to cell AL55,

Type: AL55
Press: ⮐

Your display screen should be similar to Figure 1-6.

FIGURE 1-6

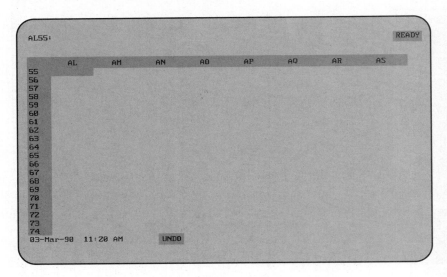

The cell pointer is positioned in cell AL55. The cell you specified at the GOTO prompt is placed in the upper left-hand corner of the window.

Using Scroll Lock

Move to: AP60

Rather than moving the cell pointer around the screen, the cell pointer can remain stationary while the worksheet columns and rows move. This is done by using the (SCROLL LOCK) key (located at the upper right-hand corner of the keyboard).

Press: (SCROLL LOCK)

The status indicator "SCROLL" appears in the status line. It tells you that this key is in effect.

Press: ↑ (3 times)

The cell pointer remained in cell AP60 while the rows moved in the direction indicated by the pointer-movement keys.

Press: ⟶ (4 times)

The cell pointer is still in cell AP60 while the columns moved four columns to the right.

To turn off (SCROLL LOCK),

Press: (SCROLL LOCK)

The SCROLL status indicator is no longer displayed. Pressing (SCROLL LOCK) acts as a toggle to turn on and off the scroll feature. You will find the scroll lock feature helpful if you want to bring into view an area of the worksheet a few rows or columns outside the window without moving the cell pointer from the current cell.

To review, the following keys are used to move around the worksheet:

Key	Action
↓ ↑ ⟶ ⟵	Move cell pointer one cell in direction of arrow
(TAB) or (CTRL) - ⟶	Moves cell pointer right one full window
(SHIFT) - (TAB) or (CTRL) - ⟵	Moves cell pointer left one full window
(PGDN)	Moves cell pointer down one full window
(PGUP)	Moves cell pointer up one full window
(HOME)	Moves cell pointer to cell in upper left-hand corner of worksheet
(END) ↓	Moves cell pointer to last row in worksheet
(END) ⟶	Moves cell pointer to last column in worksheet
(F5) (GOTO)	Moves cell pointer to specified cell
(SCROLL LOCK)	Holds cell pointer stationary while worksheet scrolls (on)

Practice moving the cell pointer around the worksheet using each of the keys presented above.

When you are ready to go on,

Move to: A1

Entering Labels

Now that you know how to move around the worksheet, you will begin creating the cafe budget. By the end of this lab, you will have entered part of the cafe budget as shown in Figure 1-7 on the next page.

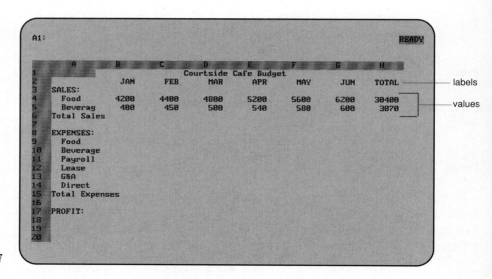

FIGURE 1-7

Entries into a worksheet are defined as either a label or a value. **Labels** create the structure of the worksheet and describe other worksheet entries. The months in row 2 are labels. **Values** are numbers (data) or results of formulas or functions. The entry in cell B4, 4200, is a value.

The column labels in this worksheet consist of the months (January through June) and a Total (sum of entries over 6 months) located in row 2, columns B through H.

The row labels in column A describe the following:

Sales:
Food	Income from sales of food items
Beverage	Income from sales of beverages
Total Sales	Sum of food and beverage sales

Expenses:
Food	Cost of food supplies
Beverage	Cost of beverage supplies
Payroll	Hourly personnel expenses
Lease	Monthly cost of space used in club
G & A	General and Administrative
Direct	Other expenses (insurance, utilities, etc.)
Total Expenses	Sum of Food, Beverage, Payroll, Lease, G&A, and Direct Expenses

Profit:	Total Sales minus Total Expenses

To create the structure for this worksheet, you will begin by entering the column labels. The column label for January will be entered in cell B2. Type the label exactly as it appears below.

Move to: B2

Type: january

Your display screen should be similar to Figure 1-8.

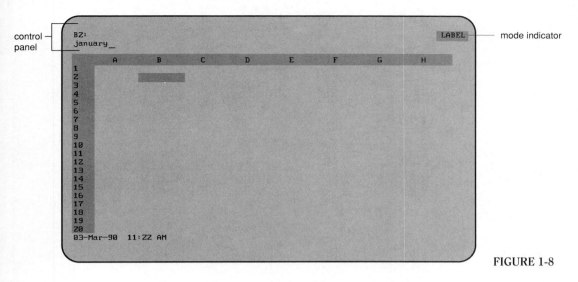

FIGURE 1-8

Several changes have occurred on the display screen. As you type, the second line in the control panel displays each character. It should display "january." The blinking cursor marks your location on the line.

Note: If you made an error while typing the label, use the (**Bksp**) key (the left-facing arrow key located above the (⏎) key) to erase the characters back to the error. Then retype the entry correctly.

Look at the mode indicator next. It changed from READY to LABEL as the current mode of operation in the worksheet. This tells you that the entry in this cell is defined as a label.

The first character of an entry into a cell determines whether the cell contents are defined as a label or a value. All entries beginning with a space, an alphabetic character (A to Z), ', ", ^, or any other characters not considered a value, define a cell as a label. All entries beginning with a number from 0 to 9, + , - , ., (, @, #, and $ define a cell entry as a value. The entry in cell B2 is defined as a label because it begins with the alphabetic character "j."

Although the label is displayed in the control panel, it has not yet been entered into cell B2 of the worksheet. To actually enter the label into cell B2,

Press:

Your display screen should be similar to Figure 1-9.

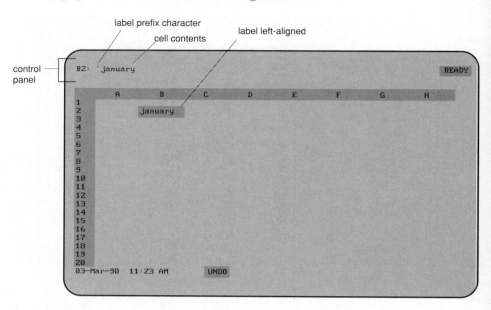

FIGURE 1-9

The label "january" is displayed in cell B2. Notice that the label is placed flush with the left side of the cell space.

Note: If you find that the entry in the cell is not correct or that it is in the wrong cell, you can cancel the entry by immediately pressing (ALT) - (F4). This is called the UNDO feature. The UNDO indicator in the status line must be displayed for this feature to work. This command will be discussed in greater detail later in the lab.

Following the cell address in the control panel, the contents of the cell are displayed. The apostrophe (') preceding the label is a **label prefix character**, which is automatically entered by Lotus 1-2-3. The label prefix character determines how the label will be displayed in the cell space. A label can be displayed flush with the left side of the cell space, centered within the cell space, or flush with the right side of the cell space. The three label prefix characters that control the placement of a label in a cell are:

Character	Alignment
'(apostrophe)	Flush left (this is the default)
" (quotes)	Flush right
^(caret)	Centered

The apostrophe is the **default** label prefix character. Defaults are options or settings automatically provided by 1-2-3. Generally they are the most commonly used settings. The apostrophe is automatically placed before any label entry unless one of the other label prefixes is entered. Notice how the label entry "january" is aligned to the left side of the cell space. The apostrophe positioned the label flush left within the cell space.

Editing a Cell Entry

Paula would like to change the label from "january" to "Jan."

An entry in a cell can be changed or edited in either the READY mode or the EDIT mode. To use the READY mode, simply retype the entry the way you want it to appear. For example, with the cell pointer on cell B2,

Type: **Jan**

Press: ⏎

Your display screen should be similar to Figure 1-10.

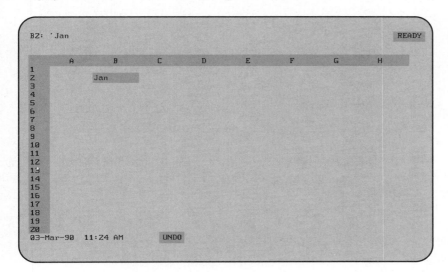

FIGURE 1-10

The new label "Jan" is entered into cell B2, replacing "january."

Next Paula wants to change the placement of the label in the cell. She wants it to be displayed flush with the right side of the cell space. To do this, she needs to change the apostrophe to quotes.

Rather than retyping the entire contents of the cell again, she can use the EDIT mode. The EDIT function key, (F2), is used to edit a cell.

Press: (F2) EDIT

Your display screen should be similar to Figure 1-11.

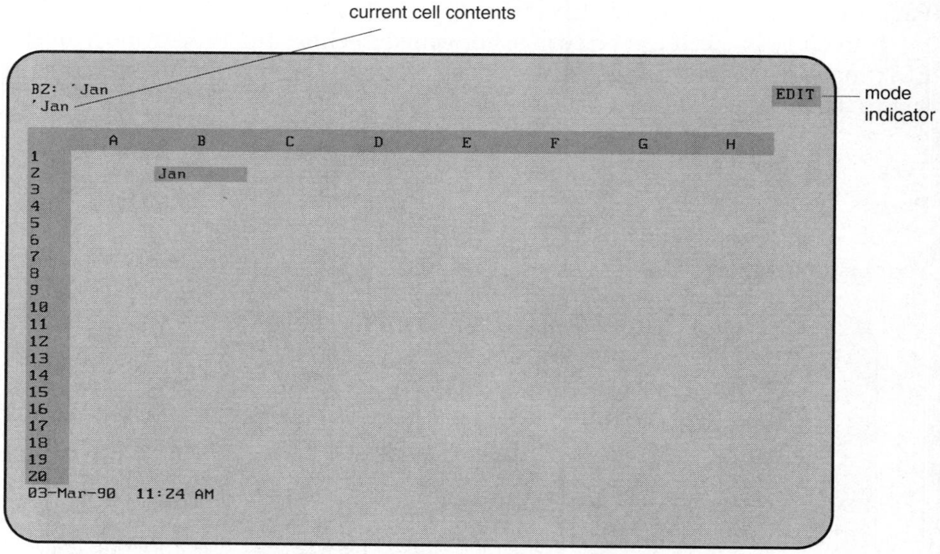

current cell contents

B2: ' Jan
' Jan

EDIT — mode
indicator

FIGURE 1-11

The control panel displays the current cell contents, and the mode indicator shows the new mode of operation as EDIT. The cursor is positioned at the end of the label in the control panel.

In the EDIT mode, the following keys can be used:

Key	Action
(HOME)	Moves cursor to beginning of entry
(END)	Moves cursor to end of entry
(DEL)	Erases character at cursor
(Bksp)	Erases character to left of cursor
(INS)	Overwrite mode in effect when on
(TAB)	Moves cursor 5 characters to right
(SHIFT) - (TAB)	Moves cursor 5 characters to left
(→)	Moves cursor 1 character right
(←)	Moves cursor 1 character left

To change the label prefix character at the beginning of the label from an apostrophe (') to quotes ("),

Press: (HOME)

The cursor moves to the beginning of the cell entry.

Press: (DEL)

The apostrophe is removed.

Type: "

Press: ⏎

Your display screen should be similar to Figure 1-12.

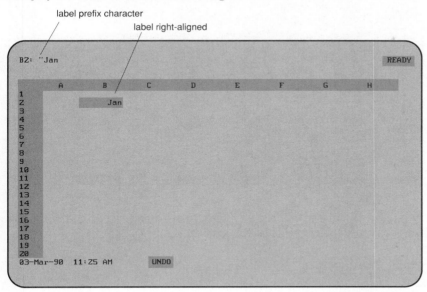

FIGURE 1-12

The label is placed to the right side of the cell. As you can see, editing would be particularly useful with long or complicated entries.

Finally, Paula wants the labels to be in all capital letters.

Press: (CAPS LOCK)

Notice that the CAPS indicator appears in the status line. The (CAPS LOCK) key affects only the letter keys. To produce the characters above the number or punctuation keys, you must use the (SHIFT) key.

Using the EDIT mode, you will change "Jan" to "JAN."

Press: (F2) EDIT

Press: (Bksp) (2 times)

The letters "an" are erased.

Type: AN

The characters "AN" are inserted into the label.

Press: ⏎

To turn off (CAPS LOCK),

Press: (CAPS LOCK)

Your display screen should be similar to Figure 1-13.

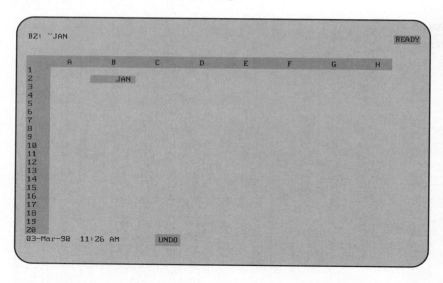

FIGURE 1-13

The next label to be entered is "FEB." You will practice using the READY and EDIT modes while entering this label in cell C2 as follows:

Move to: C2
Type: february
Press: ⏎

To change "february" to "Feb" in the READY mode,

Type: Feb
Press: ⏎

Using the EDIT mode next, change "Feb" to "FEB." First position the label flush right in the cell as follows:

Press: (F2) EDIT
Press: (HOME)

Another way to replace the apostrophe is to type over it with the quotes. This is done by pressing (INS).

Press: (INS)
Type: "

Pressing (INS) changes the entry of characters into a cell to overwrite. Anything you type will write over existing text that is already in the cell. The status indicator OVR is displayed whenever (INS) is pressed. Overwrite is turned off when you leave the EDIT mode or by pressing (INS) again.

To change the label to all capital letters,

Press: $\rightarrow$
Press: CAPS LOCK
Type: **EB**
Press: $\hookleftarrow$

Your display screen should be similar to Figure 1-14.

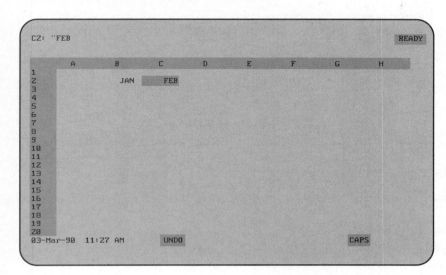

FIGURE 1-14

Notice that the OVR status indicator has disappeared. The CAPS status indicator is still displayed, showing that the CAPS LOCK key is still on.

The label for March needs to be entered in cell D2 next.

Move to: D2
Type: **"MAR**
Press: $\rightarrow$

Using the $\rightarrow$ key entered the label into the cell. It also moved the cell pointer one cell to the right. You are now ready to enter the label for April into cell E2. Moving the cell pointer to any other cell will both enter the label or value into the cell and move the cell pointer in the direction of the arrow.

The labels "APR," "MAY," "JUN," and "TOTAL" need to be entered into the worksheet in cells E2 through H2. Enter them in all capital letters. They should be displayed flush right in the cell. After typing the label "TOTAL," use $\hookleftarrow$ rather than the arrow key to enter the label into the cell, and then turn off CAPS LOCK.

Your display screen should be similar to Figure 1-15.

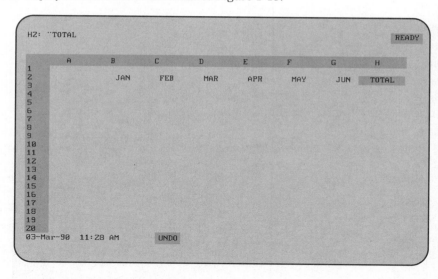

FIGURE 1-15

Using the UNDO Feature

Above the column headings, in row 1, Paula wants to enter a title for the worksheet.

Move to: D1
Type: **Courtside Cafe Budget**
Press: ⏎

Your display screen should be similar to Figure 1-16.

FIGURE 1-16

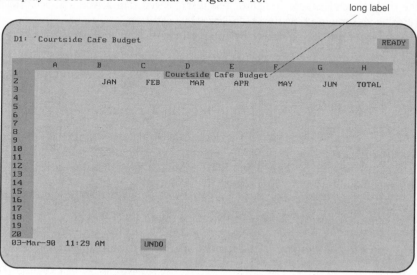

Notice that the worksheet title is longer than the 9 spaces in cell D1. When a label is longer than the cell's column width, it is called a **long label**. 1-2-3 will display as much of the label as it can. If the cells to the right are empty, the whole label will be displayed. If the cells to the right contain an entry, the overlapping part of the label will not be displayed.

Note: If UNDO is not displayed in the status line, this feature has been turned off. Consult your instructor for directions to turn on this feature, or skip to the next section, "Using 1-2-3 Menus."

Paula thinks the worksheet title is not descriptive enough.

Use the EDIT mode to change the title in cell D1 to "Estimated Budget for the Courtside Cafe."

After looking at the new title, Paula feels the first title looked better. Rather than reentering the first title, you can cancel the most recent operation that changed worksheet data or settings by using the UNDO function key ((ALT) - (F4)). This feature restores the worksheet to the way it was the last time 1-2-3 was in the READY mode.

Press: (ALT) - (F4) UNDO

The original worksheet title is redisplayed. The worksheet appears exactly as it did before you entered the last label. The UNDO key, like (SCROLL LOCK), acts as a toggle to jump back and forth between the two most recent operations. To see how this works,

Press: (ALT) - (F4) UNDO

The worksheet displays the previous title. You just undid the effect of the UNDO operation.

Press: (ALT) - (F4) UNDO

The worksheet is redisplayed with the title the way Paula wants it to appear. In order to do this, 1-2-3 creates a temporary backup copy of the worksheet each time you press a key that might lead to a worksheet change. In this way, each time you press UNDO, you are switching between the backup copy and the current worksheet.

Using 1-2-3 Menus

The row labels are entered into the worksheet in a similar manner to entering column labels. The only difference is that they are entered down column A rather than across row 2. We have already entered the row labels for you and saved them in a file on your data diskette.

To see the file containing the row labels, you will need to retrieve the file named ROWS.WK1 using the **Main menu**. This menu is accessed by pressing the slash (/) key. (Be careful not to use the backslash (\) key.)

Press: /

Your display screen should be similar to Figure 1-17.

menu pointer

mode indicator

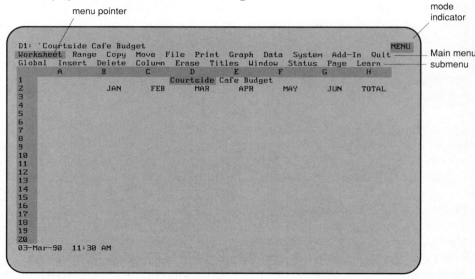

Main menu
submenu

FIGURE 1-17

The second line of the control panel now displays a list or menu of 11 commands, beginning with Worksheet and ending with Quit. The **menu pointer** is the rectangular highlight, which is currently positioned over Worksheet.

The third line of the control panel displays 10 **submenu** commands, beginning with Global and ending with Learn. The submenu commands currently displayed are associated with the highlighted main menu command, Worksheet.

To tell you that you are using the 1-2-3 menus, the mode indicator displays "MENU."

Press: →

The menu pointer moves to the right and is positioned over Range. The third line of the control panel now displays the /Range submenu. The commands listed in the submenu are the lower-level commands associated with the main menu command, Range.

Press: →

The menu pointer is highlighting Copy. A brief description of the Copy command is displayed in the third line of the control panel. This is because there are no submenu commands associated with the highlighted main menu command.

Look at the submenus or descriptions associated with each main menu command as you

Press: → (slowly 9 times)

The menu pointer has moved through the list of commands in a circular fashion and is positioned back on Worksheet.

The menu pointer can also be quickly moved to the first or last command from any location in the menu using (HOME) and (END).

Press: (END)

The menu pointer is positioned on Quit. To move back to Worksheet, the first command in the menu,

Press: (HOME)

Using the Help System

Lotus 1-2-3 has a very useful Help system to provide information about any part of the program you are using. The Help function key ((F1)) is used to access the Help system.

Press: (F1) Help

Note: If you are using a 5-1/4 inch disk, follow the directions on your screen to replace the System Disk with the Help Disk. You can run the 1-2-3 program without having the System Disk in the drive, because the entire program has been copied into your computer's memory. However, you cannot use Help unless the Help Disk is in the drive.

Your display screen should be similar to Figure 1-18.

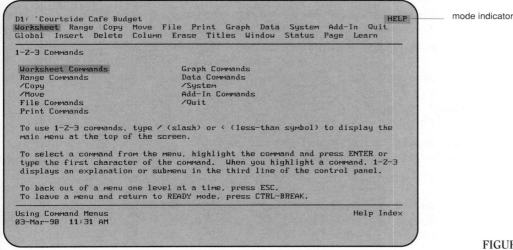

mode indicator

FIGURE 1-18

The worksheet temporarily disappears and a Help screen appears. The mode indicator now displays "HELP." Since you are using the main menu, the Help screen provides information about this feature. This Help screen tells you about the Lotus 1-2-3 commands listed in the control panel and how to select or cancel a command.

More detailed information can be obtained by moving the highlight bar with the arrow keys to any highlighted items and pressing (←). Since you want to retrieve a file, to get more help on the File command,

Move to: File Commands
Press: (←)

Your display screen should be similar to Figure 1-19.

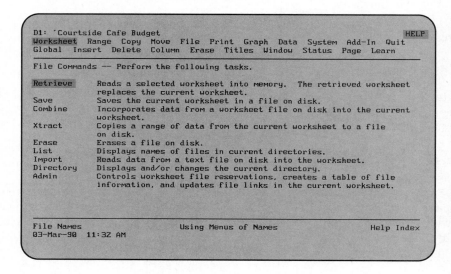

FIGURE 1-19

Information about the /File submenu commands is displayed. Read the information about this command carefully. Since you want to retrieve a file and the highlight is already over "Retrieve," to obtain more information about this command,

Press: ⏎

After reading this screen, to leave the Help screen and return to the worksheet,

Press: (ESC)

After leaving the Help screen, you are returned to the same place in the worksheet you were before accessing Help. The Main menu is displayed in the control panel. The mode indicator displays MENU again.

Note: If you are using 5-1/4 inch disks, you do not need to remove the Help Disk from the drive. This way, if you want to use Help again, you will not need to swap disks.

Retrieving a File

You are now ready to retrieve the file ROWS.WK1. To select a Main menu command or submenu option, you can use any of the following methods:

- Type the first character of the command name.
- Use → or ← to move the menu pointer to the menu item or submenu option and press ⏎ .
- Use any combination of the above methods.

Generally the method that takes the fewest keystrokes is to type the first character of the command name. This is the recommended method.

Note: If you accidentally select the wrong command or submenu option, press the (ESC) key. It will cancel the command selection and take you back one step in the command sequence. Then select the correct Main menu or submenu command. To return directly to the READY mode, press (CTRL) - (BREAK).

Since the Main menu is already displayed, to select File,

Type: F

Your display screen should be similar to Figure 1-20.

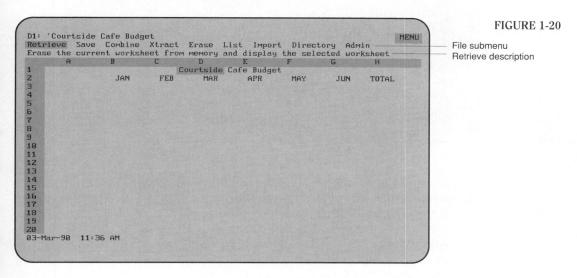

FIGURE 1-20

— File submenu
— Retrieve description

The /File submenu which was displayed in the third line of the control panel is now displayed on the second line. The third line now presents a brief description of the highlighted command, Retrieve.

Again using (→) and (←), slowly move the menu pointer to each submenu command. Either a description of the highlighted command or more submenu commands (if available) are displayed in the third line of the control panel.

To retrieve a file,

Select: Retrieve

Note: If the message "Disk drive not ready" is displayed, check that your data diskette is properly inserted in the drive and that the disk drive door is completely closed. Press (ESC) to clear the message, and reenter the command.

Your display screen should be similar to Figure 1-21.

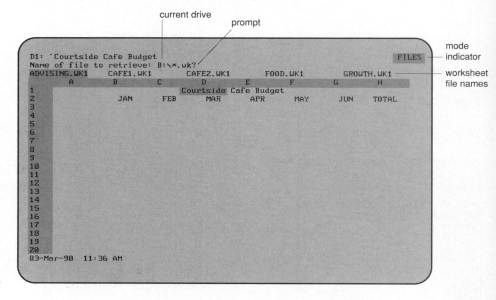

FIGURE 1-21

The second line of the control panel displays the prompt "Name of file to retrieve:." The prompt is followed by the drive that the program will search to locate your data files. If the drive letter displayed following the prompt is not the correct drive for your system, consult your instructor for further directions.

Also notice that the mode indicator has changed from MENU to FILES. This is because 1-2-3 is displaying the names of the available worksheet files in the third line of the control panel. The file names are displayed in alphabetical order. Because there is not enough room on the line to display all the file names, only the first five worksheet file names are listed. If there are more than five files in the directory, more lines of file names can be displayed by using ⬇ and ⬆. To move the menu pointer along a line of file names, use → and ←.

You want to read into memory the file ROWS.WK1. In response to the prompt for the name of the file you want to retrieve, you can type the full file name following the prompt, or you can move the menu pointer to the file name and press ↵ to select the file. Using the menu pointer to select the file,

Move to: ROWS.WK1

Press: ↵

Note: If the file name ROWS.WK1 is not displayed in the directory of file names, ask your instructor for help.

Your display screen should be similar to Figure 1-22.

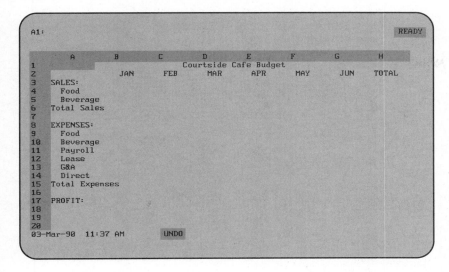

FIGURE 1-22

The current worksheet is erased from the screen and from the computer's memory. The retrieved worksheet file, ROWS.WK1, containing the row and column labels, is displayed.

To review, the command sequence used to retrieve the file ROWS.WK1 was **/F**ile **R**etrieve **ROWS.WK1** ⏎. Throughout the rest of the Lotus 1-2-3 labs, command sequences will be presented as just shown. The character(s) to type will be printed in boldface type.

Entering Values

The next step is to enter the data or values into the cells.

Remember, values can be numbers or the result of a formula or function. All values must begin with a number 0 through 9, or with any one of the **numeric symbols**: + , - , ., @, (, #, or $.

Paula has estimated that the sales of food items during the month of January will be $4,200. To enter the value 4200 into cell B4,

Move to: B4
Type: 4200

The mode indicator displays the new mode of operation as VALUE. Lotus 1-2-3 has interpreted this entry as a value because the first character entered into the cell is the number 4. Do not enter a space before a value. If you do, the cell contents will be interpreted as a label rather than a value.

Press: ⏎

Your display screen should be similar to Figure 1-23.

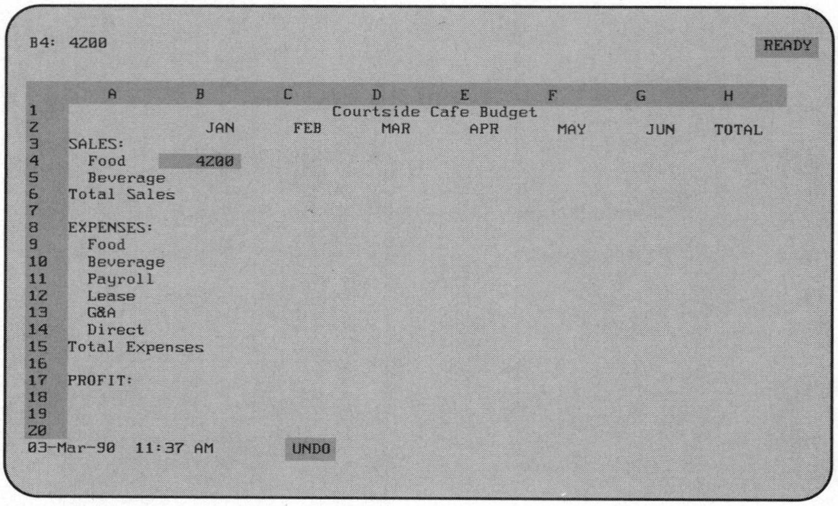

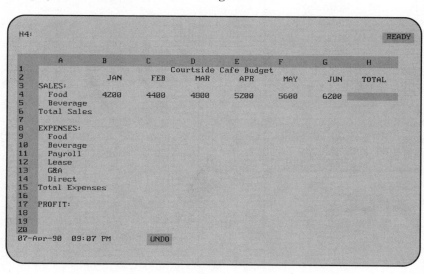

FIGURE 1-23

The value 4200 is displayed in cell B4. The value is displayed almost flush right in its cell space. One space to the right of the value is left blank. It is reserved for special numeric displays such as a ")." Unlike labels, the display of a value in a cell cannot be changed. Values are always displayed to the right side of the cell space.

To complete the data for food sales (row 4), enter the following values into the cells indicated. Use ⟶ to enter the value and move to the next cell.

> cell C4—**4400**
> cell D4—**4800**
> cell E4—**5200**
> cell F4—**5600**
> cell G4—**6200**

Your display screen should be similar to Figure 1-24.

FIGURE 1-24

Entering Formulas

A **formula** is an entry that performs a calculation. The result of the calculation is displayed in the worksheet cell. Numeric values or cell addresses can be used in a formula. If cell addresses are used, the calculation is performed using the contents of the cell addresses. As the values in the referenced cell(s) change, the value calculated by the formula is automatically recalculated. A formula is the power behind the worksheet.

Three types of formulas can be entered in a worksheet: numeric, string, and logical. You will use a numeric formula to calculate the sum of the food sales for January through June. To enter a numeric formula, the following **arithmetic operators** are used:

+   for addition

-    for subtraction

/   for division

*   for multiplication

^   for exponentiation

A formula must begin with a number or one of the numeric symbols which defines an entry as a value. If a formula begins with a cell address, the cell address must be preceded with a character that defines the cell as a value. Since the formula you will enter will sum the values in cells B4 through G4, you will use a + to begin the entry. Cell addresses can be typed in either upper- or lowercase letters. If you enter a formula incorrectly, Lotus 1-2-3 will beep and change to the EDIT mode to let you correct your entry.

The cells containing the values for food sales for January through June are cells B4 through G4. To sum the values in these cells and display the calculated value in cell H4,

Move to: H4

Type: +B4+C4+D4+E4+F4+G4

Press: ⏎

Your display screen should be similar to Figure 1-25.

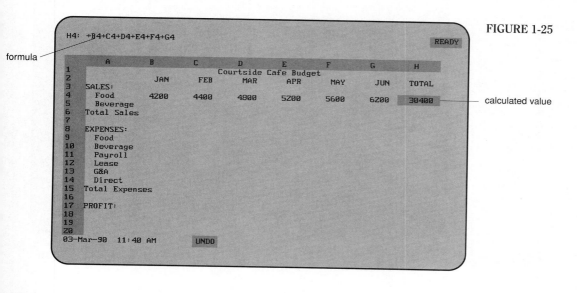

FIGURE 1-25

The formula appears in the control panel. The result of the formula, 30400, is displayed in cell H4.

The values for beverage sales need to be entered into cells B5 through G5 next.

Move to: B5
Type: 400
Press: ⏎

Notice that the label in cell A5 is now displayed as "Beverag." This is because the label exceeds the cell width of 9 spaces. The new entry in cell B5 causes the label to be interrupted after 9 characters.

Move to: A5

The control panel shows the complete row label as entered into the cell. Only the display of the label in cell A5 has been interrupted. You will learn how to change the width of a column in the next lab so that the entire label can be displayed.

Continue entering the values for beverage sales in the cells indicated:

> C5—**450**
> D5—**500**
> E5—**540**
> F5—**560**
> G5—**600**

Recalculating the Worksheet

Finally, the formula to calculate the total beverage sales needs to be entered in cell H5. It will sum the values in cells B5 through G5. Enter the formula to make this calculation in cell H5. When you are done, your display screen should be similar to Figure 1-26.

interrupted row label

FIGURE 1-26

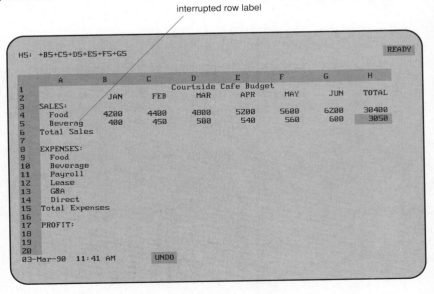

The total for beverage sales, 3050, is displayed in H5.

Paula feels that she has underestimated the beverage sales for the month of May. She wants to change this value to 580.

Move to: F5

Type: 580

Press: ⏎

The formula in cell H5 has automatically recalculated the total. The value displayed is now 3070. The automatic recalculation of a formula when a value in a referenced cell in the formula changes is one of the most powerful features of electronic worksheets. When 1-2-3 recalculates a worksheet, only those formulas directly affected by a change in the data are recalculated. This is called **minimal recalculation**. Without this feature, in large worksheets it could take several minutes to recalculate all formulas each time a value is changed in the worksheet. The minimal recalculation feature decreases the recalculation time by only recalculating affected formulas.

In the next lab you will complete the worksheet by entering the other values and formulas. Before saving the worksheet, enter your first initial and last name in cell A1. Put the date in cell A2. Don't forget to precede it with a label prefix character (for example, "9/08/91).

Saving a Worksheet

To save the current worksheet in a file on the diskette in drive B, you use the File Save command. Always save your current worksheet before retrieving another file or leaving the Lotus 1-2-3 program.

Select: / File Save

The file name of the file you retrieved, ROWS.WK1, is displayed following the prompt "File to be Saved:." The 1-2-3 program has suggested a response to this prompt by displaying the name of the file you retrieved. In response to this prompt you must specify a file name either by accepting the default name, editing the default name, or typing a new name. You will give the file a new name. To save the worksheet as it appears on the display in a new file named CAFE,

Type: CAFE

Press: ⏎

The worksheet data which was on your screen and in the computer's memory is now saved on your data diskette in a new file called CAFE.WK1. A 1-2-3 file name should not be longer than eight characters. It can include any combination of letters, numbers, underscores, and hyphens. However, it cannot contain blank spaces. It is automatically saved with the file extension .WK1. This file extension identifies this file as a worksheet file. Lotus 1-2-3 uses several different file extensions for different types of files that are created using the program.

To see a list of all the worksheet (.WK1) files on the data diskette,

Select: / File List

The first three options, Worksheet, Print, and Graph, list all files of that type in the current directory. These files are differentiated by their file extensions: .WK1, .PRN, and .PIC, respectively. The Other option lists all files regardless of the type of file in the current directory. The Linked option lists all files on the disk that are linked to the current worksheet. You will learn about these other types of files in later labs.

To display all the worksheet files,

Select: Worksheet

Your display screen should be similar to Figure 1-27.

FIGURE 1-27

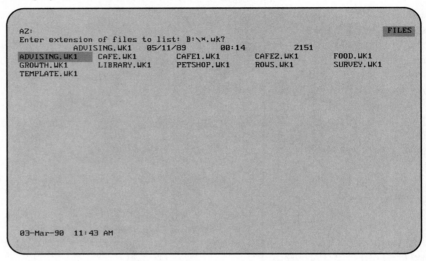

The files ROWS.WK1 and CAFE.WK1 are both listed, along with several other worksheet files you will be using in the next labs.

To return directly to the worksheet,

Press: (CTRL) - (BREAK)

The file CAFE.WK1 can be retrieved like any other worksheet file. To erase the current worksheet from the display and from the computer's memory,

Select: / Worksheet Erase

As a safety precaution, Lotus requires that you confirm that you want to erase the worksheet. Since you have already saved the current worksheet on the diskette, to confirm that you want to erase the worksheet from the screen and the computer's memory,

Type: Y

A blank worksheet screen is displayed. To retrieve the file CAFE.WK1,

Select: / File Retrieve **CAFE.WK1** ⏎

The worksheet as saved is loaded into memory and displayed. Even the cell pointer is in the cell you left it in when you saved the file.

Be very careful before erasing a worksheet, retrieving a file, or quitting Lotus 1-2-3 that you have saved the current worksheet. Otherwise your hard work will be lost.

Printing a Worksheet

If you have printer capability, you can print a copy of the worksheet. If necessary, turn the printer on and check to see that it is online. Adjust the paper so that the perforation is just above the printer scale (behind the ribbon).

Select: / Print

Two print options are displayed in the control panel, Printer and File. The output can be sent directly to a printer for immediate printing or to a file for printing later. You want to send it to the printer.

Select: Printer

Your display screen should be similar to Figure 1-28.

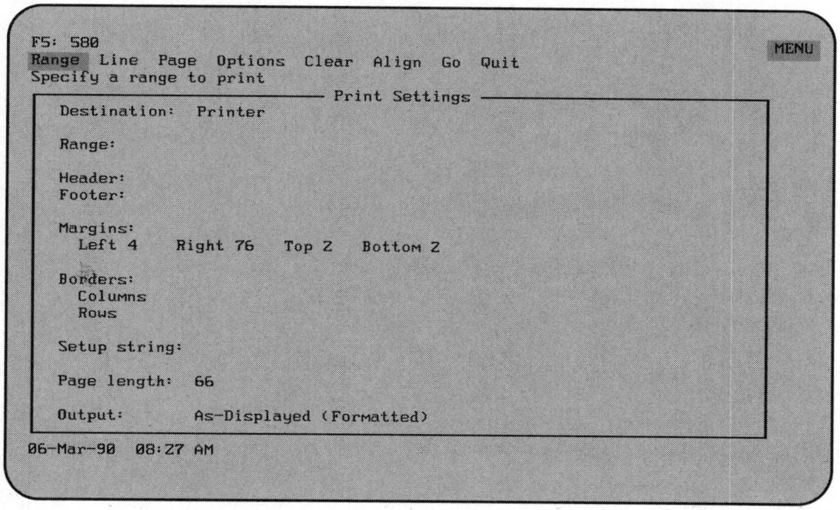

FIGURE 1-28

```
F5: 580
Range  Line  Page  Options  Clear  Align  Go  Quit                    MENU
Specify a range to print
                           ── Print Settings ──
         Destination:  Printer

         Range:

         Header:
         Footer:

         Margins:
           Left 4    Right 76   Top 2   Bottom 2

         Borders:
           Columns
           Rows

         Setup string:

         Page length:  66

         Output:      As-Displayed (Formatted)

 06-Mar-90  08:27 AM
```

The worksheet is temporarily replaced by the Print Settings sheet. As a part of many commands, 1-2-3 will display a **settings sheet** to help you keep track of the current settings for the options associated with the command you are using. To change the settings displayed in the settings sheet, you must select the appropriate commands from the menu that appears above the settings sheet. The Print Settings sheet currently displays the default print settings.There are many print settings and options available which you will use in future labs. The only print submenu command setting which must be specified is Range.

The Range option specifies the area of cells in the worksheet to be printed. You want the entire worksheet printed from cell A1 through cell H17. A **range** can be a single cell or any rectangular group of adjoining cells in the worksheet. The range is specified by entering the cell addresses of the two most distant cells in the range, separated by a period. Typically this will be the upper left corner cell (in this case, A1) and the lower right corner cell (in this case, H17) of the range.

Select: Range

The worksheet is redisplayed to let you see the range of cells you want to specify.

Type: A1.H17
Press: ⏎

The Print Settings sheet is displayed again, and the specified range has been entered following "Range" in the settings sheet.

Next, to tell the program that the alignment of the paper is at the top of the page and to begin printing,

Select: Align Go

Your printer should be printing out the worksheet. Your printed output should look like Figure 1-29.

FIGURE 1-29

	JAN	FEB	MAR	APR	MAY	JUN	TOTAL
Courtside Cafe Budget							
SALES:							
Food	4200	4400	4800	5200	5600	6200	30400
Beverag	400	450	500	540	580	600	3070
Total Sales							
EXPENSES:							
Food							
Beverage							
Payroll							
Lease							
G&A							
Direct							
Total Expenses							
PROFIT:							

When printing is finished,

Select: Page

This command advances the paper to the top of the next page.

To return to the READY mode,

Select: Quit

If you want to quit or exit the Lotus 1-2-3 program at this time,

Select: **/ Quit Yes**

The DOS prompt appears on the display screen. If it does not, follow the directions on the screen, by replacing the disk in drive A with the disk containing the COMMAND.COM file (usually your DOS disk). Remember, always save your current worksheet before quitting Lotus 1-2-3.

Key Terms

worksheet	mode	default
worksheet area	status line	long label
row	date-and-time indicator	Main menu
column	error message	menu pointer
row number	status indicator	submenu
column letter	pointer-movement keys	numeric symbols
cell	window	formula
cell pointer	scroll	arithmetic operators
current cell	prompt	minimal recalculation
control panel	label	settings sheet
cell address	value	range
mode indicator	label prefix character	

Matching

1. /   _____ **a.** moves the cell pointer to a specified cell

2. ^   _____ **b.** accesses EDIT mode

3. (F5)   _____ **c.** displays the Main menu

4. (INS)   _____ **d.** centers a label

5. .WK1   _____ **e.** a cell address

6. (F2)   _____ **f.** a number or result of a formula or function

7. +C19-A21   _____ **g.** an arithmetic operator

8. *   _____ **h.** switches between overwrite and insert

9. D11   _____ **i.** a formula subtracting two cells

10. value   _____ **j.** a worksheet file extension

Print - Ctrl-Alt , Prt Screen.

Sets up - /FDA :
on A Directory

Retrieve - /FRA :
Lotus Files

F1 - Help Key

Save File - /FS

Practice Exercises

1. Identify the parts of the worksheet screen shown below. The first item has been completed for you.

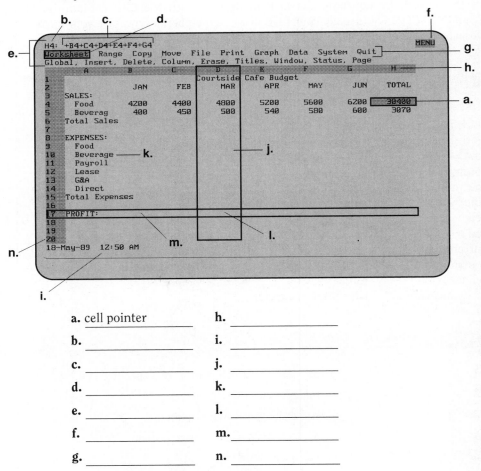

a. cell pointer _____

b. _____

c. _____

d. _____

e. _____

f. _____

g. _____

h. _____

i. _____

j. _____

k. _____

l. _____

m. _____

n. _____

2. Retrieve the worksheet file SURVEY.WK1. This worksheet contains data from a survey conducted over the years 1978 to 1986. It shows the percentage of college freshmen who expressed interest in careers in computers, education, and business. It contains many errors which you will correct as follows:

■ Change the title in cell D2 to all uppercase characters.

■ Change the title in cell D4 to Percent of College Freshmen.

■ Change the column labels in row 8 to be displayed flush right.

■ Change the values in the following cells:

    D10—5

    C14—19

    F12—5.5

    G14—24

- Check the formulas in row 16. Correct as needed.
- Enter your name in cell A1. Enter the date in cell A2.
- Save the file as SURVEY1.
- Print a copy of the file.

3. You have just finished paying off the loan on your old car and you are considering purchasing a new 1991 model car. The new car costs $12,300 and the trade-in value on your old car is $3,700. You can borrow the difference with a four-year loan of 8.9 percent. You decide to create a worksheet to help you analyze whether you should keep the old car or trade it in on a new car.

- Create the worksheet as shown below by entering the labels and values in the cells indicated. Place flush right the Old Car and New Car labels.

```
        A         B         C         D        E        F        G        H
 1   Student Name          Four Year Cost of Ownership
 2   Date                  Old Car   New Car
 3
 4   Expenses:
 5
 6   Loan payment              0      10200
 7   Gas and oil            3428       3000
 8   Insurance              2213       2403
 9   Repairs                2562       1383
10
11   Total Expenses:
12   Trade-in value:
13
14   Net cost of ownership:
15
16   Saved by not trading in:
17
18
19
20
```

- Enter the formulas to calculate the Total Expenses for the old and new cars.
- Save the worksheet as COST.
- Print the worksheet.
- You will complete this worksheet as Practice Exercise 3 in Lab 2.

4. You are the manager of Fine Things Jewelry Store. You are having a sales campaign that will reward the salesperson who has the largest average sales over a 4-week period. The winner of the contest will receive a bonus of 5 percent on all sales made during the 4 weeks. The regular percent earned is 10 percent. The campaign has been in progress 2 weeks already.

Create the following worksheet to keep track of the sales. The column labels are all flush right. Enter the formula to calculate the total sales for the 2 weeks.

```
              A         B         C         D         E         F         G         H
 1    Student Name        FINE THINGS JEWELRY STORE
 2    Date                          WEEK
 3
 4                    Week 1    Week 2    Week 3    Week 4    Total   Average   Percent
 5    Sally           1975      3608
 6    Martin          1500      5298
 7    Phillip         4295      1400
 8    Dorothy         2730      2895
 9    Alyce           4129      2568
10
11    TOTAL           14629     15769
12
13
14
15
16
17
18
19
20
```

You will complete the worksheet as Practice Exercise 1 in Lab 2. Enter your name in cell A1 and the date in cell A2. Save your completed worksheet as JEWELRY. Print a copy of the worksheet.

5. The Assistant Director of the zoo wants to prepare a financial summary for the years 1988, 1989, and 1990.

■   Create the worksheet shown below by entering the labels and values in the cells indicated. Right-align the column labels.

```
              A         B         C         D         E         F         G         H
 1    Student Name                    Zoological Society Financial Statement
 2    Date                          1988      1989      1990    TOTAL   AVERAGE
 3    Support & Revenues
 4    Operating                     5613504   6509754   7250692
 5    Fund Raising                  997676    538208    720715
 6    Supporting Org.               137070    252963    177066
 7    Interest Income               110154    154771    189723
 8    Total Support & Revenues
 9    Applications/Expenses
10    Operating                     5133565   6247933   6984207
11    Capital Projects              1150000   744631    871201
12    Fund Raising                  227640    173270    159302
13    Operating Reserve
14    Total Applications/Expenses
15
16
17
18
19
20
```

■ Edit the row labels indicated:

    A3 — All capital letters

    A4 through A7 — Enter 5 blank spaces before each label

    A8 — TOTAL S & R

    A9 — All capital letters

    A10 through A13 — Enter 5 blank spaces before each label

    A14 — TOTAL A/E

■ Enter formulas to calculate the TOTAL S & R (D8) and TOTAL A/E (D14) for 1988 only.

■ Enter the following formula in cell D13: +D8-D10-D11-D12.

■ Save the worksheet as ZOOFINAN.

■ Print the worksheet.

You will complete this worksheet as Practice Exercise 4 in Lab 2.

Creating a Worksheet: Part 2

2

OBJECTIVES

In this lab you will learn how to:

1. Copy cell contents.

2. Highlight and copy a range.

3. Enter @functions.

4. Erase cell contents.

5. Change column widths.

6. Set cell display format.

7. Insert and delete rows.

8. Use the character repeat prefix.

9. Insert and delete columns.

10. Save and replace a file.

CASE STUDY

During Lab 1 Paula Nichols, the manager of the Courtside Cafe at the Sports Club, defined the row and column labels for the cafe budget worksheet. She entered the expected food and beverage sales figures, and she entered formulas to calculate the total sales for food and beverages.

In Lab 2 you will continue to build the worksheet for the cafe. The data for the expenses needs to be entered into the worksheet. The formulas to calculate the total sales, expenses, and profit also need to be entered into the worksheet. The physical appearance of the worksheet will be improved. This will be done by adjusting column widths, inserting and deleting rows and columns, and underlining the column labels.

Using the Copy Command

Load the Lotus 1-2-3 Release 2.2 program. Your data diskette should be in the B drive (or in the appropriate drive for your computer system).

To retrieve the worksheet CAFE1.WK1,

Select: / File Retrieve **CAFE1.WK1** ⏎

Your display screen should be similar to Figure 2-1.

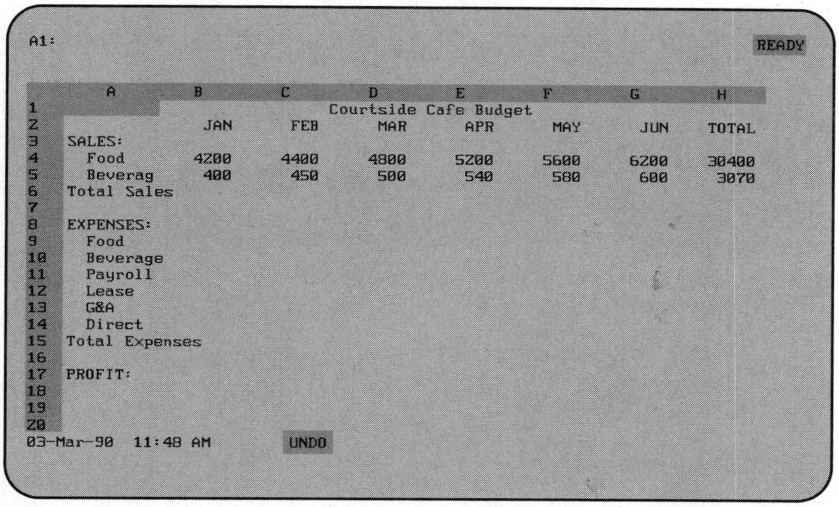

FIGURE 2-1

This worksheet should be the same as the worksheet you created in Lab 1 and saved as CAFE.WK1 on your data diskette.

Paula needs to enter the values for the expenses (rows 9 through 14) into the worksheet. The food and beverage costs are estimated by using a formula to calculate the value as a percent of sales. The remaining expenses are estimated over the 6-month period. They are the same for each month.

In Lab 1 the food and beverage sales values for January through June were entered individually into each cell because the value changed from month to month. But sometimes a value or formula in a cell is the same across several cells. Then it is faster to enter the information by using the Copy command.

Paula will begin by entering the estimated expenses for payroll first. She estimates that payroll expenses, based on the average hourly rate of pay and the number of hours needed per month to operate the cafe, will be $2,250 per month.

Move to: B11
Type: 2250
Press: ⏎

The value in cell B11 is the same value that needs to be entered in cells C11 through G11 for February through June. You could type the same amount into each month, or you could **copy** the value in B11 into the other cells. This is done using the Copy command.

To use the Copy command, with the cell pointer in cell B11,

Select: / Copy

Your display screen should be similar to Figure 2-2.

FIGURE 2-2

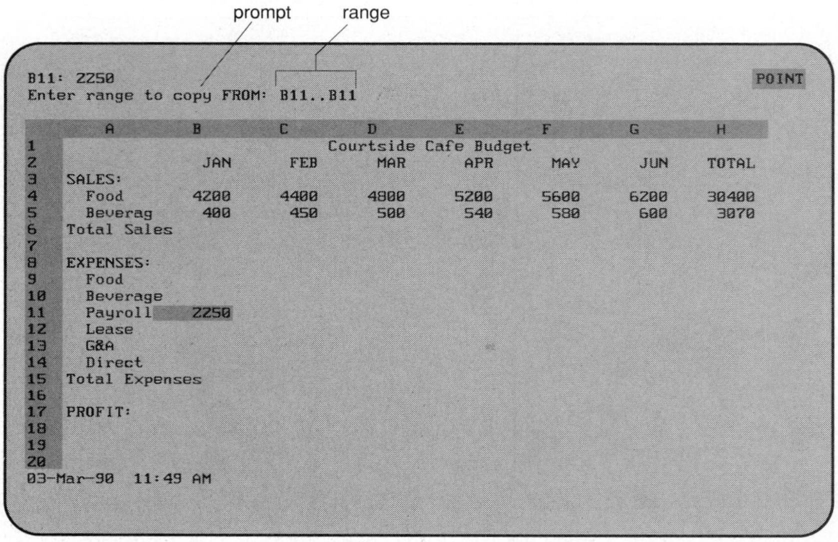

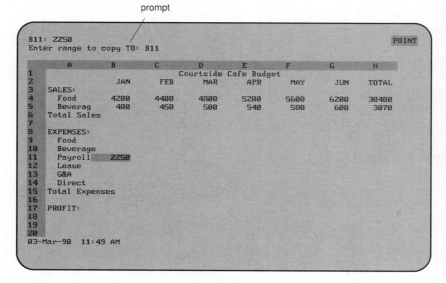

The control panel displays the prompt "Enter range to copy FROM:". Remember, a **range** is a cell or rectangular group of adjoining cells in the worksheet. The FROM range is the cell or cells whose contents you want to copy.

Following the prompt, Lotus 1-2-3 automatically enters the current cell pointer location (B11) as the default response to the prompt. Even though this is a single cell, it is displayed as a range (B11..B11). 1-2-3 always displays a range with the upper left-hand and lower right-hand cell addresses of the range separated by two periods.

If the current cell pointer position is not the cell whose contents you want to copy, you can enter the correct range following the prompt. However, since B11 is the cell whose contents you want to copy, to accept the range as displayed,

Press: ⏎

Your display screen should be similar to Figure 2-3.

FIGURE 2-3

A second prompt appears in the control panel: "Enter range to copy TO:". The range to copy TO is the cell(s) in the worksheet where you want the contents of the FROM range copied. Again 1-2-3 entered the current cell pointer position (B11) following the prompt.

Since you do not want to copy *to* B11, you need to enter the correct range, C11 through G11. To specify this range by typing in the cell addresses,

Type: C11.G11
Press: ⏎

Note: You can enter one or two periods in the range. 1-2-3 will always display a range with two periods. The cell address can be entered in either upper- or lower-case letters.

Your display screen should be similar to Figure 2-4.

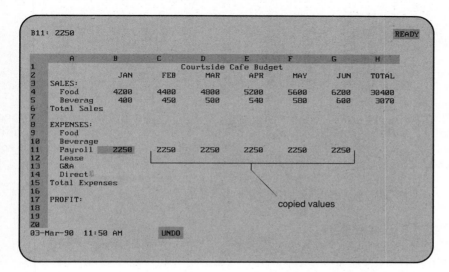

FIGURE 2-4

The value 2250 is quickly entered into cells C11 through G11. As you can see, using the Copy command is very fast. It also eliminates the possibility of typing errors.

Highlighting a Range

Next you will enter the value 500 for the lease expense for January in cell B12 and copy it across row 12 for February through June. To do this,

Move to: B12
Type: 500
Press: ⏎

To copy this value, with the cell pointer positioned in cell B12,

Select: / Copy

To accept the cell range to copy as B12,

Press:

Another way to specify a data range is by highlighting it using the POINT mode. To do this, the pointer-movement keys are used to expand the cell pointer to highlight the cell or range of cells you want to specify. Whenever 1-2-3 displays "POINT" in the mode indicator, this method can be used. To see how this works, to specify the range to copy TO, C12 through G12,

Press:

The cell pointer is positioned in cell C12. The cell address, C12, is displayed following the prompt as the first cell in the range to copy TO. Before you can highlight the range, you must **anchor** the cell pointer in the corner cell of the range. To anchor this cell,

Type: . (period)

The period stops the cell pointer from leaving cell C12 and specifies this cell as the beginning or **anchor cell** of the range. You can tell if the cell pointer is anchored by looking at how it is displayed following the prompt. If just a cell address, such as C12, is displayed, it means the cell pointer is not anchored; if, however, a range address, such as C12..C12, is displayed, it means the cell pointer is anchored. If the cell pointer is anchored in the wrong cell, press (ESC) to release it, move to the correct cell, then type a period to anchor it again.

The cell ending the range to copy TO, G12, must be entered next. To specify the range by highlighting,

Press: (→) (4 times)

Your display screen should be similar to Figure 2-5.

FIGURE 2-5

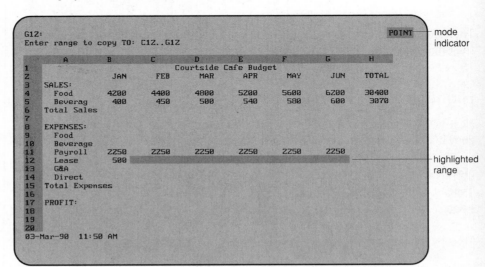

The range to copy TO is highlighted on the display screen. Each time you moved the cell pointer, the highlight bar expanded to cover the entire range of cells from the anchor cell to the cell the pointer is on. The beginning and ending cells of the range (C12..G12) are entered following the prompt in the control panel.

To enter the range as highlighted and complete the command sequence,

Press: ⏎

The value 500 is copied into cells C12 through G12. Using highlighting to specify a range is especially helpful when you have a large worksheet and the entire range is not visible on the screen. Also, highlighting avoids the entry of an incorrect range due to typing errors.

The values for G&A (General & Administrative) and direct expenses need to be entered next. For January enter the values of 175 for G&A expense and 975 for direct expenses as follows:

Move to: B13
Type: 175
Move to: B14
Type: 975
Press: ⏎

To copy the contents of cells B13 and B14 at the same time,

Select: **/ Copy**

Notice that the cell range is anchored already. To highlight the range to include cell B14,

Press: ↑
Press: ⏎

To specify the range to copy TO as the direct and G&A expenses for February through June (cells C14, the lower-left corner cell of the range, through G13, the upper-right corner cell of the range),

Move to: C14
Type: .
Move to: G13
Press: ⏎

Your display screen should be similar to Figure 2-6.

FIGURE 2-6

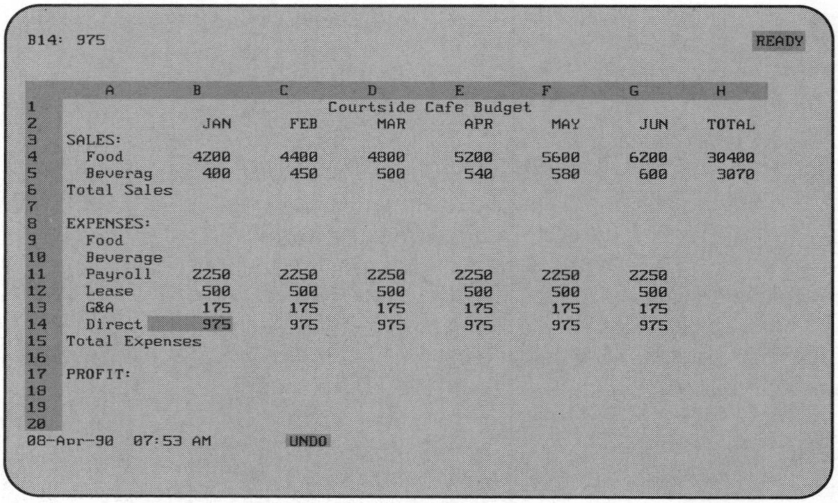
B14: 975 READY

	A	B	C	D	E	F	G	H
1				Courtside Cafe Budget				
2		JAN	FEB	MAR	APR	MAY	JUN	TOTAL
3	SALES:							
4	Food	4200	4400	4800	5200	5600	6200	30400
5	Beverag	400	450	500	540	580	600	3070
6	Total Sales							
7								
8	EXPENSES:							
9	Food							
10	Beverage							
11	Payroll	2250	2250	2250	2250	2250	2250	
12	Lease	500	500	500	500	500	500	
13	G&A	175	175	175	175	175	175	
14	Direct	975	975	975	975	975	975	
15	Total Expenses							
16								
17	PROFIT:							
18								
19								
20								

08-Apr-90 07:53 AM UNDO

The values for January G&A and direct expenses (cells B13 and B14) were quickly copied into the February through June G&A and direct expense cells (C13 through G13 and C14 through G14.)

Copying Formulas

The final two expenses that need to be entered into the worksheet are for food and beverage expenses. Paula has estimated that the cost of food and beverage supplies will be 30 percent of sales each month.

The formulas to calculate these values are:

Food expense = monthly food sales * 30%

Beverage expense = monthly beverage sales * 30%

To enter the formula to calculate the food expense for January,

Move to: B9
Type: **+B4*30%**
Press: ↵

The calculated value of 1260 is displayed in cell B9, and the formula is displayed in the control panel. 1-2-3 automatically converts the percentage in the formula to its decimal equivilant. You could also have entered .30 instead of 30% and the same result would be calculated.

The formulas to calculate the February through June food expenses (C9 through G9) need to be entered next. **Copy the formula from the January expense cell (B9) to make these calculations, using highlighting to specify the range.**

The calculated values are displayed in the specified cell range. Let's look at the formulas as they were copied into the cells.

Move to: C9

Your display screen should be similar to Figure 2-7.

FIGURE 2-7

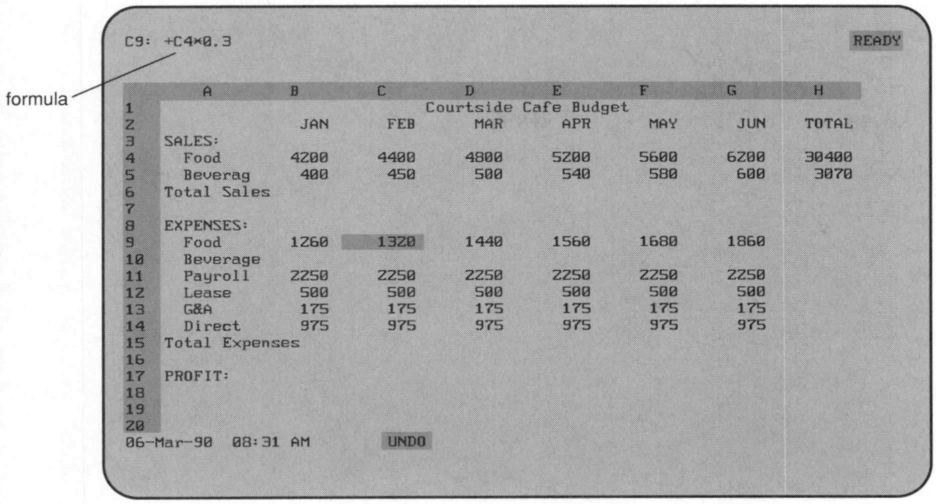

The value 1320 is displayed in the cell. Look at the formula displayed in the control panel. It is +C4*.3. The formula to calculate the February food expense is not an exact duplicate of the formula used to calculate the January food expense (+B4*.3). Instead, the cell address referenced in the formula has been changed to reflect the new column location. This is because the formula uses a **relative cell reference**. A relative cell reference is a cell or range address in a formula whose location is interpreted by 1-2-3 as relative to the cell that contains the formula. When the formula in B9 was copied, the referenced cell in the formula was automatically adjusted to reflect the new column location so that the relative relationship between the referenced cell and the new column location is maintained.

Look at the formulas as they appear in the control panel as you move to cells D9 through G9. The formula has changed to reflect the new column location in each, and it appropriately calculates the value based on the food sales for each month.

The same formula will be used to calculate beverage expenses. This formula, however, will take the monthly beverage sales values in row 5 and multiply them by 30 percent. You could enter the formula in cell B10 as +B5*30% and then copy it across row 10. Instead you will copy the formula used to calculate the January food expense (B9) to calculate the January through June beverage expenses (B10 through G10) in one step.

Move to: B9

Copy the formula in the January food expense cell to the January thorugh June beverage expense cells, using highlighting to specify the range.

Let's look at how the formulas in these cells have adjusted relative to their new location in the worksheet.

Move to: B10

Your display screen should be similar to Figure 2-8.

```
B10: +B5*0.3                                                          READY

            A        B        C        D        E        F        G        H
  1                           Courtside Cafe Budget
  2                  JAN      FEB      MAR      APR      MAY      JUN      TOTAL
  3   SALES:
  4      Food       4200     4400     4800     5200     5600     6200     30400
  5      Beverag     400      450      500      540      580      600      3070
  6   Total Sales
  7
  8   EXPENSES:
  9      Food       1260     1320     1440     1560     1680     1860
 10      Beverag     120      135      150      162      174      180
 11      Payroll    2250     2250     2250     2250     2250     2250
 12      Lease       500      500      500      500      500      500
 13      G&A         175      175      175      175      175      175
 14      Direct      975      975      975      975      975      975
 15   Total Expenses
 16
 17   PROFIT:
 18
 19
 20
 06-Mar-90  08:32 AM          UNDO
```

FIGURE 2-8

The value 120 is displayed in the cell as the cost of beverages. The formula in the control panel has been adjusted relative to the new row. It correctly calculates the value based on the contents of the referenced cell, January beverage sales (B5). **Move across the row and look at how the formulas have been adjusted to reflect both the new row and column location.**

All the expenses have been entered into the worksheet. The total for sales and expenses can be calculated now.

The formula to calculate total sales for January (+B4+B5) needs to be entered in cell B6. Highlighting can also be used to specify the cells in a formula. To do this,

Move to: B6
Type: +

To extend the cell pointer to the cell containing the January food sales, cell B4,

Press: ⬆ (2 times)

Cell B4 is entered following the + sign in the control panel. The mode indicator displays "POINT." To continue the formula, the next operator is entered.

Type: +

The cell pointer returns to the cell in which you entered the formula. To move the cell pointer to the cell containing the January beverage sales, cell B5,

Press: ⬆

Then to complete the formula,

Press: ⏎

The calculated value of 4600 is displayed in cell B6. The formula +B4+B5 is displayed in the control panel. **Copy the formula in this cell to calculate the total sales values for February through June, using highlighting to specify the range.**

Your display screen should be similar to Figure 2-9.

FIGURE 2-9

```
B6:  +B4+B5                                                    READY

          A         B        C        D        E        F        G        H
                                Courtside Cafe Budget
1
2                   JAN      FEB      MAR      APR      MAY      JUN      TOTAL
3      SALES:
4         Food      4200     4400     4800     5200     5600     6200     30400
5         Beverag    400      450      500      540      580      600      3070
6      Total Sal    4600     4850     5300     5740     6180     6800
7
8      EXPENSES:
9         Food      1260     1320     1440     1560     1680     1860
10        Beverag    120      135      150      162      174      180
11        Payroll   2250     2250     2250     2250     2250     2250
12        Lease      500      500      500      500      500      500
13        G&A        175      175      175      175      175      175
14        Direct     975      975      975      975      975      975
15     Total Expenses
16
17     PROFIT:
18
19
20
03-Mar-90   11:55 AM          UNDO
```

Entering an @Function

Next the formula to calculate the total expenses for January needs to be entered in the worksheet in cell B15 and copied across the row through June.

Move to: B15

You could use a formula similar to the formulas used to calculate the total food and beverage sales (H4 and H5). The formula would be +B9+B10+B11+B12+B13+B14. But there is a shorter way to write this formula.

1-2-3 has a set of built-in formulas called **@functions** ("at functions") that perform certain types of calculations automatically. The @function you will use to calculate a sum of a range of cells is @SUM (list). Let's take a moment to look at the way this function is written.

The structure, or **syntax**, of an @function is:

@function name (argument1, argument2...)

All @functions begin with the @ ("at") character, followed by the function name. After the function name may come one or more **arguments** enclosed in parentheses. An argument is the data the @function uses to perform the calculation. It can be a number, a cell address, or a range of cells.

In the @SUM (list) function, "SUM" is the @function name, and "list" is the argument. The term **list** means an individual cell, a range of cells, or a combination of these, each separated by a comma. A list is one of many different arguments that may be required by the @function.

The @function can be entered in either upper- or lowercase characters. There is no space between the @ sign and the @function name or between the @function name and the arguments. Like a formula, if you incorrectly enter an @function,

Lotus 1-2-3 will beep and change to the EDIT mode to allow you to correct your entry. Alternatively, you could press (ESC) to clear the entry and retype it correctly.

To enter the @function to calculate the total expenses for January in cell B15, using highlighting to specify the range,

Type:	**@SUM(**
Move to:	B9
Type:	.
Move to:	B14
Type:	)
Press:	⏎

The value 5280, calculated by the @function, is displayed in cell B15.

Copy the @function in the January total expense cell to the February through June total expense cells, using highlighting to specify the range.

The calculated values for the total expenses for January through June are displayed in cells C15 through G15 as specified.

Move to: C15

Your screen should be similar to Figure 2-10.

@function

FIGURE 2-10

```
C15: @SUM(C9..C14)                                                    READY

         A          B         C         D         E         F         G         H
 1                           Courtside Cafe Budget
 2                  JAN       FEB       MAR       APR       MAY       JUN       TOTAL
 3      SALES:
 4        Food     4200      4400      4800      5200      5600      6200      30400
 5        Beverag   400       450       500       540       580       600       3070
 6      Total Sal  4600      4850      5300      5740      6180      6800
 7
 8      EXPENSES:
 9        Food     1260      1320      1440      1560      1680      1860
10        Beverag   120       135       150       162       174       180
11        Payroll  2250      2250      2250      2250      2250      2250
12        Lease     500       500       500       500       500       500
13        G&A       175       175       175       175       175       175
14        Direct    975       975       975       975       975       975
15      Total Exp  5280      5355      5490      5622      5754      5940
16
17      PROFIT:
18
19
20
03-Mar-90   11:56 AM            UNDO
```

The value 5355 is displayed in the cell. Look at the @function as displayed in the control panel. It is @SUM(C9..C14). When an @function is copied, it is adjusted relative to the new cell location just like a formula.

Now that the total sales and expenses are calculated, the formula to calculate profit can be entered in cell B17 and copied across the row through G17. The formula to calculate profit is the difference between monthly total expenses and monthly total sales.

In the January profit cell (B17), enter the formula +B6-B15, using highlighting to specify the cell addresses. Then copy the formula to calculate the February through June profits, using highlighting to specify the range.

Your display screen should be similar to Figure 2-11.

FIGURE 2-11

The profit for January, February, and March shows a loss. Paula is not too concerned about this. In the first few months of operation of the new cafe she does not expect to make a profit.

Using the Erase Command

Finally, the @function to calculate the total sales over the 6 months, @SUM(B6.G6), needs to be entered in cell H6. This @function can then be copied to calculate the total expenses in cells H9 through H17.

Move to: H6

Enter the @function to make this calculation, using highlighting to specify the range. Copy it to calculate the total expenses in cells H9 through H17, using highlighting to specify the range. Your display screen should be similar to Figure 2-12.

FIGURE 2-12

Move to: H16

Look at the contents of cell H16. It displays a zero. The @function was copied into a cell that references empty cells. The command to erase, or remove, the contents of a cell or range of cells is an option under the Range command. To erase the @function from cell H16,

Select: **/ R**ange

The eleven /Range commands affect specific cells or ranges of cells. You will be using many of these commands in the next lab.

Select: Erase

The prompt "Enter range to erase:" is displayed in the control panel. As in the Copy command, the range (H16..H16) entered following the prompt is the current location of the cell pointer. To accept the range,

Press: ⏎

The @function is erased from the cell and consequently the value 0 is no longer displayed in the cell. Highlighting can also be used to specify a range of cells whose contents you may want to erase. Do not remove the contents of a cell by entering a blank space. If you do this, although the cell appears empty, it still contains the label prefix character and the cell is considered occupied.

Changing Column Widths

The worksheet is complete. However, Paula wants to improve the appearance of the worksheet. She can do this by adjusting the column widths, inserting and deleting blank rows and columns, using underlining, and displaying dollar signs and commas.

After entering the values for January in column B, many of the long labels in column A were interrupted because they were longer than the 9 spaces available. To allow the long labels to be fully displayed, you can increase the **column width** of column A.

To change the width of an individual column or a range of columns, the Worksheet Column command is used. Begin by positioning the cell pointer anywhere in the column whose width you want to change. You will move to cell A15 which contains the longest label in column A.

Move to: A15
Select: **/ W**orksheet

Ten Worksheet submenu commands are displayed in the second line of the control panel. The Worksheet commands let you control the display and organization of the worksheet. The command you want to use to change the width of specified columns in the worksheet is Column.

Select: Column

Five Column submenu commands are displayed in the control panel. They have the following effects:

Set-Width   specifies the width of the column that contains the cell pointer

Reset-Width   returns the current column width to the default width of 9 spaces

Hide   hides one or more columns to prevent them from being displayed and printed

Display   redisplays hidden columns

Column-Range   changes the width of a range of columns

The quickest way to change the width of a single column is to use the Set-Width command.

Select: Set-Width

The prompt asks you to enter the number of spaces you want to make the new column width. The current width, 9, is displayed following the prompt. The column width can be any value from 1 to 240. If you know the width you want to change the column to, you can simply type in the value following the prompt. However, if you are not sure how much you need to increase the column width, you can press the ⟶ or ⟵ key to increase or decrease the column width. To increase the column width,

Press: ⟶ (slowly 5 times)

Each time ⟶ is pressed, the width of column A expands one space, the value following the prompt increases by one, and the columns to the right of the current column move to the right one space. The label "Total Expenses" is fully displayed in the cell space, and the prompt displays 14 as the column width.

Press: ⟵

Your display screen should be similar to Figure 2-13.

column width
setting
14
spaces

FIGURE 2-13

A15: [W14] 'Total Expenses   READY

	A	B	C	D	E	F	G
1			Courtside Cafe Budget			
2		JAN	FEB	MAR	APR	MAY	JUN
3	SALES:						
4	Food	4200	4400	4800	5200	5600	6200
5	Beverage	400	450	500	540	580	600
6	Total Sales	4600	4850	5300	5740	6180	6800
7							
8	EXPENSES:						
9	Food	1260	1320	1440	1560	1680	1860
10	Beverage	120	135	150	162	174	180
11	Payroll	2250	2250	2250	2250	2250	2250
12	Lease	500	500	500	500	500	500
13	G&A	175	175	175	175	175	175
14	Direct	975	975	975	975	975	975
15	Total Expenses	5280	5355	5490	5622	5754	5940
16							
17	PROFIT:	-680	-505	-190	118	426	860
18							
19							
20							

03-Mar-90 12:01 PM   UNDO

Notice that the new column width setting, [W14], is displayed in the control panel following the cell address. Also notice that the Total column, column H, is no longer visible in the window. It was pushed to the right to make space for the increased width of column A.

To bring the Total column back into view in the window, you will decrease the column widths of all other columns in the workhsheet. To do this,

Select: / Worksheet Global

Your screen should be similar to Figure 2-14.

FIGURE 2-14

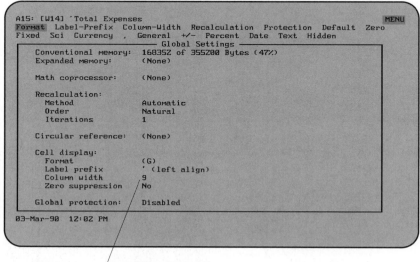

current global column width

The worksheet has been replaced by the Global Settings sheet. Like the Print Settings sheet you saw in Lab 1, the Global Settings sheet is used to help you keep track of the current settings for the options associated with the command you are using. The Global Settings sheet displays the current global settings for the worksheet. **Global** settings are settings that affect the entire worksheet. The setting you want to change is the column width. The Global Settings sheet shows that the current setting for all columns in the worksheet (except those set using the / Worksheet Column command) is 9.

To change the global column width setting, continue the command sequence as follows.

Select: Column-Width

The worksheet is redisplayed. The prompt "Enter global column width (1..240):" is displayed. To decrease the column width to 8 and see the effect on the worksheet display,

Press: ⬅

The Total column is now visible in the window. Paula wants to see how narrow she can make the columns. To decrease the column widths even more,

Press: ⬅ (3 times)

Your display should be similar to Figure 2-15.

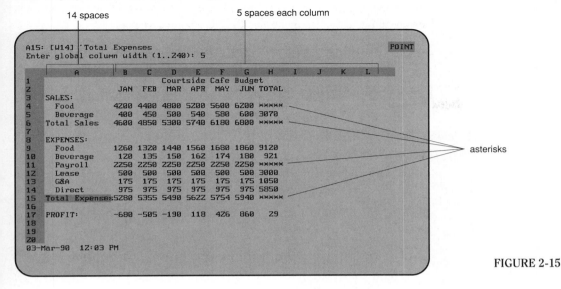

FIGURE 2-15

A series of asterisks (*****) is displayed in cells H4, H6, H11, and H15. Whenever the width of a cell is too small to display the entire value in that cell, a series of asterisks is displayed. To increase the column width back to 7,

Press: ⟶ (2 times)

Paula thinks this column width setting looks pretty good. To complete the command,

Press: ⟵

All column widths have changed to 7 except for column A, which was set using the Worksheet Column Set-Width command to 14 spaces. The Worksheet command settings always override the Worksheet Global command settings. To see the change in the Global Settings sheet,

Select: / Worksheet Global

The Global Settings sheet shows the new global column width of 7. To cancel this command and return to the READY mode,

Press: (CTRL) - (BREAK)

Formatting a Value

Next Paula wants to improve the appearance or **format** of values in the worksheet. The format of values can be changed using the Worksheet Global Format command. Since this is a global command, it will affect all worksheet cells.

Select: / Worksheet Global Format

The Global Settings sheet shows the default format setting is General (G). The 10 format options are listed in the control panel. For an explanation of these options, use the Help system.

Press: F1

The first Help screen discusses cell formats in general. To see a Help screen on numeric formats,

Move to: Numeric Formats
Press: ⏎

The two Format options Paula wants to try are Comma and Currency. After reading this screen of information, return to the worksheet.

Press: ESC

First Paula wants to see how the comma (,) format will look. To change the worksheet format to this setting,

Select: ,

The prompt in the control panel asks you to specify the number of decimal places you want displayed. To specify no decimal places,

Type: 0
Press: ⏎

Your display screen should be similar to Figure 2-16.

FIGURE 2-16

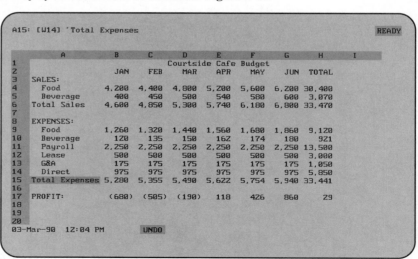

The values in the worksheet are displayed with commas where appropriate and no decimal places. Also notice the use of parentheses in cells C19, D19, and E19 to show that they contain negative values.

Next Paula wants to see how the worksheet would look with the format set to Currency. This option will display dollar signs, commas, and decimal places.

Select: / **W**orksheet **G**lobal **F**ormat **C**urrency

The prompt in the control panel asks you to specify the number of decimal places you want displayed. To display 0 decimal places,

Type: 0

Press: ⏎

Your screen should be similar to Figure 2-17.

FIGURE 2-17

```
A15: [W14] 'Total Expenses                                           READY

         A         B       C       D       E       F       G       H      I
1                         Courtside Cafe Budget
2                  JAN     FEB     MAR     APR     MAY     JUN    TOTAL
3    SALES:
4      Food      $4,200  $4,400  $4,800  $5,200  $5,600  $6,200  *******
5      Beverage   $400    $450    $500    $540    $580    $600   $3,070
6    Total Sales $4,600  $4,850  $5,300  $5,740  $6,180  $6,800  *******
7
8    EXPENSES:
9      Food      $1,260  $1,320  $1,440  $1,560  $1,680  $1,860  $9,120
10     Beverage   $120    $135    $150    $162    $174    $180    $921
11     Payroll   $2,250  $2,250  $2,250  $2,250  $2,250  $2,250  *******
12     Lease      $500    $500    $500    $500    $500    $500   $3,000
13     G&A        $175    $175    $175    $175    $175    $175   $1,050
14     Direct     $975    $975    $975    $975    $975    $975   $5,850
15   Total Expenses$5,280 $5,355  $5,490  $5,622  $5,754  $5,940 *******
16
17   PROFIT:     ($680)  ($505)  ($190)   $118    $426    $860    $29
18
19
20
08-Apr-90  08:35 AM         UNDO
```

Now the worksheet displays dollar signs and commas in all cells displaying a value. However, a series of asterisks appears in many of the cells. This indicates that the cell width is too small to fully display the value. The additional characters used to display currency (dollar sign and comma) have caused this problem. Before changing the column width, Paula wants to decide which format she prefers. You can switch back and forth between the two formats using the UNDO feature.

Note: Consult your instructor if UNDO is not displayed in the status line.

Press: ALT - F4

The comma format is displayed. To see the currency format again,

Press: ALT - F4

The UNDO feature is useful not only for undoing errors but for switching back and forth between two worksheet settings. You will recall that the UNDO feature works by creating a temporary backup copy of the worksheet each time you begin a command, start an entry, or use certain function keys that affect the worksheet data. The backup copy is stored in memory. When you use UNDO, it displays the worksheet that was stored in memory. Since 1-2-3 does not wait until the command or entry is complete before backing up the worksheet, you must use the UNDO feature immediately after executing the command or making the entry that you want to undo. A backup worksheet is not created if the key you press does not cause a change in worksheet data.

The UNDO feature is an important safeguard against mistakes that may take a lot of time to fix. However, be careful when using this command as you may get some unexpected results.

After looking at the two different formats of the worksheet, Paula decides she likes the currency format best after all. The currency format should be displayed on your screen.

Now she needs to increase the column width to allow display of all the values in their cells. To take a look at how these values are displayed, move the cell pointer to the last-used cell in the row, H15, as follows.

Press: (END)
Press: (→)

The formula used to calculate the total expenses for 6 months is displayed in the control panel. In order for the calculated value to be displayed, the width of the cell needs to be increased. Additionally, Paula thinks the columns look crowded because of the extra space required to display the currency format. To increase the width of columns B through H, the Worksheet Column Column-Range command is used.

Select: / Worksheet Column Column-Range Set-Width

In response to the prompt in the control panel you must specify the range of columns whose width you want to change. In response to the prompt, 1-2-3 displays the cell address of the current cell as the default response to range. Notice that the default response is anchored already.

To specify the range of columns, any row can be used. **Since the cell pointer is already on row 15, use highlighting to specify columns B through H as the range.**

The default response was cleared and the new range is displayed following the prompt.

To increase the column width,

Press: (→)

The width of columns B through H each changed to 8 spaces, and the values in cells H4, H6, H11, and H15 are fully displayed.

Press: (↵)

The new column width setting, [W8], is displayed in the control panel because the width of these columns was changed using the Worksheet Column command. The column width for all columns to the right of column H remain at 7 spaces, as they were set using the Global Column-Width command and were not changed when the Worksheet Column Column-Range command was used.

Inserting Rows

The appearance of the worksheet is greatly improved already. However, Paula still feels that it looks crowded. She wants a blank row entered below the worksheet title as row 2.

To insert a blank row into the worksheet, begin by moving the cell pointer to the row where the new blank row will be inserted.

Move to: H2

Select: **/ Worksheet Insert Row** ⏎

Your display screen should be similar to Figure 2-18.

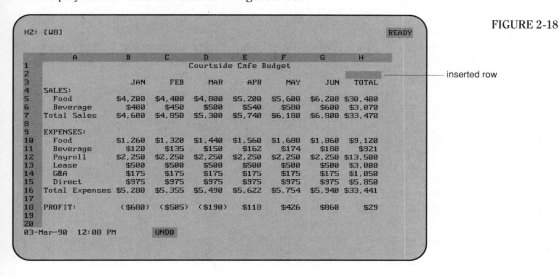

FIGURE 2-18

— inserted row

A new blank row has been inserted into the worksheet at the cell pointer location. Everything below row 2 has moved down one row. All formulas and functions have been automatically adjusted to their new row locations.

Next Paula wants to enter a blank row below the column labels. Then she will be able to underline the column labels.

Move to: H4

Insert a blank row in row 4. The rows below row 4 have moved down one row to make space for the blank row. All formulas and functions have again been readjusted.

To delete a row, use the same procedure, except select Delete rather than Insert. Be very careful when using the Delete option because any information in the range specified will be deleted.

Using the Repeat Label Prefix Character

Paula would like the month labels to be offset from the worksheet values by a series of underline characters.

To underline the column heading "TOTAL," with the cell pointer in cell H4, press the minus sign character 8 times as follows:

Type: ` - - - - - - - - `

Notice the mode indicator displays "VALUE."

Press: ⏎

The computer beeped and placed the worksheet in the EDIT mode. This is because Lotus 1-2-3 has determined that this is not a valid cell entry and wants you to edit the cell contents.

The first character entered into this cell was a minus sign. This character defined the cell entry as a value. A series of minus signs is not a valid numeric entry. If you want a character that Lotus 1-2-3 interprets as a value to be interpreted as a label, precede it by an apostrophe.

To correct this entry,

Press: (HOME)
Type: '
Press: ⏎

A series of underline characters fills the cell.

Another way to fill a cell with a repeated character is by using the fourth label prefix character, a backslash (\).

Move to: G4
Type: \

To specify the character to be used to fill the cell,

Type: -
Press: ⏎

The character following the \ fills the entire cell width. It was not necessary to enter an apostrophe before the minus character because the \ defined the cell contents as a label. The backslash can be used to fill a cell with any repeated characters.

Using the Copy command, underline the January through May column labels.

Your display screen should be similar to Figure 2-19.

prefix character

```
G4: [W8] \-                                                         READY

             A        B       C       D       E       F       G       H
 1                               Courtside Cafe Budget
 2
 3                    JAN     FEB     MAR     APR     MAY     JUN    TOTAL
 4
 5  SALES:
 6     Food        $4,200  $4,400  $4,800  $5,200  $5,600  $6,200 $30,400
 7     Beverage      $400    $450    $500    $540    $580    $600  $3,070
 8  Total Sales   $4,600  $4,850  $5,300  $5,740  $6,180  $6,800 $33,470
 9
10  EXPENSES:
11     Food        $1,260  $1,320  $1,440  $1,560  $1,680  $1,860  $9,120
12     Beverage      $120    $135    $150    $162    $174    $180    $921
13     Payroll     $2,250  $2,250  $2,250  $2,250  $2,250  $2,250 $13,500
14     Lease         $500    $500    $500    $500    $500    $500  $3,000
15     G&A           $175    $175    $175    $175    $175    $175  $1,050
16     Direct        $975    $975    $975    $975    $975    $975  $5,850
17  Total Expenses $5,280  $5,355  $5,490  $5,622  $5,754  $5,940 $33,441
18
19  PROFIT:       ($680)  ($505)  ($190)   $118    $426    $860     $29
20
03-Mar-90  12:10 PM        UNDO
```

FIGURE 2-19

Inserting Columns

Next Paula wants to separate the row labels from the months by inserting a blank column between column A and column B. The blank column will be column B.

Move to: B4

Select: **/W**orksheet **I**nsert **C**olumn ⏎

Your display screen should be similar to Figure 2-20.

inserted column

FIGURE 2-20

```
B4:                                                                 READY

             A        B      C       D       E       F       G       H
 1                               Courtside Cafe Budget
 2
 3                           JAN     FEB     MAR     APR     MAY     JUN
 4
 5  SALES:
 6     Food               $4,200  $4,400  $4,800  $5,200  $5,600  $6,200
 7     Beverage             $400    $450    $500    $540    $580    $600
 8  Total Sales          $4,600  $4,850  $5,300  $5,740  $6,180  $6,800
 9
10  EXPENSES:
11     Food               $1,260  $1,320  $1,440  $1,560  $1,680  $1,860
12     Beverage             $120    $135    $150    $162    $174    $180
13     Payroll            $2,250  $2,250  $2,250  $2,250  $2,250  $2,250
14     Lease                $500    $500    $500    $500    $500    $500
15     G&A                  $175    $175    $175    $175    $175    $175
16     Direct               $975    $975    $975    $975    $975    $975
17  Total Expenses        $5,280  $5,355  $5,490  $5,622  $5,754  $5,940
18
19  PROFIT:               ($680)  ($505)  ($190)   $118    $426    $860
20
03-Mar-90  12:10 PM        UNDO
```

A blank column has been inserted into the worksheet as column B.

Notice that the Total column, I, is no longer visible on the display. The inserted column forced it to the right of the window.

To see the rest of the worksheet, using the ⟶ key,

Move to: I4

Your display screen should be similar to Figure 2-21.

FIGURE 2-21

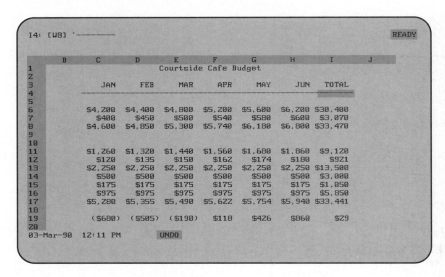

Column I is now visible on the display, but the row labels in column A are not. This makes reading the worksheet difficult, since it is hard to know what the figures mean. You will learn how to handle a worksheet that is larger than a window in the next lab.

A column can also be deleted using the same procedure, except the Delete option is selected rather than Insert. Again, be careful when deleting a column that you do not accidentally delete a column of important information.

Before saving and printing the worksheet, enter your name in cell A1 and the date in cell A2.

Saving and Replacing a File

Whenever you are finished working on a file, be sure to save the current version of the file displayed on the screen to the diskette. If you retrieve another file or leave the Lotus 1-2-3 program without saving the current version of the worksheet, you will lose all your hard work.

When you save a worksheet file you will either give the worksheet a new file name or write over the contents of an existing worksheet file using an old file name.

Before Lotus 1-2-3 saves any worksheet files, it checks to see whether the file name already exists on the diskette. If it does not exist, the worksheet is automatically saved with the new file name. If it does exist, the program asks you to specify whether you want to replace (write over) the contents of the old file with the current worksheet.

You no longer need the file you created at the end of Lab 1, CAFE.WK1. So you will reuse the file name and replace the file contents with the current worksheet.

Select: / File Save

The current worksheet file name, CAFE1.WK1, is displayed after the prompt. To enter a different file name,

Type: CAFE
Press: ⏎

The 1-2-3 program checked the diskette and found that another file already exists with the file name CAFE.WK1. The prompt in the control panel displays three options:

Cancel	returns 1-2-3 to READY mode without saving the worksheet. You can then reissue the command to save the file using a new file name.
Replace	writes over the worksheet file on disk with a copy of the current worksheet.
Backup	saves the current worksheet using the existing file name and creates a backup copy of the existing file on disk, using the same file name but with the file extension .BAK.

Select: Replace

The file is saved as CAFE.WK1. The Cancel and Replace options are a protection against accidentally writing over a file with the same name.

Printing a File

If you have printer capability, you can print a copy of the worksheet. First turn the printer on and check to see that it is online. Adjust the paper so that the perforation is just above the printer scale.

Press: (HOME)
Select: / Print Printer Range

The entire worksheet range can be specified using highlighting. To anchor the current cell and move the cell pointer to the last used cell in the worksheet,

Type: .
Press: (END)
Press: (HOME)

The range A1..I19 is entered following the prompt.

Press: ⏎

Next, to tell 1-2-3 that the paper is aligned with the top of the page and to begin printing,

Select: Align Go

After the worksheet is printed, to advance the page and leave the print menu,

Select: Page Quit

Your printout requires two pages to display the entire width of the worksheet. In the next lab you will learn how to print a large worksheet on one page.

If you are ready to leave Lotus 1-2-3, issue the Quit command.

Key Terms

copy	argument
anchor	list
anchor cell	column width
relative cell reference	global
@function	format
syntax	

Matching

1. @   _____ **a.** globally sets column width

2. \   _____ **b.** inserts a column

3. POINT   _____ **c.** erases a range of cells

4. / C   _____ **d.** indicates insufficient cell width

5. @AVG(list)   _____ **e.** method of entering cell range

6. / R E   _____ **f.** character used at the beginning of an "at" function

7. / W G C   _____ **g.** moves cursor to last-used cell

8. / W I C   _____ **h.** fills cell with repeated character

9. *********   _____ **i.** averages a range of cells

10. (END) - (HOME)   _____ **j.** copies the contents of a cell or a range of cells

Practice Exercises

1.   To complete this problem you must have created the worksheet in Lab 1, Practice Exercise 4. If you have done so already, retrieve the file JEWELRY.WK1. You will continue to build the worksheet for the jewelry store sales campaign. Enter the following sales figures:

	Week 3	Week 4
Sally	2275	3602
Martin	1898	5900
Phillip	3342	4688
Dorothy	4198	4975
Alyce	3604	2800

■   Copy the weekly total formula in cell C11 to cells D11 through H11.

- Enter @functions to calculate the total sales and average sales for each salesperson.

- The winner of the contest is the salesperson with the largest average sales over the 4 weeks. That person will earn 15 percent on their total sales. All other salespersons will earn 10 percent on their total sales. Enter the formulas to calculate the appropriate percent earned.

- Enter the current date in cell A2. Save the worksheet as JEWELRY.

- Print the worksheet.

2. To complete this problem you must have completed Practice Exercise 1 above. Retrieve the file JEWELRY.WK1. You will improve the appearance of this worksheet by inserting rows, changing column widths, and displaying currency.

- Insert a blank row at row 1. Insert another blank row below the worksheet title. Finally, insert two blank rows below the column headings for the weeks.

- Underline the column heading in row 6.

- Globally format the worksheet to display currency with 2 decimal places.

- Increase the column widths of the range of columns necessary to fully display the values.

- Move your name to cell A1.

- Erase the date from A4.

- Enter the current date in cell A2. Save the worksheet as CONTEST.

- Print the worksheet.

3. To complete this problem you must have created the worksheet in Practice Exercise 2 of Lab 1. Retrieve the file COST.WK1. You will continue to build the worksheet for the cost analysis of purchasing a new car versus keeping the old car.

- Enter the trade-in value for the old car as 924 and for the new car as 4637 after 4 years of ownership.

- Enter the formula to calculate the net cost of ownership for the old car. This formula is the difference between the total expenses and the trade-in value. Copy this formula to calculate the net cost of ownership for the new car.

- Enter a formula to calculate the "Saved by not trading in" value. This formula is the difference between the net cost of ownership for the old and new car. This value should be displayed in the old-car column.

- Format the worksheet to display currency with 2 decimal places. If necessary, increase the column width globally to fully display all values.

- Insert a blank row below the worksheet title and the column headings. Delete row 7.

- Underline the column headings. Enter underline in cell B11 and C11. Enter double underline (use the = character) in cell B14 and C14.

- Increase the column width of A to completely display all row labels. Right-align the labels in cells A7 through A10.

■ Enter the current date in cell A2, and erase the old date from cell A3.

■ Save the worksheet using the same file name, COST.

■ Print the worksheet.

4. To complete this problem you must have created the worksheet in Practice Exercise 5 of Lab 1. Retrieve the file ZOOFINAN.WK1. You will continue to build the worksheet for the 3-year financial statement for the zoo.

■ To make the worksheet easier to read, you will insert blank rows and columns. Insert a blank row between the worksheet title and the column headings. The blank row will be row 2.

■ Insert a blank row below the column headings. Underline the column headings.

■ Enter blank rows as rows 10, 12, and 18 (in that order.)

■ Enter underline characters (-) in rows 10 and 18 in columns D through H.

■ Delete column B.

■ Increase the column width of A to completely display all row labels.

■ Change the column width of column B to 4 spaces.

■ Copy the formulas used to calculate TOTAL S & R and TOTAL A/E for 1988 to calculate these values for 1989 and 1990. Also copy the formula used to calculate operating reserve for 1989 and 1990.

■ Enter @functions to calculate the TOTAL and AVERAGE in cells G6 and H6 respectively. Copy the @functions down the column. Erase the @function from those cells which reference empty cells, and replace the underline where appropriate.

■ Erase the old date from cell A3 and enter the current date in cell A2.

■ Save the worksheet using the same file name, ZOOFINAN.

■ Print the worksheet.

3 Managing a Large Worksheet

CASE STUDY

Paula Nichols, the manager of the Courtside Cafe at the Sports Club, presented the completed worksheet of the estimated operating budget for the proposed Courtside Cafe expansion to the board of directors. Although the board was pleased with the 6-month analysis, it asked her to extend the budget to cover a full year period. The board also wants her to calculate the profit margin for the proposed cafe expansion over the 12 months. At the end of 12 months the profit margin should be 20 percent. You will follow Paula as she makes the adjustments in the budget.

Locating and Correcting a Circular Reference

After presenting the budget to the board, Paula revised the worksheet, making several of the changes requested.

When responding to the DOS date prompt, be sure to enter the current date. Load Lotus 1-2-3. The data diskette should be in the B drive (or the appropriate drive for your computer system). To see what Paula has done so far, retrieve the file CAFE2.WK1.

OBJECTIVES

In this lab you will learn how to:

1. Correct a circular reference
2. Freeze row and column titles
3. Create and use windows.
4. Set window synchronization
5. Perform what-if analysis.
6. Use an absolute cell reference
7. Extract worksheet data.
8. Link worksheet data
9. Enter the system date
10. Justify text
11. Use compressed printing

Your display screen should be similar to Figure 3-1.

```
A1: [W15]                                                              READY

            A         B       C       D       E       F       G       H
 1
 2
 3                                                  Courtside Cafe Budget
 4
 5
 6                     JAN     FEB     MAR     APR     MAY     JUN     JUL
 7
 8
 9    SALES:
10      Food        $4,200  $4,400  $4,800  $5,200  $5,600  $6,200  $7,000
11      Beverage      $400    $450    $500    $540    $580    $600    $700
12    Total Sales   $4,600  $4,850  $5,300  $5,740  $6,180  $6,800  $7,700
13
14    EXPENSES:
15      Food        $1,260  $1,320  $1,440  $1,560  $1,680  $1,860  $2,100
16      Beverage      $120    $135    $150    $162    $174    $180    $210
17      Payroll     $2,250  $2,250  $2,250  $2,250  $2,250  $2,250  $2,250
18      Lease         $500    $500    $500    $500    $500    $500    $500
19      G & A         $175    $175    $175    $175    $175    $175    $175
20      Direct        $975    $975    $975    $975    $975    $975    $975
03-Mar-90  12:16 PM           UNDO                    CIRC
```

FIGURE 3-1

The worksheet now contains values for 12 months and a new row label for profit margin. The worksheet extends beyond column H and below row 20.

Note: Although there are quicker ways to move to cells in the worksheet, use the arrow keys when directed. Your display will then show the same rows and columns as the figures in the text.

To see the rest of the row labels, using ⬇ ,

Move to: A25

The row label "PROFIT MARGIN:" is now visible on the display. The formula to calculate this value still needs to be entered into the worksheet.
To see the rest of the worksheet to the right of column H, using ➡ ,

Move to: N25

Your display screen should be similar to Figure 3-2.

FIGURE 3-2

```
N25: [W8]                                                              READY

         F       G       H       I       J       K       L       M       N
 6      MAY     JUN     JUL     AUG    SEPT     OCT     NOV     DEC    TOTAL
 7
 8
 9
10    $5,600  $6,200  $7,000  $5,500  $6,400  $5,500  $6,500  $7,520 $68,820
11      $580    $600    $700    $500    $750    $800    $650    $775  $7,245
12    $6,180  $6,800  $7,700  $6,000  $7,150  $6,300  $7,150  $8,295 $76,065
13
14
15    $1,680  $1,860  $2,100  $1,650  $1,920  $1,650  $1,950  $2,256 $20,646
16      $174    $180    $210    $150    $225    $240    $195    $233  $2,174
17    $2,250  $2,250  $2,250  $2,250  $2,250  $2,250  $2,250  $2,250 $27,000
18      $500    $500    $500    $500    $500    $500    $500    $500  $6,000
19      $175    $175    $175    $175    $175    $175    $175    $175  $2,100
20      $975    $975    $975    $975    $975    $975    $975    $975 $11,700
21    $5,754  $5,940  $6,210  $5,700  $6,045  $5,790  $6,045  $6,389 $69,620
22
23      $426    $860  $1,490    $300  $1,105    $510  $1,105  $8,295 $12,834
24
25
03-Mar-90  12:16 PM           UNDO                    CIRC
```

— circular reference indicator

The TOTAL column and the values for the months of May through December are now visible. Notice the message "CIRC" displayed on the bottom line of the window. This message is a warning that a **circular reference** has been located in the worksheet. This means that a formula in a cell either directly or indirectly references itself. For some special applications, a formula containing a circular reference may be valid. These cases, however, are not very common. Whenever you see this message displayed, stop and locate the cell or cells containing the reference.

Locating the formula containing a circular reference in a worksheet can be very difficult. However, Lotus 1-2-3 has made it easy by providing a status screen. It tells you the specific cell containing the circular reference. The status screen is displayed by using the Worksheet Status command.

Select: / Worksheet Status

The Global Settings sheet is displayed. When using the Worksheet Status command, this settings sheeet is displayed to provide information about available memory, recalculation, cell display format, circular references, and global protection. To make changes to the global settings you would need to use the appropriate command. You are interested in the Circular Reference status. It tells you that the cell containing the circular reference is M23.

To clear the settings sheet and return to the worksheet,

Press: any key

Let's look at the formula in cell M23.

Move to: M23

The value in this cell is 8295. Look at the formula in the control panel. It is +M12-M23. The formula in cell M23 incorrectly references itself, M23, as part of the computation.

The formula in this cell should calculate the profit for December using the formula +M12-M21. **Correct the formula in cell M23 to be +M12-M21.**

Your display screen should be similar to Figure 3-3.

FIGURE 3-3

	F	G	H	I	J	K	L	M	N
M23: [W8] +M12-M21									READY
6	MAY	JUN	JUL	AUG	SEPT	OCT	NOV	DEC	TOTAL
10	$5,600	$6,200	$7,000	$5,500	$6,400	$5,500	$6,500	$7,520	$68,820
11	$580	$600	$700	$500	$750	$800	$650	$775	$7,245
12	$6,180	$6,800	$7,700	$6,000	$7,150	$6,300	$7,150	$8,295	$76,065
15	$1,680	$1,860	$2,100	$1,650	$1,920	$1,650	$1,950	$2,256	$20,646
16	$174	$180	$210	$150	$225	$240	$195	$233	$2,174
17	$2,250	$2,250	$2,250	$2,250	$2,250	$2,250	$2,250	$2,250	$27,000
18	$500	$500	$500	$500	$500	$500	$500	$500	$6,000
19	$175	$175	$175	$175	$175	$175	$175	$175	$2,100
20	$975	$975	$975	$975	$975	$975	$975	$975	$11,700
21	$5,754	$5,940	$6,210	$5,700	$6,045	$5,790	$6,045	$6,389	$69,620
23	$426	$860	$1,490	$300	$1,105	$510	$1,105	$1,907	$6,446
03-Mar-90 12:19 PM			UNDO						

The CIRC message has disappeared, and the affected worksheet formulas were recalculated. The new calculated value, 1907, is displayed in cell M23. This was a simple example of a circular reference error; others may be much more complex. In any case, whenever this message appears, display the status screen to locate the circular reference and determine whether it is valid or not.

Freezing Titles

Looking at the values in the worksheet, you may find it difficult to remember what the values stand for when the row labels in column A are not visible on the display screen. For example,

Move to: M19

The value in this cell is 175. Is this value a lease expense or a beverage expense or a direct expense? Without seeing the row labels, it is difficult for you to know. To see the row labels in column A,

Press: (END)
Press: (←)

Although the row labels are visible again, you cannot see the values in columns I through N. To keep the row labels visible in the window all the time while viewing the values in columns I through N, you will **freeze** column A in the window.

The Worksheet Titles command lets you fix, or freeze, specified rows or columns (or both) on the window while you scroll to other areas of the worksheet. The "titles" can consist of any number of columns or rows along the top or left edge of the window.

To freeze a column of titles, move the cursor one column to the right of the column you want frozen. Since you want to freeze column A on the window,

Move to: B23
Select: / Worksheet Titles

The Titles submenu options in the control panel have the following effects:

Both	freezes both the horizontal and vertical titles
Horizontal	freezes only the horizontal titles
Vertical	freezes only the vertical titles
Clear	unfreezes all titles

The row labels in column A run vertically down the worksheet. To freeze the vertical column of titles (A),

Select: Vertical

Nothing appears different on the display screen until you move the cell pointer.

Press: (←)

Lotus 1-2-3 beeped. It will not let you move the cell pointer into column A because it is frozen.

Watch the movement of the columns on the display screen as you use (→) to,

Move to: N23

Your display screen should be similar to Figure 3-4.

FIGURE 3-4

frozen column

```
N23:  [W8] @SUM(B23..M23)                                        READY

          A         H       I       J       K       L       M       N
 6                 JUL     AUG    SEPT     OCT     NOV     DEC    TOTAL
 7
 8
 9    SALES:
10      Food      $7,000  $5,500  $6,400  $5,500  $6,500  $7,520 $68,820
11      Beverage    $700    $500    $750    $800    $650    $775  $7,245
12    Total Sales $7,700  $6,000  $7,150  $6,300  $7,150  $8,295 $76,065
13
14    EXPENSES:
15      Food      $2,100  $1,650  $1,920  $1,650  $1,950  $2,256 $20,646
16      Beverage    $210    $150    $225    $240    $195    $233  $2,174
17      Payroll   $2,250  $2,250  $2,250  $2,250  $2,250  $2,250 $27,000
18      Lease       $500    $500    $500    $500    $500    $500  $6,000
19      G & A       $175    $175    $175    $175    $175    $175  $2,100
20      Direct      $975    $975    $975    $975    $975    $975 $11,700
21    Total Expenses $6,210 $5,700 $6,045  $5,790  $6,045  $6,389 $69,620
22
23    PROFIT:     $1,490    $300  $1,105    $510  $1,105  $1,907  $6,446
24
25    PROFIT MARGIN:
03-Mar-90  12:20 PM          UNDO
```

Column A has remained fixed in the window while columns H through N scroll into view. This makes reading the worksheet much easier.
To unfreeze, or clear, the frozen column,

Select: / **Worksheet Titles Clear**

Column A is no longer visible on the display. To further confirm that column A is unfrozen, to move to cell A23,

Press: (END)
Press: (←)

Since column A is no longer frozen, the cell pointer can be positioned in cell A23.

Titles can also be frozen horizontally, or across a row, as easily as they are frozen vertically down a column. Paula would like to freeze the month labels and the underlining in rows 6 and 7 in the window. The row to freeze is marked by positioning the cell pointer one row below the row to be frozen.

Using (↑),

Move to: A8
Select: / **Worksheet Titles Horizontal**
Press: (↑)

Again the cell pointer movement is restricted to unfrozen cells.
Using ⬇ ,

Move to: A29

Your display screen should be similar to Figure 3-5.

FIGURE 3-5

frozen rows ——

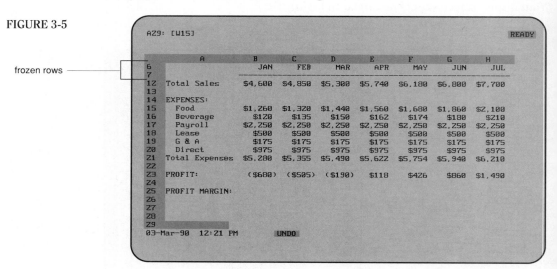

```
A29: [W15]                                                    READY

          A        B       C       D       E       F       G       H
 6                JAN     FEB     MAR     APR     MAY     JUN     JUL
 7
12  Total Sales  $4,600  $4,850  $5,300  $5,740  $6,180  $6,800  $7,700
13
14  EXPENSES:
15     Food      $1,260  $1,320  $1,440  $1,560  $1,680  $1,860  $2,100
16     Beverage    $120    $135    $150    $162    $174    $180    $210
17     Payroll   $2,250  $2,250  $2,250  $2,250  $2,250  $2,250  $2,250
18     Lease       $500    $500    $500    $500    $500    $500    $500
19     G & A       $175    $175    $175    $175    $175    $175    $175
20     Direct      $975    $975    $975    $975    $975    $975    $975
21  Total Expenses $5,280 $5,355 $5,490 $5,622 $5,754 $5,940 $6,210
22
23  PROFIT:      ($680)  ($505)  ($190)   $118    $426    $860  $1,490
24
25  PROFIT MARGIN:
26
27
28
29
03-Mar-90  12:21 PM       UNDO
```

Rows 6 and 7 remained stationary in the window as you scrolled down through the worksheet.
Using ➡,

Move to: N29

Although the month labels have remained stationary in the window with the row labels unfrozen, it is again difficult to read the worksheet. Conveniently, both column and row titles can be frozen at the same time.

Press: (HOME)

Notice that the Home position is the upper left-hand corner of the unfrozen worksheet cells rather than cell A1, which is frozen.
Clear the frozen horizontal titles.
To freeze both the horizontal and vertical titles at the same time, position the cell pointer one row below the row to be frozen and one column to the right of the column to be frozen.

Move to: B8
Select: / **W**orksheet **T**itles **B**oth
Press: ⬅
Press: ⬆

The rows above and the column to the left of the cell pointer position are frozen. Watch your display carefully as you use your arrow keys to

Move to: N8

Move to: N29

Your display screen should be similar to Figure 3-6.

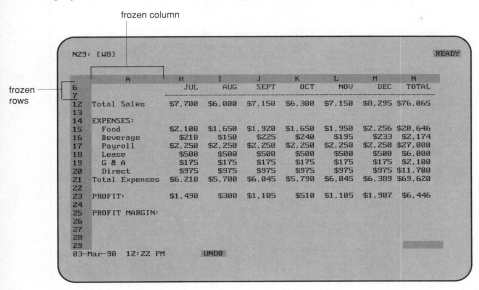

FIGURE 3-6

Both the vertical and horizontal titles remain stationary in the window as you scroll through the worksheet.

Press: (HOME)

The Home position is now the upper left-hand corner of the unfrozen rows and columns, cell B8.

Creating and Scrolling Windows

The frozen titles greatly improve the readability of the worksheet. However, it is still difficult to compare the values in columns that cannot be viewed in the same window. For example, to compare the values in each month to the values in the TOTAL column or to certain other months is difficult. This is because as one column comes into view on the display screen, the other may scroll off due to lack of space in the window.

You could freeze the leftmost column you want to compare and then scroll the worksheet until the column on the right comes into view. But then you would not be able to make any changes or see the other columns to the left of the frozen column. The solution is to create a second window on the display.

Worksheets are viewed through a **window**. The part of the worksheet you can see on your display screen is a window. So far you have had only one window, the full size of the display screen, on the worksheet. The Worksheet Windows command lets you create a second window on the screen through which you can view different areas of the worksheet at the same time.

To easily compare the values in each month to the values in column N, TOTAL, you will create a second window. This window will divide the display vertically.

Use ⟶ to,

Move to: N8

Select: / **W**orksheet **W**indow **V**ertical

Your display screen should be similar to Figure 3-7.

FIGURE 3-7

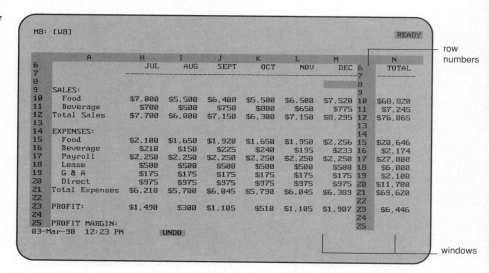

The screen is split vertically into two windows. A new border of row numbers separates the two windows. The cell pointer is positioned in the left window. This is the **active window**.

Watch your display screen carefully as you use ⟵ to,

Move to: B8

Your display screen should be similar to Figure 3-8.

FIGURE 3-8

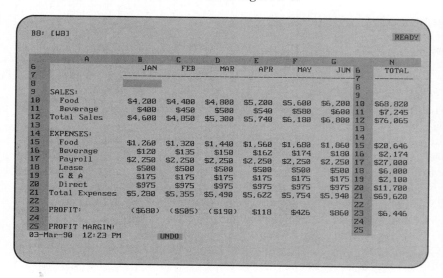

The columns in the left window move into view as the cell pointer moves across the row. The right window did not change. Now the values in January through June can easily be compared to the total values displayed in the right window.
Using ⬇,

Move to: B29

The rows scrolled together in both windows. When you scroll vertically through a vertical window, the rows in the other window will scroll at the same time, keeping the rows even in both windows. This is called **synchronized** scrolling. If a horizontal window were created on the screen, scrolling horizontally through the window would move the columns together in both windows. This is the default setting for windows in Lotus 1-2-3.

Press: (HOME)

The cell pointer can be moved from one window to the other using the Window function key, (F6)

Press: (F6) Window

The cell pointer is positioned in cell N8 in the right window.
Windows can be changed to scroll independently, or **unsynchronized**. To change to unsynchronized scrolling,

Select: / Worksheet Window Unsync

Using ⬇,

Move to: N29

The rows in the right window moved. The rows in the left window did not move.
Since a window lets you view different parts of the same worksheet, any changes made in one window are made to the entire worksheet and will be seen in either window.
Before continuing, to clear the vertical window,

Select: / Worksheet Window Clear

The display screen returns to one window.

Displaying a Percent

Now that Paula knows how to move around and manage a large worksheet, she needs to enter the formula to calculate the profit margin in cell B25. Using ⬇,

Move to: B25

The formula to calculate profit margin is:

Profit/Total sales*100%

In cell B25, enter the formula +B23/B12 using pointing. Do not multiply it times 100 percent.

Your display screen should be similar to Figure 3-9.

FIGURE 3-9

```
B25: [W8] +B23/B12                                              READY

              A          B        C        D        E        F        G        H
6                       JAN      FEB      MAR      APR      MAY      JUN      JUL
7
8
9        SALES:
10          Food       $4,200   $4,400   $4,800   $5,200   $5,600   $6,200   $7,000
11          Beverage     $400     $450     $500     $540     $580     $600     $700
12       Total Sales   $4,600   $4,850   $5,300   $5,740   $6,180   $6,800   $7,700
13
14       EXPENSES:
15          Food       $1,260   $1,320   $1,440   $1,560   $1,680   $1,860   $2,100
16          Beverage     $120     $135     $150     $162     $174     $180     $210
17          Payroll    $2,250   $2,250   $2,250   $2,250   $2,250   $2,250   $2,250
18          Lease        $500     $500     $500     $500     $500     $500     $500
19          G & A        $175     $175     $175     $175     $175     $175     $175
20          Direct       $975     $975     $975     $975     $975     $975     $975
21       Total Expenses $5,280   $5,355   $5,490   $5,622   $5,754   $5,940   $6,210
22
23       PROFIT:        ($680)   ($505)   ($190)    $118     $426     $860   $1,490
24
25       PROFIT MARGIN:   ($0)
03-Mar-90  12:25 PM              UNDO
```

The value "($0)" is displayed in cell B25. To display the value in this cell as a percent, you need to change the cell format from currency (set globally in Lab 2) to a percent with zero decimal places. Setting the cell format to percent will also multiply the formula in the cell times 100.

In Lab 2 you learned how to change the format of values with the Worksheet Global Format command. The format of a cell or range of cells can also be changed using the Range Format command. This command will affect the display of values in a specified cell or range of cells only. This setting will override the cell format previously set globally.

Select: **/ R**ange **F**ormat **P**ercent **0** ⏎ ⏎

Your display screen should be similar to Figure 3-10.

FIGURE 3-10

cell format

```
B25: (P0) [W8] +B23/B12                                         READY

              A          B        C        D        E        F        G        H
6                       JAN      FEB      MAR      APR      MAY      JUN      JUL
7
8
9        SALES:
10          Food       $4,200   $4,400   $4,800   $5,200   $5,600   $6,200   $7,000
11          Beverage     $400     $450     $500     $540     $580     $600     $700
12       Total Sales   $4,600   $4,850   $5,300   $5,740   $6,180   $6,800   $7,700
13
14       EXPENSES:
15          Food       $1,260   $1,320   $1,440   $1,560   $1,680   $1,860   $2,100
16          Beverage     $120     $135     $150     $162     $174     $180     $210
17          Payroll    $2,250   $2,250   $2,250   $2,250   $2,250   $2,250   $2,250
18          Lease        $500     $500     $500     $500     $500     $500     $500
19          G & A        $175     $175     $175     $175     $175     $175     $175
20          Direct       $975     $975     $975     $975     $975     $975     $975
21       Total Expenses $5,280   $5,355   $5,490   $5,622   $5,754   $5,940   $6,210
22
23       PROFIT:        ($680)   ($505)   ($190)    $118     $426     $860   $1,490
24
25       PROFIT MARGIN:  -15%
03-Mar-90  12:26 PM              UNDO
```

The profit margin displayed for January is "-15%."

Setting the cell format to a percent takes the value in the cell and multiplies it by 100. The value is displayed with a percent sign (%). Also notice that when the cell format is specified using the Range Format command, the setting "(P0)" is displayed in the control panel.

Copy the formula in cell B25 across the row through the end of the worksheet, using highlighting to specify the range.

Your screen should be similar to Figure 3-11.

FIGURE 3-11

Notice that not only was the formula copied but also the cell format.

To see what the total profit margin for the year is, move to cell N25.

Press: (END)
Press: (→)

The total profit margin for the year is "8%." The board of directors wants the proposed cafe expansion to show a 20 percent total profit margin during the first year of operation. The total profit margin, using the figures as budgeted for the year, is much below this objective.

Using What-If Analysis

After some consideration, Paula decides that the only way to increase the total profit margin is to reduce expenses. She feels she can reduce payroll by more carefully scheduling the number of hours the employees work. She can decrease the number of employee work hours by scheduling fewer employees to work during slow periods.

The process of evaluating what effect reducing the payroll expenses will have on the total profit margin is called **what-if analysis**. What-if analysis is a technique used to evaluate the effects of changing selected factors in a worksheet. Paula wants to know what would happen if payroll expenses decreased a set amount each month.

Before you begin, to make the worksheet easier to handle, you will create a vertical window large enough to display two columns of information. To do this,

Move to: M25
Select: **/ W**orksheet **W**indow **V**ertical

Your display screen should be similar to Figure 3-12.

FIGURE 3-12

```
L25: (P0) [W8] +L23/L12                                              READY

       A        H        I        J        K        L        M        N
 6             JUL      AUG     SEPT      OCT      NOV  6     DEC    TOTAL
 7           ──────────────────────────────────────── 7
 8                                                      8
 9    SALES:                                            9
10      Food    $7,000   $5,500   $6,400   $5,500   $6,500 10    $7,520 $68,820
11      Beverage  $700     $500     $750     $800     $650 11      $775  $7,245
12    Total Sales $7,700 $6,000   $7,150   $6,300   $7,150 12    $8,295 $76,065
13                                                     13
14    EXPENSES:                                        14
15      Food    $2,100   $1,650   $1,920   $1,650   $1,950 15    $2,256 $20,646
16      Beverage  $210     $150     $225     $240     $195 16      $233  $2,174
17      Payroll $2,250   $2,250   $2,250   $2,250   $2,250 17    $2,250 $27,000
18      Lease    $500     $500     $500     $500     $500 18      $500  $6,000
19      G & A    $175     $175     $175     $175     $175 19      $175  $2,100
20      Direct   $975     $975     $975     $975     $975 20      $975 $11,700
21    Total Expenses $6,210 $5,700 $6,045   $5,790   $6,045 21    $6,389 $69,620
22                                                     22
23    PROFIT:  $1,490     $300   $1,105     $510   $1,105 23    $1,907  $6,446
24                                                     24
25    PROFIT MARGIN:  19%       5%      15%       8%     15%25      23%      8%
03-Mar-90   12:27 PM          UNDO
```

First Paula would like to see the effect of reducing the payroll expenses to $2,100 per month.

Move to: B17
Type: **2100**
Press: ⏎

The profit margin for January (B25) changed from -15 to -12 percent. **To see the effect of reducing the payroll expenses to $2,100 for each month on the total profit margin, copy the January payroll value to the February through December payroll cells, using highlighting to specify the range.**

The worksheet has been recalculated. The new total profit margin is displayed in cell N25 in the right window. Reducing the payroll expenses to $2,100 per month has increased the total profit margin from 8 to 11 percent. This is still not enough.

Paula realizes that it may take her several tries before she reduces the payroll expenses enough to arrive at a total profit margin of 20 percent. Each time she changes the payroll expense, she has to copy the values across the entire row. A quicker way to enter different payroll expense values into the worksheet is by using a **work cell.** Any blank cell outside of the worksheet area can be used as a work cell.

Paula will use cell O17 in the right window as the work cell.

Press: (F6) Window

The cell pointer should be in cell M25 in the right window.

Move to: O17

This time Paula will decrease the payroll expense value to 1900 per month.

Type: 1900
Press: ⏎

The value in the work cell needs to be copied into the payroll expense cells in the worksheet. To do this, a formula referencing the work cell is entered in the payroll expense cells. This formula will tell the program to add the value in cell O17 to the cell contents.

Press: F6 Window

The cell pointer should be in cell B17. Enter the formula +O17 in cell B17 as follows:

Type: +
Press: F6 Window

The cell pointer should be in cell O17.

Press: ⏎

Your display screen should be similar to Figure 3-13.

FIGURE 3-13

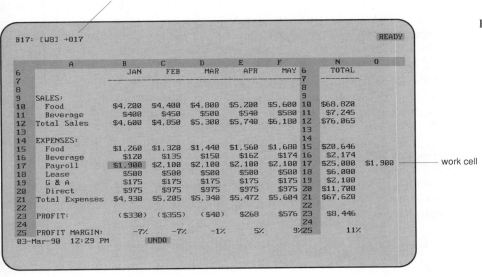

formula

work cell

The value "$1,900" is entered in cell B17. The formula in B17 tells Lotus 1-2-3 to place the value in cell O17 in cell B17.

Copy the formula in the January payroll cell to the February through December payroll cells, using highlighting to specify the range.

Your display screen should be similar to Figure 3-14.

```
B17: [W8] +017                                                    READY

           A          B        C        D        E        F     N         O
6                    JAN      FEB      MAR      APR      MAY 6  TOTAL
7      ────────────────────────────────────────────────────7────────
8                                                           8
9    SALES:                                                 9
10     Food       $4,200   $4,400   $4,800   $5,200   $5,600 10  $68,820
11     Beverage     $400     $450     $500     $540     $580 11   $7,245
12   Total Sales  $4,600   $4,850   $5,300   $5,740   $6,180 12  $76,065
13                                                          13
14   EXPENSES:                                              14
15     Food       $1,260   $1,320   $1,440   $1,560   $1,680 15  $20,646
16     Beverage     $120     $135     $150     $162     $174 16   $2,174
17     Payroll    $1,900       $0       $0       $0       $0 17   $1,900    $1,900
18     Lease        $500     $500     $500     $500     $500 18   $6,000
19     G & A        $175     $175     $175     $175     $175 19   $2,100
20     Direct       $975     $975     $975     $975     $975 20  $11,700
21   Total Expenses $4,930   $3,105   $3,240   $3,372   $3,504 21  $44,520
22                                                          22
23   PROFIT:      ($330)   $1,745   $2,060   $2,368   $2,676 23  $31,546
24                                                          24
25   PROFIT MARGIN:  -7%      36%      39%      41%      43%/25    41%
03-Mar-90  12:29 PM       UNDO
```

FIGURE 3-14

The worksheet again has been recalculated. However, there is something wrong. The value "$1,900" should appear in cells C17 through M17. Instead the value "$0" appears in those cells.

Move to: C17

The control panel shows the formula in this cell is +P17. This is a blank cell. Since it contains nothing, the value of 0 is entered in C17.

Move to cells D17, E17, and F17. Look at how the formula changes from +P17 to +Q17, +R17, and +S17. The column letter has been adjusted relative to the new column location of the formula in row 17. Each of the formulas in the cells references the cell one column to the right of the previous formula. They were adjusted relative to their location in the worksheet. As you learned in Lab 2, the formula was copied using relative cell references.

Using an Absolute Cell Reference

The formula in B17 needs to be entered so that the column in the referenced cell, O17, will not change when the formula is copied. To do this, you will use an **absolute cell reference**.

Move to: B17
Press: (F2) EDIT

To change the formula in B17 to have an absolute cell reference, enter a $ (dollar sign) character in front of the column letter. You can enter the dollar sign character by typing it in directly or you can use the ABS (Absolute) key, (F4).

When using the ABS key, first position the cursor on or immediately to the right of the cell address you want to change. Since this is the only cell address in this entry, the cursor is already appropriately positioned. To change this cell address to absolute,

Press: (F4) ABS

The cell address now displays a $ character before both the column letter and row number (O17). Because a dollar sign is entered before both the column letter and row number, this cell address is absolute. If this formula were copied to another row and column location in the worksheet, the copied formula would be an exact duplicate of the original formula (O17).

Pressing ABS repeatedly cycles a cell address through all possible combinations of cell reference types.

Press: (F4) ABS

The cell address has changed to display a dollar sign before the row number only (O$17). This is a **mixed cell reference** because only the row number is preceded by an absolute address, not the column letter. A mixed cell reference contains both relative and absolute cell references. If this formula were copied to another column and row, the column in the referenced cell in the formula would be adjusted relative to its new location in the worksheet, but the row number would not change. For example, if the formula in B17 (O$17) were copied from B17 to E13, the formula in E13 would be R$17.

Press: (F4) ABS

Again this is a mixed cell reference. This time the $ character precedes the column letter. Consequently, if this formula were copied to another row and column, the row in the referenced cell in the formula would be adjusted relative to its new location in the worksheet, and the column would not change. For example, the formula in B17 ($O17) would change to $O13 if it were copied to cell B13.

Press: (F4) ABS

The formula returns to relative cell references. You have cycled the cell address through all possible combinations of cell references.

To stop the relative adjustment of the column in the formula when it is copied from one column location to another in the same row, the formula needs to be a mixed cell reference with the column letter absolute. To make this change,

Press: (F4) ABS (3 times)

To accept the formula as displayed in the control panel (+$O17),

Press: (⏎)

Copy this formula from the January payroll cell to the February through December payroll cells, using highlighting to specify the range.

The value "$1,900" appears in each cell in row 17.

Move to: C17

Your display screen should be similar to Figure 3-15.

```
C17: [W8] +$O17                                                    READY

              A         B        C        D        E        F    N         O
       6                JAN      FEB      MAR      APR      MAY 6 TOTAL
       7                                                       7
       8                                                       8
       9    SALES:                                             9
      10      Food      $4,200   $4,400   $4,800   $5,200   $5,600 10 $68,820
      11      Beverage    $400     $450     $500     $540     $580 11  $7,245
      12    Total Sales $4,600   $4,850   $5,300   $5,740   $6,180 12 $76,065
      13                                                      13
      14    EXPENSES:                                         14
      15      Food      $1,260   $1,320   $1,440   $1,560   $1,680 15 $20,646
      16      Beverage    $120     $135     $150     $162     $174 16  $2,174
      17      Payroll   $1,900   $1,900   $1,900   $1,900   $1,900 17 $22,800      $1,900
      18      Lease       $500     $500     $500     $500     $500 18  $6,000
      19      G & A       $175     $175     $175     $175     $175 19  $2,100
      20      Direct      $975     $975     $975     $975     $975 20 $11,700
      21    Total Expenses $4,930 $5,005   $5,140   $5,272   $5,404 21 $65,420
      22                                                      22
      23    PROFIT:     ($330)   ($155)    $160     $468     $776 23 $10,646
      24                                                      24
      25    PROFIT MARGIN:  -7%     -3%      3%       8%      13%/25       14%
      06-Mar-90  08:39 AM          UNDO
```

FIGURE 3-15

The formula displayed in the control panel is an exact duplicate of the formula in
B17. It references the cell O17. Using an absolute cell reference easily solved the
problem. The absolute cell reference stopped the relative adjustment of the cells in
the copied formula by maintaining the particular cell coordinates.

Decreasing the payroll expenses to $1,900 each month has increased the total
profit margin to 14 percent (cell N25). This is closer to the 20 percent management
objective. But it's still not good enough.

Decrease the payroll expense to $1,700 per month as follows:

Press: (F6) Window

The cell pointer should be in cell O17.

Type: **1700**
Press: (⏎)

Your display screen should be similar to Figure 3-16.

FIGURE 3-16

```
O17: [W8] 1700                                                    READY

              A         B        C        D        E        F    N         O
       6                JAN      FEB      MAR      APR      MAY 6 TOTAL
       7                                                       7
       8                                                       8
       9    SALES:                                             9
      10      Food      $4,200   $4,400   $4,800   $5,200   $5,600 10 $68,820
      11      Beverage    $400     $450     $500     $540     $580 11  $7,245
      12    Total Sales $4,600   $4,850   $5,300   $5,740   $6,180 12 $76,065
      13                                                      13
      14    EXPENSES:                                         14
      15      Food      $1,260   $1,320   $1,440   $1,560   $1,680 15 $20,646
      16      Beverage    $120     $135     $150     $162     $174 16  $2,174
      17      Payroll   $1,700   $1,700   $1,700   $1,700   $1,700 17 $20,400      $1,700
      18      Lease       $500     $500     $500     $500     $500 18  $6,000
      19      G & A       $175     $175     $175     $175     $175 19  $2,100
      20      Direct      $975     $975     $975     $975     $975 20 $11,700
      21    Total Expenses $4,730 $4,805   $4,940   $5,072   $5,204 21 $63,020
      22                                                      22
      23    PROFIT:     ($130)     $45     $360     $668     $976 23 $13,046
      24                                                      24
      25    PROFIT MARGIN:  -3%      1%      7%      12%      16%/25       17%
      03-Mar-90  12:31 PM          UNDO
```

The value in O17 was quickly entered into the payroll expense cells in row 17 for each month, and the worksheet was recalculated.

By using a work cell and referencing the work cell in a formula in the worksheet using absolute cell referencing, changing the what-if value becomes a simple process.

The total profit margin is now 17 percent. This is still not enough. **Try 1400.** The total profit margin is now 22 percent. That's too high. You know the appropriate payroll expense level is between 1700 and 1400. **Now try 1500.** Your display screen should be similar to Figure 3-17.

FIGURE 3-17

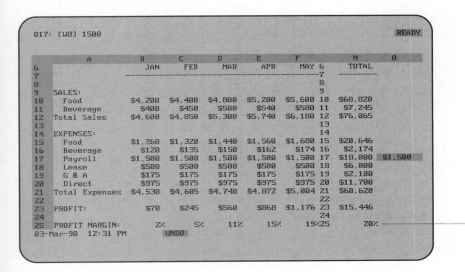

total profit margin

That's it! The total profit margin is 20 percent if payroll expenses are reduced to $1,500 per month.

Clear the vertical window and then unfreeze the titles.

Press: (HOME)

Extracting Worksheet Data

After looking at the values in the annual budget, Paula is concerned that she may have underestimated some values. She wants the club manager to review the figures before she submits the final budget to the board of directors. She decides to create a summary of the annual budget for him to look at which will contain the worksheet labels and the total values only.

Paula could create this new worksheet by entering the row labels into another worksheet. A quicker way, however, is to save the row labels in column A from the current worksheet to a new worksheet file on disk. The new worksheet file will be named CAFESUM. Figure 3-18 on the next page illustrates this process. (It will not appear this way on your screen, however.)

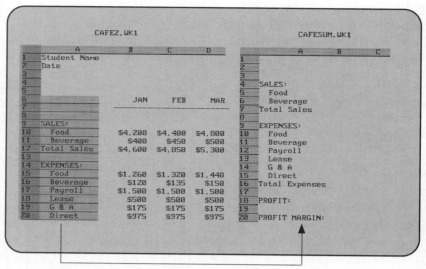

FIGURE 3-18

label extracted from CAFE2.WK1
and copied to CAFESUM.WK1

The command which will save a range of data from the current worksheet to a new worksheet file on disk is / File Xtract.

Select: / File Xtract

Two options, Formulas and Values, are displayed in the control panel. If you select Formulas, 1-2-3 copies all labels, numbers, formulas, and worksheet settings in the specified range. If you select Values, 1-2-3 performs the same function except that the values of formulas are copied, not the formulas themselves. Since the row entries are all labels, either response is acceptable. To accept the default,

Press: ⏎

In response to the next prompt to enter a file name for the extracted file,

Type: CAFESUM
Press: ⏎

Next you must specify the range to be extracted, A6 through A25 (includes three blank rows). Specify this range using highlighting. You will need to press ESC to unanchor the cell address first.

After a few moments the defined range is copied to the new file. The current file is not affected.

Save the current worksheet as CAFE3.

Retrieve the new worksheet file, CAFESUM.

Your screen should be similar to Figure 3-19.

extracted
labels

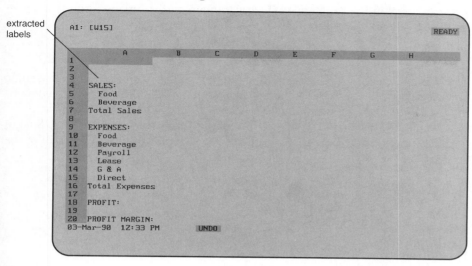

FIGURE 3-19

The column of extracted labels is displayed in the worksheet. 1-2-3 enters the extracted range in the file beginning in cell A1.

File Linking

Next Paula needs to enter the values from the CAFE3 file TOTAL column (N10 through N25) into the CAFESUM worksheet. She decides this may be a good time to see how the **file linking** feature of Lotus 1-2-3 works. This feature allows you to use values from cells in other worksheets in the current worksheet. A linking formula is entered in one file that refers to a cell in another file. When data in a linked cell changes, the worksheet that is affected by this change is automatically updated whenever it is retrieved. The file that receives the value is the **target file,** and the file that supplies the data is the **source file.** The CAFE3 file will be the source file and the CAFESUM file will be the target file. The file-linking process is illustrated in Figure 3-20.

FIGURE 3-20

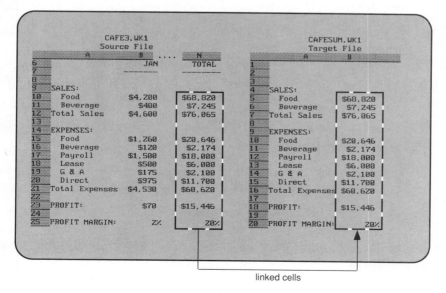

linked cells

To create a link between two files, you enter a **linking formula** in the target file that refers to a cell in the source file. The cell containing the linking formula is called the **target cell**. A linking formula uses the following format:

+<<file reference>>cell reference

The "file reference" is the file name of the source file; it is enclosed in double angle brackets. The "cell reference" is the cell address of the cell in the source file containing the value to be copied into the target file.

Paula needs to enter a linking formula for each row item The first linking formula will be entered in cell B5 of the target file and will link to cell N10 of the source file.

Move to: B5
Type: +<<CAFE3>>N10
Press: ⏎

Your screen should be similar to Figure 3-21.

FIGURE 3-21

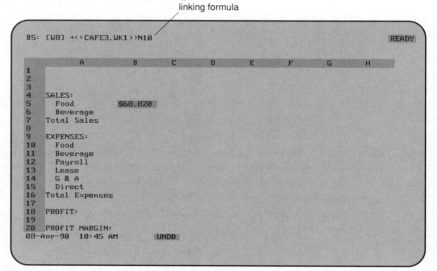

linking formula

The current value in cell N10, $68,820, was copied from the source file into the target file and displayed in cell B5.

The remaining linking formulas will reference cells N11 through N25 of the source file. Like any other formula, linking formulas can be copied, and the cell addresses will adjust relative to their new location in the worksheet.

Copy the linking formula for food sales down column B through cell B20, using highlighting to specify the range.

Notice that the values are displayed in currency format. When the Xtract command was used, the global worksheet settings were copied along with the column labels.

Erase the formulas in cells B8, B9, B17, and B19.

Correct the cell format of B20 so that the value is displayed as a percent with no decimal places.

Enter the column title "TOTAL" in cell B3. It should be right-aligned.

Enter the worksheet title "Courtside Cafe Budget" in cell A1 and "(Consolidated)" in cell A2. Precede the label in cell A2 with four blank spaces to center it beneath the label in cell A1.

Your screen should be similar to Figure 3-22.

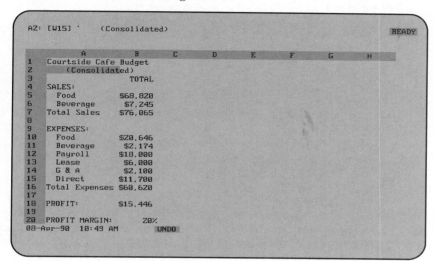

FIGURE 3-22

Save (Replace) the file as CAFESUM.

Paula shows the consolidated worksheet and the annual worksheet to the club manager. He anticipates that the lease expense for the cafe will increase by 10 percent.

To reflect this change in the budget, retrieve the worksheet file CAFE3 and change the lease expense for January through December to $550.

All affected worksheet formulas are recalculated.

Move to: N18

The total lease expense increases to $6,600.

Move to: N25

The total profit margin is still at 20 percent. To see if the consolidated worksheet, CAFESUM, reflects this change in data, the file needs to be retrieved.

First, enter your name in the current worksheet in cell A1 and the date in cell A2, and save the current file as CAFE3.

Retrieve CAFESUM.

Move to: B13

Your screen should be similar to Figure 3-23.

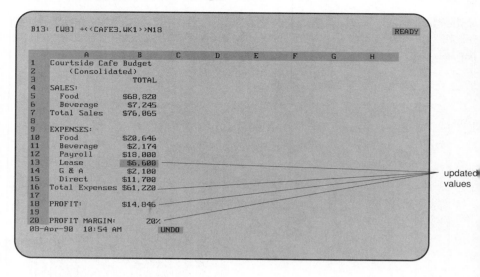

FIGURE 3-23

The target file has been recalculated using the new data. The total lease expense in cell B13, the total expense in cell B16, and the total profit margin have been updated to reflect the change of data in the linked worksheet cells.

Once a linking formula is entered in a worksheet, whenever a value(s) in the cell referenced in the source file changes, the target file is automatically updated when it is retrieved. Another way to update the source file is to use the command **/ F**ile **A**dmin **L**ink-Refresh. This command will immediately update the linked cells.

Paula likes how the file linking feature works. Now, if the board of directors request that she change other worksheet data, it will be quickly reflected in the consolidated budget worksheet.

Entering the System Date

Paula feels that the proposed budget is ready to present to the board of directors again. She would like to include a brief memo of explanation below the consolidated worksheet. Using the arrow keys,

Move to:	A24
Type:	**TO:**
Move to:	B24
Type:	**Board of Directors**
Move to:	A25
Type:	**FROM:**
Move to:	B25
Type:	**Paula Nichols**
Move to:	A26
Type:	**DATE:**
Move to:	B26

The date can be entered automatically into a worksheet using the @NOW function. This @function will display the system date entered at the DOS prompt into the worksheet. The @function calculates the date by assigning an integer to each of the 73,050 days from January 1, 1900 through December 31, 2099. The integers are assigned consecutively beginning with 1 and ending with 73,050. They are called **date numbers**.

Type: @NOW

Press: ⏎

Your display screen should be similar to Figure 3-24.

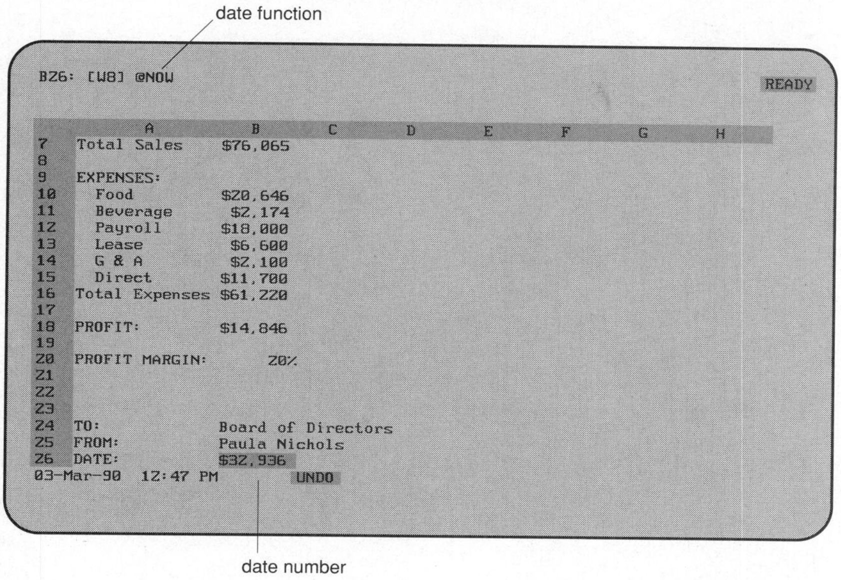

date function

FIGURE 3-24

```
B26: [W8] @NOW                                           READY

        A          B         C      D      E      F      G      H
7    Total Sales   $76,065
8
9    EXPENSES:
10     Food        $20,646
11     Beverage     $2,174
12     Payroll     $18,000
13     Lease        $6,600
14     G & A        $2,100
15     Direct      $11,700
16   Total Expenses $61,220
17
18   PROFIT:       $14,846
19
20   PROFIT MARGIN:    20%
21
22
23
24   TO:          Board of Directors
25   FROM:        Paula Nichols
26   DATE:        $32,936
03-Mar-90  12:47 PM       UNDO
```

date number

The value displayed in C32 is the date number calculated by the @NOW function displayed in currency format.

Note: The value in this cell will differ depending on the system date you entered at the DOS prompt.

To change the display of this one cell from currency to a date format, you use the Range Format Date command.

Select: / Range Format Date

Options 1 through 5 let you specify how the date will be displayed. The Time option will display the current time as recorded by DOS. You want the date displayed as mm/dd/yy. Use the Help system for information on the different date formats. The option which will display a date as Month/Day/Year is 4 (Long Intn'l).

Select: 4

To accept the range to format as B26,

Press: ⏎

A series of asterisks appears in the cell, indicating the column width is not large enough to display the value. The date format setting is displayed in the control panel as "(D4)."

> **Use the Worksheet Column Set-Width command to increase the width of column B to 9 spaces to display the date.**

Your display screen should be similar to Figure 3-25.

FIGURE 3-25

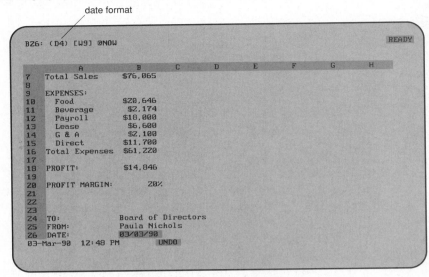

Increasing the column width by one space is all that is needed to display the date.

Note: If you did not enter a date at the DOS date prompt, the DOS default date is entered.

Justifying Text

Continue the memo below. Do not press ⏎ until directed.

Move to: A28

Type: Above is a consolidated budget for the year for the proposed expansion of the Courtside Cafe. The monthly breakdown of this budget is on the following page.

Press: ⏎

The text you have entered is a long label which is displayed as a single line of text. To change this long label into a paragraph of several lines of text no longer than a specified width, the Range Justify command is used. This command rearranges or **justifies** labels to fit within a width you specify. Using highlighting to specify the range,

Select: / Range Justify A28..F28 ⏎
Move to: A32

Your display screen should be similar to Figure 3-26.

FIGURE 3-26

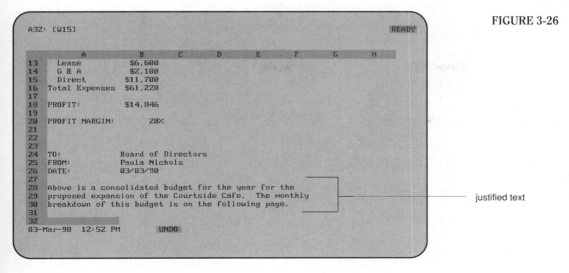

———— justified text

The long label of text in A28 has been divided into three lines of text contained in cells A28 and A30. Neither line extends beyond column F.

To enter the following sentence in cell A32,

Type: **To meet the objective of a 20% Total Profit Margin, the payroll expenses were reduced to $1,500 per month.**

Press: ⏎

Justify this label using the same range setting as above.

For a better view of the worksheet,

Move to: A35

Your display screen should be similar to Figure 3-27.

FIGURE 3-27

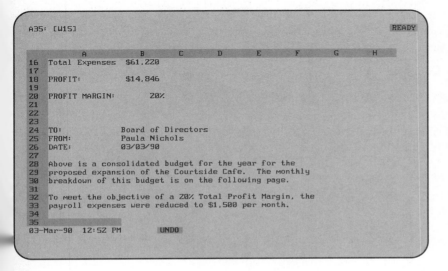

The second paragraph of the memo is now entered into the worksheet.
The worksheet is ready to be printed.

Before saving and printing the worksheet, enter your name in cell A35.

Save and Replace this worksheet using the file name CAFESUM.
Print the worksheet.

Next you need to print CAFE3. **Retrieve this file.**

Using Compressed Printing

Because of the width of the worksheet, it will require two pages of paper to print it out. To print the worksheet on one page, the print can be **compressed** by reducing the space between the letters.

Note: The following procedure works on most printers. However, it may not work on yours. Consult your instructor for the correct settings if the following does not produce the proper results.

When defining the print range, make sure the work cell O17 is not included in the range.

Select: **/ Print Printer Range**

Specify the entire worksheet, excluding cell O17, as the print range, using high-lighting.

Select: **Options**

The 8 Print options let you specify how the printed document will appear on the page. The Setup option lets you change the print size.

Select: **Setup**

The prompt to enter a setup string appears in the control panel. (A string is any sequence of characters.) Compressed print is turned on by entering the string \015.

Type: **\015** (use the number zero, not the letter O)
Press: ⏎

The Print Options submenu is still displayed in the control panel to allow you to select other options. The settings sheet displays the setup string you specified.

Select: **Margins**

When specifying compressed print, move the right margin to the right the maximum number of spaces, 132. This will allow the maximum number of characters to be printed on a line.

Select: Right
Type: 132
Press: ⏎

Your screen should be similar to Figure 3-28.

FIGURE 3-28

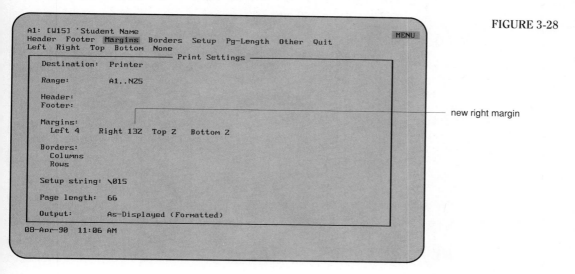

new right margin

To leave the Print Options submenu,

Select: Quit

To continue the Print command sequence,

Select: Align Go

Your worksheet should be printing. After it has completed printing, to advance the page and return to the READY mode,

Select: Page Quit

Your printed output should be similar to Figure 3-29 on the next page.

Quit Lotus 1-2-3.

Range Format
/RFC 2 A1. C10

Student Name

Date

Courtside Cafe Budget

	JAN	FEB	MAR	APR	MAY	JUN	JUL	AUG	SEPT	OCT	NOV	DEC	TOTAL
SALES:													
Food	$4,200	$4,400	$4,800	$5,200	$5,600	$6,200	$7,000	$5,500	$6,400	$5,500	$6,500	$7,520	$68,820
Beverage	$400	$450	$500	$540	$580	$600	$700	$500	$750	$800	$650	$775	$7,245
Total Sales	$4,600	$4,850	$5,300	$5,740	$6,180	$6,800	$7,700	$6,000	$7,150	$6,300	$7,150	$8,295	$76,065
EXPENSES:													
Food	$1,260	$1,320	$1,440	$1,560	$1,680	$1,860	$2,100	$1,650	$1,920	$1,650	$1,950	$2,256	$20,646
Beverage	$120	$135	$150	$162	$174	$180	$210	$150	$225	$240	$195	$233	$2,174
Payroll	$1,500	$1,500	$1,500	$1,500	$1,500	$1,500	$1,500	$1,500	$1,500	$1,500	$1,500	$1,500	$18,000
Lease	$150	$150	$150	$150	$150	$150	$150	$150	$150	$150	$150	$150	$6,600
G & A	$175	$175	$175	$175	$175	$175	$175	$175	$175	$175	$175	$175	$2,100
Direct	$975	$975	$975	$975	$975	$975	$975	$975	$975	$975	$975	$975	$11,700
Total Expenses	$4,580	$4,655	$4,790	$4,922	$5,054	$5,240	$5,510	$5,000	$5,345	$5,090	$5,345	$5,689	$61,220
PROFIT:	$20	$195	$510	$818	$1,126	$1,560	$2,190	$1,000	$1,805	$1,210	$1,805	$2,607	$14,846
PROFIT MARGIN:	0%	4%	10%	14%	18%	23%	28%	17%	25%	19%	25%	31%	20%

FIGURE 3-29

Key Terms

circular reference	mixed cell reference
freeze	file linking
window	target file
active window	source file
synchronized	linking formula
unsynchronized	target cell
what-if analysis	date numbers
work cell	justify
absolute cell reference	compressed

Matching

1. \015	_____ **a.**	absolute cell reference
2. @NOW	_____ **b.**	justifies a range of text
3. CIRC	_____ **c.**	moves cell pointer to other window
4. / W T B	_____ **d.**	enters system date
5. / W W V	_____ **e.**	causes compressed printing
6. target file	_____ **f.**	displays a range as a percent
7. +C25	_____ **g.**	the file that receives the data in a linking formula
8. / R J	_____ **h.**	freezes both horizontal and vertical titles
9. (F6)	_____ **i.**	creates a vertical window
10. / R F P	_____ **j.**	status indicator for circular reference

1. Retrieve the file PETSHOP.WK1. This is a worksheet of an income statement for the Pet Supply Shop. The formulas in the worksheet are:

Row 11   Gross margin = Sales - Cost of goods sold
Row 17   Total expense = Marketing + Administrative + Miscellaneous
          expenses
Row 19   Net income before taxes = Gross margin - Total expense
Row 20   Federal taxes = Net income before taxes * .52
Row 22   Net income after taxes = Net income before taxes - Federal taxes
Column N Total = Sum over 12 months

- Locate and correct the formula or @function causing the CIRC reference to be displayed in the worksheet (there may be more than one).

The owner of the Pet Supply Shop wants to change the worksheet to calculate the cost of goods sold as a percent of sales. He estimates that the cost of goods sold is about 45 percent of sales. You will use a work cell to hold the percent value and change the values in row 9 to be computed using this value as follows:

- Freeze both titles so that rows 6 through 25 are displayed in the window. Freeze everything above row 7 and to the left of column B.

- Move to column N. Create a vertical window at column M. Move to column N.

- Switch to the left window. Move to column B. Scroll rows 22 to 28 into view. Cell B25 is your work cell. A label has already been entered in cell A25 to identify the value you will enter in B25.

- Enter the value .45 in cell B25. Change the format of this cell to fixed with 2 decimal places.

- Enter the formula to calculate the cost of goods sold (B8*B25) in cell B9.

- Copy the formula in B9 to cells C9 through M9. To see how this change has affected the total net income after taxes, look at the value in N22 (right window). What is the value N22?

- The manager feels he may have been too high in his estimate for the percent cost value. He wants to see the effect on the total of changing the value in cell B25. Change the value in cell B25 to .40. What is the value in cell N22 now?

Next the manager would like to see the effect of changing the marketing, administrative, and miscellaneous expenses. By calculating these values as a percent of the gross margin, he feels he will be able to plan and budget better for the future.

- Enter the following values in the cells specified:

	Cell	Value
MKT	B26	.15
ADM	B27	.28
MISC	B28	.08

- Format cells B26, B27, and B28 to be displayed as fixed with 2 decimal places.

- Change the contents of cells B13 through B15 to be calculated using a formula referencing cells B26 through B28. Copy the formulas from B13..B15 through C13..M15. What is the total net income after taxes (N22) now?

- Leave the percent value for cost at .40. Change the other percent values to arrive at a net total income (N22) value as close to 5500 as possible. What total net income after taxes did you get? What were the percentages used?

- Clear the windows and titles.

- Enter your name in cell A1 and the date in cell A2. Save the worksheet as PETSHOP2.

- Print the worksheet using compressed printing.

2.   To complete this problem, you must have created the worksheet in Practice Exercise 4 of Lab 2. Retrieve the file ZOOFINAN. You will extend and expand the worksheet for the 3-year financial statement for the zoo. The assistant director of the zoo would like to project the financial statement for the next three years, 1991, 1992 and 1993.

- Format the worksheet to globally display currency with 0 decimal places. Globally adjust the column width to 13 in order to fully display the values.

- Insert 3 columns between 1990 and TOTAL for the projected years. Enter column headings for the 3 years (columns F, G, and H). Underline the new headings, and extend the underlines in the rest of the worksheet to cover the new columns.

- Insert another blank row above the column headings. Enter the heading "========Projected========" centered above the years 1991 through 1993.

- Freeze the row labels and column headings.

- Enter formulas to calculate the projected income values for the years 1991-1993. The Support & Revenues projections are: operating expenses increase 15 percent over the previous year, supporting organizations 20 percent and Interest income 22 percent. The fund -raising projected income is directly related to the amount of money allocated to fund-raising activities (cell F16). For each dollar allocated they expect to raise $4.25.

- Enter formulas to calculate the projected applications and expenses for the years 1991-1993. Operating expenses are expected to increase 17 percent each year over the previous year, capital projects 17 percent and fund raising 5 percent. The operating reserve is calculated using the same formula as in previous years.

- Copy the formula for TOTAL S & R, and TOTAL A/E for the years 1991 - 1993.

- Change the formulas used to calculate TOTAL and AVERAGE to include the new columns.
- Create a vertical window at column J. Display the years 1991 and 1992 in the left window, and TOTAL in the right window. Print your display screen (SHIFT) - (Prt scr).

In 1994 the zoo plans on adding a new jungle exhibit, which will cost $1.5 million. After looking at the results of the projected statement on the operating reserve, they realize that they will not have enough money for the new project. Currently the amount allocated toward fund raising is based upon a 5 percent increase over the previous year.

- Create a work cell a few rows below TOTAL A/E in cell F22. Format this cell to display fixed format, with 2 decimal places.
- Reference this cell to calculate the percentage increase for money allocated to fund raising in the years 1991 - 1993. Adjust the value in this cell until the total operating reserve is at least $1.5 million by the end of 1993.
- Clear the windows and titles.
- Erase the old date from cell A3, enter the current date in cell A2, and save the worksheet as ZOOFIN3.
- Print the worksheet using compressed printing. Do not include the work cell.

3.   As part of an assignment in a nutrition class, you have created a worksheet comparing four foods and the amount of exercise time it takes to burn off the calories from these foods. To see this worksheet, retrieve the file FOOD.WK1.

- In cell C16 enter the following text:

    As part of my research project on calorie burnoff, I have listed four common food items and the number of calories in each.

- Justify this line of text so that it does not extend beyond column G.
- In cell C20 enter:

    I then calculated the number of minutes needed to burn off the calories according to the type of exercise.

- Justify this line of text so that it does not extend beyond column G.
- Enter the system date in cell C24. Format the date to be displayed as Day-Month-Year (12-Jan-88).
- Enter your name in cell A1 and the date in cell A2. Save the worksheet as FOOD2.
- Print the worksheet.

4.   To complete this problem, retrieve the file COST created in Practice Problem 3 in Lab 2.

- Enter the following memo below the worksheet in column A.

The main finding of the data used in this worksheet is that by keeping the old car, the owner would save over $5,000. This is despite the estimate by expert analysts that in four years of steady driving (60,000 miles), repair costs would exceed those of the new car by $1,179 and that the old car would consume more gas.

The offsetting economies are that the old car would have lower insurance premiums and that there would be no financing costs for the old car. These two items are enough to account for nearly 55% of the costs of keeping a new car during the first four years. Therefore, it is better to keep the heap!

- Justify the text so that it is displayed below columns A through D.
- Enter the system date in cell A2. Format the date to be displayed as MM/DD/YY.
- Print the worksheet.
- Save the worksheet as COSTMEMO.

CASE STUDY

The Sports Club annual membership promotion month is in January. As preparation, the board of directors have asked the membership coordinator, Fred Morris, to present a report on the membership growth over the last 5 years.

Fred has maintained the membership data for the past 5 years. He has entered the data into a worksheet using Lotus 1-2-3. Although the data in the worksheet shows the club's growth, he feels the use of several graphs would make it easier for the board of directors to see the trends and growth patterns over the 5 years.

You will follow Fred as he creates several different graphs of the membership data.

Using the Access System

In this lab you will be using 1-2-3 to create graphs, and PrintGraph to print graphs. To make it easier to switch between 1-2-3 and PrintGraph, you will use the 1-2-3 Access system to load the 1-2-3 program. Turn on your computer and load DOS. Your 1-2-3 System disk should be in the A drive and the data diskette should be in the B drive.

To use the Access system to load 1-2-3, at the A>,

Type: **LOTUS**
Press: ⏎

OBJECTIVES

In this lab you will learn how to:

1. Use the Access System.
2. Create a line graph.
3. Specify the X axis labels.
4. Specify data to be graphed.
5. Enter graph titles.
6. Enter legends.
7. Name and save the graph.
8. Create a bar and a stacked-bar graph.
9. Create a pie chart.
10. Shade and explode the pie chart.
11. Print a graph.

Your screen should be similar to Figure 4-1

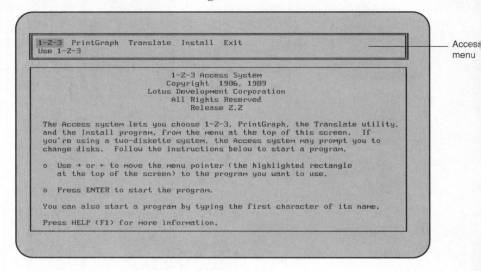

Access menu

FIGURE 4-1

The Access menu appears at the top of the screen. A description of the highlighted command appears in the next line. Read the information below the menu about how to use the Access system. To load 1-2-3, with the highlight over 1-2-3,

Press: ⏎

The 1-2-3 program is loaded in the usual manner.
To see the worksheet of membership data,

Select: / File Retrieve

Although the files to retrieve are listed in the control panel, only one line of file names can be seen at a time. To display all the files on the screen at once, use the (F3) Name key.

Press: (F3) Name

A menu of worksheet files is displayed on the screen. The name of the highlighted file and information about its size and date of creation are displayed on the third line of the control panel. To select a file from the menu, use the arrow keys to highlight the file name of your choice and press ⏎ .

Continue the command sequence by selecting GROWTH.WK1.

Your display screen should be similar to Figure 4-2.

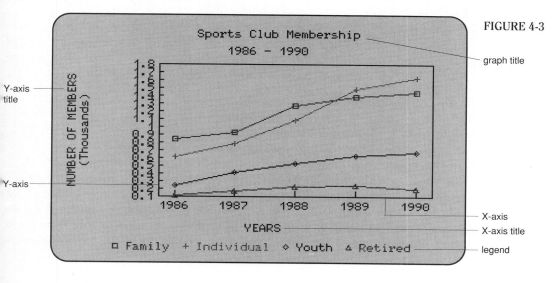

```
A1:                                                              READY

        A        B         C        D        E        F        G
1
2
3                            Sports Club Membership
4                               1986 - 1990
5
6                     1986     1987     1988     1989     1990
7                   ─────────────────────────────────────────
8
9        Family      840      930     1274     1380     1442
10       Individual  615      779     1089     1488     1635
11       Youth       250      408      535      628      675
12       Retired     114      168      232      250      198
13                  =====    =====    =====    =====    =====
14
15       Total      1819     2285     3130     3746     3950
16
17
18
19
20
06-Jul-90  01:29 PM        UNDO
```

FIGURE 4-2

The worksheet lists the four membership categories offered by the Sports Club as row labels in cells B9 through B12. They are defined as follows:

Family	spouse and dependent children
Individual	one-person membership
Youth	individual under 18 years of age
Retired	individual over 55 years of age

The total in row 15 is the sum of the four membership categories. The column labels in row 6 represent the years 1986 through 1990.

Although the worksheet shows the values for each membership category, it is hard to see how the different categories have changed over time. A visual representation of data in the form of a **graph** would convey that information in an easy-to-understand and attractive manner.

Lotus 1-2-3 can produce five types of graphs: line, bar, stacked-bar, XY, and pie. All graph types, except the pie, have some basic similarities. The basic parts of a line or bar graph are illustrated in Figure 4-3.

FIGURE 4-3

The bottom boundary of the graph is the **X axis**. It is used to label the data being graphed, such as a value of time or a category.

The left boundary of the graph is the **Y axis**. This axis is a numbered scale whose values are determined by the data used in the graph.

The worksheet data is visually displayed within the X- and Y-axis boundaries. It can be displayed as a line, bar, or stacked bar. Each group of data that is displayed is represented by a symbol. A **legend** at the bottom of the graph describes the symbols used within the graph.

A graph can also contain several different **titles**, which are used to explain the contents of the graph. In Lotus 1-2-3, the two title lines at the top of the graph are called the first and second title lines. Titles can also be used to label the X and Y axes.

In pie charts there are no X or Y axes. Instead, the worksheet data that is graphed is displayed as slices in a circle or pie. Each slice is labeled. A first and second title line can be used; however, legends and X- and Y-axis titles are not used.

Selecting the Type of Graph

The first graph Fred would like to create is a **line graph** to show the total membership growth pattern over 5 years. A line graph represents data as a set of points along a line.

All graphs are drawn from data contained in a worksheet. To graph worksheet data, the Graph menu is used. To open this menu,

Select: **/ Graph**

Your display screen should be similar to Figure 4-4.

FIGURE 4-4

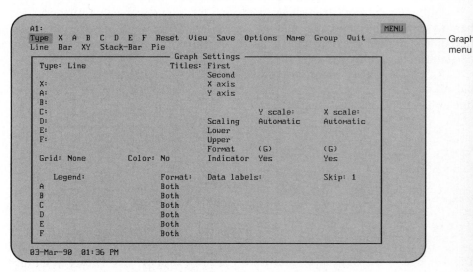

The Graph Settings sheet is displayed on the screen. Like the other settings sheets you have seen, the Graph Settings sheet helps you keep track of the choices you have made. The Graph Settings sheet shows you the current graph settings for the Graph commands displayed in the menu above the settings sheet. Since there are no graph settings specified yet, the settings sheet is empty except for the names of the graph settings and for any default graph settings.

There are 15 Graph menu commands, beginning with Type and ending with Quit. To briefly preview the Graph commands using the Help system,

Press: (F1) Help

Read this screen carefully as it describes each of the graph commands you will be using in this lab.

The first graph command you will use is Type. For further information about this command,

Press: (⏎)

The Help screen now tells you about the five types of graphs you can create using 1-2-3. After reading the information on this screen, to return to the Graph menu,

Press: (ESC)

The first step in creating a graph is to specify the type of graph you want to create. To do this,

Select: Type

Your display screen should be similar to Figure 4-5.

default
setting   graph types

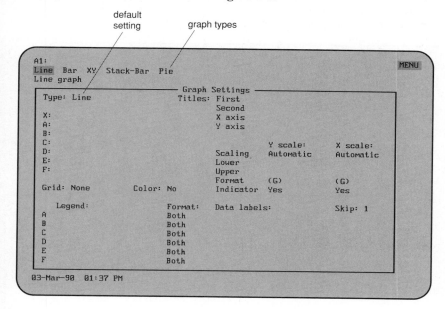

FIGURE 4-5

The five graph types are displayed in the second line of the control panel. The menu pointer is positioned on Line. As you can see from the settings sheet, the default graph type is a line graph. Since this is the type of graph you want to create, to accept the default,

Press: (⏎)

If you do not select Type from the Graph menu, a line graph is created by default.

Notice that you are returned to the Graph menu rather than the READY mode so that you can continue defining your graph settings.

Labeling the X Axis

The next step is to specify the labels to be entered along the horizontal or X axis of the graph. In a line graph the X axis usually represents some block of time, such as days, weeks, months, or years. The X axis for Fred's line graph will display the year labels, 1986 through 1990, located in cells C6 through G6.

To define the years as the X-axis labels,

Select: **X**

The Graph Settings sheet is cleared from the screen and the worksheet is displayed. Now you can see the range of cells in the worksheet containing the data to be specified as the X data range. The prompt "Enter x-axis range:" is displayed in the control panel. The current cell pointer position, A1, is displayed following the prompt. You can specify the range by typing the cell addresses or by highlighting.

Highlight the range of cells containing the year labels 1986 through 1990 as the X-axis labels.

Your screen should be similar to similar to Figure 4-6.

FIGURE 4-6

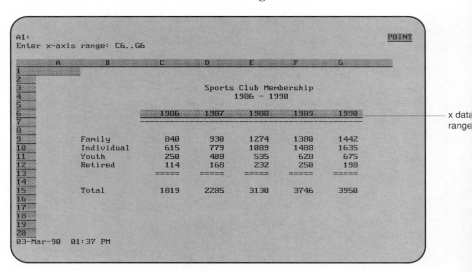

To enter the highlighted range as the X-axis labels,

Press: ⏎

The Graph Settings sheet is displayed again. The range of cells you specified for the X data range is displayed in the settings sheet. If your settings sheet does not display the X data range as C6..G6, respecify the correct X range.

Specifying the Data to Be Graphed

The range of data in the worksheet that contains the numbers to be graphed is specified next. The letters A through F in the Graph menu allow you to specify up to six data ranges to be displayed in the graph.

Fred wants to graph the values that show total membership growth over the 5-year period. This data is in cells C15 through G15. The first range of data you want to graph is entered as the A range. The same procedure you used to specify the X-axis range is used to specify a data range.

Select: **A**

The prompt "Enter first data range: A1" appears in the control panel. Again, you can type the range or highlight it.

Using highlighting, specify the range of cells containing the total membership growth for the 5 years as the A data range.

Your display screen should be similar to Figure 4-7.

FIGURE 4-7

```
G12: 198                                                              MENU
Type  X  A  B  C  D  E  F  Reset  View  Save  Options  Name  Group  Quit
Set first data range
                              ─ Graph Settings ─
   Type: Line                     Titles: First
                                           Second
   X: C6..G6                              X axis
   A: C15..G15                            Y axis
   B:
   C:                                             Y scale:      X scale:
   D:                              Scaling       Automatic     Automatic
   E:                              Lower
   F:                              Upper
                                   Format        (G)           (G)
   Grid: None        Color: No     Indicator     Yes           Yes

     Legend:          Format:      Data labels:                Skip: 1
   A                    Both
   B                    Both
   C                    Both
   D                    Both
   E                    Both
   F                    Both


 09-Apr-90   09:48 AM
```

You are again returned to the Graph Settings sheet, and the A data range setting you specified (C15..G15) is displayed.

Note: All graph data ranges (X and A-F) can be specified in one step using the Graph Group command. However, this command can only be used if the data ranges are in consecutive rows or columns.

Viewing the Graph

Once a data range and the X range have been specified, you can view the graph.

Note: To display graphs you must have a graphics adapter card that is supported by Lotus 1-2-3 and have properly installed the 1-2-3 program. See your instructor if your graph is not displayed.

Select: View

Your display screen should be similar to Figure 4-8.

FIGURE 4-8

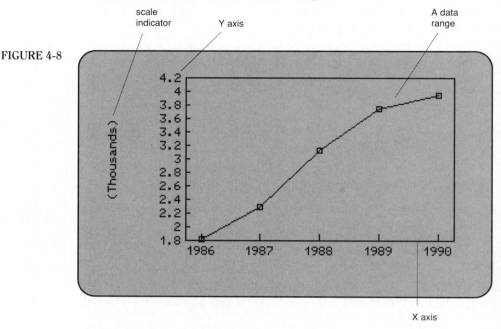

The years are displayed along the X axis. The data for total membership is displayed within the graph boundaries. Each data point is marked by a square symbol and connected by a line.

The values on the Y axis begin at 1.8 and end at 4.2. The Y axis is automatically set by Lotus 1-2-3 as a scale of values determined by the lowest and highest values in the data range. The notation "(Thousands)" appears along the Y axis to show that the Y-axis values represent numbers in the thousands. This notation is called a **scale indicator**. Scale indicators will appear when appropriate along the X or Y axis to clarify the values displayed along the axis.

The total membership growth pattern over the 5 years is now easy to see. The graph, however, still is not easy to understand. You know what the data stands for because you defined the graph settings. However, someone else would not have any idea what the graph means. The addition of titles to the graph will help explain the graph contents.

To clear the graph from the display and return to the Graph menu,

Press: any key

Entering Graph Titles

Graph titles are not required graph settings. However, without titles, the meaning of the data displayed in the graph is not clear.

Titles can be entered at the top of the graph (two lines) and along the X and Y axes. The command to add titles is a submenu option found in the Graph Options menu. The Graph Options menu is used to refine the appearance of a graph.

Select: Options

Your display screen should be similar to Figure 4-9.

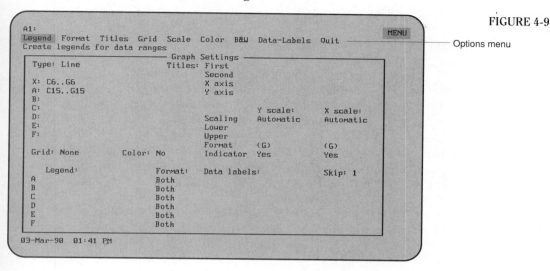

FIGURE 4-9

Options menu

The Options submenu contains eight commands that enhance the appearance of a graph or make it easier to understand. For an explanation of the meaning of these options,

Press: (F1) Help

Your display screen should be similar to Figure 4-10.

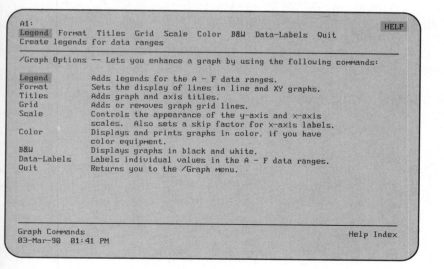

FIGURE 4-10

The Help screen describes the eight graph options. After reading this screen, to return to the Graph Settings sheet,

Press: (ESC)

To add titles to a graph,

Select: Titles

The four title alternatives are displayed in the control panel. They have the following effect:

First	puts centered text at the top of the graph
Second	centers a second line of text at the top of the graph
X-Axis	places text along the horizontal axis
Y-Axis	places text along the vertical axis

The same titles used in the worksheet can be copied into the graph, or entirely new titles can be used. The worksheet titles "Sports Club Membership" in cell D3 and "1986-1990" in cell E4 would be appropriate for labeling this graph. Each title can be a maximum of 39 characters long.

To display the worksheet screen so that you can easily refer to cells in the worksheet while specifying the graph title,

Press: (F6) Window

Whenever a settings sheet is displayed on the screen, the (F6) Window key can be used to clear the settings sheet and display the worksheet. The worksheet will continue to be displayed until the (F6) key is pressed again to redisplay the settings sheet.

To enter the first title line of the graph,

Select: First

At the prompt "Enter first line of graph title:" you can type any title exactly as you want it to appear in the graph. Alternatively, you can copy a title used in the worksheet. You want to use the same title as the one displayed in the worksheet in cell D3. To copy the contents of a cell into the graph as a title line, you type a backslash (\) character followed by the cell address containing the label. To do this,

Type: \D3

Your display screen should be similar to Figure 4-11.

cell address

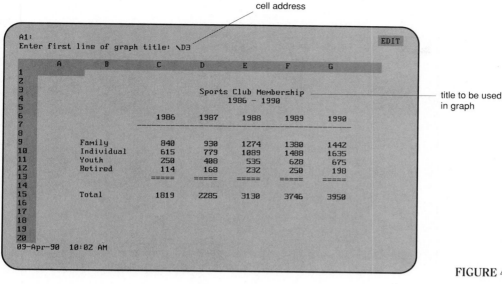

title to be used
in graph

FIGURE 4-11

Press: ⏎

The Graph Options menu is displayed in the control panel again to allow you to continue specifying other options. To redisplay the Graph Settings sheet,

Press: (F6) Window

The cell address containing the label you want to use as the first title line of the graph is displayed following "Title: First" in the settings sheet.

The second title line needs to be entered into the graph. It will be the same as the worksheet title in cell E4. To enter a second title,

Select: Titles
Press: (F6) Window
Select: Second \E4 ⏎

To leave this menu and view the graph with the title lines as specified,

Select: Quit View

Your display screen should be similar to Figure 4-12.

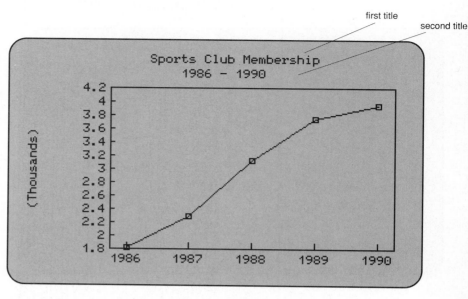

first title

second title

FIGURE 4-12

The two title lines are displayed centered above the graph. Using titles within the graph greatly improves the appearance and meaning of the line graph.

To return to the Graph menu,

Press: any key

The title lines to describe the X and Y axes need to be entered next. The X axis shows the growth in membership over the 5 years. The Y axis shows the number of members. You will label the X axis "YEARS," and the Y axis "NUMBER OF MEM-BERS."

The axis titles you want to use in the graph are not labels that are used in the worksheet. Therefore the titles must be typed following the prompt as part of the command sequence. Type the title in all capital letters. A title is displayed in the graph exactly as entered in the command sequence. To redisplay the settings sheet and enter the X- and Y-axis title lines,

Press: (F6) Window
Select: **O**ptions **T**itles **X**-Axis **YEARS** (⏎)
         Titles **Y**-Axis **NUMBER OF MEMBERS** (⏎)

The titles as you entered them are displayed in the settings sheet.

To leave the Options submenu and view the graph,

Select: **Q**uit **V**iew

Your display screen should be similar to Figure 4-13.

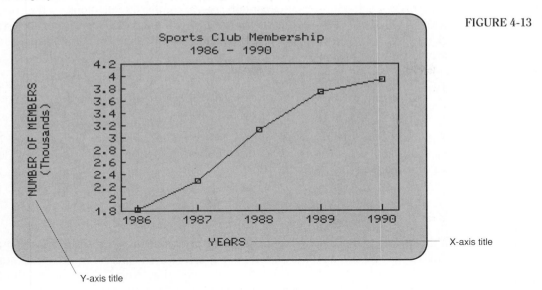

The title "YEARS" is displayed along the horizontal X axis. The title "NUMBER OF MEMBERS" is displayed along the vertical Y axis.

To return to the Graph menu,

Press: any key

Naming the Graph Settings

The line graph is the first graph created using the data in the worksheet. Many different graphs can be created and stored in a worksheet. To create more than one graph in a worksheet, each graph must be named. Naming the graph settings allows the current graph settings to be stored in the worksheet and recalled for later use. If the current graph settings are not named, the new graph settings as they are defined will write over the current settings.

To assign the current graph settings a name the Graph Name command is used.

Select: Name

The five Name options are:

Use	makes a named graph the current graph
Create	creates or modifies a named graph by storing the current graph settings with the name you specify
Delete	deletes a named graph
Reset	deletes all named graphs in the worksheet
Table	creates a table of named graphs in the worksheet

To store the current line graph settings using the name LINE,

Select: Create

A graph name can be up to 14 characters long and should be descriptive of the contents of the graph. It cannot contain spaces, commas, semicolons, or the characters +, -, /, &, >, <, @, *, #. It can be entered using either uppercase or lowercase characters. 1-2-3 will always display the graph name in uppercase. In response to the prompt to enter the name of the graph,

Type: **LINE**
Press: (⏎)

The line graph settings are stored in the computer's memory for later use. The named graph is not permanently saved on the diskette until the worksheet file is saved using the File Save command.

Saving Graphs for Printing

Although the graph is named, it cannot be printed using the PrintGraph program unless it is also saved on the diskette in a **graph file**. The picture image of the graph is saved on this file. The graph file is distinguished from other files by the file extension .PIC, which is added to the file name by the program.

Before saving this graph for printing, to identify this graph as the graph you created, change the second title line to "By [Your Name]." To do this, use the **/ G**raph **O**ptions **T**itles **S**econd command. Then to clear the exisiting second title, press (ESC). You can then enter a new second title.

To save this graph as a graph file on your data disk,

Select: Save **LINE** (⏎)

After a few seconds the graph is saved on the data diskette. You now have a named graph called LINE and a graph saved for printing called LINE.PIC. Using the same name for both the graph file name and the named graph is perfectly acceptable.

Switching the Graph Type

Once the current graph settings are named, another graph can be created using the worksheet data without erasing the previous graph settings.

Fred would like to see how the same data displayed in the line graph would look as a bar graph. This can easily be done by changing the type of graph to bar. Since the line graph settings are named, you can change the type of graph to a bar graph without destroying the line graph settings.

Select: Type **Bar** View

Your display screen should be similar to Figure 4-14.

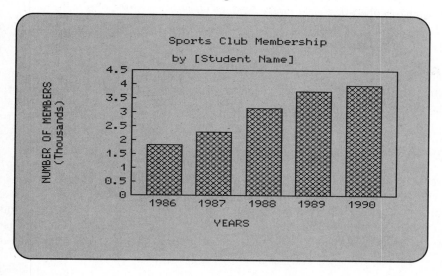

FIGURE 4-14

The data range defined in the line graph for total membership growth over the 5 years is displayed as a **bar graph**. A bar graph displays data as a set of evenly spaced bars. Each bar represents a value in the range. The Y-axis scale is different from the scale used when the data was displayed as a line graph because a bar graph must begin with the scale set at 0.

The only setting that changed was the type of graph. The bar graph is now the **current graph** because it is the one that can be viewed.

To return to the Graph menu,

Press: any key

Resetting Graph Specifications

Fred feels that a better use of the bar graph would be to show growth patterns for the four membership categories rather than the total membership growth.

To display a different range of data in the A range, the A data range needs to be canceled or reset. The Graph Reset command is used to cancel current graph settings.

Select: Reset

The Reset command options are displayed in the control panel. The Reset menu lets you cancel all the current graph settings (Graph), individual data ranges (X and A-F), all data ranges (Ranges), or all graph options (Options).

To cancel the A data range and return to the Graph menu,

Select: A Quit

The Graph Settings sheet shows you that the A data range is no longer defined. To see what has happened to the current bar graph,

Select: View

The computer beeps and a blank screen is displayed. The A data range has been erased, and consequently a graph cannot be viewed.

Press: any key

Be very careful when using the Reset command that you select the correct submenu command. It can very quickly cancel many graph settings that are very time consuming to respecify.

Defining Multiple Data Ranges

Fred wants the graph to compare the membership growth over the 5 year period for each category of membership (Family, Individual, Youth, and Retired). The A data range will contain the data for family memberships, the B data range will contain the individual membership data, the C data range will contain the youth membership data, and the D data range will contain the retired category of membership data.

Select each data range (A, B, C, and D) to define, and then, using highlighting, specify the appropriate worksheet range.

Note: If you have a color monitor, you can view your graphs in color by issuing the following command sequence: **/ G**raph **O**ptions **C**olor **Q**uit.

To view the graph,

Select: View

Your display screen should be similar to Figure 4-15.

FIGURE 4-15

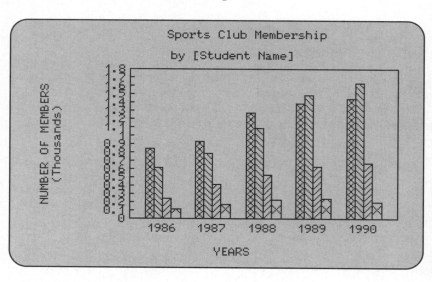

The new bar graph showing the data for each membership category in each year is displayed. Each bar represents one of the four membership categories in each year. But how do you know which bar stands for which category?

Entering Legends

When only one category was graphed, the graph was easy to understand. However, with the addition of the other three membership categories to the graph, it is difficult to distinguish among the four groups.

The use of a different **hatch pattern** (crosshatching design within the bars) or color for each of the four bars helps differentiate the groups. But how do you know which hatch pattern or color goes with which membership category?

To identify or label each hatch pattern, legends are used. A legend is a short descriptive label that helps identify the hatch patterns, or the data symbols in a line graph, that represent the A through F data ranges.

To return to the Graph menu,

Press: any key
Select: Options Legend

Each legend can be entered individually for each data range (A through F) in the same way that titles were entered. Additionally, legends can be entered as a group using the Range command. The Range command allows you to specify a range of cells in the worksheet that contain entries that you want to be the legends for the graph data ranges. 1-2-3 uses the first entry in the range as the A data range legend, the second entry as the B data range legend, and so forth. The labels must be in a continuous range, however. If a blank cell occurs between labels within the range, the blank entry will be used as a legend.

The worksheet labels—Family, Individual, Youth, and Retired— in cells B9 through B12 would be appropriate legends for the graphed data. To use the Range command to define legends for the four data ranges,

Select: Range

Specify the four worksheet labels using highlighting as the range.

The cell addresses are displayed in the settings sheet as if you had entered them individually using the backslash feature. To view the graph and see the legends,

Select: Quit View

Your display screen should be similar to Figure 4-16.

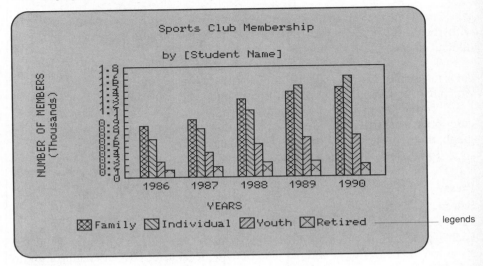

FIGURE 4-16

The four legends are displayed at the bottom of the graph to the right of the corresponding hatch symbol or color. Although 1-2-3 will accept legends up to 19 characters long, it will wrap long legends to a second line if there is insufficient space below the X axis to display the legends on a single line. To avoid this, you may want to abbreviate some of the legend labels.

The addition of legends to the graph makes reading and understanding the graph much easier.

Press: any key

The multiple-bar graph is now the current graph. Before creating another graph or recalling the line graph, the current bar graph settings must be named. Name this graph "BAR" as follows:

Select: Name Create **BAR** ⏎

Next, you will save this graph for printing as BAR.PIC.

Note: If you are viewing the bar graph in color and you do not have a color printer or plotter, set the color option back to black and white before saving the graph for printing. The command to do this is: **/ G**raph **O**ptions **B&W Q**uit. If you do not turn color off, 1-2-3 will print all ranges in solid blocks of black.

Select: **/ G**raph **S**ave **BAR** ⏎

There are now two named graphs stored in memory and two graphs saved for printing, LINE and BAR.

Creating a Stacked-Bar Graph

Fred is pleased with the bar graph, but he thinks that a **stacked-bar graph** may display the worksheet data in an even more meaningful manner. The stacked-bar graph will show

the proportion of each type of membership to the total membership in each year.
To change the bar graph to a stacked-bar graph and view it,

Select: Type Stack-Bar View

Note: If you want to view this graph in color, reselect the Color option, then
view the graph.

Your display screen should be similar to Figure 4-17.

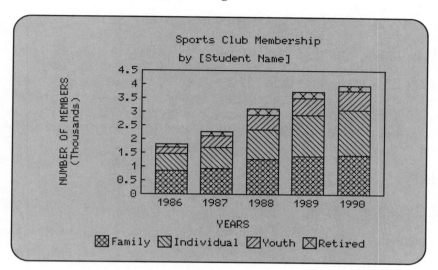

FIGURE 4-17

Rather than the bars being displayed side by side, the bars are stacked upon each
other. The Y-axis scale has changed to reflect the new range of data. The new Y-axis
range is the sum of the four membership categories, or the same as the total value
in the worksheet. It is now easy to compare how much each membership category
contributed to the total membership in each year.

Press: any key

The stacked-bar graph is now the current graph. To store the stacked-bar
graph settings using the name "STACKED," issue the following command sequence.
As you do, notice that the other two named graphs are listed in the control panel.

Select: Name Create **STACKED** ⮐

Save the graph for printing (set color to B&W first if necessary) as follows:

Select: Save **STACKED** ⮐

There are now three named graphs stored in memory: LINE, BAR, and STACKED;
and three graphs saved for printing using the same names.

Creating a Pie Chart

The final graph Fred would like to create using the worksheet data is a **pie chart**. A pie chart compares parts to the whole in a similar manner to a stacked-bar graph. However, each value in the range is a slice of the pie or circle displayed as a percentage of the total.

The use of X and A data range settings in a pie chart is different from their use in a bar or line graph. The X range labels the slices of the pie rather than the X axis. The A data range is used to create the slices in the pie. Only one data range (A) is defined in a pie chart.

To cancel all the current graph settings (stacked),

Select: Reset Graph

The settings sheet is now cleared of all graph settings.

Fred wants to compare the four membership categories for the year 1990. The labels for the slices (membership category) will be defined in the X range as B9 through B12. The A data range will be the values for 1990 in cell G9 through G12. Complete the following command sequence:

Select: Type Pie X

Specify the four membership category labels as the X range using highlighting.

Select: A

Specify the values for 1990 as the A data range using highlighting.

Select: View

Note: If you want to view the pie chart in color, you will need to turn the color option back on.

Your display screen should be similar to Figure 4-18.

FIGURE 4-18

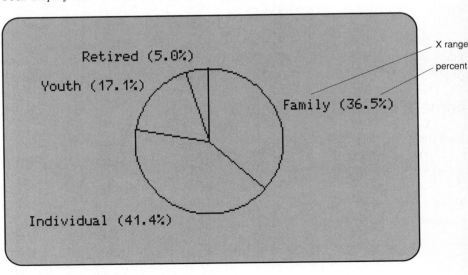

Each membership category, defined in the X range, labels each slice of the pie. Each membership category's percentage of the total membership for 1990 is displayed in parentheses next to the slice label.

To complete this graph, a title needs to be entered. Since the pie chart compares the four membership categories for the year 1990 only, the same title as used in the worksheet would not be appropriate.

Press: any key

Enter the first graph title line as "1990 Membership Comparison" and a second title line as "By [Your Name]."

View the graph.

Shading the Pie Slices

Unlike the bar graphs, the pie chart does not display hatch patterns automatically. To add this feature to a pie chart, you must create a B data range the same size as the A data range and enter a value from 1 to 8 in each cell of the B data range. These values are called **shading values**. Each value assigns a different hatch pattern or color for each slice of the pie. The number 8 leaves a pie slice as a blank. See Figure 4-19.

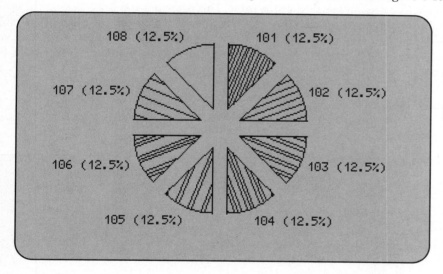

FIGURE 4-19

The shading values can be entered anywhere in the worksheet as long as they are entered as a continuous range of cells. To clear the graph and return to the READY mode,

Press: any key
Select: Quit

You will enter the shading values in column A, next to the worksheet labels.

Move to: A9

Rather than typing the numbers for the shading values into each cell, you can use the Data Fill command to fill the column with a sequence of numbers. To do this,

Select: / Data Fill

First you need to specify the range of cells to fill.

Type: A9..A12
Press: ⏎

Next the prompt asks you to enter the **start value**. This is the value you want to be the first number entered in the range. To begin the range using the number 1,

Type: 1
Press: ⏎

The next prompt is to enter the **step value** or the incrememt between each value in the range. To accept the default of 1,

Press: ⏎

Finally, you need to specify the **stop value**. This is the number 1-2-3 uses as the upper limit for the sequence. Since the range contains only four cells, the end of the range will be encountered before the default stop value (8191) is reached. Therefore, you could enter the number 4 as the stop value or accept the default. To accept the default,

Press: ⏎

Your screen should look similar to Figure 4.20.

FIGURE 4-20

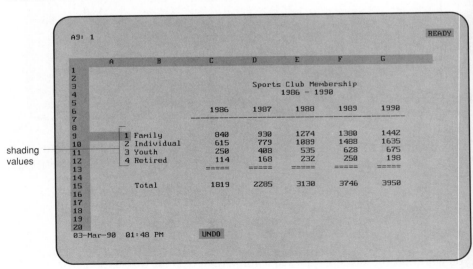

The numbers 1 through 4 are entered in the specified range. As you can see, using the Data Fill command is a real time saver whenever a range of cells needs to be filled with an incremental sequence of numbers.

Now you are ready to define the values you just entered as the B data range values for the pie chart. To do this,

Select: / Graph **B**

Specify the shading values as the B data range.

The B data range is displayed in the settings sheet. To view the change in the pie chart,

Select: View

Your screen should be similar to Figure 4-21.

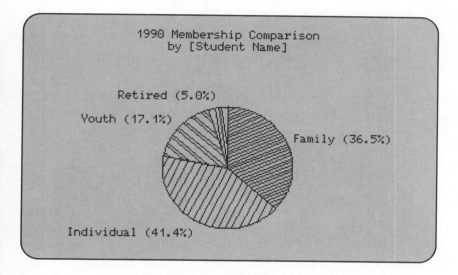

FIGURE 4-21

The shading values in the B data range determine the hatch pattern (or color if you are viewing your graph in color) for each slice of the pie. If you changed the values in the worksheet, the hatch patterns or colors would change accordingly.

Exploding a Slice of the Pie

A slice or several slices of a pie chart can be **exploded** or separated slightly from the other slices in the pie. This lets you emphasize a particular part of the pie chart. To explode a slice, add 100 to the B data range value that corresponds to the slice you want to explode.

To clear the graph and return to the READY mode,

Press: any key
Select: Quit

To explode the slice of the pie containing the data for the Retired membership category,

Move to: A12
Type: 104
Press: ⏎

The last digit (4) still determines the shading for the exploded slice.
To see the change in the pie chart, you need to view the graph. The current graph can be viewed from the READY mode by using the Graph function key, [F10].

Press: (F10) Graph

Your display screen should be similar to Figure 4-22.

FIGURE 4-22

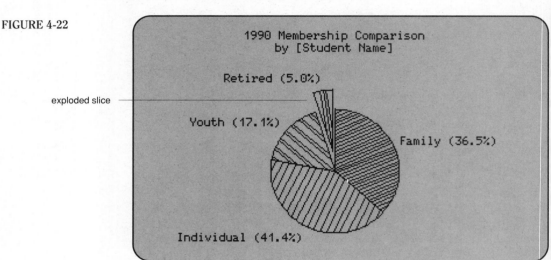

1990 Membership Comparison
by [Student Name]

Retired (5.0%)

exploded slice

Youth (17.1%)

Family (36.5%)

Individual (41.4%)

The slice of the pie representing the Retired category is exploded or separated from the other slices of the pie chart.

Fred notices that the Retired membership category represents only 5 percent of the total. He thinks this figure is a little low. To check the data entered in the worksheet for this category, return to the worksheet.

Press: any key

The value in cell G12 is 198. After checking his records, Fred sees that it was entered incorrectly into the worksheet. It should be 298. To change this figure in the worksheet,

Move to: G12
Type: 298
Press: ⏎

The worksheet has been recalculated. But what about the graphs and pie chart using the value in this cell as part of a data range? Do they change to reflect the new value?

To quickly view the current graph again,

Press: (F10) Graph

The pie chart is redrawn to reflect the change in the worksheet value for the Retired membership group. The Retired membership category for 1990 is now 7.4 percent of the total membership. The other percentages have been adjusted accordingly.

Using graphs to visually display the effects of performing what-if analysis in a worksheet is another powerful management tool.

Press: any key

Name the current pie chart settings "PIE."
Save the pie chart for printing (first set the color option to B&W if necessary) as PIE.PIC.

Recalling Named Graphs

There are now four named graphs stored in memory and four graphs saved for printing: LINE, BAR, STACKED, and PIE.

To recall a named graph and view it,

Select: Name Use

The named graphs are displayed in the third line of the control panel. To select a graph to view, move the menu pointer to the graph name and press ⏎ or type in the graph name at the prompt and press ⏎ .

To view the line graph,

Select: LINE ⏎

Your display screen should be similar to Figure 4-23.

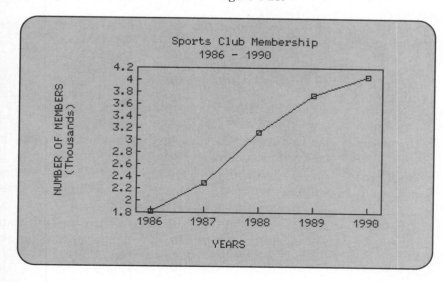

FIGURE 4-23

The line graph whose settings were named and stored in memory is displayed on the screen. Notice that this graph also reflects the change in the data in cell G12. The named graph stores only the settings, not the data in the worksheet. As a result, changes to the worksheet data are automatically reflected in the graph. However, if you change the graph settings, you would need to rename the graph.

To return to the Graph menu,

Press:　any key

To view the other two graphs (remember to erase the graph from the display after viewing it by pressing any key),

Select:　Name Use **BAR** ⏎
Name Use **STACKED** ⏎

Naming graphs is an important feature that allows you to have more than one set of graph settings in a single worksheet. The graph you view on the screen or recalled last is the current graph.

If you have not cleared the graph from the screen,

Press:　any key

To leave the Graph menu,

Select:　Quit

Saving the Worksheet

To print a graph using Lotus 1-2-3 requires that you leave the 1-2-3 program and then use the PrintGraph program disk. Before leaving 1-2-3 you should save your worksheet containing all the named graph settings. If you do not save the worksheet, the graphs you created and named will be erased from memory when you leave the Lotus program.

To save the named graphs (currently stored only in memory) with the worksheet in a new file called GRAPHS.WK1,

Select:　/ File Save **GRAPHS.WK1** ⏎

It is important to understand the differences between naming a graph, saving a graph for printing, and saving a worksheet. To review:

/ Graph Save	saves a picture of the graph on a file on the diskette with the file extension .PIC for use when the graph is printed.
/ Graph Name	assigns a name to the current graph settings so that these settings can be recalled and used at a later time. The graph settings are stored in temporary memory.
/ File Save	saves the worksheet file with the file extension .WK1 along with any named graphs. The current graph settings are also saved even if they have not been named.

To leave 1-2-3,

Select: / Quit Yes

Printing a Graph

Note: To complete this section, you must have properly installed the PrintGraph program and established the correct hardware setup for your system. Consult your instructor for details.

In a few moments, you are returned to the Access menu rather than to the DOS prompt. The Access menu lets you select the utility program you want to use. To select PrintGraph,

Type: P

If you are using 5-1/4 inch-disks, replace the 1-2-3 disk with the Printgraph disk as directed on the screen and press ⏎.

Note: If you need to load the PrintGraph program directly from the DOS prompt, insert the PrintGraph diskette in drive A. At the A>, type: PGRAPH and press ⏎.

After a few moments your display screen should be similar to Figure 4-24.

FIGURE 4-24

```
Copyright 1986, 1989 Lotus Development Corp.  All Rights Reserved. V2.2    MENU

Select graphs to print or preview
Image-Select  Settings  Go  Align  Page  Exit

   GRAPHS    IMAGE SETTINGS                    HARDWARE SETTINGS
   TO PRINT    Size           Range colors      Graphs directory
                Top      .395  X Black             B:\
                Left     .750  A Black           Fonts directory
                Width   6.500  B Black             A:\
                Height  4.691  C Black           Interface
                Rotation .000  D Black             Parallel 1
                               E Black           Printer
              Font             F Black             Eps FX,RX/lo
              1  BLOCK1                          Paper size
              2  BLOCK1                            Width     8.500
                                                  Length   11.000

                                               ACTION SETTINGS
                                                 Pause  No  Eject  No
```

This is the PrintGraph main screen. The PrintGraph menu is displayed in the third line of the control panel, and a description of the highlighted command is displayed in the second line. It is not necessary to press / to display the PrintGraph menu. A PrintGraph menu option is selected in the same way a 1-2-3 menu option is selected.

Note: The hardware settings on your display may differ from those in Figure 4-24.

To print a graph, first you will select the graph to print. Then you will prepare the printer, and finally you will print the graph.

First, to select the graph to print,

Select: Image-Select

Your display screen should be similar to Figure 4-25.

FIGURE 4-25

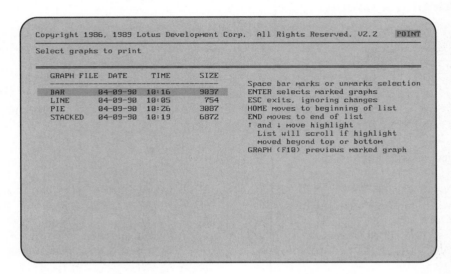

```
Copyright 1986, 1989 Lotus Development Corp.  All Rights Reserved. V2.2   POINT

Select graphs to print


  GRAPH FILE  DATE     TIME     SIZE
  ──────────────────────────────────        Space bar marks or unmarks selection
  BAR         04-09-90  10:16    9037        ENTER selects marked graphs
  LINE        04-09-90  10:05     754        ESC exits, ignoring changes
  PIE         04-09-90  10:26    3087        HOME moves to beginning of list
  STACKED     04-09-90  10:19    6872        END moves to end of list
                                             ↑ and ↓ move highlight
                                               List will scroll if highlight
                                               moved beyond top or bottom
                                             GRAPH (F10) previews marked graph
```

Note: If your screen tells you there are no graph files on the disk, check to see that the directory that PrintGraph is searching is properly defined for your system (Settings Hardware Graphs-Directory) or that the correct disk is in the drive.

The four graph files you saved for printing are listed.

The highlight bar is positioned over the first .PIC file. To select a graph to print, move the highlight bar to the file name and press the space bar.

Select: **STACKED.PIC**

A # sign appears to the left of the graph name. This indicates it has been selected for printing. If you wanted to cancel a selection, you would press the space bar again, and the # would disappear.

Before printing a graph, it can be previewed on the screen.

Press: (F10) Graph

The stacked-bar graph is displayed on the screen. The settings for this graph cannot be altered at this point.

To clear the graph from the display,

Press: any key

Note: If your instructor wants you to print more than one graph, select the additional graph names from the list of names.

When you have selected all the graphs you want to print, to return to the main PrintGraph menu,

Press: ⏎

Your display screen should reflect the graphs you have chosen to print. Turn on the printer. Check to see that it is online and that the perforation in the paper is aligned with the printer scale.

To actually print the selected graph(s),

Select: Align Go

After a few moments, your printed graph should be similar to Figure 4-26.

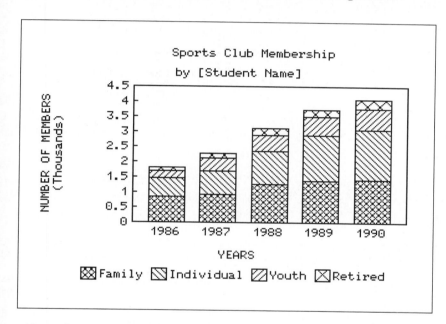

FIGURE 4-26

Note: If your screen tells you there are no graphics printers active, check to see that you have defined and selected the appropriate printer (Settings Hardware Printer).

To advance the paper to the top of the next page and to leave the PrintGraph program,

Select: Page Exit Yes

Again you are returned to the Access menu. To leave the Access system and return to the DOS prompt,

Select: Exit

Key Terms

graph	current graph
X axis	hatch patterns
Y axis	stacked-bar graph
legend	pie chart
titles	shading values
line graph	start value
scale indicator	step value
graph file	stop value
bar graph	explode

Matching

1. (F10)   _____ **a.** specifies the kind of graph

2. PIE   _____ **b.** calls up a named graph for use

3. PIC   _____ **c.** defines the data ranges to graph

4. legend   _____ **d.** displays the current graph on the screen

5. X   _____ **e.** describes the graph

6. A B C D E F   _____ **f.** displays symbols and descriptive labels of the dat

7. View   _____ **g.** picture file extension

8. title   _____ **h.** labels the horizontal axis

9. type   _____ **i.** a type of graph

10. / G N U   _____ **j.** displays the current graph from READY mode

Practice Exercises

1. The American dream of owning your own home has become elusive, in par
because the prices of homes in most places have risen faster than incomes. Th
following data shows the average price of a home and the average family incom
levels from 1976 to 1986.

HOUSING PRICES vs. PERSONAL INCOME
(in thousands of dollars)

	1976	1980	1986
Avg. Home	37	55	89
Personal Income	15	22	30

- Create a worksheet displaying this data. Use the titles and row and colum
  labels shown.
- Create a line graph showing the change in the average cost of a hom
  and family income over the years 1976 to 1986.
- Enter a first title line using the title displayed in the worksheet. Enter
  second title line: "By [Your Name]."
- Label the X axis "Years." Label the Y axis "In thousands of dollars."

- Enter legends.
- Name the line graph HOUSING.
- Save the line graph for printing as HOUSING.PIC.
- Save the worksheet as HOME.
- Print the line graph, HOUSING.PIC.

2.   Financial planners generally recommend that you allocate your capital into five categories: cash, fixed income producers (bonds), real estate, equities, and precious metals. They also recommend changing how much you allocate to each category as you reach different stages of life.

On the average, financial planners recommend that the following percentages of your capital be allocated to the five categories according to three age groups:

PERCENT ASSET ALLOCATION
(by age group)

Asset	In your 20's	In your 40's	In your 60's
Cash	22	9	5
Fixed Income	25	33	45
Real Estate	0	15	25
Equities	53	33	20
Precious Metals	0	0	5

- Create a worksheet using the titles, row and column labels, and data shown above. Do not leave blank columns between columns of data.
- Create a bar graph showing the age group as the X axis label and the percent allocation across the age groups as the data ranges. Specify the legends. Enter a first title line using the worksheet title. Enter a second title line using your name. Enter an X axis title line, "Age Group," and a Y axis title of "Percent Allocation." Name the bar graph BAR3. Save the graph to be printed as BAR3.PIC.
- Change the bar graph to a stacked-bar graph. Name the graph STACKED3. Save it to be printed as STACKED3.PIC.
- Create a pie chart to display the asset allocation for people in their 20's. Enter a first and second (use your name) title line. Add shading to the pie chart and explode the Equities slice. Name the pie chart PIE20S. Save it for printing as PIE20S.PIC.
- Create two more pie charts showing the suggested asset allocation for people in their 40's and 60's. Add shading to the pie charts. Explode the slice(s) with the largest percent allocation. Name them PIE40S and PIE60S. Save them for printing as PIE40S.PIC and PIE60S.PIC.
- Save the worksheet file with the graph settings as ASSETS.
- Print all the graphs you have saved.

3. The U.S. athletic footware market showed continued growth during the years 1983 to 1987. The data presented below shows this growth.

U.S. Athletic Footware Market Retail Sales
(in billions of dollars)

1983	4.03
1984	4.15
1985	5.01
1986	6.87
1987	8.12

- Create a worksheet of this data.
- Create a line graph of this data. It should have two title lines, and an X- and Y-axis title. The second title line should contain your name. Name and save the graph for printing as SHOESL.
- Create a bar graph of this data. It should have two title lines, and an X- and Y-axis title. The second title line should contain your name. Name and save the graph for printing as SHOESB.

In the same worksheet file, create a second worksheet of the following data showing the top five manufacturers of athletic footware and their sales for first half of 1987 compared to the first half of 1988.

1987 First Half Sales vs. 1988 First Half Sales
(in millions of dollars)

	1987	1988
Reebok	488.87	589
Nike	104.16	434
Converse	112.24	140.3
Avia	44.55	99
Adidas	70.52	82

- Create a bar graph of this data comparing the 1987 and 1988 sales figures. Specify legends. It should have two title lines. The second title line should contain your name. Create X- and Y-axis titles. Name and save the graph for printing as SALES.
- Create two pie charts of this data, one for each year. They should have two title lines. The second title line should contain your name. Add shading to the pie charts. Explode the Nike slice. Name and save the graphs for printing as PIE87 and PIE88.
- Save the worksheet as SHOES.
- Print the graphs.

4. It appears that the exercise boom is losing its strength. Since 1984 the number of Americans participating in athletic activities has plunged. The two activities that have shown an increase are Walking and Bicycling. The following data shows this change.

1984 vs. 1987 Fitness Comparison
(in millions of participants)

Activity:	1984	1987
Running	29.9	27.5
Swimming	74.6	66
Aerobics	23.2	22.8
Tennis	19.9	18.2
Walking	41.1	58.9
Bicycling	50.7	52.2

- Create a worksheet of this data. Do not leave blank columns between columns of data.

- Create a line graph of this data. It should have two title lines, and an X- and Y-axis title. The second title line should contain your name. Specify the legends. Name and save the graph for printing as FITNESSL.

- Create a bar graph of this data. It should have two title lines, and an X- and Y-axis title. The second title line should contain your name. Specify the legends. Name and save the graph for printing as FITNESSB.

- Create two pie charts of this data, one for each year. It should have two title lines. The second title line should contain your name. Add shading to the pie charts. Explode the Swimming slice. Name and save the graphs for printing as FITNES84 and FITNES87.

- Save the worksheet as DECLINE.

- Print the graphs.

Creating Templates and Macros

5

OBJECTIVES

In this lab you will learn how to:

1. Name a range.

2. Use an @IF function.

3. Create a template.

4. Create an interactive macro.

5. Debug a macro.

6. Use a repetition factor.

7. Document a macro.

8. Use the Learn feature.

9. Protect worksheet cells.

10. Create an autoexecute macro.

CASE STUDY

Fred Morris, the membership coordinator for the Sports Club, would like his assistant to maintain a biweekly membership enrollment report. To help his assistant enter this data, Fred wants to create a worksheet template using Lotus 1-2-3. He also plans to create several macros to simplify and speedup the data entry and report generation process. You will follow Fred as he completes the template and creates the macros.

Naming a Range

Fred has already created much of the worksheet to be used to enter the weekly enrollment data. To see what he has done so far, **load 1-2-3 and retrieve the file TEMPLATE.**

This worksheet displays in column A the names of the three employees who are responsible for membership enrollment: Donna, Pete, and Sue. The five membership categories, Family, Single, Student, Junior and Senior, are displayed across row 5. He also entered some sample data for Donna. It shows that she enrolled three family memberships and two memberships in each of the other categories during this time period.

The worksheet also includes several formulas.

Move to: B11

The formula in this cell calculates the total enrollment for the family membership category. It has been copied across the row through cell H11.

The second formula he entered calculates the total enrollment value earned by each person. To see this formula,

Move to: G7

Your screen should be similar to Figure 5-1.

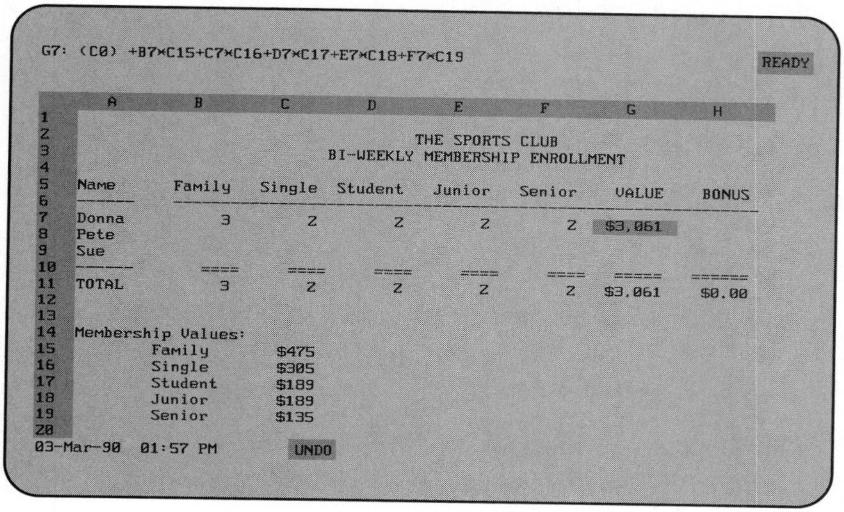

FIGURE 5-1

```
G7: (C0) +B7×C15+C7×C16+D7×C17+E7×C18+F7×C19                    READY
```

	A	B	C	D	E	F	G	H
1								
2				THE SPORTS CLUB				
3				BI—WEEKLY MEMBERSHIP ENROLLMENT				
4								
5	Name	Family	Single	Student	Junior	Senior	VALUE	BONUS
6								
7	Donna	3	2	2	2	2	$3,061	
8	Pete							
9	Sue							
10	————	====	====	====	====	====	=====	======
11	TOTAL	3	2	2	2	2	$3,061	$0.00
12								
13								
14	Membership Values:							
15		Family	$475					
16		Single	$305					
17		Student	$189					
18		Junior	$189					
19		Senior	$135					
20								

```
03-Mar-90  01:57 PM      UNDO
```

The VALUE is the sum of the enrollment value of the five membership categories for each person. The enrollment value for each category is calculated by multiplying the number of enrollments times the appropriate membership value.

The membership value for each category is the initiation fee plus one month's dues. This value is calculated and displayed for each category in cells C15 through C19. For example, the family membership value ($475) in cell C15 is the sum of the initiation fee of $400 and one month's dues of $75.

The formula in cell G7 calculates and sums the enrollment value for the five membership categories earned during the two-week period for Donna.

The formula in cell G7, however, is difficult to read because it refers to many different cells in the spreadsheet. To help clarify the meaning of a formula and to simplify entering formulas that repeatedly refer to the same cells or ranges of cells, a name can be assigned to the cell or range of cells. Once a cell or range of cells is named, the name can be used in a formula instead of the cell address. To see how this works you will assign the name Family to cell C15.

Select: / Range Name

Your screen should be similar to Figure 5-2.

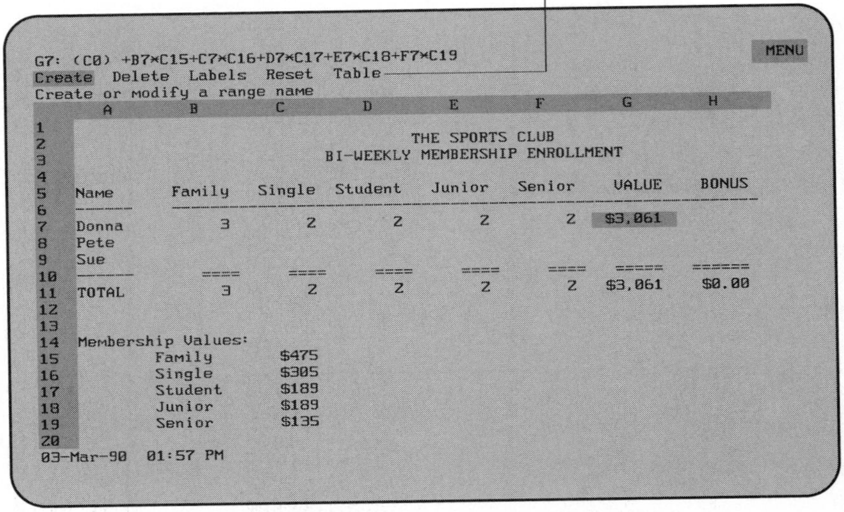

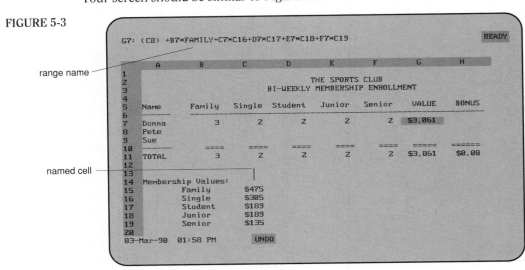

FIGURE 5-2

There are five Range Name menu options. To assign the name FAMILY to cell C15,

Select: Create

The prompt "Enter name:" is displayed. A range name can be up to 15 characters long and should be descriptive of the contents of the cell or range of cells. To enter the name,

Type: family
Press: ⏎

The next prompt asks you to specify the cell or range of cells to be named.

Type: C15
Press: ⏎

Your screen should be similar to Figure 5-3.

FIGURE 5-3

Look at the formula in cell G7 as it is displayed in the control panel. The range name Family has replaced the cell address C15. Using a range name makes the formula easier to understand.

The remaining four membership values in cells C16 through C19 need to be named next. Rather than typing in the range name, an existing spreadsheet label can be used. You will name these cells using the spreadsheet labels displayed in cells B16 through B19. For example, the membership value for the Single category in cell C16 will be named SINGLE.

First the cell pointer must be positioned on one of the corner cells in the range of labels to be used as the range names.

Move to: B16
Select: / **R**ange **N**ame **L**abels

This option displays four menu choices: Right, Down, Left, and Up. Your selection from this menu depends upon the location of the cell to be named in relation to labels. In this case, the cells to be named are located to the right of the labels.

Select: **R**ight

The prompt to enter the label range is displayed. Enter the range B16..B19 using highlighting.

You are returned to the READY mode. To see the use of the named ranges in the formula,

Move to: G7

Your screen should be similar to Figure 5-4.

FIGURE 5-4

```
G7: (C0) +B7×FAMILY+C7×SINGLE+D7×STUDENT+E7×JUNIOR+F7×SENIOR          READY

         A        B        C        D        E        F        G        H
1
2                                  THE SPORTS CLUB
3                            BI-WEEKLY MEMBERSHIP ENROLLMENT
4
5    Name      Family   Single   Student  Junior   Senior    VALUE   BONUS
6
7    Donna       3        2        2        2        2     $3,061
8    Pete
9    Sue
10   -------    ====     ====     ====     ====     ====    ======   =======
11   TOTAL       3        2        2        2        2     $3,061    $0.00
12
13
14   Membership Values:
15          Family    $475
16          Single    $305
17          Student   $189
18          Junior    $189
19          Senior    $135
20
03-Mar-90  01:58 PM       UNDO
```

The labels in cells B16 through B19 have been used to name the cells to their right. The range names are displayed in the formula.

The only time you can use the Labels option to name a cell is if the range to be named is a single-cell range and the labels are located in a cell adjacent to the cells to be named.

A range name can be used in place of cell addresses anytime a range is requested as part of a command or when using the range in a formula or @function.

The three Range Name menu options you have not used are Delete, Reset, and Table. Delete removes an individual range name from the worksheet. Reset deletes all the range names in a worksheet. The Table option creates an alphabetical list of all range names in a worksheet and their corresponding addresses. To see how the Table option works,

Move to: E15
Select: **/ R**ange **N**ame **T**able ⏎

Your screen should be similar to Figure 5-5.

FIGURE 5-5

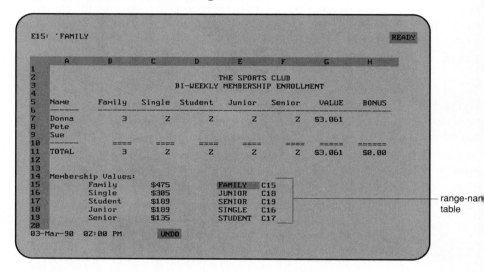

The range names and cell addresses are alphabetically displayed. This option is especially useful to someone who is not familiar with the worksheet. They can quickly see all the named ranges and associated addresses used in the worksheet.

When using this option be sure to specify an empty area of the worksheet for display of the table, as it will write over any existing data in the range.

To remove the table, erase the range E15..F19.

Finally, the formula in cell G7 needs to be copied to cells G8 and G9. Since the range names refer to specific cells that you do not want adjusted relative to the new location of the formula when it is copied, the range names must be made absolute.

Move to: G7
Press: (F2) EDIT

The cell addresses, rather than the range names, are displayed in the formula in the second line of control panel.

Since the edit cursor is to the right of C19, to change this cell address to absolute,

Press: (F4) ABS

The cell address C19 now displays the range name preceded by a $ character. A named range can only be relative or absolute, not mixed.

To complete the edit of this formula, change the cell addresses for C15, C16, C17, and C18 to absolute using the ABS key. Remember to position the edit cursor appropriately before pressing (F4).

Copy the formula, which calculates the VALUE for Donna, to calculate the VALUE for Pete and Sue.

Move to: G8

Look at the formula in the control panel. The range names appear exactly as they did in the formula in cell G7. They were copied using absolute cell referencing. The other cell addresses in the formula correctly adjusted relative to the new location in the worksheet.

Using the @IF Function

Next Fred needs to enter a formula in cell H7 to calculate the bonus earned. The club gives a 15 percent bonus on total enrollment values over $3000 and a 10 percent bonus on total enrollment values under $3000 in a two week period.

Lotus 1-2-3 has a special @function, the @IF function, that can check to see if certain conditions are met and then take action based upon the results of the check. The format for this @function is @IF(condition,true,false). This @function contains three arguments: condition, true, and false.

Condition lets you set up an equation to check against. To make this comparison, **logical operators** are used. Logical operators are used in formulas and @functions that compare values in two or more cells. The result of the comparison is either true (the conditions are met) or false (the conditions are not met).

The logical operators are:

Symbol	Meaning
=	equal to
<	less than
>	greater than
<=	less than or equal to
>=	greater than or equal to
<>	not equal to
#NOT#	logical NOT
#AND#	logical AND
#OR#	logical OR

In this case, the condition is whether the total enrollment VALUE (G7) is greater than (>) 3000. The condition argument will be G7>3000.

The true argument contains the instructions that are executed if the condition is true. In this case, if VALUE (G7) is greater than 3000 (true), then G7 is multiplied times 15 percent (G7*15%).

The false argument contains instructions that are executed if the condition is not true, or false. If VALUE (G7) is less than 3000 (false), then G7 is multiplied times 10 percent (G7*10%).

To enter the @IF function,

Move to: H7

Type: @IF(G7>3000,G7*15%,G7*10%)

Press: ⏎

Your screen should be similar to Figure 5-6.

FIGURE 5-6

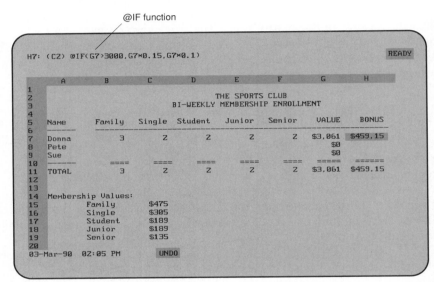

The BONUS earned using the sample data for Donna is $459.15. Since the value in cell G7 was greater than 3000, the bonus was calculated using 15%. To check that the @IF statement is calculating correctly, you will decrease the value in cell G7 to less than 3000 by decreasing the number of Family enrollments to 2.

Move to: B7

Type: 2

Press: ⏎

The value in cell G7 is now $2,586, and the calculated bonus in cell H7 is $258.60 or 10% of the value in cell G7. The @IF function is operating correctly.

Copy the @function used to calculate the BONUS for Donna to calculate the BONUS for Pete and Sue.

Creating a Template

The worksheet is complete. Now Fred is ready to create a blank **template**, or entry form, for his assistant to use for data entry.

Erase the sample membership enrollment data for Donna (B7 through F7).

Press: (HOME)

Your screen should be similar to Figure 5-7.

FIGURE 5-7

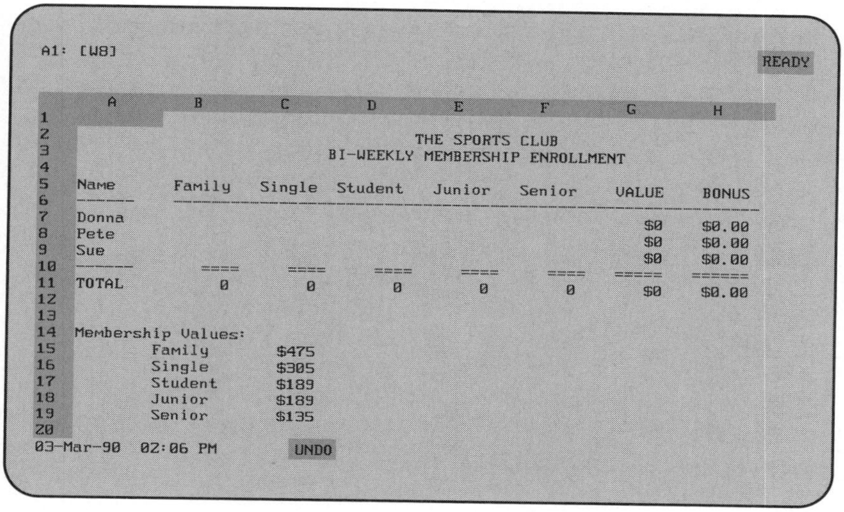

This is how the blank **template** will appear when Fred's assistant uses it to enter the biweekly enrollment figures. A template is simply a prewritten worksheet that contains blank spaces for entry of data. Templates are useful in any application where input and output is required using the same format. The template saves the user time by not having to redesign the same worksheet form each time the report is needed. The original design can be used repeatedly by saving the worksheet containing the data using a different file name than the file name used to save the template.

Creating an Interactive Macro

To speed the data entry process, Fred will create a macro that will help enter the data into the report. A **macro** is a series of keystrokes and commands that are stored as labels in a worksheet. When the macro is run or executed the series of keystrokes or commands is performed automatically.

Some macros are very simple and are merely a duplication of a series of keystrokes. For example, a macro can be written that moves the cell pointer to the left one cell. A more complex macro may perform a command, such as copying data from one cell to another or changing cell widths. Even more complex macros can be written that let you create and display your own menu and perform conditional tests.

Macros are very useful for replacing a series of commands or keystrokes that are performed repeatedly. Instead of manually entering each keystroke every time

you need to perform the same task, you use the macro, which performs the ke
strokes automatically for you.

The simplest type of macro represents keys on the keyboard. The macro con
mands consist of **keystroke instructions** which can be a single-character key or **key nam**
enclosed in braces ({key name}). The single-character keystroke instructions represen
typewriter keys on the keyboard and are identical to the keys they represent. The on
exception to this is the ⏎ key. The single-character key which represents ⏎ is th
~ (tilde). Many of the keystroke instructions that consist of a key name enclosed
braces are shown below.

Keyboard Key	Macro Keystroke Instruction
↑	{U} or {UP}
↓	{D} or {DOWN}
→	{R} or {RIGHT}
←	{L} or {LEFT}
HOME	{HOME}
END	{END}
PGUP	{PGUP}
PGDN	{PGDN}
DELETE	{DEL}
ESC	{ESC}
Bksp	{BS}
⏎	~
Waits for keyboard entry (pause)	{?}
F2	{EDIT}
F3	{NAME}
F4	{ABS}
F5	{GOTO}
F6	{WINDOW}
F7	{QUERY}
F8	{TABLE}
F9	{CALC}
F10	{GRAPH}

Creating a macro follows several steps: planning, entering, naming, testing, ar
editing. You will create a macro to enter data following these steps.

Planning the Macro

The first step in creating a macro is to plan the macro. A good way to plan a mac
is to perform the task you want it to do manually, and write down every step c
paper as you are doing it. This way you are less likely to forget a step or to perform
step out of sequence.

To demonstrate, you will enter some sample membership enrollment data fo
Donna manually.

Press:	(F5) GOTO
Type:	**B7**
Press:	(⏎)
Type:	**2**
Press:	(→)
Type:	**4**
Press:	(→)
Type:	**2**
Press:	(→)
Type:	**0**
Press:	(→)
Type:	**1**
Press:	(⏎)

You will enter a macro in the worksheet to perform each of the keystrokes you just used to enter the data for Donna. The only difference will be that, in place of the numbers that will be entered each time the report is completed, you will enter in the macro a ? character to show that the user should enter data. The recorded keystrokes on paper then would be: (F5), GOTO, B7, (⏎), ?, (→), ?, (→), ?, (→), ?, (→), ?, (⏎).

Entering the Macro

The second step is to enter the series of keystrokes as a label entry in the worksheet. The text representing the keystrokes is a macro. A macro is usually placed in an area outside of the active area of the worksheet that would not be affected by the later addition or deletion of rows and columns in the worksheet. In a large and complex worksheet, the bottom right-hand corner of the worksheet would be the best place to enter the macro statements. However, to demonstrate the macro creation process more easily, you will use an open area of the worksheet in the same window as the active area of the worksheet.

Several rules should be followed when entering a macro in a worksheet:

- Enter the macro in an empty area of the worksheet.

- Enter the macro as a label. If the macro statement begins with a non-text character, such as a number, a numeric symbol, or a /, use a label prefix character before entering the character so that 1-2-3 will interpret the entry as a label.

- Enter the macro commands using either upper- or lowercase letters. Many people use uppercase letters when entering the key names enclosed in braces and cell addresses. They use lowercase letters for macros that represent the use of the command menu. This makes reading the macro easier.

- Enter the macro in a single cell or in a vertical column of cells.

The first macro command will move the cell pointer to cell B7 using the GOTO (F5) feature. The keystroke instruction that represents the F5 function key is {GOTO}.

Move to: E14
Type: {GOTO}

Because the first character in this macro command begins with a {, the entry is interpreted as a label. Therefore it was not necessary to begin the macro with a label prefix character.

Next the cell location to move the cell pointer to must be specified.

Type: B7

To complete the GOTO command, the ⏎ macro symbol (~) must be entered.

Type: ~

The next macro statement allows you to enter data. The keystroke instruction that will do this is {?}. A macro that uses this keystroke instruction is called an **interactive macro** because it temporarily stops the action of the macro to allow the user to enter data into the worksheet.

Type: {?}

Next you want the macro to both enter the data and move right one cell. To do this,

Type: {RIGHT}

To enter the macro into the cell,

Press: ⏎

Your screen should be similar to Figure 5-8.

FIGURE 5-8

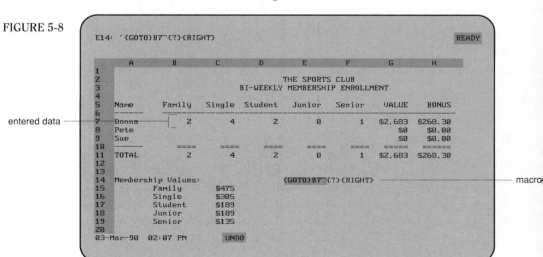

The remaining macro commands could be added to cell E14 as one long label, or they can be placed in a series of continuous cells in a single column. It is often easier to enter the macro commands in segments as a column of cells. This makes it easier to correct or edit the macro later.

Move to: E15

The next series of macro statements allow you to enter data and move the cell pointer. This time you will use the short version of the {RIGHT} macro key name, {R}.

Type: {?}{R}{?}{R}{?}{R}{?}~
Press: ⏎

Your screen should be similar to Figure 5-9.

FIGURE 5-9

```
E15:  '{?}{R}{?}{R}{?}{R}{?}~                                        READY

        A         B        C        D        E        F        G        H
1
2                                      THE SPORTS CLUB
3                           BI-WEEKLY MEMBERSHIP ENROLLMENT
4
5     Name      Family   Single   Student   Junior   Senior   VALUE    BONUS
6
7     Donna        2        4        2         0        1     $2,683   $268.30
8     Pete                                                       $0     $0.00
9     Sue                                                        $0     $0.00
10               ====     ====     ====      ====     ====    =====    =======
11    TOTAL        2        4        2         0        1     $2,683   $268.30
12
13
14    Membership Values:                     {GOTO}B7~{?}{RIGHT}
15            Family    $475                  {?}{R}{?}{R}{?}{R}{?}~
16            Single    $305
17            Student   $189
18            Junior    $189
19            Senior    $135
20
03-Mar-90  02:08 PM        UNDO
```

Be sure you entered the macro commands exactly as they appear in cells E14 and E15 in Figure 5-9. If they are different, correct your entry by editing the cell as you would any other entry.

Naming the Macro

The macro commands to enter data in the first row of the report should now be complete. The next step is to name the macro. Macros are named using the Range Name Create command.

Move to: E14
Select: / Range Name Create

The prompt to enter a name is displayed in the control panel. Notice that all the range names you entered earlier are also displayed in the control panel.

There are two ways to name a macro. The first method consists of a backslash (\) character followed by a single letter (A to Z). The second method follows the same rules for naming a range. That is, the name can consist of any combination of 15 characters.

You will use the first method to name this macro. When assigning a macro a single-letter name, it is a good idea to use a letter which is descriptive of the action of the macro.

Since this macro allows **d**ata entry to the right, you will name it \D.

Type: \D
Press: ⏎

The prompt to enter the range of cells to be named is displayed in the control panel. When naming a macro, only the cell containing the first macro statement needs to be entered. Since the cell pointer is positioned on this cell, to accept the default,

Press: ⏎

Each macro you create in a worksheet needs to be assigned a name. If you use a single-letter name, you cannot use the same letter more than once.

Testing the Macro

The fourth step is to test or run the macro. When a macro is run, it executes the commands in the first cell of the range specified when the macro was named, from left to right. It will continue executing the commands in the next cell in the same column until it reaches a blank cell, a numeric cell, or a Quit command.

To run a macro whose name consists of a \ and a single letter, the ⒜ⓛⓣ key is held down while pressing the letter key you named the macro (D).

Press: ⒜ⓛⓣ - D

The first command, {GOTO}B7~, has been executed and the cell pointer is positioned in cell B7. Notice the indicator "CMD" displayed at the bottom of the screen. This tells you that a macro is in progress and is pausing for user input. The next command, {?}, temporarily stopped execution of the macro to allow you to enter data into the cell.

Type: 3

To resume execution of the macro commands following a {?}, you must press ⏎ .

Press: ⏎

The macro continues execution by performing the next command, {RIGHT}. The cell pointer moved to the right one cell. It continues execution by performing the commands in cell E15 next from left to right. The first command in this cell, {?} causes the macro to pause and await user input.

Continue using the macro by entering the following data (remember to press ⏎) to resume macro execution after entering the data):

Cell	Value
C7	4
D7	1
E7	2
F7	0

Your screen should be similar to Figure 5-10.

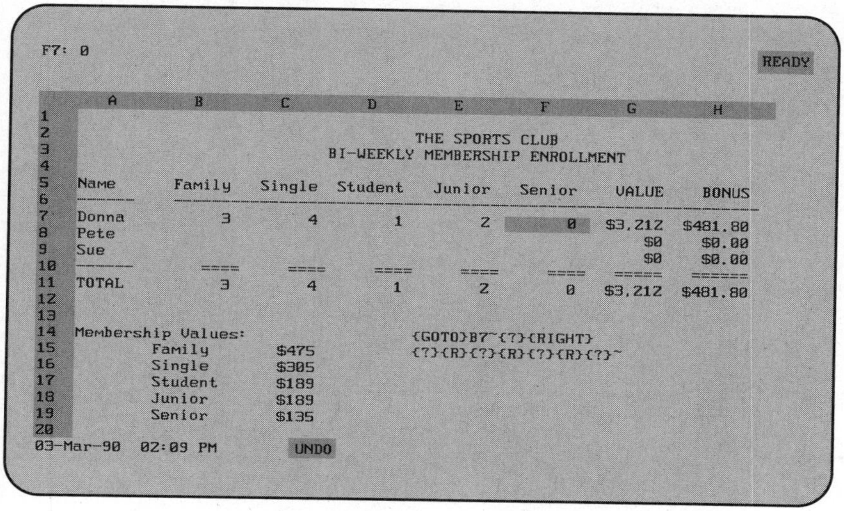

FIGURE 5-10

Editing the Macro

If you are very careful when entering a macro, it will execute properly the first time. Then you will not need to make corrections to the macro, or **debug** it, so that it performs correctly. However, not all macros will run correctly the first time. Some common errors are missing commands, and misplaced spaces and tildes.

To demonstrate an error and how to correct it, you will enter three errors in the macro you just created. The first error will demonstrate the effect of a misspelled keystroke instruction.

Move to: E14

Edit this macro so that {RIGHT} is spelled {RIGH}.

Move to: E15

The second error will demonstrate the effect of a missing command, and the third error will show the effect of an extra space.

Edit the macro in cell E15 by deleting the third {?} and entering a space before the last {?}. When edited, this macro should look like: **{?}{R}{?}{R}{R} {?}~.**

To see what happens when a macro contains an error, you will run the macro.

Press: (ALT) - **D**
Type: **4**
Press: ⏎

Your screen should be similar to Figure 5-11.

FIGURE 5-11

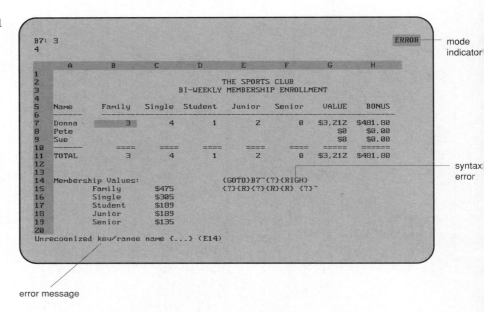

error message

Macro execution has been interrupted and the mode indicator flashes "ERROR," The error message displayed in the status line tells you that the error is due to an unrecognized key or range name and that the location of the error is in cell E14. To clear the message,

Press: (ESC)

You are returned to the READY mode. This type of error is called a **syntax error**. It is an error that is the result of a technical mistake made when entering the command. Another common mistake that causes a syntax error is a missing { or }.

A macro can be edited like any other cell entry. Since you know the cause of this error, simply change {RIGH} to {RIGHT} in cell E14.

To see how the errors in cell E15 affect the macro, invoke the macro again.

Press: (ALT) - **D**

Enter **4** as the enrollment figure for the first three categories for Donna.

You should now be about to enter the enrollment figure for the Junior category. However, the cursor is positioned on cell F7 waiting for entry of the data for the Senior category. This time an error message is not displayed and the macro continues execution.

The macro performed exactly as it should have by moving the cell pointer two cells to the right. After entering the value for the student category in cell D7, the cell pointer moved two cells right, skipping the junior category (E7). This is because the macro reads {R}{R}. The error in this macro command is a **logic error**. Because the macro is syntactically correct, an error message does not interrupt the macro execution. The macro executed the command exactly as entered in the cell.

Now watch your screen carefully as you enter the value in cell F7.

Type: **4**

Press: ⏎

Your screen should be similar to Figure 5-12.

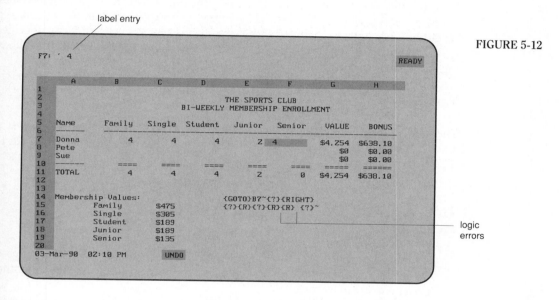

FIGURE 5-12

The entry in cell F7 begins on the left side of the cell space with a blank space, followed by 4. This is because the blank space in the macro had the same effect as beginning a cell entry with a space, that is, the mode changes to LABEL and a blank space is the first character entered in the cell. Therefore, the next character entered, 4, is interpreted as a label.

In both cases, although an error message was not displayed, the macro did not execute as intended due to a logic error. If you need to interrupt the execution of a macro because it is not performing correctly, press (CTRL) - (BREAK). "ERROR" will flash in the mode indicator. To clear the error message and return to the READY mode, press (ESC).

You have demonstrated two types of errors to be aware of: a syntax error that produces an error message, and a logic error. The macro containing a logic error may be syntactically correct, therefore Lotus 1-2-3 does not interrupt the macro execution. However, the intended task is not performed correctly.

Correct the macro in cell E15 to be: {?}{R}{?}{R}{?}{R}{?}~.

The macro should now appear as it was originally entered and it should run correctly.

Using a Repetition Factor

Next Fred wants to add to the macro to allow entry of the data for Pete in row 8
After entering the last value for Donna in cell F7, he needs to move down a row and
left four cells to begin entry of the values for Pete in row 8.

Move to: E16

The macro key that moves the cell pointer down is {D}.

Type: {D}

Next, to move the cell pointer left four cells, the macro key {L} could be typed four
times. However, whenever you need to repeat a macro key a number of times,
repetition factor can be included within the macro key. A repetition factor specifie
how many times to repeat the use of the same key. A space must be entered follow
ing the macro key name before entering the repetition factor number.

Type: {L 4}

The number 4 within the macro key tells 1-2-3 to repeat the command four times.
If the macro were executing, the cell pointer would now be in cell B8. Next, t
allow entry of data in this cell and to move right one cell space, continue the macr
as follows:

Type: {?}{R}
Press: ⬇

To continue the macro to allow the entry of data in row 8, the same sequence of
keys as in the macro commands in cell E15 can be used. A macro, like any othe
worksheet entry, can be copied.

Copy the macro in cell E15 to cell E17.

To complete the macro so that the data for Sue can be entered, the macr
commands in cells E16 and E17 can be used.

Copy the contents of E16 and E17 to E18.

Your screen should be similar to Figure 5-13.

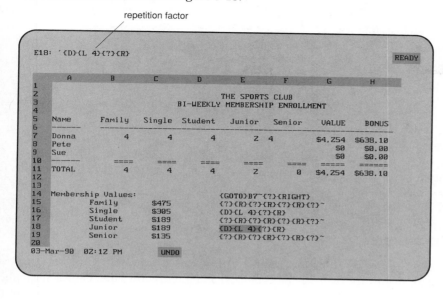

FIGURE 5-13

You have extended the macro so that it now consists of the commands in cells E14 through E19. Although you have added several lines to the original macro named \D, it is not necessary to rename the macro. By entering the additional macro commands into the cells immediately below the original commands, the macro will automatically continue executing the commands.

To test the macro,

Press: (ALT)-D

Enter 3 as the enrollment figure for all categories for Donna, 2 for all categories for Pete, and 1 for all categories for Sue. If your macro does not run correctly, locate and correct the error and rerun the macro.

Your screen should be similar to Figure 5-14.

FIGURE 5-14

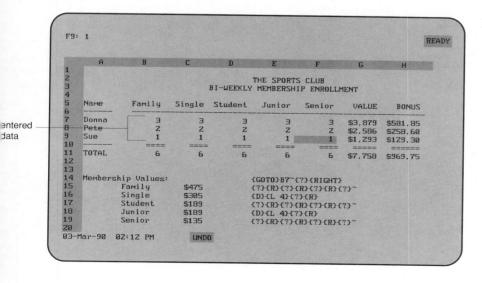

Fred feels this macro will help his assistant enter the data for the report easily.

Now that the macro is complete, you will move it out of the worksheet window to cell B25 as follows:

Move to: E14

Select: / Move **E14..E19** ⬡ **B25** ⬡

To see the new location of the macro statements,

Press: (PGDN)

Lotus 1-2-3 automatically adjusts the macro range to its new location in the worksheet.

Documenting the Macro

A macro tells 1-2-3 to perform certain commands and procedures. A worksheet can contain many macros. To avoid confusion and inform other users of the meaning of the macros in a worksheet, it is important to document the macros. Usually the name assigned to the macro is displayed to the left of the macro, and explanatory text is placed to the right.

Move to: A25

Type: \D

Move to: F25

Type: **Enrollment Data Entry**

Press: ⬡

Your screen should be similar to Figure 5-15.

FIGURE 5-15

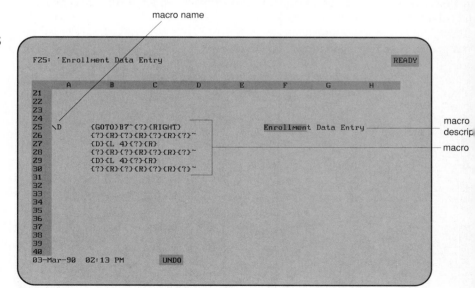

Using the Learn Feature

Next Fred would like to create a macro that will print a copy of the report after the data has been entered and save the worksheet using a new file name.

Move to: B32

First you will enter the macro to print the report. The command sequence to print the report is: **/ P**rint **P**rinter **R**ange **A1..H11** ⟵ **A**lign **G**o **P**age **Q**uit. The macro statement to perform this command is the same as the keystrokes you would use to enter the command manually. In addition to typing macros directly into worksheet cells, you can use the Learn feature to record your keystrokes as a macro at the same time as you perform them.

Before using this feature you must define a range in the worksheet where the macro commands will be recorded. This is called the **learn range**. This range is a single-column range which needs to be large enough to contain all the macro instructions. When specifying the learn range, specify a range that is much larger than you think you will need and in an area of the worksheet which will not interfere with other worksheet data.

To define the range,

Select: **/ W**orksheet **L**earn **R**ange **B32..B40** ⟵

To have 1-2-3 record your keystrokes as a macro, turn on the Learn feature by pressing the Learn key, (ALT) - (F5).

Press: (ALT) - (F5)

Your screen should look similar to Figure 5-16.

FIGURE 5-16

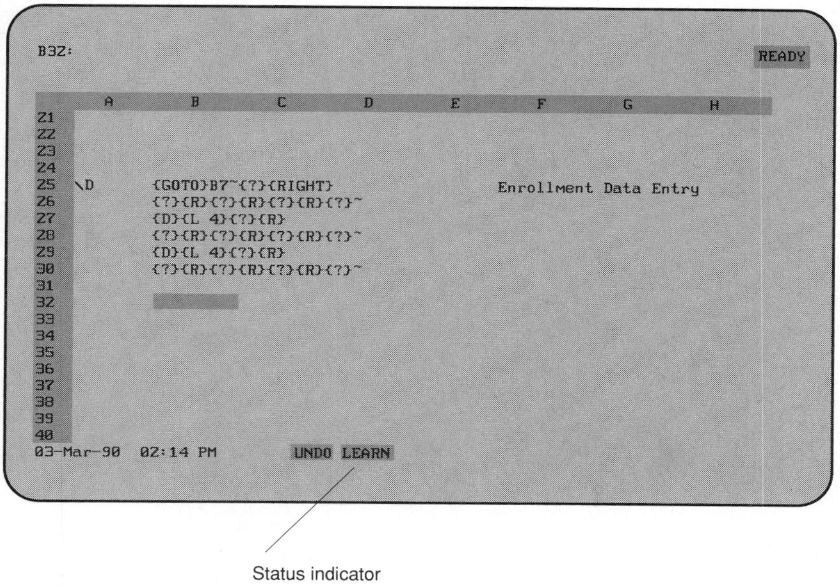

Status indicator

Notice the status indicator displays "LEARN." Now anything you type or any commands you enter will be recorded as a macro. To create the macro to print the worksheet,

Select: / Print Printer

To define the first cell of the range to print,

Select: Range
Press: (HOME)
Press: . (period)

To define the area of the worksheet to print,

Press: (↓) (10 times)
Press: (→) (7 times)
Press: (⏎)

To tell the printer to align to the top of the page, print the report, advance to the top of the next page, and then leave the print menu,

Select: Align Go Page Quit

The report should be printing. The keystrokes to print the report have also been recorded as a macro in the learn range. To turn off the Learn feature,

Press: (ALT) - (F5)

The LEARN indicator is no longer displayed. The macro instructions as they were recorded using the Learn feature have been entered in the learn range. To display all the macro statements,

Move to: B34

Your screen should be similar to Figure 5-17.

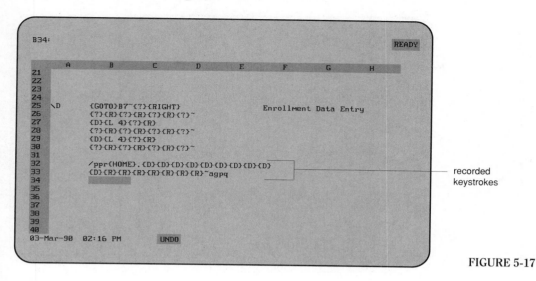

recorded
keystrokes

FIGURE 5-17

The macro commands are displayed in the learn range. Notice that it records each {D} and each {R} key name individually. The Learn feature cannot use a repetition factor within key names. Consequently the macro takes up much more worksheet space.

If you enter more characters than your learn range can hold, 1-2-3 will turn off the Learn feature and tell you the learn range is full. The learn range will contain all the macro instructions entered up to that point. You can erase the contents of the range, define a larger range, and begin again; or you can define a larger range and start where you left off.

Now you are ready to name the macro. The second method of naming a macro lets you assign a name up to 15 characters long. Again the name should be descriptive of the function of the macro. You will name the macro PRINT.

Move to: B32

Select: / Range Name Create **PRINT** ⏎ ⏎

Document the macro statement by putting the macro name in cell A32 and a short description of the macro, such as "Prints the Report," in cell G32.

Your screen should be similar to Figure 5-18.

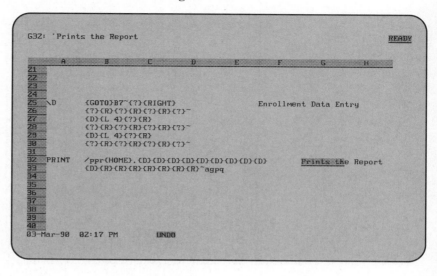

G32: 'Prints the Report   READY

```
        A          B          C          D       E       F       G          H
21
22
23
24
25   \D        {GOTO}B7~{?}{RIGHT}                      Enrollment Data Entry
26             {?}{R}{?}{R}{?}{R}{?}~
27             {D}{L 4}{?}{R}
28             {?}{R}{?}{R}{?}{R}{?}~
29             {D}{L 4}{?}{R}
30             {?}{R}{?}{R}{?}{R}{?}~
31
32   PRINT     /ppr{HOME}.{D}{D}{D}{D}{D}{D}{D}{D}{D}          Prints the Report
33             {D}{R}{R}{R}{R}{R}{R}{R}~agpq
34
35
36
37
38
39
40
03-Mar-90  02:17 PM            UNDO
```

FIGURE 5-18

To run a macro which has been named using the second method, you must use the
Run ((ALT) - (F3)) key. The Run key can be used to run any macros, including those
named with the backslash character.

Press: (ALT) - (F3)

The prompt "Select the macro to run:" is displayed in the second line of the control
panel, and all the range names used in the worksheet are listed in the third line. This
makes it difficult to distinguish between range names and macro names. To help
distinguish between the two types of range names, you may want to begin all macro
names in a worksheet with the same character, such as a \, to help you distinguish the
macro names from the range names.

The macro named PRINT is the third range name listed. To see additional
range names,

Press: (↓)

An additional line of range names is displayed. The \D macro name is the last range
name.

Rather than leave the macro name as PRINT, you will change it to \PRINT. To
cancel the Run command,

Press: (CTRL) - (BREAK)

To delete the macro name PRINT and create the macro name \PRINT,

Select: **/ R**ange Name Delete **PRINT** ⏎
Select: **/ R**ange Name Create **\PRINT** ⏎ **B32** ⏎

To run the \PRINT macro,

Press: (ALT) - (F3)

Press: (↓)

Your screen should be similar to Figure 5-19.

FIGURE 5-19

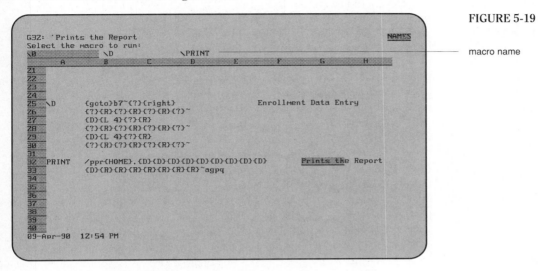

macro name

```
G32: 'Prints the Report                                        NAMES
Select the macro to run:
\D              \D              \PRINT
        A       B       C       D       E       F       G       H
Z1
Z2
Z3
Z4
Z5    \D        {goto}b7~{?}{right}          Enrollment Data Entry
Z6              {?}{R}{?}{R}{?}{R}{?}~
Z7              {D}{L 4}{?}{R}
Z8              {?}{R}{?}{R}{?}{R}{?}~
Z9              {D}{L 4}{?}{R}
Z0              {?}{R}{?}{R}{?}{R}{?}~
Z1
Z2    PRINT     /ppr{HOME}.{D}{D}{D}{D}{D}{D}{D}{D}{D}    Prints the Report
Z3              {D}{R}{R}{R}{R}{R}{R}{R}~agpq
Z4
Z5
Z6
Z7
Z8
Z9
Z0
09-Apr-90  12:54 PM
```

Now both the macros appear at the end of the named ranges and begin with a \
character.

Select: \PRINT

The printer should be printing the report. If your macro did not operate correctly,
locate and correct the error and retest the macro.

The next macro command will save the worksheet using a new file name.
Since each report is for a different two-week period in a month, Fred wants his
assistant to name the file using the name of the month that the report covers
followed by a 1 or a 2 to indicate the first or second two-week period. For example,
JAN1 would be the file name for the report covering the first two weeks in January.

The command sequence to save a file with a new file name is: **/ F**ile **S**ave file name
(↵). You will enter this macro into the worksheet directly by typing the macro commands. Since the file name will change each time the report is saved, the {?} macro
keystroke instruction is used in place of the file name.

When entering a macro that begins with a /, you must begin the entry with an
apostrophe to indicate that a label is being entered in this cell. If you do not begin
the macro statement with a label prefix character, when you press /, the main menu
will appear in the control panel rather than a / being entered in the cell. Also be
careful not to enter any blank spaces in the command sequence, as a blank in a
command sequence can stop the macro execution.

Move to: B34

Type: '/fs{?}~

Press: (↵)

The macro commands to save the worksheet will continue as part of the PRINT macro. Therefore it is not necessary to assign the save macro commands a new macro name.

Enter a description of the macro, such as "Saves the worksheet," in cell G34.

Your screen should be similar to Figure 5-20.

FIGURE 5-20

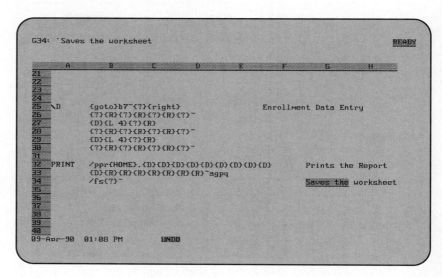

Enter your name in cell A1 and the current date in A2.

To review, the following steps should be followed when developing a macro.

Plan   Careful planning of the steps you want the macro to perform is essential to the macro development process. Writing down the steps while you are actually performing the task will greatly improve the accuracy of the macro you enter.

Enter   The macro is entered as a label in any open area of the worksheet. It is recommended that this area be outside the active worksheet space. It must be entered in a continuous range of vertical cells. A macro can also be entered by defining a learn range (/ Worksheet Learn Range) and then using the Learn feature ((ALT) - (F5)) to record your keystrokes as a macro.

Name   A macro is assigned a name using the Range Name Create command. A macro name can consist of a \ (backslash) followed by a single letter or any combination of up to 15 characters.

Test   To see if the macro is operating correctly and to locate any errors, run the macro. If the macro name consists of a \ and a single letter, press the (ALT) key and the letter name of the macro to execute the macro. If the macro name consists of any combination of characters, press (ALT) - (F3) (the Run key) and select the appropriate macro name. Testing the macro is also known as debugging, since the purpose is to locate both syntax and logic errors.

Edit   If errors are located or if you need to change a macro, it can be edited like any other worksheet entry.

Before testing this macro, Fred wants to make a few other adjustments to the worksheet.

Protecting Cells

Fred is concerned that the formulas and the macro statements in the worksheet may be accidentally altered or erased. To prevent this from happening, he will protect those cells from changes by enabling the Worksheet Protection feature.
   To turn on the Worksheet Cell Protection feature,

Select: / Worksheet Global

The Global Settings sheet tells you that global protection is disabled. This is the default. To turn protection on,

Select: Protection Enable

When this feature is used, all cells in the worksheet are protected. This means that you cannot enter or change an entry in any cell in the worksheet. Notice that "PR" is displayed in the control panel to show you that the current cell is protected.
   To allow his assistant to enter data into the worksheet, Fred needs to unprotect the range of cells where the data will be entered. To see this area of the worksheet,

Press: (HOME)
Move to: B7

To show the effect of trying to enter data into a protected cell,

Type: 5
Press: (↵)

The computer beeped and "ERROR" flashed in the mode indicator. The message in the status line tells you that this is a protected cell.
   To clear the message,

Press: (ESC)

To unprotect the range of cells to be used to enter data, B7 through F9,

Select: / Range Unprot B7..F9 (↵)

Your screen should be similar to Figure 5-21.

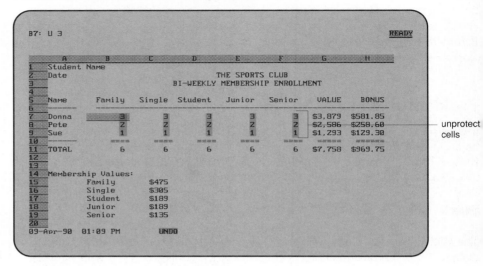

FIGURE 5-21

Notice that the control panel now displays "U" to show that these are unprotected cells. Whenever worksheet protection is enabled, the control panel will display either PR or U. The unprotected cells may also appear highlighted on your screen.

Next Fred needs to erase the sample data in the worksheet.

Select: / Range Erase **B7..F9** ⏎

He now has a blank template that can be used by his assistant to enter the biweekly enrollment data. Each time this worksheet is retrieved it will contain a blank entry template with the macro commands. His assistant will save the worksheet with the data entered in it using a different file name each time. Therefore the template will always be blank.

Creating an Autoexecute Macro

The final change Fred wants to make to the worksheet is to have the \D macro automatically begin execution as soon as the file is retrieved. This is called an **autoexecute macro**. To do this a special macro name is used, \0 (zero). Only one macro in a worksheet can be named \0. To make the \D macro to an autoexecute macro,

Select: / Range Name Create **\0** ⏎ **B25** ⏎

This macro is now named both \D and \0. Before testing the macro execution, with the cell pointer in cell A1, save your revised worksheet using the file name ENROLL.

Fred has the enrollment data for the first two weeks in October. He will use this data to demonstrate to his assistant how to use the template.

Retrieve the file ENROLL.

The data entry macro automatically began execution and the cell pointer is positioned in cell B7.

Enter the following data:

	Family	Single	Student	Junior	Senior
Donna	3	5	2	0	0
Pete	2	1	0	3	1
Sue	4	2	0	0	0

If you made an error when entering the data, either rerun the entire macro using \D or edit the cell containing the error.

To print the report and save the worksheet as OCT1,

Press: (ALT) - (F3)
Select: \PRINT
Type: OCT1
Press: (↵)

By using the template named ENROLL and saving the completed report using a new file name, the template will always be retrieved with empty cells in the worksheet space for entry of the new data.

It is also good procedure when creating a template for others to use to include documentation within the worksheet. Many templates use the HOME position in the worksheet for this documentation. It should include:

Template identification Information such as the name of the template, who designed it, the date it was last revised, and a contact person for assistance if problems occur.

Template purpose Should briefly describe what information is needed to complete the template and what output is generated from the template.

Template instructions Should briefly discuss steps for completing the template, such as the names of any macros that need to be used and what they do, how to move to different areas of the worksheet, and how to interrupt a macro.

Template procedures Should describe how to name and save the report file so that the original template is not destroyed.

Figure 5-22 shows an example of template documentation.

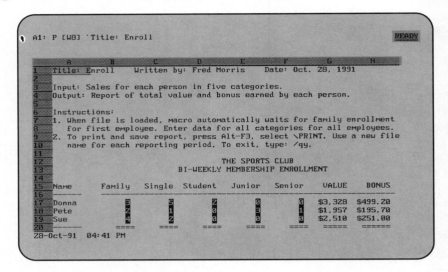

FIGURE 5-22

Always make a backup copy of the original template in case it is accidentally erased, overwritten, or lost.

Quit 1-2-3.

Key Terms

logical operators	debug
template	syntax error
macro	logic error
keystroke instruction	repetition factor
key name	learn range
interactive macro	autoexecute macro

Matching

1. / R N L L   _____ **a.** less than or equal to

2. / R N T   _____ **b.** enters the / character as a label in a cell

3. <=   _____ **c.** creates a table of range names

4. {?}   _____ **d.** the range name for an autoexecute macro

5. ~   _____ **e.** invokes the macro named \S

6. {Up 5}   _____ **f.** enables worksheet protection

7. \0   _____ **g.** allows user input during a macro

8. Alt-S   _____ **h.** assigns labels to the left of the cell pointer position as range names

9. / W G P E   _____ **i.** moves cell pointer up 5 cells

10. '/   _____ **j.** macro command for ⏎

Practice Exercises

1. The DMAB Publishing Company pays its book salespeople a base salary plus a bonus based upon an annual quota of $500,000 of sales. You will create a worksheet to be used as a template to calculate the annual salary of these employees. Set up the worksheet as if there were only 5 book salespeople, using the following information:

The base salary and annual sales for the 5 employees are:

Employee	Base Salary	Sales
A	39958	625211
B	26500	265479
C	23400	525863
D	32650	341982
E	21985	456989

The company uses two methods to calculate the bonus. The first method awards $3,000 to all salespeople who achieve 90 percent of the quota, but do not reach quota, The second method is used for all employees who achieve quota. They earn a bonus of 3 percent on the $500,000 quota minimuim plus 5 percent on the amount of sales over quota. If a salesperson does not fit either category, no bonus is paid.

- Create a worksheet calculating the bonus earned for the five employees. You should have 6 column heads: Employee, Base Salary, Sales, Annual Bonus (1), Annual Bonus (2), Total Salary.

- Enter the percents earned that determine the bonus and the quota amount as cell values. Enter descriptive labels to identify the cell values. For example:

Quota	500000
Achieve	3%
Over	5%

- Name these ranges using the Range Name Labels command. Use the named ranges in the formulas.

- Enter the formula for Annual Bonus (1) to calculate the bonus earned by salespeople that achieve quota. The formula for Annual Bonus (2) will calculate the bonus earned if the employee met 90% of quota (but less than quota).

- Enter the formula to calculate the total salary.

- Format the display of the worksheet.

- Enter a title for the worksheet. Put your name in cell A1 and the current date in cell A2.

- Save the worksheet as QUOTA.

- Print the worksheet.

2. Begin this problem with a blank worksheet. You will create a macro following the steps below.

- In cell C12 enter the macro command to move the cell pointer to cell A1.

- In cell C13 enter the macro command to enter the phrase "This was typed by a macro" into cell A1.

- Name the macro \N.

- Execute the macro. If necessary debug and reexecute the macro until it works correctly.

- In cell C14 enter the macro command to increase the width of column A to 26 spaces.

- Execute the macro. If necessary debug and reexecute the macro until it works correctly.

- In cell C15 enter the macro command to move down one cell (to cell A2) and enter your name in cell A2.

- In cell C16 enter the macro command to move to cell A3, format the cell to display a date as MM/DD/YY, and enter the current date into cell A3 using the date function.

- Execute the macro. If necessary debug and reexecute the macro until it works correctly.

- In cell C17 enter the macro to copy your name in cell A2 to cells A4.. A10 using highlighting.

- Execute the macro. If necessary debug and reexecute the macro until it works correctly.

- Edit the macro so that your name is displayed right-aligned in the cell space.

- Edit the macro so that it is more efficient. (Hint: eliminate the unnecessary tildes (~).)

- Execute the macro. If necessary debug and re-execute the macro until it works correctly.

- Save the worksheet as [YOURNAME].

- Print the entire worksheet.

3. Begin this problem with a blank worksheet. You will create a macro using the Learn feature following the steps below.

- Specify a learn range as C12..C25

Turn on the Learn feature and perform the following:

- Move the cell pointer to cell A1 and enter the label "This was typed by a macro."

- Increase the width of column A to 26 spaces.

- Move down one cell (to cell A2) and enter your name (right-aligned) in cell A2.

- Move to cell A3, format the cell to display a date as MM/DD/YY, and enter the current date into cell A3 using the date function.

- Copy your name in cell A2 to cells A4.. A10.

Turn off the Learn feature and do the following:

- Erase the contents of cells A1 through A10. Set the width of column A back to 9.

- If you made mistakes while using the Learn feature to record your keystrokes, edit the macro.

■ Name the macro and run it again.

■ If necessary debug and reexecute the macro until it works correctly.

■ Save the worksheet as LEARN.

■ Print the entire worksheet.

4. Retrieve the file ADVISING.WK1. This is a blank template used by the college advising office to track the flow of students. The worksheet row headings list the four main categories of advising. The academic advisors maintain a daily checksheet of the number of students they advise and the reason for the appointment. Each month the checksheets are totaled and the values entered into this template.

The advising coordinator wants to improve the worksheet by creating several macros which will automate the process of entering the data.

■ Each month the blank template needs to be copied to allow entry of the next month's data. Create a macro to the right of the worksheet that will copy the blank template for January (cells A5 through G15) to rows A19 through G27. Assume the cell pointer is on cell A6 when you begin the Copy command. Use pointing. The month heading for February is already entered in the worksheet. Name and document the macro.

■ Use this macro again to copy the template to allow entry for data for March. Enter the March month heading.

■ The second macro will assist in the entry of the data to complete each month's report. Write a macro that will move the cell pointer and pause for user entry of data. Assume that the cell pointer is positioned on the first category to be entered before the macro is executed. Name and document the macro.

■ Use the macro to enter data of your choice for January and February.

■ Enter your name in cell A1 and the current date in cell A2.

■ Write a macro to save and replace the worksheet using the same file name. Execute and document the macro.

■ Print the entire worksheet.

5. In this problem you will create 12 very common and handy macros. These macros can be copied into other worksheets using the / File Combine command. This saves having to recreate the same macros each time you create a new worksheet. The file containing your frequently used macros is called a macro library.

To begin this problem, retrieve the file named LIBRARY. This file contains data in columns A, B, and C that you will use to test the macros as your create them. A duplicate set of data is available beginning in cell A40. This is provided as a backup in case your macro damages the data in rows 1 through 20 as you are testing the macros.

You will use column D to display the macro name, column E to contain the macro commands, and column F to display a description of each macro. You will enter the first macro in cell E1. Remember to leave a blank cell between each macro.

■ Enter a macro to name a macro in cell E1. Assume the cell pointer is on the first cell in the macro to be named. Name it \N. You will test this macro by using it to name the next macro you will create. Use this macro to name all the other macros you will create.

■ Enter a macro beginning in cell E3 to move the cell pointer to cell A1 and enter your name in that cell. Name this macro \Y using the \N macro. Execute the macro. Debug and edit if necessary.

■ Enter a macro in cell E6 to format a cell to display a date as MM/DD/YY and enter the current date using the date function. Name it \D. Test the macro by moving to cell A2 and executing the macro.

■ Write a macro beginning in cell E9 that will change the column width. Use the interactive macro key {?} to allow you to enter the new width setting. Test the macro by changing the column width of column B to 4 and column E to 14.

■ Many macro commands can be open-ended. This means the macro begins the command sequence, and the user finishes the command by completing a range or specifying information at the prompt. The Copy command can be used in this manner. Enter a macro in cell E11 that will copy the contents of the cell that the cell pointer is on. Leave it open-ended so that the range to copy TO can vary. Test your macro by copying the value in cell A11 to B11..B12.

■ Enter a macro in cell E13 to help you fill a cell with a double-ruled line and copy it to a range. Name it \L. Test this macro by moving to cell A13 and executing the macro. Copy the line through cell C13.

■ Enter a macro in cell E15 to help you fill a cell with a single ruled line and copy it across a range. Name it \M. Test this macro by moving to cell A15 and executing the macro. Copy the line through cell C15.

■ Enter a macro in cell E17 to erase a range. Use the {?} macro command to allow you to specify the range to erase. Name it \E. Test the macro by erasing the contents of cells A17.. A18.

■ Enter a macro in cell E19 to format a cell to currency with 0 decimal places. Name it \F. Test the macro by formatting the value in cell A19.

■ Enter a macro in cell E21 to format a range to currency with 0 decimal places. Name it \R. Test the macro by formatting the values in cells A21..C21.

■ Enter a macro in cell E23 to save and replace a file. Name it \S. Test the macro by saving and replacing this file.

■ Enter a macro in cell E25 to print an entire worksheet. Since the Print command retains previous settings, such as the range, it is a good idea to clear all previous print settings as part of this macro. The print option to clear settings is Clear All. Include this option in your macro. You will also want the macro to advance the page before you quit the command. Name it \Print. Test this macro by printing your current worksheet.

To use this list of macros in another worksheet, you will want to erase all the test data in the worksheet. Then move the macro commands and documentation so they begin in cell A1. Then you can use the / File Combine command to copy the macros into the current worksheet. For information about this command use the Help system. Check with your instructor before making these changes to your file if you want to use the same file name. Otherwise assign the file a new name when saving it so that the current file remains unchanged on your diskette.

Lotus 1-2-3
Release 2.2

Glossary of Key Terms

Absolute cell reference: A $ character entered before the column letter or row number (or both) of a cell address in a formula will make the cell address remain the same (absolute) when copied.

Anchor: To freeze the cell pointer in the corner cell of a range when specifying the range using highlighting.

Anchor cell: The beginning cell of a range.

Argument: The data the @function can work on. It can be a number, a cell address, or a range of cells.

Arithmetic operators: Arithmetic signs (+, −, /, *, and ^) entered in a formula that control the arithmetic function to be performed in the formula.

Autoexecute macro: A macro that begins execution as soon as the file is retrieved. It must be named \0.

Bar graph: The data values displayed as a set of evenly spaced bars. Each bar represents a value in the range.

Cell: The space created by the intersection of a vertical column and a horizontal row.

Cell address: The column letter and row number displayed in the control panel that tells the user the current location of the cell pointer in the worksheet.

Cell pointer: A highlighted bar that shows the current cell being used.

Circular reference: A formula in a cell that directly or indirectly references itself.

Column: A vertical block of cells, one cell wide, in the worksheet.

Column width: The number of characters that the cells in a column can display.

Compressed: Printed text that is reduced in size by making the space between lines and letters smaller.

Control panel: The top three lines of the worksheet screen that display cell addresses, cell contents, program prompts, and command menus.

Copy: To duplicate the contents of a cell to other cells.

Date numbers: The integers assigned to the days from January 1, 1900 through December 31, 2099.

Date-and-time indicator: The current date and time maintained by DOS is displayed in the status line.

Debug: To run a macro to locate and correct errors.

Default: Worksheet settings automatically provided by 1-2-3.

Erase: To remove or delete the contents of a cell.

Error message: A message displayed in the status line to tell you the program detects an error or cannot perform a task.

Exploded: The slice of a pie chart is separated slightly from the other slices in the pie.

Format: The appearance or display of numeric values in the worksheet.

Formula: A mathematical expression that yields a numeric value based on the relationship between two or more cells in the worksheet.

Freeze: To hold specified rows or columns (or both) in place on the screen when scrolling.

@function: A set of built-in formulas that performs a calculation automatically.

Global: Settings that affect the entire worksheet.

Graph: The visual representation of data in a worksheet.

Graph file: A file containing the picture image of the graph used to print the graph. It has a .PIC extension.

Hatch patterns: The crosshatch designs used in bar or pie charts to differentiate the bars or slices when the graph is being viewed with a black and white monitor.

Interactive macro: A macro that temporarily stops to allow the user to enter data.

Justify: To take a long label of text and break it into several lines of text no longer than a specified number of columns.

Key name: Special words or symbols that represent specific keys on the keyboard. They are enclosed in curley braces ({keyname}).

Keystroke instruction: Macro instructions that represent keystrokes.

Label: A cell entry that begins with an alphabetic character or a label prefix character.

Label prefix character: A character that precedes a label and controls the display of the label within the cell space. A label can be displayed flush left, centered, or flush right in the cell.

Learn range: A single-column range where macro commands are recorded when using the Learn feature to enter the macro.

Legend: A brief description of the symbols used in a graph to represent the data ranges.

Line graph: Data represented in a graph as a set of points along a line.

Linking formula: A formula entered in the target file that refers to a cell in the source file, creating a link between two files.

List: An argument used in an @function that could be a cell, a range of cells, a range name, or a combination of these.

Logic error: A macro that is syntactically correct; however, it does not perform the intended task.

Logical operators: Symbols used in formulas that compare values in two or more cells.

Long label: A label entry in a worksheet that extends beyond the width of the cell it is entered in.

Macro: A series of keystrokes and commands that are stored as labels in a worksheet. When the macro is run, the keystrokes and commands are performed automatically.

Main menu: The Lotus 1-2-3 commands displayed in the second line of the control panel when the / key is pressed.

Menu pointer: The highlight bar used to select a command from the command menu.

Minimal recalculation: The recalculation of only the formulas in a worksheet that are affected by a change of data.

Mixed cell reference: A cell address that is part absolute and part relative.

Mode indicator: The condition or state of operation of the program displayed in the upper right-hand corner of the worksheet.

Numeric symbol: Any of the symbols +, -, ., @, (, #, or $ that define an entry as a value.

Pie chart: A graph that compares parts to the whole. Each value in the data range is a wedge of the pie (circle).

Point: To use the cell pointer to define the beginning and ending cells of a range.

Pointer-movement keys: The keyboard keys consisting of (↓), (↑), (→), (←), (HOME), (PGUP), (PGDN), and (TAB), which move the cell pointer around the worksheet.

Prompt: A program message displayed in the control panel which shows that the program is waiting for user input.

Range: A single cell or any rectangular group of adjoining cells in the worksheet.

Relative cell reference: The automatic adjustment of the cell addresses in a formula to its new location in a worksheet when the formula is copied or moved.

Repetition factor: A numerical entry following a macro keystroke instruction that specifies how many times to repeat the keystroke.

Reset: To cancel all graph settings or specified data ranges.

Row: A horizontal block of cells, one cell long, in the worksheet.

Run: To invoke or execute the macro commands.

Scale indicator: The notation that appears next to an axis to clarify the values displayed along the axis.

Scroll: To move more than one screen at a time horizontally or vertically through the worksheet.

Settings sheet: Displays the current settings for the options associated with the command you are using.

Shading values: Values assigned as the B data range in a pie chart that determine the hatch pattern or color for each slice of the pie.

Source cell: The file that supplies the data in a linking formula.

Stacked-bar graph: A graph that displays the data values as bars stacked upon each other.

Start value: The value that begins the range in the Data Fill command.

Status indicator: A message displayed in the bottom line of the screen that tells the user a particular key or program condition is in effect.

Status line: A line located at the bottom of the worksheet screen that displays the date-and-time indicator, status indicators, and error messages.

Step value: The increment between values in the range in the Data Fill command.

Stop value: The upper limit for the sequence of values in the range in the Data Fill command.

Submenu: The commands that are subordinate to the main menu commands.

Synchronized: Simultaneous scrolling of rows or columns in both windows at the same time.

Syntax: The structure or format for entering an @function.

Syntax error: An error that is the result of a technical mistake made when entering a command.

Target file: The file that receives the values from the linking formula.

Template: A prewritten blank worksheet that is used repeatedly to enter data.

Title: A descriptive label used in a graph at the top of the graph and/or along the X axis and Y axis lines.

Unsynchronized: Independent scrolling of rows or columns when there are two windows on the display.

Value: A number (0 to 9) or the result of a formula or an @function.

What-if analysis: A technique used to evaluate the effect of changing certain values in the worksheet to see what effect it has on other values in the worksheet.

Window: The portion of the worksheet that can be seen at any one time on the display screen.

Worksheet: A grid of vertical columns and horizontal rows used to enter and manipulate data.

Worksheet area: The largest area of the worksheet screen, located between the control panel and the status line and used to enter information.

X axis: The horizontal axis of a graph.

Y axis: The vertical axis of a graph.

Functional Summary of Selected Lotus 1-2-3 Commands

Function	Command	Action
Change appearance of the worksheet	/ Range Label	Change label alignment
	/ Range Format	Change the appearance of numbers
	/ Worksheet Global Label-Prefix	Change alignment of labels for the entire worksheet
	/ Worksheet Global Format	Change the appearance of numbers for the entire worksheet
	/ Worksheet Global Column-Width	Change the column widths for the entire worksheet
	/ Worksheet Column Set-Width	Change column width for a specified column
	/ Worksheet Column Column-Range Set-width	Change the width of a range of columns
	/ Copy	Copy part of the worksheet to another part
	/ Range Format Text	Display the formulas used in each cell
	/ Worksheet Column Hide	Hide a column from view
	/ Worksheet Insert	Insert blank columns or rows
	/ Worksheet Titles	Freeze rows or columns on the screen
	/ Move	Move data from one part of the worksheet to another

Function	Command	Action
Change appearance of the worksheet (*continued*)	/ **R**ange **J**ustify	Justify a range of text
	/ **W**orksheet **D**elete	Delete rows or columns
	/ **W**orksheet **W**indow	Split the display into two windows
Copying data	/ **C**opy	Copy part of the worksheet to another area
	/ **F**ile **I**mport	Incorporate data from a text (ASCII) file
	/ **F**ile **C**ombine	Incorporate data from another worksheet file
Erasing data	/ **W**orksheet **D**elete	Delete rows or columns
	/ **F**ile **E**rase	Erase a file from diskette
	/ **R**ange **E**rase	Erase a range of the worksheet
	/ **W**orksheet **E**rase	Erase the entire worksheet
Graphing data	/ **G**raph **O**ptions **L**egend	Add descriptive legends
	/ **G**raph **O**ptions **T**itles	Add descriptive titles
	/ **G**raph **O**ptions **D**ata-Labels	Label individual data points
	/ **G**raph **O**ptions **G**rid	Overlay a horizontal and/or vertical grid on the graph
	/ **G**raph **O**ptions **S**cale	Specify the numeric scale of the X and Y axes
	/ **G**raph **R**eset	Erase all graph settings
	/ **G**raph **V**iew	Display the graph on the screen
	/ **F**ile **L**ist **G**raph	Display a list of graph (.PIC) files
	/ **G**raph **N**ame	Save the current graph settings for later use
	/ **G**raph **X, A–F**	Define the data ranges to graph
	/ **G**raph **G**roup	Specifies the X and A-F data ranges in a graph in one step
	/ **G**raph **S**ave	Save the current graph as .PIC file
	/ **G**raph **T**ype	Define the type of graph
Hiding data	/ **W**orksheet **C**olumn **H**ide	Hide entire column from view
	/ **W**orksheet **C**olumn **D**isplay	Redisplay a hidden column
	/ **R**ange **F**ormat **H**idden	Hide contents of a cell
Loading data	/ **F**ile **I**mport	Incorporate text (ASCII) file into worksheet
	/ **F**ile **C**ombine	Incorporate data from another worksheet
	/ **F**ile **R**etrieve	Load a worksheet file
Moving data	/ **M**ove	Move data to another part of the worksheet
	/ **F**ile **X**tract	Save specified data in a separate worksheet file
Printing your work	/ **P**rint **P**rinter **L**ine	Advance printer paper one line
	/ **P**rint **P**rinter **P**age	Advance printer paper to the top of the page

Function	Command	Action
Printing your work (*continued*)	/ **P**rint **P**rinter **G**o	Begin printing
	/ **P**rint **P**rinter **O**ptions	Change printer settings
	/ **P**rint **P**rinter **O**ptions **O**ther **C**ell-Formulas	Print cell formulas instead of cell values
	/ **W**orksheet **C**olumn **H**ide	Hide certain columns
	/ **P**rint **P**rinter **C**lear	Remove current printer settings
	/ **P**rint **F**ile	Send worksheet data to a text (ASCII) file
	/ **P**rint **P**rinter **O**ptions **H**eader/**F**ooter	Set header/footer for printed page
	/ **P**rint **P**rinter **O**ptions **M**argins	Set margins for printed page
	/ **P**rint **P**rinter **A**lign	Set paper to top of page
	/ **P**rint **P**rinter **R**ange	Specify range of the worksheet to print
	PrintGraph Program	Print a graph
Protecting data	/ **F**ile **S**ave P	Assign a password to a worksheet
	/ **W**orksheet **G**lobal **P**rotection **E**nable	Turn on protection facility
	/ **R**ange **P**rotect	Prevent changes to a range of cells
	/ **R**ange **U**nprotect	Remove protection of certain cells
	/ **R**ange **I**nput	Restrict cell pointer to movement among unprotected cells
Saving your work	/ **F**ile **X**tract	Extract and save part of the worksheet
	/ **G**raph **S**ave	Save a graph as a .PIC file for printing
	/ **F**ile **S**ave	Assign a password to the worksheet
	/ **F**ile **S**ave **B**ackup	Save current worksheet and create a backup file with a .BAK extension
	/ **P**rint **F**ile	Save the worksheet as a text (ASCII) file
Working with files	/ **F**ile **L**ist	Display the names of files in the current directory
	/ **W**orksheet **G**lobal **D**efault **U**pdate	Save default settings in 1-2-3 configuration file
	/ **F**ile **D**irectory	Specify directory where 1-2-3 will look for files this session
	/ **W**orksheet **G**lobal **D**efault **D**irectory **U**pdate	Specify directory where 1-2-3 will look for files in future sessions
Miscellaneous	/ **W**orksheet **S**tatus	Display current worksheet settings
	/ **W**orksheet **G**lobal **D**efault **S**tatus	Display configuration settings for printer, current directory, etc.
	/ **Q**uit	Exit 1-2-3

Function	Command	Action
Miscellaneous (*continued*)	/ **W**orksheet **G**lobal **D**efault	Specify configuration settings for printer, current directory, etc.
	/ **W**orksheet **G**lobal **R**ecalculation	Specify how and when to recalculate formulas
	/ **F**ile **A**dmin **L**ink-Refresh	Immediately updates the linked cells in the worksheet files.
	/ **D**ata **F**ill	Fills a range of cells with a sequence of numbers.
	/ **W**orksheet **L**earn **R**ange	Defines range of cells where the macro commands will be recorded when using the Learn feature.

Function Keys

Key	Name	Action
(F1)	HELP	Displays a 1-2-3 Help screen.
(F2)	EDIT	Puts 1-2-3 in EDIT mode and displays the contents of the current cell in the control panel.
(F3)	NAME	Displays a menu of range names.
(F4)	ABS	Cycles a cell or range address between relative, absolute, and mixed.
(F5)	GOTO	Moves cell pointer directly to a particular cell.
(F6)	WINDOW	Moves cell pointer between two windows. Turns off the display of setting sheets (MENU mode only).
(F7)	QUERY	Repeats most recent /Data Query operation.
(F8)	TABLE	Repeats most recent /Data Table operation.
(F9)	CALC	Recalculates all formulas (READY mode only). Converts formula to its value (VALUE and EDIT modes).
(F10)	GRAPH	Draws a graph using current graph settings.
(ALT) - (F1)	COMPOSE	When used with alphanumeric keys, creates characters you cannot enter directly from the keyboard.
(ALT) - (F2)	STEP	Turns on STEP mode, which executes macros one step at a time for the purpose of debugging.
(ALT) - (F3)	RUN	Displays a menu of named ranges in the worksheet so you can select the name of a macro to run.
(ALT) - (F4)	UNDO	Cancels any changes made to the worksheet since 1-2-3 was last in READY mode. Press again to redo changes.
(ALT) - (F5)	LEARN	Turns Learn feature on and records keystrokes in the learn range. Press again to turn off the Learn feature.
(ALT) - (F7)	APP1	Activates add-in program assigned to key, if any.
(ALT) - (F8)	APP2	Activates add-in program assigned to key, if any.
(ALT) - (F9)	APP3	Activates add-in program assigned to key, if any.
(ALT) - (F10)	APP4	Activates add-in program assigned to key, if any, or displays /Add-In meu if there is no add-in assigned to keys.

INDEX

Absolute cell address:
  defined, SS4
  and range names, SS138
  using, SS82-85
Addition, in worksheets, SS31
Address, cell:
  absolute, SS4, SS82-85
  defined, SS7
  mixed, SS83
  range name used in place of, SS138
  relative, SS5, SS49
  typing, SS31
Analysis, what-if:
  defined, SS5
  using, SS79-82
Apostrophe, for flush left labels, SS16, SS17, SS18
Arguments:
  in @functions, SS51-52
  in @IF functions, SS139-40
Arithmetic operators, SS4, SS31
Arrow keys, SS8
Asterisks, displayed in cells, SS57
@functions:
  arguments in, SS51-52
  copying, SS52-53
  correcting errors in, SS51
  defined, SS51
  entering, SS51-53
  @IF, SS139-40
  @NOW, SS91
  statistical, SS50
  @SUM, SS51
  types of, SS51
Autoexecute macros, SS160-62
Automatic recalculation, SS4
Axes on graphs:
  defined, SS104
  labeling, SS106-7, SS112-13

Backslash (\):
  in macro names, SS145
  to repeat characters, SS62-63
Bar graphs:
  creating, SS115
  crosshatching designs on, SS117-18
  entering legends on, SS117-18
  multiple ranges for, SS116
  stacked-bar graphs, SS118-19
Booting up, SS6-7
Braces for macros key names, SS142

Canceling command selection, SS27
Capital letters for labels, SS19
Caret for centering labels, SS16
Cell addresses:
  absolute, SS4, SS82-85, SS139
  defined, SS7

mixed, SS83
range names used in place of, SS138
relative, SS5, SS49
typing, SS31
Cell pointer, SS7, SS13
Cells:
  asterisks displayed in, SS57
  defined, SS4, SS7
  editing entries in, SS17-22
  protecting, SS159-60
  work, SS80
Character repeat label prefix, SS61-63
Charts, pie, SS120-21
Circular references:
  defined, SS4
  locating and correcting, SS69-72
Color, viewing graphs in, SS116
Columns:
  defined, SS4, SS7
  deleting, SS64
  entering labels for, SS13-16
  freezing, SS72-75
  inserting, SS63-64
  letter labels for, SS11
  widths, changing, SS54-57
Command macros, SS153-59
Commands:
  canceling, SS27
  Copy, SS42-45, SS170, SS171
  for copying data, SS171
  Erase, SS53-54
  for erasing data, SS171
  File, SS26
  File List, SS33
  File Retrieve, SS34
  File Save, SS33, SS126
  Graph, SS104-6
  for graphing data, SS171
  for hiding data, SS171
  Justify, SS92
  for loading data, SS171
  for moving data, SS171-72
  Print, SS35, SS65, SS94
  for printing, SS172
  for protecting data, SS172
  Quit, SS36
  Range, SS54
  Range Erase, SS54, SS160
  Range Format Date, SS91
  Range Format Percent, SS78
  Range Justify, SS92
  Range Name, SS135-39, SS145, SS160
  Range Unprotect, SS159
  for saving, SS172
  summary of, SS170-73
  Worksheet Column, SS54
  Worksheet Erase, SS34
  Worksheet Global Column-Width, SS56-58

Worksheet Global Format, SS57
Worksheet Global Protection Enable, SS159
Worksheet Insert Column, SS63
Worksheet Insert Row, SS61
Worksheet Status, SS71
Worksheet Titles, SS72-74
Worksheet Window, SS75-77, SS80
Compressed printing, SS94-95
Control panel, SS7
Copy command, SS42-45, SS171
Copying:
  @ functions, SS52-53
  commands for, SS171
  defined, SS4
  underline, SS62-63
  values, SS43-45
Currency format, SS58

Data, specifying for graphs, SS107
Date, entering, SS90-92
Debugging macros, SS147-49
Deleting. See Erasing
Displaying:
  filenames, SS26
  graphs, SS108, SS116
  negative values, SS58
  percents, SS77-79
Division in worksheets, SS31
Documentation:
  for macros, SS152
  for templates, SS161
Dollar sign in formulas, SS82-83

EDIT mode, SS17, SS19
Editing:
  cell entries, SS17-22
  labels, SS17-22
  macros, SS147-49
Electronic spreadsheets:
  advantages of using, SS3-4
  defined, SS3
  terminology for, SS4-5, SS167-70
Entering:
  @functions, SS51-53
  date, SS90-92
  formulas, SS31-32, SS48-50
  graph titles, SS108-12
  labels, SS13-16
  labels for X axis, SS106
  legends on graphs, SS117-18
  macros, SS143-45
  system date, SS90-92
  titles on graphs, SS108-13
  titles for worksheets, SS22-23
  values, SS29-30
Erase command, SS53-54
Erasing:
  columns, SS64

commands for, SS171
  a range, SS54, SS160
  worksheets, SS34
Errors, correcting:
  in @functions, SS51
  circular references, SS69-72
  in command selection, SS25
  logic, SS148-49
  in macros, SS147-49
  syntax, SS148-49
Executing macros, SS141
Exponentiation in worksheets, SS31

File command, SS26
File List command, SS33
File Retrieve command, SS34
File Save command, SS33, SS126
Filenames:
  displaying, SS26
  .PIC extension, SS114
  writing over, SS65
Files:
  picture, SS114
  printing, SS65
  replacing, SS64-65
  retrieving, SS26-29
  saving, SS64-65, SS114, SS147
Formatting:
  as currency, SS58
  defined, SS4
  as percents, SS77-79
  values, SS57-60
Formulas:
  absolute cell address in, SS82-85
  defined, SS4, SS31
  entering, SS31-32, SS48-50
  for percents, SS77-79
  types of, SS31
Freezing:
  defined, SS5
  titles, SS72-75
Function keys:
  (F1) (Help), SS25
  (F2) (Edit), SS17
  (F5) (GOTO), SS11
Functions, @:
  defined, SS5
  entering, SS51-53
  @IF, SS139-40
  @NOW, SS91
  @SUM, SS51
  types of, SS51

Global commands. *See* Worksheet commands
GOTO key ((F5)), SS11
Graph command, SS104-6
Graphics adapter card, SS108
Graphs:
  adapter card, for displaying, SS108
  for analysis, SS4
  axes on, SS100, SS106-7, SS112-13
  bar, SS115-18
  canceling settings, SS120
  commands for creating, SS171

creating, SS101-27
  crosshatching designs on, SS117-18
  data for, specifying, SS107
  defined, SS5
  displaying, SS108, SS116
  labeling the axes, SS106-7, SS112-13
  legends, entering, SS117-18
  line, SS104-14
  multiple ranges for, SS116
  naming settings, SS113-14
  options for, SS109
  pie charts, SS120-21
  printing, SS127-29
  recalling, SS125-26
  saving, for printing, SS114
  selecting type of, SS104-6
  specifying data for, SS107
  stacked-bar, SS118-19
  titles on, SS104, SS108-13
  types of, SS103
  viewing, in color, SS116

Hardware:
  color monitor, SS116
  graphics adapter card, SS108
HELP mode, SS25
Help system:
  accessing with (F1), SS25
  using, SS25-26
Hiding data, commands for, SS171
Highlighting, SS45-48
Home position, SS8-9, SS24

@IF function, SS139-40
Inserting:
  columns, SS63-6
  rows, SS61
Interactive worksheets, SS141

Justify command, SS92
Justifying:
  defined, SS5
  text, SS92-94

Key names in macros:
  entering, SS143-44
  errors in, SS147
  repetition factor in, SS150-52
Keys:
  arrow, SS8
  backslash (\), SS62-63, SS145
  (CAPS LOCK), SS19
  in EDIT mode, SS17
  (END), SS10, SS24
  (ESC), SS27, SS52
  GOTO, SS11
  (HOME), SS8-9, SS24
  (INS), SS18, SS20
  for moving around worksheets, SS13
  (PGUP) and (PGDN), SS10
  (SCROLL LOCK), SS12
  slash (/), SS22
  See also Function keys; Key names
Keystroke instructions in macros, SS142

Label prefix characters, SS16, SS17
Labels:
  defined, SS5, SS14
  editing, SS17-22
  entering, SS13-16
  position in cells, SS16
  for X axis on graphs, SS106
  See also Titles
Learn feature, using, SS153-59
Legends on graphs:
  defined, SS104
  entering, SS117-18
Line graphs:
  entering titles, SS108-13
  labeling the X axis, SS106-7
  specifying, SS100-1
  specifying data for, SS107
List in @functions, SS51
Loading data, commands for, SS171
Loading Lotus 1-2-3, SS6-7
Logic errors in macros, SS147-49
Logical operators, SS139-40
Lotus 1-2-3:
  loading, SS6-7
  maximum size of worksheet, SS9
  quitting, SS36

Macros:
  autoexecute, SS160-62
  automating with, SS134-66
  command, SS146-47
  creating, SS134, SS146-47
  debugging, SS147
  documenting, SS152
  editing, SS147-49
  entering, SS143-45
  errors in, SS147-49
  executing, SS141
  interactive, SS141, SS144
  key names in, SS142-43
  keystroke instructions in, SS142
  moving, in worksheets, SS152
  naming, SS145-46
  planning, SS142-43
  for printing, SS153-59
  protecting macro cells, SS159-60
  repetition factor in, SS150-52
  testing, SS146-47
Main menu, using, SS23-24
Manual recalculation, SS5
Memos in worksheets, SS92-94
MENU mode, SS22
Menu pointer, SS22
Menu, Main, SS23-25
Mixed cell addresses, SS83
Mode indicator, SS7
Modes:
  defined, SS5
  EDIT, SS17, SS19
  HELP, SS25
  Highlight, SS45
  MENU, SS24
  mode indicator, SS7
  overwrite, SS17, SS19

Modes: (*continued*)
    READY, SS7, SS20
    VALUE, SS29-30
Move command:
    defined, SS5
    to move macros, SS152
Moving data, commands for, SS171-72
Multiplication in worksheets, SS31

Naming:
    graph settings, SS113-14
    macros, SS145-46
    ranges, SS134-39
Negative values, displaying, SS58
@NOW function, SS91
Numeric formats, SS58
Numeric keypad, SS8

Operators:
    arithmetic, SS4, SS31
    logical, SS139-40
Overwriting, to edit, SS17, SS19

Percents, displaying, SS77-79
Picture files, SS114
Pie charts, SS120-25
Pointing ranges
    for copying, SS46-48
    for printing, SS65
Print command, SS35, SS65, SS94
PrintGraph program, SS127-28
Printing:
    commands for, SS172
    compressed, SS94-95
    files, SS65
    graphs, SS127-29
    macros for, SS153-59
    ranges for, SS35, SS65, SS94
    saving graphs for, SS114
    worksheets, SS35-37, SS65
Prompts, defined, SS12
Protecting cells, SS159-60, SS172

Question mark, in macros, SS144
Quitting, SS36

Range command, SS54
Range Erase command, SS54, SS160
Range Format Date command, SS91
Range Format Percent command, SS78
Range Justify command, SS92
Range Name command, SS135-39, SS145, SS160
Range Name table, SS138-39
Range Unprotect command, SS159
Ranges:
    for copying values, SS44-45
    defined, SS5
    erasing, SS54, SS160
    formatting as percents, SS77-79

justifying, SS92-94
moving, SS152
multiple, for graphs, SS116
naming, SS134-39
pointing, SS46-49
for printing, SS35, SS65, SS94
protecting, SS150-60
unprotecting, SS160
READY mode, SS7, SS20
Recalculation:
    automatic, SS4
    manual, SS5
References, circular:
    defined, SS4
    locating and correcting, SS69-72
Relative cell addressing, SS5, SS49
Repeating characters, SS61-63
Repetition factor in macros, SS150-52
Replacing files, SS64-65
Retrieving files, SS26-29
Rows:
    defined, SS5, SS7
    freezing, SS72-75
    inserting, SS61

Saving:
    commands for, SS172
    files, SS64-65, SS114, SS147
    graph settings, SS113-14
    graphs for printing, SS119
    macros for, SS157-58
    worksheets, SS33-35, SS126-27
    worksheets with graph settings, SS126-27
Screens, split, SS76-77, SS80
Scroll Lock, SS12
Scrolling:
    defined, SS10
    with (SCROLL LOCK), SS12
    synchronized, SS77
    unsynchronized, SS77
    windows, SS75-77
Slash key (/), SS22
Spreadsheets. *See* Worksheets
Stacked-bar graphs, SS118-19
Status indicator, SS10
Status window, displaying, SS71
Subtraction in worksheets, SS31
@SUM function, SS51
Synchronized scrolling, SS77
Syntax errors in macros, SS148-49
System date, entering, SS86-89

Templates for data entry:
    creating, SS141, SS160-61
    documenting, SS161
Terminology for worksheets, SS4-5, SS167-70
Testing macros, SS146-47
Text, justifying, SS92-94
Tilde (~) as macro key name, SS142

Titles:
    entering on worksheets, SS21
    freezing, SS72-75
    on graphs, SS104, SS108-13
    longer than cell, SS22
    See also Labels

Underlining headings, SS61-63
Unprotecting cells, SS160
Unsynchronized scrolling, SS77

VALUE mode, SS29-30
Values:
    copying, SS43-45
    defined, SS5, SS14
    entering, SS29-30
    formatting, SS57-60
    negative, displaying, SS58
    percent, displaying, SS77-79
    See also Formulas

What-if analysis:
    defined, SS5
    using, SS79-82
Windows:
    defined, SS9
    moving around in, SS9-10
    scrolling, SS75-77
    split-screen, SS76-77, SS80
    status, displaying, SS71
Work cells, using, SS80
Worksheet Column command, SS54
Worksheet Erase command, SS34
Worksheet Global Column-Width command, SS56-SS58
Worksheet Global Format command, SS57
Worksheet Global Protection Enable command, SS159
Worksheet Insert Column command, SS63
Worksheet Insert Row command, SS61
Worksheet Status command, SS71
Worksheet Titles command, SS72-74
Worksheet Window command, SS75-77, SS80
Worksheets:
    advantages of using, SS3-4
    autoexecuting, SS160-61
    automating, SS134-66
    defined, SS3, SS7
    erasing, SS34
    interactive, SS141, SS144
    macros in, SS134-66
    maximum size of, SS9
    memos in, SS92-94
    moving around, SS8-13
    printing, SS35-37, SS65
    printing compressed, SS94-95
    protecting cells in, SS159-60, SS172
    saving, SS33-35, SS126-27
    saving, with graph settings, SS126-27
    terminology for, SS4-5, SS167-70

dBASE III PLUS

7 8 9 0   KGP KGP   9 5 4 3

P/N 047884-8

ORDER INFORMATION:
ISBN 0-07-047884-8

CONTENTS

Overview   Database DB3
Definition of Database   DB3
Advantages of Using a Database   DB4
Database Terminology   DB4
Case Study for Labs 1–4   DB5

Lab 1   Creating a Database   DB6
Starting dBASE III PLUS on a
    Two-Disk System   DB7
Starting dBASE III PLUS on a
    Hard-Disk System   DB7
Using the Dot Prompt   DB8
Using The Assistant   DB9
Defining the Database File Structure   DB12
Creating Field Names   DB16
Inputting Records   DB23
Appending Records to the Database   DB30
Printing the Database   DB31
Quitting dBASE III PLUS   DB33
Key Terms   DB33
Matching   DB33
Practice Exercises   DB34

**Lab 2   Modifying, Editing, and
    Viewing a Database   DB37**
Opening a Database File   DB37
Modifying the Database Structure   DB39
Browsing the Database Records   DB42
Editing Database Records   DB49
Marking Records for Deletion   DB50
Positioning the Record Pointer   DB51
Displaying Database Records   DB59
Recalling Records Marked for Deletion   DB61
Listing Database Records   DB61
Removing Records Marked for Deletion   DB62
Printing Selected Records   DB62
Key Terms   DB64
Matching   DB64
Practice Exercises   DB64

**Lab 3   Sorting, Indexing, and
    Summarizing Data   DB67**
Displaying a Disk Directory   DB67
Displaying the File Structure   DB68
Sorting the Database Records   DB70
Creating a Multilevel Sort File   DB73
Creating an Index File   DB76
Opening Index Files   DB80
Using the Seek Command   DB82
Using the Dot Prompt   DB84
Summarizing Data   DB86
Printing a Simple Report   DB88
Key Terms   DB89
Matching   DB90
Practice Exercises   DB90

**Lab 4   Creating a Professional
    Report   DB92**
Examining the Report Screen   DB92
Entering the Report Title   DB95
Specifying the Report Column   DB97
Viewing the Report   DB103
Modifying the Report   DB104
Creating Subtotals   DB112
Printing the Report   DB115
Key Terms   DB118
Matching   DB118
Practice Exercises   DB118

Summary   dBASE III PLUS   DB122
Glossary of Key Terms   DB122
Functional Summary of Selected dBASE III
    PLUS Commands   DB124

Index   DB125

Database

A word processor helps you enter and manipulate text. An electronic spreadsheet helps you enter and analyze numerical data. A computerized database helps you enter and manage information or data in record format.

Databases have been in existence for many years. Paper records organized in a filing cabinet by name or department are a database. The information in a telephone book, organized alphabetically, is a database. The records maintained by a school of teachers, classes, and students is a database.

Before computers, most database records were kept on paper. With computers, the same data is entered and stored on a diskette. The big difference is that an electronic database can manipulate—sort, analyze, and display—the data quickly and efficiently. What took hours of time to pull from the paper files can be extracted in a matter of seconds using a computerized database.

Definition of a Database

A **database** is an organized collection of related data that is stored in a file. The data is entered as a record which consists of several fields of data. Each record contains the same fields. For example, a school has a database of student records. Each record may contain the following fields of data: name, address, social security number, phone number, classes, and grades. All the records for each student in the school are stored in a single file.

Some **database** programs only access and manipulate the data in a single file. Others allow the user to access and relate several files at one time. For example, the school may have a second database file containing data for each student's current class schedule. At the end of the semester the grades are posted in this file for each student. The data in one file can then be merged into the other file by using a common field, such as the student's name, to link the two files.

The database program contains commands that allow the user to design the structure of the database records and enter the data for each record into the file. This is the physical storage of the data. How this data is retrieved, organized, and manipulated is the conceptual use of the data.

Advantages of Using a Database

A computerized database system does not save time by making the data quicker to enter. This, as in most programs, is a function of the typing speed of the user and his or her knowledge of the program.

One of the main advantages to using a computerized database system is the speed of locating the records, updating and adding records to the file, and organizing the records to meet varying needs.

Once data is entered into the database file, the data can be located very quickly by record number or field data. In a manual system, usually a record can be located by knowing one key piece of information. For example, if the records are organized by last name, to find a record you must know the last name. In a computerized database, even if the records were organized by last name, the record could still be located without knowing the last name. Any other field, such as address or social security number, could be used to locate the record. Because specific records can be located quickly, the data in the fields can easily be edited and updated.

A second advantage to a computerized database system is its ability to arrange the records in the file according to different fields of data. The records can be organized by name, department, pay, class, or whatever else is needed at a particular time. This ability to produce multiple file arrangements helps provide information in a more meaningful manner. The same records can provide information to different departments for different purposes.

A third advantage is the ability to perform calculations on different fields of data. Instead of pulling each record from a filing cabinet, recording the piece of data you want to use, and then calculating a total for the field, you can simply have the database program sum all the values in the specified field. It can even selectively use in the calculation only those records meeting certain requirements. Information that was once costly and time-consuming to get is now quickly and readily available.

Finally, a database program can produce either very simple or complex professional-looking reports. A simple report can be created by asking for a listing of specified fields of data and restricting the listing to records meeting specified conditions. A more complex professional report can be created using the same restrictions or conditions as the simple report. But the data can be displayed in columnar format, with titles, headings, subtotals, and totals.

In manual systems, there are often several files containing some of the same data. A computerized database system can allow access by more than one department to the same data. Common updating of the data can be done by any department. The elimination of duplicate information saves space and time.

Database Terminology

Create: The process of defining the database file structure.
Delete: To remove a record from the database file.
Edit: To change or update the data in a field.
Field: A collection of related characters, such as last name.
File: A database of records.
Index: The display of records in a file according to a specified key field.
Record: A collection of related fields, such as class time, class name, or grade.
Report: A listing of specified fields of data for specified records in the file.
Scope: The number of records in a file to be processed by the command.

2000 Records
256 characters in a field

Date
characters   *Date field*
numeric   *memo field*
logical

Search: To locate a specific record in a file.

Sort: To arrange the records in a file in a specified order.

Structure: The attributes (name, type, width) and order of fields in the record.

Type: The content of a field can be Character (alphanumeric), Numeric, Logical, or Date.

Case Study for Labs 1–4

Two separate cases are used in the dBASE III PLUS labs. The first case study demonstrates the basic features of creating, updating, and finding records in a database file. The second case study emphasizes organizing and using records to produce information and reports.

Labs 1 and 2   The Sports Club membership is growing rapidly. Their current method of maintaining membership data consists of a filing system of 3 × 5 index cards. This system was fine when the club was small. But now that the club has grown so much, the system no longer works.

The membership coordinator, Fred Morris, recently purchased dBASE III PLUS. He will use the program to create a database file of member records. We will follow Fred as he creates the database file structure, enters records, and edits, deletes, and locates records in the file. He will also retrieve and print a listing of specified records from the database file.

Labs 3 and 4   In the second case, Donna McIntyre, the assistant manager of the Sports Club, has a dBASE III PLUS file of employee records. We will follow Donna as she organizes the records in the file using sorting and indexing. The records are analyzed using the three numeric functions in dBASE III PLUS—Count, Add, and Average. A simple report is produced in Lab 3. Lab 4 deals exclusively with the Report Generation program of dBASE III PLUS. First a report is created listing all employees alphabetically, the rate of pay, hours worked, and weekly pay. A second report is produced summarizing the same employee data by job category.

Creating a Database

1

OBJECTIVES

In this lab you will learn how to:

1. Load dBASE III PLUS.

2. Issue commands at the dot prompt.

3. Use The Assistant to issue commands.

4. Use the Help facility.

5. Define the database structure.

6. Input records to a database.

7. Append records to a database.

8. Use the editing keys.

9. Print the database records.

10. Quit dBASE III PLUS.

CASE STUDY

Fred Morris is the membership coordinator for the Sports Club. One of Fred's responsibilities is to keep track of all the club's membership records. Currently, this information is stored on 3×5 note cards like the one shown below.

```
Account No:    1001
Membership Date:    May 21, 1983
First Name:    Edward
Last Name:    Becker
Street:    1036 W. 5th Place
City:    Mesa
State:    AZ
Zipcode:    85205
Age:    45
Auto Payment:    Yes
```

This system was fine when the club was small. Now, however, the club is much larger, and Fred is having problems with this manual database system.

To automate the membership records, Fred has purchased dBASE III PLUS. We will follow him as he learns how to use dBASE III PLUS to create a membership database, insert records, and print the database.

Starting dBASE III PLUS on a Two-Disk System

Load DOS and respond to the date and time prompts. The A> should appear on the display screen. Remove the DOS diskette from drive A.

Place the Special Educational Version of dBASE III PLUS Disk 1 (hereafter called the "dBASE III PLUS Sampler Disk 1 or 2") in drive A. To start the dBASE III PLUS program, in upper- or lowercase letters,

Type: **DBASE**

Press: ⏎

Starting dBASE III PLUS on a Hard-Disk System

The dBASE III PLUS program should have already been installed on your hard disk. It is assumed that the program files are on the C drive in the subdirectory \DBASE and that your data diskette drive is A. If your setup is different, substitute the appropriate drive and subdirectory name in the directions below.

The drive door(s) should be open. Turn on your computer and, if necessary, respond to the date and time prompts. The DOS C> should be displayed.

Put your data disk in drive A, and if necessary, close the drive door.

To load the dBASE program, begin by changing the default disk drive to A. At the C>,

Type: **A:**

Press: ⏎

Drive A is now the default drive. This means that the diskette in the A drive will be used to save and retrieve files. Now you are ready to load the dBASE program. The command, DBASE, will load the program into memory. You must include the drive and subdirectory path as part of the command to tell the system where to find the dBASE files. To do this,

Type: **C:\DBASE\DBASE**

Press: ⏎

After a few moments your display screen should look similar to Figure 1-1.

FIGURE 1-1

```
                 dBASE III PLUS  version 1.0  IBM/MSDOS DEMO
     Copyright (c) Ashton-Tate 1984, 1985, 1986.  All Rights Reserved.
            dBASE, dBASE III, dBASE III PLUS, and Ashton-Tate
                      are trademarks of Ashton-Tate


     You may use the dBASE III PLUS software and  printed materials in
     the dBASE III PLUS software package under the terms  of the dBASE
     III  PLUS  Software  License Agreement.   In summary, Ashton-Tate
     grants you a paid-up, non-transferable,  personal license to use
     dBASE III PLUS on one  microcomputer or workstation.   You do not
     become the owner of  the package,  nor do  you have  the right to
     copy or alter the software or printed materials.  You are legally
     accountable for any violation of  the  License  Agreement  or of
     copyright, trademark, or trade secret laws.




Command Line     ||<B:>||                                        |
Insert Sampler Disk 2 in drive A and a Data Disk in drive B, and press ENTER
                    or press Ctrl-C to abort.              _
```

This screen discusses the license agreement for using the dBASE III PLUS program.

Note: Throughout the labs the screens will reflect use of the B drive as the drive containing your data diskette.

Following the instructions at the bottom of the screen, remove the sample Disk 1 from drive A and insert the sampler Disk 2 in drive A. Your data diskette should be in drive B.

Your display screen should look similar to Figure 1-2.

menu
bar

pull-down
menu

action
line

status bar
navigation line

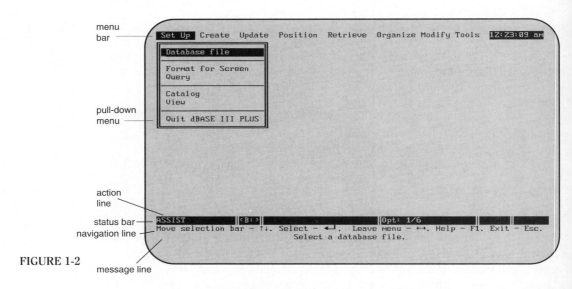

FIGURE 1-2

message line

This is The Assistant. **The Assistant** is a collection of menus that help you perform dBASE III PLUS commands and operations. There are two ways to issue commands in dBASE III PLUS. One way is to use The Assistant to select and build the commands. The other way is to use the dot prompt to directly enter the commands.

Using the Dot Prompt

To leave The Assistant and display the dot prompt,

Press: (ESC)

Your display screen should be similar to Figure 1-3.

FIGURE 1-3

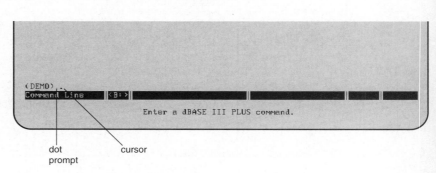

dot   cursor
prompt

The Assistant has been replaced by a nearly blank display screen. Near the bottom of the screen, immediately following "(DEMO)", is the **dot prompt** (a period) followed by a blinking cursor.

dBASE III PLUS commands are entered following the dot prompt. The cursor shows you where the next character you type will appear as you enter the command. For example, the dBASE III PLUS dot command "Assist" will return you to The Assistant from the dot prompt.

To issue this command, in either upper- or lowercase letters,

Type: **ASSIST**
Press: ⏎

Note: If an error message appears on your display screen, you probably made an error entering the command. Press (ESC) and type the command again.

You should be returned to The Assistant. Your display screen should be similar once again to Figure 1-2.

Many experienced dBASE III PLUS users prefer using the dot prompt to issue commands. After you have completed these labs, you may also find it quicker to use the dot prompt to issue many commands.

However, the Assistant eliminates many typing and other kinds of potential errors. Beginners (as well as many more experienced users) find that The Assistant is a very effective means of issuing commands. Next we will learn how to use The Assistant to issue dBASE III PLUS commands. Throughout this series of labs we will use The Assistant rather than the dot prompt to issue most commands.

Using the Assistant

The Assistant is a menu-driven tool used to issue dBASE III PLUS commands. As selections are made from The Assistant menu, the dBASE III PLUS dot command is created and displayed.

The top line of the screen, beginning with "Set Up" and ending with "Tools," is called the **menu bar.** It lists the eight **menus** that can be opened.

Directly below the menu bar is a box containing a **pull-down menu** of options that are available for selection.

At the bottom of the screen there are four lines of information: the action line (currently blank), the status bar, the navigation line, and the message line.

We will be discussing in detail the different areas of The Assistant screen as we use them throughout the lab.

The **menu highlight bar,** currently over "Set Up" in the menu bar, allows you to select and open a menu. The current open menu is Set Up.

The pull-down menu lists the six menu **options** associated with the open Set Up Menu that can be selected. Within the pull-down menu, the **selection bar** is currently highlighting "Database file". Notice that the **message line** (the last line on the screen) displays a brief description of the highlighted menu option.

The ⟵ and ⟶ keys, located on the numeric keypad, are used to select and open a menu from the menu bar. Watch your display screen as you

Press: ⟶

Your display screen should be similar to Figure 1-4.

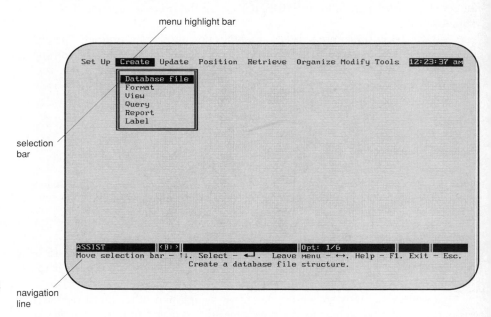

FIGURE 1-4

The menu highlight bar is now positioned over "Create" and a new pull-down menu appears in a box below the open menu. This box displays the six menu options that are associated with the open Create Menu.

Each time ⟶ is pressed, the menu highlight bar moves to the right to open the next menu. The pull-down menu of options associated with the highlighted (open) menu is displayed. To open the other six menus and see the associated pull-down menu of options, slowly

Press: ⟶ (6 times)

The menu highlight bar should be positioned over "Tools". To move quickly back to the beginning of the menu bar, watch your display screen as you

Press: ⟶

The menu highlight bar wraps around to the beginning of the menu bar. It should be positioned over "Set Up" again.

The menu highlight bar can also move to the left through the menu by using ⟵. Watch your display screen as you

Press: ⟵ (4 times)

The highlight bar moves one menu to the left each time ⟵ is pressed. It should be positioned over "Retrieve".

The (HOME) and (END) keys can be used to move the menu highlight bar to the first menu, Set Up, or to the last menu, Tools, from any location in the menu bar. To demonstrate,

Press: (HOME)

The menu highlight bar moved quickly to Set Up when (HOME) was pressed.

Press: (END)

Although we were at the beginning of the menu when (END) was pressed, using the (END) key will take you to Tools from any location in the menu bar.

To quickly move the menu highlight bar to open a specific menu, the first letter of the menu name can be typed. To quickly move back to Create,

Type: C

The Create Menu is open. The selection bar is positioned over the Database file option in the pull-down menu.

Instructions on how to move the selection bar are given in the **navigation line** (second line from the bottom of the screen). It tells you that the selection bar is moved by using the ⬆ and ⬇ keys. (The ⬆⬇ displayed in the navigation line represents the ⬆ and ⬇ keys.)

To move the selection bar to the Format option,

Press: ⬇

Your display screen should be similar to Figure 1-5.

FIGURE 1-5

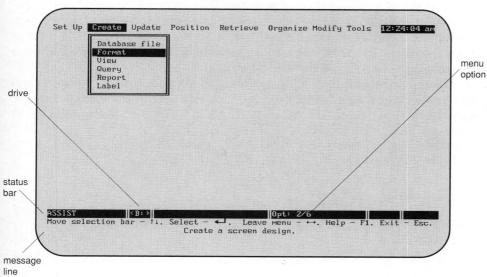

The selection bar is positioned over the Format option. The message line briefly tells you that this option will let you "Create a screen design".

Notice that the information in the status bar (highlighted bar at the bottom of the screen) has changed. The **status bar** is divided into six areas. It tells you where you are in the menu and the state of various optional settings. As the settings change, the information displayed in the boxes changes.

Right now the first box in the status bar tells you that you are using The Assistant. The second box displays the drive you are using. The third box is blank until a file is in use, at which time it will display the filename. The fourth box displays "Opt: 2/6". The highlighted option, Format, is the second (2) of six (6) options available. Each time the selection bar moves, the option number changes. The last two boxes are blank. They will display the status of the (INS), (CAPS LOCK), and (NUM LOCK) keys when they are on.

Note the changes in the message line and the status bar as you

Press: (↓) (slowly, 5 times)

The selection bar moved down through the options and back up to "Database file". It wrapped around through the options in a manner similar to the movement of the menu highlight bar.

To move the selection bar quickly to the last option in a pull-down menu,

Press: (↑)

Like the menu highlight bar, the selection bar can move in either direction through the options and wraps around its menu. Unlike the menu highlight bar, however, the selection bar cannot be moved by typing the first letter of the desired option name.

Defining the Database File Structure

Now that you are familiar with how to move the menu highlight bar and the selection bar, we will follow Fred as he defines the structure for the database.

A database file consists of rows (records) and columns (fields) of information. A **field** is a collection of related characters, such as a person's name. The column titles are called **field names.** A **record** is a collection of related fields, such as a person's name, address, and phone number.

Fred's first step is to do a little planning. Fred decides that each member will be represented as a record in his database. Each member's record will consist of the same 10 pieces of information that are currently stored on 3 × 5 index cards. The 10 fields will be:

> Account Number
> Membership Date
> First Name
> Last Name
> Street
> City
> State
> Zipcode
> Age
> Fee Payment Method—Automatic Payment

Once the fields are determined, the database structure can be defined. A database file is created and the fields are defined using the Create Database file command.

The Create Menu should be open, and if the selection bar is not already on the Database file option,

Move to: Database file

Each of the six pull-down menu options in the Create Menu corresponds to a different type of file that can be created in dBASE III PLUS. Although the message line gives you a brief description of each option, more detailed information is provided by pressing the Help ((F1)) key.

With the selection bar on the option you want more information about, in this case Database file,

Press: (F1)

Your display screen should be similar to Figure 1-6.

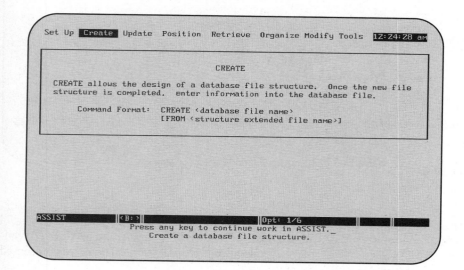

FIGURE 1-6

Information about the Create Database file command and the format for entering this command at the dot prompt are displayed. You can access information about each pull-down menu option from The Assistant screen simply by pressing (F1), Help.

To clear the information and return to The Assistant screen,

Press: any key

For information on how to select a pull-down menu option, refer to the navigation line. First the selection bar is moved to the option you want to use. Following the directions in the navigation line select the option by pressing (⏎). (The ⏎ displayed on the navigation line represents the (⏎) key.)

With the menu pointer on Create and the selection bar on Database file,

Press: (⏎)

Note: If you accidentally select an incorrect menu option, press (ESC) to cancel the selection and return to the previous selection.

Your display screen should be similar to Figure 1-7.

FIGURE 1-7

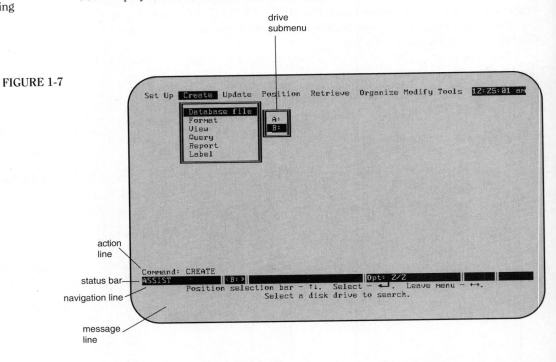

There are several changes on the screen. Now, another box appears displaying a **submenu** of options. The two options, "A:" and "B:", represent the disk drives available. (Your screen may display several more drive selections. The drives presented will reflect your particular system.)

The **action line** (above the status bar) displays the dBASE III PLUS command "CREATE". As pull-down menu and submenu options are selected using The Assistant, the action line will display the dBASE III PLUS dot command as it is being built.

The status bar displays "Opt: 2/2". This means that the selection bar is on the second of two possible submenu options.

The message line provides information concerning the submenu. In this case, we must specify the disk drive where the database file will be saved. The disk drive we want to use to hold the new file is the B drive. (Your system may be different. Consult your instructor if you are not sure of the drive to select.)

Move to the drive containing your data diskette.

To select the drive, following the directions in the navigation line,

Press:

Your display screen should be similar to Figure 1-8.

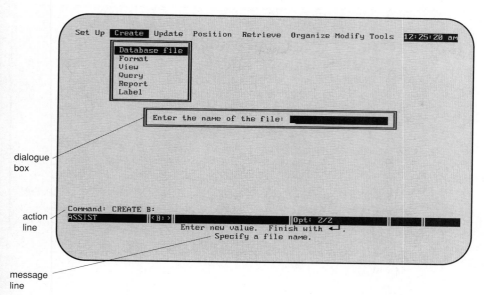

dialogue
box

action
line

message
line

FIGURE 1-8

The action line now shows the dot command "CREATE B:". Another box appears on the display screen. It replaces the drive selection submenu box. This box is called a **dialogue box** because it contains a **prompt.** A prompt is a dBASE III PLUS message that requires a user response. In this case, the dialogue box wants you to "Enter the name of the file:". The message line tells you to specify a filename.

The filename should be descriptive of the contents of the database. It cannot be longer than eight characters. Nor can it include any blank spaces, periods, or special characters. Do not enter a filename extension. dBASE III PLUS automatically assigns a special extension to the filename.

Since Fred's database file will contain information on each club member, he has decided to name the file MEMBERS. In either upper- or lowercase characters,

Type: MEMBERS

If you made an error, use the (Bksp) key to delete the characters back to the error. Then retype the filename correctly. Watch the action line closely to see the complete dBASE III PLUS command as you

Press: (↵)

The complete command in the action line was CREATE B: MEMBERS. If you used the dot prompt to directly enter the command to create a database file, it would be entered exactly as displayed in the action line.

The Assistant, through the use of menu and submenu options, help information, and dialogue boxes, helps the user to build and execute the dBASE III PLUS commands. The actual dot commands are displayed in the action line as the user selects options from the menus.

Your display screen should be similar to Figure 1-9.

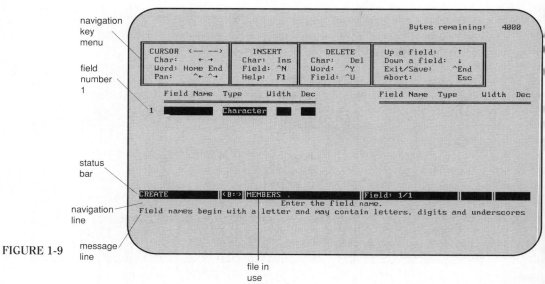

navigation
key
menu

field
number
1

status
bar

navigation
line

FIGURE 1-9   message
line

file in
use

The Assistant screen has been replaced by the Create screen. This screen is used to define the structure of your database file.

The **navigation key menu** across the top of the screen contains editing and cursor navigation keys to use while in the Create screen.

The central area of the screen contains two identical sets of column headings: Field Name, Type, Width, and Dec (decimal places). These are the four pieces of information that are needed to define each field in the record.

Under the left set of column headings is a highlighted area beginning with the number 1. This is where the first field will be defined.

The first three boxes in the status bar now tell you that the Create Menu is the current menu, the B drive is in use, and the filename is MEMBERS. The fourth box, which used to display the menu option number, now tells you which field the highlight bar is on, "Field: 1/1".

The navigation line tells you that dBASE III PLUS wants you to enter a field name. The message line briefly defines the characteristics of a field name.

Creating Field Names

The first field to be defined is Account Number. The field name needs to be entered first. It should be descriptive of the contents of the field data. It can be up to 10 characters long and may contain letters, digits, and underscores. It cannot contain blank spaces. The blinking underscore or cursor will show where each character will appear as you type.

Fred has decided to use the field name ACCT_NUM. The name can be typed in either upper- or lowercase letters. dBASE III PLUS will display them as all uppercase. An underscore is entered by using the (SHIFT) key and the dash (the key to the right of 0).

Type: ACC_NUM

Fred sees that he has made an error already. He forgot the "T" in "ACCT". Look at the navigation key menu. The "CURSOR" (left) section shows that the ⟵ and ⟶ keys will move the cursor character by character. The other three sections of the navigation key menu tell you how to insert and delete characters and fields, how to move between fields, and how to save your work or abort the command.

To correct the entry, we will move the cursor back to the location of the error and retype it correctly as follows:

Press: ⟵ (4 times)
Type: T_NUM

Your display screen should be similar to Figure 1-10.

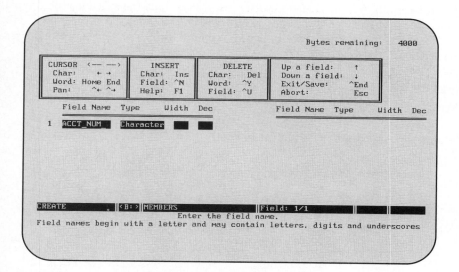

FIGURE 1-10

The new characters typed over the existing letters.

Now that the field name is correct, to indicate you are finished defining the field name,

Press: ⟵

The cursor skips to the Type column and waits for input. The field type, "Character", is already displayed in this space because it is the default setting. There are five **field type** choices:

Character (C) contains any alphanumeric characters (letters, punctuation, numbers that are not used in calculations).

Numeric (N) contains only digits, a decimal point, and a sign. All numbers that will be used in calculations or will be sorted.

Logical (L) contains either a Yes (Y) or No (N) or True (T) or False (F) response.

Date (D) contains a numeric date entry.

Memo (M) contains free-form text.

Although the account number is a numeric entry, no calculations will be made using it. Therefore, Fred decides to define it as a Character field type.

The field type can be selected in two ways. One way is to type the first letter of the field type.

Type: C

(Since "Character" was already displayed, we could also have simply pressed ⏎ to accept the default setting.)

The cursor moves to the next column, Width. **Field width** is the number of spaces needed to hold the largest possible entry into that field.

A Character field can be 1 space to 254 spaces wide as noted in the message line. Logical, Date, and Memo field types are automatically assigned field widths by dBASE III PLUS. A numeric field width must also include the space for the decimal point, the number of decimal places, and the sign.

Fred has determined that the largest account number will occupy four spaces. To specify 4 as the field width,

Type: 4
Press: ⏎

Your display screen should be similar to Figure 1-11.

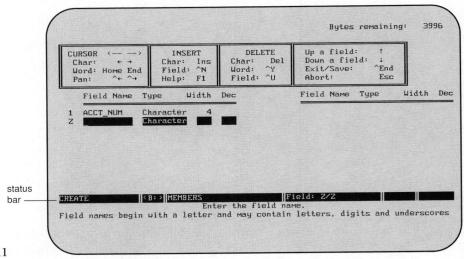

FIGURE 1-11

The cursor skips the Dec (decimal) column because the field type was not defined as numeric. The program waits for you to enter the field name of the second field. Notice that the status bar shows that you are working on the second field of a total of two fields ("Field: 2/2").

The second field is the Membership Date (MEMB_DATE). To enter the second field name,

Type: **MEMB_DATE**
Press: ⏎

The program is waiting for definition of the field type. This field will display the date the member joined the club in the form of month/day/year. The field type choice which will display the date in this format is Date.

For the last field type specification, we typed the first letter (C for Character) of the field type. An alternative way is to use the space bar to change the default choice. Watch the field type change as you

Press: space bar (5 times)

To set the field type to Date, press the space bar until Date appears, and then,

Press: ⏎

Your display screen should be similar to Figure 1-12.

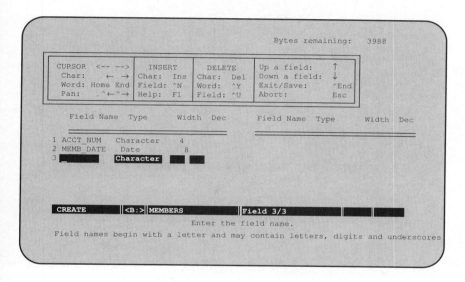

FIGURE 1-12

Notice that the field width for the Date type was automatically entered as eight (mm/dd/yy) spaces by dBASE III PLUS. The program is now waiting for the definition of the third field.

The third field will hold the member's last name. The field name is LAST_NAME. The field type is Character, and the field width is 18 spaces. Complete the third field specifications as follows:

Type: LAST_NAME
Press: ⏎
Press: ⏎
Type: 18
Press: ⏎

The fourth field is FIRST_NAME, Character, 15.

Type: FIRST_NAME

dBASE III PLUS beeped and moved the cursor to the Type column. This occurred because the field name was the maximum length of 10 characters. Whenever a field entry equals the maximum allowable space, the cursor will automatically move to the next column.

Continue defining the field characteristics for FIRST_NAME as follows:

Press: ⏎
Type: 15
Press: ⏎

Your display screen should be similar to Figure 1-13.

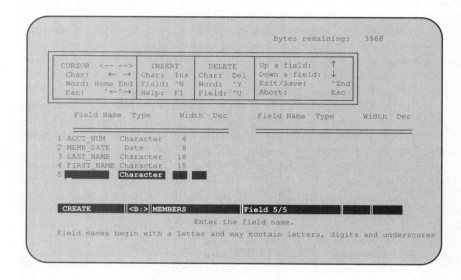

FIGURE 1-13

Enter the information for the next four fields. They are defined as follows:

Field Name	Type	Width	Dec
STREET	C	22	
CITY	C	15	
STATE	C	2	
ZIPCODE	C	5	

You will notice that the field type for ZIPCODE is defined as Character. Again, although this field contains numbers, it will not be used in calculations. Also, by specifying the type as Character, any leading 0s (for example, the zipcode 07739) will be preserved. Leading 0s in a Numeric type field are dropped (which would incorrectly make this zipcode 7739).

When you have completed the four fields, your display screen should be similar to Figure 1-14.

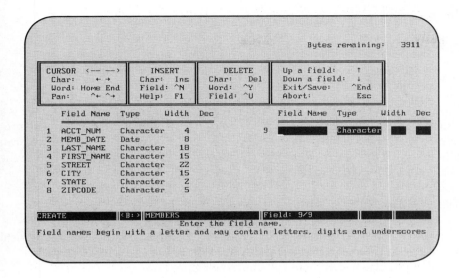

FIGURE 1-14

The cursor has moved over to the right-hand column under Field Name. The program is waiting for you to define the ninth field.

To enter the field information for the ninth field, Age,

Type: AGE

Press: ⏎

Type: N

Numeric is displayed in the Type column. This field is defined as a Numeric type because the data may be used to perform calculations. The cursor skipped to the field width column. The maximum number of spaces needed in this field is two.

Type: 2

Press: ⏎

Since the field type is defined as Numeric, the program is waiting for the Dec column to be defined. The member's age is a whole number. Therefore, we want zero decimal places displayed.

Type: 0

Press: ⏎

Simply pressing ⏎ would also have entered the default decimal place setting of zero.

The last field, 10, will indicate whether the member participates in the automatic fee payment program.

To enter the field name,

Type: AUTO_FEE

Fred decides this is not a good field name for this field. He wants to change it to AUTO_PAYMT. To erase the last three letters, "FEE,"

Press: (Bksp) (3 times)

(Bksp) erases the characters to the left of the cursor.

Type: **PAYMT**

The AUTO_PAYMT field type is Logical. The data that will be entered in this field is a response to the question "Is the member using the automatic fee payment program?" The answer will be either a true/yes or a false/no entry. Remember, you can either type the first letter of the type (L) or you can use the space bar to display the field types and press ⏎ to select it.

Select: Logical

dBASE III PLUS automatically defines the field width as 1 space for a Logical field type. The data entered in this field is displayed as a single character, T/Y or F/N.

Your display screen should be similar to Figure 1-15.

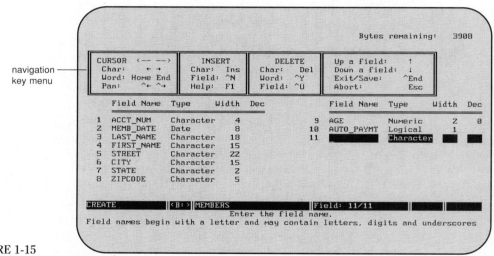

navigation key menu

FIGURE 1-15

After looking over the database file structure, Fred decides to increase the STREET field width from 22 to 25 spaces. Again, referring to the navigation key menu, ⊕ and ⊕ are used to move up or down between fields. To move right one word (END) is used, and to move left one word (HOME) is used.

Press ⊕ to move the highlight bar to field 5, STREET.

To move the cursor to the field width column,

Press   (END) (2 times)

You can also use ⏎ to move the highlight bar to the next field to the right.

Finally, to change the STREET field width to 25 spaces,

Type: 25

Press:

Your display screen should be similar to Figure 1-16.

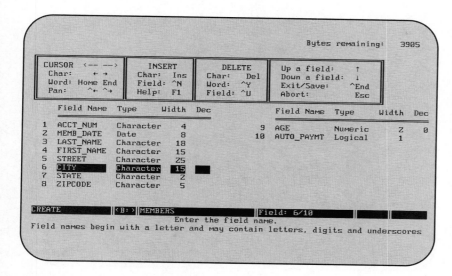

FIGURE 1-16

Carefully check your screen to ensure that all field names, types, and widths match exactly those in Figure 1-16. If your screen does not match, correct it now.

Once you are satisfied that your field entries are correct, the database file structure needs to be saved to the diskette. The navigation key menu shows you that the key sequence to Exit and Save is ^End (the ^ stands for the (CTRL) key). The (CTRL) key is held down while pressing the (END) key.

Press (CTRL)-(END)

The navigation line instructs you to press ⏎ to confirm that you want to leave the Create screen. If you wanted to continue in the Create screen, you would press any other key. To leave the Create screen,

Press: ⏎

The drive light goes on briefly, and the structure for your file is saved on the diskette using the filename MEMBERS.

Inputting Records

The next prompt in the action line from dBASE III PLUS is "Input data records now? (Y/N)". You can enter records immediately after specifying the database structure by responding "Yes" (Y) to the prompt. Or you can return to The Assistant by responding "No" (N).

Fred has a meeting to go to in just a few minutes, but he would like to enter a few records before leaving. To enter records, in response to the prompt,

Type: Y

Your display screen should look similar to Figure 1-17.

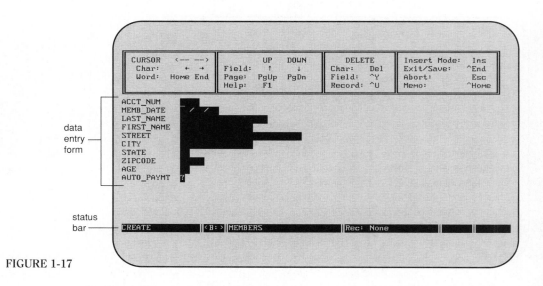

FIGURE 1-17

The main area of the screen displays a blank **data entry** form. It consists of the 10 field names you just defined and a shaded area following each field name. The size of the shaded area corresponds to the width of the field.

The MEMB_DATE field displays slashes (/) to separate the month, day, and year. The AUTO_PAYMT field contains a "?". This means that no response has been entered into this field yet and that the field has been defined as Logical.

The status bar shows "Rec: None". This area of the status bar will display the total number of records in a file and the number of the record that dBASE III PLUS is positioned on.

The data for the first record is:

Field Name	Field Data
ACCT_NUM	1001
MEM_DATE	May 21, 1983
LAST_NAME	Becker
FIRST_NAME	Edward
STREET	1036 West 5th Place
CITY	Mesa
STATE	AZ
ZIPCODE	85205
AGE	45
AUTO_PAYMT	Y

The cursor is positioned to accept entry of the data for the first field, ACCT_NUM.

Type: 1001

dBASE III PLUS beeped and automatically moved the cursor to the next field. The program will do this when the contents of the field fill all the spaces.
Complete the MEMB_DATE field as follows:

Type: 054183

Your display screen should be similar to Figure 1-18.

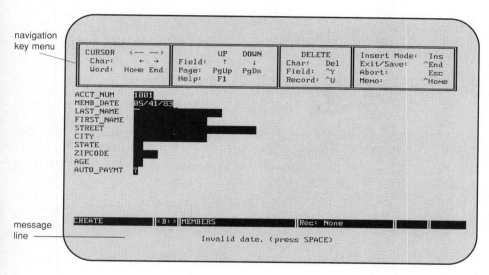

FIGURE 1-18

dBASE III PLUS beeped again. However, this time it did not move the cursor to the next field. Notice the message line. It tells you that this is an invalid date. dBASE III PLUS makes some logic checks on the data entered. In this case, the date entered (05/41/83) could not be correct—no month has 41 days.
To correct the date entry, following the directions in the message line,

Press: space bar

The cursor moves to the beginning of the date field. To correct the date,

Press: ⟶ (2 times)
Type: 2
Press: ⟵

The data you enter in a record must be typed just as you want it to appear. Unlike field names, which are displayed in all uppercase letters (even if you typed the field name in all lowercase characters), the field data you enter for each record is displayed just as you type it. It is very important to be consistent when entering field data. It should be entered the same way for every record. For example, if you decide to use all uppercase characters to enter the LAST_NAME field data, then every record should have the last name entered in all uppercase characters. Also, be careful not to enter a blank space before or after a field entry. This can cause problems when using the database to locate records.

Enter the LAST_NAME data exactly as shown below:

Type: **Becker**

Press: ⏎

Enter the FIRST_NAME data as follows:

Type: **Edward**

Press: ⏎

The STREET field is next.

Type: **1026 W 50th Place**

Press: ⏎

Fred notices that he entered the address incorrectly. It should be **1036 West 5th Place.**

To correct this entry, we will use several of the cursor-movement and editing keys shown in the navigation key menu.

To move back up to the STREET field,

Press: ⬆

First the house number needs to be corrected. To move the cursor under the "2" and change it to a "3",

Press   → (2 times)

Type: 3

The "3" replaced the "2" in the house number.

The cursor can move word by word to the right or left by using (HOME) and (END). To position the cursor on the space after the "W",

Press: (END)

Press: →

Next, we want to add the letters "est" to make the word "West". To insert characters into existing text, turn on the Insert mode as follows.

Press: (INS)

The status bar displays the message "Ins" to tell you that this mode is in operation. While Ins is on, characters you type are inserted into existing text. They do not type over the existing text.

Type: est

The characters were inserted into the existing text by moving the existing text to the right to make space.

To turn off the Insert mode,

Press: (INS)

To correct the rest of the street address,

Press: (→) (2 times)
Press: (DEL)

The "0" and the space it occupied are deleted. The (DEL) key deletes the character at the cursor location.

To move to the next field,

Press: (↵)

Enter the data into the CITY field as follows:

Type: Scottsdale
Press: (↵)

Another error. Fred was looking at the wrong record when typing in the city. It should be Mesa. To completely delete the field entry, the (CTRL)-Y key combination is used (hold down (CTRL) while pressing Y).

Press: (↑)
Press: (CTRL)-Y

This editing command deletes all characters from the cursor location to the right. Since the cursor was positioned at the beginning of the entry, the entire entry was deleted. It can be used to delete part of an entry by moving the cursor to the place in the entry where you want everything to the right deleted.

Type: Mesa
Press: (↵)

Enter the data for the remaining fields, typing the information exactly as it appears below. If you make typing errors, practice using the editing keys demonstrated above.

Field Name	Field Data
STATE	AZ
ZIPCODE	85205
AGE	45
AUTO_PAYMT	Y

The data for the first record is now complete. A second blank data entry form is displayed on the screen. The status bar displays the message "EOF/1". This means that the program is currently viewing a blank record at the **E**nd **O**f the **F**ile (EOF) and that there is one record in the file (/1). dBASE III PLUS assigns each record in the file a **record number.** The record number is determined by the order the record is entered into the file. Since this is the first record entered into the file, it is assigned record number 1. The program also keeps track of its location in the file by using a **record pointer.** Only one record can be used or displayed at a time. The record pointer is positioned on the record in use. In this case, the record pointer is positioned on a blank record located at the end of the file.

To review, the cursor-movement and editing keys that we have used are shown below.

Key	Result
(←⎯)	Moves cursor to next field
(⎯→)	Moves cursor one space forward
(←⎯)	Moves cursor one space backward
(↑)	Moves cursor up one field
(HOME)	Moves cursor one word forward
(END)	Moves cursor one word backward
(DEL)	Deletes character at cursor
(INS)	Turns Insert mode on or off
(Bksp)	Deletes character left of cursor
(CTRL)-Y	Deletes all characters from the cursor to the right

Fred has just enough time to enter a second record before going to his meeting. Enter the following data into the second record.

Field Name	Field Data
ACCT_NUM	0683
MEMB_DATE	February 24, 1986
LAST_NAME	Christianson
FIRST_NAME	Phillip
STREET	1766 N. Extension #17-24
CITY	Scottsdale
STATE	AZ
ZIPCODE	85205
AGE	26
AUTO_PAYMT	Y

When you have completed entering the data for the second record, a blank data entry form is displayed on the screen again. The program is ready for input of data for the third record. The status bar displays "EOF/2". This means the record pointer is located at the end of the file on a blank data entry form and there are two records in the file. The second record has been assigned the record number 2.

To view the contents of record number 1,

Press: (PGUP) (2 times)

Your display screen should be similar to Figure 1-19.

navigation
key menu

status
bar

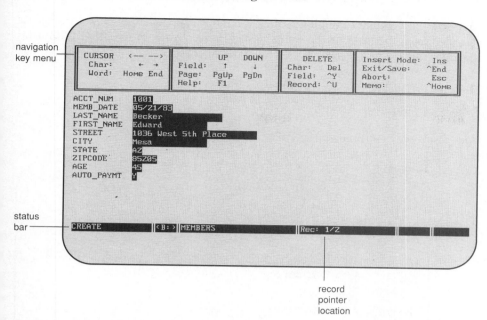

FIGURE 1-19

record
pointer
location

The membership information for Edward Becker, record number 1, is displayed on the screen. Look at the status bar. It shows that the record pointer is positioned on the first of two records ("Rec: 1/2"). Pressing (PGUP) or (PGDN) will move the record pointer up or down through the records in the file and display the record the pointer is positioned on.

Check your record entries carefully. Edit if necessary.

Fred has to go to his meeting and wants to end the process of adding records to the file. The navigation key menu shows that the command to exit and save is (CTRL)-(END). This is the same key sequence you used to save the file structure to the diskette. Before you use this command, make sure the record pointer is not on a blank data entry form. If it is on a blank data entry form when the records are saved to the diskette using (CTRL)-(END), a blank data entry form will be saved as a record.

Move to any completed record in the database.

To end the process of adding records to the file, to save the last record entered onto the diskette, and to return to The Assistant,

Press: (CTRL)-(END)

Note: You may have noticed that when you moved the record pointer to another record, the drive light went on briefly. By moving to another record, the program automatically saves the last record entered to the diskette.

Another way to end the process of adding records to the file is to simply press (⏎) when the record pointer is on the EOF (blank entry form). The blank entry form will not be saved as a record in the file.

If you did not want to save changes made to the current record, press (ESC) to exit.

Appending Records to the Database

Fred left the computer running while he attended his meeting. Now that he has returned from the meeting, he wants to add more records to the MEMBERS database file. To add more records to the end of the database file,

Move to: Update
Select: Append

Your display screen should look similar to Figure 1-20.

FIGURE 1-20

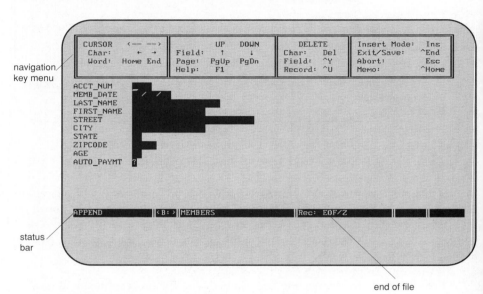

navigation
key menu

status
bar

end of file

This is the Append screen. It is the same screen we used to enter records immediately after creating and saving the file structure. A blank data entry form is displayed on the screen. The status bar shows that the record pointer is on the end of the file and that there are two records in the file.

The navigation key menu at the top of the screen is the same as the one in the Create screen. It tells you how to move around the screen and edit entries.

Enter the following two records into the database.

Field	Record #3	Record #4
ACCT_NUM	0728	0839
MEMB_DATE	October 10, 1982	March 3, 1984
LAST_NAME	Salvana	Johnson
FIRST_NAME	Lori	William
STREET	2061 Winchester Rd.	1622 E. Donner Dr.
CITY	Apache Junction	Tempe
STATE	AZ	AZ
ZIPCODE	85220	85284
AGE	31	23
AUTO_PAYMT	N	N

After you have inserted records 3 and 4, move to each of the records and check them for accuracy. Edit any entries that are incorrect.

Remember, do not have the record pointer on the end of the file (blank record) when you save and exit the Append screen. If you do, a blank record will be saved to your file.

Press: (CTRL)-(END)

You are returned to The Assistant.

Printing the Database

Fred would like to view and print a hard copy of the four records in his file. The Retrieve Menu options let you view and print a database file. The List option will scroll the records in the file on the display screen and will also let you print the records. Using the menu highlight bar and the selection bar,

Select: Retrieve
Select: List

Your display screen should be similar to Figure 1-21.

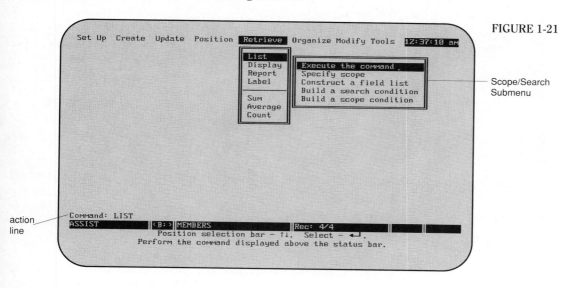

FIGURE 1-21

Scope/Search Submenu

action line

A new submenu is displayed. It lists options for limiting the **scope** (range or number of records) and specifying conditions for the List command to follow. We will be using and explaining many of the options in the Scope/Search submenu in the next lab.

Notice the dot command in the action line. It is simply "LIST". Watch the action line to see the dot command as you continue the command sequence using The Assistant.

To list all the records and all the fields in each record in the database file (the default setting),

Select: Execute the command

A dialogue box appears containing the prompt "Direct the output to the printer? [Y/N]".

If you have printer capability, make sure the printer is on. To specify that you want the output to be printed,

Type: Y

If you do not have printer capability (or if you simply do not want a printed copy of the records),

Type: N

Regardless of your response to this prompt, you will still see the output on the display screen. Your display screen should be similar to Figure 1-22.

FIGURE 1-22

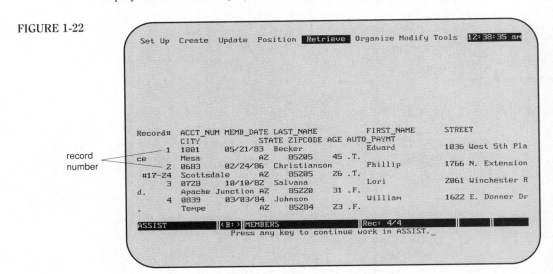

The four records are listed on the display screen and printed if specified. The field names and the contents of each record wrap around to a second line because the record length is too long to fit on one line. This makes reading a listing of records difficult. The next lab will demonstrate other ways of specifying and displaying the contents of a file.

The record number assigned to each record as it was entered into the file is displayed in the first column. Notice that the data entered in the AUTO_PAYMT field is either a T or an F. Even though we entered Y and N, dBASE III PLUS will display the data in a logical field as a T or an F.

To clear the display screen and return to The Assistant,

Press: any key

Notice in the status bar that the record pointer position is now "Rec: EOF/4". After the contents of a file have been listed, the record pointer is placed at the end of the file.

Quitting dBASE III PLUS

We will continue to follow Fred as he builds and uses his database file of membership records in the next lab. The command to end a dBASE III PLUS session is an option in the Set Up Menu.

Select: Set Up

To quit dBASE III PLUS,

Select: Quit dBASE III PLUS

Quit closes all open database files and returns you to the DOS prompt. Always use Quit when ending a dBASE III PLUS session. If you end the session by turning off or rebooting your computer without selecting Quit, you may damage the open database file. This could cause loss of data.

Key Terms

The Assistant	field name
dot prompt	record
menu bar	submenu
menu	action line
pull-down menu	dialogue box
menu highlight bar	prompt
options	navigation key menu
selection bar	field type
message line	field width
navigation line	record number
status bar	record pointer
field	scope

Matching

1. Rec: 4/4

2. Dot prompt

3. Opt: 1/6

4. Create

5. (F1)

6. (CTRL)-(END)

7. Append

8. (CTRL)-Y

9. EOF/12

10. scope

_____ a. defines the range or number of records to be used

_____ b. record pointer is on the end of the file containing 12 records

_____ c. Assistant command to add records

_____ d. accesses Help

_____ e. deletes characters from cursor to right

_____ f. shows location of selection bar

_____ g. allows direct entry of command

_____ h. exits and saves work to diskette

_____ i. record pointer is on record 4 of a total of four records in a file

_____ j. Assistant command to enter the file structure

Practice Exercises

1. Identify the parts of the dBASE III PLUS screen by entering the appropriate letters in the blanks below.

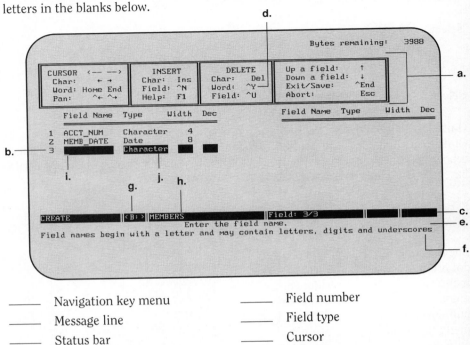

_____ Navigation key menu	_____ Field number
_____ Message line	_____ Field type
_____ Status bar	_____ Cursor
_____ Navigation line	_____ Disk drive
_____ Database filename	_____ Deletes word

2. Susannah owns a small business that sells custom-made ceramic tiles. She currently keeps her client orders and payment records in a small accounting ledger. Her business has grown considerably since she first started it a year ago, and she decided to invest in a computer. She wants to keep track of her client orders and payments using dBASE III PLUS. She has defined the fields as follows:

Field Name	Type	Width	Dec
LAST_NAME	C	12	
FIRST_NAME	C	10	
ADDRESS	C	20	
CITY	C	12	
STATE	C	2	
ZIP	C	5	
PHONE	C	8	
DATE	D		
UNIT_COST	N	5	2
QUANTITY	N	4	
PAID	L		

- Load dBASE III PLUS.
- Create a database file using the field information defined above. Name the file TILES.
- Enter the two records shown below.

Record 1	Record 2
Doyle	Miller
Marilyn	Phillip
298 Winding Way	46 South View
Fairview	Albion
PA	PA
07392	09523
298-1374	468-9238
02-12-89	03-21-89
3.75	4.85
125	75
N	N

- Enter your name and appropriate information as the third record using Append.
- Print a copy of the three records.
- Exit dBASE III PLUS.

3.   Joe is a full-time college student. He is in his third full semester of school. He wants to create a database file of all the courses he has taken to date. His fields are:

COURSE_NUM   Character 6
TITLE   Character 20
SEMESTER   Character 4
GRADE   Numeric 1

The semester is entered as f=fall, sp=spring, followed by the year. The year is entered as "88" for 1988.

The grade is on a 4.00 grading scale with 4=A, 3=B, 2=C, 1=D, 0=F.

- Load dBASE III PLUS.
- Create a database file named SCHOOL using the fields as defined above.
- Enter the data below in numbered order (shown in parenthesis). You will have 10 records. Check your data carefully before saving and exiting.

(1)   ENG101   (6)   ENG102
       Freshman English   Freshman English
       F 88   Sp 89
       C   B

(2)   MAT 210   (7)   MAT210
       Calculus   Calculus
       F 88   Sp 89
       D   C

(3) BUS 100
     Intro to Business
     F 88
     B

(4) PSY 100
     Intro to Psychology
     F 88
     B

(5) PED101
     Physical Education
     F88
     A

(8) ACC 120
     Accounting 1
     Sp 89
     B

(9) ART 100
     World Art
     Sp 89
     B

(10) PED102
     Physical Education
     Sp89
     A

For the eleventh record, enter your name in the field TITLE and leave the other fields blank.

- ■ Print a copy of the database records.
- ■ Exit dBASE III PLUS.

4. Lynne is the recording secretary for the Future Entrepreneurs Club. To help keep track of the club members, she decides to create a database to include each member's full name, complete address, home telephone number, and major.

- ■ Load dBASE III PLUS.
- ■ Create a database file named ENTRE.
- ■ Define a record structure appropriate for Lynne's needs using 9 fields.
- ■ Enter your name and appropriate related information in the first record.
- ■ Enter 19 additional records using either real or fictitious data.
- ■ Print a copy of the database records.
- ■ Exit dBASE III PLUS.

2

Modifying, Editing, and Viewing a Database

CASE STUDY

Fred continued to work on appending records to the database file. After a short period of time, he had 20 records in the file. Before adding more records, he wants to show the club manager a printout of the records in the file. The manager suggests that another field, SEX, may be useful in analysis of the membership records. We will follow Fred as he modifies the database structure to include this new field of data.

Throughout the day Fred receives several notes asking him for information or telling him about changes that need to be made to various member records. Updating records and providing information to other staff members from the membership data is a routine part of his job. We will follow Fred as he locates, edits, adds, and deletes records in the database file.

Finally, he has one last job for the day. The accounting department would like a list of members participating in the automatic fee payment program. Fred will use dBASE III PLUS to produce this list.

Opening a Database File

Load dBASE III PLUS. Follow the directions in Lab 1 if you are uncertain of the procedure.

Note: Many of the commands in dBASE III PLUS are made of a sequence of selections from The Assistant. The command sequences you are to issue will appear on a

OBJECTIVES

In this lab you will learn how to:

1. Open a database file.

2. Modify the database structure.

3. Browse the database records.

4. Edit the database records.

5. Mark records for deletion.

6. Position the record pointer.

7. Display database records.

8. Recall records marked for deletion.

9. List all and selected records.

10. Delete records from the file.

11. Print selected records.

single line following the word "Select:". Each command selection will be separated
by a slash (/). If the menu item can be selected by typing the first letter of the
command, the first letter will appear in boldface. Anything you are to type will also
appear in boldface text.

To use or **open** an existing database file,

Select: **S**et Up / Database file / B:

Your display screen should be similar to Figure 2-1.

FIGURE 2-1

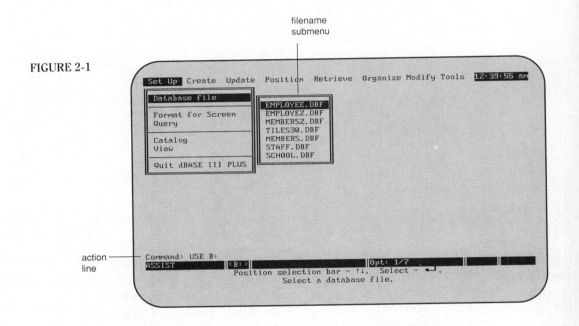

The names of all the database files on the data diskette are displayed in the
submenu. Notice the file extension .DBF following the file names. This extension is
automatically added to a database file name by dBASE III PLUS. The extension
identifies the file as a database file. The file you created in Lab 1, MEMBERS.DBF, as
well as several others we will be using in the next two labs, are listed.

Note: The file names listed on your screen may be different from those in Figure 2-1
depending upon the homework problems you have completed.

The file with 20 member records in it is MEMBERS2.DBF. It is the same as the
file MEMBERS.DBF you created in Lab 1, except that it now contains 20 records.

Select: MEMBERS2.DBF

Your display screen should be similar to Figure 2-2.

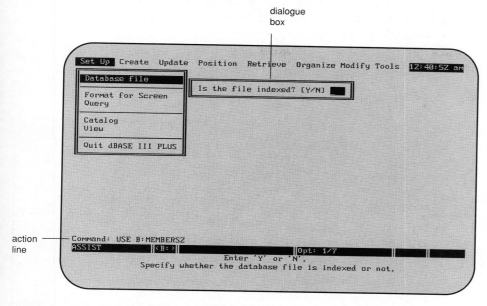

FIGURE 2-2

Notice the command in the action line, "USE B:MEMBERS2". If you used the dot prompt to issue the command to open a database file, the command would be entered exactly as displayed in the action line.

The dialogue box prompt "Is this file Indexed?" is waiting for a response of either Yes (Y) or No (N). We will be explaining file indexing in the next lab. For now the response is No.

You can either type the letter **N** or press ⏎. Pressing ⏎ will respond to the prompt as if **N** had been typed. Whenever a Yes or No response is needed in a dBASE III PLUS command, the default is No.

Type: N (or press ⏎)

After a few seconds the file is read from the diskette and becomes the open database file. The Assistant Menu is available for selections.

The status bar shows that the file MEMBERS2 is open and that the record pointer is on record 1 of 20 (Rec: 1/20). Whenever a file is opened, the record pointer is automatically placed on the first record in the file.

Modifying the Database Structure

First Fred wants to add the new field, SEX, to the database file structure. To change, or **modify,** the structure of a database file, use the Modify Menu.

Move to: Modify

The six Modify Menu options are displayed. The Modify Menu allows you to edit the structure of a dBASE III PLUS file. The Modify Menu options are the same six options listed under the Create Menu. Any files you create can be modified.

To modify a database file,

Select: Database file

Your display screen should be similar to Figure 2-3.

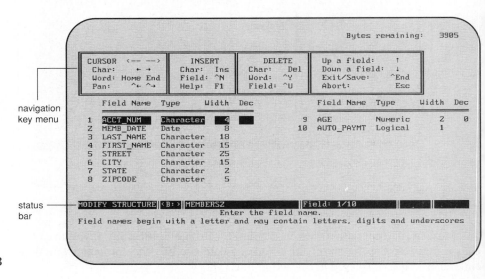

FIGURE 2-3

This screen should be familiar to you. It is the same screen that was displayed when you created the database file structure. The only difference is that it contains the data you entered to define the field structure. However, the status bar shows that the screen form in use is Modify Structure rather than Create.

After looking at the order of the fields, Fred decides that he wants to add the new field, SEX, between the eighth field, ZIPCODE, and the ninth field, AGE. The new field will be field number 9.

To add a new field to the file structure, a blank field line must be inserted into the structure. The navigation key menu displays the command to insert a field. It is ^N ((CTRL)-N).

First move to the location in the structure where you want the field inserted. To quickly move the highlight bar to field 9, AGE,

Press: (CTRL)-(→)

To insert a blank field line,

Press: (CTRL)-N

Your display screen should be similar to Figure 2-4.

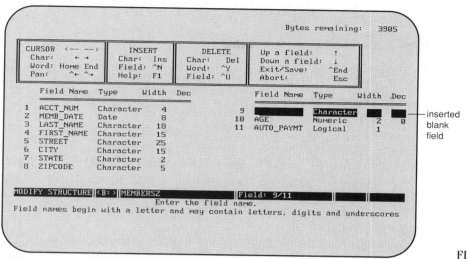

FIGURE 2-4

The AGE field has moved down one line to become field number 10. A blank field line is ready to be defined as field number 9.

Enter the following new field information:

Field name: **SEX**
Type: **C**haracter
Width: **1**

Your display screen should be similar to Figure 2-5.

FIGURE 2-5

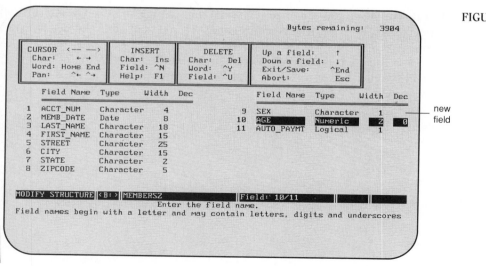

The new field has been added to the database file structure. To exit the Modify Structure screen, to save the structure changes to the diskette, and to return to The Assistant,

Press: (CTRL)-(END)

In response to the prompt, to confirm or save the changes made to the file,

Press: (⏎)

The disk drive light goes on briefly as the changes to the file structure are saved on the diskette. Saving the changes to the file structure does two things. dBASE III PLUS creates a new file with the new file structure using the original file name. Then it changes the original file to a backup file using the file extension .BAK. The records that were in the original file are copied into the new file. As the records are copied to the new structure, the progress of the number added is displayed on the bottom of the screen,

You can modify the structure of your database at any time if you are careful. Sometimes, however, certain changes can cause loss of all data or of data in that field. For example, if you change the field name, do not change its width or type at the same time. If you do, data will be lost. Also, do not delete or insert new fields and change field names at the same time. Data will be lost.

Browsing the Database Records

Next, Fred needs to add the data for the new field, SEX, to the records in the database.

Select: Update

The Update Menu has commands that let you display and change information in your database file. Eight submenu options let you add, edit, and delete data and records.

The Browse command allows full-screen viewing and editing of multiple records in the file. It is especially useful for changing the data in the same field for many records.

Select: Browse

Your display screen should be similar to Figure 2-6.

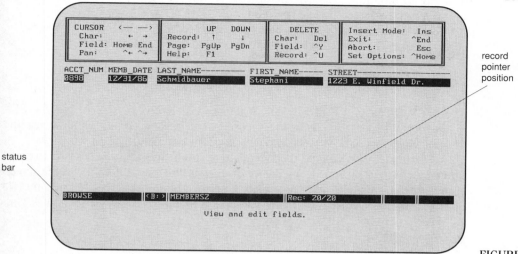

FIGURE 2-6

The status bar shows that we are using the Browse command and that the record pointer is located on record 20, the last record in the file. The data for record 20, Stephani Schmidbauer, is displayed. To display a full screen of records,

Press: (PGUP)

Eleven records are displayed on the screen. Browse displays as many records as possible on a screen. Each record occupies one line. The highlight bar indicates the record pointer location, and the blinking cursor shows your location in that record. The record number is not displayed.

The last field visible on the screen is STREET. To see the fields to the right of STREET, watch your screen closely as you

Press: (CTRL)-(⟶) (4 times)

Your display screen should be similar to Figure 2-7.

FIGURE 2-7

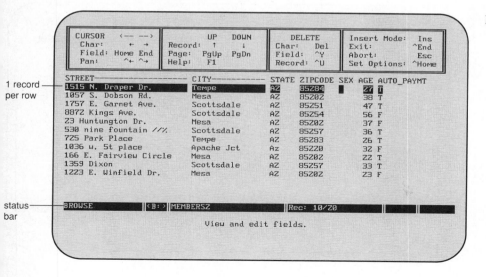

The remaining fields are displayed on the screen. However, the fields to the left of STREET are no longer visible. The process of moving right and left to bring a field into view on the screen is called **panning.**

The column of data for the SEX field needs to be entered for each record. The contents for each record can be determined by looking at the member's name.

Press: (CTRL)⎯ (2 times)

The LAST_NAME and FIRST_NAME fields are visible on the screen, but the SEX field is not. Whenever the fields in a record extend beyond a single window, reading and knowing what data belongs with which record is difficult.

Fortunately, Browse has its own menu of commands to make it easier to move around and see particular fields. Before displaying this menu, let's make the screen easier to read and allow more records to be displayed on the screen at one time. To do this, turn off the display of the navigation key menu.

Press: (F1)

Once a menu item has been selected, the (F1) key no longer displays a Help screen. It now turns on or off the navigation key menu. To completely fill the screen with records,

Press: (PGUP)

Seventeen records are displayed on the screen. The highlight bar is positioned on record 1, Becker. The navigation key menu can be turned back on by pressing (F1) at any time.

To access the Browse Menu,

Press: (F10)

Your display screen should be similar to Figure 2-8.

FIGURE 2-8

Browse
Menu

message
line

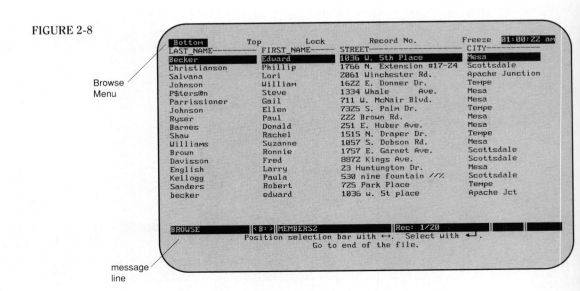

The Browse menu bar appears at the top of the screen. You can select a menu item by moving the highlight bar to the option and pressing ⏎. Or you can type the first letter of the menu item.

Read the message line as you slowly

Press: ⏎ (5 times)

The six menu items have the following effect:

Bottom   moves cursor to the last record in the file

Top   moves cursor to the first record in the file

Lock   stops the scrolling of specified fields

Record No.   moves cursor to a specified record number

Freeze   specifies a single field to edit

Fred needs to enter the data for the SEX field to every record. To do this, he needs to be able to see the FIRST_NAME and LAST_NAME fields while entering the data in the SEX field for each member.

To stop the scrolling of, or **lock,** these two fields on the screen when he moves to the SEX field to enter the data,

Select: Lock

A dialogue box appears prompting you to enter the number of columns to lock. Counting from the left side of the screen, LAST_NAME and FIRST_NAME occupy the first two columns. To lock these fields,

Type: 2

Press: ⏎

The Browse menu bar disappears from the screen. Watch your screen carefully as you pan to the right.

Press: CTRL-→ (4 times)

Your display screen should be similar to Figure 2-9.

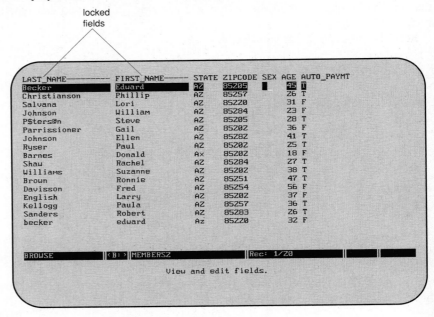

FIGURE 2-9

The two locked fields have remained stationary on the screen while the fields to the right have scrolled into view. The SEX field column can now be viewed at the same time as the name fields.

Fred can now easily look at the FIRST_NAME field data and complete the data for the SEX field.

The Browse Menu option Freeze allows you to restrict, or **freeze,** the movement of the cursor to a single field. To call up the Browse menu bar again and select this option,

Press: (F10)
Select: Freeze

In response to the prompt in the dialogue box to "Enter the field name to freeze:", in either upper- or lowercase letters,

Type: SEX
Press: (⏎)

Your display screen should be similar to Figure 2-10.

frozen field

```
LAST_NAME————— FIRST_NAME————— STATE ZIPCODE SEX AGE AUTO_PAYMT
Becker          Edward          AZ    85205   ▮   45 T
Christianson    Phillip         AZ    85257       26 T
Salvana         Lori            AZ    85220       31 F
Johnson         William         AZ    85284       23 F
P$ters@n        Steve           AZ    85205       28 T
Parrissioner    Gail            AZ    85202       36 F
Johnson         Ellen           AZ    85282       41 T
Ryser           Paul            AZ    85202       25 T
Barnes          Donald          Ax    85202       18 F
Shaw            Rachel          AZ    85284       27 T
Williams        Suzanne         AZ    85202       38 T
Brown           Ronnie          AZ    85251       47 T
Davisson        Fred            AZ    85254       56 F
English         Larry           AZ    85202       37 F
Kellogg         Paula           AZ    85257       36 T
Sanders         Robert          AZ    85283       26 T
becker          edward          Az    85220       32 F


BROWSE        |<B:>|MEMBERS2           |Rec: 1/20       |      |
                       View and edit fields.
```

FIGURE 2-10

The cursor jumps to the specified field, SEX. The member in the first record is a male. To enter this data as a capital letter,

Press: (CAPS LOCK)

Type: M

dBASE III PLUS beeped, the disk drive light went on, and the cursor skipped to the next record.

Continue entering the data for this field, looking at the FIRST_NAME field to determine whether the member is male or female. When you complete the data for the last record displayed on the screen, another record will scroll into view to be edited. This continues until the last record in the database file is displayed.

After entering the sex for the last record, your display screen should be similar to Figure 2-11.

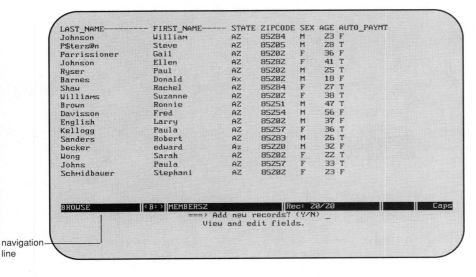

```
LAST_NAME————— FIRST_NAME————— STATE ZIPCODE SEX AGE AUTO_PAYMT
Johnson         William         AZ    85284   M   23 F
P$ters@n        Steve           AZ    85205   M   28 T
Parrissioner    Gail            AZ    85202   F   36 F
Johnson         Ellen           AZ    85282   F   41 T
Ryser           Paul            AZ    85202   M   25 T
Barnes          Donald          Ax    85202   M   18 F
Shaw            Rachel          AZ    85284   F   27 T
Williams        Suzanne         AZ    85202   F   38 T
Brown           Ronnie          AZ    85251   M   47 T
Davisson        Fred            AZ    85254   M   56 F
English         Larry           AZ    85202   M   37 F
Kellogg         Paula           AZ    85257   F   36 T
Sanders         Robert          AZ    85283   M   26 T
becker          edward          Az    85220   M   32 F
Wong            Sarah           AZ    85202   F   22 T
Johns           Paula           AZ    85257   F   33 T
Schmidbauer     Stephani        AZ    85202   F   23 F


BROWSE        |<B:>|MEMBERS2           |Rec: 20/20      |      |Caps
              ===> Add new records? (Y/N) _
                       View and edit fields.
```

FIGURE 2-11

navigation line

The prompt in the message line asks "Add new records?". While in Browse, new records can be added to the end of the file. Since we do not need to add any new records at this time,

Type: N (or press ⏎)

Did you notice several errors in the records as you were entering the data in the SEX field? For example, the second record displayed on the screen has several errors in the LAST_NAME. Fred also noticed that he entered the data for Edward Becker twice, as record number 1 and as record number 17. Record 17, however, contains several errors. He figures there are probably several other errors in other fields that are not visible on the screen.

Editing a single field column in Browse is easy. However, editing fields that span more than a single screen display becomes awkward. You have to keep panning the screen. An alternative method of editing data is to use Edit.

Let's leave Browse to use Edit to correct the errors in the other records. First move the record pointer to the top of the file and unfreeze and unlock the fields as follows:

Press: F10
Select: Top

The cursor is positioned on the first record in the file. To unfreeze the SEX field,

Press: F10
Select: Freeze
Press: ⏎

The SEX field is unfrozen. You can now move the cursor to any field.
Unlock the columns in a similar manner.

Press: F10
Select: Lock
Press: ⏎

To verify that the fields are unlocked and unfrozen, pan the screen to the left.

Press: CTRL-⏎ (6 times)

The ACCT_NUM column should be visible on the screen again.
Finally, turn on the display of the navigation key menu and turn off CAPS LOCK as follows:

Press: F1
Press: CAPS LOCK

To save the changes made while using Browse and to return to The Assistant,

Press: CTRL-END

Another method of leaving Browse is to press ESC. However, if the cursor is still on the record you last made changes to, the changes to that record will not be saved.

Editing Database Records

Fred wants to correct the errors and delete the duplicate record in the database file. To do this, he will use the **Edit** command. This is another option in the Update Menu.

Select: Edit

Your display screen should be similar to Figure 2-12.

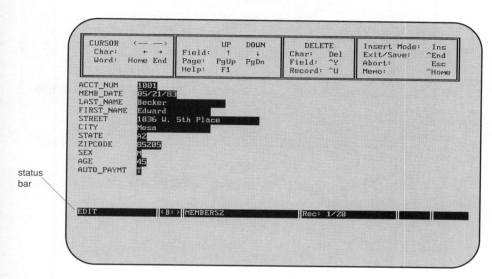

FIGURE 2-12

This screen should look familiar. It is identical to the Append screen. The status bar shows that we are using Edit and that the record pointer is on record number 1. The record displayed by the Edit command will always be the record the record pointer is positioned on at the time the command is issued.

You cannot see more than one record at a time using Edit. But you can see and edit the fields more easily within a record.

To move up and down through the records, the (PGUP) and (PGDN) keys are used.

Move to: Record 5

This is the first record containing several errors. The same editing and cursor-movement keys that are used in Append are used in Edit. They are displayed in the navigation key menu.

Correct the LAST_NAME to **Paterson** and the street to **1334 W. Hale Ave.**

Your display screen should be similar to Figure 2-13.

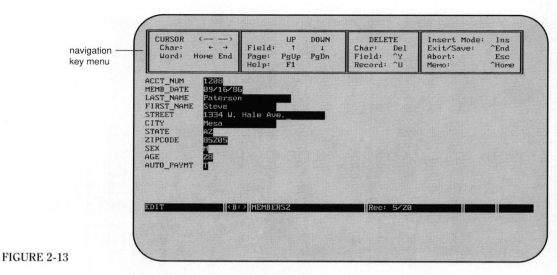

navigation key menu

FIGURE 2-13

Examine the other records as you move to records 9 and 15. Make the corrections to the two records shown below:

Record 9   STATE should be **AZ**
Record 15   STREET should be **530 Nine Fountains Dr.**

Marking Records for Deletion

The duplicate record for Becker is record 17. To remove, or **delete,** an entire record from a file is a two-step process. The first step is to mark the record for deletion. The second step is to actually remove the record from the database file.

The navigation key menu shows you that the command to delete a record is ^U ((CTRL)-U). First, the record pointer must be on the record to be deleted.

Move to: Record number 17

When marking a record for deletion, the cursor can be on any field in that record. To mark the record for deletion,

Press: (CTRL)-U

Your display screen should be similar to Figure 2-14.

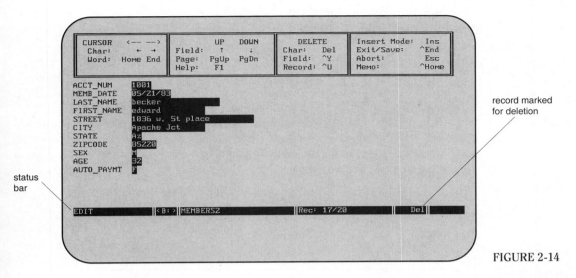

status
bar

record marked
for deletion

FIGURE 2-14

The status bar displays "Del" to show that this record is marked for deletion. A record can be marked for deletion in the same manner while using Browse and Append.

The "Del" marking can be removed from a record by pressing (CTRL)-U a second time. The record pointer must be on the record marked for deletion.

To save the changes made in Edit and return to The Assistant,

Press: (CTRL)-(END)

Fred has completed the first step in removing a record from a database file by marking it for deletion. The record is still part of the file until the second step, which will actually remove the record from the database file, is completed. The second step is accomplished by using the Pack command in the Update Menu. Before Fred uses the Pack command to actually remove this record from the database file, he has several other changes he wants to make to other database records. They are to:

- Change Ellen Johnson's last name to Foran.
- Delete record 5 for Paul Ryser, who canceled his membership.
- Display record 15 to get address information.

You will learn how to make these changes next.

Positioning the Record Pointer

To make the changes to these records, Fred needs to find the specific records in the database file. He could use Edit to move the record pointer to each record. However, that can take a lot of time, especially if the database is large. Instead he will use the dBASE III PLUS Position Menu options to quickly locate a specific record in a database. Once the record is located it can then be updated or displayed.

The first change Fred needs to make is a name change. Ellen Johnson married and her last name changed to Foran. To quickly locate this record,

Select: Position

There are five Position Menu options. Notice that "Seek" and "Continue" are displayed in dimmed letters and that you cannot move the selection bar to those options. In order to use these options, certain other conditions must be met first. "Locate", "Skip", and "Goto Record", however, are available for selection.

The Skip and Goto Record options require that you know the record number. Fred does not know the record number for Ellen Johnson, only her name. However, the Locate option will find a record by searching the database file for specific data in a field that matches the data you specify in the command.

Select: Locate

Your display screen should be similar to Figure 2-15.

FIGURE 2-15

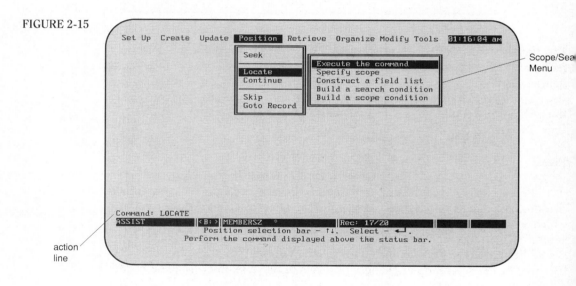

Five submenu options are displayed which allow you to specify the scope (range) of records in the database to search or the criteria (conditions) to search on. This is the same Scope/Search Menu that was displayed when you used the Retrieve List command in Lab 1.

Fred needs to specify the field content, or **search condition,** for the command to use.

Select: Build a search condition

Your display screen should be similar to Figure 2-16.

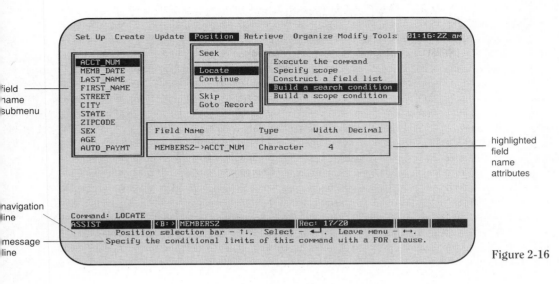

Figure 2-16

The field name submenu on the left lists all the field names in the database. The information box in the center displays the field name and attributes of the highlighted field. The message line asks you to specify the conditional limits of the search condition with a FOR clause.

This may all sound very confusing. However, it is really quite simple. First, the command wants you to select from the field submenu the field name you want to use to locate the record. Then, it wants you to enter the specific data within the selected field that you want the program to find in the database file. Fred wants to locate the record using the field LAST_NAME. To select a field name, following the directions in the navigation line, move the selection bar with ⊙ and ⊙ and press ⟸.

Select: LAST_NAME

Your display screen should be similar to Figure 2-17.

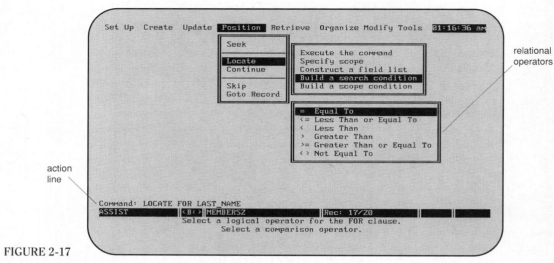

FIGURE 2-17

Another submenu appears displaying six **relational operators.** Relational operators allow the program to compare character or numeric data in a field to the data specified as part of the command. In this case, Fred wants to search FOR LAST_NAME *equal to* the character string "Johnson".

Select: = Equal To

A dialogue box appears prompting you to enter the condition to search on. The search condition must be a character string because the selected field, LAST_NAME, is defined as a Character type. It must be entered exactly as it appears in the record.

Type: **Johnson**
Press: ⏎

A submenu of **logical operators** is displayed. This submenu will allow you to specify a second search condition which can be compared to the first condition. To indicate that this is the only field to search on,

Select: No more conditions

The action line displays the completed command as "LOCATE FOR LAST_NAME='Johnson' ". If you were entering this command at the dot prompt, it would be entered exactly as displayed in the action line.

The Scope/Search Menu is again available for selections. We want dBASE III PLUS to search all records in the database file until it locates a record matching the search condition. Since this is the default scope setting, it is not necessary to select Specify scope from the Scope/Search Menu.

We are now ready to tell the Locate command to begin the search. The selection bar can be moved quickly to the first option or last option in a submenu, using (PGUP) or (PGDN). To move to and select "Execute the command",

Press: (PGUP)
Press: (⏎)

Your display screen should be similar to Figure 2-18.

FIGURE 2-18

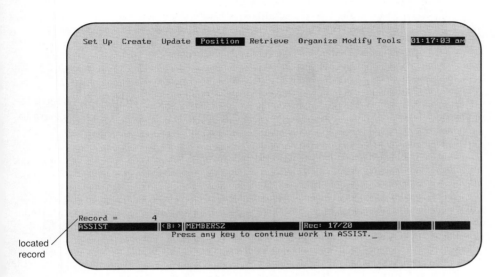

located
record

The first record in the file to exactly match the specified search condition of "LAST_NAME Equal To Johnson" is record number 4. Only the record number is displayed at the bottom of the screen.

Note: If your command did not locate this record, reissue the command and make sure you enter the name Johnson exactly as shown.

To return to The Assistant,

Press: any key

Notice that the record pointer is now positioned on record number 4.

What if there are other records in the database with a last name of Johnson? Notice that the "Continue" option is no longer in dimmed letters, indicating that this option can now be selected. The Continue option can be used to look for the next record that meets the conditions specified in the Locate command.

To continue searching the file to locate the next record that meets the same search conditions,

Select: Continue

The next record meeting the Locate conditions is record number 7. Are there others?

Press: any key
Select: Continue

The screen display shows the message "End of LOCATE scope". This means that all
the records in the file have been searched and there are no more records meeting
the Locate search condition.

Now Fred knows that record numbers 4 and 7 both have last names of Johnson.
How can he find out which is Ellen Johnson? He could go into Edit and look at both
records. But that defeats the purpose of using Locate.

What he will do is make his conditions more specific. He will search for both
last and first names.

To return to The Assistant,

Press: any key
Select: Locate / Build a search condition / LAST_NAME /
= Equal To / **Johnson** ⏎

Reminder: Command sequences that combine several menu selections will appear as
written above. The slash (/) separates the menu selections. Letters in boldface are to
be typed.

Your display screen should be similar to Figure 2-19.

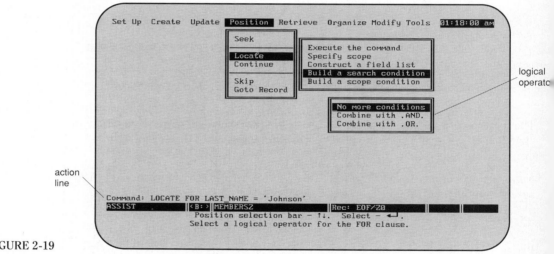

FIGURE 2-19

The submenu of logical operators is displayed. To specify a second search condition,
LAST_NAME can be combined with either an AND or an OR to a second condition.

Select: Combine with .AND.

Watch the action line as you continue to build this command.

Select: FIRST_NAME / = Equal To / **Ellen** ⏎ /
No more conditions / Execute the command

Record number 7 is displayed on the screen. Since there were only two Johnsons, there is no need to select Continue. The more specific the conditions are in the search, the more accurate and efficient the Locate command can be.

To return to The Assistant,

Press: any key

Notice that the record pointer is on record number 7. To edit this record,

Select: Update / Edit

Ellen Johnson's record is displayed. The Edit option will display the record that the record pointer is currently on.

Change LAST_NAME to **Foran.**

Press: (CTRL)-(END)

The second note on Fred's desk asks him to delete record number 5 for Paul Ryser. If the record number is known, then the Goto Record command is the quickest way to position the record pointer.

Select: Position
Select: Goto Record

Your display screen should be similar to Figure 2-20.

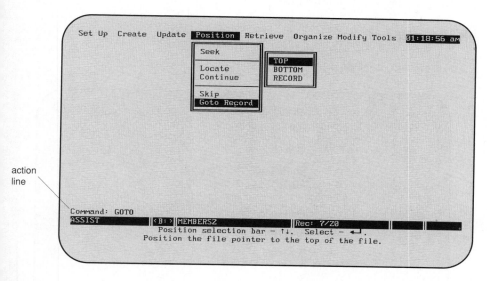

FIGURE 2-20

action
line

Your choices are to position the record pointer to the TOP (first record) or BOTTOM (last record) of the file or to a specific RECORD number. We want to move the pointer to record number 5.

Select: RECORD
Type: 5
Press: (⏎)

The completed command in the action line was "GOTO RECORD 5". This would have been a simple command to enter at the dot prompt.

The status bar indicates that the record pointer is positioned on record 5. Since the record pointer is on the record we want to remove, a quick way to mark that record for deletion is to use the Delete option in the Update Menu.

Select: Update / Delete

The default setting for the Delete command is to mark for deletion the current record, number 5. The Scope/Search Menu is displayed. Since record number 5 is the record we want to delete, we do not need to specify conditions or scope. Using the Delete option is also useful for marking for deletion a number of records with common data in a field. You would do this by specifying scope and search conditions.

Select: Execute the command

The screen shows that one record has been marked for deletion. The command in the action line was simply "DELETE". Many times, using the dot prompt to issue commands is faster.

To return to The Assistant,

Press: any key

The last note on Fred's desk asks for the address of record number 15. Another way to move the record pointer is Skip.

Select: Position / Skip

Your display screen should be similar to Figure 2-21.

FIGURE 2-21

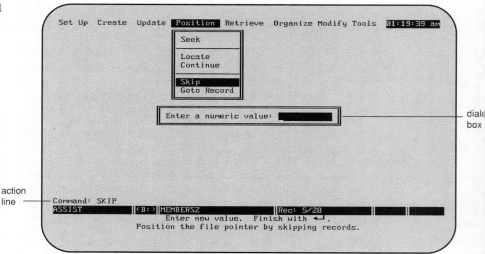

The record pointer is currently on record number 5. Fred wants to move the pointer to record number 15, which is 10 records past the current record pointer location.

In response to the prompt in the dialogue box,

Type: **10**

Press: ⏎

The status bar shows that the record pointer is now on record number 15. The command in the action line was "SKIP 10".

Displaying Database Records

Fred does not need to change the data in this record, he just needs to get the address information. He can quickly do this using Display, an option under the Retrieve Menu.

Select: Retrieve / Display

The Scope/Search Menu is displayed again. We do not need to specify a search condition or scope because the default setting for Display is to display the current record.

Select: Execute the command

Your display screen should look similar to Figure 2-22.

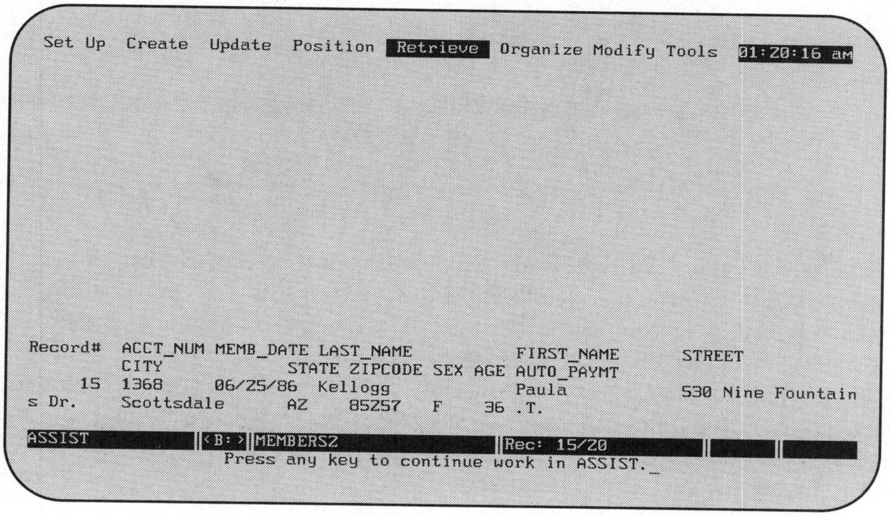

FIGURE 2-22

```
 Set Up  Create  Update  Position  Retrieve  Organize Modify Tools  01:20:16 am




 Record#  ACCT_NUM MEMB_DATE LAST_NAME        FIRST_NAME       STREET
          CITY            STATE ZIPCODE SEX AGE AUTO_PAYMT
      15  1368     06/25/86  Kellogg          Paula            530 Nine Fountain
 s Dr.    Scottsdale      AZ    85257   F   36 .T.
 ASSIST                 <B:> MEMBERS2              Rec: 15/20
                  Press any key to continue work in ASSIST._
```

The data for record 15 is displayed on the screen. Fred can now respond to the request for address information.

To return to The Assistant,

Press: any key

Before Fred uses the Pack command to remove the two records marked for deletion from the file, he would like to see a list of all the records. It is always a good

idea to check the records you have marked for deletion before using the Pack
command. Once Pack is selected, the records are gone for good.

Select: Display / Specify scope

The options in the Scope submenu allow you to specify how many records in the file
will be processed. Move the highlight bar to each of the options. Read the message
line for a description of each. The default scope setting for Display is the current
record.

To display all the records,

Select: ALL / Execute the command

Your display screen should be similar to Figure 2-23.

FIGURE 2-23

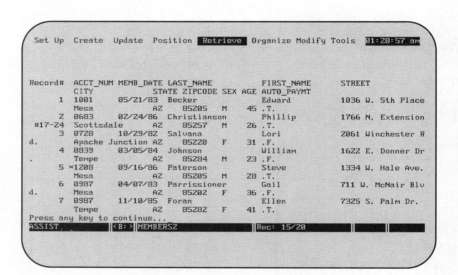

Record numbers 1 through 7 are displayed on the screen. Display automatically
pauses the scrolling of the records when the screen is full.

Look at record number 5. The asterisk between record number and the data in
the first field shows that this record is marked for deletion. Fred sees, however, that
this is the record for Steve Paterson, not Paul Ryser. He must have been given an
incorrect record number. There is no need to panic. The delete marking can be
easily removed, as we'll demonstrate shortly.

To see the next screenful of records,

Press: any key

The next screenful of records is displayed. The field names appear at the top of each
column. Notice that Paul Ryser's record, number 8, is not marked for deletion as it
should be.

Press: any key

The last screenful of records is displayed. Note that the duplicate record for Becker,
number 17, is correctly marked for deletion.

To return to The Assistant,

Press: any key

After displaying all the records, the record pointer is positioned on the end of the file.

Recalling Records Marked for Deletion

Fortunately Fred had only marked the records for deletion and, as you can see, the records are still in the file.

dBASE III PLUS allows you to easily **recall,** or remove, the delete marking with the Recall option in the Update Menu.

Select: Update / Recall

The Scope/Search Menu is displayed. Since Fred wants to reinstate only one of the two records he has marked for deletion, he needs to specify the record to be recalled.

Select: Specify Scope / Record / 5 ⏎ / Execute the command

The message on the screen tells you that one record has been recalled.

Press: any key

To mark Paul Ryser's record, number 8, for deletion,

Select: Delete / Specify Scope / Record / 8 ⏎ /
Execute the command

As you can see, it is always a good idea to check that the correct records are marked for deletion before issuing the Pack command.

Listing Database Records

Since we want to see all the records, we will use the List command to verify that the records for Becker and Ryser are still marked for deletion and that Paterson's record has been recalled,

Press: any key
Select: Retrieve / List / Execute the command / N

The List command quickly scrolls the records in the file without pausing, as the Display command did. If you watched carefully, you could see that the two records marked for deletion were correct and that record 5 was not marked for deletion.

Press: any key

If you missed seeing the marked records, reissue the command and use (CTRL)-S to stop the scrolling of the records when the screen is full. Press any key to continue scrolling.

Removing Records Marked for Deletion

Finally, Fred is ready to remove the marked records from the database. The step which actually erases a marked record from the database is Pack.

Select: Update / Pack

The command is executed immediately. The disk drive light goes on while the command is executed, and after a few moments your display screen should be similar to Figure 2-24.

FIGURE 2-24

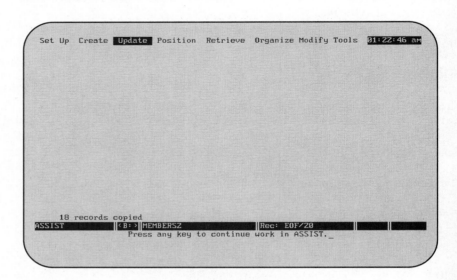

```
  Set Up  Create  Update  Position  Retrieve  Organize Modify Tools  01:22:46 am




            18 records copied
ASSIST          <B:> MEMBERS2                    Rec: EOF/20
                  Press any key to continue work in ASSIST._
```

The message displayed, "18 records copied", tells you that the two marked records have been removed from the database. Pack also renumbers the remaining records to fill in the empty spaces left by the deleted records.

To return to The Assistant,

Press: any key

Printing Selected Records

Fred still has one last thing to do, for the accounting department. He needs to print a list of the records in the database of all members who are using the automatic payment program. To do this,

Select: Retrieve / List / Build a search condition / AUTO_PAYMT

The submenu of relational operators is not displayed. This is because AUTO_PAYMT is a logical field, and dBASE III PLUS assumes you want the true condition.

To continue the command sequence,

Select: No more conditions / Execute the command

If you have printer capability,

Type: Y

If you do not have printer capability,

Type: N

Your printed output should be similar to Figure 2-25.

FIGURE 2-25

```
RECORD#  ACCT_NUM  MEMB_DATE  LAST_NAME           FIRST NAME    STREET
         CITY            STATE  ZIPCODE SEX  AGE  AUTO_PAYMT
      1  1001      05/21/83   Becker              Edward        1036 W. 5th Place
         Mesa           AZ      85205   M    45   .T.
      2  683       02/24/86   Christianson        Phillip       1766 N. Extension
#17-24   Scottsdale     AZ      85257   M    26   .T.
      5  1208      09/16/86   Paterson            Steve         1334 W. Hale Ave.
         Mesa           AZ      85205   M    28   .T.
      7  987       11/10/85   Foran               Ellen         7325 S. Palm Dr.
         Tempe          AZ      85282   F    41   .T.
      9  756       08/07/83   Shaw                Rachel        1057 S. Dobson Rd
         Tempe          AZ      85284   F    27   .T.
     10  756       08/07/83   Williams            Suzanne       1057 S. Dobson Rd
         Mesa           AZ      85202   F    38   .T.
     11  755       06/10/84   Brown               Ronnie        1757 E. Garnet Av
e.       Scottsdale     AZ      85251   M    47   .T.
     14  1368      06/25/86   Kellog              Paula         530 Nine Fountain
s Dr.    Scottsdale     AZ      8527    F    36   .T.
     15  357       02/17/83   Sanders             Robert        725 Parl Place
         Tempe          AZ      85202   F    26   .T.
     16  876       05/28/84   Wong                Sarah         166 E. Fairview
Circle
         Mesa           AZ      85202   F    22   .T.
     17  1599      07/18/87   Johns               Paula         1359 Dixon
         Scottsdale     AZ      85257   F    33   .T.
```

Only the records whose AUTO_PAYMT field contents are true are listed.

Although the database of member records is far from complete, the sample list will show the accounting department the type of report that dBASE III PLUS is capable of producing.

To return to The Assistant,

Press: any key

To leave dBASE III PLUS,

Select: Set Up / Quit dBASE III PLUS

Key Terms

open   delete
modify   search condition
panning   relational operators
lock   logical operator
freeze   recall

Matching

1. (CTRL)-N   _____ a.   accesses the Browse Menu
2. (F1)   _____ b.   stops scrolling of records
3. (F10)   _____ c.   unmarks record marked for deletion
4. Freeze   _____ d.   identifies record marked for deletion
5. (CTRL)-(→)   _____ e.   marks record for deletion
6. (CTRL)-U   _____ f.   inserts a blank field line
7. Pack   _____ g.   stops display of navigation key menu
8. (CTRL)-S   _____ h.   allows edit of a single field
9. Recall   _____ i.   removes records marked for deletion from file
10. *   _____ j.   pans screen to right

Practice Exercises

1.   This problem requires that you have completed Lab 2 and have modified the
file MEMBERS2.DBF as specified in that lab.

- Edit record 1 by entering your first and last name in the appropriate
  fields.
- Print the entire database.
- Mark records 4, 5 and 15 for deletion, and change Rachael Shaw's age
  to 28.
- Print the entire database.
- Recall record 4.
- Remove all records that are marked for deletion.
- Print only those records for male members.
- Print all records for members whose age is less than 35 and zip code is
  85202.

2.   Open the database file TILES30.DBF. This file has the same database structure
as the file created in Practice Exercise 2 in Lab 1 and saved as TILES.DBF. Susannah
continued to enter her clients' information into her database file. It now contains 30
records.

Edit record 1 by entering your first and last name.

- Edit the following records:

Record 3	FIRST NAME is Thomas
Record 12	ADDRESS is 8903 W. Longmore
Record 20	CITY is Hightown
Record 25	UNIT_COST is 12.50
Record 28	STATE is PA
Record 29	PAID is True (T)

- While in Edit, mark records 23 and 28 for deletion.
- Use your name and address information as a new record to be added to the database file. Today, you have ordered 56 tiles at a cost of $3.25 each. Your account is not paid.
- Use the Position Menu to Locate the record for Carol King. Display the record. How many tiles were ordered and what was the unit cost?
- Skip eight records. Display this record. What is the quantity ordered for this record?
- Recall record 10.
- Goto Record 24. What is the client's last name?
- List all the records. How many are marked for deletion? What is the total number of records?
- Recall the record marked for deletion with a last name of Reed.
- Remove the marked records from the file. How many records are in the file now?
- Print all records having a city of Albion.

3.   This problem requires that you have completed Practice Exercise 3 in Lab 1, by creating the database file named SCHOOL.DBF. Open the database file SCHOOL.DBF.

- Confirm that your name has been entered as record 11. If it has not, enter your name in the field TITLE and leave the other fields blank.
- Joe has decided that he needs to add another field of data to his file structure. This field will contain the number of credit hours earned for each class taken. Insert this new field as field number 4. The field name is HOURS. It is a Numeric field with a field width of 1 and 0 decimal places.
- Use the Freeze command in the Browse submenu to enter the data for the HOURS field for each record in the file. All the classes are 3 credit hours except MAT210 which is 5 credit hours and Ped101 and Ped102 which are each 1 credit hour. Do not enter data for record 11.
- Enter the courses you took and the grades you earned last semester as new records in this file. Begin with record 12.
- Remove the record for MAT210 taken in Fall 1988 from the database file.
- Print a list of all the classes in which a grade of B was earned.

4.   Bob is a manager for a small manufacturing company. One of his responsibilities is to keep weekly records for each of the company's 20 employees. Bob has created a database using dBASE III PLUS to help him.

- Open the database file STAFF.DBF.
- Edit record 1 by entering your first and last name.
- Modify the structure to include a new field SEX to be inserted between the existing fields PAY and HRS.
- Based on the FIRST_NAME for each employee, enter either F or M for SEX. If you cannot determine whether the first name is for a male or female, enter a question mark (?).
- Edit the following records:

  Record 5   FIRST_NAME is Robert
  Record 17   Hours is 35

- Delete records 3, 7, and 10.
- Print the entire database.
- Print only those employees who work in Accounting and earn less than $4.75.

3

Sorting, Indexing, and Summarizing Data

CASE STUDY

Donna McIntyre is the assistant manager of the Sports Club. As part of her responsibilities she maintains all employee records and produces weekly and monthly employee status reports.

The database structure and all the hourly employee data have been entered into a file using dBASE III PLUS by her assistant. We will follow Donna as she organizes the records in the file, analyzes the information in the database, and produces a simple report.

Displaying a Disk Directory

Donna's assistant created the database file of hourly employee records. He left the diskette and a note containing a description of the file structure in Donna's in-basket before leaving on vacation.

Upon seeing the diskette and note, Donna decides to take a look at the file. However, she realizes her assistant neglected to tell her the name of the file. Donna hopes that by looking at a list of all the files on the diskette, she will be able to pick out the file.

Load dBASE III PLUS.

To see a listing of all the files on the diskette,

Select: Tools

The Tools Menu performs mostly operating system functions such as setting the disk drive, listing the disk files (directory), copying, erasing, and renaming files.

Note: If you are using a drive other than B to hold your data files, select the appropriate drive from the drive submenu.

To see a directory of files on the diskette in the B drive,

Select: Directory / B:

OBJECTIVES

In this lab you will learn how to:

1. Display the disk directory.

2. Create a sorted database file.

3. Create a multilevel sorted file.

4. Create an index file.

5. Open index files.

6. Use the Seek command.

7. Use the dot prompt.

8. Perform basic numeric calculations.

9. Create and print a simple report.

Your display screen should be similar to Figure 3-1.

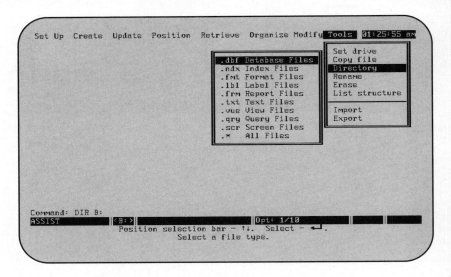

FIGURE 3-1

The nine types of files that can be created using dBASE III PLUS and the file extensions associated with each type are displayed in the submenu. We created and used database files (.DBF) in Labs 1 and 2. In this lab we will create index files, which have an .NDX file extension. This submenu allows you to view only the files with a specific file extension or to view all the files on the diskette.

To see a complete list of files on the diskette (use (PGDN)),

Select: .*   All Files

All files on the diskette are listed. This includes files that are accessed by other types of software, such as files created by a word processor, as well as the files created by dBASE III PLUS.

This screen also shows the total number of bytes used by the files, total number of files on the diskette, and the total number of bytes remaining on the diskette.

Donna looks through the list of file names and sees a database file named EMPLOYEE.DBF. This file name is descriptive of the contents of the file she is looking for.

To return to The Assistant,

Press: any key

Note: Throughout the rest of this text, if you are using a drive other than B to hold your data diskette, select the appropriate drive for your system.

Displaying the File Structure

Donna wants to open the EMPLOYEE.DBF file and then view its structure to confirm that this is the file she wants to use.

Select: Set Up / Database file / B: / EMPLOYEE.DBF / **N**

The EMPLOYEE.DBF file is open. The List structure option in the Tools Menu lets you display and print the structure of the open database file. To display, but not print, the structure of this file,

Select: Tools / List structure / **N**

Your display screen should be similar to Figure 3-2.

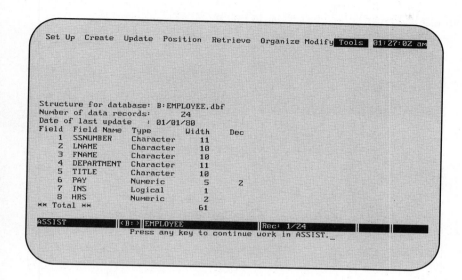

FIGURE 3-2

The first three lines display the name and drive location of the database file (B:EMPLOYEE.dbf), the number of database records (24) in the file, and the date of last update.

The eight field names and their attributes are displayed next. Below the list of field names the total number of bytes (spaces), plus 1, used by the eight fields is displayed. dBASE III PLUS adds one extra space for marking records for deletion.

The EMPLOYEE.DBF file contains eight fields of data. The written description left by Donna's assistant of each field (shown below) confirms that this is the correct file.

SSNUMBER   The employee's social security number. This field is defined as a Character field since no numeric calculations would be made using it. The width was set at 11 to allow for two dashes within the nine-digit number.

LNAME   The employee's last name.

FNAME   The employee's first name.

DEPARTMENT   The division of the club the employee works in.

TITLE   The employee's job title.

PAY   The employee's hourly rate of pay. This is a Numeric field, displaying two decimal places.

INS   This field indicates whether the employees chose to participate in the insurance program offered by theclub. It is a Logical field.

HRS   The number of hours per week the employee works. This is a Numeric field with no decimal places.

To return to The Assistant,

Press: any key

To view the records in the database file,

Select: **R**etrieve / **L**ist / **E**xecute the command / **N**

Your display screen should be similar to Figure 3-3.

FIGURE 3-3

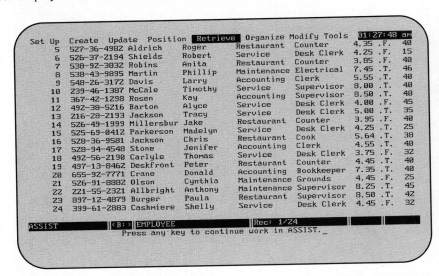

Each record occupies only a single line because the record length is short enough to be completely displayed in a window. The Sports Club has 24 hourly employees. Notice that the records are not ordered in any sequence other than the original record number order they were assigned as the data was entered into the file.

To return to The Assistant,

Press: any key

Sorting the Database Records

Donna would like to organize the records in the database file in a more meaningful way. She wants the records **organized,** or arranged, in alphabetical order by last name. To do this, the Organize Menu is used. The Organize Menu helps you arrange the order of records in your file.

Select: Organize

There are three menu options: Index, Sort, and Copy. The Index and Sort commands allow you to change the order of records in a file. The Copy command makes a copy of all or selected portions of the file.

To sort the records in the file by last name,

Select: Sort

Your display screen should be similar to Figure 3-4.

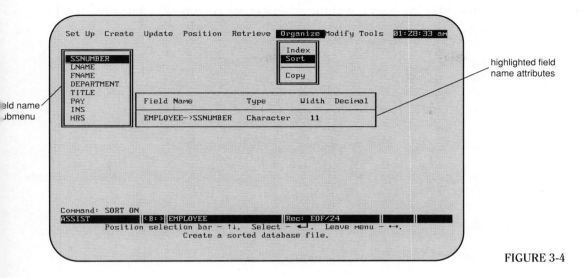

FIGURE 3-4

A field name submenu is displayed. Donna wants the records arranged in alphabetical order by LNAME. The field on which a database is sorted is called the **key field.** To select a key field, following the instructions in the navigation line, move the highlight bar to the field name and press ⏎.

Select: LNAME

To leave the field name submenu,

Press: ⟶

The Sort command creates a new database file. It contains a duplicate of all the records in the original database file arranged in the order specified. To specify the drive to create the new sorted file on,

Select: B:

The new file needs a file name. Enter the file name for the new sorted database file as follows:

Type: LASTNAME
Press: ⏎

The completed command shown in the action line was "SORT ON LNAME TO B:LASTNAME".

The B disk drive light goes on, and the file is sorted and saved on the diskette. After a few moments your display will tell you the percentage and number of records sorted.

The new database file is a duplicate of the original EMPLOYEE.DBF file. It has been saved as LASTNAME.DBF on the diskette in the B drive. The only difference between the two files is that the records in the new file are arranged alphabetically by last name.

To return to The Assistant,

Press: any key

To open the new database file of sorted records,

Select: Set Up / Database file / B: / LASTNAME.DBF / **N**

The status bar shows that the database file in use is LASTNAME. To view the records in this file,

Select: **R**etrieve / Display / Specify scope / All / Execute the command

Your display screen should be similar to Figure 3-5.

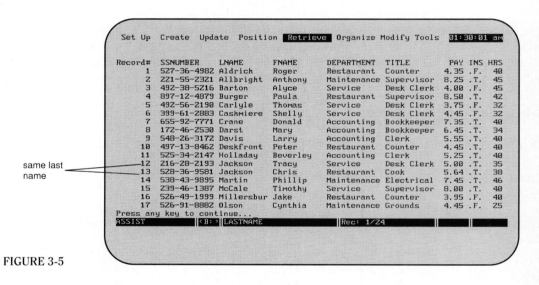

same last
name

```
 Set Up   Create   Update   Position   Retrieve   Organize  Modify  Tools   01:30:01 am


 Record#  SSNUMBER    LNAME      FNAME      DEPARTMENT   TITLE        PAY  INS  HRS
       1  527-36-4982 Aldrich    Roger      Restaurant   Counter      4.35 .F.  40
       2  221-55-2321 Allbright  Anthony    Maintenance  Supervisor   8.25 .T.  45
       3  492-38-5216 Barton     Alyce      Service      Desk Clerk   4.00 .F.  45
       4  897-12-4879 Burger     Paula      Restaurant   Supervisor   8.50 .T.  42
       5  492-56-2190 Carlyle    Thomas     Service      Desk Clerk   3.75 .F.  32
       6  399-61-2883 Cashmiere  Shelly     Service      Desk Clerk   4.45 .F.  32
       7  655-92-7771 Crane      Donald     Accounting   Bookkeeper   7.35 .T.  40
       8  172-46-2530 Darst      Mary       Accounting   Bookkeeper   6.45 .T.  34
       9  548-26-3172 Davis      Larry      Accounting   Clerk        5.55 .T.  40
      10  497-13-8462 Deskfront  Peter      Restaurant   Counter      4.45 .T.  40
      11  525-34-2147 Holladay   Beverley   Accounting   Clerk        5.25 .T.  40
      12  216-28-2193 Jackson    Tracy      Service      Desk Clerk   5.00 .T.  35
      13  528-36-9581 Jackson    Chris      Restaurant   Cook         5.64 .T.  38
      14  538-43-9895 Martin     Phillip    Maintenance  Electrical   7.45 .T.  46
      15  239-46-1387 McCale     Timothy    Service      Supervisor   8.00 .T.  40
      16  526-49-1999 Millersbur Jake       Restaurant   Counter      3.95 .F.  40
      17  526-91-8882 Olson      Cynthia    Maintenance  Grounds      4.45 .F.  25
 Press any key to continue...
 ASSIST            <B:> LASTNAME                   Rec: 1/24
```

FIGURE 3-5

The sorted database file, LASTNAME.DBF, contains the same data as the original file, EMPLOYEE.DBF. But the records in the sorted database are listed in ascending alphabetical order by last name. Notice that the records have been renumbered.

Look at record numbers 12 and 13. Both the employees have the same last name, Jackson. Donna would like the records to be sorted so that the first names are alphabetized within same last names. This would change the order so that Chris Jackson's record would come before Tracy Jackson's.

To see the next screenful of records,

Press: any key

To return to The Assistant,

Press: any key

Creating a Multilevel Sort File

A file can also be sorted on more than one key field. This is called a **multilevel sort.**
To alphabetize the employees' first names within identical last names, two key fields,
LNAME and FNAME, are specified.

Select: Organize / Sort /

To select more than one key field, simply move the selection bar to each field you
want to select from the field name submenu and press ⏎. When sorting on multiple key fields, the most important key field is selected first.

Move to: **LNAME**
Press: ⏎
Move to: **FNAME**
Press: ⏎
Press: →
Select: **B: / Namesort** ⏎

The action line displays the command as "SORT ON LNAME, FNAME TO
B:NAMESORT". Multiple key fields are separated by commas in the dot command.
   To return to The Assistant and open the file NAMESORT.DBF,

Press: any key
Select: Set Up / Database file / B: / NAMESORT.DBF/ **N**

The open database file is now NAMESORT.DBF. To view the records in their
new sorted order,

Select: Retrieve / List

Rather than displaying all the fields in each record, you can restrict the listing
to display only the fields we are interested in seeing, i.e., LNAME and FNAME. To
specify which fields to display,

Select: Construct a field list

Your display screen should be similar to Figure 3-6.

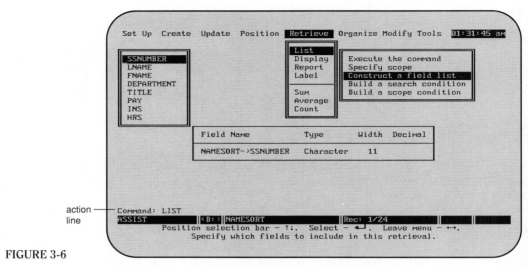

FIGURE 3-6

The field name submenu is displayed. The order in which the fields are selected from the field name submenu will determine the order they are displayed on the screen.

Select:	FNAME
Select:	LNAME
Press:	(→)
Select:	Execute the command / **N**

The command in the action line was "LIST FNAME, LNAME".
Your display screen should be similar to Figure 3-7.

FIGURE 3-7

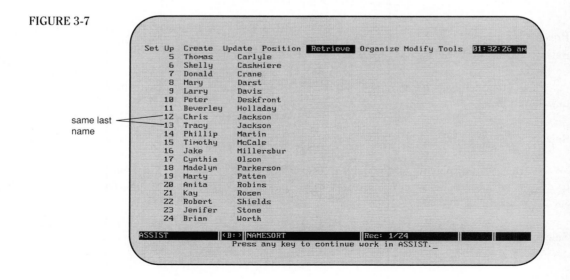

The employee names are displayed with the first name before the last name. Chris Jackson's record is now number 12. It comes before Tracy Jackson's record, which is number 13. Donna is pleased with the results of the multilevel sort.

To return to The Assistant,

Press: any key

Donna needs to update the open database file, NAMESORT.DBF, by adding a new employee record.

Select: Update / Append

A blank entry form is displayed on the Append screen. The record pointer should be positioned on EOF/ 24.

Enter the following data:

Field Name	Field Data
SSNUMBER	187-49-0213
LNAME	Fischer
FNAME	Sarah
DEPARTMENT	Service
TITLE	Desk Clerk
PAY	3.55
INS	N
HRS	40

Another blank entry form is displayed. To verify that the data for Sarah Fischer was entered correctly,

Press: (PGUP)

Record number 25 is displayed on the screen. Edit if necessary.

To save the new record and exit the Append screen,

Press: (CTRL)-(END)

Do not press (CTRL)-(END) when a blank record form is displayed on the screen. If you do, a blank record will be added to the file.

To view the records in the file,

Select: **R**etrieve / List / Execute the command / **N**

The record for Sarah Fischer is the last record in the file. Each time a record is added to a file using Append, it is added to the end of the file. The file would need to be resorted in order to have the records arranged in alphabetical order.

In addition, the original file, EMPLOYEE.DBF, and the other sorted database file, LASTNAME.DBF, do not contain the record for Sarah Fischer. Her record would need to be added to each of these files to make them up to date.

Press: any key

As you can see, the Sort command has some serious drawbacks:

- Each time a file is sorted using the Sort command, a new duplicate file is created. With a large database, this duplication of data uses a lot of your diskette space.

- The renumbering of the records in the sorted file makes locating a record by record number unlikely. Each time the file is sorted, the record number may change.

- Sorting a large database takes a lot of time, sometimes several hours.

- Each time a change, addition, or deletion to the original file is made, the sorted file becomes out of date. The original file would need to be re-sorted, or the sorted file would need to be updated.

For these reasons, using the Sort command is usually limited to files that do not change frequently. Donna feels that the file of employee records will change frequently as people are added and deleted and changes are made to individual records. Many of these problems can be resolved by creating index files.

Creating an Index File

Donna wants to create an index file using the file EMPLOYEE.DBF.

To close the sorted file, NAMESORT.DBF, and open the original unsorted file, EMPLOYEE.DBF,

Select: Set Up / Database file / B: / EMPLOYEE.DBF / **N**
Select: **O**rganize

To use Help for information on the Index option,

Press: F1

Your display screen should be similar to Figure 3-8.

FIGURE 3-8

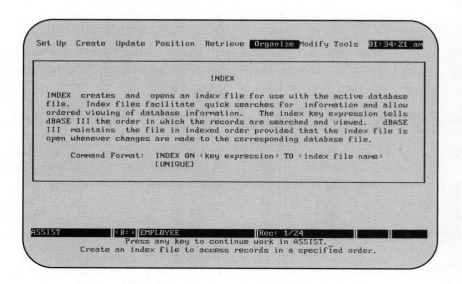

Read this screen carefully. The Index command is used to create index files which control the order of display of records in the open database file.

　　To return to The Assistant,

Press:　any key

To use the Index option to arrange the records ordered alphabetically by last name and first name.

Select:　Index

Your display screen should be similar to Figure 3-9.

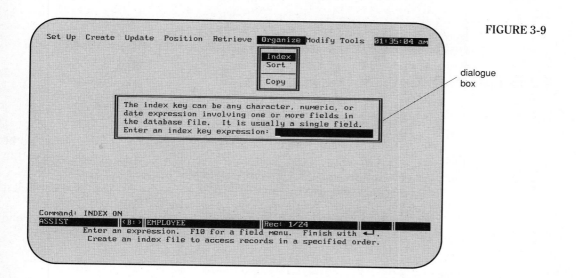

FIGURE 3-9

The message in the dialogue box prompts you to enter a **key expression.** In the Sort command, the key field to sort on was specified. Here, the index key expression must be specified. This is simply the field or fields that will determine the order of the records.

　　There are two ways to enter the index key expression. You can type the field name exactly as it appears in the database file following the prompt in the dialogue box. Or you can select the field name from a field name submenu. To display the field name submenu,

Press:　F10

As in previous screens where the field name submenu is displayed, move the selection bar to the desired field name and press ⏎ to select it.

Select:　LNAME

Your display screen should be similar to Figure 3-10.

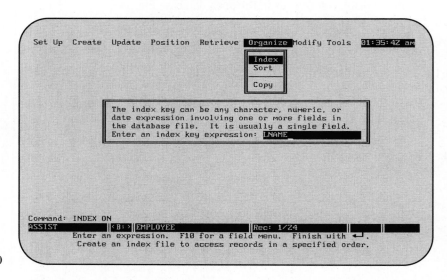

FIGURE 3-10

LNAME is entered as the key expression in the dialogue box. The field name sub-menu is no longer displayed.

To complete the entry Donna could simply press ⏎, and the file would be indexed on the LNAME field only. However, to have first names alphabetized within same last names, a second index key expression must be specified.

In a manner similar to the multilevel sort, we will index the file on both last name and first name. This is called **multilevel indexing.**

The cursor is positioned after LNAME in the dialogue box. To add a second index key expression,

Type: +
Press: (F10)
Select: FNAME

Your display screen should be similar to Figure 3-11.

FIGURE 3-11

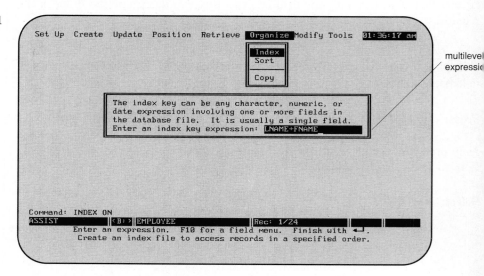

multilevel
expressio

Both fields are displayed as key expressions in the dialogue box. To end the specification of the key expressions,

Press: ⏎

The Index command creates a new file with a file extension.NDX. To complete the command sequence, enter the drive where the indexed file will be saved and the file name for the indexed file as follows:

Select: B: / **EMPNAME** ⏎

The completed command in the action line was "INDEX ON LNAME+FNAME TO B:EMPNAME".

The action line shows that 100 percent of the records have been indexed. To return to The Assistant,

Press: any key

As soon as an index file is created, the records in the EMPLOYEE.DBF database file are reordered according to the key expressions. The index file does not need to be opened, as the sortfile did. It is put into use immediately. To view the records in the EMPLOYEE.DBF file,

Select: **R**etrieve / Display / Specify scope / All / Execute the command

Your display screen should be similar to Figure 3-12.

FIGURE 3-12

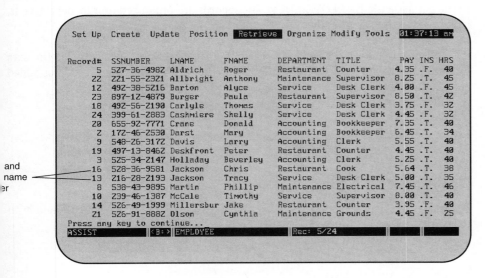

```
  Set Up  Create  Update  Position  Retrieve  Organize Modify Tools  01:37:13 am

  Record#  SSNUMBER    LNAME      FNAME     DEPARTMENT  TITLE        PAY INS HRS
        5  527-36-498Z Aldrich    Roger     Restaurant  Counter      4.35 .F.  40
       22  221-55-23Z1 Allbright  Anthony   Maintenance Supervisor   8.25 .T.  45
       12  492-38-5Z16 Barton     Alyce     Service     Desk Clerk   4.00 .F.  45
       23  897-12-4879 Burger     Paula     Restaurant  Supervisor   8.50 .T.  42
       18  492-56-Z190 Carlyle    Thomas    Service     Desk Clerk   3.75 .F.  32
       24  399-61-Z883 Cashmiere  Shelly    Service     Desk Clerk   4.45 .F.  3Z
       20  655-92-7771 Crane      Donald    Accounting  Bookkeeper   7.35 .T.  40
        Z  172-46-Z530 Darst      Mary      Accounting  Bookkeeper   6.45 .T.  34
        9  548-Z6-317Z Davis      Larry     Accounting  Clerk        5.55 .T.  40
       19  497-13-846Z Deskfront  Peter     Restaurant  Counter      4.45 .T.  40
        3  525-34-2147 Holladay   Beverley  Accounting  Clerk        5.25 .T.  40
       16  528-36-9581 Jackson    Chris     Restaurant  Cook         5.64 .T.  38
       13  216-28-Z193 Jackson    Tracy     Service     Desk Clerk   5.00 .T.  35
        8  538-43-9895 Martin     Phillip   Maintenance Electrical   7.45 .T.  46
       10  239-46-1387 McCale     Timothy   Service     Supervisor   8.00 .T.  40
       14  526-49-1999 Millersbur Jake      Restaurant  Counter      3.95 .F.  40
       21  526-91-888Z Olson      Cynthia   Maintenance Grounds      4.45 .F.  25
  Press any key to continue...
  ASSIST          <B:> EMPLOYEE                   Rec: 5/24
```

and name

The index file has taken control over the order of display of the records of the open database file, EMPLOYEE.DBF. The records are arranged in the same order as in the multilevel sort file NAMESORT.DBF. The records for the two Jacksons are in alphabetical order by last and first names.

Each record still has the original record number it was assigned when it was entered into the database file. The records have not been physically reordered in the file as they were when the Sort command was used. Indexing uses an index **pointer** which controls the order of display of the records in the EMPLOYEE.DBF file.

The Sort command creates a duplicate database file. The records are physically reordered and renumbered. The Index command creates an index file containing pointers (the index key expression values and corresponding record numbers) to records in the open database file. Since the entire record is not copied into the index file, this file takes up much less diskette space.

To continue to view the rest of the file and return to The Assistant,

Press: any key (2 times)

The club manager has asked Donna for a list of all employees by department. To do this, Donna needs to create a second index file. This one will arrange the employee records alphabetically within departments. The most important key expression is selected first.

Select: Organize / Index / **DEPARTMENT+LNAME+FNAME** /
B: / **EMPDEPT** ⏎

To return to The Assistant and view the records in the new index order,

Press: any key
Select: **Retrieve** / List / Execute the command / **N**

The new index file, EMPDEPT.NDX, now controls the order of display of the records in the database file EMPLOYEE.DBF. The records are organized first by department, next by last name, and finally by first name.

The first index file, EMPNAME.NDX, is closed.

Before preparing the report for the club manager, Donna needs to add the data for Sarah Fischer to the EMPLOYEE.DBF file. (Remember that her record was added only to the sorted database file, NAMESORT.DBF.)

To clear the list,

Press: any key

Opening Index Files

The new record can be added to the original database file, EMPLOYEE.DBF and both index files at the same time. To do this, both index files must be open.

To open both index files,

Select: Set Up / Database file / B: / EMPLOYEE.DBF

This time in response to the prompt "Is the file indexed?",

Type: Y

Your display screen should be similar to Figure 3-13.

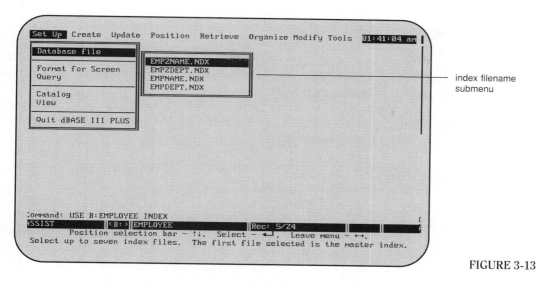

index filename
submenu

FIGURE 3-13

An index file name submenu appears. It displays all the index files on this diskette (including index files you will use in the next lab). To open an index file, move the selection bar to the index file name and press ⏎.

Select: EMPNAME.NDX

Your display screen should be similar to Figure 3-14.

FIGURE 3-14

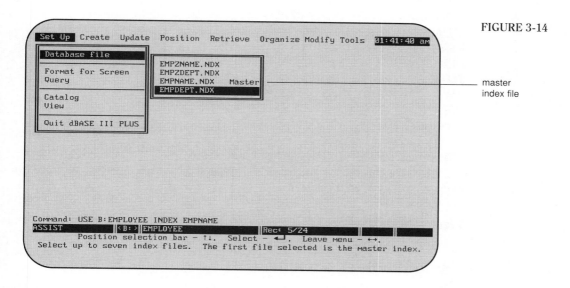

master
index file

The word "Master" appears next to the file name. The first index file that is opened is called the **master index.** This index file will control the order of display of the records in the EMPLOYEE.DBF file.

To open the second index file,

Select: EMPDEPT.NDX

As additional index files are selected they are numbered 2, 3, and so on. They are open, but they are not in control of the order of display of records on the screen. They are called **secondary indexes.**

The command in the action line is "USE B:EMPLOYEE INDEX EMPNAME, EMPDEPT".

To leave the index submenu,

Press: ⊙→

Whenever a file is updated, it is important that all related index files are open so that they will be automatically updated at the same time. dBASE III PLUS will update open index files *only*. You can open as many as seven index files at once. Of course, the more index files that are open, the longer the update process takes because each index file has to be updated at the same time.

If you wanted to use the EMPLOYEE.DBF file without using an index file, you would respond "No" to the prompt "Is your file indexed?".

Add the data for Sarah Fischer to the database file as follows:

Select: Update / Append

Enter the data below exactly as it appears:

Field Name	Field Data
SSNUMBER	187-49-0213
LNAME	Fischer
FNAME	Sarah
DEPARTMENT	Service
TITLE	Desk Clerk
PAY	3.55
INS	N
HRS	40

Check the record for accuracy and edit if necessary.

To save the record and leave the Append screen (remember, do not have a blank record form on the screen),

Press: CTRL-END

Using the Seek Command

To verify that Sarah Fischer's record was added to the master index file, the Seek option in the Position menu can be used. This command can be used only on files that are indexed. If an index file is not open, this option will not be available for selection through The Assistant.

To quickly locate the record,

Select: Position / Seek

Your display screen should be similar to Figure 3-15.

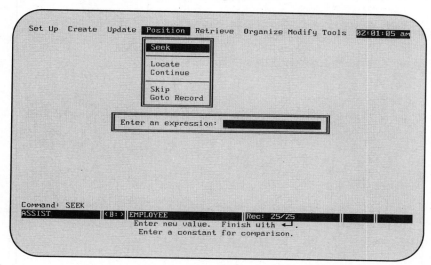

FIGURE 3-15

A dialogue box appears prompting you to "Enter an expression:". Any key expression field value entry that matches the first index key expression in the master index file can be entered. The first index key for the master file is LNAME. The expression to enter in this Seek command can be any last name in the EMPLOYEE.DBF file. You will enter the last name, Fischer, of the record we want to locate, as the seek expression.

The expression must be entered exactly as it appears in the file. dBASE III PLUS is case-sensitive, which means it searches for strings exactly as they are entered in the dialogue box—uppercase, lowercase, or a combination of the two. For this reason, when entering your data into the file, you need to be consistent with your use of upper- and lowercase letters.

If the expression is a character field, it must be enclosed in quotes (') or brackets([ ]).

Type: 'Fisher'
Press: ⏎

The message displayed at the bottom of the screen tells you that there are no records in the file that match the expression. Donna notices that she spelled the last name incorrectly. To try it again,

Press: any key
Select: Seek / **'Fischer'**
Press: ⏎

No error message is displayed this time. Although nothing appears to have happened, the record was found. The pointer is now located on that record. The Seek command quickly locates the first record in an indexed file that matches the specified expression.

To return to The Assistant,

Press: any key

To display the record located by the Seek command,

Select: **R**etrieve / Display / Execute the command

Your display screen should be similar to Figure 3-16.

FIGURE 3-16

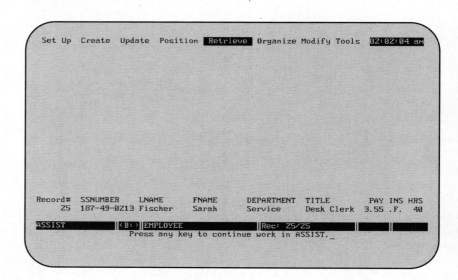

```
    Set Up  Create  Update  Position  Retrieve  Organize Modify Tools   02:02:04 am




    Record#  SSNUMBER     LNAME       FNAME       DEPARTMENT  TITLE       PAY INS HRS
        25  187-49-0213 Fischer     Sarah        Service     Desk Clerk  3.55 .F.  40
ASSIST          |<B:>||EMPLOYEE                  ||Rec: 25/25
                    Press any key to continue work in ASSIST.
```

The record for Sarah Fischer is displayed. Although not apparent with this small database, using Seek to find a record in a large indexed file is faster and more efficient than using Locate.
To return to The Assistant,

Press: any key

Next, we want to verify that Sarah Fischer's record was added to the other index file. To do so, we need to change the master index file to EMPDEPT.NDX. We could use The Assistant to select Set Up / Database file / B: / EMPLOYEE.DBF / Y / EMPDEPT.NDX EMPNAME.NDX. However, changing the master index file can be done easily and more quickly at the dot prompt.

Using the Dot Prompt

To get to the dot prompt screen,

Press: (ESC)

A dBASE III PLUS dot command can be typed in either upper- or lowercase letters.

To enter the command to change the order of the index files so that the secondary index file, number 2, becomes the master index file,

Type: ‎ **SET ORDER TO 2**
Press: ⏎

The message displayed on the screen tells you that the master index file is EMPDEPT.NDX.

Note: If you entered the command incorrectly and have an error message on the screen, press (ESC) and retype the command.

This is easy, assuming you remember the index filenames and the order the index files were opened. In case you do not remember the index file names, you can have a directory of index files displayed as follows.

Type: ‎ **DIR *.NDX**
Press: ⏎

Your display screen should be similar to Figure 3-17.

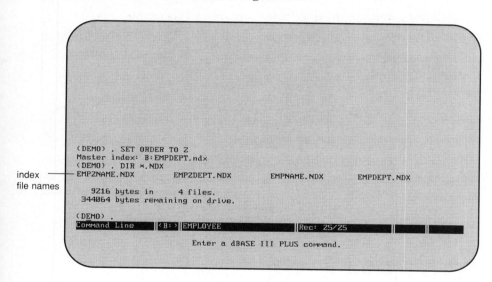

FIGURE 3-17

index file names

All the index files on the diskette are displayed. If you do not remember the order you used to open the index files,

Type: ‎ **DISPLAY STATUS**
Press: ⏎

We are interested only in the first four lines following the command. It tells you the current database file in use, the master index file, and other open index files. The keys used in the indexed files are also displayed.

There is a lot of other information about the current dBASE III PLUS session provided using this command. To see the next screen of information and return to the dot prompt,

Press: ‎ any key

To return to The Assistant, you can type ASSIST or use the (F2) key.

Press: (F2)

The master index file is EMPDEPT.NDX. The records will be displayed in order by department, last name, and first name.

To verify that Sarah Fischer's record was added to this index file,

Select: **R**etrieve / List / Execute the command / **N**

Your display screen should be similar to Figure 3-18.

FIGURE 3-18

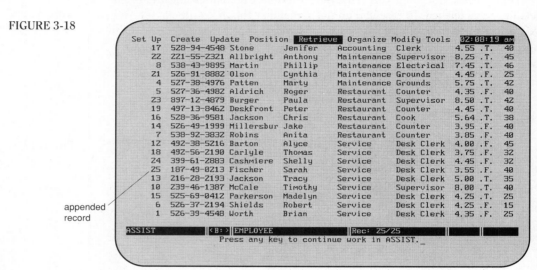

appended record

Sarah Fischer, record number 25, is displayed alphabetically within the service department. Since both index files were open at the time the record was added to the EMPLOYEE.DBF file, both index files were updated with the new record.

To return to The Assistant,

Press: any key

Using indexed files has many advantages over Sort.

- Accessing records is faster with Seek.
- The indexed file takes up much less diskette space because only the pointers to records in the database are stored in the file.
- All open index files are automatically updated if changes are made in the database file.

Summarizing Data

The club manager wants to know the number of employees, average pay rate, and total hours worked for all employees in the service department.

Now that the database is up to date, Donna can proceed to analyze the data. To do this, Donna will use the dBASE III PLUS **numeric functions.** These functions can average, sum, or count the specified records in a database.

To find out how many employees there are in the service department, use the Count command. This is an option under the Retrieve Menu.

Select: **R**etrieve / Count / Build a search condition / DEPARTMENT /
= Equal To / **Service** / No more conditions / Execute the command

Your display screen should be similar to Figure 3-19.

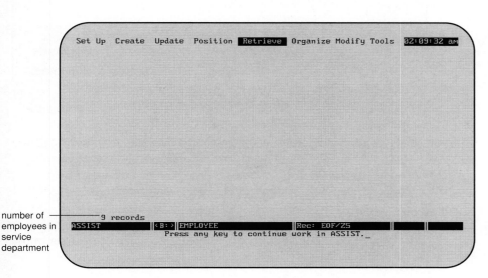

FIGURE 3-19

number of employees in service department

The number of records (9) meeting the specifications is displayed.
To return to The Assistant,

Press: any key

To find the average hourly rate of pay for all employees in the service department,

Select: Average / Construct a field list

Notice that only the Numeric fields are available for selection from the field name submenu.

Select: Pay / Build a search condition / DEPARTMENT / = Equal To /
Service / No more conditions / Execute the command

Your display screen should appear similar to Figure 3-20.

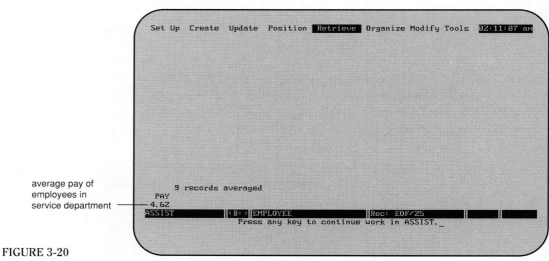

average pay of
employees in
service department

FIGURE 3-20

The number of records averaged and the computed average pay rate of 4.62 are displayed.

To return to The Assistant,

Press: any key

To calculate the total number of hours worked last week by employees in the service department,

Select: Sum / Construct a field list / HRS / Build a search condition /
DEPARTMENT / = Equal To / **Service** / No more conditions /
Execute the command

The number of records summed and the total number of hours worked by all employees in the service department, 289, are displayed.

To return to The Assistant,

Press: any key

Printing a Simple Report

Donna is ready to create the report listing all employees by department for the club manager. The only fields of data he wants to see in the list are department, last and first names, job title, and rate of pay.

The master index file is EMPDEPT.NDX. Therefore, the display of records will be in the desired order.

To produce a printed report of this information,

Select: **R**etrieve / List / Construct a field list /
DEPARTMENT, LNAME, FNAME, TITLE, PAY / Execute the command

If you have printer capability,

Type: Y

If you do not have printer capability,

Type: N

Your printed output should be similar to Figure 3-21.

FIGURE 3-21

```
Record#   DEPARTMENT    LNAME       FNAME      TITLE        PAY
     20   Accounting    Crane       Donald     Bookkeeper   7.35
      2   Accounting    Darst       Mary       Bookkeeper   6.45
      9   Accounting    Davis       Larry      Clerk        5.55
      3   Accounting    Holladay    Beverly    Clerk        5.25
     11   Accounting    Rosen       Kay        Supervisor   8.50
     17   Accounting    Stone       Jenifer    Clerk        5.25
     22   Maintenance   Albright    Anthony    Supervisor   4.55
      8   Maintenance   Martin      Phillip    Electrical   7.45
     21   Maintenance   Olson       Cynthia    Grounds      4.45
      4   Maintenance   Patten      Marty      Grounds      5.75
      5   Restaurant    Aldrich     Roger      Counter      4.35
     23   Restaurant    Burger      Paula      Supervisor   8.50
     19   Restaurant    Deskfront   Peter      Counter      4.45
     16   Restaurant    Jackson     Chris      Cook         5.64
     14   Restaurant    Millersbur  Jake       Counter      3.95
      7   Restaurant    Robins      Anita      Counter      3.85
     12   Service       Barton      Alyce      Desk Clerk   4.00
     18   Service       Carlyle     Thomas     Desk Clerk   3.75
     24   Service       Cashmiere   Shelly     Desk Clerk   4.45
     25   Service       Fischer     Sarah      Desk Clerk   3.55
     13   Service       Jackson     Tracy      Desk Clerk   5.00
     10   Service       McCale      Timothy    Supervisor   8.00
     15   Service       Parkerson   Madelyn    Desk Clerk   4.25
      6   Service       Sheilds     Robert     Desk Clerk   4.25
      1   Service       Worth       Brian      Desk Clerk   4.35
```

Donna is pleased with the report she has created. However, she would like the report to look more professional. We will demonstrate how to prepare a professional report in the next lab.

To return to The Assistant,

Press: any key

To quit dBASE III PLUS,

Select: Set Up / Quit dBASE III PLUS

Key Terms

index	pointer
key field	organize
multilevel sort	master index
key expression	secondary index
multilevel indexing	numeric functions

Matching

1. .NDX
2. DIR *.DBF
3. SET ORDER TO 4
4. DISPLAY STATUS
5. (F2)
6. master
7. Sort
8. Index
9. Count
10. pointer

_____ a. a numeric function that counts the number of records in a file

_____ b. index key values and record numbers contained in the index file

_____ c. displays The Assistant

_____ d. dot command to display a directory of database files

_____ e. dot command to change the open index file 4 to the master

_____ f. file extension for indexed files

_____ g. dot command that provides information about the current dBASE III PLUS session

_____ h. the index file opened first

_____ i. organizes a file on a key expression

_____ j. creates an index file

Practice Exercises

1.   This problem requires that you have completed Lab 3 and have created the indexed files as specified in that lab. Open EMPLOYEE.DBF with the index file EMPNAME.NDX.

- Edit record 1 by entering your first and last name in the appropriate fields.
- Sort the records by TITLE and LAST_NAME. Name the sorted file STITLE.
- Print the database file STITLE.
- Index the file EMPLOYEE on TITLE. Name the index file EMPTITLE.
- Change EMPLOYEE's master file to EMPTITLE.
- Print the database file EMPLOYEE.DBF.
- Print a report displaying FIRST_NAME, LAST_NAME, DEPARTMENT, and TITLE, organized by TITLE.

2.   To complete this problem you must first have completed Practice Exercise 2 in Lab 2. Open the database file TILES30.DBF.

- Use the LOCATE command to confirm that your name has been entered into the database. If it has not, enter your first and last name as a record.
- Index the file on UNIT_COST. Name the index file COST. What is the unit cost of the tile that is ordered most often?
- Index the file on DATE. Name the index file DATE. How many orders were placed in September?
- Sort the records by LAST_NAME and FIRST_NAME. Name the sorted file TILESORT. Open the sorted file. How many records have a last name of King?
- Open the file TILES30.DBF. Open the index file COST.NDX first and DATE.NDX second.

- Using the dot command, change the order of the index files so that DATE.NDX is the master index file.

- Print a list of all paid accounts displaying the LAST_NAME, QUANTITY, and UNIT_COST fields only, organized by date.

3. To complete this problem, you must first have completed Practice Exercise 3 in Lab 2. Open the database file SCHOOL.DBF.

- Use the LOCATE command to confirm that your name has been entered into the database. If it has not, enter your name in the field TITLE of record 11.

- Index the file on COURSE_NUM. Name the index file COURSE.

- Index the file on GRADE. Name the index file GRADE.

- Use the Sum function to calculate the total number of hours earned. What is Joe's total hours earned?

- Use the Count function to calculate how many B's Joe has earned. How many B's has Joe earned?

- Print a simple report showing the course TITLE and GRADE, categorized by GRADE.

- Print another report displaying COURSE_NUM and HOURS organized by COURSE_NUM.

4. To complete this problem you must first have completed Practice Exercise 4 in Lab 3. Open the database file STAFF.DBF.

- Use the LOCATE command to confirm that your name has been entered into the database. If it has not, enter your first and last name as a record.

- Sort the file on DEPARTMENT. Name the sorted file DEPTSTAF.

- Print the file STAFF.DBF.

- Print the file DEPTSTAF.DBF.

- Index the file STAFF on DEPARTMENT and TITLE. Name the index file DEPT.

- Print the file STAFF.DBF.

- Use the number functions to determine:

a. The number of people in the Accounting department.

b. The average pay in the Maintenance department.

c. The total number of hours worked (for all departments).

- Print a simple report displaying LAST_NAME and DEPARTMENT, by DEPARTMENT.

- Print a report displaying FIRST_NAME, LAST_NAME, DEPARTMENT, and TITLE organized by DEPARTMENT.

4

Creating a Professional Report

OBJECTIVES

In this lab you will learn how to:

1. Use the report generator feature.

2. Specify a title for a report.

3. Specify report columns.

4. View the report.

5. Modify a report.

6. Define subtotals.

7. Print a report.

CASE STUDY

The club manager is pleased with the data analysis and report Donna produced. Next, he would like a weekly report listing the employee's name, hourly pay rate, hours worked, and weekly pay. He would also like a second report on a monthly basis. This report will list the employees by department, hourly pay, hours worked, and monthly pay. To create the reports, Donna will use the dBASE III PLUS report generator.

Examining the Report Screen

At the end of Lab 3, Donna McIntyre, the assistant manager of the Sports Club, had updated the EMPLOYEE.DBF file, sorted and indexed the file, and performed some basic analysis of the data. We will use the database file EMPLOYE2.DBF in this lab. This file should be the same as the file EMPLOYEE.DBF after you completed Lab 3.

Load dBASE III PLUS.

Reminder: Throughout the rest of this text, if you are using a drive other than B to hold your data diskette, select the appropriate drive for your system.

Open the file EMPLOYE2.DBF as follows:

Select: Set Up / Database file / B: / EMPLOYE2.DBF

Donna will open the index file EMP2NAME.NDX. This index file arranges the records by last name and first name. This is the order in which she wants the names to be arranged in the report.

To complete the command sequence,

Select: Y / EMP2NAME.NDX ⟶

The basic format of a report consists of:

Margin settings   top, bottom, left, and right

Page title   up to four lines of text, displayed at the top of each report page

Column titles   up to four lines of text, displayed over each column of information

Column contents   the fields of data to display in the column

Column totals   the sum of the column contents displayed beneath each column of data

The first report Donna needs to create is the weekly report listing each employee's name, pay rate, hours worked, and weekly pay. It will look like the report shown in Figure 4-1.

```
                    Employee Payroll Report                        ──── page title
                    Week of May 16,  1994

    Last Name      First Name    Pay      Hours        Weekly       ──── column title
                                          Worked         Pay

    Aldrich        Roger         4.35       40         174.00
    Allbright      Anthony       8.25       45         371.25
    Barton         Alyce         4.00       45         180.00
    Burger         Paula         8.50       42         357.00
    Carlyle        Thomas        3.75       32         120.00
    Cashmiere      Shelly        4.45       32         142.40
    Crane          Donald        7.35       40         294.00
    Darst          Mary          6.45       34         219.00
    Davis          Larry         5.55       40         222.00
    Eberley        Peter         4.45       40         178.00
    Fisher         Sarah         3.55       40         142.00
    Holladay       Beverley      5.25       40         210.00
    Jackson        Chris         5.64       38         214.32      ──── column content
    Jackson        Tracy         5.00       35         175.00
    Martin         Phillip       7.45       46         342.70
    McCale         Timothy       8.00       40         320.00
    Millersbur     Jake          3.95       40         158.00
    Olson          Cynthia       4.45       25         111.25
    Parkerson      Madelyn       4.25       25         106.25
    Patten         Marty         5.75       42         241.50
    Robins         Anita         3.85       40         154.00
    Rosen          Kay           8.50       40         340.00
    Shields        Robert        4.25       15          63.75
    Stone          Jennifer      4.55       40         182.00
    Worth          Brian         4.35       25         108.75
    *** TOTAL ***

                                           921        5127.47      ──── column total
```

FIGURE 4-1

The Create Report command is used to specify and save the various settings for the report in a **report format file.** The file extension used by dBASE III PLUS to identify a report format file is .FRM. To use this command and to specify the filename for the report format file as EMPWEEK,

Select: Create / Report / B: / **EMPWEEK** ⮐

Your display screen should be similar to Figure 4-2.

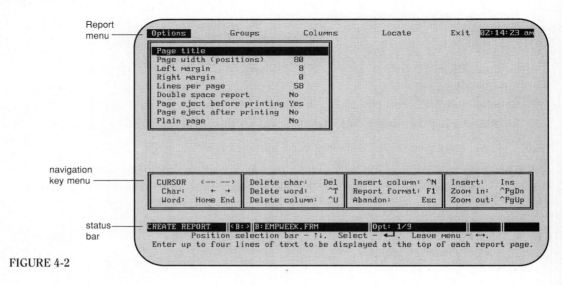

Report
menu

navigation
key menu

status
bar

FIGURE 4-2

This is the Create Report screen. The status bar shows that you are using the Create Report command and that the file being created is called EMPWEEK.FRM. The filename extension, .FRM, identifies the file as a report format file.

Across the top of the screen is a menu bar. It contains five menu choices: Options, Groups, Columns, Locate, and Exit. Each of the five menu items assists in building the report form as follows:

Options   allows you to specify the title for the report, page width and length, margins, and spacing

Groups   specifies what data fields and headings will be used for subtotals

Columns   specifies each column of data that will appear in the report and the column heading for each

Locate   allows you to move to and edit a specific column while designing the report

Exit   saves the report form and returns you to The Assistant

The Report menu bar works just like The Assistant menu bar. As a menu item is opened, a pull-down menu of options appears in a box for selection. A series of submenus and entry areas (similar to dialogue boxes) appear frequently to assist in creating the report.

At the bottom of the screen a navigation key menu is displayed.

Press: [F1]

Your display screen should be similar to Figure 4-3.

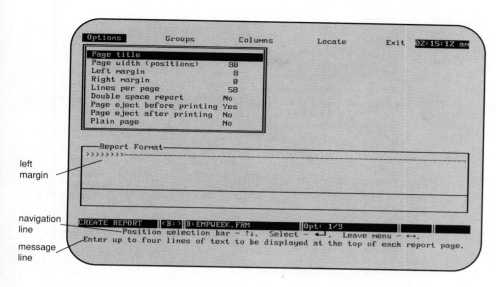

left
margin

navigation
line

message
line

FIGURE 4-3

The navigation key menu is cleared from the screen. The Report Format box is displayed. This box will display a coded diagram of the layout of the report as it is being created. The only **code** currently displayed in the Report Format box is a series of >>>'s on the left side of the box. This code shows the location and size of the left margin. Pressing (F1) changes this area of the Create Report screen to display either the navigation key menu or the Report Format box.

The navigation line and message line work the same as they do in The Assistant.

Entering the Report Title

The title of this report will be "Employee Payroll Report for the Week of May 16, 1994." A menu option is selected by moving the selection bar to the item and pressing (⏎). Use the navigation line for help in making selections and moving around the screen.

Select: Options / Page title

An empty box, called an **entry area,** appears on the screen. These blank entry areas will appear frequently while creating the report. They are used to enter the information needed by the selected menu option. The blinking cursor within the entry area shows you where the next character you type will appear. If you make an error while typing the entry, use the (Bksp) key to erase the characters back to the error. Then retype the entry correctly.

Type: **Employee Payroll Report**
Press: ⏎

The cursor moved to the second line. To enter the rest of the title as a second title line,

Type: **for the Week of May 16, 1994**

Your display screen should be similar to Figure 4-4.
The title occupies two lines in the entry area. You can have up to four lines of title

FIGURE 4-4

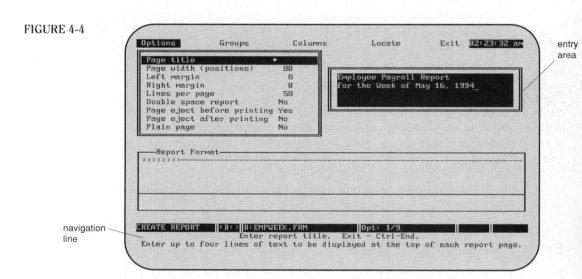

displayed in a report. Although the text is left-justified in the entry area, dBASE III PLUS will center each title line on the page when the report is displayed or printed.

Notice that the navigation line shows that the command to exit this menu is the (CTRL)-(END) key combination.

Press: (CTRL)-(END)

You are returned to the Options Menu. The first eight letters of the title are displayed following the Page title option in the pull-down menu.

The other selections under Options allow you to set the page width, margins, spacing, and page eject options. The default values displayed next to each option are acceptable for now. They are appropriate for most purposes.

Specifying the Report Column

Next the contents, heading, and size of each column of data to appear in the report are specified.

Select: Columns

Your display screen should be similar to Figure 4-5.

FIGURE 4-5

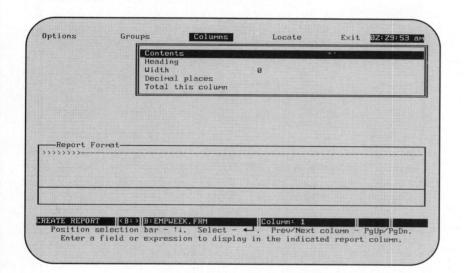

The first three menu options, Contents, Heading, and Width, are displayed in high intensity. They can be selected and defined immediately. The last two, Decimal places and Total this column, are displayed in regular intensity. They are not available for selection yet.

Each column of data that will appear in the report must be defined. The status bar shows that the current column being used is "Column: 1". First the field of data from the database file that will appear as the **column contents** is specified by selecting the Contents option. The first column will display the information in the LNAME field.

Select: Contents

The entry area for the column contents is the space to the right of the option name. A triangle followed by a blinking cursor appears in the entry area to show that the option is waiting to be defined. There are two ways that you can enter the column contents. The first is to type the field name exactly as it appears in the database file. The second is to select the field name from a field name submenu. Using the field name submenu eliminates the possibility of typing errors and incorrect field names.

To display the field name submenu,

Press: (F10)

Your display screen should be similar to Figure 4-6.

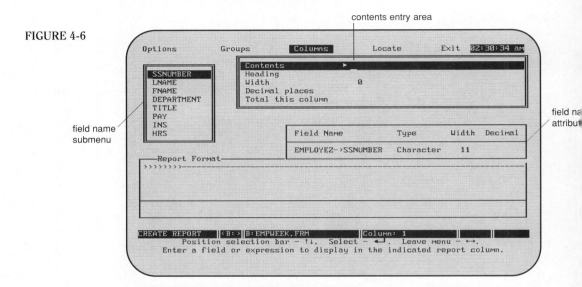

FIGURE 4-6

A field name submenu and a box showing the highlighted field name attributes are displayed.

Move to: LNAME

Notice that the attribute box shows the field width for the LNAME field is 10 spaces.

Press: ⟵

LNAME is entered at the cursor location on the contents entry area. To accept this field as the contents to be displayed in column 1,

Press: ⟵

Your display screen should be similar to Figure 4-7.

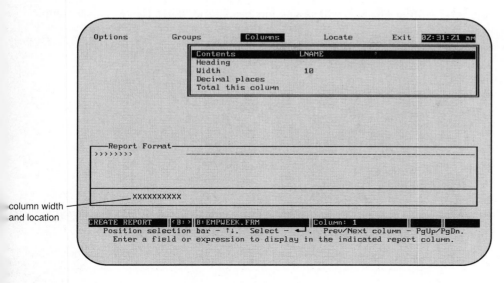

column width and location

FIGURE 4-7

Notice that the **column width** has been defined as 10. dBASE III PLUS automatically enters the field width from the database file structure as the column width.

The Report Format box displays a series of X's. This code marks the location of the first column of data. The number of X's corresponds to the width of the field.

The next Column setting to be specified is Heading. The **column heading** is the column title which will describe the data in the column.

Select: Heading

Another blank entry area appears on the screen. The column heading will be entered in this space. It can be up to four lines of text.

Type: **Last Name**
Press: (CTRL)-(END)

The column heading is displayed in the heading line. The Report Format box also displays the heading over the column.

The third option, Width, is acceptable as displayed. The column width will be 10 spaces. This is the same as the field width for the LNAME field in the database file.

The last two options, "Decimal places" and "Total this column", are not available for specification. They can be specified only when the contents of the column is a numeric field type of data.

Press: (PGDN)

A blank Column menu box appears for entry of information for the second column. The status bar shows that you are working on "Column: 2". The contents of column 2 will be FNAME, with a column heading of "First Name" and a column width of 10 spaces.

Define the second column as follows:

Select:	Contents
Press:	(F10)
Select:	FNAME
Press:	(⏎)
Select:	Heading
Type:	**First Name**
Press:	(CTRL)-(END)

When you have completed defining the second report column, your display screen should be similar to Figure 4-8.

FIGURE 4-8

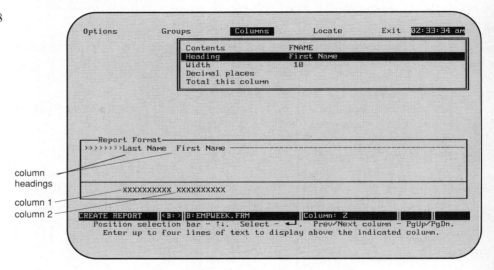

The first two columns of data have been defined. The Report Format box shows how they will appear in the report. dBASE III PLUS automatically inserts one blank space between the columns. The next column of data will hold the hourly rate of pay.

Press: (PGDN)

Following the above procedure, define column 3 as follows:

Contents: **PAY**
Heading: **Pay**

Your display screen should be similar to Figure 4-9.

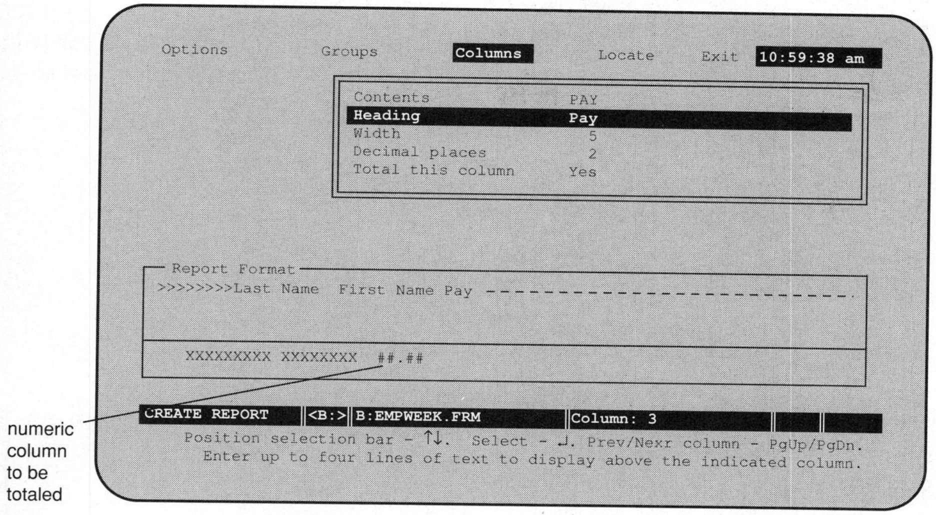

numeric
column
to be
totaled

FIGURE 4-9

The settings for Width, Decimal places, and Total this column were automatically defined by dBASE III PLUS. Width is set for five spaces, allowing for two decimal places and a period. The setting for Decimal places is 2. These are the same as the settings used for the PAY field in the database file structure. Both these settings are acceptable.

The setting in Total this column is "Yes". Also notice the display of # # . # # in the Report Format box. This means that the values in this column will be totaled in the report. dBASE III PLUS automatically totals numeric columns unless you tell it not to. However, we do not want the column of hourly pay rates totaled. To change the setting in "Total this column" to "No".

Select: Total this column

Simply selecting this menu option automatically changed the setting to "No." The code of # # . # # in the Report Format box has changed to 99.99. This code means this is a numeric column that is not to be totaled.

Press: (PGDN)

Define column 4 using the following information. (Refer to the navigation line if you need assistance while making selections.)

Contents: HRS
Heading: **Hours Worked**
Width: 12
Decimal places: 0
Total this column: Yes

Notice that the width of the column was determined this time by the number of characters in the column heading and not the field width. The larger of the two will determine the column width setting.

The final column of data, which will display the weekly pay, is a calculated field. To calculate the values that will be displayed in the column requires that the hours worked be multiplied by the hourly rate of pay (HRS*PAY).

Press: (PGDN)
Select: Contents
Press: (F10)
Select: PAY

The field PAY is entered in the Contents entry area. To multiply (*) the PAY by HRS,

Type: *
Press: (F10)
Select: HRS
Press: (⏎)

Enter the column heading as Weekly Pay.
Your display screen should be similar to Figure 4-10.

FIGURE 4-10

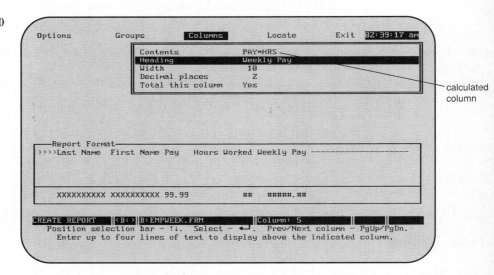

calculated column

The settings for Width, Decimal places, and Total this column are acceptable.

We have defined the five columns of data. Now we are ready to see how the report looks.

Select: Exit

To save the report format on the diskette,

Select: Save

After a few seconds, the file is saved and you are returned to The Assistant.

Viewing the Report

Donna would like to view the report before printing out a copy of it in case there is anything she wants to change.

Select: **R**etrieve / Report / B: / EMPWEEK.FRM / Execute the command / **N**

The report scrolls onto the screen. When "Page No." appears at the top of the screen, to stop the scrolling of the screen,

Press: (CTRL)-S

Your display screen should be similar to Figure 4-11.

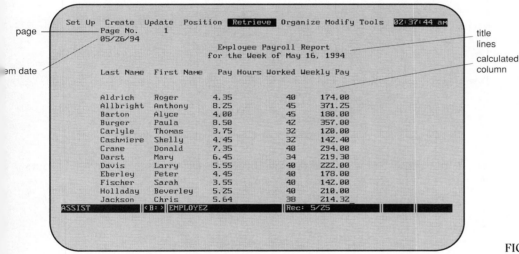

FIGURE 4-11

The page number and system date are displayed in the upper left-hand corner of the report. Donna would like to eliminate these two lines.

The title lines are centered in the middle of the page. However, because the columns of data are not evenly spaced on the page, the title looks off-center.

The report title would look better if it just read "Employee Payroll Report" on the first line and "Week of May 16, 1994" on the second line.

The employee names are listed in alphabetical order. The order of records in the database file is controlled by the master index file, EMPNAME.NDX. The report will display the column data in the same order as the master index file.

The Weekly Pay column values were calculated according to the formula entered as the Weekly Pay column contents.

The column headings for Hours Worked and Weekly Pay would look better if entered on two lines.

To see the rest of the report,

Press: any key

Your display screen should be similar to Figure 4-12.

FIGURE 4-12

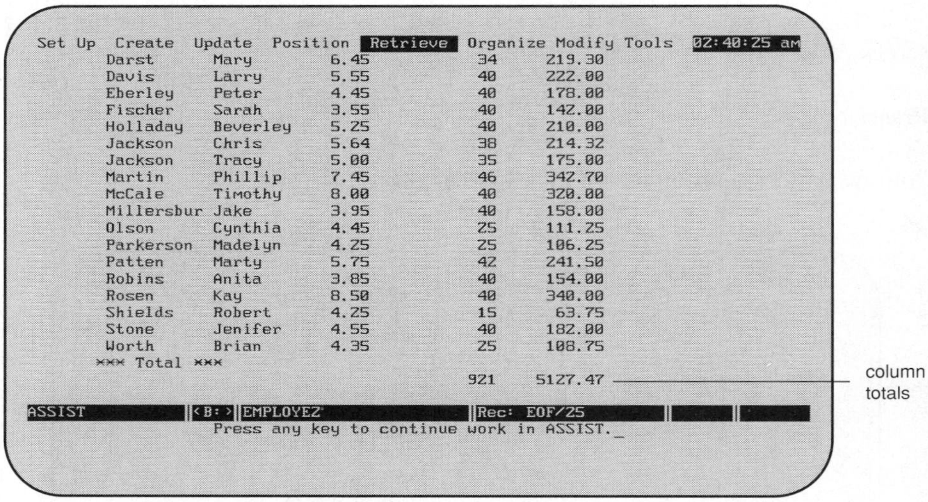

The bottom line of the report displays the total for the Weekly Pay and Hours Worked columns as specified. The Pay column is not totaled.

Modifying the Report

Donna would like to make several changes to the layout of the report format file.

To return to The Assistant,

Press: any key

To modify the report format file,

Select: Modify / Report / B: / EMPWEEK.FRM

Your display screen should be similar to Figure 4-13.

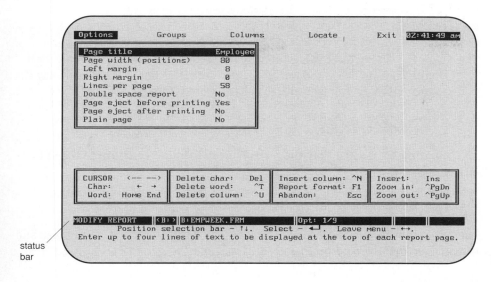

status
bar

FIGURE 4-13

The Modify Report screen is displayed. It is the same as the Create Report screen except that it contains the specifications for the report file EMPWEEK.FRM. The navigation key menu is displayed at the bottom of the screen.

Donna wants to change the report title first.

Select: Page title

Your display screen should be similar to Figure 4-14.

FIGURE 4-14

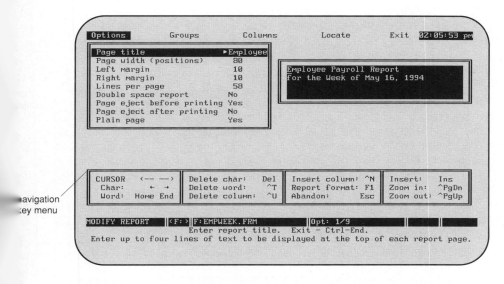

navigation
key menu

The current title is displayed in the entry area. To change the second line of the title to "Week of May 16, 1994,"

Press: ⏎

The cursor is positioned at the beginning of the second title line.

Donna wants to delete the words "for the" from this line. Notice in the navigation key menu that the key sequence to delete a word is CTRL-T.

Press: CTRL-T (2 times)

The two words are deleted from the second line of the title. To return to the Options Menu,

Press: CTRL-END

The option which allows Donna to turn off the display of the page number and system date from the report is Plain page. To change the setting from "No" to "Yes",

Press: PGDN
Select: Plain page

Simply selecting this option changed the setting to "Yes". The report will not display page numbers and the system date. Changing this setting to "Yes" will also stop the printing of a report title on each page of the report. It will be printed on the first page only.

Next, Donna would like to change the column headings for the Hours Worked and Weekly Pay columns. To quickly locate a specific column,

Select: Locate

Your display screen should be similar to Figure 4-15.

FIGURE 4-15

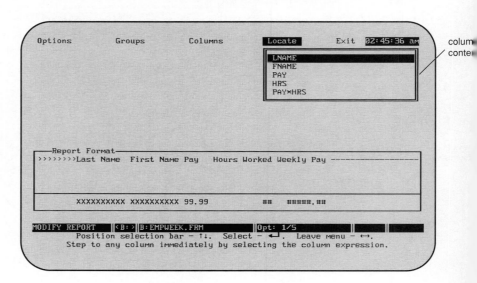

The five field names specified as the column contents for the five columns are displayed in the menu box.

Select: HRS

The menu highlight bar jumped to the Columns Menu. The Hours Worked column information is now displayed in the box. The Report Format box replaces the navigation key menu on the screen.

Using Locate is especially helpful with a report that has many columns. This is because it eliminates paging down through all the column screens to locate the column you want to use.

Select: Heading

Donna wants to change the title so that "Hours" is on the first line and "Worked" is on the second line.

To move the cursor to the beginning of the word "Worked",

Press: (END)

To delete the word "Worked" from the first line,

Press: (CTRL)-T

To move to the second line and enter the word "Worked" on this line,

Press: (⏎)
Type: **Worked**
Press: (CTRL)-(END)

Your display screen should be similar to Figure 4-16.

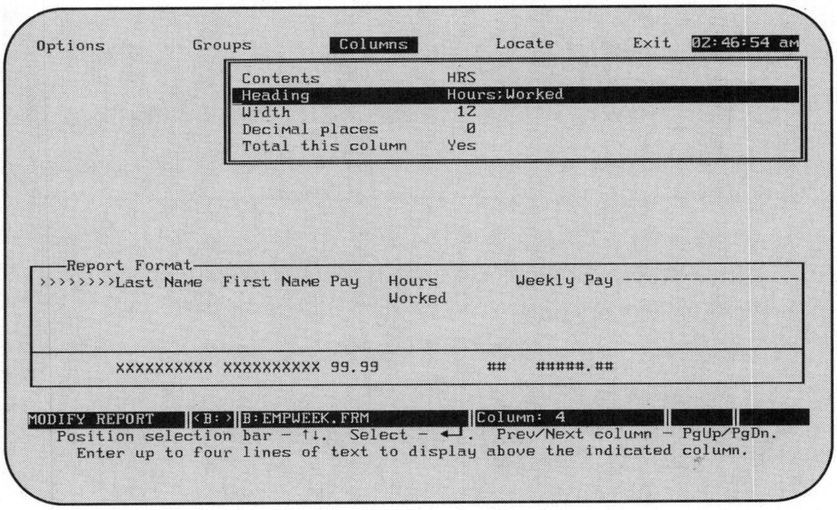

FIGURE 4-16

Notice that a semicolon is displayed between the two words in the Heading entry area. The semicolon indicates a carriage return and the end of the first line.

The column width is still 12. It did not change to reflect the smaller length of the title line.

The Report Format box displays the new column heading on two lines. Notice, however, that because the column width is still set at 12, the code, # #, marking the location of the column contents, is not displayed below the column heading.

To correct this, change the column width to six spaces (the number of characters in the word "Worked") as follows:

Select: Width
Type: 6
Press: ⟵

The contents of the Hours Worked column are now displayed under the column heading.

Press: (PGDN)

In the same manner, change the column heading for the Weekly Pay column so that it is displayed on two lines. Set the column width to seven spaces. When you are done, your display screen should be similar to Figure 4-17.

FIGURE 4-17

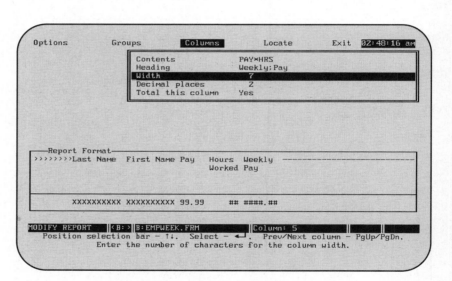

Look at the Report Format box. Donna is still not happy with the layout of the columns. They are not evenly spaced across the width of the page.

To evenly space the columns on the page, we will enter six blank spaces in front of the column headings for the Pay, Hours Worked, and Weekly Pay columns.

Press: (PGUP) (2 times)

The Pay column information is displayed.

Select: Heading
Press: (INS)
Press: space bar (6 times)
Press: (CTRL)-(END)

Your display screen should be similar to Figure 4-18.

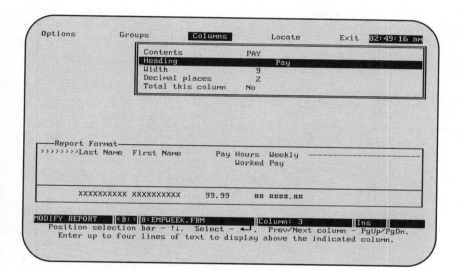

FIGURE 4-18

The column width has increased to nine spaces. As you can see in the Report Format box, the entire column has moved to the right six spaces on the page.

Press: (PGDN)

Enter six blank spaces before the Hours Worked and Weekly Pay column headings as follows:

Select: Heading
Press: space bar (6 times)
Press: ⏎
Press: space bar (6 times)
Press: CTRL-END

Press: PGDN
Select: Heading
Press: space bar (6 times)
Press: ⏎
Press: space bar (6 times)
Press: CTRL-END

To turn off the Insert mode,

Press: INS

When you have finished, your display screen should be similar to Figure 4-19.

FIGURE 4-19

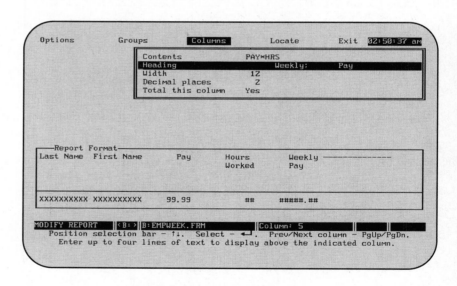

Notice that the column widths automatically adjusted to reflect the increased size of the column headings.

The columns appear more evenly spaced across the width of the page, as you can see in the Report Format box.

Next, to center the columns on the page, the right- and left-margin settings will be increased to 10 spaces. The command to change margins is under Options.

Select: Options / Left margin / **10** ⏎
Select: Right margin / **10** ⏎

Your display screen should be similar to Figure 4-20.

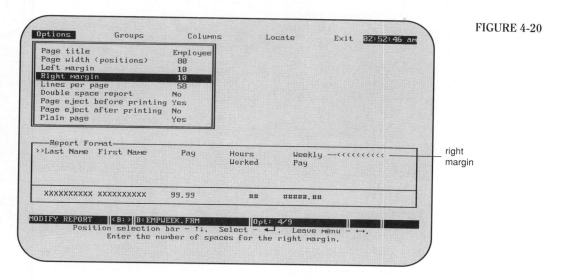

FIGURE 4-20

The Report Format box displays the new layout of the report. The entire width of the page cannot be displayed at one time in the Report Format box. Therefore, the left-margin setting shows only two >'s, while the right-margin setting displays all 10 <'s.

Finally, to turn off Page eject before printing the report,

Select: Page eject before printing

Donna thinks this will be a lot better. To save these changes,

Select: Exit / Save

The Assistant is displayed on the screen again.

To view the report,

Select: Retrieve / Report / B: / EMPWEEK.FRM / Execute the command / **N**

Press (CTRL)-**S** to stop the scrolling of the report as soon as the report title scrolls to the top of the screen.

Your display screen should be similar to Figure 4-21.

```
 Set Up   Create  Update  Position  Retrieve  Organize Modify Tools   02:53:42 am
                        Employee Payroll Report
                         Week of May 16, 1994

             Last Name  First Name      Pay       Hours       Weekly
                                                   Worked        Pay


             Aldrich    Roger          4.35         40        174.00
             Allbright  Anthony        8.25         45        371.25
             Barton     Alyce          4.00         45        180.00
             Burger     Paula          8.50         42        357.00
             Carlyle    Thomas         3.75         32        120.00
             Cashmiere  Shelly         4.45         32        142.40
             Crane      Donald         7.35         40        294.00
             Darst      Mary           6.45         34        219.30
             Davis      Larry          5.55         40        222.00
             Eberley    Peter          4.45         40        178.00
             Fischer    Sarah          3.55         40        142.00
             Holladay   Beverley       5.25         40        210.00
             Jackson    Chris          5.64         38        214.32
             Jackson    Tracy          5.00         35        175.00
 ASSIST          <B:> EMPLOYEZ                 Rec: EOF/25
```

FIGURE 4-21

Well, that's an improvement over the first time!

After viewing the entire report, press any key to return to The Assistant.

Creating Subtotals

The second report Donna needs to produce is a monthly report of all employees by department. It will show each department's monthly totals for hours worked and monthly pay.

Many of the same columns of data will be used in this report as are used in the weekly report. Rather than redefine many of the same columns and headings, Donna can modify the current report format to meet the new report specifications. To do this, she needs to make a copy of the EMPWEEK.FRM file. She can then change the copy of the report format file to create the new monthly report format file. The command to copy a file is an option in the Tools Menu. She will name the new file EMPMONTH.FRM.

Complete the command sequence below.

Select: Tools / Copy file / B: / EMPWEEK.FRM / B: / **EMPMONTH.FRM** ⏎

To modify the report file,

Select: Modify / Report / B: / EMPMONTH.FRM

Change the Page title to:

Employee Payroll Report
for May, 1994

The data in this report will be **grouped,** or organized, by department. Each numeric column of data within the group will display a subtotal if the Total this column option is "Yes".

Select: Groups
Select: Group on expression

The field name to group the data by is entered on this line. To call up a field name submenu,

Press: (F10)
Select: **DEPARTMENT**
Press: (↵)

The printed heading that will appear at the start of each group in the report is entered next.

Select: Group heading
Type: **Department**
Press: (↵)

The last change Donna needs to make to the report format is in the Weekly Pay column. The formula to compute the monthly pay rate and the column heading need to be changed.

Select: Locate / PAY*HRS / Contents

We will change the formula in this column to be Pay*Hrs*4 (number of weeks in a month). Since the cursor is located at the end of the formula, to edit the formula,

Type: *4
Press: (↵)

To change the column heading to Monthly Pay,

Select: Heading
Press: (END)
Press: (CTRL)-T
Type: Monthly
Press: (CTRL)-(END)

Save the changes and view the new report as follows:

Select: Exit / Save / Retrieve / Report / B: /
EMPMONTH.FRM / Execute the command / N

Watch the screen as the department titles scroll past. Stop the scrolling several times using CTRL-S for a better look at the report. The last screen of the report should be similar to Figure 4-22.

```
 Set Up   Create  Update  Position  Retrieve  Organize Modify Tools  03:02:21 am
          ** Department Accounting
            Rosen      Kay          8.50              40        1360.00
          ** Subtotal **
                                                      40        1360.00

          ** Department Service
            Shields    Robert       4.25              15         255.00
          ** Subtotal **
                                                      15         255.00

          ** Department Accounting
            Stone      Jenifer      4.55              40         728.00
          ** Subtotal **
                                                      40         728.00

          ** Department Service
            Worth      Brian        4.35              25         435.00
          ** Subtotal **
                                                      25         435.00

          *** Total ***
                                                     921       20509.88

 ASSIST          < B: > EMPLOYEZ              Rec: 5/25
                    Press any key to continue work in ASSIST. _
```

FIGURE 4-22

The employees are grouped, or categorized, by departments. However, many of the departments are displayed more than once. Consequently, the subtotals are all incorrect. This is because the wrong master index file was in control at the time the report was run. Whenever groups are specified in a report format file, the database file in use must be indexed or sorted by the same field that is selected for the group expression.

To return to The Assistant,

Press: any key

To access the dot prompt and change the master index file to EMP2DEPT.NDX, which is indexed by department,

Press: (ESC)
Type: **Set index to EMP2DEPT.NDX**
Press: (⏎)
Press: (F2)

To view the report again,

Select: **R**etrieve / Report / B: / EMPMONTH.FRM / Execute the command / **N**

Stop the scrolling of the screen as soon as the title reaches the top line of the screen. Your display screen should be similar to Figure 4-23.

```
  Set Up   Create   Update   Position   Retrieve  Organize Modify Tools   03:04:41 am
                          Employee Payroll Report
                             for May, 1994

           Last Name  First Name        Pay        Hours       Monthly
                                                    Worked         Pay

          ** Department Accounting
           Crane      Donald           7.35            40      1176.00
           Darst      Mary             6.45            34       877.20
           Davis      Larry            5.55            40       888.00
           Holladay   Beverley         5.25            40       840.00
           Rosen      Kay              8.50            40      1360.00
           Stone      Jenifer          4.55            40       728.00
          ** Subtotal **
                                                      234      5869.20


          ** Department Maintenance
           Allbright  Anthony          8.25            45      1485.00
           Martin     Phillip          7.45            46      1370.80
           Olson      Cynthia          4.45            25       445.00
  ASSIST            <B:> EMPLOYE2              Rec: EOF/25
                  Press any key to continue work in ASSIST. _
```

FIGURE 4-23

Notice that now each department is listed only once. The subtotals under each department are accurate. This report will provide the management of the club much valuable information.

Continue to scroll the report on the screen. Press any key to return to The Assistant.

Printing the Reports

If you have printer capability, print a copy of the monthly employee report as follows:

Select: Retrieve / Report / B: / EMPMONTH.FRM / Execute the command / Y

Your printed output should be similar to Figure 4-24.

```
                        Employee Payroll Report
                          Week of May, 1994

        Last Name          First Name      Pay        Hours         Monthly
                                                       Worked            Pay

        ** Department Accounting
        Crane              Donald          7.35          40         1176.00
        Darst              Mary            6.45          34          877.20
        Davis              Larry           5.55          40          888.00
        Holladay           Beverley        5.25          40          840.00
        Rosen              Kay             8.50          40         1360.00
        Stone              Jennifer        4.55          40          728.00
        *** Subtotal ***
                                                        234         5869.20


        ** Department Maintenance
        Allbright          Anthony         8.25          45         1485.00
        Martin             Phillip         7.45          46         1370.80
        Olson              Cynthia         4.45          25          445.00
        Patten             Marty           5.75          42          241.50
        *** Subtotal ***


        ** Department Restaurant
        Aldrich            Roger           4.35          40          696.00
        Burger             Paula           8.50          42         1428.00
        Eberley            Peter           4.45          40          712.00
        Jackson            Chris           5.64          38          857.28
        Millersbur         Jake            3.95          40          632.00
        Robins             Anita           3.85          40          616.00
        *** Subtotal ***


        ** Department Service
        Barton             Alyce           4.00          45          720.00
        Carlyle            Thomas          3.75          32          480.00
        Cashmiere          Shelly          4.45          32          569.60
        Fisher             Sarah           3.55          40          568.00
        Jackson            Tracy           5.00          35          700.00
        McCale             Timothy         8.00          40         1280.00
        Parkerson          Madelyn         4.25          25          425.00
        Shields            Robert          4.25          15          255.00
        Worth              Brian           4.35          25          435.00
        *** Subtotal ***
                                                        289         5432.60

        *** Total ***
                                                        921        20509.88
```

FIGURE 4-24

Next, change the master index file to EMPNAME.NDX and print the weekly employee report as follows:

Select: **R**etrieve / Report / B: / EMPWEEK.FRM / Execute the command / **Y**

Your printed output should be similar to Figure 4-25.

```
                    Employee Payroll Report
                    Week of May 16, 1994

   Last Name      First Name     Pay        Hours          Weekly
                                            Worked            Pay

   Aldrich        Roger          4.35         40          174.00
   Allbright      Anthony        8.25         45          371.25
   Barton         Alyce          4.00         45          180.00
   Burger         Paula          8.50         42          357.00
   Carlyle        Thomas         3.75         32          120.00
   Cashmiere      Shelly         4.45         32          142.40
   Crane          Donald         7.35         40          294.00
   Darst          Mary           6.45         34          219.00
   Davis          Larry          5.55         40          222.00
   Eberley        Peter          4.45         40          178.00
   Fisher         Sarah          3.55         40          142.00
   Holladay       Beverley       5.25         40          210.00
   Jackson        Chris          5.64         38          214.32
   Jackson        Tracy          5.00         35          175.00
   Martin         Phillip        7.45         46          342.70
   McCale         Timothy        8.00         40          320.00
   Millersbur     Jake           3.95         40          158.00
   Olson          Cynthia        4.45         25          111.25
   Parkerson      Madelyn        4.25         25          106.25
   Patten         Marty          5.75         42          241.50
   Robins         Anita          3.85         40          154.00
   Rosen          Kay            8.50         40          340.00
   Shields        Robert         4.25         15           63.75
   Stone          Jennifer       4.55         40          182.00
   Worth          Brian          4.35         25          108.75
   *** TOTAL ***
                                             921         5127.47
```

FIGURE 4-25

To review, the following steps are used when creating a report:

- Open the Create Report screen and specify a filename.
- Define the options—report title, line spacing, margins, and so on.
- Define Groups if you want the data categorized and subtotals displayed.
- Define the Column Contents, Headings, and Width.
- Save the report format file.
- View the report.
- Modify the report format file if necessary.
- Print the report.

To leave dBASE III PLUS,

Select: Set Up / Quit dBASE III PLUS

Or from the dot prompt,

Type: Quit

Key Terms

report format file   column heading
code   column width
entry area   group
column contents

Matching

1. .FRM	_____	a.	multiplication
2. >>>>>	_____	b.	code for a numeric column to be totaled
3. 99.99	_____	c.	deletes word
4. XXXX	_____	d.	right margin code
5. (F1)	_____	e.	report format file extension
6. column: 4	_____	f.	displays field name submenu
7. (F10)	_____	g.	code for column width
8. # #. # #	_____	h.	displays Report Format box or navigation key menu
9. (CTRL)-T	_____	i.	code for a numeric column not to be totaled
10. *	_____	j.	current column position

Practice Exercises

1.   This problem requires that you make a copy of the file EMPLOYE2.DBF. Name this new file PROB1.DBF.

- Open the file PROB1.DBF.
- Index this file by TITLE and name the indexed file JOBTITLE.
- With the index set to JOBTITLE.NDX, create a report format file named JOBANAL.
- Enter the first line of the page
  Title: Job Class Analysis.
  Enter the second line: (Enter your name).
- Set the column contents to be TITLE, PAY, DEPARTMENT, FNAME, and LNAME to have the headings Job, Wage, Department, First Name, and Last Name respectively. Wage is to be displayed with two decimal places.
- View this report. Modify it (*do not,* however, turn off the page number and system date) to improve the appearance of the reportby adjusting headings and column widths. Set the left and right margins to 8. Change the Option "Page eject before printing" to "NO". Save and print the report.
- Index PROB1 by DEPARTMENT and name the indexed file JOBDEPT.
- With the index set to JOBDEPT.NDX, create another report file named DEPTANAL by copying JOBANAL.FRM into DEPTANAL.FRM.

- Modify DEPTANAL.FRM by: Changing the first title line to "Job Class Analysis by Department", group the data by department, and specify the group heading to be "Department".

- View this report: Modify it (do turn off the page number and system date) to improve the appearance of the report: Save and print the report.

2.   To complete this problem you must first have completed Practice Exercise 2 in Lab 3. Open the database file TILES30.DBF. Using the data in this file and the index files DATE.NDX and COST.NDX, you will create and print two report files.

- The first report Susannah wants to create will display last names, phone numbers, amount owed (unit cost*quantity), and whether the account is paid or not. The data in this report will be organized by date.

- Name this report file AMTDUE.

- Enter the title for the report on two lines. The title is AMOUNT DUE REPORT; BY DATE ORDERED.

- There will be five columns. Accept the default column width. Do not total column 4. Enter the following column information:

Column Number	Column Contents	Column Heading
1	DATE	DATE;ORDERED
2	LAST_NAME	LAST NAME
3	PHONE	PHONE;NUMBER
4	UNIT_COST*QUANTITY	AMOUNT;OWED (Do not total column.)
5	PAID	PAID

- Save the report format.

- View the report.

- Modify it if necessary to be displayed so that it looks balanced on the page. Change column 4 to be totaled. Change "Page eject before printing" to "NO".

- Print the report.

- The second report Susannah wants to create will show her the unit cost, quantity ordered, and total due (unit_cost*quantity). The data in this report will be categorized by the unit cost.

- Name this report file ORDERS.

- Title the report COST AND QUANTITY DATA; your name.

- Group the data by UNIT_COST.

- Title the group heading UNIT COST.

- There will be three columns of data. Accept the default column widths. Do not total column 1. Enter the following column information:

Column Number	Column Contents	Column Heading
1	UNIT_COST	UNIT COST (Do not total this column.)
2	QUANTITY	AMOUNT;ORDERED
3	UNIT_COST*QUANTITY	TOTAL

- Save the report.
- View the report.
- Modify the report by adjusting the column placement and margins.
- Do not have a page number displayed. Turn off page eject before printing.
- Save, view, and print the report.

3.   To complete this problem, you will need to have completed Practice Exercise 3 in Lab 3. Using the data and index files in SCHOOL.DBF, create and print a report showing the course title, hours, and grade earned as follows:

- Name the report file GRADES.
- Title the report COURSES AND GRADES EARNED: Your Name.
- The columns should contain the course title, hours, and grade. Enter appropriate column headings. Total where needed. Adjust headings, column width and margins as needed. (Turn off "Page eject before printing."
- Save, view, and print the report.
- Modify GRADES.FRM to group on Semester. Title the group heading appropriately.
- Index the file on SEMESTER. Name the index file SEMESTER.
- View the report. Modify it if necessary.
- Print the report.

4.   Tom has a modest but growing library of 20 books. He wants to create a database file to record the title, author, publisher, category (i.e. fiction, biography, reference and textbook) copyright, date, and page length for each book.

- Create a database file LIB.DBF.
- Appropriately define the structure.
- Use either your personal library or your school's library to enter data for records 1 through 20.
- Create a report format file named LIBLIST.
- Page Title: Personal Library; (enter your name)
- Specify the column headings to be TITLE, AUTHOR, PUBLISHER, COPYRIGHT.
- Order the records alphabetically by the author's name.

- View this report, modify (*do* turn off the page number and system date) to improve the appearance of the report. Turn off page eject before printing. Print the report.

- Create another report file named CATEGORY.

- Copy LIBLIST.FRM into CATEGORY.FRM.

- Modify CATEGORY by changing the first page title line to "Personal Library by Category." Group the data by category, and specify the group heading to be Category.

- View the repor: Modify it (*do* turn off the page number and system date) to improve the appearance of the report. Print the report.

dBASE III PLUS

Glossary of Key Terms

Action line: Displays the dBASE III PLUS command as it is built while you are selecting menu options from The Assistant.

The Assistant: A menu driven method of entering dBASE III PLUS commands.

Column contents: The field of data that will determine the contents of a column in a report format file.

Column heading: Specifies the label that will appear above each column of data defined in a report format file.

Column width: The number of spaces each column in a report format file can display.

Codes: The characters displayed in the report format box which symbolize the location and format of the columns in a report format file.

Delete: To mark a record to be removed from the database file when the Pack command is used.

Dialogue box: An entry area that appears on the screen to allow entry of information in response to a command selection or prompt.

Dot prompt: The dBASE III PLUS prompt, represented by a dot, that allows direct entry of commands.

Edit: Allows updating of a single record at a time.

Entry area: A blank area that allows entry of report format specifications.

Field: A collection of related characters, such as a person's name, that makes up a single item in a record.

Field name: The name assigned to a field of information in a record. It can be up to 10 characters long, consisting of letters, numbers, and underscores. It cannot contain any blank spaces and must begin with a letter.

Field type: Determines the type of data that can be entered in a field. The five types are Character, Date, Numeric, Logical, and Memo.

Field width: The number of spaces assigned to a field.

Freeze: A Browse Menu item that restricts cursor movement to a specified field column only.

Groups: Specifies the fields to be grouped together and subtotaled in a report format file.

Index file: Organizes the records in a file according to the specified index key expression. Affects only the display of the records in the database file.

Key expression: The field or fields used to determine the order of records in an index file.

Key field: A field used in sorting the database. It determines the order of records in the sorted file.

Lock: To hold in place specified fields at the left edge of the screen when panning the screen in Browse.

Logical operator: Used to relate logical expressions by selecting either .AND., .OR., or .NOT..

Master index file: The first index file opened. It controls the display of the records in the database file.

Mathematical operators: Used to generate numeric results. They are + for addition, – for subtraction, * for multiplication, and / for division.

Menu: The list of commands displayed in the menu bar.

Menu bar: A selection of menu items, displayed at the top of The Assistant screen, from which you select the operation or command you want to use.

Menu highlight bar: The highlight bar that is used to select the menu you want to use.

Message line: Displays information on the highlighted menu option.

Modify: To make changes to the structure of existing dBASE III PLUS files using the Modify Menu.

Multilevel index: An index file that controls the arrangement of the records in a database file using more than one key expression.

Multilevel sort: A sorted file whose records are organized by the first key field specified and within that by the second key field.

Navigation key menu: Displays the edit and cursor-movement keys available for use.

Navigation line: The line of information at the bottom of the screen that tells you how to move around the menu display.

Numeric functions: A set of built-in formulas that allow calculations on numeric fields of data. They are Sum, Average, and Count.

Open: To use a dBASE III PLUS file.

Options: Command choices available when a menu is opened.

Organize: Arranges the records in a file according to the order specified.

Pan: To scroll into view in the window fields that are off-screen to the right or left while in Browse.

Pointer: The index key values and record numbers of the records in a database file that make up the index file.

Prompt: A message displayed in a dialogue box that requires a user response.

Pull-down menu: A list of options that is displayed when a menu is opened.

Recall: To remove the delete marking from a record.

Record: A collection of related fields of information.

Record number: A unique number automatically assigned by dBASE III PLUS to each record as it is entered into a file.

Record pointer: The number of the current database record.

Relational operators: Used to generate logical results. They are > for greater than, < for less than, = for equals, <> for not equal, <= for less than or equal to, >= for greater than or equal to, $ for substring comparison.

Report format box: Displays a coded layout of the report as columns are defined and options selected.

Report format file: The file created to hold the report specifications. It has an .FRM extension.

Scope: Limits the records to be searched in a file to the range specified.

Search condition: A way to locate records in a file whose field contents meet the specification.

Secondary index: An index file that is opened after the master index file has been selected. It will be updated, but it does not determine the display of records.

Selection bar: The highlighted bar that is used to select pull-down menu options and submenu options when using The Assistant.

Status bar: A highlighted bar at the bottom of the screen that is divided into six areas. It keeps you posted on where you are in The Assistant screen and tells you the state of various optional settings.

Submenu: A list of options that appears when a selection is made from the pull-down menu.

Functional Summary of Selected dBASE III PLUS Commands

dBASE: Starts dBASE III PLUS.

Execute the command: Performs the command as displayed in the action line.

Specify scope: Specifies the range of records in the file to be processed when the command is executed.

Construct a field list: Specifies the fields to include in the retrieval when the command is executed.

Build a search condition: Specifies the conditional limits of the command with a FOR clause.

Build a scope condition: Specifies the conditional limits of the scope condition with a WHILE clause.

Function	Command	Action
Set Up	Database file	Opens an existing database file for use.
	Quit dBASE III PLUS	Quits the dBASE III PLUS program, closes all open files, and returns you to DOS.
Create	Database file	Creates a new database file (.DBF).
	Report	Creates a report format file (.FRM).
Update	Append	Adds new records to the open database file.
	Edit	Allows you to change the contents of a record. One record at a time is displayed on the screen.
	Browse	Allows you to change the contents using full-screen editing. Up to 17 records can be displayed at one time, one record per row.
	Delete	Marks record(s) for deletion.
	Recall	Reinstates all or selected records marked for deletion.
	Pack	Permanently removes all records marked for deletion.
Position	Seek	Locates the first record in an indexed file that matches the key expression.
	Locate; Continue	Moves the record pointer to the first record that matches the specified expression. Continue is then used to find subsequent records.
	Skip	Moves the record pointer forward or backward a specified number of records.
	Goto Record	Moves the record pointer to a specified record number.

Function	Command	Action
Retrieve	List	Lets you view and print all or selected fields and records. Does not pause when screen is full.
	Display	Lets you view all or selected fields and records. Pauses when screen is full.
	Report	Lets you display or print a report using the report format file.
	Sum	Computes the sum of numeric fields.
	Average	Computes the average of numeric fields.
	Count	Counts the number of records meeting a specified condition.
Organize	Sort	Creates a database file (.DBF) that physically rear ranges the records in a database based on specified key fields.
Modify	Database file	Allows changes to the field structure of an existing database file.
	Report	Allows changes to the settings stored in a report file.
Tools	Set drive	Changes the default drive for the program to locate the data files.
	Copy file	Duplicates the contents of any type of file to another file.
	Directory	Displays a listing of files on a specified disk drive.
	List structure	Displays and prints the file structure of the open database file.

INDEX

Action line, DB8, DB9
Analysis of database data, DB86-DB88
Appending records, DB30-DB31, DB75, DB82
Assistant, The:
    and dot commands, DB9
    screen for, DB8
    using, DB9-DB12
Averaging data, DB87

Browsing records, DB42-DB48

Character field type:
    advantages for using, DB20
    defined, DB17-DB18
Code, in Report Format box, DB95
Columns, in reports:
    contents of, DB97-DB98
    headings for, DB99
    modifying layout of, DB108-DB111
    numeric, DB101
    specifying, DB97-DB103
    subtotals for, DB112-DB115
    width of, DB99

Commands:
    Append, DB30-DB31, DB75, DB82
    Assist, DB9
    Browse, DB42-DB48
    Continue, DB52, DB55
    Copy, DB70
    Copy file, DB112
    Count, DB87
    Create Report, DB94
    Database file (Create), DB10, DB12, DB23
    Database file (Modify), DB39-DB42
    Database file (Set UP), DB38-DB39, DB80
    Delete, DB50-DB51, DB58
    Directory, DB67-DB68, DB85
    Display, DB59, DB60, DB79, DB84
    Edit, DB49-DB50, DB57
    entering, DB9, DB37-38
    Goto Record, DB52, DB57
    Index, DB76-DB80
    List, DB31, DB61, DB62-DB63, DB70, DB73,
       DB75, DB80, DB86, DB88
    List structure, DB69
    Locate, DB52, DB55-DB56

Pack, DB59-DB60, DB62
Quit, DB33, DB117
Recall, DB61
Report (Create), DB93
Report (Modify), DB104-DB112
Report (Retrieve), DB103, DB111, DB113, DB114, DB115-DB116
Retrieve, DB59
Seek, DB52, DB82-DB84
Set drive, DB125
Skip, DB52, DB58
Sort, DB70-DB76
summary of, DB124
Conditional searching, DB52-DB56
Copying files, DB70, DB112
Counting records, DB87
Create Menu:
    Database file, DB10, DB12, DB23
    Report, DB93
Create Report screen:
    Columns, DB97-DB103
    Exit, DB111, DB113
    Groups, DB113
    Locate, DB106, DB113
    Options, DB95, DB111
Creating file structure:
    defined, DB4
    entering field names, DB16-DB23
Cursor:
    freezing movement of, DB46
    unfreezing, DB48

Data:
    analyzing, DB86-DB88
    grouped, in reports, DB113
Data entry (see Inputting records)
Database files (see Files)
Databases:
    advantages of using, DB4
    defined, DB3
    See also Structure, file
Date field type:
    defined. DB17, DB19
    entering invalid dates, DB25
dBASE III PLUS:
    loading, DB7-DB8
    quitting, DB33, DB63, DB69, DB117
    report generator, DB92-DB117
    See also Assistant, The
Deleting characters, DB15
Deleting records:
    defined, DB4
    marking for deletion, DB50-DB51, DB58
    packing to remove, DB59-DB60, DB62
    undeleting, DB51, DB61
Dialogue boxes, DB15
Directories, disk, displaying, DB67-DB68, DB85
Disk directories, displaying, DB67-DB68
Disk drives, specifying, DB14, DB125
Displaying:
    disk directories, DB67-DB68
    file structures, DB68-DB70
    indexed records, DB79, DB80
    records with List, DB31
    reports, DB103-DB104, DB114-DB115
    specific records, DB59-DB60, DB79, DB84

Dot prompt, DB8-DB9

Editing:
    defined, DB4
    during data entry, DB26-DB27
    previously entered records, DB49-DB50, DB57
Entry areas, on Report screen, DB95
EOF/1 (End Of the File) message, DB27
Errors, correcting, DB15, DB17
    during data entry, DB26-DB27
    in report generator, DB96

Fields:
    character, DB17, DB18, DB20
    date, DB17, DB19, DB25
    defined, DB4, DB12
    defining, DB12-DB23
    key, DB71, DB73
    locking, DB45
    logical, DB17, DB22
    memo, DB17
    names for, DB16
    numeric, DB17, DB21, DB87, DB101
    panning, DB44
    and searching for records, DB53
    submenu, DB53-54
    types of, DB5, DB17
    width of, DB22
File names:
    for database files, DB15, DB38
    for index files, DB68
    for report format files, DB93
File structure:
    defining, DB12-DB23
    displaying, DB68-DB70
    saving, DB23, DB42
Files:
    appending to, DB30-DB31, DB75, DB82
    copying, DB70, DB112
    creating, DB10, DB12, DB23
    defined, DB4
    index, DB79, DB80-DB82, DB85, DB88
    indexing, DB4, DB68, DB76-DB82, DB86
    modifying, DB39-DB42
    opening, DB37-DB39, DB68, DB72, DB73, DB80, DB92
    printing, DB31-DB32
    quitting, DB33, DB63, DB89, DB117
    report format, DB93, DB104
    sorting, DB70-DB76
    See also File names, File structure
Formatting reports, DB93
Freezing cursor movement, DB46
    unfreezing, DB48
Function keys:
    F1, DB13, DB44
    F10, DB48, DB98

Goto Record command, DB52, DB57
Grouped data, in reports, DB113

Help function (F1), DB13, DB44

Index files:
    displaying directory of, DB85
    filename extension for, DB79

master, DB82
opening, DB80-DB82
printing reports with, DB88-DB89
secondary, DB82
Indexing:
advantages over sorting, DB86
defined, DB4
filename extension used, DB68
on multiple key fields, DB76-DB80
Inputting records, DB23-DB29
appending records, DB30-DB31
consistency in, DB25
correcting errors, DB26-DB27
editing when entering, DB26-DB27
saving and existing, DB29
Insert mode, DB26, DB110

Key expressions, DB77
Key fields:
multiple, DB73
for sorting, DB71
Keys:
Backspace, DB15, DB28
Ctrl-Y, DB27, DB28
cursor, DB9-DB12, DB17, DB28
Del, DB27, DB28
for editing, DB26-DB27, DB28
End, DB10, DB11, DB26, DB28
Esc, DB13, DB29
Home, DB10, DB28
Ins, DB26-DB27, DB28
for modifying structure, DB40
Pgdn, DB31, DB68
Pgup, DB28, DB31, DB43
See also Function keys

Listing:
file structures, DB69
records, DB31, DB61, DB62-DB63, DB70,
DB73, DB75, DB80, DB86, DB88
Loading dBASE III PLUS, DB7-DB8
Locating records, DB55-DB56
Locking fields, DB45
Logical field type:
defined, DB17
creating, DB22
Logical operators, DB54

Master index, DB82
Mathematical operators, DB123
Memo field type, defined, DB17
Menu bar:
for The Assistant, DB9
for Browse, DB45
for Report screen, DB94
Menu highlight bar, DB9, DB10
Menus:
action line, DB8, DB9
Browse, DB45
canceling selection, DB13
menu bar, DB8, DB9
message line, DB8, DB9
navigation line, DB8, DB9, DB10, DB16
pull-down, DB8, DB9
selecting and opening, DB9-DB10
selection bar, DB9, DB10

status bar, DB8, DB9
submenus, DB14
summary of functions, DB124-DB125
See also individual menus: The Assistant,
Create, Modify, Organize, Position,
Retrieve, Set Up, Tools, Update
Message line, DB8, DB9
Modes (*See* Insert mode)
Modify Menu:
Database file, DB39-DB42
Report, DB104-DB112
Modifying database structure, DB39-DB42
Modifying reports, DB104-DB112
Multilevel:
indexes, DB76-DB80
sorts, DB73-DB76

Navigation key menu, DB27, DB22, DB40, DB49,
DB94
Navigation line, DB8, DB9, DB10, DB16
Numeric field types:
creating, DB21
defined, DB17
and numeric functions, DB87
in reports, DB101
Numeric functions, DB87

Opening files:
database, DB37-DB39, DB68, DB72, DB73,
DB80, DB92
index, DB80-DB82
Operators:
logical, DB54
mathematical, DB123
relational, DB54
Options, scope, DB31
Organize Menu:
Copy, DB70
Index, DB76-DB82
Sort, DB70-DB76

Packing records, DB59-DB60, DB62
Panning fields, DB44
Pointer:
index, DB80
record, DB28, DB32, DB51-DB61
Position Menu:
Continue, DB52, DB55
Goto Record, DB52, DB57
Locate, DB52, DB55-DB56
options, DB52-DB52
Seek, DB52, DB82-DB84
Skip, DB52, DB58
Printing:
database files, DB31-DB32
reports, DB88-DB89, DB115-DB117
selected records, DB62-DB63
Prompts:
in dialogue boxes, DB15
dot, DB8-DB9
Pull-down menus, DB8, DB9
Quitting dBASE III PLUS, DB33, DB63, DB69,
DB117

Recalling deleted records, DB61

Records:
  analyzing data in, DB86-DB88
  appending, DB30-DB31
  blank forms, DB75
  browsing, DB42-DB48
  counting, DB87
  defined, DB4, DB12
  deleting, DB4, DB50-DB51, DB58, DB62
  displaying with List, DB31
  editing, DB49-DB50, DB57
  finding, DB51-DB61
  indexing, DB4, DB68, DB76-DB80, DB86
  inputting, DB23-DB29, DB30-DB31
  listing, DB31, DB61, DB62-DB63, DB70, DB73,
    DB75, DB80, DB86, DB88
  locating, DB55-DB56
  marking for deletion, DB50-DB51, DB58
  numbers for, DB28
  packing to remove, DB59-DB60, DB62
  printing, DB31-DB32, DB62-DB63
  recalling deleted records, DB61
  record pointer, DB28, DB32, DB51-DB61
  removing delete marks, DB51, DB61
  saving, DB29
  scope options, DB31, DB60-DB61
  searching for, DB51-DB59, DB82-DB84
  sorting, DB5, DB70-DB76, DB86
  summing, DB87-DB88
Relational operators, DB54
Report format box, DB95
Report format file
  file name extension for, DB93
  modifying, DB104-DB112
Report generator, DB92-DB117
Reports:
  columns in, DB97-DB103
  creating, DB92-DB117
  defined, DB4
  displaying, DB103-DB104, DB114-DB115
  entering the title, DB95-DB97
  formatting, DB93
  modifying, DB104-DB112
  numeric functions in, DB101
  printing with index file, DB88-DB89, DB115-
    DB117
  retrieving, DB103, DB111, DB113-DB116
  subtotals in, DB112-DB115
Retrieve Menu:
  Count, DB87
  Display, DB59, DB60, DB79, DB84
  List, DB31, DB61, DB62-DB63, DB70, DB73,
    DB75, DB80, DB86, DB88
  Report, DB103, DB111, DB113, DB114, DB115-
    DB116

Saving:
  changes to file structure, DB42
  file structure, DB23, DB42
  files, DB29

records entered, DB29
Scope/Search submenu:
  options, DB31, DB60
  for recalling deleted records, DB61
  scope defined, DB4
Screens:
  Append, DB30
  The Assistant, DB8
  Columns, DB97
  Create, DB16, DB23
  Create Report, DB94
  Modify, DB40
  Modify Report, DB105
  panning records on, DB44
  Report, DB92-DB95
Scrolling:
  with List option, DB31
  locking fields, DB45
  in reports, DB103, DB114
  See also Browsing records
Search condition, DB52-DB56
Searching:
  conditional, DB52-DB56
  defined, DB5
Secondary indexes, DB82
Selection bar, DB9
Set Up Menu:
  Database file, DB38-DB39, DB80
  Quit, DB33, DB117
Slash, in commands, DB38, DB56
Sorting records:
  compared to indexing, DB86
  defined, DB5
  disadvantages of, DB76
  multilevel, DB73-DB76
  on one field, DB70-DB73
Status bar, DB8, DB9
Structure, file:
  defined, DB5
  defining, DB12-DB23
  listing, DB69
  modifying, DB39-DB42
Summing records, DB87-DB88

Tools Menu:
  Copy file, DB112
  Directory, DB67-DB68, DB85
  List structure, DB69
  Set drive, DB125
Type, field (*see* Field type)

Update menu:
  Append, DB30-DB31, DB75, DB82
  Browse, DB42-DB48
  Delete, DB50-DB51, DB58
  Edit, DB49-DB50, DB57
  Pack, DB59-DB60, DB62
  Recall, DB61